1 MONTH OF
FREE
READING

at

www.ForgottenBooks.com

By purchasing this book you are eligible for one month membership to ForgottenBooks.com, giving you unlimited access to our entire collection of over 1,000,000 titles via our web site and mobile apps.

To claim your free month visit:

www.forgottenbooks.com/free194693

ISBN 978-0-483-23023-1
PIBN 10194693

THE

PRESBYTERIAN QUARTERLY

AND

PRINCETON REVIEW.

EDITORS:

LYMAN H. ATWATER; JAMES M. SHERWOOD.

NEW SERIES,—VOL. VI.

1877.

NEW YORK:
Published by J. M. SHERWOOD,
21 BARCLAY STREET.
PRINCETON: McGINNESS & RUNYAN.
PHILADELPHIA: PRESBYTERIAN BOARD OF PUBLICATION, 1334 Chestnut St.
AMERICAN NEWS CO., NEW YORK NEWS CO., *General Agents*.

Press of ROGERS & SHERWOOD, 21 Barclay Street, New York.

THE PRESBYTERIAN QUARTERLY

AND

PRINCETON REVIEW.

1877. 20698.

CONTENTS OF THE JANUARY NUMBER.

CONTENTS OF THE APRIL NUMBER.

CONTENTS OF THE JULY NUMBER.

CONTENTS OF THE OCTOBER NUMBER.

THE

PRESBYTERIAN QUARTERLY

AND

PRINCETON REVIEW.

NEW SERIES, No. 21.—JANUARY, 1877.

Art. I.—EXEGETICAL THEOLOGY, ESPECIALLY OF THE OLD TESTAMENT.*

By CHARLES A. BRIGGS, D.D., Prof. in Union Theological Seminary, N. Y.

EXEGETICAL THEOLOGY is one of the four grand divisions of Theological Science. It is related to the other divisions, historical, systematic, and practical, as the primary and fundamental discipline upon which the others depend, and from which they derive their chief materials. Exegetical Theology has to do especially with the sacred Scriptures, their origin, history, character, exposition, doctrines, and rules of life. It is true that the other branches of theology have likewise to do with the sacred writings, in that their chief material is derived therefrom, but they differ from Exegetical Theology, not only in their *methods* of using this material, but likewise in the fact, that they do not *themselves* search out and gather this material, directly from the holy writings, but depend upon Exegetical Theology therefor ; whilst their energies are directed in Historical Theology in tracing the development of that material as the determining element in the history of the people of God ; in Systematic Theology, in arranging that material in the form most appropriate for systematic study, for attack and defense, in accordance with the needs of the age ; in Practical Theology, in. directing that material to the conversion of souls, and training them in the holy life.

---

* The substance of this article was delivered 'as an Inaugural Address, by occasion of the induction of Dr. Briggs (Sept. 21, 1876) into the chair of Hebrew and the Cognate Languages in the Union Theological Seminary, N. Y.

Thus the whole of theology depends upon the exegesis of the Scriptures, and unless this department be thoroughly wrought out and established, the whole structure of theological truth will be weak and frail, for it will be found, in the critical hour, resting on the shifting sands of human opinion and practice, rather than on the rock of infallible divine truth.

The work of Exegetical Theology is all the more important, that each age has its own peculiar phase or department of truth to elaborate in the theological conception and in the life. Unless, therefore, theology freshen its life by ever-repeated draughts from the Holy Scriptures, it will be unequal to the tasks imposed upon it. It will not solve the problems of the thoughtful, dissolve the doubts of the cautious, or disarm the objections of the enemies of the truth. History will not, with her experience, unless she grasp the torch of divine revelation, which alone can illuminate the future and clear up the dark places of the present and the past. Systematic Theology will not satisfy the demands of the age if she appear in the worn-out armor or antiquated costume of former generations. She must beat out for herself a new suit of armor from Biblical material which is ever new; she must weave to herself a fresh and sacred costume of doctrine from the Scriptures which never disappoint the requirements of mankind; and thus armed and equipped with the weapons of the Living One, she will prove them quick and powerful, convincing and invincible, in her training of the disciple, and her conflicts with the infidel and heretic. And so Practical Theology will never be able to convert the world to Christ, and sanctify the church, without ever renewing its life from the Bible fountain; and so pervading our liturgy, hymnology, catechetical instruction, pastoral work and preaching, with the pure, noble, and soul-satisfying truths of God's word, that the necessities of the age may be supplied, for "man shall not live by bread alone, but by every word that proceedeth out of the mouth of God." (Matt. iv: 4; Deut. viii: 3.)

And the history of the church, and, indeed, Christian experience, has shown that in so far as the other branches of Theology, have separated themselves from this fundamental discipline, and in proportion to the neglect of Exegetical Theology the church has fallen into a dead orthodoxy of scholasticism, has lost its hold upon the masses of mankind, so that with its foundations undermined, it has yielded but feeble resistance to the onsets of infidelity. And it has ever been that the reformation or revival has come through the resort to the sacred oracles, and the organization of a freshly stated body of doctrine, and fresh methods of evangelization derived therefrom. We thus have reason to thank God, that heresy and unbelief so often drive us to our citadel, the sacred Scriptures, and force us back to the impregnable fortress of divine truth, in order that, depending no longer merely upon human weapons and defenses, we may use rather the divine, and thus reconquer all that may have been lost, and advance a stage onward in our victorious progress toward the end. Our adversaries may overthrow our systems of theology, our confessions and catechisms, our church organizations and methods of work, for these are, after all, human productions, the hastily thrown up out-works of the truth ; but they can never contend successfully against the word of God that liveth and abideth forever (1 Peter i : 23), which, though the heavens fall and the earth pass away, will not fail in one jot or tittle from the most complete fulfillment (Matt. v : 18), which will shine in new beauty and glory as its parts are one by one searchingly examined, which will prove itself not only invincible but all-conquering, as point after point is most holy contested, until at last it claims universal obedience as the pure and faultless mirror of him who is himself the brightness of the Father's glory and the express image of his person. (2 Cor. iii : 18; Heb. i : 3.)

Now it is an important characteristic of our Reformed and Calvinistic churches, that they give the sacred Scriptures such a fundamental position in their confessions and catechisms, and lay so much stress upon the so-called *formal* principle of the Protestant Reformation. Thus in both Helvetic confessions and the Westminster they constitute the first article*, whilst in the Heidelberg and Westminster catechisms they are placed at the foundation, in the former as the source of our knowledge of sin and misery, and of salvation (Quest. iii, xix), in the latter as dividing the catechism into two parts, teaching "what

---

* Niemeyer, *Collectio Confess.*, pp. 115, 467.

man is to believe concerning God, and what duty God requires of man."—(*Larger Catechism*, Quest. v; *Shorter Catechism*, Quest. iii.) And the authority of the word of God as "the *only* rule of faith and obedience" (*Larger Catechism*, Quest. v), has ever been maintained in our churches and seminaries.

Exegetical Theology being thus according to its *idea* the fundamental theological discipline, and all *important* as the fruitful source of theology, it must be thoroughly elaborated in all its parts according to exact and well-defined scientific *methods*. The *methods* proper to Exegetical Theology are the synthetic and the historical, the relative importance of which has been hotly contested. The importance of the historical method is so great that not a few have regarded the discipline, as a whole, as at once a primary division of Historical Theology. The examination of the Bible sources, the sacred writings being of the same essential character as the examination of other historical documents, they should be considered simply as the sources of Biblical history, and thus the writings themselves would be most appropriately treated under a history of Biblical literature (Hupfeld, Reuss, Fuerst, *et al.*), and the doctrines under a history of Biblical doctrine (the school of Baur).* But the sacred writings are not merely sources of historical information; they are the sources of the faith to be believed and the morals to be practiced by all the world; they are of everlasting value as the sum total of sacred doctrine and law for mankind, being not only for the past, but for the present and the future, as God's holy word to the human race, so that their value as historical documents becomes entirely subordinate to their value as a canon of Holy Scripture, the norm and rule of faith and life. Hence the synthetic method must predominate over the historical, as the proper exegetical method, and induction rule in all departments of the work; for it is the office of Exegetical Theology to gather from these sacred writings, as the storehouse of divine truth, the holy material, in order to arrange it by a process of induction and generalization into the generic forms that may best express the generic conceptions of the sacred Scriptures themselves. From this point of view it is clear, that the analytic method

---

* Compare my article on Biblical Theology, *Am. Presb. Review*, 1870; p. 122, *seq.*

can have but a very subordinate place in our branch of theology. It may be necessary in the work of separating the material, in the work of gathering it, but this is only in order to the synthetic process, which must ever prevail. It is to the improper application of the analytic method to exegesis, that such sad mistakes have been made in interpreting the word of God, making exegesis the slave of dogmatics and tradition, when she can only thrive as the free-born daughter of truth, whose word does not yield to dogmatics, but is divinely authoritative over dogmatics, and before whose voice tradition must ever give way; for exegesis cannot go to the text with preconceived opinions and dogmatic views that will constrain the text to accord with them, but rather with a living faith in the perspicuity and power of the word of God *alone, of itself*, to pursuade and convince; and with reverential fear of the voice of him who speaks through it, which involves assurance of the truth, and submission and prompt obedience to his will. Thus, exegesis does not start from the unity to investigate the variety, but from the variety to find the unity. It does not seek the author's view and the divine doctrine through an analysis of the writing, the chapter, the verse, down to the word; but, inversely, it starts with the word and the clause, pursuing its way through the verse, paragraph, section, chapter, writing, collection of writings, the entire Bible, until the whole word of God is displayed before the mind, from the summit that has been attained after a long and arduous climbing.

Thus Exegetical Theology at least is a science, whose premises and materials are no less clear and tangible than those with which any other science has to do, and whose results are vastly more important than all other sciences combined, as they concern our salvation and everlasting welfare; and if, furthermore, this material with which we have to do be what it claims to be—the very word of God to man,—it is clear that here alone we have a science that deals with immutable facts and infallible truths, so that our science may take its place in the circle of sciences, despite all the efforts of false science to cast it out, as the royal, yes, the divine science. But let it be remembered that this position will be accorded it by the sciences only in so far as theology as a whole is true to the spirit

and character of its fundamental discipline, and does not assume a false position of dogmatism and traditional prejudice,
or attempt to tyrannize over the other sciences in their earnest
researches after the truth.

Exegetical Theology being thus fundamental and important,
having such thorough-going scientific methods, it must have
manifold *divisions* and subdivisions of its work. These, in
their order and mutual relation, are determined by a proper
adjustment of its methods and the subordination of the historical to the inductive process. Thus at the outset there are
imposed upon those who would enter upon the study of the
sacred Scriptures certain primary and fundamental questions
respecting the holy writings, such as : Which are the sacred
writings ? why do we call them *sacred ?* whence did they originate ? under what historical circumstances ? who were their
authors ? to whom were they addressed ? what was their design ?
are the writings that have come down to us genuine ? is the text
reliable ? and the like. These questions may be referred to the
general department of *Biblical Introduction.* Then the text
itself is to be interpreted according to correct principles and
by all the instrumentalities at hand, with all the light that
the study of centuries may throw upon it. This is *Biblical
Exegesis.* Finally, the results of this exegetical process are to
be gathered into one organic whole. This is *Biblical Theology.*
These then are the three grand divisions into which Exegetical Theology naturally divides itself, each in turn having its
appropriate subordinate departments.

I. BIBLICAL INTRODUCTION has as its work to determine all
those introductory questions that may arise respecting the sacred writings, preliminary to the work of exegesis. These questions are various, yet may be grouped in accordance with a
general principle. But it is, first of all, necessary to limit the
bounds of our department and exclude from it all that does not
properly come within its sphere. Thus Hagenbach* brings into
consideration here certain questions which he assigns to the
auxiliary disciplines of Sacred Philology, Sacred Archæology,
and Sacred Canonics. But it is difficult to see why, if these
are in any essential relation to our department, they should not

---

Encyklopädie. 9te Auf. s. 40.

be logically incorporated; whilst if they do not stand in such close relations, why they should not be referred to their own proper departments of study. Thus Sacred Canonics clearly belongs to our discipline, whilst Sacred Archæology no less certainly belongs to the historical department; and as for Sacred Philology, it should not be classed with theology at all, for the languages of the Bible are not sacred from any inherent virtue in them, but only for the reason, that they have been selected as the vehicle of divine revelation, and thus their connection with the scriptures is accidental rather than necessary. And still further we are to remark, that all departments of theology are in mutual relation to one another, and in a higher scale all the departments of learning act and react upon one another—such as theology, philosophy, philology, and history. Hence, that one department of study is related to another does not imply that it should be made auxiliary thereto. Thus the languages of scripture are to be studied precisely as the other languages, as a part of General Philology. The Hellenistic Greek is a dialect of the Greek language, which is itself a prominent member of the Indo-Germanic family, whilst the Hebrew and Chaldee are sisters with the Assyrian and Syriac, the Arabic and Ethiopic, the Phœnician and Samaritan, of the Shemitic family. The study of these languages, as languages, properly belongs to the college or university course, and has no appropriate place in the theological seminary. Valuable time is consumed in these studies that is taken from Exegetical Theology itself and never compensated for. The Shemitic languages are constantly rising into prominence, over against the Indo-Germanic family, and demand their appropriate place in the curriculum of a liberal education. The time has fully come when philologists and theologians should unitedly insist that a place should be found for them in the college course ; and that this valuable department of knowledge, upon the pursuit of which so much depends for the history of the Orient, the origin of civilization and mankind, as well as the whole subject of the three great religions of the world, should not give way to the physical sciences, which, whilst properly of subordinate importance as dealing mainly with material things, have already assumed an undue prominence in our institutions of learning over against philology, history, and philosophy, that

deal with higher and nobler problems. German theology has a
great advantage, in that the theological student is already prepared in the gymnasium for the university with a knowledge of
Hebrew relatively equivalent to his Greek. The Presbyterians of
Scotland have advanced beyond us in this respect, by requiring an elementary knowledge of Hebrew, in order to entrance
upon the seminary course, at the same time providing such
elementary training during the seminary vacation.   This is a
step in which we might readily follow them. We cannot afford to
wait until all the colleges follow the noble lead of the University
of Virginia, Lafayette, and others, in giving their students the
option of Hebrew instruction; but must use all our influence to
constrain them to fulfill their duty of preparing students for the
study of theology, as well as of the other professions. We might,
at least for the present, provide in our larger seminaries a special preparatory course of study, of say three months in the
summer in which instruction might be given in Hebrew,
Hellenistic Greek, and Philosophy. Now this or some other plan
must be adopted, if the study of the Old Testament is to assume
its proper place in our theological instruction ; if our church is
to successfully meet and overcome the assaults, daily becoming
more frequent and bitter, not only from without, but from
within (*vide Scribner's Monthly*, Sept., 1876., Art.—"Protestant
Vaticanism"), upon the Old Testament foundations of our
faith.   .

Still further it is to be noticed, that there can henceforth be
no thorough mastery of the Hebrew tongue by clinging reverently to the skirts of the Jew. We might as well expect to
master the classic Latin from the language of the monks,
or acquire evangelical doctrine from Rome.   The cognate languages are indispensable. And it is just here that a rich treasure,
prepared by divine Providence for these times, is pouring into
our laps, if we will only use it.   The Assyrian alone, as recently
brought to light, and established in her position as one of the
oldest sisters, is of inestimable value, not to speak of the Arabic
and Syriac, the Ethiopic, Phœnician, Samaritan, and the lesser
languages and dialects that the monuments are constantly
revealing. Immense material is now at hand, and is still being
gathered from these sources, that will considerably modify our
views of the Hebrew language, and of the history and religion

of the Hebrews in relation to the other peoples of the Orient. We are only beginning to learn that the Hebrew language has such a thing as a syntax, and that it is a highly organized and wonderfully flexible and beautiful tongue, the result of centuries of development.   As the bands of Massoretic tradition are one after another falling off, the inner spirit and life of the language are being discovered; the dry bones are clothing themselves with flesh, and rich, warm blood is animating the frame, giving to the features nobility and beauty.*   If the Presbyterian Church is to be renowned for its mastery of the Bible, if the symbols and the life of the church are to harmonize, we must advance and occupy this rich and fruitful field for the Lord, and not wait for the unbelievers to occupy it before us, and then be compelled to contend at a disavantage, they having the prestige of knowledge and success.†

Whilst, therefore, we exclude the study of the Hebrew and cognate languages from the range of Exegetical Theology, we magnify their importance, not only to the theological student, but also to the entire field of scholarship. Other scholars may do without them, but for the theologian these studies are indispensable, and we must at the very beginning strain all our energies to the mastery of the Hebrew tongue. If we have not done it out of the seminaries, we must do it in the seminaries. We must take our disadvantages as we find them, and make up by severity of study for the lack of time ; and whilst we cannot at present do justice to the requirements of the Exegetical Theology of the Old Testament, though for the present she must be the little sister in the seminary course, yet we must not undervalue her ; we must form a proper conception of her, employ faithfully her methods, cover the ground of her divisions, even if but thinly, and she will grow upon our hands and prove herself one of the excellent ones.   For though we can only deal with *selections*, and study the broad outlines of our discipline, and have but a

---

*It is exceedingly gratifying that our American students are eagerly entering upon these studies.   The large classes in the cognate languages, not only in our seminary (the Syriac class of 1875 was 9, the Arabic class of 1876 is 19), but also at Princeton, promise great things for the future in this regard.

†The church should be very grateful that the Assyrian researches have fallen at once into Christian hands, and not, like the Egyptian, been the storehouse at the start for the enemies of the truth.

fragmentary course at the best, yet we may taste of some of the tit-bits of Scripture and enjoy them to the full, and thus learn the richness of the word of God as the true soul food. We may be prepared by little things for greater things, and, above all, learning to love our methods and our work, we may devote our lives to it for the glory of God and the good of our race.

Having excluded Sacred Philology from Exegetical Theology and from Biblical Introduction, we now have to define more closely the proper field of Biblical Introduction. *Biblical Introduction* has to do with all introductory questions respecting the sacred Scriptures, all the introductory work that may be necessary to prepare the way of Biblical Exegesis. Looking at the sacred Scriptures as the *sources* to be investigated, we see three fields of inquiry presenting themselves : the individual writings, the collection or canon, and the text ; or, in more detail the three groups of questions : 1. As to the origin, authorship, time of composition, character, design, and direction of the *individual writings* that claim, or are claimed, to belong to the sacred Scriptures. 2. As to the idea, extent, character, and authority of the *Canon*, into which these writings have been collected as the sacred Scriptures of the church. 3. As to the *text* of which the Canon is composed, the MSS. in which it is preserved, the *translations* of it and *citations* from it. These subordinate branches of Biblical Introduction may be called sacred Isagogics, sacred Canonics, and sacred Criticism.

Now with reference to these departments in detail : (1) *Sacred Isagogics* is in itself a kind of introduction to Biblical Introduction, dealing with those questions that are most fundamental. Here we have to do with individual writings and groups of writings. The parts are ever to be investigated before the wholes, the individual writings before the collected ones. With reference to each writing, or, it may be, part of a writing, we have to determine the historical origin and authorship, the original readers, the design and character of the composition, and its relation to other writings of its group. These questions must be settled partly by *external historical* evidence, but chiefly by *internal* evidence, such as the language, style of composition, archæological and historical traces, the conceptions of the author respecting the various subjects of human thought, and the like. Now with reference to such questions as these, it is manifest that we have nothing to do with traditional views or dogmatic opinions. Whatever may have been the prevailing views in the church with reference to the Pentateuch, Psalter, or any other book of Scripture, they will not deter the conscientious exegete an instant from accepting and teaching the results of a historical and critical study of the writings themselves. It is just here that Christian theologians have greatly injured the cause of the truth and the Bible by dogmatizing in a department where it is least of all appropriate, and, indeed, to the highest degree improper, as if our faith depended at all upon these human opinions respecting the word of God ; as if the Scriptures could be benefited by defending the indefensible, whereas by these frequent and shameful defeats and routs these traditionalists bring disgrace and alarm even into the impregnable fortress itself, and prejudice the sincere inquirer against the Scriptures, as if these were questions of orthodoxy or piety, or of allegiance to the word of God or the symbols of the church. Our standards teach that "the word of God is the only rule of faith and obedience,* and that "the authority of the Holy Scripture, for which it ought to be believed and obeyed, dependeth not upon the testimony of any man or church, but wholly upon God, the the author thereof."† How unorthodox it is therefore to set up another rule of prevalent opinion as a stumbling block to those who would accept the authority of the word of God alone. So long as the word of God is honored, and its decisions regarded as final, what matters it if a certain book be detached from the name of one holy man and ascribed to another, or classed among those with unknown authors? Are the laws of the Pentateuch any less divine, if it should be proved that they are the product of the experience of God's people from Moses to Josiah? ‡ Is the Psalter to be esteemed any the less precious that the Psalms should be regarded as the product of many poets singing through many centuries the sacred melodies of God-fearing souls, responding from their hearts, as from a thousand-stringed lyre, to the touch of the Holy One of Israel? Is the book of Job less majestic and sublime, as, the noblest monument of sacred poetry, it stands before us in its solitariness, with un-

---

* *Larger Catechism,* Quest. iii.   † *Confess. of Faith,* Chap. i: 4.
‡ *British and Foreign Evang. Review,* July, 1868, Art. "The Progress of Old Testament Studies."

known author, unknown birthplace, and from an unknown period of history? Are the ethical teachings of the Proverbs, the Song of songs, and Ecclesiastes, any the less solemn and weighty, that they may not be the product of Solomon's wisdom alone, but of the reflection of many holy wise men of different epochs, gathered about Solomon as their head? Is the epistle to the Hebrews any less valuable for its clear presentation of the fulfillment of the Old Testament priesthood and sacrifice in the work of Christ, that it must detached from the name of Paul? Let us not be so presumptuous, so irreverent to the Word of God, so unbelieving with reference to its inherent power of convincing and assuring the seekers for the truth, as to condemn any sincere and candid inquirer as a heretic or a rationalist, because he may differ from us on such questions as these? The internal evidence must be decisive in all questions of Biblical Isagogics and we must not fear but that the *truth*, whatever it may be, will be most in accordance with God's Word and for the glory of God and the interest of the church.

The individual writings having been examined in detail and in their inter-relation, we now have to consider them as collected writings in the canon of the church.

(2) *Sacred Canonics* considers the *Canon* of sacred Scripture as to its *idea* in its historical formation, its extent, character, authority, and historical influence. These inquiries, like those in the previous department, are to be made in accordance with the historical and synthetic methods. We are not to start with preconceived dogmatic views as to the *idea* of the canon, but derive this *idea* by induction from the sacred writings themselves; and in the same manner decide all other questions that may arise. Thus the extent of the Canon is not to be determined by the consensus of the churches, * or by the citation and reverent use of them in the fathers, and their recognition by the earliest standard authorities,† for these historical evidences, so important in Historical Theology, have no value in Exegetical Theology,

---

* Indeed, they do not agree with reference to its extent whether it includes the Apocryphal books or not, and, still further, they differ in the matter of distinguishing within the canon, between writings of primary and secondary authority.

†These, indeed, are not entirely agreed, and if they were, could only give us a human and fallible authority.

as they had no influence in the formation of the Canon itself; nor, indeed, by their accord with orthodoxy or the rule of faith,* for it is not only too broad, in that other writings than sacred are orthodox, but again too narrow, in that the standard is the shifting one of subjective opinion, or external human authority, which, indeed, presupposes the Canon itself as an object of criticism; and all these external reasons, historical and dogmatic, after all, can have but a provisional and temporary authority— but the only authoritative and final decision of these questions is from the internal marks and characteristics of the Scriptures, their recognition of one another, their harmony with the idea, character, and development of a divine revelation, as it is derived from the Scriptures themselves, as well as their own well-tested and critically examined claims to inspiration and authority. These reasons, and these alone, gave them their historical position and authority as a Canon; and these alone can have their place in the department of Exegetical Theology. And it is only on this basis that the historical and dogmatic questions may be properly considered, with respect to their recognition by Jew and Christian, and their authority in the church. The writings having thus been considered individually and collectively, we are prepared for the third step, the examination of the text itself.

(3) *Sacred Criticism* considers the text of the sacred Scriptures both as a whole and in detail. The sacred writings have shared the fate of all human productions in their transmission from hand to hand, and in the multiplication of copies. Hence, through the mistakes of copyists, the intentional corruption of the heretic, and supposed improvement of the over-anxious orthodox, the MSS. that have been preserved betray differences of reading; and questions arise with respect to certain parts of writings, or, indeed, whole writings, whether they are genuine or spurious. This department has a wide field of investigation. First of all, the peculiarities of the Bible language must be studied, and the idiomatic individualities of the respective authors. Then the age of the various MSS. must be determined, their peculiarities, and relative importance. The ancient versions

---

*It was in accordance with this subjective standard that Luther rejected the epistle of James and Esther. Comp. *Dorner, Gesch der Protest. Theologie*, s. 234, *seq.*

now come into the field, especially the Septuagint, the Chaldee and Samaritan Targums, the Syriac Pechito, and the Vulgate, which again, each in turn, has to go through the same sifting as to the critical value of its own text. Here, especially in the Old Testament, we go back of any MSS. and are brought face to face with differences that can be accounted for only on the supposition of original MSS., whose peculiarities have been lost. To these may be added the citations of the original text in the works of rabbins, and Christian scholars. Then we have the still more difficult comparison of parallel passages, where differences of text show a difference in MSS. reaching far back of any historical MSS., or even version.* Now, it is manifest that Biblical Criticism has to meet all these difficulties and answer all these questions, and harmonize and adjust all these differences, in order that the genuine, original, pure, and uncorrupted text of the word of God may be gained, as it proceeded directly from the original authors to the original readers. And the exegetical method will begin with the differences of the Scripture texts, before it enters upon the study of MSS. and versions. This department of study is all the more difficult for the Old Testament, that the field is so immense, the writings so numerous, various, and ancient, the languages so little understood in their historical peculiarities, and, still further, in that we have to overcome the prejudices of the Massoretic system, which, whilst faithful and reliable so far as the knowledge of the times went, yet, as resting simply on tradition, without critical or historical investigation, and without any proper conception of the general principles of grammar and comparative philology, cannot be accepted as final ; for the time has long since passed when the vowel points and accents can be deemed inspired. We have to go back of them, to the unpointed text, for all purposes of criticism.

Thus the work of *Biblical Introduction* ends, by giving us all that it can learn respecting the individual writings, their collection in the Canon, and their text, by presenting to us

---

*Comp. Psalm xiv with Psalm liii ; Psalm xviii with 2 Samuel xxii, and the books of Samuel and Kings on one hand, with the books of the Chronicles on the other, and indeed, throughout. Compare also the Canonical books of Ezra, Nehemiah, and Daniel, with the Apocryphal additions and supplements in the Septuagint version, and finally the citation of earlier writings in the later ones, especially in the New Testament.

the sacred Scriptures as the holy word of God, all the errors and improvements of men having been eliminated, in a text so far as possible, as it came from holy men who "spake as they were moved by the Holy Ghost" (2 Peter i: 21), so that we are brought into the closest possible relations with the living God through his word, having in our hands the *very form* that contains the very *substance* of divine revelation ; so that with reverence and submission to his will we may enter upon the work of interpretation, confidently expecting to be assured of the truth in the work of Biblical Exegesis.

II. BIBLICAL EXEGESIS. And now first of all we have to lay down certain general principles derived from the study of the word of God, upon which this exegesis itself is to be conducted. These principles must accord with the proper *methods* of Exegetical Theology and the nature of the work to be done. The work of establishing these principles belongs to the introductory department of *Biblical Hermeneutics.* The Scriptures are human productions, and yet truly divine. They must be interpreted as other human writings, and yet their peculiarities and differences from other human writings must be recognized,* especially the supreme determining difference of their inspiration by the Spirit of God, in accordance with which they require not only a sympathy with the human element in the sound judgment and practical sense of the grammarian, the critical investigation of the historian, and the æsthetic taste of the man of letters ; but also a sympathy with the divine element, an inquiring, reverent spirit, to be enlightened by the Spirit of God, without which no exposition of the Scriptures as sacred, inspired writings is possible. It is this feature that distinguishes the discipline from the other corresponding ones, as *Sacred Hermeneutics.* Thus we have to take into the account the inspiration of the Scriptures, their *harmony*, their unity in variety, their sweet simplicity, and their sublime mystery ; and all this not to override the principles of grammar, logic, and rhetoric, but to supplement them, yes, rather, infuse them with a new life and vigor, making them sacred grammar, sacred logic, and sacred rhetoric. And just here it is highly important that the *history of exegesis* should come

---

* Comp. Immer, *Hermeneutik der N. T.* s. 9.

into the field of study in order to show us the abuses of false **principles** of interpretation as a warning; and the **advantages of** correct principles as an encouragement.*

After this preliminary labor, the exegete is prepared for his work in detail, and, indeed, the immensity of these details is at once over-powering and discouraging. The extent, the richness, the variety of the sacred writings, poetry, history, and prophecy, extending through so many centuries, and from such a great number of authors, known and unknown, the inherent difficulty of interpreting the sacred mysteries, the things of God—who is sufficient for these things? who would venture upon this holy ground without a quick sense of his incapacity to grasp the divine ideas, and an absolute dependence upon the Holy Spirit to show them unto him! (John xvi: 15.) Truly, here is a work for multitudes, for ages, for the most profound and devout study of all mankind, for here we have to do with the *whole word of God to man.* The exegete is like the miner of Job xxviii.†

> "To (nature's) darkness man is setting bounds;
> Unto the end he searcheth every thing,—
> The stones of darkness and the shade of death
> Breaks from the settlers' view the deep ravine;
> And there, forgotten of the foot-worn path,
> They let them down—from men they roam afar."

For the exegete must free himself as far as possible from all traditionalism and dogmatic prejudice, must leave the haunts of human opinion, and bury himself in the word of God. He must descend beneath the surface of the word into its depths. The letter must be broken through to get at the precious idea. The dry rubbish of misconception must be thrown out, and a shaft forced through every obstacle to get at the truth. And whilst faithful in the employment of all these powers of the human intellect and will, the true exegete fears the Lord, and only thereby hopes through his intimacy with the Lord for the revelation of wisdom.‡

1. The exegete begins his work with *Grammatical Exegesis.* Here he has to do with the *form,* the dress of the revelation,

---

*Compare especially Diestel, *Gesch. d. A. T. in der Christ. Kirche,* Jena, 1869.

†Taylor Lewis' version *Lange's Commentaries,* Volume on Job. N. Y., 1874.

‡Job xxviii: 28; Psalm xxv: 14; Proverbs viii: 17, *seq.*

which is not to be disregarded or undervalued, for it is the form in which God has seen fit to convey his truth, the dress in which alone we can approach her and know her. Hebrew grammar must therefore be mastered in its etymology and syntax, or grammatical exegesis will be impossible. Here patience, exactness, sound judgment, and keen discernment are required, for every word is to be examined by itself, etymologically and historically, not etymologically alone, for Greek and Hebrew roots have not unfrequently been made to teach very false doctrines, forgetting that a word is a living thing, and having, besides its root, the still more important *stem*, branches, and products—indeed, a history of meanings. The word is then to be considered in its syntactical relations in the clause ; and thus step by step the *grammatical sense* is to be ascertained, the false interpretations eliminated, and the various possible ones correctly presented and classified. Now, without this patient study of words and clauses no accurate translation is possible, no trustworthy exposition can be made.* It is true that grammatical exegesis leaves us in doubt between many possible constructions of the sense ; but these doubts will be solved as the work of exegesis goes on, and then, on the other hand, it eliminates many views as ungrammatical which have been hastily formed, and effectually prevents that jumping at conclusions to which the indolent and impetuous are alike inclined.

2. The second step in exegesis is *Logical* and *Rhetorical Exegesis*. The words and clauses must be interpreted in accordance with the context, the development of the author's thought and purpose ; and also in accordance with the principles of rhetoric, discriminating plain language from figurative, poetry from prose, history from prophecy, and the various kinds of history, poetry, and prophecy from one another. This is to be done not after an arbitrary manner, but in accordance with the general laws of logic and rhetoric that apply to all writings whatever. Now it is clear, that whilst the use of figurative language has given occasion to the mystic and the dogmatist

---

*Yes, we may say that no translation can be thoroughly understood after the generation in which it was made, without this resort to the original text, which alone can determine in many cases the meaning of the translators themselves, when we come upon obsolete terms, or words whose meanings have become modified or lost.

for the most arbitrary and senseless exegesis, yet the laws of
logic and rhetoric, correctly applied to the text, will clip the
wings of the fanciful, and destroy the foundations of the dogmatist, and, still further, will serve to determine many questions that grammar alone cannot decide, and hence, more narrowly define the meaning of the text.

3. The third step in exegesis is *Historical Exegesis.* The
author must be interpreted in accordance with his historical surroundings. We must apply to the text the knowledge of the author's times, derived from archæology, geography, chronology,
and general history. Thus only will we be able to enter upon
the *scenery* of the text. It is not necessary to resort to the history of exegesis; one's own observation is sufficient to show the
absurdities and the outrageous errors into which a neglect of
this principle leads many earnest but ignorant men. No one can
present the Bible narrative in the dress of modern every-day
life without making the story ridiculous. And it must be so
from the very nature of the case. Historical circumstances
are essential to the truthfulness and vividness of the narrative.
Instead of our transporting Scripture events to our scenery,
we must transport ourselves to their scenery, if we would correctly understand them and realize them. If we wish to
apply Scripture truth we may, after having correctly apprehended it, eliminate it from its historical circumstances, and
then give it a new and appropriate form for practical purposes;
but we can never interpret Scripture without historical exegesis. This will serve to more narrowly define the meaning
of the text, and to eliminate from the results thus far attained
in the exegetical process.

4. The fourth step in exegesis is *Comparative Exegesis.* The
results already gained with reference to any particular passage
are to be compared with the results attained in a like manner
in other similar passages of the same author, or other authors
of the period, and in some cases from other periods of divine
revelation. Thus, by a comparison of Scripture with Scripture,
mutual light will be thrown upon the passage, the true conception will be distinguished from the false, and the results
attained adequately supported.

5. The fifth step in exegesis is one of vast importance,
which, for lack of a better name, may be called *Literary*

Exegesis. Great light is thrown upon the text by the study of the views of those who, through the centuries, in the various lands, and from the various stand-points, have studied the Scriptures. Here in this battle ground of interpretation we see almost every view assailed and defended, so that multitudes of opinions have been overthrown, never to reappear; others are weak and tottering—comparatively few still maintain the field. Manifestly it is among these latter that we must in the main find the true interpretation. This is the *furnace* into which the results thus far attained by the exegete must be thrown, that its fires may consume the hay, straw, and stubble, and leave the pure gold thoroughly refined. Christian divines, Jewish rabbins, and even unbelieving writers, have not studied the word of God for so many centuries in vain. No true scholar can be so presumptuous as to neglect their labors. No interpreter can claim originality or freshness of conception, who has not familiarized himself with this *mass* of material that others have wrought out. Nay, on the other hand, it is the best check to presumption, to know that every view that is worth anything must pass through the furnace. Any exegete who will accomplish anything, must know that he is to expose himself to the fire that centres upon any combatant that will enter upon this hotly-contested field. Thus, as from the study of the Scriptures he *first* comes into contact with human views, traditional opinions, and dogmatic prejudices; whilst on the one side these will severely criticize and overthrow many of his results, on the other side the results of his faithful study of the word of God will be a fresh test of the correctness of those human views that have hitherto prevailed, so that, from the acting and reacting influences of this conflict, the truth of God will maintain itself, and it *alone* will prevail.

I have thus far described these various steps of exegesis, in order that a clear and definite conception may be formed of its field of work—not that they are ever to be represented by themselves in any commentary, or even carried on independently by the exegete himself, but that they should be regarded as the component parts of any thorough exegetical process, and that although as a rule naught but the results are to be pre-

sented to the public, yet these results imply that no part of
the process has been neglected, but that all have harmonized
in them, if these are true and reliable results.

In advancing now to the higher processes of exegesis,
we have to observe a marked difference from the previous processes, in that the former have had to do with
the entire text, these with only select portions of it.
And still further we are to remark, that whilst in these processes, the results are to be attained which will be most
profitable to the great masses of mankind, we must severely
criticize those who, without having gone through the previous
processes themselves, either use the labors of the faithful
exegete without acknowledgment, or else, accepting without
examination traditional views, build on an unknown foundation; for the world does not need theological castles in the
air, or theories of Christian life, but a solid structure of divine
truth as the home of the soul, and an infallible guide for living
and dying.

6. The sixth step in exegesis is *Doctrinal Exegesis*, which
considers the material thus far gathered in order to derive therefrom the ideas of the author respecting faith and morals.
These ideas are then to be considered in their relation to one
another in the section and chapter. Thus we get the doctrine
that the author would teach, and are prepared for a comparison of it with the doctrines of other passages and authors.
Here we have to contend with a false method of searching
for the so-called *spiritual sense*, as if the doctrine could be
independent of the form in which it is revealed, or, indeed,
so loosely attached to it, that the grammar and logic should
teach one thing, and the spiritual sense another thing. There
can be no spiritual sense that does not accord with the results
thus far attained in the exegetical process. The true spiritual
sense comes before the inquiring soul as the product of the
true exegetical methods that have been described. As the
differences of material become manifest in the handling of it,
the doctrine stands forth as divine and infallible in its own
light. Any other spiritual sense is false to the word of God,
whether it be the conceit of Jewish cabbalists or Christian
mystics.

7. The seventh and final effort of exegesis is *Practical Exe-*

gesis—that is, the text is now to be given its application to the faith and life of the present. And here we must eliminate not only the temporal bearings of the text from the eternal, but also those elements that apply to other persons and circumstances than those in hand. And here all depends upon the character of the work, whether it be catechetical, homiletical, evangelistic, or pastoral. *All* Scripture may be said to be *practical* for *some* purpose, but not every Scripture for *every* purpose. Hence, practical exegesis must not only give the true *meaning* of the text, but also the true *application* of the text to the matter in hand. Here we have again to deal with a false method of seeking *edification* and deriving pious *reflections* from every passage, thus constraining the text to meanings that it cannot bear, doing violence to the word of God, which is not only not to be added to or taken from as a whole, but also as to all its parts. This spirit of interpretation, whilst nominally most reverential, is really very irreverential. It originates from a lack of knowledge of the Scriptures, and a negligence to use the proper methods of exegesis, as if the Holy Spirit would reveal the sacred mysteries to the indolent, even if they should be pious; for whilst he may hide the truth from the irreverential critic, he cannot be expected to reveal it except to those who not only have piety, but also search for it as for hidden treasures. This indolence and presumptuous reliance upon the Holy Spirit, which too often proves to be a dependence upon one's own conceits and fancies, has brought disgrace upon the word of God, as if it could be manifold in sense, or was able to prove anything that might be asked of it. Nay, still worse, it leads the preacher to burden his discourse with material which, however good it may be in itself, not only has no connection with the text, but no practical application to the circumstances of the hour, or the needs of the congregation. Over against this abuse of the Scriptures, the exegete learns to use it properly, and whilst he cannot find everywhere what he needs, yet he can find by searching for it, far more and better than he needs; yes, he will learn, as he studies the word, that it needs no forcing, but aptly and exactly satisfies with appropriate material every phase of Christian experience, gently clears away every shadow of difficulty that may disturb the inquiring spirit, proving itself *sufficient* for each and every one, and abundantly ample for all mankind.

.We thus have endeavored to consider the various processes
of exegesis by which results are attained of essential importance to all the other departments of theology.   The work of
the exegete is foundation work.   It is the work of the study,
and not of the pulpit, or the platform.   It brings forth treasures new and old from the word of God, to enrich the more
prominent and public branches of theology.   It finds the
nugget of gold that they are to coin into the current conceptions of the times.   It brings forth ore that they are to work
into the vessels or ornaments, that may minister comfort ito
the household and adorn the home and the person.   It gains
the precious gems that are to be set by these jewelers, in order that their lustre and beauty may become manifest and
admired of all.   Some think it strange that the word of God
does not at once reveal a *system of theology,* or give us a
confession of faith, or *catechism.*   But experience shows us
that no body of divinity can answer more than its generation ;
no catechism or confession of faith but what will in time
become obsolete and powerless, remaining as historical monuments and symbols, as the worn and tattered banners that
our veterans or honored sires have carried victoriously through
the campaigns of the past—but not suited entirely for their descendants. Each age has its own peculiar work and needs, and
it is not too much to say, that not even the Bible could devote
itself to the entire satisfaction of the wants of any particular age, without thereby sacrificing its value as the
book of all ages. It is sufficient that the Bible gives us the
material for all ages, and leaves to man the noble task of
shaping that material so as to suit the wants of his own time.
The word of God thus is given to us in the Bible, as his
truth is displayed in physical nature—in an immense and
varied store-house of material.   We must search in order to
find what we require for our soul's food, not expecting to
employ the whole, but recognizing that as there is enough
for us, so there is sufficient for all mankind and for all ages, in
its diversities appropriate for the various types of human
character, the various phases of human experience, so that no
race, no generation, no man, woman, or child, but what may
find in the Scriptures the true soul-food, material of abounding
wealth, surpassing all the powers of human thought and all the
requirements of human life.

The work of Exegetical Theology does not end, however, with the work of Biblical Exegesis, but advances to its conclusion in *Biblical Theology*. Exegetical Theology not only in the department of Biblical Exegesis produces the material to be used in the other department of theology in a confused and chaotic state, but it has its own highest problem to solve, in the thorough arrangement of that material in accordance with its own synthetic method. As there is a history in the Bible, an unfolding of divine revelation, a unity, and a wonderful variety, so Exegetical Theology cannot stop until it has arranged the Biblical material in accordance with its historical position, and its relative value in the one structure of divine revelation. And here, first, we see the culmination of the exegetical process, as all its departments pour their treasures into this basin, where they flow together and become compacted into one organic whole—for Biblical Theology rises from the exegesis of verses, sections, and chapters, to the higher exegesis of writings, authors, periods, and of the Old and New Testaments as wholes, until the Bible is discerned as an organism, complete and symmetrical, *one* as God is one, and yet as *various* as mankind is various, and thus only divino-human as the complete revelation of the God-man.

In this respect Biblical Theology demands its place in theological study as the highest attainment of exegesis. It is true that it has been claimed that the history of Biblical Doctrine, as a subordinate branch of Historical Theology, fully answers its purpose; and again, that Biblical Dogmatics, as the fundamental part of Systematic Theology, covers its ground; and, indeed, these branches of the sister grand divisions of theology do deal with many of its questions and handle much of its material. But this is simply for the reason, that Biblical Theology is the highest point of exegesis, where the most suitable transition is made to the other departments; but it does not, it cannot, belong to either of them. As Biblical Theology was not the product of Historical or Systematic Theology, but was born in the throes of the exegetical process of the last century, so it is the child of exegesis, and can flourish only in her own home. The idea, methods, aims, and, indeed, *results*, are entirely different from those presented in the above-mentioned parts of Historical and Systematic Theology. It does not give us a *history* of doctrine, although it does not neglect the historical method in the unfolding of the doctrine. It does not seek the *history* of the doctrine, but the *formation*, the *organization*, of the doctrine in history. It does not aim to present the Systematic Theology of the Bible, and thus arrange Biblical doctrine in the forms that Systematic Theology must assume for the purposes of the day; but in accordance with its synthetic method of seeking the unity in the variety, it endeavors to show the *Biblical system* of doctrine, the form assumed by theology in the Bible itself, the organization of the doctrines of faith and morals in the historical divine revelation. It thus considers the doctrine at its first historical appearance, examines its formation and its relation to others in the structure, then traces the formation as it unfolds in history, sees it evolving by its own inherent vitality, as well as receiving constant accretions, ever assuming fuller, richer, grander proportions, until in the revelation of the New Testament the organization has become complete and finished. It thus not only distinguishes a theology of periods, but a theology of authors and writings, and shows how they harmonize in the *one* complete revelation of God.* Now it is manifest that it is only from this elevated standpoint that many important questions can be settled, such as the *relation of the Old Testament to the New Testament*—a fundamental question for all departments of theology. It is only when we recognize the New Testament as not only the historical fulfillment of the Old Testament, but also as its *exegetical* completion, that the *unity* and the *harmony*, all the grander for the variety and the diversity of the Scriptures, become more and more manifest and evident. It is only from this standpoint that the apparently contradictory views, as, for instance, of Paul and James, in the article of justification, may be reconciled in their difference of types. It is only here that a true doctrine of inspiration can be given, properly distinguishing the divine and human elements, and yet recognizing them in their *union*. It is only thereby that the *weight of authority* of the Scripture can be fully felt, and the consistency of the infallible Canon invincibly maintained. It is only in this

---

* See my article on Biblical Theology, in *Am. Presb. Review*, 1870.

culminating work that the preliminary processes of exegesis may be delivered from all the imperfections and errors that still cling to the most faithful work of the exegete. It is only from these hands that history receives its true keys, systematic theology its indestructible pillars, and practical theology its all-conquering weapons.

Thus Exegetical Theology is a theological discipline, which, in its various departments, presents an inexhaustible field of labor, where the most ambitious may work with a sure prospect of success, and where the faithful disciple of the Lord may rejoice in the most *intimate* fellowship with the Master, divine truths being received immediately from the divine hand, old truths being illuminated with fresh meaning, new truths filling the soul with indescribable delight. The Bible is not a field whose treasures have been exhausted, for they are inexhaustible, As in the past holy men have found among these treasures jewels of priceless value; as Athanasius, Augustine, Anselm, Luther, and Calvin, have derived therefrom *new* doctrines that have given shape not only to the church, but to the world; so it is not too much to expect that even greater saints than these may yet go forth from their retirement, where they have been *alone* in communion with God through his word, holding up before the world some *new* doctrine, freshly derived from the ancient writings, which, although hitherto overlooked, will prove to be the necessary complement of all the previous knowledge of the church, and, indeed, no less essential to its life, growth, and progress than the Athanasian doctrine of the Trinity, the Augustinian doctrine of sin, or the Protestant doctrine of justification through faith.

Art. II.—THE EARLY RELIGION OF IRELAND.

By Rev. Wm. Hamilton, D.D., Northfield, O.

Prince Ælfrid's Itinerary through Ireland, A.D. 684.

I. I found in Inisfail the fair, in Ireland, while in exile there,
Women of worth, both grave and gay men, many clerics and many laymen.

II. I travelled its fruitful provinces round, and in every one of the five* I found,
Alike in church and in palace hall, abundant apparel and food for all.

III. Gold and silver I found, and money, plenty of wheat and plenty of honey ;
I found God's people rich in pity, found many a feast and many a city.

IV. I also found in Armagh the splendid, meekness, wisdom, and prudence blessed,
Fasting, as Christ hath recommended, and noble counsellors untranscended.

V. I found in each great church, moreo'er, whether on island or on shore,
Piety, learning, fond affection, holy welcome and kind protection.

VI. I found the good lay monks and brothers, ever beseeching help for others,
And in their keeping the holy word, pure as it came from Jesus the Lord.

VII. I found in Connaught the just, redundance of riches, milk in lavish abundance,
Hospitality, vigor, fame, in Cruachan's land of heroic name.

VIII. I found in the country of Connell the glorious, bravest warriors, ever victorious ;
Fair complexioned men and warlike, Ireland's lights, the high, the star-like !

IX. I found in Munster unfettered of any, kings and queens and poets a many—
Poets well skilled in music and measure, prosperous doings, mirth, and pleasure.

X. I found in Ulster, from hill to glen, hardy warriors, resolute men ;
Beauty that bloomed when youth was gone, and strength transmitted from sire to son.

XIII. I found from Ara to Glea, in the broad rich country of Ossorie,
Sweet fruits, good laws for all and each, great chess-players, men of truthful speech.

---

* Meath, which is now part of Leinster, was then a separate province.

XIV.	I found in Meath's fair principality, virtue, vigor, and hospitality;
	Candor, joyfulness, bravery, purity, Ireland's bulwark and security.*
XV.	I found strict morals in age and youth, I found historians recording truth,
	The things I sing of in verse unsmooth, I found them all—I have written, sooth.

NOTHING has greater influence in forming national character than religion. In the British Islands there are three distinct types of religious principle, and, consequently, three equally distinct varieties of national character—Romanism in Ireland, Protestant Episcopacy in England, and Presbyterianism in Scotland and in Ulster, or the North of Ireland. Each of these may easily be seen in the varying character of the people.

But in all the diversities of habit and temperament which may be found in Great Britain and Ireland, we can scarcely discover anywhere a greater difference than between the native or aboriginal Irish, and the Scottish Highlanders: and yet they were originally the same people. History shows them both to be Celtic. The writer of this article, just before leaving the old country for Canada, thirty years ago, called on the Rev. Walter McGilvray, of Glasgow, a minister of distinguished reputation as a preacher, both in Gaelic and English. In the course of conversation on missions, Mr. McGilvray mentioned that he had at one time seriously thought of accepting a call which he had to Dublin, that he might become the means of·introducing Highland ministers into Ireland to act as missionaries among the Roman Catholic Irish-speaking population of the West and South. "The Gaelic language," said he, "and the Irish are so much alike, that a preacher who knew Gaelic, could, in three or four weeks easily learn to preach in Irish."

And yet how different now are the Celtic Irishman and the Scottish Highlander, as well in character as in religion. Each is, indeed, of warm and earnest temperament, and each is devotedly attached to the religious system he professes; but the Highlander is among the bluest of Presbyterians, while there is no more zealous and bigoted partisan of Popery than the Irishman. The history of the two countries explains and accounts

---

* The allusion here is to the palace of Tara, the residence of the Supreme Monarch.

for the difference.   The Church of Scotland performed her duty to the brave and hardy mountaineers, but the government and Church of England perpetrated in Ireland an almost unbroken succession of cruelties, crimes, and blunders for centuries, so that Protestantism became in that unhappy country a synonym for oppression, and Popery the symbol of patriotic resistance to innumerable wrongs.   The Protestant clergyman was a tithe-lifter, the priest an angel of consolation.

We live, however, in an age of revolutions.   The changes that have been wrought within the memory of men who are still living are wonderful.   It is but a few years since the Church of Scotland was quietly, by Act of Parliament, delivered from the incubus of patronage, which had century after century produced repeated secessions in that land of martyrs. Ireland has also felt the genial influence of the age.   The oppressive yoke of the established church has been broken, the power of the landlords, by which that yoke had been maintained, has been overthrown, the political disabilities of Irish Roman Catholics have been removed, so that now they stand on a footing of perfect equality with their fellow subjects. Three-fourths of the twelve judges in Ireland were lately Roman Catholics, and one-half of the Board of National Education profess the same creed.   We mention these things as significant facts, without intending to justify the policy of proceeding so far in liberalism.   The accumulated wrongs of seven centuries have been removed, and nothing of the kind now really remains but their bitter recollection.   The system of Romanism still survives, as a bar to improvement and an incentive to disaffection and disturbance ; but the Roman Catholic Irishman has no more real political grievances now than his Protestant fellow subject.   Still Ireland is to England, though from a different cause, what the South is to the American Union.

In such circumstances it becomes a matter of most interesting inquiry : What was the original Christianity of Ireland, and how has she come into her present religious and political condition ?

We propose to enter briefly into these inquiries.   The venerable records of the book of Genesis point to the East as the cradle of the human race.   Greeks, Romans, and northern barbarians may be traced back to oriental sources. The evidence comes partly from languages which indicate a common origin, and partly from traditionary history. The evidence for the eastern origin of the ancient Irish is varied and ample. Julius Cæsar, in his commentaries on the wars, mentions the Celts, or, more properly, the Kelts, as being in his day among the most formidable tribes in Gaul. The Irish language is the best preserved dialect of the ancient Celtic. It is, as we have said, the same as the Gaelic spoken in the Highlands of Scotland. The Irish alphabet is also identical with the Phœnician, which was brought by Cadmus from Phœnicia to Greece. But we can go still further in this direction. In a drama written by the old Latin poet, Plautus, there are twenty-five lines of a foreign tongue, supposed to be spoken by Hanno, a Phœnician, but quite unintelligible to modern scholars, until it was discovered that the words gave a suitable meaning in Irish. This indicates clearly that Ireland was peopled or colonized from Phœnicia, whose inhabitants, we know, were early addicted to sea-faring and colonization. Another remarkable proof is, that the first of May has always been observed in Ireland with great festivity, under the name of Beltine or Bealtine, which means the fire of Baal or Bel, the false god of Phœnicia, so often mentioned in the Old Testament. The sun and moon were worshipped under the names of Bel and Samen, and O'Halloran, in his History of Ireland, says, that the most cordial wish of blessing and courtesy among the Irish peasantry used to be : "The blessing of Samen and Bel be with you!" One of the lines of Plautus, to which reference has been made, is "O! that the good Balsamen may favor them!" Is not this a remarkable coincidence?

No other country in Europe boasts of a longer line o ancient monarchs than Ireland. Martin Haverty's history of that country, published in 1865, goes back one thousand seven hundred years before the Christian era; but there is one melancholy feature of the history, whether true or fabulous, that nearly all the kings died by violence, either in war or by assassination. The early inhabitants were shepherds or agriculturalists. On the tops of hills, which have lain uucultivated as long as the oldest traditions can testify, there are found, at the present day, manifest traces of ancient husbandry. Immense numbers of beautifully wrought golden ornaments have been found buried in Irish bogs. The gold for making these must have been imported in ages of some commerce and refinement. Music was in earlier times much cultivated in that country. The bards were famous for their minstrelsy. Some of the finest Irish melodies are of the greatest antiquity.

The conquest of Great Britain by the Romans neither included the Highlands of Scotland nor extended to Ireland. In the life of Agricola, by Tacitus, mention is made of an invitation from Ireland, by an expelled chieftian of that country, for the Romans to invade and conquer that island. But the Roman eagles were never displayed there. After the Romans left England the Britains were hard pressed by the Picts and Scotts from North Britain; so that they invited the warlike Saxons to come from the continent and aid them, which they did ; but when they had driven back the enemy, they likewise drove off their allies, the British, into Wales and Cornwall. Thus England and the Lowlands of Scotland became Saxon; while the Irish, or, as they called the Scotts, a people of Eastern origin, occupied Ireland and the Highlands of Scotland.

We have now briefly indicated the origin and history of the early inhabitants of Ireland. So much seemed necessary to introduce our special subject.

The time, at which Christianity was first introduced into Ireland is not known with any degree of exactness. That it had made some progress before the time of St. Patrick is admitted by Roman Catholic writers to be "without doubt." Frequent mention is made of four Christian bishops, as laboring among the Irish people before the arrival of St. Patrick. But this is a question of far less importance than the question, whether the great missionary was commissioned by the Church of Rome and subordinated to her authority. To disentangle the real facts of St. Patrick's life from the tissue of fabulous legends with which monkish ingenuity has interwoven them, is extremely difficult; but we shall endeavor to present the leading features of his career as correctly and briefly as possible.

The great Apostle of Ireland, as Patrick has been called,

was born in 387 A. D. This appears from his own writings. Some say that his birth-place was Dunbarton or Kilpatrick, in Scotland. Others, with more probability, say that he was a native of the West of France. The circumstances of his early life agree better with the latter locality. When he was only sixteen years of age he was taken captive by freebooters from Ireland, who had been sent on a marauding expedition by the celebrated King Niall of the Nine Hostages. Patrick was sold into captivity to a chief named Milcho, who dwelt in the county Antrim, near the mouutain of Slieve Mis, now called Slemish. Here he spent six years as a shepherd. He describes the manner of his life at the period in his book— "*Patrick's Confession.*" "My constant business," he says, "was to feed the flocks"; "I was frequent in prayer; the love and fear of God more and more inflamed my heart; my faith was enlarged, and my spirit augmented; so that I said a hundred prayers before day, in the snow, in the frost, in the rain; and yet I received no damage; nor was I affected with slothfulness; for the spirit of God was warm within me."

How simply beautiful and pious is this language! How unlike the superstitious utterances of Romish saint-worship! It bears every mark of genuine faith and Christian piety. Such is the uniform character of St. Patrick's book. There is no special honor to the Virgin Mary, no worship of saints or angels; nothing but simple piety and the love of Jesus. Here is one of the most convincing evidences by which we can ascertain the character of St. Patrick's labors.

At the end of six years he obtained his freedom. His account of the manner of his escape is told in his own words in the *Confession.* "I was warned," he says, "in a dream, to return home; and I arose and betook myself to flight, and left the man with whom I had lived six years." After a month's travelling, he was again seized; and again he escaped after six months' captivity. Within three months more he reached home; but he had a dream, in which he saw a man coming to him, called Victorinus, with a great number of letters. He gave Patrick one to read, which began "Vox Hibernianorum." While he was reading, he heard a voice coming from a neighboring wood, and crying to him: "We entreat thee, holy youth, to come and walk among us."

This dream, whatever may have been its origin, determined him to prepare for the work of the ministry among the Irish. It was not, however, till he was forty-five years of age that he accomplished his purpose. In the mean time little is known of his history. Former missionaries had been driven away from Ireland by the opposition of the Pagan priesthood and by the fierceness of the people. But Patrick, accompanied by more than twenty young men, landed at Dundrum, in the county Down, and was received more favorably. During thirty years he labored in all parts of Ireland with astonishing success; and at the age of seventy-eight, he died near Downpatrick, on the 17th day of March, A. D. 465, at a place called Sabhul, or Saul, full of age and honors. The last work he performed was the writing of his "Confession," a simple, unpretending, Christian document, in which no trace of Romanism appears.

The next person of much note in the ecclesiastical history of Ireland is Columb-kill, the chief leader of the Culdees, and the founder of the so-called monastery of Hy or Iona, in a small island of the same name on the west of Scotland. He was born at Garten, in the county Donegall, in 521, and died in 577. In his days England had been reduced almost to barbarism by the Anglo-Saxon wars. But in the sixth and seventh centuries Ireland was renowned throughout Europe as the home of piety and learning, and the refuge of the persecuted and oppressed. Among the galaxy of eminent men in Ireland, none was more eminent than Columb-kill. The first forty-three years of his life were spent in his native country. Being connected with the royal family of the O'Neills, he was enabled to found many schools or monasteries, among which that of Derry was the most illustrious. The college at Armagh had been founded by St. Patrick, and was in those days attended by thousands of students from all parts of Europe. Roman Catholic writers particularly mention that Columb-kill never consented to be ordained as a prelate. He was content with priest's orders. Is not this a significant fact, showing the system he followed? The learned Selden maintains that the Culdees were strict Presbyterians; and Bede, an English Roman Catholic writer, says, "that they preached only such works of charity as they could learn from the prophetical, evangelical, and apostolic writings," that is, in short, *from the Word of God.*

Civil wars having broken out in Ireland, Columb-kill turned his attention to the conversion of the barbarous Picts in the north of Scotland, now called the Highlands. Colonies of Scotts from the north of Ireland had already settled in that region and established their influence over the Picts. Conall, king of the Irish Scotts in the Highlands, gave Columb-kill, who was his relative, the small island of Iona for the location of his monastery. It was, at that time, occupied by the Druids, whose memorials may still be traced there. Having expelled the Druids, Columb-kill made Iona the headquarters —the Mount Zion of Culdeeism. His missionary operations began in the wild regions of Scotland, north of the Grampian mountains. Brude, the king of that part of the country, was converted, and his people, as was usual in those days, embraced the same faith as their chieftain.

It does not belong to our present design to enter, at any length, into the history of Culdeeism in Scotland and the north of England. It has been our purpose, in this article, merely to show the connection between Ireland and the Culdees; that we may from their principles and practice infer the character and condition of the country from which they emigrated. Culdeeism owed its origin to Ireland, and was an evidence of the pure Christianity that had been established there.

Still, we may be permitted to linger awhile amidst the recollections of that ancient Christian colony planted amidst the isles of Scotland. Iona is one of the few places in the world whose wealth consists entirely in their memorials. The traveller who visits that rocky and barren isle sees no towering remains of gorgeous temples; no classic fragments of marble pillars and statues ; no high-raised mound of mouldering warriors but the rude, spacious church edifice and the humble, now roofless dwellings of those who preached the pure and simple gospel to the poor twelve hundred years ago.

It was no wonder that the learned and pious Dr. Samuel Johnson, knowing, as he did, the sacred recollectious of that hallowed isle, made a pilgrimage from London to Iona in the last century, when there were neither steamboats nor railroad to make the journey commodious. In the following beautiful passage he gives expression to the feelings he experienced in Iona :

" We were now treading that illustrious island which was once the luminary of the Caledonian regions, whence savage clans and roving barbarians derived the benefits of knowledge and the blessings of religion. To abstract the mind from all knowledge would be impossible if it were endeavored, and would be foolish if it were possible. Whatever draws us from the power of the senses, whatever makes the past, the distant, or the future, predominate over the present, advances us in the dignity of thinking beings. Far from me and my friends be such frigid philosophy as may conduct us indifferent or unmoved over any ground which has been dignified by wisdom, bravery, or virtue. That man is little to be envied whose patriotism would not gain force upon the plain of Marathon, or whose piety would not grow warmer among the ruins of Iona."

Johnson was a tory, but his heart was in the right place.

Two reflections are suggested by this concise account of the Early History of Ireland :

1. It is remarkable how truth, though long obscured and hidden, will, on careful examination, shine forth from the very midst of error. The lives of St. Patrick and St. Columb-kill, as written by the monks, are full of absurd fictions ; but the Confessions of Patrick and the grand mission-work of Columb-kill, with the occasional hints of Roman Catholic writers, enable us to discover that they were real men of God—beacon lights amid the darkness. So it is ever with Christ and his Apostles. When we look back into the ages of ancient Christianity we see already the gathering clouds of Papal superstition; but when we come to the age of the Apostles—the age of saints and martyrs—we find in the Apostolic Fathers but little, and in the Scriptures themselves nothing, of Romish corruption. " The Bible, and the Bible alone, is the religion of Protestants," and of the primitive Christian Church.

2. The history of Ireland shows that the influence of Rome has been the bane of that country. It must, indeed, be the ruin of any country in which it gains the ascendancy. In a few centuries after the time of St. Patrick, Ireland was the home of religion and learning. The Bible was taught in her schools, and copied in her monasteries. Thousands of stu-

dents from all parts of Europe crowded to her seminaries of education, and were received with open arms and splendid hospitality. An interesting memorial of all this is still preserved by Prince Ælfrid,[*] of Northumberland, of which we have given, at the head of this article, a rarely beautiful and very exact translation, by James Clarence Mangan.

Art. III.—DALE ON BAPTISM.[†]

By Rev. W. J. Beecher, Professor in Theological Seminary, Auburn, N. Y.

Baptist writers have been accustomed to insist that a word has but a single meaning, which always clings to it, and from which it cannot be dissevered. Upon the application of this claim to *baptizo* they have largely depended. This word, they say, has one signification, and only one, throughout the Greek literature. Their opponents have generally deemed it quite important to dislodge them from this position. They have dealt largely in the instances in which the secondary significations of words have virtually become new significations. They have fortified the position, that even if *immerse* could be proved to be the original and classical meaning of *baptizo*, the word may, nevertheless, in its technical use in describing religious rites, have become independent of that primary meaning. In Dr. Dale's controversial attitude all this is changed.

---

[*] This Ælfrid must not be confounded with Alfred the Great, who reigned more than a century afterward in the south of England.

[†] *Classic Baptism. An Inquiry into the Meaning of the word* $BA\Pi TIZ\Omega$, *as Determined by the Usage of Classical Greek Writers.*

An Inquiry into the Usage of $BA\Pi TIZ\Omega$, *and the Nature of Judaic Baptism, as Shown by Jewish and Patristic Writings.*

An Inquiry into the Usage of $BA\Pi TIZ\Omega$, *and the Nature of Johannic Baptism, as Exhibited in the Holy Scriptures.*

An Inquiry into the Usage of $BA\Pi TIZ\Omega$, *and the Nature of Christic and Patristic Baptism, as Exhibited in the Holy Scriptures and Patristic Writings.* By James W. Dale, D.D., Pastor of Wayne Presb. Church, Delaware Co., Pa. Philadelphia : Wm. Rutter & Co., 1871-74.

Instead of insisting that Baptists adhere too rigidly to the physical signification of the word, hei nsists that they have never been half rigid enough. Instead of asking leave to vary from the generic meaning which they have assigned, he narrows this to the limits of a specific meaning. Instead of complaining that they make the word too scant, he complains that they make it too wide. He claims that it means only a part of what they count it to mean; and that the *other* part is that from which all their conclusions are drawn.

Other controversialists on his side of the question have been accustomed to say, 'A word may have secondary meanings: therefore, our opponents *may be* mistaken ; and the facts show that they *are* mistaken.' Dr. Dale says, 'Our opponents *must be* mistaken, because the primary meaning of the word is so specific as to contradict their conclusions. By it their views are not only not proved, but disproved. Most of the propositions which men on our side of the question are accustomed to hold, as ascertained by induction, may not only be reconciled with the strict meaning of the word, but positively deduced from it.'

Some Baptist writers give *baptizo* a sufficiently broad scope of meaning to make it include the *condition* of being within a receptive element, as well as the *act* of coming within, or putting something within, such an element. Others, in terms, confine it to the act, and deny that it can be used to express the mere condition ; although nearly all of these sometimes use the word in the latter sense, and inconsistently with their own definitions. In other words, some of them say, "dip, and nothing but dip," and others say "dip, or immerse." Against both Dr. Dale sets up the opposing definition, "immerse, or rather, *merse*, as distinguished from dip." The difference he affirms to be radical in two respects. First, dip expresses action, rather than condition ; but merse, condition, rather than action. Secondly, the act of dipping is always brief, quickly terminated, unless the contrary appears from additional statements, or from circumstances ; while the condition of mersion, unless the contrary appears from circumstances, or from additional statements, is not terminated at all, but is permanent. Physical baptism is, in all the extent of this distinction, not dipping, and not dipping or immersion, but mersion, as distinguished from dipping. But Dr. Dale is careful to

explain that he does not employ the word merse as the equivalent of baptize, but only to distinguish the *intusposition* which
constitutes baptism, from all the inconsistent notions with
which his opponents have confounded it.

It absolutely follows that the water used in the rite of baptism cannot possibly be the receptive element within which
the baptized person is placed. If the distinctions just made
are correct, then, in the natural meaning of words, to baptize
one within water, as distinguished from dipping him, would be
to drown him. The *intusposition*, in ritual baptism, must needs
be into something else than the water,—something within
which the baptized person can stay ; and the use of the water
must be for something else than an enveloping element.

This accords with the constructions which ordinarily follow
baptizo. Eis with the accusative, denotes the receptive element
within which that which is baptized is brought by baptism.
The dative, or in Hebraized Greek, *ἐν* with the dative, denotes
some special agency used in the baptism. In purely physical
baptisms the agency may be the same with the receptive
element, or may be different. In other baptisms, the receptive element, expressed by *eis* with the accusative, is the new
condition of character, or of relation to other beings, within
which that which is baptized is placed by the baptism ; while
the agency, expressed by the dative, with or without *ἐν*, may
be either water, fire, Holy Ghost, wine, ashes, stones, tear
drops, blood drops, opiate pills, or something else, according
to the character of the particular baptism in hand ; and may
be used by dipping, pouring, sprinkling, swallowing, or otherwise, according to the circumstances.

Hence, ritual baptism is not the placing of a person within
the water, or fire, or Holy Ghost, or ashes, and taking him out
again, which is contrary to the established meaning of the word
baptize ; but the putting of the person into certain new
conditions or relations, and leaving him there,—this being done
by the appropriate symbolical use of water or other agencies.

Has Dr. Dale succeeded in establishing his position ?

He begins with the question, whether the results heretofore reached by Baptist investigators are so satisfactory as to
preclude the need of further investigation ? This question
he answers in the negative, on merely *prima facie* grounds.

First, these investigators confound the two words, *bapto* and *baptizo*, which is presumptively contrary to the analogies of language. Secondly, to the two words thus confounded, they attribute various and irreconcilable meanings and uses. They define them by "dip, and nothing but dip," plunge, sink, overwhelm, cover by flowing, by rising up, by pouring over, immerse, immerge, submerge, plunge, imbathe, whelm, and a multitude of other incongruous terms, some indicating act, some indicating condition, some changing with juggler-like agility from act to condition, and back again.

Having found these former investigations thus unsatisfactory, Dr. Dale enters upon an independent inquiry. In the following synopsis, the attempt is made to retain the essential substance of his argument, though, for the sake of brevity, an entirely different order of arrangement is adopted.

I. Dr. Dale sustains his opinion, first, from the presumption that the Greek language, having already the word *bapto* to express the act of momentary intusposition, would not gratuitously form another word from the same root for exactly the the same use. This presumption is certainly very strong. Synonyms, and especially those formed by ordinary processes, from the same root, are almost invariably formed for the distinct object of expressing differences as well as resemblances. These differences seldom fade out, because they constitute the very reason of being of the new word. No other differences between words are so persistently maintained. It is extremely improbable, then, at the outset, that the difference between *bapto* and *baptizo* was either originally so slight, or has so vanished from view, as to leave the two words with practically the same use and signification.

Some of the lexicons call *baptizo* the frequentative of *bapto*, and give "to immerse repeatedly" as its primary meaning. This definition Dr. Dale distinctly repudiates. Probably he would not object to designating *baptizo* as the intensive of *bapto*, so dipping its object that it will stay dipped. If his opponents prefer to call it causative, they must still admit that causative and intensive forms, in different languages, are often interchangeable, and may be so in this instance. Make the word *bapto*, therefore, causative-intensive, or intensive-causative, by the formative appendage, *izo*, and you have, as a natural grammatical result, even if it is not a result absolutely inevitable, that *baptizo* should cause its object permanently to assume the condition which, in being *bapted*, it would assume momentarily. Form the derivative in this way, according to the usual analogies, and all vestiges of modal act and of brevity in the act at once vanish. The condition reached by the object becomes the one important fact under consideration. It is no longer of the least consequence how that condition came to be, or whether it will ever cease to be.

II. Dr. Dale further argues from the analogy of the use of two distinct classes of words in various languages. One class, like *bapto*, call attention to the act by which a given condition is secured. The other class, like *baptizo*, call attention to the securing of the condition, without reference to the form of the act by which it is secured. Among the words currently used in the Baptistic controversy, for example, dip, dive, plunge, tingo, etc., belong to the former class; bury, whelm, merse, steep, drench, drown, etc., to the latter class.

Verbs of the first of these two classes differ among themselves in the form of the act they describe. Dip presents a quiet, momentary act; plunge, a violent, momentary act; dive, an act more prolonged. When used intransitively, the motion of the act is performed by the subject of the verb. The *boy* dives. The *oar* dips in the water. The *sailor* plunges overboard. When used transitively, the motion of the act is performed by the object of the verb, "He dips the *oar*." It is still the oar that moves, though oar is now the object of the verb, and no longer its subject. "The pirate plunges the *sailor* overboard." The object that moves is the sailor. In words of this sort, in fine, the differences and changes of meaning belong to the act described. Except through the act, they have no reference to the condition secured by the act. Their primary meaning in the passive voice precisely corresponds to their meaning in the active.

On the other hand, the words of the second of the two classes, differ among themselves in regard to the condition in which the object is placed. The animal immersed in water is simply within the water, and if it happens to be a fish, may enjoy itself there.   The animal whelmed in the water is somewhat under the destructive power of the water, as well as within it.   Drowned in the water, it has come wholly under its destructive power.   When these verbs are used transitively, it makes no difference whether the motion called for be performed by the object of the verb, or by something else.   You bury a seed, either by putting the seed in the earth, or by putting the earth over the seed.   A boat is equally whelmed, whether a whirlpool pulls it under water, or a storm pushes the waves over it.   A potato in a pan of water is equally immersed, whether you first pour in the water, and then drop in the potato, or first put in the potato, and then pour in the water.   A man may be drenched, or drowned, or soaked, indifferently, by moving him into water, or by moving water upon him.   In these words the differences and changes of meaning belong to 'the condition to be secured.   Except through the condition they have no reference to the securing act.   In the active voice, they make demand for some act, but not for one particular form of action rather than another.   In the passive they may even cease to imply any securing act whatever.   A pebble in the lake may be just as much immersed as the knife that fell upon it, though the pebble be thought of as having always been there, and so as never having come there by any act of any kind.   We speak of veins of coal buried in the earth, without bringing into consciousness any idea as to the act of burial—simply having in mind the mere condition of burial.   We may not in the least think how the coal came to be there, or whether it ever came to be there at all.   We only think of the fact of it being in that condition.

Now it is characteristic of words of the first of these two classes, to avoid expressing the continuance of the condition which they initiate.   They either express or suggest its speedy discontinuance, or else refuse to express or suggest anything in regard to it.   When you hear of a thing dipping into water, you expect its instant emergence.   When you hear of a person diving, you expect that he will emerge before long.   When you hear of something plunged into water, you have no expectation at all as to whether it will emerge or not.   In no case does the word itself lead you to a definite expectation that the condi-

tion reached will continue. You may expect that the diver
will stay under water because you know that he is weighted,
but never from the mere fact of his diving.

As the words which express the form of the act by which
a given condition was arrived at, thus refuse to express the
continued condition itself, so do the words which express condition refuse to express either the form of the act by which
the condition was reached, or the discontinuance of the condition itself. To say that a thing is buried, or whelmed, or mersed,
or drenched, or drowned, gives you no information as to the
particular process by which it came so, and awakens no expectation of its ever ceasing to be so. The mode in which the
condition was produced, or the discontinuance of the condition itself, may be suggested by something in connection with
the use of the word, never by the word itself.

Since the word _bapto_ evidently belongs to the first of these
two classes, and is, by the laws of language, confined to the
first, it leaves a clear field for its intensive, _baptizo_, to occupy,
in representing the same line of thought in the second. And
a word of this meaning in the second class is imperatively
needed. Is it credible, therefore, that _baptizo_, if it ever came
into use, should forsake its own proper realm, and usurp that
already occupied by its primitive? And since _baptizo_ is thus
essentially a word which expresses condition rather than the
act by which the condition was arrived at, it is likely to share
the peculiarity of its class in persistently retaining its own
proper character, and refusing to denote a definite act performed in a certain prescribed mode.

III. This position Dr. Dale fortifies by citations from many
of the best Baptist scholars.

On pages 126 and 238 of _Classic Baptism_, Dr. Gale is quoted
as saying, "Besides, the word _baptizo_, perhaps, does not so necessarily express the action of putting under water, as in general, a thing's being in that condition, no matter how it comes
so, whether it is put into the water, or the water comes over it."

On page 56, _Classic Baptism_, Cox is quoted as assuming that
bapto and _baptizo_ are equivalent, and saying of the dew with
which Nebuchadnezzar was _bapted_—Dan. iv: 33—"The verb,
does not imply the _manner_ in which the effect was produced,

but the *effect* itself; not the *mode* by which the body of the king was wetted, but its *condition*."

On page 58, Morell is quoted as saying, that the most usual meaning of *baptizo* is to dip. " But it appears quite evident that the word also bears the sense of *covering by superfusion.* This is admitted by Dr. Cox, who says, 'A person may be immersed by pouring; but immersion is the being plunged into water, or overwhelmed by it. Was the water to ascend from the earth, it would still be baptism, were the person wholly covered by it.' Thus far we surrender the question of immersion, and in doing so, feel no small pleasure in finding ourselves in such good company as that of Dr. Cox."

In *Judaic Baptism*, page 47, the *Religious Herald* is quoted as saying, in its review of *Classic Baptism:* " It is conceded that the Greeks called drunkenness baptism; and in this baptism there was no envelopment. An intoxicated man was baptized by wine. It was not the drinking of wine, nor the operation of it, but the condition—the intoxication resulting from its use—that was called the baptism."

These citations certainly seem to support Dr. Dale's opinion. A baptism is not an act of a certain peculiar form. It is not even, necessarily, an act of any form. It may be a mere condition.

In *Classic Baptism*, page 71, and in numerous other places, Dr. Conant is quoted as conceding that physical baptism does not require any particular form of act, although clinging to the idea that it requires act of some form. " The ground idea expressed by this word is, to put into or under water (or other penetrable substance), so as entirely to immerse or submerge ; that this act is always expressed in the literal application of the word, and is the basis of its metaphorical use."

To the same effect, Ingham, of London, is cited in *Johannic Baptism*, page 46; "Admitting that *bapto* may more exclusively retain the idea of putting any thing *into* another, whilst *baptizo* means to immerse, not only when the object is put into the element, but, as in occasional instances on record, when the element is brought upon and around the object."

To the effect that *baptizo* differs from *bapto* and all like words, in that it leaves its object within the receptive element where it has placed it, our author quotes, on page 45 of *Classic Bap-*

tism, from Dr. Dagg: *"Bapto* more frequently denotes slight or temporary immerson than *baptizo."* "In nearly one-half of the examples in which *baptizo* occurs in the literal sense, it signifies the immersion which attends drowning and the sinking of ships."

On page 95, Dr. Conant is cited as saying: " The idea of emersion is not included in the Greek word. It means simply to put into or under water, without determining whether the object immersed sinks to the bottom, or floats in the liquid, or is immediatly taken out."

In *Judaic Baptism,* p. 25, our author cites from the review of *Classic Baptism* in the *National Baptist,* to the effect, that "he," Dr. Dale, "has established a difference in use between *bapto* and *baptizo.* His *statement* of that difference seems to us defective, but that there is a difference is evident. He has, also, brought clearly out, what our own examination had before proved, that the word *baptizo* does not of itself involve the lifting out from the fluid of that which is put in."

On page 49, he quotes Dr. Kendrick: *"Baptizo* became naturally applied ordinarily to immersions of a more formal and longer character, while *bapto* ordinarily denoted the lighter and shorter." "Granted that *bapto always* engages to take its subject out of the water (which we do not believe), and that *baptizo never* does engage to take its subject out of the water (which we readily admit). We let *baptizo* take us into the water, and can trust to men's instinctive love of life, their common sense, their power of volition and normal *muscular* action, to bring them safely out."

On page 90, several short quotations are given from Carson, as follows. " The classical meaning of the word is in no instance *overwhelm."* When drunkenness is called baptism, "Literally, it is *immersed in* wine." Yet " There is no likeness between the *action* of drinking and immersion." " The likeness is between their effects." "Between a man completely under the influence of wine, and an object completely subjected to a liquid, in which it is wholly immersed."

Passages like these certainly leave Dr. Dale very little to desire in the way of concessions. There is no great room for difference between him and his opponents, except in regard to the true bearing of the conceded facts.

IV. But the most important argument, of course, is **that** from usage. In Classic Baptism, our author cites one hundred and thirteen passages in which *baptizo* is used. On page **135** he says of these, "Every passage of what may be termed *Classical Greek* (liberally interpreted) which I have met with, either as the fruit of my own direct examination, or that of others, has been adduced. The period embraced within these quotations is about one thousand years." · The subsequent volumes give lists equally exhaustive from the writers of Hebraized Greek, and full extracts from the Patristic writers

Of these instances, this article will now present those which must, of necessity, control the whole argument, namely, those in which *baptizo* is followed by *εἰς* with the accusative, or by the dative with or without *ἐν*. The design is, within this limit, to give all the instances which Dr. Dale cites as classic, all the instances which he cites from the Jewish writers of Greek and from the New Testament and a sufficient number from the Christian fathers. For the translations Dr. Dale is mainly responsible, except in the cases of the italicized words, and of the New Testament passages. The passages not designated are from the classic Greek lists of the volume on Classic Baptism.

In the following list *baptizo* is followed by *εἰς* with the accusative, and by no dative. Three exceptional instances are deferred to a subsequent list. *Into* is uniformly given as the translation of *εἰς*. Notice, that in every instance the accusative following *εἰς* describes the receptive element within which the person or thing baptized is placed by its baptism. In all the cases of ritual baptism, and in many of the others, this receptive element is a new condition or relation, and not water or any other physical element. Notice, also, that in absolutely every case, the baptizing leaves that which is baptized within the element, and in nearly every case, with a positive certainty that it will remain there for some prolonged period of time.

"I found Cupid among the roses, and holding him by the wings, I *baptized* him *into* the wine, and took and drank him."

"But when the Sun had *baptized himself into* the ocean flood,"

. "They *baptize*, therefore, a pole *into* the water."

"*Baptizing* others *into* the lake."

"Nobly *baptizing himself into* the lake Copais."

These two are cases of drowning.

"Then dipping into oil" "apply it during the day, and, as soon as it stings, take it away, and *baptize* it, again, *into* woman's milk."

"He gathered the shields of the slain foe, and, having *baptized* his hand *into* the blood, he reared a trophy and wrote upon it."

"The water is incrusted so easily about every thing *baptized into* it, that they draw up crowns of salt, when they let down a rush circle."

"And stretching out his right hand, so as to escape notice by none, he *baptized* the entire sword *into* his throat."—*Josephus, Jewish Wars*, ii : 18.

"And *baptized* by (ὑπο) drunkenness *into* insensibility and sleep."—*Josephus, Ant.* x : 9.

Symmachus translates Psalm lxix : 2.—("I sink in deep mire, where there is no standing")—"I am *baptized into* boundless depths, and there is no standing."

The Septuagint translates Isaiah xxi : 4.—"My heart wanders ; iniquity *baptizes* me ; my soul is put *into* fear."

"And preaching a *baptism* of repentance *into* remission of sins."—*Mark* i : 4 ; *Luke* iii : 3.

"But he said to them, *into* what then were ye *baptized*? But they said *into* the baptism of John."—*Acts* xix : 3.

"But hearing, they were *baptized into* the name of the Lord Jesus."—*Acts* xix : 5.

"Know ye not that as many of us as were *baptized into* Jesus Christ, were *baptized into* his death?"—*Rom.* vi : 3.

"Therefore, we were buried with him through the *baptism into* the death."—*Rom.* vi : 4.

"Repent ye, and let every one of you be *baptized* upon the name of Jesus Christ *into* remission of sins."—*Acts* ii : 38.

"Only they were *baptized into* the name of the Lord Jesus."—*Acts* viii : 16.

"Or were ye *baptized into* the name of Paul?"—1 *Cor.* i : 13.

"*Baptizing* them *into* the name of the Father, and of the Son, and of the Holy Ghost."—*Matt.* xxviii : 19.

"For as many of you as were *baptized into* Christ, put on Christ."—*Gal.* iii : 27.

Speaking of John the Baptist, comparing his own water

baptism with that of the Holy Ghost and of fire, Basil the Great says (ii : 341): " Since then the Lord conjoined both that from (ἐν) water *into* repentance, and that from the Spirit *into* regeneration, the Scripture, also, foreshadows both these *baptisms*."

Clemens Alex. says (ii : 1212): "They *baptize* out of chastity *into* fornication, teaching to indulge in pleasures and passions."

Most of these instances, and perhaps all, so far imply modal act, that what is baptized is represented as moved into the receptive element. This suggests that there may be some limits within which *baptizo*, either by its own force, or by that of its combinations with other words, calls for some kind of act ; and that the current claim of Baptist writers to this effect may, within these limits, be established. That no such force, however, is regularly and necessarily inherent in the word itself, will sufficiently appear as we advance.

Before giving the instances in which *baptizo* is followed by the dative, we cite a few, taken at random from among many, in which the word may be said to be absolutely used. This article has already noticed the conceded fact, that a Greek was often said to be baptized, with the meaning that he was drunk. It is similarly conceded that one was said to be baptized, with the meaning that he was bewildered, or senseless, or helpless, or destroyed, or otherwise in a ruinous condition ; and that cities and other things were said to be baptized when they were badly damaged or ruined. In most of these instances, the primary physical meaning of the word can doubtless be traced in some form, and its adjuncts supplied. But to all practical purposes, its use was evidently absolute, and without any thought of the adjunct. All this is conceded, but the cases of this kind throw so much light on those in which the dative is employed, that it is desirable to examine a few of them, for the sake of distinctness of impression. Notice, also, that these instances are all such as imply permanence of condition, and that they are such as call for various forms of modal act.

The following passage is from Achilles Tatius : " For what is sudden, all at once and unexpected, astounds the soul, falling on it unawares, and has *catabaptized* it." The soul is here said to be catabaptized, not by being put into something sudden, but by having something sudden fall upon it. It would doubtless be possible to complete the regimen by saying catabaptized *into* amazement. But this is unnecessary. The sense is sufficiently complete if we call the use of the word virtually absolute. The soul is simply said to be *catabaptized*, that is, bewildered.

"If I purpose to see all the rivers, my life will be *catabaptized*, not seeing Glycera." That is, if the love-sick fellow shall be absent from Glycera long enough to see all the rivers, his life will *be made thoroughly miserable.*

"Misfortunes befalling *baptize* us"—that is, ruin us, or tend to ruin us.

"This is he, who, having found the miserable Cimon *baptized* (distressed) and forsaken, did not overlook him."

"One heavy-headed and *baptized*"—that is, drunk.

"I myself am of those who, yesterday, were *baptized*"—that is, drunk.

"A lofty billow, rising above, baptized them" (*Jos., Jewish Wars,* iii: 9); that is, destroyed the vessels by sinking them. Here are two modal acts. The vessels are poured upon by the baptising agency, the billow, and are moved into the receptive element, the sea. But the thing prominently meant is, that the ships were destroyed in the storm. And one might sufficiently catch this meaning without at all attending to either of the modal acts by which the destruction was effected.

This appears yet more distinctly in our next example. "Already being *baptized* and ready to go down, some of the pirates at first attempted to pass into their own boat." Here the pirates are said to be baptized when they and their ship are ruined, and before either sink into the water.

"Who, independently of the sedition, afterward *baptized* the city.—(*Jos. Jewish Wars,* iv: 3)—that is, *ruined the city by famine.*

There are dozens of similar instances. It is possible, of course, to trace the primitive meaning of *baptizo* through them all, and so classify each, under some long name, as an instance of some sort of rhetorical figure. But as a matter of fact, people who spoke Greek went through no such process when they said of a person or thing that was drunk, or drowned, or destroyed, or ruined, or badly injured, or bewildered, or miserable, that he or it was baptized.

Dr. Dale admits that the classic dative, following ἐν, may, like εἰς, with the accusative, denote the receptive element of a baptism. He claims however, that the classic dative without ἐν, and the Hebraic dative with or without ἐν, regularly denote, not receptive element, but agency or instrument. He cites some instances where this is certainly the case, even when the thing denoted by the dative is water or other penetrable substance, which might, in other circumstances, be used as the enveloping element. And if this is sometimes so, even in physical baptism, much more may it be usually so in ritual baptism.

But when we bring all the instances together, and examine them in detail, we find that, without an exception that is properly such, the dative after *baptizo*, classic or Hebraic, with or without ἐν, denotes something that might be conceived of as enveloping that which is baptized. With equal uniformity, it denotes agency, rather than envelopment, in the case actually in hand. In no case, probably, does it denote the receptive element as such; although, in some cases, the receptive element is the same with the baptizing agency.

We begin with the most numerous class of instances—those in which the classic dative occurs without ἐν. *By* is used, in every instance, as the sign of the dative.

"And dying, they filled the lake with dead bodies; so that to the present many barbaric arrows, and helmets, and pieces of iron breastplates, and swords, *embaptized by* the marshes, are found." The marshes are something that might conceivably envelop the armor of the men who perished in them. One might try the experiment of governing the dative here by ἐν understood, and translating, "embaptized in the marshes," making the passage mean that the old pieces of armor were found sunk in the mud and water of the marshes, and covered by them. This makes good sense, and doubtless comes very near the true sense of the passage. But it gives a still better meaning in this case, and a meaning imperatively required, as we shall see, by the analogy of the succeeding instances, to count the dative as denoting agency, and translate "embaptized by the marshes." The marshes are spoken of as that which embaptizes the old armor; whether *into* their own mud and water where it was found, or into the ruinous condition in which it

was found, or into yet some other physical or ideal receptive
element, is not stated.

"Although the spear should fall out into the sea, it is not
lost; for it is constructed out of both oak and pine, so that the
oaken part being *baptized by* weight, the rest is floating and
easily recovered." Weight might conceivably be spoken of as
a quality enveloping its substance; but is here actually spoken
of, not as enveloping it, but as an agency baptizing it into
something else, namely, the sea, as an enveloping element.

"They have the soul very much *baptized by* the body, and
therefore the seminal element, partaking in the highest degree
of the rational and physical power, makes its offspring more
intelligent." The body may be conceived of as enveloping the
soul. Evidently, however, it is here represented, not as enveloping the soul, but as acting upon it, baptizing it into something else as an enveloping element, namely, into the condition
of being able to transmit its qualities to posterity.

"Shall I not ridicule one *baptizing* his ship *by* much freight,
the blaming the sea for sinking it full?" It is entirely possible to form a mental picture of freight so piled on and around
a ship as literally to inclose it. But that is not at all the picture presented here. The freight is agency, and baptizes the
ship into something else, namely, into the sea, or into ruin, as
the enveloping element.

"The others, *baptizing* the attacking ships *by* stones and
engines from above." Not enclosing them within a covering
of stones and other missiles shot from engines, although this is
a conceivable notion; but baptizing them *by* the missiles—
into the sea, perhaps, that is, sinking them—or, perhaps, into
ruin; or, using the words absolutely, simply baptizing them,
that is, ruining them.

In these five instances, notice how perfectly unessential is
the mode of the use of the baptizing agency. The marshes
baptize the armor by envelopment, or, perhaps, by corrosion.
The weight baptizes the spear by pulling it down. The body
baptizes the soul by interpenetration. The man baptizes his
ship by freight, by loading the freight on. The defenders
baptize their assailants by missiles, by shooting.

Substantially the same comments apply to all the following
instances:

"But I, *baptizing* you *by* sea waves, will destroy with bitterer billows."

To make a pickle, "*baptize* many *by* strong brine, after dipping in boiling water."

"To be *baptized by* such a multitude of evils."

Love contending with anger in the same bosom, "*baptized by* anger, is subdued."

Of Æsop's fox, it is said, "*baptizing* tow *by* oil, binding it to her tail, he set it on fire."

"On account of the abundant revenue from these sources, they do not *baptize* the people *by* taxes."

"Cnemon, perceiving that he was deeply grieved and *baptized by* the calamity, and fearing lest he may do himself some injury, removes the sword privately."

"When midnight had *baptized* the city *by* sleep."

"But let us not be *sumbaptized*, (*co-baptized*) *by* this grief of his, nor be, unobservantly, carried away by his tears, as by torrents."

The running away of the bakers would be a great calamity, "*by* which the city would, immediately, be *baptized*, just as a ship, the sailors having deserted it."

"*Baptized by* diseases and by arts of wizards."

"Knowing him to be licentious and extravagant, and *baptized by* debts of fifty millions."

One should be cautious against overtasking studious children, "For as plants are nourished by water, in measure, but are choked by excess, after the same manner the soul grows by labors, in measure, but is *baptized by* those which are excessive."

"The Io-Bacchus, *baptized by* much wantonness, was sung in feasts and sacrifices of Bacchus."

"Whom having *catabaptized* (thoroughly baptized) *by* the same drug," is spoken of Satyrus, drugging the chamber servant of Leucippe into a stupid sleep.

To be drunk is to be "*baptized by* unmixed wine."

"Thebe exhorted to the murder, and having *baptized* and put to sleep Alexander, *by* much wine, she dismisses the guards of the bed-chamber under pretext of using the bath, and called the brothers to their work."

"Bacchus" " *baptizes by* sleep, the neighbor of death."

"Since, now, a mass of iron pervaded with fire, drawn out of the furnace, is *baptized by* water, and the heat, by its own nature quenched by water, ceases."

"You would not have seen a shield, or a helmet, or a long pike; but the soldiers *by* bowls and cups and flagons, along the whole way *baptizing*, out of large wine jars and mixing vessels pledged one another."

Didymus Alexandrinus (692) says, "*Baptism* is effected *by* every water, indiscriminately."

Clemens Alexandrinus (ii: 649) says of the repentant captain of a band of robbers, who had formerly been a disciple of the apostle John, " He wept bitterly", "being *baptized* a second time *by* the tears."

Gregory Thaumaturgus (x : 1188) records the prayer, "*Baptize* me who am about to baptize them that believe, through (διὰ with genitive) water and spirit and fire ; *by* water, possessing power to wash away the filth of sins ; *by* spirit, possessing power to make the earthly spiritual, *by* fire, possessing a nature to burn up the thorns of transgressions."

Justin Martyr says that Christ, "through being crucified," "redeemed us who were *baptized by* the most heavy sins which we had committed."

Clemens Alexandrinus says (i : 57): " The man who is *baptized by* ignorance is more stupid than a stone."

The following from Philo, as cited by Eusebius, is perhaps the only instance in a properly Judaic Greek author in which the dative without ἐν is used in regimen after *baptizo ;* except, of course, the instances hereafter to be cited, where it is used in company with certain other adjuncts. Speaking of the evils of gluttony, Philo says, " The sober and content are more intelligent, but those always filled with drink and food are least intelligent, as though the reason were *baptized by* the things coming upon it."

The dative with ἐν after *baptizo* is nearly as rare in classic and patristic Greek, as is the dative without ἐν in the Greek written by Jewish authors. This goes very far toward proving that there is no difference between the Hebraized dative with ἐν, and the classic dative without. And an examination of the instances now to be given, will show that the presence or absence of the preposition between *baptizo* and its dative makes no important difference, even in classic Greek.   Perhaps the true explanation may be, that ἐν never occurs in this position in a properly classic passage, all the instances being the result of real, though indirect, Hebraistic influence.

Origen, iv: 280, says of Elijah, " Having taken his mantle and wrapped it together, he smote the water, which divided hither and thither, and they both passed through ; to wit, he and Elisha ; for he is made more fitted to be taken up, having *baptized himself* ἐν the Jordan, seeing that Paul called, as we have before shown, a more wonderful passage through the water baptism."   He evidently means that Elijah was in some sense baptized *by* the Jordan, but certainly not within its water as an enveloping element.

Alexander, the Aphrodisian, accounts for the stupidity of brutes, " Because they have their nature and perceptive power *baptized* ἐν the depth of the body."

Plotinus says of the soul, that "death to her, even yet *baptized* ἐν the body, is to sink in matter, and to be filled of it."

Chariton says, " I saw a vessel wandering in pleasant weather, full of its own storm, and *baptized* ἐν calm."

In these three instances, Dr. Dale admits that the dative following ἐν designates the receptive element. Yet surely it does not, even here, designate the receptive element as such.   It is not being inclosed within a body that renders a soul brutish or dead, but being affected by the inclosing body.   Our attention is not so much called to the fact that the vessel is surrounded by calm, as to the fact that it is affected by the surrounding calm.   Even these instances are no exceptions to the law, that the dative after *baptizo*, with or without ἐν, expresses agency rather than receptive element, though in these, as in some other instances, the agency and the receptive element happen to coincide.

All this is strongly confirmed by the following passages, where the datives with ἐν are used interchangeably with those without.

" John indeed *baptized by* water, but ye shall be *baptized* ἐν Holy Ghost not many days hence."—Acts i : 5.

" I indeed *baptize* you *by* water," " he shall *baptize* you ἐν Holy Ghost and fire."—Luke iii : 16.

Cyril, of Alexandria, says, " We have been *baptized*, not *ἐν* bare water, nor yet *by* the ashes of a heifer."

Origen says, " Christ, therefore, did not *baptize ἐν* water, but his disciples.   He reserves to himself the *baptizing by* Holy Spirit and fire."

And if the dative with *ἐν* after *baptizo* differs so little from the pure dative, and always expresses agency rather than en- velopment, even in authors whose style is comparatively near that of the classic Greek, much more may we expect the same thing in the more Hebraic Greek of Josephus and Matthew.

Josephus says, (*Jewish War*, i : 22) describing the murder of Aristobulus : " And then, being *baptized ἐν pool* by the Gala- tians, according to command, he died," There is no article before pool.   He was baptized, not *ἐν the pool*, but *ἐν pool*. The idea is not that he was baptized *into* the pool and left there.   The context shows that he was not.   The statement is, that they baptized him absolutely ; that is, destroyed him ; or, if you please, baptized him into death, using the pool as the destroying agency.   It happens that we know that the agency was used in this case, by repeatedly ducking the head of the swimming boy under water. This we know, however, from the context, and not from the words themselves.   And if, in this instance, where we know that there was actual inclosure within the substance denoted by the dative, the dative thus denotes the instrument by which the baptism was performed, rather than the element into which the baptized person was introduced, much more is the same likely to be true in other cases, where we have no such knowledge.

Aquila translates Job ix : 31, " Even then thou wilt *bap- tize* me *ἐν* pollution."

The Septuagint translates 2 Kings v : 14, " And went down Naaman, and *baptized himself ἐν* the Jordan seven times, ac- cording to the word of Elisha."   The article here has no ef- fect on the syntax.   The translator simply follows the Hebrew usage, which regularly prefixes the article to this particular proper name.   For the rest, the natural meaning is that he baptized himself, that is, performed whatever lustrations were appropriate in the circumstances, *by the aid of* the Jordan as agency or instrumentality.   This would still remain true, even if we should admit a thing of which there is no sufficient evidence, namely, that he performed the baptism by immersing himself within the water of the river. Even in that case, the Greek still calls attention to the fact, that he baptized himself by using the river, and not to his putting himself within the river. If the translator had desired to say that Naaman baptized himself *into* the Jordan, he could easily have said it.

The remaining instances of ἐν with the dative are all instances of New Testament baptisms, and are as follows:

" He shall *baptize* you ἐν Holy Ghost and fire."—Mat. iii : 11.

"I, indeed, *baptized* you ἐν water, but he shall *baptize* you ἐν Holy Ghost."—Mark i : 8.

"I, indeed, *baptize* ἐν water."—John i : 26.

" I came *baptizing* ἐν water," or, according to some copies, ἐν the water."—John i : 31.

"And were *baptized* of him ἐν the Jordan, confessing their sins."—Mark i : 5.

" He who sent me to *baptize* εν water, the same said unto me," "He is the one *baptizing* ἐν Holy Ghost."—John i : 33.

"And he commanded them to be *baptized* ἐν the name of the Lord."—Acts x : 48.

This is the only instance of baptism "ἐν the name." Elsewhere it is uniformly "*into*" or "*upon* " the name.

That the distinction thus insisted upon between εἰς with the accusative, and the dative with or without ἐν, following *baptizo*, is not imaginary, is further confirmed by the following instances where the two constructions are employed together.

"And were all *baptized into* Moses, ἐν the cloud and εν the sea."—1 Cor. x : 2.

Origen says, and substantially many times repeats it : "Paul might say of this, I do not wish you, brethren, to be ignorant that all our fathers passed over through the Jordan, and were all *baptized into* Jesus (Joshua) ἐν the spirit and river."—iv: 277.

" Wherefore, though they were all *baptized into* Moses, by the cloud and the sea, their baptism has something bitter and unpleasant, because still fearing their enemies." "But the *baptism into* Jesus, ἐν the truly sweet and potable river, has many choice things above that." "For ἐν the *baptism into* Jesus, we know that the living God is in us. And the Lord acknowledges the reproach of Egypt to be taken away in the day of the *baptism into* Jesus, when Jesus thoroughly purified the children of Israel."

"I indeed *baptize* you ἐν water *into* repentance."—Matt. iii: 11.

"For also ἐν one Spirit, we were all *baptized into* one body."—1 Cor. xii: 13.

Can anything possibly be clearer than this difference of regimen? If baptism is immersion, then these baptized persons are said to be immersed into Moses, into repentance, into one body, into Joshua. Certain special agencies are also designated ἐν the use of which these immersions are effected. These agencies are the cloud and the sea in the first instance, water in the second, one spirit in the third, and the "truly sweet and potable river," Jordan, in the fourth. This last instance is particularly noticeable. Origen does not say that the children of Israel were baptized ἐν the *dry bed* of the Jordan. He does not even leave this open for inference. He expressly says that in their crossing the dry bed of the river, they were baptized ἐν the "sweet and potable river" itself. The modal use of the baptizing agency, in this instance, is characterized, not by its covering the baptized persons, but by it being restrained from covering them. The water is here distinctly made to baptize by positive *non*-immersion, and not by immersion. This is worthy the attention of those who so strenuously insist, on the strength of this same preposition ἐν following *baptizo*, that Naaman and John's disciples must have been physically submerged under the waters of the same Jordan.

These two forms of regimen, that with εἰς and that with ἐν might be made to follow *baptizo* in nearly or quite every instance in which it occurs. And in every such instance, correctly constructed, the distinction which has just been made will be found to hold. The accusative preceded by εἰς always denotes the receptive element. The dative, with or without ἐν always denotes instrumentality. It is peculiar instrumentality, indeed. It ordinarily differs from that denoted by the prepositions δια and ὑπο in that its nature is such that it might conceivably become enveloping element. It also usually differs from other forms of instrumentality, in that some portion of its own substance is used up with every baptism effected.

The things named in the dative are such things as water, fire, blood, missiles, and not such as the hand, a cup, a hyssop branch. But to this instrumental construction the dative after *baptizo* is rigidly confined. It never departs from it, and, consequently, never denotes the covering element as such, though, as we have seen, the covering element and the instrumental agency may, in some cases, be the same substance.

There are a few apparent (though not real) exceptions.

In the following two instances, ἐν is evidently not in special regimen after *baptizo*, but indicates mere general relation of locality.

Judith "went out nightly into the valley of Bethulia, and *baptized herself* ἐν the camp, upon the fountain of water."

"John was *baptizing* ἐν the wilderness."—Mark i: 4.

Probably the same construction most naturally explains John iii: 23, "John was also baptizing ἐν Ænon near to Salim;" and many scholars will prefer to give this construction to some of the examples cited above as instances of the ordinary regimen. Instances of this sort, of course, have no special weight on either side of the main question now under discussiom.

In the following three instances εἰς apparently indicates mere locality, instead of having its ordinary force. Perhaps, in each case the preposition properly following a verb understood, and does not really follow *baptizo*. In the first instance, it is claimed to be known that baptism was performed on the sea shore, and not within the sea.

"Call the purifying Old Woman, and *baptize thyself at* (εἰς) the sea, and remain all day sitting on the ground." Or, "[Going] *unto* the sea, baptize thyself."

"Those, therefore, defiled by a dead body, introducing a little of the ashes and hyssop-branch into a spring, and *baptizing* of this ashes (introduced) *into* the spring, they sprinkled both on the third and seventh of the days."

"Jesus came from Nazareth of Galilee, and was *baptized* of John *at* (εἰς) the Jordan."—Mark i: 9. That is, having entered *into* the Jordan region, he was baptized. If this passage stood by itself, it would be naturally translated, "baptized into" the Jordan, immersed within the water of the river. One could not object, in this instance, that Jesus would have been drowned by such a baptism, for the context, (on the supposition that he was within the water), immediately takes him out of it. It this translation of the present passage were countenanced by even any diversity of usage in other passages, it might be plausibly defended. But it is not. In absolutely every other in-

tance of ritual baptism, the element introduced by ɛἰς is ideal
and not physical. If the contrary is true here, it is true in direct
contradiction to an extended usage which is elsewhere strictly
uniform. It is much easier to suppose that here is a case of
elliptical expression. Strictly parallel expressions are common.
See, for instance, John x: 40; "And he went away again beyond Jordan, *into* the place *where* John at first *baptized*."

We have thus traversed a definite class of the instances in
which the Greek word *baptizo* occurs. The field traversed in
the volumes of Dr. Dale is much more extensive. The results
from every part agree. Baptism, by the *usus loquendi* of
the word, is never mere dipping, but always unlimited intusposition. It is entirely indifferent as to the form of the act by
which the intusposition is secured, whether by plunging, sinking, pouring, dripping, absorption, or some other. *Baptizo* is
regularly followed by ɛἰς with the accusative of that into which
the baptized object is intusposed, and by the dative, with or
without ἐν, of a certain peculiar instrumentality by which the
intusposition is effected. In physical baptisms, this instrument
tality used for effecting the intusposition may be the same as
the element into which the intusposition is effected, but is oftener
different. In ritual and spiritual baptisms the element into
which the intusposition is effected is always ideal, never physical, and always differs from the special instrumentality which
effects the intusposition.

If the mode of effecting the intusposition is indifferent, of yet
less consequence is the mode of using the special instrumentality, when the latter differs from the receptive element. If
it were granted that the baptizing of a person is the immersing
him into certain new conditions or relations, and that this must
always be done by a certain modal act,—namely, the moving of
him from a position without those relations to a position within them—it would not at all follow that the water, or Holy Ghost,
or other special instrumentality used in so moving him, must
needs go through the same forms of motion. Even if the mode
of intusposition were important, the mode of using the special
instrumentality by which the intusposition was effected might
be altogether unimportant.

According to the New Testament, the believer is baptized
by the Holy Ghost *into* Christ, and *by* water *into* visible rela-

tions with Christ. It is of no consequence under what form we
conceive of the intusposition into Christ as taking place; whether
by the believer's moving to Christ and entering him, or by
Christ's coming to the believer and surrounding him, or in some
other form of conception. No matter what the form, it is still
baptism into Christ, or, the terms being changed, baptism into
outward relations with Christ. Of yet less consequence is it
by what form of act the Holy Ghost or the water effect these
baptisms.

V. A fifth line of argument in Dr. Dale's volumes is found
in his analysis of the patristic use of the words that describe
baptism.

The doctrine and practice of the Christian fathers, in the matter
of baptism, is one thing, and their use of language, in describing their doctrine and practice, quite another thing. And since
they were better linguists than theologians, the argument from
their use of language is much stronger than that from their opinions and customs.

Most of these writers practiced baptism by immersion, in
ordinary cases. Many of them doubted whether baptism by
any other form was valid, or, at best, equally valid with that
in the form usually practiced. They held that water has been
medicated by the brooding of the Holy Ghost upon it at the
creation, or by the baptism of Jesus in it, or both, so that it
has a drug-like quality, in virtue of which it washes away sin.

They baptized men and women naked, since it was their
persons and not their clothes that needed to have the sin washed
out of them. Many of them immersed the candidate thrice in
commemoration of the Trinity, or of the three days which
Christ lay in the grave. Many of them, in baptizing, used salt
and oil and spittle, and practiced cauterization and other
superstitious additions to the rite.

Their doctrine and usage, then, were confessedly very corrupt, and cannot have great weight in determining what our
doctrine and usage should be. But this does not change the
fact that they spoke and wrote either Greek, or Latin full of
Greek technical terms. We may resort to their writings to
find the meanings of words. And if we find that their *usus
loquendi* differs from what their practices would lead us to ex-

pect, then their errors of practice may even strengthen, rather than weaken, our argument from their use of words.

Now it is remarkable that these men, although they baptized by immersion in water, do not currently speak of baptism as being immersion in water. According to their uniform ordinary use of language, Christian baptism is the passing into a condition of healing from sin, and other baptisms consist in other analogous changes of condition or character. Their baptism was not immersion in water, although, as a matter of fact, it was usually *by* immersion in water.

The Greek and Latin passages in which this usage appears, would fill a good sized volume. A few specimens must suffice.

Baptism was accounted a thorough change of character. In Basil the Great (iii : 736) is the following question and answer :

"What is the purport and power of baptism?"

"The baptized is thoroughly changed as to thought, and word, and deed, and becomes, according to the power bestowed, the same as that by which he was born."

The result of baptism was supposed to be accomplished by a medicinal quality supernaturally imparted to the waters. Ambrose (iii : 627) says, "Perhaps some one may say, 'Why did he who was holy wish to be baptized?' Hear then : Christ was therefore baptized, not that he might be sanctified by the waters, but that he might sanctify the waters, and by his own purity purify the stream which he touches; for the consecration of Christ is a greater consecration of the element. For when the Saviour is washed (*abluitur*) the whole water is cleansed (*mundatur*) for our baptism, and the fountain is purified (*purificatur*), that the grace of the washing may be supplied to the people coming after."

Tertullian (ii : 615) says, "Christ having been baptized, that is, sanctifying (*sanctificante*) the waters by his baptism."

Ignatius says, (660) "Jesus Christ was born and baptized, that he might purify the water by his passion."

Jerome (ii : 161) says, "How is the soul, which has not the Holy Spirit, purged from old defilements? For water does not wash the soul, unless it is first washed by the Holy Spirit, that it may be able spiritually to wash others. 'The Spirit of the Lord,' says Moses, 'was borne above the waters.' From which it appears that baptism is not without the Holy Spirit."

Dïdymus Alexandrinus (692) says, "Accordingly the Holy Spirit by his movement upon the waters, appears from that time to have sanctified them, and made them life-giving. For it is evident to every one, that what overlies imparts of its own quality to that which underlies, and all underlying matter is accustomed to take of the peculiarity of that which overlies. Whence baptism belongs to all water indiscriminately, in necessity, as waters are of one nature, and all are sanctified."

Tertullian (iii: 1082) argues, that there can be no baptism except within the Catholic church. "It is necessary, also, that the water be purified and sanctified first by the priest, that it may be able, *by its own baptism*, to cleanse the sins of the baptized man."

Clement of Alexandria (i: 285) declares, that "sins are remitted by one perfect drug ($\varphi\alpha\rho\mu\alpha\kappa\varphi$), spiritual baptism."

In all this, notice, it is not at all the immersion in the water that is spoken of as constituting the baptism; but the being brought by the medicinal power of the water into a state of healing from sin. Many times over, a person is said to be baptized by water, and in the same breath the water itself is said to be baptized by the brooding of the Spirit, or the descent of Jesus into Jordan, or the priestly character of the officiating minister. Evidently, the baptizing of the water was not thought of as the immersing it into the priestly character, or into the descent of Jesus, or into the brooding of the Spirit; but as the bringing it, through these agencies, into the possession of a sin-remitting power which it did not otherwise possess. So the baptizing of a person was not thought of as the immersing him in water, but as the bringing him, through the agency of the water, into the new condition of remitted sin.

This usage is confirmed by the following passages, in which tears or blood or suffering, without any idea of envelopment within either, take the place of water as the baptizing agency.

Tertullian (i: 1217) says, "We have a second washing, one and the same, to wit, of blood. These two baptisms he shed forth from the wound of his pierced side. It is this baptism which takes the place of the washing of water when it has not been received, and restores it when it has been lost." "Martyrdom will be another baptism."

Cyprian (iii : 1123) speaks of "martyrdom, when one confesses Christ before men, and is baptized by his own blood. And yet not even this baptism profits the heretic. The baptism of a public confession and of blood cannot profit a heretic unto salvation."

Origen (ii : 980) says, "It is the baptism of blood only which makes us more pure than the baptism of water. The Lord says: 'I have a baptism to be baptized with, and how am I straitened until it be accomplished?' You see that he called the pouring out of his blood, baptism." "By the baptism of water, past sins are remitted; by the baptism of blood, future sins are prevented." "If God should grant unto me that I might be washed by my own blood, that I might receive this second baptism, enduring death for Christ, I would go safe out of this world."

Augustine (ix : 276): "Petilianus says, The Saviour having been baptized by John, declared that he must be baptized again; not now by water or spirit, but by the baptism of blood, by the cross of his passion." "Blush, O persecutors! ye make martyrs like to Christ, whom, after the water of true baptism, baptizing blood sprinkles."

Jerome (iv : 35) represents the Saviour as declaring that, "instead of ancient victims, and incense, and new moons," and so forth; "the religion of the Gospel pleases me; that ye should be baptized by my blood, by the washing of regeneration, which alone can remit sin."

Clemens Romanus (837) says, of the unbaptized martyr, "Let him die without sorrow, for the suffering which is for Christ will be to him a truer baptism."

Jerome (v : 730) says, "Hear the Saviour in two passages, indicating the need of fire and knife. In one place, he says, 'I have not come to send peace upon earth, but a sword;' and in another, 'I am come to send fire upon the earth.' Therefore, the Saviour brings fire and sword, and baptizes those sins which could not be purified by the purification of the Holy Spirit."

Athanasius (iv : 644) says, "God has granted to the nature of man three baptisms, purifying from all sin whatsoever. I mean, 1. The baptism by water; 2. The baptism by our own blood through martyrdom; 3. The baptism by tears into which [baptism] the harlot was purified. And likewise Peter, the chief of the holy apostles, after his denial, having wept, was received and saved."

Now the baptism which consisted in Peter's going out and weeping bitterly was neither physical immersion, nor by physical immersion. The baptism of the woman who was baptized by washing the Saviour's feet with her tears, was neither physical immersion, nor by physical immersion. The baptism which consists in being stabbed, or torn to pieces, or burned, or strangled, or poisoned, as a martyr, is neither physical immersion, nor by physical immersion. The baptism of incorrigible sin by fire and sword is neither physical immersion, nor by physical immersion. The baptism which consists in "the suffering which is for Christ" is neither physical immersion, nor by physical immersion. The baptism wherein all believers are baptized by the Saviour's blood is neither physical immersion, nor by physical immersion. The baptism in which "baptizing blood sprinkles" is not physical immersion, nor by such immersion. Jesus, baptized "by the cross of his Passion," was not physically immersed in the cross. The baptism of which it is said "He called the pouring out of his blood baptism," and "These two baptisms he shed forth from the wound of his pierced side," is not physical immersion, nor by physical immersion. The "baptism of public confession" is neither physical immersion, nor by physical immersion. In this whole class of passages no notion of envelopment appears. The baptizing consists in being brought into healing from sin.

The same usage further appears in the passages in which clinic baptism is discussed. The form of the question is not whether the pouring or sprinkling upon a sick person, or an imprisoned martyr, is a baptism; but whether such baptism is valid, or equally valid with the more usual mode? Without any dissent, the disputants on both sides agree that it is proper enough to call this rite of sprinkling or pouring for the remission of sins, a baptism.

Yet, further, these authors constantly apply the name baptism to the sprinklings, pourings, and other forms of rite mentioned in the Old Testament, or practiced among Jews or heathen.

For instance, they repeatedly designate as baptism the emptying of the four water-pots of water upon the sacrifice of

Elijah—1 Kings xviii : 34. The following, from Origen (iv : 241), is a specimen : "For he," that is, Elijah, "commanded the priests to effect this baptism. How, then, is he coming to baptize, who did not then baptize? Christ does not baptize with water, but his disciples; but he reserves for himself the baptizing by the Holy Spirit and fire."

Ambrose (i : 875), commenting upon Psalm, li : 10—"Sprinkle me with hyssop and I shall be clean"—says : " He who wished to be cleansed by typical baptism was sprinkled with the blood of the lamb by a bunch of hyssop."

Jerome (v : 341) thus discourses upon Ezekiel xxxvi : 16. "I will pour out or sprinkle upon you clean water, and ye shall be cleansed from all your defilements. And I will give you a new heart, and I will put a right spirit within you." " I will pour out the clean water of saving baptism." "And it is to be considered, that a new heart and a new spirit may be given by the pouring out and sprinkling of water." "And I will no more pour out upon them the waters of saving baptism, but the waters of doctrine and of the word of God."

Tertullian (i : 1204) : " But the nations without the knowledge of spiritual things, attribute the same efficacy to their idols, but with unmarried waters they deceive themselves. They everywhere purify villas, houses, temples, and whole cities by sprinkling water, and are washed in the spectacles of Apollo and Eleusis." " Here we see the work of the devil emulating the things of God, since he practices even baptism among his own people."

Justin Martyr (437) says of circumcision : " What need is there of that baptism to one baptized by the Holy Spirit ?"

As a plain matter of fact, therefore, many of the operations which the early Christian literature designates as baptisms, were performed by pouring, sprinkling, cutting. or other forms of modal act. But, in every instance, the operation is thought of as causing the person or thing baptized to pass out of one condition into another and different condition,—usually out of a condition of sin-sickness into a condition of healing from sin.

VI. Dr. Dale further strengthens his argument by citing the instances in which we probably or certainly know that baptisms, recognised by the New Testament, or the early church, as proper Christian baptisms, were performed otherwise than by

immersion.   The limits of this article forbid our delaying here,
except to note, in passing, a single point, in which the logical
force of this argument differs from that of the other arguments
which we have been considering.

Admitting the position so abundantly proved, that baptism
is not immersion in water, one might still claim that immersion
in water is peculiarly fitted to be the *mode* of baptism, and
that it is the only mode sanctioned by the usage of the apostles
and of the earlier Christians.   But the fact is, that no usage can
be proved sufficiently uniform and authoritative to satisfy this
claim.

VII. Incidentally, Dr. Dale contends that many of the New
Testament instances of baptisms, commonly supposed to be
ritual, are not so, but are exclusively spiritual.   In maintaining
this view, he distinguishes between ritual baptism and *real*
baptism—that is, the baptism of the Holy Ghost.   Then he
argues, that real baptism is presumably meant wherever the
contrary is not designated.   Yet, if any one should maintain
that ritual baptism is, in its own proper kind of reality, as real
as spiritual baptism ; and that this reality, as being the one
that most people naturally think of, is the one which has the
presumption in its favor; this difference would not affect the
main issues in question.

Notably, Dr. Dale uses this kind of reasoning in disposing of
the cases where burial is mentioned in connection with baptism.
He regards these as cases of spiritual baptism, and therefore
denies all inferences drawn from them in regard to the mode
of ritual baptism.   Yet, the question which baptism is intended
in these cases, is simply the question whether Paul is arguing
from Christian experience or from Christian profession.   It is
true that believers should be dead to sin and alive to holiness,
because they have experienced the benefits of Christ's sin-aton-
ing death, that is, have been spiritually baptized into his death.
It is equally true that they should be dead to sin and alive to
holiness, because, in being ritually baptized into the death of
Christ, they have outwardly professed the experience of its
benefits.   On either supposition, the thing spoken of is the
significance of the baptism, and not the mode of it.   The
question, whether Dr. Dale is correct in here excluding ritual

baptism, is not one which greatly affects the main issues.

In its statement of the conclusion that follows from these premises, this article has constantly adhered to the direct form. Spiritual baptism into Christ is the intusposing of a person, by the agency of the Holy Ghost, into a genuine Christian condition and character, so that henceforth he shall remain enveloped in this character, and marked by it. Ritual Christian baptism is the intusposing of the person by water, as the divinely appointed agency, emblematically, into a genuine Christian character and condition, and actually into the outward character and name of Christian. Dr. Dale, however, constantly prefers a less direct form of statement, and one which involves the yet fuller discussion of the subject. He finds the word *baptizo* developing a secondary meaning. That which is intusposed comes to be controllingly under the power of the enveloping substance. Hence, *baptizo* comes to denote controlling characteristic influence, no matter whether it comes by intusposition or not. This position he maintains by an extensive examination of the analogies of the secondary meanings of *bapto*, of other analogies, and of usage. In this form he almost uniformly states his conclusion.

There is no doubt about the reality of this secondary meaning. The new mode of statement which it affords has certain advantages. Yet it is simply a new form of statement, and not a real change of meaning. To baptize one into repentance is to bring him, either actually or emblematically, under the controlling power of repentance. This is accurately the same as to introduce him into a repentant state. The same double form of statement might be everywhere employed.

It is no slight confirmation of the view taken in these volumes, that it points out distinct boundaries for several of the controversial positions heretofore held, and shows that these positions, if thus bounded, cease to be antagonistic.

For example, the great body of those who have defended baptism by other forms than immersion, have strongly insisted on the character of baptism as a purifying ordinance. Spiritual baptism is purification from sin. The ceremonial lustrations by which Jewish worshipers were purified from uncleanness were baptisms. Water is the chosen agent in baptism, because of its purifying quality. Ashes figure in other baptisms, because their alkaline quality gives them a purifying power greater than even that of pure water. Fire is the symbol of the baptism of the Holy Ghost, because it is the most intense and thorough of all purifying agencies. Jewish proselyte baptism was ritual cleansing from the defilements of idolatry. Christian baptism is an emblem of Christ's cleansing from sin,—that is, of justification; and of the Holy Ghost's cleansing from sin,—that is, of renewal and sanctification. This view they are able to support by page after page of citation from the Scripture and from the early Christian authors. All the current Greek and Latin words for washing, cleaning, purifying, laving, bathing, rinsing, are familiarly applied to baptism.

At first thought, all this seems inconsistent with the view taken by Dr. Dale. But a little reflection shows us that the new condition or character into which one is introduced by baptism is always a purified character or condition. Or, to take the other form of statement, the agency, or element, under the controlling power of which one is brought by baptism, is always a purifying, cleansing agency or element. No writer insists upon this more strenuously than Dr. Dale. He denies, indeed, that purification is the differential characteristic of baptism. But he magnifies it as the most important and essential property of baptism. In all their main features, the two views are identical, and not inconsistent. The real difference between them is simply a difference in logical nomenclature.

On the other hand, Baptist controversialists have been so impressed with the weight of the evidence they have gathered, to the effect that baptism is identical with immersion, that they have been betrayed into certain very jealous utterances regarding their opponents, who failed of being convinced by the evidence. Dr. Dale first indicates the need of a more precise definition of the term immersion—in which most Baptists of real scholarship will agree with him—and then accepts their evidence and their conclusions; merely pointing out, that the immersion, which is proved by their evidence, in the case of ritual baptisms, is always into the new religious condition entered by the candidate, and never, except incidentally, into the water or other baptismal agency.

Once more, the distinctions, so clearly drawn by Dr. Dale,

show the true bearing of the large body of evidence quoted by the advocates of the doctrine of baptismal regeneration. Spiritual baptism is regeneration, the new birth, in which one, who was formerly born outside the spiritual kingdom of God, becomes a citizen born. Ritual baptism is the outward recognition of this new birth. But in being this, it is itself ritual new birth, the being born into outward citizenship of the visible kingdom of God. This truth has been so discredited, by being associated with superstition, that we are are in danger of losing sight of its real value. Baptism is a seal as well as a sign ; and a seal of citizenship in Christ's kingdom, as well as of that purification which characterizes citizenship there. The initial seal of citizenship is baptism. It is neither some public covenant service, nor the vote of some congregation or church court, but baptism.

In fine, Christ has ordained baptism to be "a sign and seal of ingrafting into himself, of remission of sins by his blood and regeneration by his spirit; of adoption, and resurrection unto everlasting life ; and whereby the parties baptized are solemnly admitted into the visible church, and enter into an open and professed engagement to be wholly and only the Lord's."

Art. IV.—AN INDIANA PIONEER.

By the Rev. H. A. Edson, D. D , Indianapolis.

WHETHER lineage, talents, character, or usefulness be regarded, there is abundant reason for an attempt to trace the careers of the founders of Presbyterian institutions in Indiana. Todd and Balch are memorable names in Presbyterian annals. If Providence had sent William Wirt to hear "Father Martin" preach, the description of James Waddel's eloquence might fitly have had a companion-piece. Crowe and Johnston were as brave and good, as they were discreet and successful. Cameron and McGready, and Thomas Cleland, of Kentucky, gave some of their best labors to the wilderness north of the Ohio.

And among the living, Dr. Ravaud K. Rodgers and Dr. Charles C. Beatty recall with pleasure their missionary tours in the West.* Not the least worthy of recognition is the man whom Gillett describes, perhaps with justice, as "the father of the Presbyterian Church in Indiana."†

John McElroy Dickey was born in York District, South Carolina, December 16, 1789. His grandfather, of Scotch-Irish descent, came from Ireland to America about the year 1737. His father, David Dickey, was twice married, first on March 28, 1775, to Margaret Robeson, who died four months after her marriage; and subsequently, September 4, 1788, to Margaret Stephenson. John was the first-born and only son of this latter marriage. He had four sisters, of whom one died in infancy.

His parents were in humble circumstances, but of excellent Christian character. David Dickey was a man of unusual intelligence, and, according to the testimony of his son, had remarkable self-control. "I never saw him angry but once," the latter declared; "nor did I ever see him manifest peevishness or fretfulness, even in old age." No pressure of business could ever induce him to omit the customary household worship or other religious duties. For years he taught the neighborhood school, and when John was but three years of age carried him to it daily. Of such a man the wife was a true helpmeet. Like Hannah, she had given her son to God, and formally devoted him to his service. It was her habit, while at the wheel spinning flax or cotton, to gather her children about her for instruction in the Shorter Catechism. "To my mother," said Mr. Dickey, "more than to any other human being, am I indebted for what I am. In the midst of doubts, fears, discouragements, and toils, it has often been a source of consolation to know that I had a mother who, in covenant with God,

---

* Dr. Rodgers spent the winter of 1818–19 in Indiana; Dr. Beatty that of 1822-23. At the recent semi-centennial commemoration of the Synods of Indiana, (Indianapolis, October, 1876) it was observed that these two are the only survivors of all the itinerants previous to 1826. The Rev. Samuel G. Lowry, of Minnesota, became a settled minister in 1825—the only resident clergyman, previous to the Synod's organization, who still lives.

† *Gillett's History*, vol. ii: p. 307.

gave me up to him and to the work of the ministry. If all
mothers were like her, the Lord's vineyard could not long lack
laborers."

Under such a home influence, the children all grew insensi-
bly into the habits of piety, and were unable to fix the time
when their early religious experience began. The son became
familiar with the Scriptures, the Confession of Faith and Form
of Government of the Presbyterian Church—the reading books
of that day—and the foundations were permanently laid for the
clear theological views of his subsequent ministry. At four
years of age, it is said that he had read the Bible through.
Not much later he was acquiring a considerable knowledge of
mathematics, under his father's instruction, and aided by a
coal and a pine board. He eagerly improved his humble opportunities for study, until new advantages were providentially
opened to him by the removal of the family northward in 1803.
David Dickey, though reared in a slave state, looked upon
slavery as a curse, and sought to deliver his family from its influence ; but upon leaving South Carolina he found himself
obliged by circumstances to remain in Livingston County,
Kentucky. After assisting for two or three years in the labor
of clearing and cultivating his father's land, John went to study
under the direction of his cousin, the Rev. William Dickey,*
about a mile from his own home. The manse, however, had
but one room, and the proprietor had several children of his
own. Young Dickey, therefore, built a shelter near the house
where he might keep his books and study. Thus he read
Virgil and the Greek Testament, remaining with his cousin for
about eighteen months. A school was then opened by the
Rev. Dr. Nathan H. Hall, at Hardin's Creek Church, two
hundred and fifty miles distant, whither he determined to make
his way. His father was quite unable to assist him, but John
had secured a colt on the farm and raised it, so that he was

---

*The valuable notice of Mr. Dickey, in Sprague's *Annals*, is marred by
several inaccuracies. The Rev. William Dickey appears as *Wilson ;* Mr. D.'s
great-grandfather is said to have emigrated from Ireland about 1740, whereas it
was his grandfather, who came several years earlier than that date ; Muhlenburg
Presbytery is changed to *Mecklenburg ;* the date of the organization of Salem
Presbytery is set forward seven years ; Columbus, *Ohio,* is substituted for Columbus, Indiana. The appended communications from Mr. Dickey's ministerial
brethren are singularly pictorial and just.

now in possession of a fine young horse. Thus mounted, with perhaps two dollars in money, he set out upon the long journey. For board and lodging he sold his horse to a Mr. McElroy, and entered with zeal upon his studies. The horse ran away and was never recovered, but the student was already a favorite, and continued a member of the McElroy household until his course at Dr. Hall's school was completed. He gave such assistance as he could in the labors of the farm, and all further compensation was refused by the hospitable host. It was thus, that afterward, to avoid confusion often arising from the commonness of his own name, Mr. Dickey added McElroy to John. Soon becoming an assistant-teacher in the school, he was enabled to support himself, at the same time working hard at his own course of study.

Here he remained nearly two years, when he entered upon the study of theology with the cousin who had previously been his instructor, and with the Rev. John Howe, at Glasgow, Kentucky. He was licensed to preach by Muhlenburg Presbytery, August 29, 1814, in the twenty-fifth year of his age, having already, November 18th of the previous year, been united in marriage with Miss Nancy W., daughter of William and Isabel (Miller) McClesky, of Abbeville district, South Carolina.

In December, after his licensure, he made a visit to Indiana, and spent a few Sabbaths at what is now Washington, Davies County, with a church that had been constituted, in August of the same year, by the Rev. Samuel Thornton Scott, Indiana's first resident Presbyterian minister. There were now but two other organized Presbyterian societies within the limits of Indiana territory—the " Indiana " church, near Vincennes, constituted in 1806, and the Charlestown church, established in 1812. A church formed in 1807, and known as the Palmyra church, had become extinct. There were but two Presbyterian meeting-houses, both of logs, and both in the " Indiana " parish. But two Presbyterian ministers were already settled in Indiana,* Mr. Scott and the Rev. William Robinson.

Mr. Dickey engaged to return to the Washington congregation, and accordingly, in May, 1815,† still a licentiate under

---

* The Rev. Samuel Baldridge, M.D., had, in 1810, settled at Lawrenceburg, but before Mr. Dickey's arrival had removed to Ohio.

† *Dickey's Brief History*, pp. 12, 13.

the care of Muhlenburg Presbytery, he set out for his home in the wilderness, with his wife and their infant daughter. The family, and all their earthly goods, were carried on the backs of two horses. His library consisted of a Bible, Buck's Theological Dictionary, Bunyan's Pilgrim's Progress, and Fisher's Catechism. When the ferriage across the Ohio was paid, they had a single shilling left.

Now began the self-denials and struggles of pioneer life. It was impossible to expect a comfortable support from the feeble congregation.* There was little money in the neighborhood. Taxes were partly paid in raccoon skins, fox skins, and "wolf-scalps." People lived on what they could raise from the small clearings, by barter, and by hunting. Indians still occasioned annoyance and anxiety. Corn was pounded in mortars, or rubbed on tin graters. Wheat flour was seldom seen. Fruit was rare, except the wild plums, grapes, gooseberries, and paw-paws. Mr. Dickey, therefore, aided the support of his family by farming on a small scale,† teaching a singing-class, and writing deeds, wills, and advertisements. He also surveyed land, and sometimes taught school. Much of this work was done gratuitously, but it secured the friendship of the people. His average salary, including money and gifts, of which he kept a record, even to the minutest detail, for the first sixteen years was eighty dollars. In some way he secured forty acres of land, to which he subsequently added eighty acres. Twenty or thirty acres he cleared, chiefly by his own labor. With his neighbors' help he built his house in the woods. It was a small log-cabin—the floor of slabs split and hewed from oak and poplar trees ; the windows small, greased paper serving instead of glass; the chimney partly of stone and partly of sticks, and daubed with clay. In later years he erected a school-house on his farm, and made sash with his own hands for the small glass then in use. He was "handy" with tools, and fashioned the wood-work of his plows and other farming implements. Often

---

* All the pioneers were compelled by some make-shift to eke out a maintenance. Through much intermediate "weariness and painfulness" on the farm, or in the shop or school, they were glad to win their way to a Sunday pulpit, or a "sacramental meeting," or a protracted preaching tour.

† The character of the man came out, however, in the style of his farming. It was so thorough and intelligent, that the productiveness of his fields was proverbial.

would less skillful neighbors work for him in the field, while he "stalked" their plows, or made them a harrow or rake. He also had a set of shoemaker's tools, mending the shoes of his family, and often those of his neighbors. He could himself cut out and make a neat shoe, but "never liked the work, and avoided it if possible." Music he read with great facility, supplying the lack of books with his pen, several of these manuscript volumes being carefully kept by his children. He was not unaccustomed, on special occasions, to compose both music and hymns for the use of the congregation. Under his management the winter singing-school became a prominent and happy feature of the life in the wilderness.

Preaching every Sabbath, and often during the week, he was compelled to do much of his studying while at work on the farm, or as he rode on horseback from place to place. The family were too poor to afford a lamp or candles, and often, after a day of manual labor, Mr. Dickey would gather pine-knots, and having kindled a bright fire, would sit on the hearth and write the plans of his sermons. His best opportunities for meditation, however, came while riding to his preaching-stations, through the forests, and along the quiet roads. With his Bible, hymn-book, and Confession of Faith in the saddle-bags, and a Testament or small Concordance in his pocket ready for use, he pursued careful investigations of important themes. "On a pony that had learned to avoid the mud by going close to the rail fence," says his son,* "I have seen him riding for miles, and at every corner lifting his leg and drawing it up on the saddle to avoid the rails, too much absorbed in thought to observe what the pony or himself was doing. Occasionally returning to consciousness of things about him, he would rein the horse out into the road ; but the beast, preferring the harder ground, would soon go back to the fence, and creep so close to the sharp corners that the process of leg-lifting would begin again, and go steadily on for another hour."

At one time, returning from a preaching-tour to find the family entirely out of meal and flour, he remounted his horse, went to the mill several miles distant, procured a supply, and with the sack on the horse's back started homeward. But be-

---

* The Rev. Ninian Steele Dickey, to whom the writer is under many obligations, for the facts of this article, and for the use of MSS.

coming engaged in meditation, the sack fell off without his notice. The hungry children, who had made several meals of potatoes, saw with dismay that he was returning without the supplies, and calling their mother, met him as he rode up to the gate. A single question was enough to reveal the state of the case, and wheeling about, half-amused and half-ashamed, he hurried back to find the sack at the roadside. He often said, that to think closely he must be on his horse. There was no subject engaging the attention of the world which he did not ponder as thoroughly as his opportunities allowed. He was well informed on questions of public policy, and sometimes addressed communications to those in power, always urging that " righteousness exalteth a nation." These communications were kindly received, and often elicited respectful replies.

Mr. Dickey's cheerful labors were overshadowed, however, and sometimes wholly interrupted, by the alarming diseases common in such new settlements. At first his own family escaped, but before a year had passed all were prostrated, and on October 2, 1816, Mrs. Dickey died. Added to these personal sorrows was the discouragement arising from frequent removals of his people to other neighborhoods. There was, moreover, no suitable place of worship. This latter want was soon supplied, however. Though it was difficult to select a site against which no one would object, scattered as his congregation were along White River, upon a tract sixteen miles long by ten wide, they finally united upon a piece of "Congress land," "whose sterile soil would not be likely soon to tempt a purchaser to dispossess them. The members of the little society met on a day appointed, and cut logs twenty feet in length, which, with their native covering of bark and moss, were laid together. The minister was present to encourage his people, and some of the logs were notched by his own hands. The roof was of clap-boards. The earth formed both floor and carpet. The seats were hewed puncheons. On this log meeting-house, the third, it would seem, which the Indiana Presbyterians possessed, the people looked with pride. Rude as was the humble sanctuary, it equalled, if it did not surpass, the houses in which several of the congregation lived. It continued to be the place of worship until shortly after Davies County was organized, when the county-seat was located at Washington, a temporary court-house was erected, and this then became the meeting-house."*

After four years service† in this field, Mr. Dickey removed to Lexington, Scott County, and became pastor of the New Lexington and Pisgah churches, while he also had charge of the Graham church, situated on a creek of that name between Paris and Vernon, in Jennings County. His installation, August, 1819, over the two former congregations, was the first formal Presbyterian settlement in the territory.‡ Previously, however, April 2, 1818, Mr. Dickey had married Miss Margaret Osborn Steele. This wife shared his trials and successes for nearly thirty years,† and became the mother of eleven children. The picture of the pioneer parsonage and its busy life would be sadly imperfect without the portrait of this Christian woman.

She was worthy of her husband. Much of his usefulness must be attributed to her. For the maintenance of the family she gave her full share of toil and self-denial, often living alone with her children for months together, disciplining them to industry and usefulness, while their father was absent upon long and laborious missionary journeys. She cultivated a garden which supplied many household wants. Reared as she had been on the frontier, her education was at first limited, but under her husband's tuition she became a respectable scholar, able to instruct her own and her neighbors' children. She was an adept at the spinning-wheel and loom, and for many years made with her own hands all the linen and woolen cloth and garments for the family. There were also frequent additions to the exchequer from the sale of jeans of her manufacture. Such was her trust in God, that fear never seemed to disturb her peace. She had lived for a time where the dread of. prowling savages forbade the lighting of a lamp, or of a fire at night, and ordinary trouble produced no visible

---

* MSS. of the Rev. Thomas S. Milligan, long a friend of Mr. Dickey's family, a man of studious tastes and noble character. His death (October 7, 1876) has occasioned great and sorrowful surprise.

† Dickey's Brief History, p. 4.

‡ Read's Christian Traveller, pp. 91, 213.

† Her death occurred October 24, 1847.

disturbance of her mind. In every good work she was fore-most, whether it were making husk mattresses for the students at Hanover College, gathering supplies for destitute mission-aries, or caring for the sick and unfortunate at home. The meagreness of her own household stores did not prevent her from doing much for others. In the absence of her hus-band the family altar was regularly maintained, and the Sab-bath afternoon recitations from the Shorter Catechism were by no means omitted. Though her residence was on a farm, and most of Mr. Dickey's public life was spent as pastor of a country church, the scattered homes of the people did not prevent her sustaining a woman's weekly prayer-meeting. In the Sabbath-school and at public worship her place was seldom vacant, notwithstanding the claims of so large a family. It was the custom to begin the communion services on Friday, which was often a fast-day, and to continue them through the fol-lowing Monday. Neighboring ministers and congregations attended these services in great numbers. Often was the hospitality of the parish taxed to the utmost. "Though I relished heartily the enthusiasm of these gatherings, especially the singing and the social enjoyment," says a member of Mr. Dickey's family, "I recollect that in my early days I dreaded these occasions, because I had to sleep on the floor, often without even a carpet or pillow, that room might be made for strangers. One of my father's neighbors, they used to say, had accommodation for sixty guests, while many young men and boys slept on the hay in the barns. Notwithstanding the claims of guests and the necessity of unusual work at these seasons, everything was ordered so that the women of the household might be present at all the public meetings. I do not recollect ever to have known my mother to be absent except on account of the severe illness of herself or some member of the family, and never did I hear her complain of the burden of entertaining so many strangers. I have known her to be much concerned as to suitable provision for their comfort, but what she had was cheerfully given." Is it not natural to ask, whether the dignity and gracefulness of these hospitable rites are often surpassed or equalled now? The preparations are more elaborate and the ceremonies more pretentious, but is the welcome as warm or as wise?

It is not surprising that a mother, so prudent and diligent, so religious in her denial of self and her generosity to others. aided, too, by such a husband, should be blessed with dutiful and noble children.   Her sons and daughters grew up in piety, and most of them survive in prominent and useful stations.*

In the midst of the scenes now described, Mr. Dickey's indefatigable labors continued.   He served the New Lexington and Pisgah churches until April, 1835, a period of sixteen years, when the care of the former congregation was committed to other hands, though he held the pulpit of the Pisgah Society for twelve years longer, and until the infirmities of age admonished him that the end was near.   It is not as pastor of the small country flock that his usefulness is to be measured, however.   He was a travelling bishop.   From far and near he was called to assist in special services, in revivals, at communions, and in vacant churches.   The whole southern half of the territory he often traversed in difficult horseback journeys, and frequently his mission work extended to the "regions beyond." In January and Feburary, 1823, having received an appointment from the Assembly's "Committee on Missions," he made an exploring tour to Vincennes and Crawfordsville, and returning, fulfilled appointments for preaching which he had scattered as he advanced.   "Before he had reached the end of his outward journey violent rains had fallen, and the Wabash, with its tributaries, became very high, and was for the most part without bridges.   Yet he preached thirty one sermons in thirty days, and kept all his appointments save two.   In a number of cases if the engagements had been a single day earlier or later, the

---

* It would seem that our pioneer history furnishes a notable illustration of the power of parental influence. Especially do the humble parsonages of the early days in the woods, prove what worthy children God gives to faithful fathers and mothers. Of Mr. Dickey's children nine survive, viz.: Margaret, wife of Dr. James F. Knowlton, Geneva, Kansas; Jane, wife of Dr. W. W. Britain, on the homestead, near New Washington, Clark Co., Indiana; the Rev. Ninian S., for eighteen years pastor of our church in Columbus, Indiana, now at Greenville, Illinois; John P., a Presbyterian ruling elder, and James H., in Allen County, Kansas; Nancy E., wife of Mr. Mattoon. Geneva, Kansas; Martha E., wife of Thomas Bone, Esq., Chester, Illinois; Mary E., wife of James M. Haines, Esq., New Albany, Indiana; and William Matthews, a graduate of Wabash College, a student of medicine, a prisoner at Andersonville, and now a resident of California. The oldest son died at the age of seventeen, while a student for the ministry.

impassable streams must have detained him. And so he was accustomed to say, 'the Lord delivered me out of the deep waters.' In the summer of 1824 he spent two months in the counties of Bartholomew, Rush, Shelby, and Decatur, under the direction of the Indiana Missionary Society, which a short time before he had assisted in forming. During this journey he organized the churches of Columbus and Franklin, and the church of New Providence, near Shelbyville. His custom was to make a tour of two weeks, preaching daily, and then for an equal length of time remain at home laboring in his own parish.''*

We are aided in recalling the methods and sacrifices of those days by the vivid pen of one of Mr. Dickey's fellow-laborers. "At Madison, in 1829," he says, "I first met with Father Dickey, who came to assist Mr. Johnston† during a protracted meeting. He had been delayed a little by stress of weather and bad roads; the congregation were assembled when he entered the church, fresh from his horse and journey. I seem to see his figure, of full medium height, spare and bent, marching up the aisle in a well-worn and soldier-like overcoat, and drab leggings, with saddle bags on his arm, and presenting a face, thoughtful, gentle, and earnest, expressive of an equable spirit, firm and mild. When he spoke from the pulpit he had an unnatural tone; he showed little rhetoric, little of the learning or art of the schools, but much good sense, faith, and fruit of study in prayer and love. The people listened with a kind and appreciative attention. His character evidently helped him. He was well known in Madison, and everybody felt that his words were those of a wise and disinterested friend. There I learned to revere him as one communing much with God, and ever penetrated with everlasting things; whose mind and heart were habitually conversant with the greatest interests; who sought not his own, but was revolving plans of large usefulness; a man, sober and trusty of judgment, and of organizing ability; laborious and modest; stable in the truth; candid and liberal, but not lax; fraternal and broad

---

* MSS. of the Rev. Thos. S. Milligan.

† The Rev. James H. Johnston, who died at Crawfordsville March 8, 1876, having completed the longest term of continuous service ever attained by a minister of our church in Indiana—more than fifty-one years.

in his sympathies, loving and, like Christ, loving the world.

"A few days later I found Father Dickey at Indianapolis, attending the anniversaries of the State Benevolent Societies, in establishing which he had been among the prime movers, and in which he continued to show an efficient interest. The legislature was in session, and on the Sabbath he preached to a large audience, from Jeremiah vi: 16—'Thus saith the Lord, stand ye in the ways, and see, and ask for the old paths, where is the good way, and walk therein, and ye shall find rest for your souls.' He spoke with unction and to general acceptance, notwithstanding his peculiar mode of delivery.

"Two months afterward he surprised me with a visit at my bachelor's room at an inn in Logansport. He had come on an exploring mission from his home in the southern part of the State, in February, 1830, encountering such difficulties from the roads and high waters and rude beginnings of the settlers, remote from each other, as belonged to that period, and all from a desire, preaching as he went, better to know the spiritual destitutions of the State, and more intelligently to labor in removing them.

"During a few more years I was wont to see him at synods where his presence was always valued, and notably I remember him in the General Assembly at Philadelphia, 1832. In the strifes of the times he was not a warm partisan; he knew nothing of intrigue; and beyond most men seemed to act above prejudice, and in the light of conscience and the Spirit of Christ."*

Though never of a rugged constitution, the contrast with his wife's vigor and endurance being the occasion of frequent remark on her part, indulging the hope, as she did, that she might

---

* MS. letter of the Rev. Dr. Martin M. Post, dated January 7, 1876. Born in Cornwall, Vermont, December 3, 1805; Middlebury's valedictorian in 1826; a graduate of Andover; reaching his mission field at Logansport, Indiana, December, 1829, he there continued to reside until his death, October 11, 1876. For the fathers of the Indiana Synod the semi-centennial year has been a fatal one. Johnston fell asleep March 8th, but three days before John Ross (æt. 92), these two having been the sole remaining representatives in the Synod, North, of the former times. Dr. Post's demise occurred but four days later than that of Thomas S. Milligan. Dr. Post's five sons all received a collegiate and theological training, the youngest, Roswell O., being now pastor of the flock so long cared for by his father.

be permitted to cheer him in life's decline, Mr. Dickey sustained such various labors as have been described for a long period. Not until April, 1847, was he compelled by failing health to surrender the pastorate he had held for twenty-eight years. After an interval of a few months his health was so far restored that he was able to labor in the service of the American Tract Society for nearly a year. On the termination of this work he sought no further fixed employment, but ministered in the pulpit and as a counsellor, most usefully, as opportunity came.

In 1828 Mr. Dickey had published, under the direction of the Synod, "*A Brief History of the Presbyterian Church in the State of Indiana*," now the source of our best information with regard to the early days.* This small pamphlet it was his earnest desire to enlarge and complete. "The last work of my father's life, on which his heart was set," writes his son, " was the completion of the history. He was very feeble in body at the last, but vigorous in mind, and sat at his table and wrote as long as he was able. Industry was his characteristic. I never saw him idle an hour. When forced to lay down his pen it cost him a struggle. At his request I acted as his amanuensis and prepared several sketches of churches, of which he said no other living man knew so much as he." All was, however, left quite unfinished. He lived but a day or two after laying aside his pen.†

---

* " In regard to the early history of Presbyterianism in Indiana, he was a sort of gazetteer or book of reference, from which we had rarely. if ever, occasion to appeal."— Dr. Henry Little in *Sprague's Annals*, vol. iv : pp. 518–19.

† As to the origin of the *Brief History*, and the various efforts to supplement and complete it, see *Minutes of Salem Pres.*, vol. i : p. 20 ; *Minutes of Madison Pres.*, vol. i : p. 26; *Minutes of Indiana Synod*, vol. i : pp. 13, 15, 31, 53, 59, 60, 549, 586, 612, 624 ; vol. ii : pp. 207, 225, 347, 384, 401, 419, 423, 436, 437, 446. Mr. Dickey's pamphlet, though accurate, is not infallible.   I have before me the author's copy, with his manuscript corrections.   The more important of these are the following : Page 5, as to Madison Church, read, " it was supplied by Mr. Robinson for two years. In the summer of 1819 the Rev. Thomas S. Searle located at Madison, and was installed the following year pastor of Madison and Hanover Churches ; " page 6, as to the date of the organization of Pisgah Church, read, " February 27, 1816;" the name of Daniel C. Banks is substituted for that of James McGready, as having constituted the New Albany Church, the latter having formed the church at Jeffersonville; page 7, as to the date of the Rev. Isaac Reed's settlement in Owen County, read, " October, 1822 ; " page 8, read, " Mr. Proctor labored three-fourths of his time (at Indianapolis) for a year, beginning October, 1822. Mr. George Bush commenced his labors there in June, 1824;" page 10, read, " June, 1821,"

The only meetings of the Presbytery and Synod he had failed to attend were those held at New Albany a few weeks previous to his death. He wrote to his brethren apprising them of his feebleness, and assuring them that his work was nearly done. Synod appointed a committee to suggest a suitable reply, on the reception of which Mr. Dickey was deeply moved, at the family altar with choked utterance giving thanks to God that the lines had fallen to him in such goodly places, among such loving and faithful brethren, and praying that God would greatly prosper them. Suffering intensely in the closing hours, his peace was great. Although for twenty-five years afflicted with a pulmonary disease, his endurance was remarkable. He finally fell asleep November 21, 1849. The Rev. Philip Bevan, a licentiate of Cincinnati Presbytery, at this time supplying the New Washington Church, officiated at the funeral. On the following Sabbath the Rev. Dr. Harvey Curtis, then pastor of the Second Church, Madison, preached in the New Washington Meeting-house, a commemorative discourse from the text descriptive of Barnabas: "He was a good man, and full of the Holy Ghost, and of faith."—Acts xi : 24.

Mr. Dickey's remains lie buried beside his second wife and three of his children, in the cemetery of the Pisgah (now New Washington) Church. His tombstone is a plain marble slab, inscribed with his name, age, the date of his death, and the text of the commemorative discourse.*

Of the man who so wisely and laboriously laid the foundations of Christian society in Indiana, the best estimate is pre-

---

as the date of the organization of Evansville Church ; page 11, for James Balch, substitute Nathan B. Derrow, the name of the " New Hope " Church, having been originally, and until 1825, "Hopewell."

There are such typographical errors as Samuel B. Robinson for *Robertson*, and *Martin B.* for Nathan B. Derrow.

It is also to be observed that Dickey makes no allusion to the organization of Concord Church, Orange County, Sept. 27, 1818 (by Orin Fowler), nor to the useful labors of Samuel Baldridge (1810–12), Samuel J. Mills (1814–15), William Goodell (1822), Lucius Alden (1825), and John Ross (1822-1876).

* On the announcement of his death in Synod, a movement was made to erect a monument to his memory at the expense of his brethren. The motion was opposed by Samuel Merrill, Esq., who said that he knew Mr. Dickey well enough to be sure that such display would have offended his modesty. Mr. Merrill suggested instead, that funds be raised for a hall in Wabash College. to be known as " Dickey Hall ". The suggestion met with cordial approbation, but was never carried out.

sented in the simple record of his career.   It is, however, to be observed, how sagacious and determined he was in the advocacy of views which then were new, but now are generally accepted among good men.   In his personal appearance, most unostentatious, his dress was usually homespun.   Though in his later years he wore broadcloth in the pulpit—his every-day garb was of the jeans provided by the hands of his wife and daughters.   Doubtless, the necessity of economy determined this habit, but there was also still remaining among the plain people of the frontier that prejudice against imported stuffs, which, during the Revolution, had been so violent.*   Beneath such an unassuming exterior, however, dwelt a singularly broad and self-reliant mind.

The character of the man was indicated in his early and bold advocacy of the temperance reform.   It has been asserted that he preached the first sermon in Indiana against intemperance.†   A lady, who became his daughter-in-law, relates, as illustrating the propriety of such preaching at the time, that on one occasion, when a child, she was put out a back window by her mother, and sent with great haste to one of the neighbors for whiskey, "because they saw Mr. Dickey, the preacher, coming." One of his son's earliest recollections is of a stormy onset upon him by four of his parishioners, all distillers, as they were gathered under a spreading beech, after one of his discourses against the prevailing vice.   "I expected," says the witness, "that he would give them a severe castigation, and was indignant, when afterward, with reference to the affair, he merely said, 'Why, I didn't suppose they would like the sermon.'   And yet, so great was the influence of his teaching, that two of these men never distilled whiskey afterward.   One of them would not even sell his distilling apparatus, but let it

---

* The Rev. James Dickey, of South Salem, Ohio, a cousin of "Father Dickey," went to the General Assembly at Philadelphia, dressed in homespun, and on a Sabbath was invited to fill one of the city pulpits. After ascending the pulpit the sexton first came to him, and subsequently the elders, to offer him a pew, as he was now occupying the clergyman's place. But they were soon surprised with a good sermon from the intruder. The next day the ladies of the congregation presented him with a clerical suit, but he gently declined it, saying, that where he lived the people would not hear him preach in such clothes.

† The honor seems to belong either to him, or to "Father Cravens," of the Methodist Church.

stand and rot.   In a few years, public sentiment, aided by a fire
which destroyed one of the establishments, closed the other
stills, so that intoxicating drinks were not manufactured within
the bounds of his congregation." He met the neighboring
ministers in argument upon this subject, and so ably and with
such good humor did he maintain his cause, that largely owing to his influence, the region where he lived and labored
banished intoxicating liquors from use as a beverage.   His
reputation as a debater in behalf of total abstinence was so assured, and the unpopularity of opposing him so well known,
that a young man who had represented the district in Congress,
and was an aspirant again for the position, declined to debate
the question with him, though he had issued a challenge to any
one who would meet him.

"Father Dickey" was always an earnest anti-slavery man.*
For several years he cast the only ballot in his township for
free-soil principles.   By and by, his convictions became so
strong that, though he never introduced politics into the
pulpit, privately and in debating societies he discussed the
question, and ultimately won over nearly all his people to anti-
slavery sentiments.† Living on the border where runaway
negroes were numerous, he fearlessly preached from such texts
as "Thou shalt not deliver unto his master the servant which
is escaped from his master unto thee" (Deut. xxiii: 15); and
under his instructions the better men of the community ceased
the lucrative business of hunting fugitives, although the prac
tice had been thought innocent and necessary.   The name of
"the old Abolitionist," which those "of the baser sort" gave
him, rather pleased him.   He said it would one day be popular.

"I remember Father Dickey," writes Mrs. Harriet Beecher
Stowe,‡ "chiefly through the warm praises of my brother and

---

* See Mrs. Stowe's *Men of Our Times*, p. 548 ; Cf. Reed's *Christian Traveler*,
p. 152 ; Johnson's *Forty Years in Indiana*, pp. 12, 13, 15, and 17 ; and Crowe's
Abolition Intelligencer.

† I have before me a thick, yellow manuscript, in the careful handwriting of
Father Dickey, and entitled, *An Address to Christians on the Duty of Giving
Suitable Instruction to Slaves*. The argument is tender and convincing. It is
dated December 20, 1822—a very early period for such an argument upon the
Kentucky border.

‡ From Mandarin, Florida, February 5, 1876.

my husband, who used to meet him at Synods and Presbyteries. They used to speak of him as an apostle after the primitive order—'poor, yet making many rich ; having nothing, and yet possessing all things.' He advocated the cause of the slave in the day when such advocacy exposed one to persecution and bodily danger. My husband, to whom I have appealed, says he remembers him well and loves his memory, but that he was a man that ' didn't make anecdotes ;' always constant, steady, faithful, he inspired younger ministers by his constancy and faith, and the simplicity of his devotion to Christ.* In my novel of Dred, now changed in title to Nina Gordon, the character of Father Dickson was drawn from my recollection of this good man, as described to me." †

The services Mr. Dickey rendered to the cause of education were also important. His own early opportunities for study had been secured amidst manifold difficulties, and he sought the more earnestly to provide for his children, and his neighbors' children, an easier and better way. In his first parish in Davies County he taught school.‡ Until the division of the Presbyterian Church in 1837, he was an active trustee of Hanover College.§ Chiefly through his influence a wealthy Englishman, Mr. Thomas Stevens, was induced to establish and maintain a female seminary on the Ohio River, near Bethlehem. In a suitable brick building, erected by Mr. Stevens for that purpose, Mr. Dickey resided several years, providing a home for the teachers, and securing educational privileges for his children. The first principal of the school was Miss Longly, who, after two years in the seminary, became the wife of the Rev.

---

* A clergyman, who was at one time a pastor in southern Indiana, and went back to New England after a few years' trial of the frontier, relates that on a certain occasion he saddled his horse and rode fourteen miles to lay his discouragements before Mr. Dickey, and obtain advice and sympathy. But when he observed how the latter was supporting a large family, without a thought of faltering, though in the midst of difficulties compared with which his own were trifling, he returned home without even mentioning the object of his visit.

† See Stowe's *Nina Gordon*, vol. i : pp. 300, 301, and *passim.*

‡ The Presbyterian minister was almost inevitably the schoolmaster in the early days at the West. Scott, Baldridge, Robinson, Todd, Martin, Crowe—nearly all of the earliest settled ministers taught schools.

§ It is evident that in all the first struggles of the school at Hanover, he, with Johnston, was Crowe's " brother beloved."

Dr. Riggs, of the Sioux mission. Much was accomplished by the school for the whole surrounding region.

It is not surprising that a life so variously useful, and a character so strikingly symmetrical, have elicited affectionate eulogies. "He was always spoken of with great reverence by my mother," says one who in childhood was accustomed to see him at her own home. "I met him first in Presbytery," wrote another, "and I well remember that the impression of his goodness derived from others was heightened in me by the first day's observation. . . I was never with one whose flow of feeling savored so much of heaven."* "He has left a name," said Dr. Martin M. Post, "which suggests a wise counsellor, a true worker, a thoroughly honest and godly man. May a double portion of his spirit rest on his successors in the Synods of Indiana."

Art. V.—THE SABBATH QUESTION.†

By Rev. Byron Sunderland, D. D., Washington, D. C.

One of the latest expositions of the Sabbath ordinance is the paper of Rev. S. M. Hopkins, D. D., Professor in the Auburn Theological Seminary, read before the Evangelical Alliance, at Pittsburgh, last year. He concedes a Christian *consensus* " as to the duty of consecrating one day in the week to the ends of physical rest, and moral and religious culture."

"But," he continues, "at that point the agreement ends. As respects the grounds of the obligation and the manner of performing it, there prevails a wide difference of opinion." He speaks of it as "the Sunday observance," and, beginning with the Sabbatarian Pharisees, in the time of Christ, he alludes to the dispute which then arose, and recalls the views and practice existing from that day to the present. He argues the

---

* Henry Ward Beecher, in *Sprague's Annals*, vol. iv : p. 519.
† Published at the special request of a large number of the clerical and lay members of the Baltimore Synod.

abrogation of the fourth commandment, from the teaching of Christ and of Paul, and from the testimony of Barnabas, Tertullian, Justin Martyr, Luther, Calvin, and Alford. He concludes, "that Sabbatical obligation to keep any day, whether seventh or first, was not recognized in apostolical times;" and says that the term "Sabbath" was then never applied to the day of Christian convocation.

Finally, however, he places "the sanction for a Christian Sabbath" on "the ground of custom," or, of what he terms, " a fixed, invariable usage"—"corroborated by a wide observation of its beneficial influence."

We confess that we are not satisfied with this exposition. Nor has any advocate of the Christian Sabbath, either in earlier or later times, with whose views we are acquainted, presented the subject in what seems to us to be the best form. From the days of the Christian fathers down to this hour, there is no symbol of the Sabbath doctrine which fully meets the case. Even the Westminster Confession is no exception. To much of the moralizing on the need of the day and the manner of its observance, we, of course, assent. But in regard to an ordinance of such import to mankind, it seems that there must be some expression of the will of God. The Scriptures are supposed to contain His will. If, upon a fair and candid investigation, it shall be discovered that all divine legislation on this subject has been swept away, and that we are remanded to tradition and custom, and the grounds which pertain thereto, for the only sanction of the day, then we see not how, as Christians, we are to defend the Sabbath against overwhelming assault.

Setting aside, therefore, the whole controversy, as it has stood in the history of the church and of the nations, let us go back to the Word of God.

What is the Scriptural Authority, Design, and Observance of the Christian Sabbath?

I.—AUTHORITY.

Christ asserts that he came not to destroy, but to fulfill, the law and the prophets (Matt. v : 17). Whatever may be embraced in these terms, we suppose the decalogue — that is the moral law, to be included. He says he did not come to repeal that law, but to confirm it—to expound, exemplify, and

emphasize it. The fourth commandment is a part of this moral
law; we have no right to separate it from the rest. It stands
or falls with the body to which it belongs. If the prohibition
of theft, or adultery, or murder, remains, so does the sanctity
of the Sabbath. And not only do the moral reasons of the law
remain with it, but also the *exempli gratia*, the divine example.
If the fact, that God rested from his labors on the seventh day,
was ever a reason why any man should remember the Sabbath-
day to keep it holy, that reason remains to-day in all its force.

That Christ recognized this truth in his contest with the
Pharisees is evident from his doctrine. (Mark ii: 27; Luke
vi: 5.) He claimed lordship over the institution, and declared that the Sabbath came to be through the man, not the
man through the Sabbath. And while it is true, as Prof. Hopkins suggests, that the Jewish Sabbath was appointed for the
Jewish man; this does not limit the teaching of Christ, nor
does it seem to have been in his contemplation at the time.
The Jews complained that their Sabbath had been violated by
his disciples. Christ answered, first, by a precedent specific to
the Jewish law, and, second, by the broad assertion of the relation of humanity itself to the Sabbatic institution. He
plainly teaches that this institution arises on account of human
nature, and not human nature on account of the institution.
And he crowns the whole by assuming the right, in pursuance
of the commandment, to fix not only the status, but the manner,
of observing the Sabbath ordinance. This he did by his doctrine and example. As to the obligations of the Jewish Sabbath, he did treat them as no longer binding. But did he
thereby abrogate all Sabbath law and institutions? That is the
question. Did he intend then and there to abolish the fourth
commandment, and leave his followers and the world thence-
forth without the sanction of divine authority for a Sabbath
ordinance? Others may think he did, but we can come to no
such conclusion. The lordship of the Sabbatic ordinance must
imply its existence; and the truth that it exists on account of
humanity, involves a parallel of continuance. So long as mankind remain, so long must the Sabbath remain. It is constituted by Christ, and founded in the needs of human nature.
This is not an abolition or repeal of the fourth commandment,
but rather its confirmation. That law, by the very doctrine of

Christ, is carried over the existing Sabbath in every dispensation.

If this view be correct, what shall we say of the subsequent teachings of the Apostle Paul? We cannot suppose him to contravene the doctrine of Jesus, or to assail the perpetual obligation of the moral law. Therefore, all that he says must be applicable to the Jewish system only. And what he does teach, is that this system, with its types and its calendar, is now abolished; it is no longer binding, either on Jew or Gentile. To term this "a quibble," as Prof. Hopkins does, is to fly in the face of a logical necessity.

We admit, then, that the Jewish Sabbath is abolished. Its requirements are no longer obligatory. But how do we show that the Christian Sabbath, with all the sanction of the fourth commandment, endorsed and re-endorsed by Christ himself, has supervened?

On this point we first introduce the *weekly* period. In the Mosaic cosmogony we find a provision for the measurement of time—" for signs and seasons, days and years—" but none for a *septenary*. Yet, the *week* is one of the most important divisions of time in the word of God. How does it arise? Let us take three examples, the Creation week, the Jewish week, and the Christian week. Here are three distinct cases of a division of time, consisting of six secular days, followed by a seventh and sacred day. They are each and all *founded upon and reckoned from some great providential event.* Thus, the Creation week is founded upon, and reckoned from, the providential event of the creation. The Jewish week is founded upon, and reckoned from, the falling of the manna. The Christian week is founded upon, and reckoned from, the greatest event of all, the Resurrection of Christ, the Saviour of the world! For these statements, see Gen. i and ii; Ex. xvi and xx; John xx: 1, 19-26. We have here the narrative of the origin and measurement of the weekly periods, affording, in this respect, a beautiful and striking analogy in the successive dispensations. Though in the Scriptures we find no trace of identity, or even connection, between them; yet, each is constituted on a similar principle, with a similar number of secular and sacred days, following in a similar order, while each has a special and peculiar design, and each is reckoned from a distinct and separate providential event. It hence follows, that as the Creation Sabbath was the seventh day of the Patriarchal week, and the Jewish Sabbath was the seventh day of the Levitical week; so the Lord's day, or Christian Sabbath, is the seventh day of the Christian week.

We next introduce, in the Scripture view, the change of calendar, on which we remark two things: first, that in the Bible record, *no special notice of this change is given*, either from the Creation week to the Jewish, or from the Jewish to the Christian; and, second, that in each case the narrative proceeds with the change of reckoning *as though such* notice had been given. Thus, we find in the sixteenth of Exodus an account of the Jewish reckoning, involving the Jewish calendar without the slightest allusion to the cessation of the Creation week, or to any change of calendar. What became of the Creation week or its calendar the Scriptures do not inform us. We only know from the record, that the Jewish reckoning, or calendar of weeks, began after the Exodus, and at the falling of the manna. In a similar manner we find the Scripture narrative, proceeding with the Christian calendar, or reckoning of time, after the resurrection of Christ, and this without any special notice given of the change. But that then there was such a change of calendar appears in three particulars, viz.:

(*a*) There was a change of era. Before, the year had been counted from the beginning of the world; afterward, it was counted from the birth of Christ.

(*b*) There was a change in the beginning of the day. Before, it had been at sunset; afterward, it was at midnight, as would appear from Mark xvi: 9, unless the passage be rejected as spurious; still, in that case, as a matter of fact, the Greek construction favors the change which has actually taken place, so that the day in the Christian calendar is reckoned from midnight, and not, as formerly, from sunset.

(*c*) There was a change also of the week; the Christian week displacing the Jewish week, and the Christian calendar supplanting the Jewish calendar, in all the nations of Christendom. In John xx: 26, we find the narrative proceeding with the reckoning of the first Christian week. The phrase "after eight days" is evidently equivalent to the Hebraism for a *week*.

This first Christian week, or octave of days, is inclusive of the day on which Christ rose, and the seven days following it, six of these days being secular and the seventh a Sabbath !—for the seventh day of the established week is always a Sabbath according to the instruction of the Fourth Commandment. But why, it may be asked, do we not count our week from the first seven, rather than the last seven, of this octave of days? The reason why we do not will presently more fully appear. It is sufficient now to say that a new reckoning is made, and a new calendar is adopted.

This brings us directly to the consideration of the next point of investigation, which involves the accuracy of our English version. It is said Christ arose "on the first day of the week," meaning the Jewish week. If the Jewish calendar is to be retained, then, as a matter of fact, Christ did rise on the first day of the Jewish week. And on the same principle, if the Pagan calendar is to be employed, Christ likewise rose on the Sunday of the Pagan week; and one coincidence has just as much to do with the occurrence of the event as the other; but both are wholly foreign to anything which we are able to extract from the Greek original. There are just eight passages where this English phrase, "first day of the week," appears, namely:

1. Matt. xxviii : 1—εἰς μίαν σαββάτων.
2. Mark xvi : 2—πρωὶ τῆς μιᾶς σαββάτων.
3. Mark xvi : 9—πρωὶ πρώτῃ σαββάτον.
4. Luke xxiv : 1—τῇ δὲ μιᾷ τῶν σαββάτων.
5. John xx : 1—τῇ δὲ μιᾷ τῶν σαββάτων.
6. John xx : 19—τῇ μιᾷ σαββάτων.
7. Acts xx : 7—τῇ μιᾷ τῶν σαββάτων.
8. 1 Cor. xvi : 2—κατὰ μίαν σαββάτων.

A careful examination of these passages leads us to wonder how the whole Christian world have consented to such a construction. As to the force of interpretation, all these passages may be regarded as but a *single case*, since the Greek expression, whether found in the New Testament, or cited by the Fathers, with some slight grammatical variations, is substantially the same in all; and its literal English signification is, "On one of the Sabbaths." That we are not presuming, without a precedent, to array our individual opinion, as to this rendering, against that of the entire conclave of Christian scholars, let us here observe, that no less a man than John Calvin, in his notes on I Cor. xvi : 2, gives it this identical construction—" On one of the Sabbaths !"

Where, then, is the authority in any other Greek usage for making the phrase mean " the first day of the week ?" Out of the hundreds of places where this word σάββατον occurs, both in Scripture Greek, and all other Greek, so far as we can find, there is not one single instance where the word in any of its forms has, or can have, the signification of ἑβδομάς. We are aware of the almost universal consent to give the word in these eight or nine passages of the New Testament the meaning of *week*. Scholars seem to have blindly followed one another, generation after generation. As a specimen of this arbitrary and forced construction, we may refer to Dr. Edward Robinson, one of the most eminent of modern exegetists. What does he say? Why, that wherever the word σάββατον is preceded by a numeral it has the signification of *week*. And what are his examples? Substantially *only two* in all Greek literature, namely—the eight passages already cited, which for this purpose can only be counted as *one*, and another passage in Luke xviii : 12, where the phrase, νηστεύω δὶς τοῦ σαββάτου, is translated, " I fast twice in the week." But why not give the literal rendering, which would much better suit the circumstances, " I fast twice on the Sabbath?" This constitutes the entire array of Greek precedent and usage for the present English version of the phrase. If there be any other authority or principle on which our version can be justified, we should like to see it produced. But in the absence of all such proof, we are not inclined to take any *ipse dixit*—and feel constrained, like Galileo, in his day, to reject the general opinion, and adhere to the literal version—" On one of the Sabbaths."

What then follows? Why, simply, that Christ rose on a day which is called in the Scriptures *a Sabbath* ; that on that day he first met with his disciples ; that " eight days after," which is confessedly the idiom for a *week*, he met with them again, so that the last of those days which closed the first Christian week was *the Christian Sabbath*. If Christ rose on a Sabbath, as we have shown, and on the same day met with his disciples, and then " eight days " after they met again, the second meeting must have been likewise on the Sabbath. For, counting the

Sabbath on which he rose an intercalated day, as commencing a new calendar, then the eighth day after would be another Sabbath, which with the six intervening secular days, or Christian week, fills out the octave, and gives us the demonstration required.   Hence we see why the last seven days of this octave must be counted as the first ·Christian week.   If this be correct, we have, in that narrative of John, the introduction of the new calendar and the reckoning of the first Christian week, with its seventh day for the Christian Sabbath, and so onward from that time to this.   Now, discarding our English version, which is simply discarding the Jewish calendar, which with the whole typical system, the apostle in his writing says, again and again, was abrogated, we come back to the real narrative of the Christian Sabbath, and find that, despite the frequent assertions to the contrary, this day of Christian convocation is called a *Sabbath*, and that this is the first and principal title given to it in the New Testament.   In one place (Rev. i: 10) it seems to be called "the Lord's day," $\tau\tilde{\eta}$ $\varkappa\upsilon\rho\iota\alpha\varkappa\tilde{\eta}$ $\dot{\eta}\mu\dot{\epsilon}\rho\alpha$.   In another place (Acts xiii: 42) it appears to be described as $\tau\dot{o}$ $\mu\epsilon\tau\alpha\xi\upsilon$ $\delta\dot{\alpha}\beta\beta\alpha\tau o\nu$, " the Sabbath intervening," or, between two Jewish Sabbaths, and it is never called "the first day of the week," much less "Sunday," which belongs to the Pagans.

In further confirmation of this point, look carefully at the Greek of Matt. xxviii: 1.   What is it? $\dot{o}\psi\dot{\epsilon}$ $\delta\dot{\epsilon}$ $\sigma\alpha\beta\beta\dot{\alpha}\tau\omega\nu$— literally, "but late of Sabbaths "—or, as we should say, "at the close of the Sabbaths," that is, the series of Jewish Sabbaths—$\tau\tilde{\eta}$ $\dot{\epsilon}\pi\iota\varphi\omega\sigma\varkappa o\dot{\upsilon}\sigma\eta$—literally " in the dawning ;" $\epsilon i\varsigma$ $\mu\dot{\iota}\alpha\nu$ $\sigma\alpha\beta\beta\dot{\alpha}\tau\omega\nu$—literally, "on one of the Sabbaths," that is, the new series of Sabbaths then commencing.   So far as we can see, this passage distinctly relates to the close of one series of Sabbaths and the beginning of another series, which is precisely according to the fact.   The Jewish Sabbaths were then legally closed, and the Christian Sabbaths began.   So we find two Sabbaths coming together at the Resurrection of Christ. He slumbered in the sepulchre during the Jewish Sabbath, and rose from the dead on the next day, which is styled, in a narrative inspired by the Holy Ghost, $\mu\dot{\iota}\alpha\nu$ $\tau\tilde{\omega}\nu$ $\sigma\alpha\beta\beta\dot{\alpha}\tau\omega\nu$— "one of the Sabbaths."   And this concinnity, by which the Christian Sabbath is made to supervene the Jewish Sabbath, finds a stiking parallel in the narrative of the Pass-

over and the Eucharist. At the institution of the Lord
Supper, the two feasts come together, one immediately aft
the other. From that day the yearly observance of the P
over was legally concluded, and the Lord's Supper succeed(
it. Although the Jews continued afterward the Passov
observance, it had no binding authority of law. In like ma
ner, the Christian Sabbath succeeded the Jewish, although tl
Jews continue the observance of their Sabbath to this da
Their calendar, however, is no longer in vogue but amon
themselves, and it never had any obligatory or legal forc
among the nations of Christendom. But what a gloss
on this passage has been perpetuated in our English version!
Not only does it violate the grammar of the passage, but it
gives to the second σαββάτων a meaning altogether different
from the first, and for no reason in the premises. The construction is purely arbitrary and calculated to mislead. After
thus turning the text of Scripture upside down, it is no wonder
that men deny to the Christian Sabbath its proper title.

Having now shown the clear existence and recognition of
the Christian Sabbath in the New Testament, we cannot fail
to see how completely it comes under the direct application of
the fourth commandment. " Six days shalt thou labor and do
all thy work, but the seventh is the Sabbath of the Lord thy
God." " The seventh " of what ? Certainly the seventh day of
the established week, whatever it may be. Under the Patriarchal dispensation it was the seventh day of the Creation
week; under the Jewish dispensation it was the seventh day
of the Jewish week; and now, under the Christian dispensation
it is the seventh day of the Christian week. Hence our present Christian Sabbath has all the sanction and obligation which
the fourth commandment can give to it. It is the Sabbath of
the Lord our God ; Christ is God and the Lord of the Sabbath.
He has fixed its status in the Christian era by his resurrection,
and has taught men how to observe it. The doctrine is simple
and the proof is clear. Stated from the Bible stand-point, it
seems to be impregnable.

What it obviates.

1. In the first place we avoid the old false issue, respecting
the alleged change from the seventh to the first day of the Jew-

ish week. We have nothing to do with that. The mere circumstance, that our Christian Sabbath happens to fall on the first
day of the week in the Jewish calendar, has no more to do with
its origin and establishment, than the fact that it also happens
to fall on the Sunday of the Pagan week. It is nothing more
than a coincidence of time—and we might as well call the Pagan
Sunday the first day of the Jewish week, and *vice versa*, as to
call our Christian Sabbath either "Sunday," or "the first day of
the week." It is this misapplication of Pagan and Jewish terms
to our Christian Sabbath which has brought confusion, error,
and long protracted controversy. Let us call it by the name
which is given it in the New Testament, and not by any foreign title. This point, we are glad to say, was insisted upon
in our last General Assembly. So with the falling of this old
issue falls a great part of the discussion which constitutes the
vast and tiresome literature of the Sabbath question.

2. **Again**, we thus avoid the necessity of demoralizing the
Decalogue, of conceding that the fourth commandment is
no part of the moral code. True, as applied to the observance
of the Jewish Sabbath for the Jews alone, peculiar restrictions
and rigors were added to it. (See Ex. xxxi: 13–17, and xxxv:
2–3; and Num. xv: 32–36.) Christ, however, struck these off
in the new dispensation. He distinguished between the form
and spirit of the law as it stands in the Decalogue on the one
hand, and on the other, those conditions and peculiar regulations of the Jewish Sabbath, which were designed for that people and that ordinance alone. But the abrogation of these regulations left the fourth commandment still in all its force—just
as His abrogation of the Mosaic causes of divorce left the validity
of the *one cause* unimpaired. The law which requires the sanctity of the Sabbath stands upon the same footing in the doctrine of Christ, with the law which protects the marriage state.
The seventh commandment is no more a part of the moral
code than the fourth. There is no cause for its segregation,
save and except only the supposed change from the seventh
to the first day of the Jewish week. This fruitless speculation
assails the integrity of a law which was designed to be, and is,
perpetual.

3. Again, we avoid the necessity of tracing any identity of
time between the Patriarchal, the Jewish, and the Christian

weeks—and so between their respective Sabbaths. Specious
but doubtful arguments have been adduced for their chronological identity, as though this would add to their authority.
But the question is wholly immaterial, and as we find in the
Scriptures no trace of their historic connections—as each of
them stands on the merit of its separate nature and design,
and as one supersedes the other without any special notice
of the change, it is only idle to moot the point at all.

4. Again, we avoid the necessity of answering arguments
drawn from all those notices of the Jewish Sabbath in the New
Testament, on which were held assemblies to whom Christ
and his apostles preached. Notwithstanding the Jewish Sabbaths were then legally closed, yet the Jews, by force of custom, held then, as they do now, to their Sabbath ordinance,
In the beginning it was necessary, for an effectual ministry;
that Christ and his followers should be brought in contact
with the collected people. But the fact that they used for
this purpose the Jewish days of convocation no more invalidates the origin and authority of the Christian Sabbath than
the fact that they preached to the multitudes on other days
of the week negatives the existence of the Jewish Sabbath
custom. And so all arguments drawn from this source against
the Christian Sabbath are seen to be irrelevant.

5. Again, we thus avoid the necessity of refuting arguments,
drawn from the doctrine of Paul, respecting the sacred days
of the Jewish calendar. These days in all their routine, he
plainly tells us, are no longer of divine sanction and obligation—no longer binding on the conscience, whether of Jew
or Gentile. They have all alike become indifferent—men
may keep them or not, at their pleasure. But we are not for
a moment to suppose that this teaching of Paul is designed
to abrogate the fourth commandment, or to detract from the
doctrine of Christ himself in regard to the Sabbath ordinance.
When we hear from the writer of the epistle to the Hebrews—
see iv: 9—that "there is left a Sabbath-keeping to the people
of God," and have grounds to believe that these are the
words of Paul, we must look for some principle of harmoniz-
ing one part of this statement with the other; and the only
conclusion is, that while he altogether sets aside the Levitical
economy, he plainly shows that the Sabbatic Institution

changed to a different day, by the change of the Hebrew week, is to continue in perpetuity to the people of God.

6. Again, we thus avoid all devious reasoning on the Institution of the Christian Sabbath, from the days of the early fathers until now.   We find such reasoning fanciful and inconsistent, full of assumption and contrariety, and the fruit of a capricious and fertile imagination.   It proceeds often from the confusion of subjects, from false analysis, from imperfect investigation, from dubious illustration, from a traditional credulity, from the power of custom, from the weight of great names, from the spirit of partisanship, and from the pride of victory.   One proposal is, that the law requires only one-seventh of the time—one day in seven, no matter which; another is, that the requirement is impracticable, since the antipodes cannot observe the same time—nor can the observance of any time be enforced on multitudes of human beings; another is, that there is no trace either of the name, or of the observance of *our* Christian Sabbath through the first three centuries; another is, that the day observed by Christians was never called "the Sabbath" until the time of Origen (A. D. 254); another is, that the Sabbath ordinance had its rise in the decree of Constantine the Great (A. D. 321), and so on *ad libitum*. Now we know that all these propositions are inadequate—if not unfounded; and, by simply adhering to what we find in the word of God upon the Sabbath question, we can afford to cast aside all arguments and expositions which spring from other quarters. And thus we think we show a valid Bible ground for the authority and obligation of this Christian ordinance—one of the most beneficent of God's gifts to man, and for the maintenance and defense of which we are sacredly bound to use all lawful means in our power, both with individuals and nations.

II.—DESIGN.

Time in itself is an abstraction.   It is of no value separate from life and history.   Events in their succession give to it a measurement and periodicity.   Creation, with all it contains, subsists in conditions of activity and repose.   A period of motion followed by a period of rest is the requirement of all living beings.   This is pre-eminently true of human nature, an aptitude which is recognized and utilized in the Word of God. The weekly period of labor and rest is not founded in caprice, but in the constitution of man himself. The design of the Sabbath, or seventh day of the week, is not arbitrary, but fits into the needs of mankind. The Scriptures show this design to be, physical rest and moral uses, suspension from secular and engagement in sacred things. The Sabbath is God's memorial in the earth—one of those grand religious land-marks by which the course of generations is to be traced throughout successive ages. Its design is to break the current of human affairs and create a pause for the advantage of man's higher nature. It is to grant occasion to turn away the thoughts from perishable things to those which are imperishable, from converse with the mundane to communion with the heavenly sphere, from His works of creation to God himself. In other words, the Sabbath is to be a day for those hallowed uses of all things, those humane deeds and religious acts which lift up society to a nobler plane of existence, and fit mankind for a better life here, and a sublime immortality hereafter. We surely know this both from the law and the prophets, the evangelists and apostles, and, more than all, the living Christ himself.

" And God blessed the seventh day and sanctified it, because that in it he had rested from all his work."—*Gen.* ii : 3.

" Remember the Sabbath day to keep it holy—six days shalt thou labor and do all thy work, but the seventh is the Sabbath of the Lord thy God."—*Ex.* xx : 8, 9, 10.

" Blessed is the man that doeth this ; that keepeth the Sabbath from polluting it."—*Isa.* lvi : 2.

" If thou turn away thy foot from the Sabbath, from doing thy pleasure on my holy day, and call the Sabbath a delight, the holy of the Lord—honorable—and shalt honor him, not doing thine own ways, nor finding thine own pleasure, nor speaking thine own words, then shalt thou delight thyself in the Lord, and I will cause thee to ride upon the high places of the earth and feed thee with the heritage of Jacob thy Father."—*Isa.* lviii : 13, 14.

" And it shall come to pass from one new moon to another, and from one Sabbath to another, shall all flesh come to worship before me, saith the Lord."—*Isa.* lxvi : 23.

" There remaineth therefore a *Sabbath-keeping* to the people of God."—*Heb.* iv: 9.

And to crown this testimony by showing the perpetual de﹅ sign of the Sabbath, we have both the acts and the doctrines of the ascended Saviour. The transcript of his example and the great fact of his resurrection from which our Sabbath is reckoned, and of which it is the continued memorial, is all before us. And then, as we have already seen, we have the positive instruction of his words: " the Sabbath was made for man, not man for the Sabbath..' This, as expressed in the original, is a deeply philosophical statement of the very design of the holy day. How is the Sabbath made for man? First, a seventh day, the last of the weekly period is set apart. It is so much time to be consecrated and employed for the highest and most enduring interest of our nature. Next, this time man devotes to such uses, and by such devotion it becomes a hallowed day; man keeps it holy according to the commandment. The Sabbath does not hallow the man, but the man the Sabbath. This is the order and mode in which it comes to be. In doing this man honors the Lord of the .Sabbath, and receives in return the promised blessing. The Sabbath cannot make man holy, but he can make it holy, and therein glorify God and enrich himself. This is the truth which Christ unfolded while declaring himself to be Lord of the Sabbath. It would be long, and is, perhaps, now needless, to show in how many ways the full working of this benignant design among men would benefit the world. It may be safely said that there is no real good for man, however considered, which it would not promote, and no evil which it would not tend to mitigate or remove.

III.—OBSERVANCE.

Having now shown the authority and design of the Christian Sabbath, as a divine ordinance of perpetual obligation, we come to submit some observations on the manner of its observance. What light do the Scriptures cast on this important practical subject? While the teaching of God's word is mainly general, yet it is broad enough to cover the whole question of human duty, and the obligations of individual conscience in every condition and generation of mankind. The Bible is a book of principles, as well as of institutions. The law is clearly stated, but at the same time, in its detailed application to specific acts and circumstances, much has been left to the individual conscience and judgment of men. It is here that our responsibility begins. Here we must seek to know the will of God, and to cherish the spirit of obedience.

A studious collation of Scripture hints would disclose the following particulars of a Christian observance of the Sabbath :

1. The Sabbath must be remembered.—*Ex.* xx: 8.

2. It must be hallowed.—*Ex.* xx: 8.

3. It must be secure from ordinary secular occupation, being, in this respect, a day of rest.—*Ex.* xx : 9.

4. It must be employed in divine worship—private and public—with meditation, prayer, and the preaching of the word.—*Isaiah* lxvi : 23, and *Acts* xx: 7.

5. It must be hailed as the honorable of the Lord, and held in delight as a day of gladness and of the Eucharist.—*Isaiah* lviii : 13; *Ps.* cxviii: 24; *Acts* xx : 7; 1 *Cor.* x : 16.

6. It must not be dishonored by frivolous recreation or idle pleasure.—*Isaiah* lviii: 13.

7. It must not be disturbed by unseemly noise and tumult.—*Hab.* ii : 20; Matt. 24 : 20; *Heb.* iv : 9.

8. It must not be outraged by gala spectacles and vain parades.—*Isaiah* lviii: 13; *Ps.* lxv : 1, 2, 4, 7.

9. It must not be profaned by traffic for gain or sordid industry.—*Neh.* xiii : 15-22; *Isaiah* lviii : 13.; *John* ii : 13, 17.

10. It must not be polluted by any form of vice or dissipation.—*Isaiah* lvi : 2.

11. It may be used in acts of social intercourse; spent in imperative travel ; visiting the prisoner, the sick, or the poor ; in religious instruction, and deeds of charity.—*Matt.* xii : 1, 13 ; *Luke* xiii: 10, 17, and xxiv: 13, 31.

12. It may be employed in any works of necessity or mercy. —*Mark* ii: 23, 28, *et passim.*

These conditions of Sabbatic obligation apply generally to human society. They belong alike to the individual, the family, the community, the church, and the state. They are equally binding on young and old, and find their modification only in those cases of exigency which are clearly sanctioned under some phase of Providence.

Such is the Scripture outline of a Sabbath observance which

seems equally removed from that of the Jewish synagogue, and that of a German beer-garden. A Pharisaic austerity and a French indulgence are alike excluded. In the reaction in this country from Puritan Sabbatism, the nation has been drifting to the opposite extreme of continental license, and the danger now is, that with such views as have passed current among professedly Christian teachers through many centuries, the divine ordinance, as it was left by Christ and his apostles, may be inundated and practically swept away. Are the Christian church and this favored Republic prepared for such a catastrophe?

It remains for us, in this light, to distinguish the more prevalent forms of Sabbath desecration, or Sabbath abuse, in our time, to show the consequent demoralization, and to offer an appeal for a return to the old Scripture path, wherein is the right way of prosperity and peace :

1. In the first place, the Sunday press, as conducted among us, must be regarded as a monstrous example of Sabbath desecration. Its very name denotes its Pagan origin and spirit. Under the Sabbath law, as Christ left it, the only possible justification of any Sabbath publication must be found in public necessity for the diffusion of current intelligence. It is possible that on this ground a Sabbath journalism can be made to stand. But we all know the general nature of the product of the Sunday press, and the outrage upon the quiet of the Christian Sabbath, and the public morals, which its sale inflicts. It may be truly stated as a rule, the exceptions being rare, that the reading thus furnished to the nation, and, unhappily, to large portions of the church, is of a fearfully debauching character. No possible necessity exists. It is simply a transcendant and unblushing violation of the law of God.

2. Again, Sunday parades and noisy processions in time of peace, excursions of pleasure, and open places of amusement, or dissipation, are, as a rule, clearly in conflict with the law of the Christian Sabbath. So far from securing one of the primary objects of the Sabbath—physical repose and refreshment—they tend to just the opposite result—fatigue, exhaustion, and disease of body ; a clouded mind ; a seared conscience ; and the paralysis of the whole moral man. They thus unfit their devotees for the succeeding sober and necessary duties and respon-

sibilities of life.   Their influence is every way pernicious, giving rein to disorder, and disregard for all law, human and divine. In the light of the Christian Sabbath ordinance, they must be condemned as flagrant offences against the welfare of society, both in church and state.   The specious pretexts by which they are upheld are only worthy of their heathen origin and Pagan name.   The Christian Sabbath is not a holiday for riot, and noise, and public pageantry, even though it were guised in Romish ceremonies or funeral solemnities.   The poor and friendless laboring classes may sometimes find a pitiful relief in this uncertain and transient excitement, but they will invariably pay for it in subsequent animal depression, and the utter prostration of the moral sense.   It is all very fair to talk about going forth to feel the balmy air, and bask in the clear sunlight ; about opening libraries, and furnishing art galleries, and the like, for the gratification and improvement of the lower orders, but let us not for this purpose conspire to cheat both God and man out of that day which is consecrated to our Redeemer's worship, and to the paramount interests of the human soul !

3. There is another prevalent form of Sabbath abuse, from which continual evil flows, and that is the work and travel of those who, in official station, or in a wide connection of industrial, commercial, or governmental affairs, plead necessity from lack of time or pressure of business.   It is possible that exceptional cases may exist for such a deviation from ordinary Sabbath law, but, at the very best, it is an evil without any other palliation ; and where submission to it is voluntary or habitual, it becomes an offence against the Lord's Day.   That there is a stolidity of conscience and a laxity of practice in this regard, widespread and increasing, is obvious to the most careless observer.   The whole usage is wrong and pernicious.   It is subversive of the very intent and spirit, as well as the letter, of the Sabbath law.   It perverts the Sabbath to improper uses, and prepares the mind for other and grosser forms of Sabbath violation.

At this point we may hold the government of the nation and corporate bodies responsible for every causeless infraction of the Sabbath law, either by themselves or those whom they employ ; whatever can be avoided out of respect to the divine authority of this Christian ordinance, men in every condition are bound to avoid. Whether in legislation or its execution this principle holds good, and its wanton contravention will produce unmixed evil with the growth of the country and the advance of civilization. Certain great forms of public demands have come into existence, requiring arrangements for the running of cars and the movement of vessels, for telegraphic operation, for mail transportation, and the transmission of intelligence. It is most difficult to draw the exact line of necessity about transactions of so wide a scope and so complicated a casuistry. But this one thing is plain, the principle of the Sabbath law remains, and there can be no case of rational and beneficent exertion for which it does not provide, while its sanction is withheld from all needless, selfish, or sordid application or employment of the day.

Nor are we clear that even in the church itself there has not grown to be an excessive and exhaustive labor. The necessity for preaching is as great as ever. The pulpit is more in demand than ever, but the quantity of ministration, especially in the centres of population, has been largely compensated by the changed circumstances of society. Books, periodicals, newspapers, and Sabbath-schools have, to a great extent, supplemented the work of the Gospel's ministry. Attendance upon Sabbath preaching, morning and evening, in addition to all the other duties which have their claim upon us, has become in many cases burdensome, if not impracticable. In this intense life and exacting civilization, both body and mind all the more need rest, while the demand of home life and family religion are likely to suffer neglect as well on the Sabbath as on other days of the week. Meanwhile, the labors of the Christian ministry have been augmented in many other directions. Their hands are full of appropriate work aside from pulpit preparation. And when to this is added the growing custom of Sabbath funerals, may it not be a question of the reduction of sermons to be preached on the Sabbath to the stated congregation, and of the discountenance of Sabbath funerals which but too frequently amount to a mere Sunday display.

Demoralization.

Upon a review, therefore, of the whole situation, can there be any doubt of the tendency to Sabbath desecration, and of the moral deterioration it inevitably involves? We have already seen the connection of this most beneficent ordinance of Heaven with the highest welfare of human nature; and we think there is no doubt that the most upright men among us—those of the deepest religious convictions, and the purest daily lives, other things being equal—are those on whom in childhood was impressed by a pious parentage the sanctity of the Sabbath, and the fidelity of its observance. There is a wondrous connection, as all experience and observation show, between the influence of this hallowed day, and the varied welfare of humanity. When, therefore, it is prostrated, wantonly and wickedly trampled under foot, we may expect nothing but an outbreak of irreligion, infidelity, vice and pollution on every hand. Its general disregard would be like the opening of Pandora's box. It would be hoisting the flood-gates of iniquity, to deluge the land with all forms of immorality, all deeds of turpitude and shame. The very permanence of society would be thus endangered, and the people would be fitted for such calamities and wars, as have been so often the sad maturity of human infatuation. History is full of examples of the most solemn warning. And it is no wonder that when men like Luther, the ruling spirit of the Reformation, came to tell the people of Central Europe that they are at liberty to trample down this ordinance of God—all the licentiousness of a continental Sunday should be the result—or that when men like Prof. Hopkins, eminent in the church of our own time, come to tell Americans that there is no express divine authority for the Christian Sabbath, all the grosser elements of society should hail the announcement, and prepare themselves with greater freedom for a carnival of Sunday pleasure, low and unrestrained! Such, I am sure, is not the doctrine of the holy prophets and apostles. Such is not the will of Christ himself, the Head of the church and the supreme Lawgiver of the world!

The Appeal.

When, therefore, we come to read in God's word, the blessings which fall on the keepers of the Sabbath, and the curses which overtake all those who habitually neglect or dishonor it; when to the voice of the written Revelation is joined the testimony of nature, and of man himself, the evidence of individual experience, and of national prosperity, the support of historic demonstration, and of providential care; do we not find the strongest motives to a united and earnest effort to rescue the Christian Sabbath from profanation, and to defend it from all assaults? When we recall the attitude of the founders of the Republic, the noble words they uttered for the Sabbath, and their warnings against its popular demoralization; when we remember the recent attempt to blot out the Sabbath during the progress of that grand Centennial Exposition, which is designed for a memorial alike of the birth of the Republic, the mighty deeds of our fathers, and of all the triumphs of the first great century of our national existence; an attempt which was happily frustrated by the energies of the most noble and Christian men of the country; and when, at this moment, we are reminded of the convention of European Protestants, at Geneva, during this very year, to consider in what way they may bring back their nationalities to the simple doctrine of the New Testament, upon the question of the Christian Sabbath; must we not, in all this, find a new incitement and a fresh encouragement in every honest effort to maintain the sanctity of the Lord's day, and to impress upon our government, and upon all classes of our people, an immanent sense of its overwhelming importance?

Let us then hear no more and have no more of that vain liberalism, which virtually surrenders the battle before it is begun.   But let the Christian ministry and the Christian church, let every patriot and every philanthropist, join hands together in this divine cause, and let the resolution be, never to quit the work of Sabbath Reformation, till everywhere the day shall be sincerely acknowledged, and held with reverence in every heart.

If the Sabbath of the Christian is such as we have described it, we may well feel that it is the sheet-anchor of our individual, social, and national prosperity. Its faithful observance will not alone be pleasing to God, which is the highest consideration, but will also surely entail his gracious Benediction on us, and on our children, and children's children, to the latest generations.

Art. VI.—PRESENT FACILITIES FOR EVANGELIZING THE WORLD.

By the Rev. R. G. WILDER, late Missionary to India.

AN impression is widely current that missionaries engaged in evangelizing heathen nations at the present time, labor at serious disadvantage compared with the Apostles, and their immediate successors. A recent writer, the Rev. G. H. Rouse, of Calcutta, India, has developed this idea at some length in the July number (IX) of *The Indian Evangelical Review*, and his sentiments are so generally entertained, that there is the more reason for noticing them, in speaking of present facilities for prosecuting this evangelizing work. In noticing them, however, we desire to do so, not at all in the spirit of controversy, but entirely in the interest of the work itself. The writer referred to states his proposition as follows, viz. :

"The early preachers of the Gospel enjoyed many great advantages, as compared with the preachers of the present day." And in specifying these advantages, he mentions, first, "The power of working miracles." And after giving a somewhat extended list of apostolic miracles, and dwelling on their startling and convincing effect, he removes all ambiguity, and renders his view complete and distinct by saying, "We have no such power ; therefore, we cannot be surprised if our success is not equal to that of the Apostles."

On this we remark :

1. It was the special *dis*advantages of those early preachers that made this power of working miracles in their case proper and, in a measure, necessary. Had they possessed all the facilities of the present day, and this power of working miracles superadded, we might then speak of it as a positive advantage. But such was not the case. The very fact that God gave them, and not us, this power of working miracles, justifies the inference that God saw a special reason for bestowing on them this gift. And though we may not be able to comprehend this reason in its full extent, we can see, in the special circumstances of the case, enough to justify its bestowment on the preachers of that age, rather than on those of any subsequent age.

Opposition to the Gospel was then universal. "Darkness covered the earth, and gross darkness the people." * Outside the Hebrew nation, superstition and idolatry everywhere prevailed ; while Christ encountered the most intense hatred and opposition from the Jews themselves. "He came unto his own, and his own received him not." † If the reigning idolatry and superstition were to be broken up, if that intense darkness, and the perversity of Jewish minds, even, ·were to be penetrated with divine light, the occasion, then, if ever, fully justified miraculous intervention for the mere purpose of startling and arresting attention. Besides, it was the beginning of a new dispensation. The old Mosaic ritual, finding its fulfilment in the advent of the promised Messiah, was to be abrogated. Usages which had gathered force for ages were to be discontinued. "The kingdom of heaven was at hand."‡ And the difficulty of inaugurating it, in that climax of human depravity and spiritual death, justified and, in a measure, necessitated the use of miracles, merely for their startling and convincing effect—in such measure, indeed, as does not now exist. We shall be told that the case of heathen nations now is much the same. In the fact of the darkness, idolatry, and superstition of some of them we grant it. But in the absence of any Christian nation to break the universal darkness, and, both by precept and example, hold up to them the true light of life, the condition of existing heathen is not the same. In this respect, missionaries of the present day have an immense advantage, as will appear more fully in the sequel. Hence we assume, that to those early preachers the gift of miracles, estimated only for their startling and convincing effect, was not so much an advantage over present preachers, as it was a partial compensation for their great disadvantages.

But this startling and convincing effect of miracles—the only one (save their healing efficacy) which can be urged in plea of their necessity now—was not their primary or chief object, even in Apostolic times. Their true object was to attest the Messiahship and resurrection of Jesus. The special need of miracles for this purpose is universally conceded ; as, also, the necessity of their being performed at or near the time and

---

* Isaiah lx : 2.   † John i : 11.   ‡ Mat. iv : 17.

place of Christ's advent and public ministry. Here was an occasion worthy of miracles. The union of divinity and humanity in the person of the Son of God is itself the greatest of all miracles, and required the most positive confirmation by God himself. It is not too much to say that, excepting those specially taught of God, like Simeon and Anna in the temple,[*] a readiness to receive Jesus of Nazareth as the true Messiah, without such confirmation, would have been credulity, not faith.

And so, too, in regard to the evidence of Christ's resurrection—the last and crowning proof of his Messiahship. Ordinary witnesses were not sufficient. Their testimony needed confirmation. Their veracity and credibility, in a matter of such immense moment, required to be divinely attested. God could and did attest the Messiahship of Jesus by "a voice from the excellent glory," declaring, "This is my beloved Son, in whom I am well pleased."[†] But only a few heard this voice, and, to render it of service to others, this direct testimony of God himself, like that in proof of the resurrection, depends on the veracity of the disciples. Hence the need of divine testimony to their veracity and credibility. And how was this testimony possible by other and more conclusive means than this gift to them of working miracles in Christ's name. This was bestowed in the time, place, manner, and extent most fitting in the view of God himself.

Looking at the great scheme of human redemption in its progressive development, to plead that those early preachers had advantages over those of the present age, is virtually to urge that *they* have the advantage in a most difficult enterprise, who plan and labor near its inception, rather than those who push forward the same enterprise after grand and glorious results have been achieved.

Doubtless it will be readily conceded that there was a necessity for this power of working miracles, in the case of those early preachers, not now existing—that we can conceive in no way in which the Messiahship of Jesus, and the divine commission of the Apostles, could have been established without the gift of this power. And yet, some may still urge, that could

---

* Luke ii: 25-36.   † 2 Pet. i: 17.

missionaries have this power superadded to their present facilities for evangelizing the heathen, they might hope for much
more rapid success.   To such we reply :

2. Miracles have no converting efficacy.   Such efficacy is not
claimed by the writer mentioned.   He frankly concedes, " We
do not, for a moment, say that miracles, by themselves, will
convert the soul."   The special virtue he claims for them, is
their power to arrest the attention of careless and stolid hearers.
Waiving here the question, whether God has ever bestowed
the gift of miracles *merely* or *mainly* for this purpose, or
whether it would be worthy of him to do so, it may be safely
affirmed, that of all who witnessed the miracles wrought by
Christ and the Apostles, by far the larger part disregarded
them, and lived and died in unbelief.   Even in case of that
most astounding miracle, the raising of Lazarus from the dead
—while we read "many . . believed on him ;" we also
read, " but some of them went their ways to the Pharisees,"
who "from that day forth took counsel together, to put him
to death," and even conspired to kill Lazarus also.*   The
thousands who saw the miracle of the loaves and fishes,
followed Christ, not because of the miracle, but because they
did eat of the loaves and were filled.†   So far were miracles
from having any converting or saving power, that they not unfrequently roused the most implacable hatred.   The healing of
the cripple at Lystra startled and roused the people, at first,
to such an extent, that they were ready to sacrifice to Paul
and Barnabas as gods.‡   But how evanescent this result of
the miracle !   How quickly they stoned Paul and drew him
out of the city, supposing he had been dead."   The casting
out of the "spirits of divination" from the damsel,§ instead of convincing and converting the people, proved but the
signal for a murderous attack on Paul and Silas.

Pretended miracles are not infrequent among superstitious
heathen at the present time ; and their effect on minds receiving them as veritable miracles, is probably not altogether
unlike the effect of true miracles on most of those who
witnessed them in the days of the Apostles.   At the village of
Ratrer, on the banks of the Krishna River, in India, thirty

---

* John xi : 45, 46, 53, and xii : 10.   † John vi : 26.   ‡ Acts xiv : 8-19.   § Acts
xvi : 16.

miles from the writer's home, there recently appeared a religious devotee—a Hindoo Wainegi—claiming to exercise
miraculous power in curing certain diseases. His fame spread
rapidly and widely through the whole region. Thousands
flocked to him, and scores claimed to have become healed of
their diseases by his miracles. It was estimated by intelligent
observers, who regarded him only as an impostor, that 50,000
people visited him the first month—generally the lowest and
most superstitious of the people. After the first month
curiosity subsided, the throngs rapidly diminished, and at the
end of three months, when we visited him personally, he had
not had a visitor for ten days, and was just on the point of
deserting the place for some remote region, and yet, of all the
superstitious thousands who visited him, and the scores who
claimed to have been cured of pains and diseases by him, we
were never able, before or after our visit to him, to elicit from
any one a word of doubt as to his miraculous power. Many
stoutly affirmed their previous sufferings and their positive relief on visiting the miracle-worker. But curiosity was thus
quickly sated, and he ceased to draw. Take, with this fact,
the testimony of *Merivale*, as to the influence of miracles in the
first centuries of the Christian era, viz.: "There was great
proneness to accept the claim of miracles; but, at the same
time, and *in consequence of this very proneness*, very little weight
was attached to it [this claim] as an argument of divine
power."*

We need not stop to point out the difference between such
spurious miracles and those recorded in the New Testament.
The latter had a worthy purpose aside from all healing mercy
attending them. They were to attest the Messiahship and
resurrection of Jesus, the credibility of the Apostles, and the
divine authority of their teaching; and thus to subserve the
highest good of man and the glory of God. The former furnished
credentials to no new teacher, introduced no new truth—no
moral or spiritual teaching whatever. The Wainegi's religious
character and claims were as readily admitted before as after
his pretended miracles; and his motive and object were patent
—selfishness and personal aggrandizement, fame and the offer-

---

* *Conversion of Rom. Empire*, p. 9.

ings of those who visited him ; and these latter received from him no moral or spiritual teaching, nothing of any kind which could become the germ of a new or better life. The only benefit from such miracles, wholly disconnected with moral and spiritual teaching, must be temporal good—the healing of bodily disease. But even this, in the case before us, existed only in the fancy of the superstitious persons claiming to have been healed. No benefit to them, even, was manifested to others.

The New Testament miracles, on the other hand, are inseparably linked with the most profound and vital spiritual truths ever conceived of by the human mind. Detached from these, true miracles would at once become comparatively insignificant. Linked with them, as the Apostolic miracles always are, and still it is not the miracles, but the vital truths they teach, substantiate and enforce, that produce spiritual and saving effects on human hearts. Hence, the instances of conversion as the direct results of true miracles, without preaching, are few, if any; whereas, " it pleased God by the foolishness of preaching to save them that believe."* Preaching, without miracles, was effective in Apostolic times, as well as now. At Iconium, Paul and Barnabas " *so spake* that a great multitude . . believed."† The miracle which shook the foundation of Paul and Silas' prison at midnight, struck off their manacles, and threw open their prison doors, only made the jailor unsheath his sword to kill himself. It was Paul's *preaching* that led him to cry out, " What must I do to be saved?" and led to his faith and baptism.‡ It may be doubted whether the startling miracle on the day of Pentecost would have resulted in the conversion of a single soul, but for Peter's sermon ; for it was " when they *heard this*, they were pricked in their hearts," and cried out, " What shall we do?" And " they that gladly *received his word* were baptized," and added to the church.§ The Apostle Paul ranks preaching much above the gift of tongues, even in his day.||

When we speak of our disadvantages from inability to work miracles now, it becomes us to bear in mind that a perpetual miracle is impossible in the very nature of the case. It must .

---

* 1 Cor. i: 21.   † Acts xiv: 1.   ‡ Acts xvi: 23-30.
§ Acts ii : 37, 41. || 1 Cor. xiv: 2-6.

transcend all usages and actions of known laws, or it is no miracle; and the perpetual recurrence of any event, takes from it the inherent elements of a miracle. Had God continued to send manna from Heaven, from the days of Moses to the present time, it would be no more a miracle now, than is the daily rising and setting of the sun. And, without doubt, every repetition of a miracle weakens its force, diminishes that much its startling and convincing effect, and by parity of reasoning, more or less weakens the force of any and all miracles; so that the use of miracles is limited, both by the inherent elements of a miracle, and by the very nature of the human mind.

As to the use of miracles for their startling and convincing effect, it is worthy of serious consideration, whether missionaries of the present day have not all desirable facilities for arresting the attention of their ignorant and superstitious, or careless and stolid hearers. Their foreign nationality, strange manners and customs, their different complexion and style of living, and, most of all, their marked superiority in education and knowledge of the arts and sciences, and the divine origin, character, power and sanctions of their holy faith, avail at once to attract all necessary attention. The first sight of a magic lantern, the first shock from an electric battery, the first sight of a railroad car flying thirty miles an hour, or of a message brought from the other side of the globe in a few minutes by means of a wire passing under the ocean, are really as startling and convincing to ignorant and superstitious heathen as any miracle that was ever wrought; so that the necessity of miracles for arresting the attention of the heathen can hardly be urged in this age. And in case of those whose attention has once been arrested, till they have heard the Gospel and turned away rejecting it, whether found in heathen or in Christian lands, if they desire to see miracles, they are much like those who came to Christ, seeking a sign (miracle), but whom he would not gratify.*

But would not this power of working miracles now furnish to heathen minds mighty and most desirable credentials to the character and divine authority of missionaries, and thus secure

---

* Mat. xvi : 1-4.

a ready reception of their message. Our train of remark on this point would take us over ground already traversed, and develop the comparatively barren results of miracles in the way of conversion, even in case of those performed by the Apostles, and by Christ himself. We readily admit that Christ and his Apostles needed such credentials. It was fitting and necessary that God should furnish miraculous proof of the messiahship of Christ, and of the character of the witnesses to his life, death and resurrection. But this has been done ; and in doing it, the doctrines of the Gospel have been clearly defined and established, so that its teachers and preachers now need no higher credentials than those which obtain from preaching those doctrines already stamped with the approval and seal of God. And this leads us to remark :

3. The value of every true miracle is perpetual.

Not for the people of Palestine only were the miracles of Christ and the Apostles wrought, but for the world; not for that age only, but for all subsequent time. We might as well attempt to limit the value of the resurrection, or the virtue of Christ's death, to the men of that generation, as to attempt thus to limit the design and use of the miracles of Christ and the Apostles. If matter is indestructible, how much more properly may we affirm that all moral truth is indestructible for all time and for all eternity? If God's dealings with his ancient people, the Jews, was not for them alone, but "for our admonition,"* how manifestly must this be true of every miracle of past generations? And as to the miracles wrought in proof of Christ's Messiahship, and in confirmation of the character and credibility of those early preachers and witnesses of his resurrection, we submit the inquiry, Have not the Christian preachers of the present day a special advantage? Does not the fancied advantage of those early preachers turn wholly on the startling and convincing character of miracles, already shown to be so barren of results in actual conversions? Is there not a special value in the test to which these same miracles have been subjected for eighteen centuries? Prudent and thoughtful minds are not carried away by the blaze and glare of sudden events, however startling. They will not readily be led captive by false prophets and false Christs. And who can

---

* 1 Cor. x : 11.

doubt that it is better to be slow and cautious in recognizing
and receiving truth, even, than rashly to follow Theudas and
his four hundred, to be slain, or scattered and brought to
nought ?*

And so far as the use of miracles to convince the unbelieving is concerned, could not the hearers of those early preachers,
in the very presence of their miracles, plead a better excuse
for suspending judgment or withholding faith than can be
urged by unbelievers of the present day? When the chief
priests and elders suborned the soldiers to report—" His disciples came by night and stole him away while we slept "†—had
they not a far better chance for the success of their plot than
they would have now? When Galileo first announced the
earth's motion and was compelled to recant on pain of death,
what wonder if others still doubted? But since his declaration
has endured the criticism and test of centuries, only to be
more clearly demonstrated and fully confirmed, can any one
longer doubt, or furnish any reasonable excuse for unbelief?
As we go to the heathen and supplant their false physical science with the facts and teachings of true science, demonstrated
and established beyond the possibility of a doubt by any intelligent mind, so also we take to them the facts and teachings of
the Gospel, attested and demonstrated with no less clearness
and certainty. We grant that the sight of the cross, with the
Son of God dying upon it, would move some minds more
deeply than a perusal of the recorded tragedy. But is not this
because of the more direct appeal to the passions through the
sense of sight? It is the *fact* of the sufferings and death of
the Son of God that appeals to the reason, the intellect, and
the heart, and results in repentance and saving faith, when
these obtain. Of all that multitude who followed him to Calvary, how few repented and believed, even though the sun was
darkened, the earth quaked, the rocks were rent, the graves
were opened, and many dead saints arose and went into the
city, and the centurion and they that were with him were constrained to exclaim, " Truly, this was the Son of God."‡ We
cannot doubt the profoundness of their impression, but, alas !
how transient and ineffective ! And can any one desire that

---

* Acts v: 37.   † Mat. xxviii : 13.   ‡ Mat. xxvii : 51-54.

the scenes of the crucifixion and resurrection be re-enacted for their convincing effect on careless, worldly, and stolid hearers? And is there, really, any more occasion for a repetition of one of the miracles, divinely appointed and employed for demonstrating tne Messiahship of Jesus, and attesting the character and credibility of those early preachers and witnesses? When a case has been brought into court, and all the facts and witnesses have been duly examined, and a decision has been reached after the most searching and thorough investigation and the most mature deliberation possible, if a party come and ask for a new trial, or a repetition of the testimony, must he be gratified? Is it not rather obligatory on said party to point out some error in fact or in testimony before asking a re-hearing? And, in this case, an attempt to point out such error having been repeated again and again by successive generations of infidels during a period of more than eighteen hundred years, and all in vain, are we not now entitled to consider this case finally closed?—to receive the Gospel as fully established, requiring no new proof, and no repetition of the miracles which attended Christ's advent, attesting once for all time his Messiahship and resurrection? Whether preaching to unbelievers in Christendom, or to ignorant and superstitious heathen, are we not entitled to take the Gospel as God's only remedy for sin, and the proofs by which it was established as potential and operative for all time, without any attempt or wish to re-enact them?

We would attribute no intentional impiety to those who seem to desire this power of working miracles, and regard its absence a weakness and disability in their practical ministry; and yet, do not their views and desires savor somewhat of the spirit of those who came to Jesus, saying, " Master, we would see a sign from thee," * when he had just restored the withered hand and cast out a devil, causing one blind and dumb both to see and speak? It is worthy of notice, in this connection, that Merivale mentions the " *historical testimony* " to the miracles of Christ and the Apostles as one of the chief agencies in the conversion of the Roman empire.

The *second* advantage claimed for those early preachers is

---

* Mat. xii: 38-39; x: 22.

the wide diffusion of Judaism. The language of the writer
above mentioned is, "Another great advantage which the early
heralds of the cross possessed, lay in the fact that the way had
been prepared for them by the spread of Judaism," through
"the dispersion of the Jewish people into all parts of the Roman empire."

We are ready to admit the full value of the "oracles of
God," and the highest estimate of the elements of the Gospel
as embodied in the Old Testament Scriptures, which had been
translated into Greek, and were more or less widely known in
Apostolic times. We cheerfully concede that the centurion of
Cesarea was, probably, not the only Jewish proselyte—not the
only Gentile who was "a devout man," "feared God," and
"prayed to God always." * And yet, do not all the facts on
this point, embodied in history, furnish ample proof that at
the date of Paul's conversion such devout Gentiles were
exceedingly few. Cannot every missionary in India reckon
up a larger number of such praying, God-fearing men
among the unbaptized Hindus of his acquaintance, than
history gives us any reason to believe there was in the whole
Gentile world at that date? And as to the "Hebrew Scriptures," translated into the one Greek language of that time,
but existing only in manuscript, have we not now both the Old
and New Testament translated, not only into Greek, and into
English, more widely spoken than Greek ever was, but into
some 200 of the prominent languages of the world, and printed
and circulated widely in every large unevangelized nation, in
its own native tongue?

And as to the dispersion of the Jews, those living representatives of Judaism—were they any more dispersed than
they are now? Have we not the "*Beni-Israel*" in India?
Are they not found in China and Africa, and all parts of the
known world?

And as to the help to those early preachers from Judaism
and the Jews—Is there not danger of somewhat overestimating
it? Does not the light from this source shine even more
brightly now, only that their glimmering torch pales before the
clearer shining of the full-orbed Gospel? Did the unbelieving
Jews really prove helpful to those early preachers? Who
commenced the persecution against them? Who murdered

---

* Acts x.

the first martyr, Stephen, venting their rage by gnashing on him with their teeth?* Who but Jews conspired against Paul, as soon as he was converted, "watching the gates of Damascus day and night to kill him?"† Who but Jews were those "more than forty men," who "bound themselves under a curse, saying that they would neither eat nor drink till they had killed Paul?"‡

In estimating the influence of Judaism on the Pagan mind with reference to Christianity, we must never forget that the orthodox Jews had crucified its founder, and the Pagans knew it; that every Christian sermon, like that of Peter on the day of Pentecost, charged home upon them this terrible crime, and that this new faith, at every step of its progress, impugned the national belief of the Jews. So directly opposed to Judaism, as then formulated, were the most vital elements of the Christian's faith and practice, that the Jewish priests, teachers and rulers everywhere opposed and interdicted the Christian teachers, imprisoned and scourged them, threatened them with death, stoned and beheaded them when they could, even in Pagan cities, calling in the aid of heathen magistrates, and rousing the prejudices and hatred of the heathen against the Christians, by every possible argument and influence in their power.

In prosecuting missions in India and elsewhere, we sometimes find occasion to lament the hindrance to our work from the pernicious influence of renegade Europeans and Americans, who, being nominal Christians, are looked upon by the heathen as representatives of Christianity, and yet misrepresent and belie our holy faith by their unholy lives. But let circumstances be so changed that the great mass of our countrymen, both in Christendom and in pagan lands, shall manifest the bitterest hostility to us, and persecute us with murderous hate from city to city, as the Jews did those early preachers, compassing every now and then the death of one and another of the most zealous and successful of our missionary band—let such a state of things obtain, and such events be transpiring constantly in sight of those we seek to evangelize, and should we not feel ourselves at far more serious disadvantage than we now are?

---

* Acts vii: 54.   † Acts vii: 24.   ‡ Acts xviii: 12.

With the hope of their expected Messiah still deferred, and the mighty argument of the passing centuries forcing upon the minds of the Jews the ever-recurring question, "Was not Jesus of Nazareth, after all, our promised Messiah?" Scattered, as they still are, in all lands, and their feeble remnant in Jerusalem, gathering at their "wailing place," every Friday, to kiss and bathe with tears the fragment of their broken temple-walls, and chant their bitter lamentations and penitential prayers to their father's God, whose chastenings they no longer fail to recognise—with Jewish converts to Christianity multiplying at such a rate, that in the Protestant countries of Europe there are now more than three hundred of them in clerical orders, preaching Christ and him crucified, as the true Messiah ; must we not feel that from this very source, Judaism and the Jews, we have an immense advantage over those early preachers?

The *third* advantage specified is, that " those early preachers had not to contend with such compact and mighty systems of idolatry as we have to meet at the present day in India or China."

There is nothing in China, or any other part of the world but India, that, in compactness, massive strength, grossness or intensity of superstition and cruel rites, can make good any claim to pre-eminence over Greek and Roman idolatry. The one peculiarity of Hinduism, which gives it compactness and strength above all other religions invented by man, is *caste.* Hindu idolatry has nothing, in its origin, elements, universality, or the blind devotion of its votaries, at all more formidable than those systems of idolatry with which those early preachers had to contend. But *caste has* proved Satan's master-piece. This has been the cement of Hinduism and the source of its special power of resistance. But it is worthy of notice, that to make good his position, in regard to India, even to his own mind, our writer goes back nearly a century, and takes Hinduism, not as it *is*, but as it *was*, in the days of Carey's and Marshman's first aggression upon it, at almost the first contact of Christianity with it. Surely there has been a mighty change in Hinduism since that day ; and the proposition to be demonstrated required the comparison to be restricted to " preachers of the *present day*." Of those early preachers our writer says: "The religions they had to assail were long past their prime; they were already on the wane." Is not the same true of Hinduism, to-day? And of every other false religion known? If pagan philosophy had weakened the systems of idolatry prevalent in the Roman Empire in the days of the Apostles, has not the Gospel done vastly more than this to the idolatrous systems of the present day? If the educated of Apostolic times had become "skeptics," is it not equally true now that educated young Hindus, by the thousand, have no more faith in their 330,000,000 gods, than the missionaries themselves have? At the very time this article referred to was passing through the press in Bombay, was not the educated, non-Christian Brahmin, Dyaram, preaching against idolatry to thousands of his co-religionists in Poona, the capital of the old Marathi Empire, and the stronghold of the Brahman faith? Wielding his eloquence with such effect, that some of his idolatrous hearers who were convinced broke in pieces their idol gods, and threw them into the gutter? And what of the thousands of educated young Hindoos, represented by the *Kurta Bhojas*, of Northern India, the *Bhramo-Somaj*, of Bengal, and the *Prarthna Subha*, of Bombay? Do they not abjure and preach against idolatry? And do not the adherents of the two latter societies condemn and discard caste also? Is not this cement of Hindooism already crumbling under their vigorous blows? Do they not publicly condemn infant marriages, and nearly the whole list of Hindu abominations? And advocate female education, remarriage of Hindu widows, and most of the rites and usages of Christian civilization? Were there any organizations like these in Apostolic times, marking the decay of idolatry and the progress of enlightenment?

And what of our converts, as fellow-laborers in the work of the Gospel? Is it true that those early preachers were favored above us in this respect? Paul tells us of the Greek Titus, and of the Eurasian Timothy—both worthy helpers, we may well believe, from his account of them. But in all that is said of Gentile preachers in Apostolic times, do we find any comparable to our noble band of native brethren and co-workers in India—scores of them, in education, social position, birth, and brains, ranking with the highest of their countrymen, and in piety and devotion to their work, with the most zealous and efficient of the missionaries. That any one can think those early preachers had better facilities than we in India have, for establishing independent, self-supporting churches, with native pastors and elders, is simply a marvel. So far as the finding of suitable men for pastors and church officers among our far more numerous converts, the advantage is largely ours.

As to the decay and weakness of idolatry in Apostolic times, our writer speaks more correctly when he says: " Not, however, that idolatry was a weak enemy at the time of the Apostles—very far from it. It had its worship and its priests, and the common people still were its adherents. It was patronized by the emperor and court," etc. Here is a frank admission of the almost unbroken prestige and power of idolatry throughout the Roman Empire in the life-time of the Apostles. The great mass of the people were wedded to their gods—"in all things too superstitious "* (excessively devoted), as Paul says to the people of Athens. The emperors and nobles favored and patronized idolatry, and the philosophers, despite all that can be said of their skepticism, loved to have it so, and did what they could to keep it up for the sake of the common people, and for its political use and influence, if not from their own convictions. In his " *Conversion of the Roman Empire*," Merivale describes the elements of the then prevalent paganism, and emphatically testifies: " It was a formidable foe to the Gospel. It not only dwelt in the hearts and persuasions of the people, but was supported by all the powers of political interest; it glowed with the powers of ceremonial observances; it was hallowed by the charm of long possession, by its pretended appeal to actual experience, and the demonstration it affected to derive from the worldly success of the Roman Empire. It was still a living and active principle, for it was capable of a marked revival, a new growth and development, as proved more than once in the course of the Roman history.†

Another advantage claimed for those early preachers is, " The gospel spread at first among the inhabitants of the countries bordering on the Mediterranean, whose moral stamina was far superior to that of the Hindus." That the low

---

* Acts xvii: 22.   † *Conversion of the Roman Empire*, p. 58.

caste people of India are greatly wanting in moral stamina we admit. That the descendants of the genuine Aryans, the Hindus proper, fail to exhibit the highest moral principle and character in their heathen state, we also admit. That they possess or exhibit less moral stamina than did the Gentiles bordering on the Mediterranean, to whom those early preachers first carried the gospel, we do not believe. We feel certain that an impartial balancing of all the facts in both cases would bring out results decidedly in favor of the Hindus. Let those who think differently, and are inclined to endorse the views of our writer on this point, read again Paul's description of those same Gentiles in his day, as left on record in the first chapter of his Epistles to the Romans. Let them read again his epistles to the other churches he himself had planted, and weigh deliberately his condemnation of sins and enormities such as never yet have been known among the converts of our India churches. Let them study Roman society, even during "the brilliant age of Augustus and the Antonines;" yea, in the great Emperor Augustus himself, begging money through the streets of Rome in obedience to his dreams, and wearing the skin of a sea-calf as an amulet against lightning in a thunderstorm. What darker, fouler element of Pagan superstition or human depravity ever existed than prevailed among the upper classes of Rome in the reign of Domitian, as painted in the 6th and 9th *Satires of Juvenal*, when "fetid licentiousness frothed even in the imperial palace?" No, from close observation during some thirty years spent among the Hindus, and from some knowledge of their history for twenty-five centuries past, we are constrained to dissent very decidedly from the opinion that they are at all inferior in moral stamina to the inhabitants of the countries bordering on the Mediterranean in the early days of Christianity.

From the facts and data thus far developed, may we not then assume it as clearly demonstrated, that [the missionaries of the present day, instead of being at any *dis*advantage, really possess a very decided advantage over those early preachers in these very points where the advantage has been claimed for them; with the single exception of the gift of miracles, which had its special and appropriate use in their day, and which would be out of place and, to say the least, of very doubtful utility at the present time?

From this standpoint let us consider a little more in detail, some of the advantages of our missionaries now laboring in in this work—some of the facilities of the present age for evangelizing the world. If we glance at physical and material facilities, it is obvious to remark ;

1. *Rapid aud easy travel* is an advantage.to our present missionaries unknown to the apostolic and early preachers.

The conveniences and safety of travel throughout the Roman Empire in the days of the apostles are often mentioned as one of their advantages in disseminating the gospel. And yet any and every part of the world is now practically nearer to London or to New York than the outlying provinces of the Roman Empire then were to their capital. A missionary now can visit his antipodes from any point on the globe in half the time it took Paul to go from Cesærea to Rome. This advantage of our missionaries is not limited to the mere rapidity and comfort of travel to themselves personally. It has to do with intercommunication in all its phases—the frequent visits of their Christian friends and countrymen to the mission fields, the visits of intelligent Hindus, Chinese, Japanese, and other unevangelized races to the Christian lands, and the rapid exchange of letters and telegrams, bringing all lands and peoples into close intercommunion and literally realizing the prophet's vision, "many shall run to and fro, and knowledge shall be increased." *

We are aware that the same facilities of locomotion and intercommunication may be enlisted in the cause of error, false doctrine, and irreligion. But the grosser forms of heathen superstition rarely leave their habitats to seek new climes and conquests by these modern facilities of travel. Like the evil spirits cast out by Jesus, they pray rather to be let alone in their possessions. The special work of the missionary is to let in heaven's light into these dark and stagnant cess-pools of superstition—to teach all nations the blessed gospel, knowing it will prove "a savor of death unto death" to some, but of "life unto life" to all who receive it into good and honest hearts. Confident in the power of God's truth to secure the final victory over all forms of error and superstition, the

---

* Dan. xii : 4.

church may well regard these wonderful facilities for travel and intercommunication as a special dispensation to aid her in evangelizing the world, a work dearer to God than all the secular enterprises of the race.

2. *The world is open to the Gospel.*

We do not attach so much importance to this advantage as some minds seem inclined to. This world has always belonged to Christ and for more than eighteen centuries his disciples have lacked neither authority nor ability to invade and subdue any part of it, and to bring it all back to his allegiance. In the long and drowsy prayers of many for the removal of interdicts and opposition to the Gospel in heathen lands—prayers savoring more of an apology for the neglect of known duty, than of an ardent desire to press forward in the path of duty at all hazards, as abundantly shown by the failure of the church to occupy heathen lands when every hindrance has been removed—is there not much in tone and spirit which, to Christ and holy angels, must seem a solemn mockery? There never has been a time or a people since the crucifixion, when the Gospel of God's grace was not divinely adapted to become the power of God to salvation ; and nowhere has it been faithfully preached, under whatever interdicts and opposition, without winning souls to Christ. When the divine commission was given, " Go ye into all the world and preach the Gospel to every creature," * it was not added, " where kings and rulers do not interdict you." Such qualifying clause was not appended, even in parenthesis. Rather were the disciples duly notified, " If they have persecuted me, they will also persecute you." † And still they were to go and teach all nations—not those only which should be opened to their efforts by some miraculous Providence, but those among whom they should encounter opposition and persecution, even unto death. Those first disciples obeyed, and the result was, that in a few centuries Christianity supplanted all forms of paganism and superstition, and triumphed throughout the Roman empire, despite the most persistent efforts of her rulers to oppose and destroy it. Here is early and ample proof that the church need never have hesitated to enter China, or India, or any other part of the

---

* Mark xvi : 15.   † John xv : 20.

world, because of governmental interdicts and opposition. The teaching of Christ anticipates and provides for all such emergencies—" For whosoever will save his life shall lose it ; but whosoever will lose his life for my sake, the same shall find it."† The relaxing of this spirit in the church marked her weakness and degeneracy. It is the shame and disgrace of the Christian church of the seventeenth and eighteenth centuries, that a commercial stock-jobbing company of Protestant England was allowed, from sheer greed of gold and lust of power, to exclude the Gospel from their heathen subjects under their rapidly extending rule in India, more than two hundred years, without a single Christian martyr suffering the penalty of violating their unrighteous interdict. It is the special glory of the church of this nineteenth century, that God raised up a band of Christian young men, so inspired with the love of Jesus and the true type and spirit of primitive Christianity, that they dared to disregard that unrighteous interdict, and to go and make efforts to preach the Gospel to those perishing idolaters at any peril. It is a severe rebuke to the small faith of our Christian Israel, that *one* stripling, David, was able so quickly to conquer a giant so mighty—that Gordon Hall, single-handed, while held in durance by Sir Evan Napier, in Bombay, under strict orders of banishment, and waiting a ship to convey him forever from India, was helped of God to pen words and move moral and spiritual forces which speedily broke down the barriers and opened all India to the Gospel ; while this glorious result of high-daring in the cause of Christ becomes a beacon-light on which the church may well turn her eye in every like emergency.

The result of Judson's noble daring, in throwing himself into Burma, under native rule, when banished from British India, and, with much privation and suffering, commencing single-handed a work which has developed into scores of churches and thousands of converts won to Christ ; the labors of Swartz and Ziegenbuld in the native states of Southern India, as also of Moffat and Livingstone in Africa, and noble workers in other mission fields, furnish abundant evidence that the church, or individual Christians, need not wait for the permission of human rulers to obey Christ. In their legitimate work of sav-

---

* Luke ix : 24.

ing souls they may trust God in any and all perils; and his special care of all true workers in this service, inclining capricious rulers to extend toleration to them, and often shielding from cruel plots and murderous hands, deserves the thoughtful study, both of humble saints and scornful sinners. Even the Jesuits, in Japan, found toleration and protection from the native rulers till, discarding the teaching of their divine Master—" My kingdom is not of this world "*—they embroiled themselves in politics, and thereby incurred deserved banishment.

But though, in this important sense, belonging to Christ, and being wholly embraced in the "Great Commission," the world has ever been open to the Gospel, and the church has had no valid excuse for leaving one nation or tribe of the race unevangelized; yet, in the recent removal of all interdicts and barriers, and the universal toleration of Protestant missionaries in all lands and nations, there is a significance which marks a special Providence in the progress of this work. Those who covered their paltry gifts and puny efforts under long and languid prayers for the removal of these interdicts, are now confronted with needy millions and nations, no longer resisting, but inviting, nay, challenging, their largest efforts and most generous gifts for making known to them the blessings of the Gospel. Those who have been most sincere and earnest in their supplications have now the rich joy and inspiration of answered prayers, showing God's readiness to hear and bless, and inciting to continuance in well-doing, on a scale more commensurate with the magnitude of this world-wide enterprise.

Contrast this present state of the world with what it was in Apostolic times, when the Gospel was bound so far as human powers could bind it, when Christians were everywhere spoken against and persecuted, were often flying from place to place at peril of their lives, and often suffering imprisonment and torture, even unto death; and can we speak of the advantages of those early preachers over the missionaries of the present day? Is not the advantage wholly with those now laboring to evangelize the world?

3. *The most influential and powerful nations are now Christian.*

---

* John xviii: 36.

Taking Christianity in its widèst limits, embracing the Greek,
Roman, and Protestant branches of the Christian church, and
though still outnumbered by the thronging millions of the
Pagan and Moslem races, yet with whom is the balance of
power among the nations? We need not enumerate "the five
great powers of Europe," or speak of the prestige and influence of our own country—the United States—these six Christian nations holding the unquestioned dictatorship of the world.
Their influence is felt and acknowledged in every land. Not
only are the influence and prestige of Great Britain felt throughout Europe. British America and Australia own her dominion,
and glory in it; while her rule over 300,000,000 Hindus and
Moslem, in India, is well nigh absolute ; and her growing power
in China and Central Asia, in Southern and Eastern Africa,
New Zealand, and scores of the islands of Oceanica, is undisputed. The few Pagan nations of any note still existing seem
conscious of their impotence. The Sultan of Turkey—the
head of the whole Moslem race—holds his throne and power
only by leave of these Christian nations, and the Khedive of
Egypt listens meekly to their advice. Japan and China—the
latter holding in check her pride of celestial birthright and
prerogatives, are sending their youth into the very heart of
Christendom to learn true science, civilization, and government, and study the genius of our Christian institutions.

We need not express our grief at the imperfection, nay, positive evils and wrongs, still manifest in the rule of these Christian nations—the favor and support of idolatry and-false religions, the enforced opium traffic, the pernicious licensing of
the grossest vice and intemperance, and kindred national
crimes and enormities, still tolerated and practised by our
rulers. Let the forces of the Christian church be summoned
to correct these evils, and make the rule of these Christian
powers such as shall everywhere bless humanity and honor
God.

We need not recall the fact, that the sources of prosperity
and power among these nations are in Christianity itself. This
fact but intensifies the arguments and motives for enlisting the
utmost energies of the church in efforts to make the Gospel
the controlling force in the mind and heart of every ruler, and
in every act of the governing body; while, at the same time,

it makes manifest the certainty, that in proportion as Christianity permeates the body politic of these nations, just in the same proportion will their influence and rule be extended and perpetuated over the whole world.   But taking things as they now exist—the actual status of Christian and Pagan nations to-day—and what a mighty contrast rises to view between the advantages—nay, the difficulties and hindrances, the buffetings and cruel persecutions, the crucifixions and beheadings, of those early preachers, and the grand vantage-ground of the church and her missionaries at the present time.

4. *True science, education, and literary culture, are mainly in the hands of Christians.*

This fact is too manifest to require demonstration.   It is felt and conceded wherever Christian missionaries go among the heathen.   It gives them a mighty vantage-ground for overturning systems of superstition and false religion, mixed, as they always are, with false science.   Even Brahmanism, the most compact and impregnable religious system ever yet invented by human genius or Satanic cunning, becomes stultified and impotent under the teaching of true science.

This is an advantage of present missionaries quite unknown to those early preachers.   They were, mostly, uneducated. Paul, the only one of literary culture among the early disciples, recognizes this fact, and, for special reasons, glories in it, affirming : " God hath chosen the foolish things of the world to confound the wise ; and God hath chosen the weak things of the world to confound the things which are mighty."* He would have Christ and his cross receive all the glory of those early triumphs of Christianity.   And all the glory of her triumphs must and will be his forever.   But no proper source of influence and power for arresting and impressing minds in favor the Gospel need be despised or rejected.   This source of influence is just as legitimate now as was the power to work miracles in Apostolic times.   And who shall say it is not equally potent?   Converting efficacy inheres in neither.

The contrast here is very marked.   Those early preachers went forth comparatively ignorant.   The highest development of science, and the profoundest erudition of that age, were the heritage, mainly, of Jewish rabbis, and of the schools and

---

* 1 Cor. i: 27.

philosophers of Greece and Rome. From their prouder literary eminence both Jews and Pagans looked down upon Christians with scorn, ready to exclaim, "Thou wast altogether born in sin, and dost *thou* teach us?" * Now, Christian missionaries go forth from the best institutions of learning the world has ever known, thoroughly versed in profane and sacred lore, and in the latest scientific discoveries and investigations; able at once to explain many of the dark problems and mysteries in life and nature which perplex the heathen, and thereby to explode the cruel superstitions which have held them all their lifetimes in bondage. Wielding this potent influence, and seeing its effect on ignorant and superstitious minds, and the still mightier influence of the Gospel itself, why should we desire the gift of miracles, even if God were willing to bestow it?

5. *The wealth of the world is largely in the hands of Christians.*

We would not unduly exalt this advantage. Experience has abundantly shown that both wealth and power may prove a curse, instead of a blessing—may weaken and demoralize the church herself, instead of extending her influence and spiritual conquests over others. Paul did vastly more to evangelize the world at his own charges, while supporting himself and those that were with him by tent-making, than many a modern missionary does, sustained with large resources furnished by the church.

And yet the economy of the Gospel recognizes the value of wealth laid on God's altar for his service and glory. In no other way can wealth be so invested with vital and spiritual elements, in no other way be so made to promote spiritual and eternal interests, as in making it aid in this work—in teaching to the ignorant and perishing Christ and him crucified. Given the men and women of Christ-like spirit and zeal in this work, and the great want is the means for sustaining them and their schools and labors in the foreign field. And the marvel is, that Christian men and women do not discern and seize their opportunity for thus transmuting their gold into eternal treasure, by making it subserve God's glory in enlightening and saving souls. The amount of wealth in the Christian church is immense. With all her imperfections of Christian

---

* John ix: 34.

character and practice, she has still proved the truth of Apostolic teaching, that "Godliness is profitable unto all things; having promise of the life that now is," as well as "of that which is to come." As so-called Christian nations hold the chief power, so also do they hold the greater portions of the world's wealth.   Unevangelized nations occupy portions of the world equally rich, doubtless, in universal and natural resources, but these are largely undeveloped.   The great accumulations of developed resources are found in Christendom.   If professing Christians would use their wealth in evangelizing the world with the fierceness, fixed purpose, energy, and effectiveness with which they use it in carrying on wars, building manufactories, railroads, telegraphs, and commercial navies, *ten years* would suffice to bring the Gospel to the intelligent understanding of every dweller on our globe.   The accomplishment of an object so dear to Jesus, and in itself so good and glorious, ought to be an incitement sufficient to nerve every Christian heart to the putting forth of the utmost ability and effort ; while the immense gifts of the heathen in support of their false religions, like the $2,000,000 expended every year on one single feast to Doorga, in Calcutta, rise to view as if to shame and reproach Christians for the smallness of their gifts and efforts in the service of him, who gave his own life a ransom for them.

Contrast this wealth of the church now with the weakness and poverty of the Apostolic church, when Christians who had a little property felt constrained to sell it, and place all avails in a common treasury to meet the wants of the needy and suffering of their own number; and can we speak of the advantage of those early preachers over those of the present day on this point ?   Must we not rather take shame to ourselves, that despite this immense advantage in our favor, they so far surpassed us in benevolence, zeal, devotion, self-sacrifice, and earnest, persistent effort in the service of the Gospel ?

6. *The wide diffusion of the English language.*

The value of this advantage turns on the fact, that English is the language of the most influential Protestant nations, and embodies most of the Protestant Christian literature of the world.   The general prevalence of the Greek language in Apostolic times, and the translation of the Old Testament into

Greek, is claimed as a special advantage of those early preachers. But English is vastly more prevalent now than Greek
was then; and the amount of Christian literature it carries
over the world with it is beyond all comparison. The English
language is a common medium of communication now the
world over. It is used on every continent, and on almost every
island of the ocean. The natives of every land and clime have
come to know something of the paramount power and influence of the English-speaking-race, and develop a wonderful
eagerness to master the language of a people so active, enterprising, and powerful. In the different countries of South
America, in all the more prosperous settlements begirting the
continent of Africa, in the seaports and commercial centres of
Japan and China, and in all the large towns and cities of India,
hundreds and thousands of the native inhabitants use the
English language fluently and correctly enough for all practical
purposes, while many use it with much accuracy and beauty.
And having gained the key to treasures so vast and valuable
as are to be found in our Christian science and literature, they
are not likely to leave them unexplored. Thousands of
heathen youth are exploring them, and in doing so, are
brought under influences, and into relations with their Christian teachers, most favorable to Christianity and fatal to
superstition. The venerable Dr. Duff has labored some thirty
years for Hindoo youth in the metropolis of India, all in English, finding no necessity to learn a vernacular language.
Drs. Somerville, Seeley, and others, fresh from Scotland and
America, have visited the large cities of India, preaching and
lecturing to the educated young Hindus in the English
language. Such a wide success and controlling influence has
this language gained over the entire world, that in the work of
evangelizing the nations, we venture to assume that we have,
in this language, an advantage far greater than those early
preachers had in the gift of tongues.

7. *Foundations are now laid.*

And here we approach a class of advantages which can obtain only in the progress of an enterprise—advantages wholly
unknown to those early workers. In the completed canon of
sacred Scriptures—the possession of the New Testament—who
can estimate our advantage over the Apostolic church?—an

advantage in itself far surpassing the gift of miracles for any
other purpose than to attest the Messiahship of Jesus and furnish Apostolic credentials.

But in the entire work of laying foundations, the mind is
almost overwhelmed with the magnitude and multiplicity of
the considerations to be weighed, and shrinks from the attempt
to form any adequate impression of the immense advantages
we now have over those who laid the foundations of the
Christian church under the New Testament dispensation, and
over all who have borne their part in building and bringing
it to its present status.   Even in the case of Peter, notwithstanding the special teaching for years of Christ himself, it
required God's intervention to make him extend the narrow
foundations, on which he began to build, far enough to make
room for the centurion Cornelius; while it cost Paul and
Barnabas the long journey from Antioch to Jerusalem, and
the solemn deliberations of the whole Apostolic college there,
to decide the terms of church membership for Gentile converts.

But viewing the difficult problems which were cropping up
ever and again in those early centuries; the repeated church
councils for eliminating and guarding against heresy, and determining the creeds and practice of the church; the contrast
between the state of things at the inception of the modern
missionary enterprise, only some sixty years ago, and the
present time, reveals an immense advantage in our favor.
Then, everything was tentative; the languages of the heathen
were to be learned, and, in most cases, to be learned under
gravest disadvantages—in many cases, to be learned from vocal
sounds, their elements to be first determined, and then reduced
to writing.   And the languages once acquired, they were still
destitute of Christian ideas.   The herculean labor of translating the Bible, preparing text-books, and creating a Christian
literature was still to be accomplished.   This work is not yet
perfected.   Languages have still to be learned by each new
worker, but special helps greatly lessen this toil; while the
Bible, faithfully translated, published, and circulated more or
less widely in some 200 of the principal languages and dialects
of the heathen, and a Christian literature, embracing scores and
hundreds of volumes in these various languages, disclose an

immense amount of labor, the full harvest of which we and our
successors are yet to reap and garner, and mark, somewhat
our grand vantage-ground over our predecessors over sixty
years ago, and still, moreover, those early preachers toiling at
the foundations of their work, without even the cost of printing
to aid them in disseminating Christian truth.   Carry out the
parallel in all the other foundations laid—the schools and
printing-presses established, the Christian communities and
churches organized, and the hundreds of places in every
part of the unevangelized world, whose Gospel light has been
kindled, and how is it possible, for a moment, to compare our
position with that of those early preachers at the inception of
their mighty work, without feeling that God has given us
facilities for carrying it forward to completion, of which they
were able to catch but the feeblest glimpse, and this only in
prophetic vision !

Art. VII.—PRESBYTERIAN COLLEGES, AS RELATED TO THE GROWTH OF OUR MINISTRY.*

By REV. A. A. E. TAYLOR, D.D., President of Wooster University, Ohio.

THE preaching of the Gospel is conceded to be the divinely
ordained method of propagating true religion upon the earth.
It, therefore, becomes one of the fundamental duties of the
church to provide the supply of ministers needful for the task,
of course subject to the action of the personal divine call to
the ministry.   There are two principal reasons that make this
labor on the part of the church incessant, as they require a
constant supply of new candidates for the pulpit.   These are,
first, the natural waste of the clergy by retirement from active

---

* *Annual Catalogues of Allegheny, Auburn, Chicago, Danville, Lane, Princeton,
and Union (N. Y.) Theological Seminaries, for* 1875-76.

*Annual Reports of the Board of Education, and Annual Minutes of the General
Assembly.*

duty, by dismission to other branches of Christian work, and such like causes, and by death; and, second, the ever enlarging demand arising from the steadfast increase in number of home churches to be supplied, and in the expansion of the missionary work. In our rapidly developing nation, the home cause of itself requires a large, constant increase of ministers.

Confining our attention in this article to the " Presbyterian Church of the United States of America," as distinguished from other Presbyterian bodies, let us take the Minutes of its General Assembly for the current year as the basis of some estimates relating to the demand and supply of its ministry. So doing, we herein discover that during the past ecclesiastical year 85 ministers have died, and 27 have been dismissed to other denominations, while there has been an increase of 78 in the number of the churches. This creates the need for 190 new ministers, not taking into account now the question of any surplus number that may be already on hand. As an offset to this loss, we have, during the same period, ordinations, 137 ; ministers received from other churches, 53 ; in all, precisely 190, thus so far balancing these accounts. There is left, therefore, as the deficiency for the year, exactly that number lost to the church by retirement to other duties, or to rest from active labors, and the increased requirement of new missionary fields during the year. This number of retiring clergymen is difficult to estimate with any approximate accuracy from lack of proper data, but that it must be very considerable is shown by the fact, that *fully one-fourth of our enrolled ministry is not engaged in direct supply* of our churches, and that one-fifth of our churches now stand vacant.*

That there is a serious falling off in the proportionate supply of our ministry, the following comparison will show, as drawn from the Minutes of the following respective years:

1876.	Ministers, 4,744	Churches, 5,077	Members, 535,210
1871.	" 4,346	" 4,616	" 455,378
Gain	" 398	" 461	" 79,832

Here we find that in five years there have been 63 more

---

*By an accurate count in the Minutes of Assembly of 1875, it is found that of 4,706 ministers, 1,153 are reckoned as either retired, teaching, acting as agents, or

churches added than ministers, and, also, that while the general
average at present yields about 112 communicants for each
minister enrolled, the comparative increase of these five years
has been but one minister to each 200 communicants. Taking
into account, however, the fact already mentioned, that one-
fourth of the ministry is out of the pulpit, it leaves the present
average of one active minister to each 150 members. Thus
we have a falling off in these five years in the supply of ministers of at least 25 per cent., or 5 per cent. per annum, in proportion to the increase of membership. If it be suggested that
this is no serious loss, since it is remedied by the average increase of membership in each church, the reply is evident that
this distribution of increase cannot go on very long, the churches
being, on the average, quite large enough for the strength of
the ministry now, and it will not do to depend upon it for any
length of time, or otherwise than as a temporary expedient.
The above result is also indicated by the valuable tables of
comparative increase in churches and ministry in the last report of the Board of Education, wherein it is proved, that
while the increase of membership for the past five years has
been 7 per cent. per annum, the increase of the ministry for
the same period has been but 2 per cent. per annum. The
comparison of the tables for the last ten years yields a still
greater disproportion, while as we run our eye still further back,
comparing the growth of the church by decades, the steadfast
decline of both ministry and membership is really alarming.

If we now turn to the direct means used for the supply of
ministers, we find that our church has made liberal and efficient
provision for the *theological* training of candidates, fully equal
in all respects to the demand likely to be imposed upon her.
We have eight theological seminaries in active operation. Of
these the Pacific Seminary has as yet but very few students
(seven last year), and in the absence of a printed catalogue, its
data are beyond our reach, and have not been estimated or
taken into our account at all.

---

supplies for churches in other connections. Beside these, many are designated as
Evangelists, which seems now to be the popular phrase, of whom a goodly number
are agents, or preach but rarely, and without regular appointments. Also, out of our
5,077 churches, the Minutes show 1,074 to be vacant in 1876.

The remaining seminaries report for the last year, as follows:

Union (N. Y.)	Professors and Teachers,	7	Students,	142
Princeton	"	7	"	120
Allegheny	"	7	"	85
Auburn	"	6	"	48
Lane	"	5	"	38
Chicago	"	6	"	24
Danville	"	4	"	20
Total		42		477

These figures show an average of about 11 students to each instructor. However, the first mentioned four seminaries having 27 teachers and 395 students, have nearly 15 students to each professor; while the remaining three seminaries, with 15 teachers and 82 students, average but five and a half students to a professor.

It is aside from our present purpose or desire to comment on these figures, further than to say, that if the church lack candidates it is evidently not from want of sufficient provision under able and renowned professors, and with large endowments and means of pecuniary assistance in the theological schools. Twice the present number of students might be therein accommodated. But now, taking the number of students in these seminaries, and dividing by three, which is the number of years in the seminary course of study, we have resulting a prospective yearly increase of candidates from this source of about 160. It is, however, to be considered, as will hereafter be illustrated, that a goodly proportion of these students are candidates of various other denominations, seeking here the superior educational facilities offered by our schools, which fact seriously lessens the prospective proportion of candidates herefrom for our own supply. But, as already shown, the average annual number demanded by the wants of the church from other sources than that caused by retirement from active duties of the ministry is 190. This makes apparent the necessity of an increase for estimated demands of our churches, of certainly not less than 100, aud probably 150, ministers annually, of whom, if, as last year's figures show, 50 came from other churches, we should have to satisfy the demand of no less than 100 more theological students annually. And this estimate is based upon the present rate of progress in our church without providing for that enlargement of her work, naturally to be expected, and certainly to be prayed for and looked for in her present position.

Now the grave question inevitably arises, whence are we to reasonably expect this increase, imperatively required to meet the demand which is now steadfast, and that will constantly grow more pressing in its necessity year by year, unless the church decline?

It is a legal requirement of our system, and according to our time-honored custom and inherited principles, that candidates should be prepared, before entering upon their theological training, by a thorough collegiate course, or its full equivalent. It is, therefore, both lawful and expedient to inquire what our church has been doing meanwhile, and what she is now doing, to prepare educated material for her theological schools, by establishing, or fostering, an adequate system of collegiate training preparatory to these technical schools of theology. The answer is as evident as it is damaging, and may reveal, in large part, the secret of this growing insufficiency of candidates. It is a fact that this most important matter has been largely left to provide for itself, in the hands of private educational corporations, often representing her interests, indeed, but very feebly aided by the direct agency and efforts, and, alas! often not encouraged by the sympathies of the church itself. There are a few of these noble collegiate institutions that, through a struggle for many years, a struggle, often, for bare existence, have done most of this preliminary work; but one or two of which have been able to attain, in long years, the rank and power absolutely needed for the demand the church has ever made upon them. The sacrifice has mainly fallen upon a few self-sacrificing instructors, who have devoted their lives, and not unfrequently, besides, their individual means, to the bearing of burdens that justly belonged to the church they were serving.

Now, it is a growing conviction among many of the thoughtful and far-seeing ministers and members of the church, that she has failed, and is failing, just at this point, and that she is suffering, and must suffer more in the future, because of this failure. They feel, that before she can secure to herself such an educated ministry, as she must needs have to insure success in her labors, she must, as a church, extend her educational work further down toward youth, and lay hold with energy and enthusiasm upon the system of collegiate training. In other words, for the sake of her theological schools, and her coming ministry, not to mention the expanding need of an educated Presbyterian laity in this day of increasing lay effort, the church herself should do for the colleges, also, what has been recognized and performed as bounden duty in the case of theological training. For while we have been in large part neglecting this sphere of work altogether, except in a few special and partial instances, other and rival interests have been quietly assuming control of collegiate training, and turning its practical influence and products into other channels than the supply of the ministry.

A careful analysis of the various colleges whence students come to our theological seminaries will yield abundant light on this subject. Fortunately, the annual catalogues of these seminaries, for 1875–76, furnish us with carefully prepared tables that afford the information desired. There were, as we have already seen, 477 students in these seminaries last year, of whom ten are enrolled as post-graduates, whose colleges are not named, and who, therefore, are necessarily omitted in our count. With regard to the remaining 467 students, an exact collation of the catalogues yields the following results: There are 13 colleges represented in these lists, that are enrolled as "Presbyterian" in *Johnson's Universal Cyclopædia*, which is supposed to be the most recent and accurate authority on this point, and in which it is inferred, on substantial grounds, that the authorities of the colleges themselves have been consulted as to the statement of their denominational connections, since the special accounts of these colleges in this Cyclopædia have been avowedly prepared, in most cases, by some official connected therewith. That no injustice may be done to any, we have faithfully followed, in every case, this authority of the Cyclopædia, which is also confirmed by the Annual Reports of the Commissioner of Education. These 13 colleges labeled "Presbyterian," furnish the following number of theological students for the year 1875–76, arranged in the order of their comparative numbers: Princeton College, 64; Hamilton, 28; Washington and Jefferson, 26; Wooster, 24; Lafayette, 23;

Hanover, 20; Wabash, 18; Maryville, 13; Blackburn, 4;
Westminster (Mo.), 3; Center, 3; Highland, 2; Lincoln, 2—
total, 230 students. Thus, colleges reckoned as Presbyterian
furnish but 230 of 467 students therein—*a little less than half
the number*—leaving 237 to come from other quarters. Of this
remainder a few are enrolled as from high-school, school, collegiate institute, academy, normal school, and naval academy,
not having had any proper collegiate⁻training whatever; while
a goodly number of those from colleges named are not enrolled
as graduates, but as having been in partial attendance upon
their course; both of which facts deserve the earnest attention
of the church, and especially of the Presbyteries, in view of
Form of Government, chap. xiv: sec. 3.*

Of those students from colleges not enrolled as "Presbyterian," the following list shows those institutions represented
by numbers of four or upward: Amherst (Cong.) 18; Yale
(Cong.) 12; Westminster, Pa. (U. P.) 12; Williams (Cong.) 9;
Marietta (Undenom.) 9; Union (Undenom.) 8; Western Reserve (Undenom.) 8; Oberlin (Cong.) 7; Dartmouth (Cong.)
6: Rochester (Bap.) 5; Dalhousie 5; and the following by
four each: Allegheny (Meth.), Franklin (P. and U. P.), Mon-
mouth (U. P.), Muskingum (Undenom.), Rutgers (Ref.), Knox
(Cong.), Michigan Univ. (State), Univ. of Penn. (Undenom.),
and Waynesburg (Cumb. Pres.) These twenty colleges furnish
135 students, leaving the remainder of 102 students either non-
collegiates, or scattered among forty-five other colleges mentioned, among which, it may be stated, incidentally, for subsequent use, but eight State universities are named, which
give sixteen students in all, an average of two students for the
ministry for each State university; while of the larger secular
institutions, Cornell gives two, and Harvard but ONE. Now,
of these, about sixty students are from Congregational
colleges, and twenty others from institutions in which Presbyterians have a partial interest, while the Reserves, such as
Marietta and Western Colleges, of nearly all the other denominations, are represented. This last fact has an important

---

* "And it is recommended that the candidate (for licensure) be also required⁻to
produce a diploma of Bachelor or Master of Arts, from some college or university;
or, at least, authentic testimonials of his having gone through a regular course of
learning."

bearing on the previous estimate, made to show our delinquency of candidates; since, judging by the denomination of the colleges attended, *one-third* of the students would belong to other branches of the church. This, however, is too large an estimate, considering the fact that Presbyterian students do not unfrequently attend other denominational schools. An estimate of one-fifth of our theological students belonging to other denominations, is certainly within reasonable inference. Nor is this difference remedied by Presbyterian students in theological seminaries of other denominations. This tedious, but accurate collation of figures must assuredly fix the attention of every thoughtful and earnest member of our church upon the startling fact of the utter and lamentable inadequacy of collegiate institutions under our own control, or even influence, as related merely to the wants of the rising ministry.

It is also not impossible that this promiscuous training of half our ministry during their collegiate education, in *sixty-five* (!) non-Presbyterian institutions, may have something to do with the intimation not unfrequently heard as to the character of the coming ministry, and its relative efficiency and power as compared with that of former days; and may further assist in accounting for both the large number of vacant churches, and of unoccupied ministers.

When, however, we enlarge our view, and take into account the necessity of a laity thoroughly trained under Presbyterian influences, and the bias almost certainly given to students, and impressing them for life, by the special religious and denominational influences of the colleges' they attend, surely no one who loves our branch of the church, and has hopes for her permanence as a body of believers, can remain unimpressed with the disastrous lack of Presbyterian collegiate education.

Let us now consider some important facts bearing upon this subject, holding the coming ministry especially in view; and, afterward, inquire as to some possible modes of remedy for the evil.

First.—In the first place, it is hardly necessary to do more than mention the absorbing interest taken in the cause of collegiate education by the fathers in our church, and their indefatigable and zealous labors to secure the establishment of such institutions under their own immediate control. We might, indeed, go back to Geneva, and to Scotland, and to the Reformed Churches of the Continent generally, and show how their position in conflict with spiritual powers that held the means and instruments of education, so far as they existed at all, in their hands, opened before the Reformers, as a prime necessity of self-existence, and of ecclesiastical succession, the establishment of such institutions as would prove promotive of the Reformed principles, and under their own direction ; and, undoubtedly, under a similar pressure from the Established Church, and having the critical position and wise example of the Reformers before their eyes, did our American fathers awaken to their need of the defensive and protective power of colleges in which men after their own heart and mind might be trained. We have reaped the·fruit of their far-seeing wisdom in this respect, and, in so doing, we should consider what our ecclesiastical descendants, in turn, may require at our hands. This statement, thus made, does not need verification to those who have even the slightest familiarity with the early history of American collegiate effort. Before the middle of the last century, and when the first synod of our church numbered but fifty ministers, direct action was begun, and a school of an academical character, as preparatory to higher effort, was definitely established, to teach " languages, philosophy, and divinity." And this action was subsequent to the establishment of the Log College of Tennent, and of other schools holding a real though informal relation to the synod, as its records abundantly show. The connection of this synod subsequently with Princeton College is well known, and though, for State reasons, it was not formally recognized, yet, the sending by the synod of Gilbert Tennent and Samuel Davis abroad as agents in its behalf, and the address issued and sent by their hands to the General Assembly of the Church of Scotland, with the generous response of the National Collection ordered by the Scottish Assembly, amounting to $12,000, together with repeated ordering of collections in all the congregations of the synod for it, abundantly expound the relations existing between the synod and the college, which has also been illustrated in all their subsequent history. In those days, synod and presbytery, and in due time the assembly, in various forms and modes, all took direct action,

looking to the establishment and maintenance of Presbyterian colleges.   In Pennsylvania, Virginia, New York, North
and South Carolina, Ohio, Kentucky, Tennessee, and elsewhere, such efforts were countenanced and encouraged.   Indeed, there seemed to be but one spirit in the church on this
subject, down to a recent period, and the ablest pens of our
ministry have devoted their highest eloquence to the maintenance of these views.   Perhaps it is owing to the many
failures in these efforts, from causes usually wholly beyond
the control of the church and its courts, that the zeal of the
church herein has grown slack, and the sentiments so ardently
advocated have been permitted to find a temporary repose.

But these views, inherited from the Reformers and pressed
into activity by the demands of their own times, are no less
true and no less important in these present days.   And we
may, hereafter, attempt to show that the nature of the times
calls most loudly for their resurrection and enforcement, and
that the difficulties that interposed for their temporary abatement do now no longer exist.   If the fathers were wise in these
opinions, it certainly behooves the church to re-examine them,
and inquire whether certain evils, that are likely to befall her
interests, may not be traced to the modern neglect of a subject
deemed formerly so essential to her life.

Second.—Attention should also be further directed to the
fact, that other Christian denominations are evidently impressed
with the extreme importance of these views, and have taken
action accordingly in the foundation of institutions that represent and propagate their own doctrinal opinions.   The zeal
and activity of some of these sister churches, resulting to their
vast advantage, should afford us a stimulus for re-awakened exertion, while the comparative decline of others who have neglected them should prove a warning, lest we fall under the
same condemnation.   We may instance the American Methodist Church, whose growth and power have advanced to a degree parallel with the expansion of their educational efforts,
and who now stand in the forefront in the advocacy of the
cause of especial education for their own ecclesiastical development.   And statistics might be offered to prove, beyond a cavil,
that both the ministry and the laity of our church have suffered
seriously from the influences thus brought to bear upon our

own youth who have been subjected to the educational **direction** of other denominational institutions. The only **consolation** is, that our loss has been their gain, and that the **general** cause of Christ has not suffered as it might, had these **students** been given over to the formative power of purely secular **education**.

We may, indeed, learn some valuable lessons in this **respect** from the Romish Communion, and its unswerving maintenance of the necessity of education under its own control. *Fas est ab hoste doceri.* For without trenching upon the discussion **of** the relation of the church to the secular schools, this much **will** appear evident, that the Church of Rome is right from **its** standpoint, and only provides for its own safety by **insisting** upon holding the higher, not to speak of the lower, **education** of its youth in its own hands. What now appears as an **urgent** requirement for its self-preservation, may ere long impress **itself** upon the Protestant churches as an equal necessity for **their** existence, in these days of the boasting advocacy of **so-called** scientific opposition to the truth in many educational **quarters,** and in schools and colleges utterly beyond church control. This secret of the power of Rome and her great gains in many quarters through her educational organizations, so often **patron**ized by Protestants, may admonish us to be warned in time, while the popular growth of skeptical views largely among our youth, and mainly advanced through irreligious or non-religious educational agencies, should fix our attention upon facts and prospects, and guard us against disasters, whose approach is portended not only by hostile, but by friendly voices.

Third.—The peril in which our church is placing herself **by** neglecting direct collegiate education is to be found, not as in some former times, in the state of general ignorance that might result, at least in part, from such neglect. But the danger now is, that the rising generation may be very thoroughly instructed under influences alien, if not positively hostile to the spread of evangelical piety. Since the leaders of our church have ceased to take a prominent and persistent position on this subject— that is, within the last few years, there has been a steadily and rapidly advancing spirit of education laying hold of our Amercan youth. The development of the popular influence of our public schools, through their increasing thoroughness and scientific management in the last score of years, is something really remarkable. New and systematic methods, organized and trained teachers, lavish means of support, and adequate buildings and apparatus, have increased their efficiency tenfold. Well nigh all the children of the land have been drawn into these schools, and their courses of study have been gradually advanced until many of them land their pupils, moderately well prepared on the average, at the doors of the college course The subject of compulsory education is also now seriously discussed. Meanwhile, much of the religious education formerly gained for such of them as were of pious parentage, by a certain proportion of home education, and more largely by private schools and academies under avowedly religious teachers, is now almost entirely lost. For the average religious influence of State schools cannot rise, in the nature of the case, above the same influence in the State itself. Even were the reading of the Scriptures and opening prayer permitted—which are not every where allowed—these exercises must necessarily be but formal and general in their religious impression, to suit the views of everybody's children who attend. Thus the educational power of the primary schools has grown to be well nigh universal in the land with a religious influence necessarily infinitesimal; and the church has already lost, and probably irredeemably lost, much in this respect that it formerly held. Also, growing out of this primary education is the growing tendency of the State to enter into contest for the control of the higher education afforded by colleges and all institutions preparatory to professional or purely technical training. In the East generally, where colleges have been taking root for a century past, and where many of them have become fortified in financial means and influence and in public favor, this encroachment of State education does not seem so alarming. But in the Western States and in some parts of the East, not thoroughly furnished with collegiate advantages, the State colleges are rapidly rising into a power that endangers the very existence of all denominational or independent institutions. The vast advantage of State funds upon which to fall back for support renders their success unquestionable, allowing necessary time for growth and experience in work. There are State institutions West of the Mississippi whose annual income fully equals $30,000, besides large annual appropriations. Looking upon this subject purely in the light of popular education, the rise and growth of these universities may be matters of public congratulation. But, considering the question as purely secular, as distinguished from religious education in the colleges, and the results likely to flow to religion in the land from the grasp of the State laid upon higher education, we do most earnestly feel and contend that the result will logically and necessarily be that the church will thereby become largely shorn of the power that comes through the direction of the education of her youth, and more especially as related to the furnishing of her future ministry. We are aware that we are touching upon delicate ground, and we feel it necessary to express our respect for the general management of these State institutions thus far in their history. But we invoke the candid and foreseeing consideration of religious men to the results likely and, as we believe, inevitably to flow from the wide prevalence of this system. It is admitted that there may be, and that there are, in some, or in all, of these institutions, individual professors who are godly men, and who, from their respective chairs of languages, science, and philosophy, may exert a positive religious influence upon the students under their control. And the general impression of such institutions may be, for a time, in a positively religious direction. But certain other facts are also to be considered, as follows : *First*, from the fact of their control by the State, such colleges cannot be made sure for such a position, because they belong to the people, and are under the direction of the Legislatures, and, as every one knows, these cannot be controlled and permanently held in any religious direction. The same conditions will insure that they eventually follow in the same direction with the public schools of lower grade.

Fourth.—It is beyond dispute, and, therefore it is not invidious to mention, that in many of their chairs there are, and that in any of them there are likely to be placed, professors who are thoroughly imbued with the modern spirit of opposition to religion, which claims support from science, or, at least, to orthodox views of religion. For it is a boast openly made, that clergymen are, and should be, shut out from these chairs, as in the days of Julian, even where their qualifications may be equal to those of others, and that these institutions are to be kept free from any teachers who may impart a denominational or religious bias. And so, perhaps, it should be. But all direct religious influence is necessarily denominational to this extent,. that all religious people belong to one or other of the denominations; and the hue and cry raised against denominationalism. is made simply as the most popular appeal by which to oppose religious influence of all kinds in education. Now, as these State institutions succeed in possessing the control of higher education, do they deprive the church, in the same degree, of the influence of education for its own benefit, and obtained by such control. What colleges the church has are compelled to struggle all the more desperately for existence under the rivalry, if not with the aroused opposition, of the State institutions. The question that results therefore, is this—whether the church can succeed, as she might and ought, provided, ultimately, the higher education passes out of her hands into that of the State. We have already seen what were the views: of the Fathers upon this subject, growing out of their experience of the control of higher education by powers not in sympathy with the church. And while these State universities. have large and constantly increasing attendance, and among them sons of our ministers, and graduates numbered annually by hundreds, the statistics of the seminaries, already considered in this article, show the relatively small proportion of candidates for the ministry furnished from their walls—there being but eight of them represented in the seminaries, with an average of but two students from each institution, and sixteen in all. Looking now at the necessity of a supply, and especially of an increase, of candidates for the ministry who must come through college halls, the importance of securing institutions. under church control, in view of the failure of these State institutions to do this work, would seem to be most urgent. And the question, whether the passing of collegiate control from. the church to the State has not much to do with the comparative decrease in candidates, is one demanding most serious. examination. Leaving the State her institutions for her public uses, can the church neglect to establish and maintain her own institutions for her own use without prospect of serious peril?

Fifth.—As the counterpart of the last consideration,.

which we have endeavored to present as mildly as the circumstances of the case permit, there arises the estimate of the value of institutions under church influence, direct or indirect, to the advancement of the church, and especially to the supply of the ministry. And surely the historical argument here should be decisive without any protracted elaboration. Everyone who knows anything whatever about the subject, understands the vast religious power exercised in these church colleges upon all the youth educated therein. This power arises, first, from the presence of men of positive religious views in the several chairs, who, in the presentation of every subject, bring to bear the arguments for religion belonging to the range of that study. There is scarcely a branch taught in any department of higher education that may not be made, that is not made, consciously or unconsciously, by the professor thereof, either subversive or confirmatory of religion. Moreover, the religious character and avowed opinions of the professor create deep and abiding influence upon his pupils. And a teacher, even by incidental comment, or a sneer, and by the general tone of his instructions, without positive and openly expressed bias, will seriously affect the views of the youth in his department. Young men at the period of college education are learning to inquire for themselves into all questions, and religion with the rest. The age of inquiry is the age of natural skepticism, which is well nigh certain to affect every young mind at the point where it begins to think for itself. Inquiring too often begins with displacing the presumption of the truth of religion as the basis of examination. If the doctrine of the natural depravity of the human mind and heart, and that man has lost the image of God in knowledge, be true, it follows that the presumption naturally leans in the direction of the rejection of religion. And the youth, from this standpoint, demands that the truth of religion be demonstrated, contrary to the bent of his natural feelings. This is, then, a very dangerous period in life, and one that demands incessant and positive religious influences ever present, in every department of training, as a safeguard against the dangers of skepticism and the natural unbelief of the human heart.

The general tone and impression of religious society among students is also a very essential factor in the safeguard of collegiate education. Youth run in flocks, and where the public opinion is not vigilantly guarded and directed toward religious belief, the rush of the multitude, the force of public opinion, is a very serious danger to all subjected to its control. And then, again, the great gain made to religious ranks, both in laity and for the clergy, by those revivals of religion that so frequently appear in religious colleges, is universally conceded. There is not a college connected with our church from whose classes year after year there have not gone forth into the ministry young men who were converted within its walls, and whose attention and intention have been therein directed toward this sacred sphere of toil. Many of the brightest lights in the church, and many of its most efficient servants in all fields of her work, at home and abroad, acknowledge the direction thus given to their lives by the specific power of the college revival, and of the college influence when revivals have not appeared. Many of these ministers have been drawn from outer circles not religious, or from other denominations, and have proved a direct gain, which would not have been made but for the control of the college over their spiritual lives. Now the practical question arises, whether colleges not under religious control have done, or can do, this work for the church; and whether the church can endure to leave this kind of work undone. Be it also noted in this connection, that the revivals of religion, so extensive in our religious colleges during the past winter, did not extend, to any appreciable extent, among institutions under secular or non-religious direction; and the material increase of students for the ministry already in our theological seminaries in the present year, of itself, bears ample testimony to the correctness of these views.

Sixth—Another thought, bearing upon the increase of our candidates for the ministry, deserves attention. Connected with the more extensive education of youth in the land, and largely springing from it, is the increase of spheres for the employment of educated talent. The old limitation of the educated to the three leading professions, law, medicine, and theology, has passed away. New fields have been added quite as broad, influential, and to many far more attractive than these. The press, with the various literary occupations connected therewith, demands annually quite as many laborers as were formerly required for the three learned professions. Scientific occupations have opened in every direction, with amorous charms for the young and ambitious mind. Art has increased her spheres a hundred-fold. The building of railroads, architecture, and the working of the metals, annually demand thousands for their service. Politics have grown into a profession largely followed ; every form of manufacture and trade now invoke the aid of educated mind, as never before in the history of the world. The profession of the teacher is calling to our young men from ten thousand school-houses, even in the farthest regions of the West, while the law and medicine need their representatives in every hamlet from Maine to Oregon. The whole world meanwhile is open to missionary labor, and our home fields are but sparsely scattered over with those who carry the glad tidings of salvation. Now whence, amidst all these various calls, are the Christian fields to be supplied with sufficient laborers? The attractions of the other callings are growing every year more fascinating, as these callings are becoming more profitable, and offering increasing opportunities to ambition and love of fame and power. That the ministry suffers very seriously in the loss of the best talent formerly devoted to its service, by the rivalry of these new occupations, any one may see, and the church has already felt the loss. There is also need for renewed and utmost diligence on the part of the church, to increase and strengthen every influence by which our young men may be drawn back, against these rival forces, to her ranks. And where does the secret of her practical power in this respect lie, but in giving herself with a new and great awakening to the necessity of striking early in life, and beginning to train youth for her own heavenly uses, in the stage of collegiate education, during which the young usually decide upon their course in life ?

Seventh.—Nor do we dare omit reference to that alien spirit of the age which has reared its head aloft with so much audacity and determination in this latter time, challenging the power of the church, and defying her on every hand, to self-defense. There never has been a valuable scientific discovery, nor any seeming advance in knowledge, that has not been instantly seized by the enemies of religion, and urged on some pretext against the fundamental positions of the church. The warfare has usually been begun by the boastful declaration, that now the church will be put to her utmost strength to save herself from overthrow, and her downfall has been triumphantly proclaimed in advance. This exultation of anticipated victory carries with it the popular phrenzy, and often weakens the confidence even of believers themselves. The past is repeating itself, in this respect, in the present, and it has taken into alliance with itself all the power of the modern scientific discovery it can seduce or torture into its service; while modern popular philosophy, in its strongholds, is avowedly its guardian and high authority. The science of nature, and the science of the human mind, including the new science of society, have struck hands in an appeal to the widely educated mind of the century for the overthrow of religion, as a superstition of the past. The fickle, but powerful, spirit of the age is in danger of yielding ready submission to this organized combination, and the church has already a terrible conflict on her hands. Without dread as to the ultimate result, the church must yet see and feel that for this battle she must have a ministry fortified in the faith, and widely instructed in science. The well-nigh universal hold which the press has gained upon the public mind, both through the volume and the newspaper, avails to scatter the knowledge of evil as well as good, and to instruct all reading minds everywhere, both in the discoveries of science, and in the influences thence drawn by hostile minds against the positions of Christianity. The pulpit is no longer the only nor the main channel for the publication of opinions upon religion. And the minister preaches on the Sabbath, even in remote districts, to an audience daily fed on religious themes by other teachers, and often by those holding views contrary to his own, of science, philosophy, and religion. It follows, therefore, that the ministry of the present and future must be one versed, at least, as well as are the people upon all themes bearing upon the defence of religion, and upon the phases of its conflict with all other departments of knowledge.

These things are widely reflected upon, and often written about. But they bear with peculiar force upon the position herein defended, that such a ministry as the times demand is not likely to be forthcoming, if the church continue to rely upon secular collegiate institutions, for the supply of a ministry to be educated along the line of her necessary defence. It is a mistake common to many of our most thoughtful and penetrating minds, if it be a mistake, that the church is already seriously suffering in her highest interests from her remissness in planting and sustaining colleges for her own young men, wherein they may be trained with rigid exactness and exhaustive thoroughness, in those fundamental principles that enter into this modern phase of the contest with unbelief, and in which they may be saved to the ranks of her learned defenders. The enemies of religion have grasped much of this influence, and in many institutions of this land, abundantly patronized by Christian parents, their sons are being indoctrinated, with great subtlety, in the new views, which, beginning with scientific and philosophic skepticism, lead on to practical infidelity and ruin; and by these means, which the church seems slow to employ, her own sons are being seduced to the ranks of those who are proving themselves her most dangerous adversaries.

Eighth.—It is worth while to mention, if not to elaborate, the most popular argument urged against Christian colleges, and pressed with especial fervor by the leaders in the ranks of secular education. Assuming the position of friends of genuine religion and a pure Christianity, they display their zeal in behalf of the church by avowing themselves the particular champions of her unity, and the baptized defenders of her consolidation as against sectarian divisions. One could think, to hear them argue, that denominationalism were the highest phase of apostasy, worse than skepticism, worse than atheism— even the betrayal of Christ by his own people. In their eyes, denominational colleges are the crying evil of the day, since they tend to keep alive sectarianism and to postpone the day of consolidated unity. It is apparent to every penetrating observer that such theorists have mounted this hobby merely for the purpose of advancing their own particular schemes of education. But in this age of sincere, loving desire for unity, and for organic union among God's people, the dogmatism of these teachers and their followers affects many truly devout persons even of our branch of the church, and renders them cautious in their support of their own church institutions. We need only pause to show that this outcry against sects and sectarian institutions is pure and silly sentimentalism, unpractical and inpracticable sensationalism.   The existence of denominations representing different phases of interpretation of the meaning of the Scriptures, in the statement of its doctrinal truths, does by no means imply or necessitate mutual hostility or even enmity between these various branches of the church. Through their instrumentality and the power of their various organizations, all classes of people and nearly all nations have been reached by the gospel. We doubt whether as much could have been accomplished for Christianity by any other system of propagation. The mingling of all branches of the church into one heterogeneous mass, while their conscientious views differ as to leading truths of the gospel, would be folly, as absurd as destructive.   And to compel or persuade all Christians to the same religious convictions, while they remain in an unsanctified condition, is an Utopian dream, possible only to the most visionary theorists. What is needed is not organic union, but spiritual unity.   Experience also shows that the more zealous each Christian is in promoting his own especial theories of work, the more effectually does the general cause of pure religion advance.   The entrance of coldness and want of zeal into any denomination opens the door to liberalism and consequent feebleness in pressing on the gospel.   And the catholic spirit is invariably found to be broadest among those who maintain the greatest activity in their particular spheres of Christian toil. But looking at the matter in the only possible, practical light, we see that the various denominations do exist and are certain to endure for a considerable time to come. What then shall be done in the church meanwhile, before the boasted day of absolute unity arrives?   Shall each denomination cease its individual efforts, surrender its particular schemes of activity, and fall in with any general current that may chance to sweep it away? As for ourselves, so long as we have a Presbyterian organization, no necessity would seem more imperative than that of urgently maintaining in full power and efficiency all our own methods of self-support and advancement.   And until, as a denomination, we are prepared for surrender or death, it would be egregious folly for us to listen to the syren voices of those enthusiasts who decry denominationalism and invoke us by their delusive songs to the strait betwixt the shoals of liberalism on the one hand, and the whirlpool of absolutism on the other. · If such enemies, whom we believe to be the most dangerous foes of the true spiritual unity of the church, can persuade us to abandon the only efficient means by which our ministry, and consequently our branch of the Lord's Zion, can be maintained, they will gain an easy victory for their heresies, and strike a serious blow at the cause of Christ itself. How much of the apathy of the church as to her own educational organizations may have sprung from the wide-spread diffusion of these liberal notions of church unity we cannot tell, but that such views naturally would produce precisely such an effect, and that they have been most zealously advocated in the ears of our people, we all do know.

And this fact is especially patent as relating to our collegiate system. For while there is no question as to the vital importance of pure religious family training that precedes the college course, or as to the same necessity for denominational theological training for the ministry that follows the college work, the no less important duty in regard to the collegiate education that intervenes, seems to have fallen into disrepute and largely into neglect. That many earnest efforts formerly organized have failed, for various reasons, has undoubtedly caused the loss of heart therein. But the change of the sentiment of the times as to education in general, and especially the awakening of zeal in the endowment of educational schemes, show that the former causes of failure may now be largely remedied, and that the church may press on her collegiate system to success, if she will but apply her energies to the inviting task.

It only remains to consider what *practical means* may be employed for the reorganization of this system of collegiate instruction, and its future efficient administration. The first appeal must evidently be made to the educated ministry and laity of our church, who should carefully consider the vital bearing of this subject upon the coming life and energy of our own church organization. This is a call for personal activity and influence in support of our own organized colleges, and for the establishment of new colleges, where the future may reasonably seem to demand their existence. The ministry, from the pulpit, and in private, should bring their whole influence to bear in encouraging Presbyterian parents to shun the dangers of educating their children in other schools, and to send them where they know every lawful power will be brought to bear to save them to our own faith, and to our own church organizations.   Parents need not only instruction but example here.   And the sons of our ministers, from whom our ministerial ranks are so largely recruited, should be sent conscientiously to our own schools, in preference to all others, despite convenience of location, and other comparatively trivial advantages.   That our own institutions accomplish this training quite as efficiently and successfully, will be conceded by those who take sufficient pains to examine.   The laity of our church, who believe in her divine calling to an especial mission among men for Jesus Christ, should also be awakened, not only to encourage and support our own colleges, but to contribute liberally of their means for their endowment.   If our laity were as keenly alive to our own interests, as are those of many other denominations, there would be comparatively little difficulty in the support of our colleges.   For Presbyterians are notably an educating church, as we have ever been, and we need only to preserve our own forces within ourselves, to ensure eminent prosperity.   And we have reason to know that our own sons are urgently and systematically spirited away by exaggerated representations to other schools, even of other denominations.

That our synods and presbyteries should likewise enter with revived zeal into this cause is also apparent.   The power of their approval and support is one of the strongest aids that can be rendered, and is eagerly sought in many quarters by schools whose influence is not directly to our advantage, to say the least.   That their active sympathy and approval should be withheld from others, where thereby a disadvantage falls upon our own colleges, is evidently the first step.   After that the discussion may fairly be opened as to what measures may be taken that will best elevate and strengthen those institutions that represent their own principles, and furnish candidates for their own ministry.   The influence of local jealousies that have often proved so disastrous, and the partiality of ministers for their own alma maters, often distant from their present fields

of labor, should be considerately repressed, and, with one heart
and mind, all should unite for the maintenance of the institutions most directly advantageous to their own Presbyterial or
Synodical interests.   We feel that such counsel is not only
wise, but absolutely essential to our church extension, and that
it needs to be openly expressed, and considered carefully, in
these times of the pressure of many-sided education upon the
people at large.   The Presbyteries might likewise direct candidates for the ministry to our own schools.

But, rising to a still higher point of view, we are led to inquire what may our church do through her general agencies,
for the spread of the gospel, in the advancement of this cause.
This brings us to the discussion of a question of considerable
delicacy, and which is approached with much hesitancy, after
long and serious deliberation.   Our church has organized
certain general schemes for the direction of particular spheres
of church activity, and has committed the same to Boards,
appointed to the control of these several departments.   Among
these, is this vast educational field, with its Board of Education.   It is fair to inquire, in a friendly and thoroughly loyal
spirit, laying aside all tendency to mere criticism, what this
Board is doing, and what it may lawfully do, for the encouragement and maintenance of our colleges.   It becomes necessary,
at this point, to revert to the past.   In what may be termed
the palmy days of the educational work, under Assembly direction, when Van Rensselaer and Chester on the one side,
and Thornton A. Mills on the other, gave their enthusiasm,
and well-nigh their lives, to its promotion, the cause of denominational education was constantly and eloquently advocated throughout the bounds of the church, both by the secretaries themselves, and by the great masters in Israel, summoned to their aid.   Both the *Reviews*, of which this REVIEW
is the successor, bear abundant testimony in their pages to the
efficiency of these efforts.   The *"Home, School, and the Church,"*
an annual magazine, edited by the able and zealous Secretary,
Van Rensselaer, was conducted through ten volumes with
great power, and furnishes well nigh 2,000 pages, containing
about 200 articles bearing directly upon our own church
educational schemes.   The address of the leading educators
were therein carefully collected, and published to the church,

among them the various exhaustive discussions of the editor himself, presented previously in person before various Synods and Presbyteries and educational institutions. These volumes form, without exception, the most valuable repository of information and argument, on this subject, to be found in this country. The General Assembly was itself encouraged and rallied every year to zeal in this cause ; many institutions were organized, and others were lifted up to conditions of temporary efficiency. Had the work been pressed on to the present, in the same spirit and power, there would be less need of the argument and plea here presented. In those days, the secretaries visited the various institutions, in person, as required by the constitution of the Board, wrought among the teachers and youth, awoke a lively spirit in all hearts toward this cause, as well as toward that of personal religion, and gained many valuable accessions to the ministry, not a few of whom are now in active labor in our ranks. The course of education stood well-nigh abreast with those of Home and Foreign Missions, and the annual pleas made to the church in its behalf, presented the highest arguments, and rang with electric appeals, that the church could not resist, showing "that the educational institutions of the church have ever constituted a part of her true glory and power, from primitive times, through the Reformation, down to the present period."

In addition to this advocacy of the claims of this cause, plans were organized for the raising of funds, through this agency, to support such institutions as needed immediate assistance. And while no effort was made to raise permanent funds for endowment, in one branch of the church at least, grants were annually voted to aid professors and teachers in such institutions to reimburse them for their expenses in the education of candidates for the ministry, while collections were taken in the churches for the securing of funds to be thus used. Scholarships were also founded in various institutions through the agency of the Board and as authorized by the Assembly. Thus, for example, we have the action of the Assembly (O. S.) as follows :

1848. "*Resolved*, That colleges, as an integral part, and in their widespread relations to the best interests of society, a vitally important part, of a complete system of Christian edu-

cation, demand the fostering care of the church, and that the
Board of Education be, and hereby is, authorized to assist in
the promotion of the cause of collegiate education by means
of any funds that may be given for that purpose."

1851. " It is recommended to our churches and members to
assist, as far as possible, in the endowment of our colleges, and
to co-operate with the Board of Education in sustaining them
during the interval for which they may need aid."—*Baird's
Digest*, p. 411.

The protracted alliance of the other branch of the church
with the American Education Society, or its branches, and the
more recent organization of its own committee of education
by its General Assembly, insured large success to this cause in
that field. And the enthusiasm awakened, and the generous
offerings made in its support, need no comment. Suffice it to
say that the whole Presbyterian Church was thoroughly aroused
to the importance of constant and active exertion in its behalf,
and that its growth in both branches was steadfast, exceedingly
profitable to the church, and beneficial to the ministry. We
have the authority of the present administration of the Board
of Education for saying, that a careful examination of the
Minutes of Assembly for the present year shows that out of
4,744 ministers enrolled, 1,853—about one-third of the number
—have been aided by the Boards of our church, as constituted
before and since re-union. If we add to these those who were
assisted by local organizations in the late N. S. branch before
1862, when the Assembly's committee was organized, the proportion will be greatly increased.

In turning to consider the condition of this work in our re-
united church, a candid statement reveals the fact, that the pleas
and appeals to the church, except as to the general work of the
promotion of revivals of religion, which is the remote and indirect mode of advancing this cause of education, have fallen into
comparative desuetude ; that the visits of the representatives of
this cause to our educational institutions have well nigh ceased ;
that collections are no longer made in the churches for aid of
the academies and colleges ; that all popular enthusiasm in the
church on the subject has expired ; that the work of this Board
has fallen into an humble and subsidiary place beside the other
great agencies for the spread of the Gospel; and that no zeal

is enkindled in the Assembly in its behalf.   And all this has
come to pass while education in society and in the State has
awakened more and more the popular enthusiasm, and has advanced with liberal expenditures and rapid strides.   And we
state the literal fact when we assert, that the sphere of this
Board has been reduced well-nigh to the single agency whereby
food and clothing are doled out to a moderate number of candidates for the ministry every year.   Meanwhile, many in the
church have grown incredulous as to the propriety of even this
much effort and expenditure; influential organs of the press
have called in question the necessity and propriety of the existence of the board; for which, and other reasons, it has been
steadily losing popular favor, and the comparatively small sum
needed for its meagre and recently reduced appropriations is
with difficulty obtained.   Instead of assisting the colleges in
the support of the young men who are passing through their
course, the Board does nothing in this direction whatever, all
its funds being needed for their temporal necessities.   Every
one of our colleges in which candidates are educated has to
expend annually, in furnishing free tuition to the candidates
under the care of the Board, *fully as much money* as the Board
gives these students for the supply of their material wants—
estimating by the proportionate expense for the education of
each pupil.   The college takes care of his brains, and the Board
takes care of his body only.   Whether or not the colleges
should be required to bear this burden alone, year in and year
out, without any remuneration from the church therefor, is a
question that it would not seem difficult for justice to answer.
When the Board has the annual collections of the church to
fall back upon, and the colleges, especially in the West, wherein
so many of our candidates are educated, have only the narrow
income from very insufficient endowments upon which to draw,
it would seem but right that the church should at least lift this
burden of expenditure in her own behalf from the backs of the
colleges, through the agency of her educational administration.

Thus the broader and wider sphere of increased usefulness
may be re-opened to the Board, whereby it may enlarge its
operations, invoke new sympathies for its efforts, and increase
its usefulness to the church and to the world, in laying plans

for the establishment of scholarships, and for the payment of the tuition of the youth committed by the Presbyteries to its care, to add nothing as to the new zeal it may awaken in behalf of our colleges.   That we are justified in fixing this duty upon the Board may be seen by quoting from its constitution, as adopted by the re-united church, as follows :

"Art. II.—*Objects*. The Board of Education shall be the organ of the General Assembly of the church, for the general superintendence of the church's work in furnishing a pious, educated, and efficient ministry, in sufficient numbers to meet the calls of its congregations ; to supply the wants of the destitute classes and regions of our own country, and to go into all the world and preach the Gospel to every creature. It shall provide for the collection and judicious distribution of the funds which may be requisite in the proper education of candidates for the ministry under its care, and it shall, in co-operation with the ecclesiastical courts, do whatever may be proper and necessary to develop an active interest in education throughout the church."

Two things, by this showing, the Board is expected to do, as the organ of the church : first, to superintend the furnishing of a ministry in sufficient numbers for the demands of the church ; and, secondly, to superintend the raising of necessary funds.   And yet in the report of the Board for the current year, by the presentation of elaborate tables, it is shown, in its own words, that " the number of candidates for the ministry in the Presbyterian Church is not commensurate with the necessities and obligations of the Presbyterian Church in this country; the number of ministers is not enough for the churches and communicants, and it is relatively diminishing." The report of the last Assembly Committee on Education, in considering this report of the Board, states that there has been a falling off in the number of candidates from the previous year of 38, and from two years past, of 92 ; and adds, that "the ratio of ministers, both to the communicants of the church and to the increasing population of the country, *has continued for many years to decline.*"   The statistics presented by the Board also show, that while the present number of candidates is 460, " the probable total annual average, in both branches of the church, from 1850 to 1869, would be 572," including 155 academical students now dropped, leaving the church just where she has stood, in this respect, for the last quarter of a century, except that she has ceased her academical work. Meanwhile, the church has gone on increasing, and other boards of the church have advanced with its progress.

A comparison of the present status of the church with that of the O. S. branch alone, in 1860, will further illustrate the subject, as follows:

1876—Home Mis. $287,717 For. Mis. $517,689 Ed. $72,041 Mem. $535,210
1860— "   "   118,904 "   "   237,583 "   70,970   "   292,927

To these figures add, 1876, candidates 460; 1860, candidates 492; while the average amount annually contributed to education in the last five years is, according to the report, but $62,000.

Thus, while the mission funds have both been more than doubled, and the church membership is well-nigh doubled also, education has barely held its own; all the academical students, being one-fifth of the whole number, having been cut off; and while, in 1860, $6,340 were raised for the school-fund, not a dollar is reported as now secured for this purpose. The case would have appeared more hopeful if, in connection with this unfortunate showing of the Annual Report, some plans had been presented, by way of superintendence, for giving the cause a new impetus; had some adequate efforts been put forth for arousing the failing zeal of the church, or, at least, for putting an end to the gradual but sure decline. We believe that the figures prove that from the time when the church began to lose her zeal and to cease her activity in behalf of her own colleges, the public interest waned, the funds ceased to flow, and the plan of struggle for existence by the Board began. The church surely has a right to look for the progress of this cause in relative proportion to the progress of her other schemes of work, especially since the furnishing of a ministry lies at the basis of success in every other department.

We have no disposition, as before stated, to reflect upon the Board or its executives, past or present, we are even zealous in our sympathy. But the statement of these facts seemed absolutely necessary both for the information of the church, and for its benefit, and for the proper strength of our argument. The present time, moreover, when a change in the administration of the Board has occurred, and when there is a brief interval before full work may begin with new plans and higher purposes, seemed less offensive for the presentation of the facts, than a subsequent occasion might have proved. Under this new administration, opening with such promise of renewed vigor, may we not hope for an era of better things for church education. We have several strong colleges in the East, and quite a number on comparatively safe footing, though with very limited incomes, in the West—all are striving with much self-sacrifice on the part of capable professors to do the preliminary part of the training for the ministry that falls to their lot, conscientiously and effectively. We believe, after quite extensive examination into their condition, that they are in every respect worthy of the confidence and affection of the church. And not writing in any sense in behalf of any one of them, but sincerely desiring the success and enlargement of them all, to the utmost extent, we do with intense earnestness invoke the attention of our ministry and of our thoughtful laity to the work the institutions are doing so quietly, and to the necessity of fitting them adequately for the attainment of higher efficiency and larger results. As essential to the consecration of the purity, power, and very life of the church, as so intimately connected with the character and force of the ministry of the future, they assuredly do deserve the prayers, the cheering words, the helpful hands of all who love our Presbyterian fold. As against the encroachment of the world, as against the boasting attack of organized skeptical and materialistic forces, as against the inducements offered by other branches of the church, drawing many of our youth to their service, our colleges, though comparatively weak and much neglected, are doing duty that the future will be glad to recognize, though the present may underestimate its intrinsic value and ignore its wide extent.

The serious question, therefore, that presses upon the church in connection with their work, is not merely whether they are sufficient for the adequate supply of the ministry, provided the church do not increase but come to a stand-still, but what they are capable of doing in this direction, provided her work extend as it should.   And the other question follows, if these church colleges do not afford that supply, from whence have we any expectation, founded upon experience or reason, that the necessary supply can be elsewhere secured.

Art. VIII.—THE VOWEL-POINTS CONTROVERSY IN THE XVI, XVII, AND XVIII CENTURIES.

By Rev. B. Pick, Rochester, N. Y.

In the second half of the last century, the controversy as to the age of the Hebrew vowel-points was terminated by the general acknowledgment that they were of comparatively recent origin.   It is not our intention to review the whole range of literature treating on that subject, which is in part enumerated in Malcolm's Theological Index under *Vowels.** We will give the gist of the matter in the briefest possible manner.

As early as the ninth century, Natronai II. ben Hilai,† in reply to the question, whether it is lawful to put the points to the Synagogal Scrolls of the Pentateuch, distinctly declared the points not to be Sinaitic (*i. e.*, sacred), but invented by the sages, hence we must not put the points to the scrolls of the law.   "The same opinion as to the recent origin of the vowel-points was expressed by no less an authority than Ibn Ezra (born 1088, and died 1176), in his Hebrew Grammar, entitled *On the Purity of the Hebrew Style* (*Zathuth*, p. 79, ed. Fürth, 1827.)   From Ibn Ezra, this opinion was also espoused by some Christian scholars in the middle ages, such as the celebrated Dominican, *Raymond Martin* (died 1287), who in his *Pugis Fidei* (pars iii, dissert. iii, cap. xxi, p. 895, ed. Carpzoo, Leipzig, 1687), boldly asserted that the vowel-points in the text of the Old Testament were put there by Ben Naphtali and Ben Asher, *circa*

---

* Malcolm puts Scaliger among those who defended the antiquity of the vowel-points, but this is a mistake, as he opposed it.

† Comp. our art. *Natronai II. ben Hilai* in the Cyclop. of McClintock and Strong.

900–960 ("sed duo Judæi, quorum unus dictus est Naphtali, alter vero Ben Asher, totum rebus Testamentum punctasse leguntur.") This opinion of Raymond was confirmed by no less an authority than the celebrated *Nicolaus de Lyra* (died 1340), in his commentary on Hosea ix : 12, and it was regarded as paramount by all succeeding Catholic writers.

To invest it with an air of originality, *Jacob Perez de Valencia* (died 1491), gives the following account of the origin of the vowel-points, which we give, not on account of its intrinsic value, but on account of its amusing nature. " After the conversion of Constantine the Great, the Rabbins perceived that great multitudes of Gentiles embraced Christianity with the greatest devotion all over the globe ; that the church prospered very favorably, and, that also of the Jews an immense number became convinced of the truth by experience and miracles, whereby their gains and revenues were lessened. Roused by this wickedness, they assembled in great multitudes at the Babylon of Egypt, which is called Cairo, where they, with as much secrecy as possible, falsified and corrupted the Scriptures, and concocted about five or seven points to serve as vowels, these points having been invented by Ravina and Ravashe, two of their doctors. The same Rabbins also concocted the Talmud." (*Prolog. in Psalmos*, tract vi.) Hence, he maintains, " that as faith is to be placed in the Holy Scriptures as the Jews now interpret and punctuate them." (*Ibid.*, tract ii, fol. xxiii : " ideo nulla fides adhibenda est scripturæ sacræ sicut hodie habent (Judæi) sic interpretatum et punctuatum.")

Among Jewish commentators and grammarians, it was the general belief that the vowel-points were either given to Adam in Paradise, or communicated to Moses on Sinai, or were fixed by Ezra and the Great Synagogue. This view was deemed all the more orthodox, and the famous sabbatistical work called *Zohar*, which was believed to be a revelation from God, communicated through R. Simon ben Yorhai (*circa A.D.* 70–110), maintained it, which was adopted as final. *

This opinion, however, was assailed by no less an authority than *Elias Levita* (died 1549), who, in his *Massoreth ha Masso-*

---

* It is now admitted that the author of this cabalistical work was *Moses de Leon*, of Spain, who died in 1305; cf. our art. *Moses de Leon*, in McClintock and Strong's *Cyclop.*

reth, denied the divine origin and the antiquity of the vowel-points, and defended his heterodoxy by the most una ssailable arguments.

Levita's arguments soon became known to the Christian world through S. Münster's (died 1552) and Pellican's (died 1556) translation, and Christendom, otherwise divided, at once agreed to welcome Levita's results. The assertion made in former years by R. Martin, Nic. de Lyra, Perez de Valencia, re-echoed now in Luther (who called the vowels "neu menschen-fuendlein"), Calvin, Zwingle, Mercer, Th. Beza, Drusius, Joh. Scaliger, Gessner, Mercier, etc., who boldly disclaimed the antiquity, divine origin, and authority of the points. "The conviction of the Protestant leaders undoubtedly was, that by liberating themselves from the traditional vowel-points of the synagogue, after having discarded the traditions of the Church of Rome, they could more easily and independently prosecute their Biblical studies, without any trammels whatever," thus making the Bible, and the Bible alone, without gloss and without tradition, the rule of faith and practice. But Rome soon changed her tactics. Whilst in former years it was the hatred of the Jews which induced men like Raymond to charge the Jews with having introduced innovations and corruptions into the text of the Bible, the Church of Rome now laid hold of the admission made by Levita, in order to confute thereby her opponents. From the novelty of the points she deduced, I. "That the Bible could only be read in ancient days by the few chosen spiritual teachers;" and II. "That the Scriptures, without these points, cannot possibly be understood, apart from the traditions of the Church of Rome." This opinion soon found its way into England, and was advocated by Dr. Th. Harding (1512–1572), the celebrated antagonist of Bishop Jewel (cf. *Works of John Jewel*, ii, p. 678 ; Parker Society Edition).

Alarmed at this *modus operandi*, the defenders of Protestant-ism commenced beating a retreat. They now declared that the points were put to the text by the Prophets themselves, and that to say otherwise was *heathenish* and popish. Thus, the charge of *Gregory Martin* (*circa* 1534–82) in his work, en-titled, "*A Discovery of the Manifold Corruptions of the Holy Scripture, by the Heretics of our Days*" (reprinted in Fulke's *Defence of the Translators*, Parker Society, 1843), that Protestants in their versions follow the Hebrew vowels, which were of 'a recent origin, was rebutted by *Fulke*, with the declaration, that " seeing our Saviour hath promised that never a particle of the law shall perish, we may understand the same also of the Prophets, who have not received the vowels of the later Jews, but even of the Prophets themselves, however that heathenish opinion pleaseth you, and other papists." Among those who beat retreat are also to be found Hugh Broughton (1549–1626) in his commentary on *Daniel* ix : 26, London, 1597), and the celebrated Piscator (1546–1626) in his commentary on *Matt.* v : 18.

Hitherto, both Catholics and Protestants chiefly relied upon abusing each other. None of them thought of examining Levita's arguments, or of corroborating or refuting his statements. To be or not to be, that was the question on both sides, and besides, neither of the two parties had sufficient Talmudical learning and critical tact. The first attempt to meet Levita's book was made by the learned *Azariah de Rossi*, in 1574–5, in chapter lix, part iii, of his work, " *The Light of the Eyes*," (*Meor Agnaim*, Mantua, 1574–5, Vienna, 1829), wherein he tried to prove the antiquity of the vowel-points from the Zohar and the Talmud.

With weapons like these, the Protestants now opened a new campaign, under the leadership of *Buxtorf, the Father* (died 1629), with a display of Rabbinical bayonets. The antiquity and divinity of the vowel-points, which were formerly abandoned, were now defended, and in his *Tiberias sive Commentarius Masorethicus*, Basle, 1620, Buxtorf made use of de Rossi's arguments. Feeble as these arguments were, they nevertheless found many supporters, who ranged themselves under the leadership of Buxtorf, who, however, was not destined to carry everything before him in his first battle against Levita. The Buxtorf-de-Rossi alliance produced a counter alliance, headed by Lewis Capellus (died 1658). Before Capellus published his treatise, he sent it in manuscript to Buxtorf for examination, who returned it with the request that it might not be printed. He then sent it to Erpenius, who was so convinced by its arguments and learning, that, with the sanction of the author, he printed it at Leyden, under the title, " *The Mystery of the Points Unveiled*" (*Arcanum punctatonis revelatum*, Leyd. 1624, afterwards reprinted by his son, Amsterd. 1689, fol.)

A time of anxious suspense followed the publication of Capellus' work, during which time Father Morinus (1591-1659), formerly a Protestant, published his " Biblical Exercitations on the Hebrew and Greek Texts " (Paris, 1633), against the antiquity of the vowel-points, in which he compared " the Scriptures to a mere nose of wax, to be turned any way, to prove thereby the necessity of one infallible interpretation."

After a silence of twenty-four years, Buxtorf, the son, published, in 1648, a reply against Capellus, entitled " A Treatise on the Origin, Antiquity, and Authority of the Vowel-points and Accents in the Hebrew Scripture of the Old Testament," Basle, 1648 ; to which Capellus answered in a rejoinder, " A Vindication of the Mystery of the Vowels Unveiled," published by his son in 1689.

The consequence of this controversy was, that Protestant Christendom everywhere was divided into two hostile camps, vowelists and anti-vowelists. Soon the controversy was transplanted to England, where Levita and Capellus were represented by Walton, de Rossi and Buntorf by Lightfoot and Owen. Twelve months after the publication of Owen's work *On the Integrity and Purity of the Hebrew and Greek Text of the Naphtali*, London, 1659, vol. iv., p. 44, fol., of his collected works, London, 1823), Walton published a reply, *The Considerator Considered*, London, 1659, (reprinted by Todd in the 2d vol. of his Memoirs of Bishop Walton, London, 1821), containing more additional and valuable contributions to the literature of this controversy.

Although the antiquity of the vowel-points still found advocates in Joseph Cooper (*Dornus Mosaicæ Clavis, sive Legis Septimentum*, etc., London, 1673), Samuel Clark (*An Exercitation Concerning the Original of the Chapters and Verses in the Bible*, etc., *ibid*, 1698), Whitfield (*A Dissertation on the Hebrew Vowel-Points*, Liverpool, 1748), and Dr. Gill (*A Dissertation Concerning the Antiquity of the Hebrew Language, Letters, Vowel-Points, and Accents*, London, 1767), who published learned dissertations in defense of Dr. Owen and against Walton, yet it must be admitted that Walton's works decided the battle in England in favor of the anti-vowelists.

On the continent Wasmuth, with his *Vindiciæ Hebr. Script.* (Rostock, 1664), and others, entered the lists in support of Buxtorf, whose adherents in Switzerland exalted his views to a confessional article of belief in the *Formula Consensus*, Art. iv, Can. ii, so that a law was enacted in 1678, that no person should be licensed to preach the gospel in their churches, unless he publicly declared that he believed in the integrity of the Hebrew text and in the divinity of the vowel points and accents (*codicem Hebr. Vet.Test. tum quoad consonas tum quoad vocalia sive puncta ipsa sive punctorum saltem potestatem* Θεόπνευστον *esse.*

An intermediate course, proceeding on the assumption that there had been a simpler system of vowel-marks, either by three original vowels, or by diacritic points, was opened up by Rivetus (*Isagoge seu Introductio Generalis, Vet. et Novi Test.*, Leyd., 1627, ch. 8,§ 15, p. 104), Hottinger, and others, and was pursued especially by J. D. Michælis (*von de Alter der Hebr. Vocale*, Orient. Bibl., ix: 82ff. 88ff.), Trendelenburg (*in Eichhorn's Repertor.*), xviii, p. 78ff.), Eichhorn, Jahn, Berthold, and others.*

The controversy, which so vehemently raged for more than three centuries, may now be regarded as ended. Modern research and criticism have confirmed the arguments urged by Levita against the antiquity of the present vowel signs. It is now established beyond question, from the discovery of ancient MSS., that there were two systems of vocalization contrived almost simultaneously, the earlier or first system developed by Acha or Achai, of Irak (Babylon), about 550; the later or second system by Motha, of Tiberias, about A. D. 570.

As to the first system, representing the traditional pronunciation of the text in the East, its peculiarity consists in having signs of a different shape to represent the vowels, and that these are almost uniformly placed *above* the letter. Hence it is called the *superlineary system* and the *Babylon* or *Assyrian system*, from the fact that its contriver lived in Babylon.

The later or second system has been for centuries commonly adopted both by Jews and Christians in the pointed editions of Hebrew Bibles, and it is far more complete and extensive, and exhibits more sharply the niceties of the traditional pronunciation and intonation of the text, than does the Babylonian system, with which it competed. It is called the *Tiberian system*, and the *Palestinian* or *Western system*.

---

*Diestel, *Gesch. d. Alten Test. in der Christl. Kirche*, Jena, 1869. Pp. 253, 334ff, 401, 451, 566, 570, 595ff.

Art. XI.—CONTEMPORARY LITERATURE.

THEOLOGY.

WE have received from A. S. Barnes & Co., New York, two substantial volumes of the English "Congregational Union Lectures," for 1874 and 1876. The course for 1874 (now in its second edition) was given to a "select class of the students" of Cheshunt College, by DR. H. R. REYNOLDS, *On John the Baptist: a Contribution to Christian Evidences* (pp. 548). The other course, by E. MELLOR, D.D., has for its subject, *Priesthood in the Light of the New Testament* (pp. 423). The prelections are under the care of the Congregational Union of England and Wales. Even "the oral delivery can be dispensed with." These volumes furnish good evidence of the wisdom with which this trust is dispensed. Both of them are fundamental and vigorous discussions of important themes, in a way to meet objectors and to fortify believers. The importance of such public lectures at the present time is increasingly appreciated.

The monograph of Dr. Reynolds is not merely a life of John the Baptist, but a full survey of his times and surroundings, of his relations to the old and the new dispensations, and especially of his relations to Christ and the gospel narrative. It is a critical history, with due consideration of the difficulties and objections raised by the later criticism, especially of the German schools. It thus becomes a valuable "contribution to Christian evidences." And this thorough piece of work is all the more welcome, because it fills an almost vacant place in theological literature. The literature of the subject is found chiefly in the lives of Christ, the most important of which are freely used by Dr. Reynolds. The eight lectures are under the following heads: Significance and Sources of the Biography of John; his Nativity—examining the theories of Strauss and others; John, as the Exponent of the Old Testament Dispensation, as Priest, Ascetic, Prophet, and more than Prophet; The Preaching in the Wilderness; The Transitional Work of John; his later Ministry and Special Revelations; The Ministry of the Prison; Results, Echoes, and Lessons of the Ministry. This gives the outline for a full treatment of the subject, which is pursued with sound judgment to satisfactory results. It is an indispensable book to one who would thoroughly study the immediate antecedents of the life of our Lord.

Dr. Mellor's volume on "The Priesthood," as might be expected from the lecturer's high reputation, is an acute and vigorous presentation of the doctrine, in the light of the New Testament authority and testimony, freed from all the accretions of tradition. In the first two lectures it is shown that "the priesthood is not an order in the New Testament," and in the third, "its alleged order and lineage" are subjected to a keen criticism, while the difficulties, and, in fact, historical impossibility, of the "Episcopal Succession" are convincingly exhibited. . . . In the remaining lectures, the general doctrine is applied to the Lord's Supper, the Real Presence, and the Confessional—advocating with old and fresh arguments the ground of the Reformed churches, in the spirit of Whately, Jacob, Lightfoot, and other recent writers. We regret to miss another lecture on the connection between Sacerdotalism and Skepticism, which the writer had "hoped to prepare" for this work. The style is popular and earnest, so that it is well adapted to general reading. It lays bare, with critical anatomy, that subtle sacerdotal element, which has in so many ways perverted thc Christian system and banished Christ behind the forms and ordinances of the external church.

Jehovah-Jesus: the Oneness of God, the True Trinity, by ROBT. D. WEEKS. Dodd, Mead & Co. The doctrine of this treatise is—that Jesus is "the Supreme God, the Only Begotten Son of God, and the Son of Man"— all in one; the only Trinity is not a Trinity of Persons, but the above Trinity in Jesus. It is the Swedenborgian view, which identifies Jehovah and Jesus. The writer's proof of the divinity of Jesus is clear and forcible. His attempted proof, that there is no real personal and eternal distinction between the Father and the Son, seems to us to confound things that differ. The careful discriminations of the orthodox doctrine are not thoroughly mastered. For example, he seems to suppose that the received doctrine of the Trinity involves, or implies "the co-existence of three infinite beings," which is quite as emphatically repudiated by the orthodox as by himself.

The True Man, and other Practical Sermons, by REV. SAMUEL S. MITCHELL, D.D. New York: R. Carter & Bros. The pastor of the New York Avenue Presbyterian Church, of Washington, D. C., gives full proof in these discourses of his eminent fitness for his work and position—a workman that needeth not to be ashamed. He speaks cogently and concisely on such themes as "The Great Requirement," "Physical Conditions," "Spiritual Assimilation," "Faith Culture," "The Death of Jesus," "Life Wisdom," etc.

J. B. Lippincott & Co., Philadelphia, publish *Christ the Teacher of Men*, by A. W. PITZER, author of *Ecce Deus Homo*, in some respects the best of all the *Ecce* books. This book sets forth Christ as the divine, authoritative, and infallible teacher, in opposition to the infidelity of rationalism and materialism, within and without the church. It treats of the prophetical office of Christ. The extent and manner of his teachings, as the covenant prophet, through the Holy Ghost, by miracles and types, as well as by literal statement, together with his personal peculiarities and credentials, as the divine teacher of men. He takes occasion to explode the doctrine that Christ's teachings in the New Testament only are inspired, while the Old Testament is uninspired. He shows, what needs now to be vindicated, that Christ reaffirmed the law and the prophets, and that "all Scripture is given by inspiration of God."

In *The Different Phases of Infidelity, Including Evolution Examined and Compared with the Evidence of the Truth of Revelation*, by a LEYMAN, we recognize the hand that has enriched the pages of this REVIEW with articles which our readers will, doubtless, remember, on the Sabbath, and on the anointment of our Saviour by Mary. It is published by Brearley & Stoll, of Trenton, N. J., and it is a very creditable contribution to the apologetic literature of the day.

The same may be justly said of the Baccalaureate discourse of Dr. Asa D. Smith, President of Dartmouth College, in reference to prevalent skepticism, delivered to the last graduating class.

William Blackwood & Sons, Edinburgh and London, and Scribner, Welford & Armstrong, in this country, have published *The Christian Doctrine of Sin*, by JOHN TULLOCH, D.D., being six lectures on the Croall Foundation, delivered in Edinburgh. Whatever might be published by Principal Tulloch, on this or any theological topic, would be sure to command attention, on account of his decided eminence and theological antecedents. Theologians and Christian inquirers will eagerly look for his views on a subject which has tasked, and on many sides baffled, the profoundest thinkers of Christendom from the beginning until now.

In these lectures the author treats of evil and the sense of sin, as they are recognized in the consciousness of the most barbarous and degraded peoples, and upward through the ascending stages of moral and religious culture, till he deals with it as it arises under the different degrees of revelation; while he discusses the contents and normal authority of this revelation. These stages of revelation, which he specially considers in their relation to sin, are three—that of the Old Testament, of Christ in the Gospels, and of Paul in his Epistles. In the Old Testament representations, sin "everywhere comes forth as an act of the human will done against the divine will, or some special institution supposed to represent the divine will. . . . It is something wrong in the disposition or state of man toward the divine, something always for which man is responsible. But there is no analysis of the conception beyond the fact that, it is at variance with the divine order" (pp. 86-7). The significance of such statements in the author's presentation of the subject lies in the strong antithesis between them and every seeming or real attempt to trace the origin or authorship of sin to God. This carries us into that abyss which, as yet, the human intellect has never fully sounded—the relation of the decretive to the preceptive will of God. All will sympathize with the author's endeavor to fasten the origin of, and responsibility for, sin upon the will of the creature. Yet it is not necessary for this purpose to follow him in his reluctance to view the tempter of our first parents as the personal devil, so abundantly and manifoldly set forth in the New Testament, as he admits; or to be as chary, as he sometimes is, of connecting all events, evil included, with the divine providential purpose; lest he should thereby impute to the Most High "the abominable thing which his soul hateth." He, however, comes very near the sum and substance of Scriptural and Catholic truth on this whole subject, in the final summation, with which he closes his very able lecture on this subject.

"As a whole, we may sum up the doctrines of the Old Testament as follows, gathering into one view the results of our analysis:

"1. The Hebrew conception of evil is distinctively moral. It is the disobedience of the human will against the divine, expressed in the form of command, revelation, or law. In other words, it is what we specially mean by sin.

" 2. It is not only a rejection of divine law, but a rejection of divine good.

" 3. All sin is in its nature destructive. It bears death in it as its natural working or outcome.

" 4. It is not merely individual, but diffusive. Having once entered into human nature, it becomes a part of it, an hereditary taint, passing from generation to generation, often with accelerated force.

" 5. It is connected with a power or powers of evil outside of man, the character and influence of which are as yet but dimly revealed.

" 6. And to these several points of our summary we may add a further, which has been emphasized by certain expositors of the religion of Israel. Evil is also connected with the will of Jahveh as the supreme source of all energy and events. Facts of evil (*ra*), no less than of good, are traced upward to the Almighty Will, as the ultimate source of all things. This is true beyond all question, but it exceeds the truth to say, as (Knenen) does, that the older Israelitish prophets and historians did not hesitate to derive even moral evil from Jahveh. . . . It was, nevertheless, true, as has been clearly seen in the course of our exposition, that the essential idea of evil in the Hebrew mind was so far from associating itself with the Divine Will, that its special note or characteristic was opposition to this Will."—pp. 95-6.

When Principal Tulloch takes in hand Christ's exhibition of sin in the Gospels, he finds it to be more intense, spiritual, inner, reaching to all deviations from, or coming short of, a perfect standard ; and against a God whose perfection in love, holiness, and power are set over against it in more luminous and impressive contrast. The deformity of sin, as the free disobedience to God of the creatures of his goodness and love, becomes more conspicuous in the light of the unmatched goodness and benignity of the Being it defies.

Passing to the Pauline doctrine of sin, the main points in the author's view arrange themselves under three heads : " 1st—The universality of sin ; 2d—The nature and seat of sin; 3d—The effects or consequences of sin." As to the first, he maintains this universality. As to the second, he soundly says: " The seat of *sin* is the ' flesh.' This, in its broadest sense, is distinguished from the ' spirit.' As thus distinguished from the spirit, it represents the whole of this human nature in its estrangement from the Divine—all the activities of body and mind with which fallen man is capable of opposing the Divine." The consequences of sin are " death," in both a subjective and objective sense ; in the former as it works the destruction and misery of the sinner, in all his parts and faculties, by its own inherent tendency and influence ; in the latter, as it exposes him to all the positive penal inflictions and visitations of God's wrath against all sin and unrighteousness.

The closing lecture is on original sin. He maintains that the Scriptures teach the fall of all men in the fall of the first; and, although somewhat wavering, he in the main makes a close approach to the doctrine of our confession: " Our first parents being the root of all mankind, the *guilt of their sin* was imputed, and the same death in sin, and corrupted nature conveyed to all their posterity." He says—" I am glad to be able to quote these words for their own sake, and because of their source. They are weighty and, on the whole, sober words ; and although they necessarily take us away from the immediate atmosphere of Scripture, they do not seem to me, rightly understood, to exceed the fair meaning of St. Paul." (P. 191.) The manner in which the author touches certain collateral topics enhances the value and interest of the discussion. A few masterly strokes dispose of all manichean, fatalistic, pantheistic, or materialistic solutions of the problem. He is especially incisive in pointing out the antagonism of the evolution theory of the genesis of man and nature to morality, religion, and the Bible. Many apologists for evolution and the Bible suppose that they have removed this antagonism, when they show that there may be a theistic form of it which leaves the teleological argument for the Being of God substantially intact; and that the Creator may use antecedent forms of being as material on which he engrafts the successive and higher forms of it. But this, by no means, suffices to clear the inconsistency between it and revelation, in itself, and as including morality and religion.

In the language of Principal Tulloch:

"The favorite conceptions of modern science involve, if they do not start froms a definite view of human nature, at variance with the old Biblical or spiritual view. Man is conceived as developed—from lower forms of life by lengthened processes of natural selection. There is nothing necessarily inconsistent with enlightened Christianity in this idea, so far. The Divine mind may work out its plans by processes of growth or adaptation as readily as by any other way. Nay, as it has been recently admitted by one of the most distinguished advocates of the modern idea, the teleological conception, or the conception of design, is prominently suggested, rather than excluded, by the theory of development as a mere *modus operandi.* But, beyond question, the chief advocates of the theory mean something very different. Nature is supposed by them to be not merely the sphere of operation, but the operating power itself—beyond which there is nothing. Man is not merely, like all other things, a natural growth; but he is nothing else. There is no higher divine element in him. There is no such thing—or, at least, nothing that we can know and validly infer. Material facts and their relations, or laws, are all that we can ever know. It is this underlying sense of the theory which is at variance with the old Biblical view of human nature. It leaves no room, for example, for the idea of sin. For that which is solely a growth of nature cannot contain anything that is at variance with its own higher laws. . . The two conceptions of sin, and of development, in this materialistic sense, cannot co-exist." (Pp. 4, 5.)

While Dr. Tulloch laboriously unfolds and compares the teachings of Scripture on the subject of sin, and makes them the basis of his own doctrines to an extent seldom true of Rationalists, yet he often suggests the query—whether the statements of Scripture or the deductions of reason are the more authoritative in his view. He says: "No doctrine has come forth in complete lineaments from the Divine mind. The modern theologian does not consider doctrines to be formed by the mere analogies and co-ordination of texts. They are not only logical deductions from Scriptural data; they are vital growths within the Christian consciousness. So the business of the theologian is, not only to deduce conclusions from Scriptural premises, but to trace the vital links in the organism of Christian thought."—(Pp. 24, 25.) "If we identify Revelation with its record—in other words, with Scripture —

then it might be assumed that Divine truth was something absolutely fixed in the text of Scripture. . . But Revelation can only be conceived as a new force of spiritual light and knowledge, communicated to a spiritual intelligence. This force enters, like every other force of knowledge and morality, into the higher culture of the race, and, from a supernatural point of view-is the most powerful factor in advancing that culture."—(P. 216). According to this, the great Protestant doctrine that " The Word of God is the only and sufficient rule of faith and practice," must give way ; and reason, in, formed in some sort by it, under the title of Christian consciousness, must be installed as supreme arbiter of faith and morals in its place.

While we throw out a caution here, we do not wish it to be understood as depreciating the value of this volume as a contribution to the literature of its subject. We rate it highly in this respect.

T. & T. Clark, of Edinburgh, and Scribner, Welford & Armstrong, New York, issue at $2.50, *Messianic Prophecy; its Origin, Historical Character, and Relation to New Testament Fulfilment,* by Dr. EDWARD RHEIM, Professor of Theology in Halle ; translated from the German, with the author's approbation, by the Rev. John Jefferson—a very learned, solid, and judicious work, which cannot fail to be helpful to students of prophecy. It asserts a real significance in the mind of the prophet as to the events he predicted ; that these events thus meant by him were a part of the prophecy, whatever else they may have typified, symbolized, or foreshadowed, and they often pointed to ulterior and grander meanings to which the literal predictions bore about the same relation as the shell to the kernel. But Dr. Rheim strenuously maintains that, in order to give any due interpretation of the prophecies in their higher significance, we must first understand the intent of the prophet in using the words of the prophecy ; and that otherwise prophetic interpretation has no other safeguard to keep it from evaporating into an imaginative idealism.

While thus guarding against this extreme, he is equally strenuous against that mere literalism in prophetic interpretation which sacrifices its vital import to the letter which kills. In particular, he rejects those constructions of prophecies in regard to the future of the Jews, which looks for the consummation of Christ's kingdom on earth through their restoration to their native land, and to their former pre-eminence in God's earthly kingdom. The substance of this volume originally appeared in the form of contributions to the *Studien und Kritiken,* in the years 1865 and 1869. We should have been glad if the translation could have been rendered into more simple and idiomatic English.

The same houses in Edinburgh and New York publish, at $6.00, *The Humiliation of Christ in its Physical, Ethical, and Official Aspects,* by Dr. ALEXANDER B. BRUCE, Professor of Divinity in the Free Church College, Glasgow, which is a valuable contribution to Christological literature. It is learned, discriminating, and orthodox. It discusses the Kenosis with great thoroughness, and much to our satisfaction. He maintains it to have proceeded from the free determination of our Lord, before his abasement, to undergo it for the sake of exalting his people; and that it consisted not in emptying himself of his Godhead, either in its essence or essential properties, but in suspending some of its visible manifestations and splendors, which are separable from its essence. Yet he maintains that there was a special glory in this very Kenosis, and all the other points of Christ's humiliation, on account of the dignity of the being who bore it, and the glorious ends he sought by it. As to the physical element in his humiliation, it consisted in this Kenosis involving the assumption of true and proper manhood, with all its sinless infirmities, exposures, temptations; the scorn, derision and insults of men; the conflict with Satan; the agony of Gethsemane; the accursed death of the cross.

As to its ethical character, while it was sinless, it involved on the human side moral development along with his growth in wisdom and stature, and his temptability in all points like ourselves, yet without sin. He strenuously opposes the extravagant views of Edward Irving and others—that Christ took upon himself not only a temptable, but a sinful, human nature.

As to its official aspects, Prof. Bruce earnestly and ably insists that this humiliation was, although voluntary, yet none the less vicarious and penal in satisfaction of the violated justice and law of God. Under this head he presses a vigorous criticism of the views of Socinians, McLeod, Campbell, Bushnell, and other adversaries.

Theology as a Science, involving an Infinite Element, is the title of the Inaugural Discourse delivered before the Southern General Assembly, at Savannah, last May, by the REV. JOHN L. GIRARDEAU, D.D., Professor of Didactic and Polemic Theology in the Columbia Theological Seminary. We see in it evidences of the contact of the author's mind with some of the vexed questions which lie at the base of the psychology and metaphysics of theology. The mutual relations, and the distinctive characteristics of Faith and Knowledge, and the part which each performs in our apprehensions and convictions concerning the Infinite, are discussed in a style which has, it may be, "the promise and potency" of future clearness, when longer culture and practice in the study and teaching of these problems shall have brought the eloquent author to ripe views of this subject. But, meanwhile, the Inaugural seems to us to deliver a mass of metaphysics which only the rarest of assemblies could digest, even if presented with the clearness and brilliancy which were so characteristic of Dr. Girardeau's predecessor, Thornwell.

Scribner, Armstrong & Co. are publishing a new edition of DR. BUSH- NELL'S works, of which the *Sermons on the New Life* appear as one install- ment. They are marked by the freshness, originality, the fervent and devout spirit which characterize most of his practical works. They also, at times, startle by those doctrinal eccentricities to which he was prone, and which constitute the great drawback to his life and works. It is all the more marvellous in the case of such an eminent genius that his most important aberrations should have arisen from ignorance of catholic theology. His conception of accepted orthodoxy seems to have been determined very much by some provincial and personal forms of theologizing which had currency in his own region. His antagonism to them seems to have received its chief impulse and direction, not from any servile following, but still from the influence, of Coleridge and Schleiermacher. Curiously enough, it frequently happens that he thinks he is sapping or re-casting some article of catholic truth, when, in fact, he is battering down some narrow provincialism or idiosyncracy in theology to replace it with substantial catholic doctrine. In his sermon on regeneration, for example, he says: "The wrong is back of the act, in some habit of soul, some disposition, some *status* of character, whence the action comes. Now this something, whatever it be, is the wrong of all wrong, the sin of all sin; and this must be changed—which change is the condition of salvation." (P. 116.)

The American Tract Society publishes *Three Colloquies on Vital Matters in Religion*, between D. L. Moody and Dr. Wm. S. Plumer, which were held with very solemn effect during the meetings conducted by Mr. Moody last winter; also, *The Difference Between a Protestant and a Roman Catholic*, from the French of Roussel, in which the points of contrast are very clearly and strikingly drawn out in a dialogue between the two.

The Metropolitan Pulpit, edited by Rev. I. K. Funk, a Monthly devoted to the publication of Themes and Outlines of Sermons preached each month in New York and Brooklyn, has recently been started in this city, and we are glad to learn is meeting with encouraging success. The idea is a happy one. It meets with favor from our leading preachers of all denominations, who cheerfully lend their aid to the editor in his worthy undertaking. *The American National Preacher*, during the forty years of its existence, performed an invaluable service to the ministry and the church of this country, both as an informing and an educating power, and had no little influence on the pulpit of other lands, in which it circulated largely in its serial form and where many thousands of its bound volumes have been sold. On the whole the plan of the "Metropolitan Pulpit" is preferrable, at least to the student and the preacher, to that of the old "Preacher." These carefully prepared outlines of sermons, fresh from the lips and pens of our best preachers, as models of thought, as themes of study, as suggestive of texts, topics, and illustrations, can scarcely fail to be influential and eminently helpful to the student of sermonic literature, and to the preacher, whoever he may be and whatever his talents and acquirements, who make a judicious use of them. Each number will contain from twelve to fifteen outlines of sermons, fifty themes and texts of leading sermons. It is offered also, at a very low price.

—J. M. S.

History and Biography.

History of the Reformation in Europe in the Time of Calvin, by the Rev. J. H. Merle d'Aubigne, D.D. Translated by W. L. R. Cates. Vol. VII. Geneva, Denmark, Sweden, Norway, Hungary, Poland, Bohemia, the Netherlands. New York: R. Carter & Bros., 1877. This volume, as now published, was fully written out by Dr. Merle d'Aubigné—the editor's task consisting in verifying quotations and making slight emendations. The best and most complete part of the book is devoted to Geneva and Calvin ; the History of the Reformation in the other countries is less thorough. One more volume will complete the work. While it cannot be said that many new discoveries are made as to Calvin's character and career, yet this delineation has the merit and effect of a new and great historical picture, with striking groupings of the chief actors and a warm coloring of the canvass. So severe a critic as M. de Remusat said of the work, "That it is one of the most remarkable books in our language." The finer and softer tides of Calvin's remarkable personality are lovingly depicted. Many readers will be surprised to learn that, speaking of predestination, Calvin writes in his Institutes : "Ignorance of these things is learning, but craving to know them is a kind of madness." " It is a singular fact," adds Dr. Merle, "that what Calvin indignantly calls a madness should be named *Calvinism.*"

History of Neshaming Presbyterian Church of Warwick, Hartsville, Bucks Co., Pa., 1726–1876, by REV. D. K. TURNER. Philadelphia : Culbertson & Bache ; 8vo, pp. 370. This is the fullest and most complete local history which the Centennial year has as yet brought us. It is illustrated by engravings, including a profile likeness of Rev. Wm. Tennent, Sr. The writer was pastor of the church for twenty-five years, from 1848 to 1873, being the successor of Dr. Jas. P. Wilson, who was settled there eight years, from 1839 to 1847, and who still labors wisely and faithfully in his highly honored ministry in Newark, N. J. The other pastors were Wm. Tennent, 1726 to 1742—the founder of the famous Log College ; Chas. Beatty, for twenty-nine years, from 1743 to 1772; Nathl. Irwin, 1774 to 1812, nearly thirty-eight years; Robt. B. Belville, for twenty-five years, from 1813 to 1838 ; and the present pastor, Rev. Wm. E. Jones, since 1873. Few churches of its numbers have had an abler ministry or a wider influence. The historian has not only given an account of its ministers and elders, but also of their relatives and descendants, so that the book is a valuable biographical repertory. Six chapters are devoted to Tennent and his sons, and the history of Log College and its alumni, including such names as Samuel and John Blair, Samuel Davies, Samuel Finley, Wm. Robinson, John Rowland, and his remarkable trial. The seventh chapter is on Rev. Francis McHenry, an assistant to Mr. Tennent, who was at last installed over the "Old Lights" there. Chapters eight to eleven are upon Rev. Chas. Beatty and his descendants, one of the staunchest patriotic and Presbyterian families of the land, still represented in its best qualities in our Presbyterian ministry. Extracts from Mr. Beatty's journal, which was published in London, relating to the Indian wars and missions, are given in the ninth chapter. The pastorate of Rev. N. Irvin falls in part in the period of the War of the Revolution, and he was earnest in word and work for the good cause—as were almost all the Presbyterians of the land. They never flinched on the question of civil and religious liberty. We cannot go further into detail in respect to this excellent history, and are obliged to omit extracts which we would gladly make. It is an example of what should be written about all our prominent churches, now that there is special impulse and opportunity, as well as encouragement, for such literary labors.   The volume is beautifully got up as to paper and type; so that it is ornamental as well as useful.

Forty Years' Mission Work in Polynesia and New Guinea, from 1835 *to* 1875, by the REV. A. N. MURRAY, of the London Missionary Society.   New York : R. Carter & Bros. pp. 509.   With maps of Polynesia and New Guinea.   These artless and truthful records of a long, trying, and faithful missionary career can not be read without deep interest and sympathy.   They enlarge our view of the need and possibilities of the missionary work, of its trials and triumphs.   No tribe can prevail against Christian self-denial and love.   We need not despair of the gospel when we are witnessing its new victories among the Samoans of Manua and the Papuans of New Guinea. The latter island is the largest on the globe, excepting Australia and, possibly, Borneo.   It has not yet been fully explored.   The mission began in 1871 is full of promise.   Mr. Murray's testimony as to his work is valuable.   He went entirely unarmed and unmolested, and says : " I have found in all my experience that the rule that holds in dealing with men, whether civilized or savage, is, that *what we are to others, they are to us.*"   He also testifies, that he " never found in all his wanderings among savage tribes any who had not some idea of a future life, and of beings superior to themselves, to whom they owed some sort of homage, and whom they feared and sought in some way to propitiate.

The same publishers issue *The Judgment of Jerusalem—Predicted in Scripture, Fulfilled in History*, by the REV. WM. PATTON, D.D., pp. 231, which presents a forcible picture of the fall of Jerusalem, from Josephus and other authorities, and vindicates the accuracy of the inspired record.

Nelson & Phillips issue *The Life and Letters of the Rev. John McClintock, D.D., LL.D., Late President of Drew Theological Seminary*, by GEORGE R. CROOKS, D.D.   Dr. McClintock was, if not foremost, at least the peer of the foremost, of the recent great lights in the American Methodist Church.   Eloquent as a preacher, eminent as a scholar, a man of affairs, remarkable for practical wisdom, of devout and exemplary piety, he seldom touched anything which he did not adorn.   He excelled as an educator and an author.   The *Cyclopædia of Biblical, Theological, and Ecclesiastical Literature*, which he edited in connection with Dr. Strong, will be a lasting monument to its originators and editors.

This volume is very largely an autobiography, in which the accomplished editor lets the subject of it speak largely for himself.   It consists mostly of his correspondence, including letters to him of importance.   These give an insight into his inner life and real character.   They also show the part he took and the influence he exercised on public affairs.   The correspondence with his English friends during the late war, and especially in regard to the Trent affair, sheds much light on the British view of that subject, still a puzzle to many.

Presbyterianism in Sewickley Valley—a historical discourse delivered by JAMES ALLISON, July 16, 1876—is among the newest and most instructive of the historical discourses of which the year has been prolific.

Addresses at the Dedication of the Chapel and Library of the Presbyterian Theological Seminary of the Northwest, by DRS. HALSEY, JONATHAN ED-WARDS, and KITTREDGE, are well suited to the occasion. The chief is that of Dr. Edwards, which renders important service in rescuing from oblivion, or from an obscurity of chaotic confusion, which is hardly better, the history of this important Theological Seminary, not merely during its own life, but in those antecedent institutions which preceded and prepared the way for it.

MacMillan & Co. publish the 5th volume of that greatest of recent English Historical Works, *The History of the Norman Conquest of England; its Causes and Results.* By EDWARD A. FREEMAN, LL.D. This treats of the effects of the Norman Conquest. It is replete with the same vastness of erudition, keenness of criticism, breadth and depth of historico-philosophical insight, which have won for the previous volume a foremost and enduring place in historical literature. The present volume is especially rich and valuable in the light it sheds on the development of some of the great distinctive features of the British Constitution. It enables us to get a better understanding of them, as it brings to view their formative causes. For sale by McGinness & Runyon, Princeton.

Scribner, Armstrong & Co. have issued two more volumes of their admirable series of Epochs of History, Ancient and Modern. These are *Roman History, the Early Empire, from the Assassination of Julius Cæsar to that of Domitian,* by W. W. CAPPS, M. A., with two Maps; and in Modern Histroy, *The Early Plantagenets,* by WILLIAM STUBBS, M. A., Regius Professor of Modern History in the University of Oxford, also with two Maps. These, like their predecessors in the series, furnish facilities for acquiring a knowledge of the Epochs treated, not elsewhere accessible to the general reader. For sale by McGinness & Runyon, Princeton.

J. L. Libole, of Philadelphia, publishes a small volume of *Acrostical Pen-Portraits of the Eighteen Presidents of the United States,* by D. F. LOCHERBY. They will hardly bear criticising, being of all grades, good, bad, and indifferent, with a preponderance of the latter sort.

Centenary Memorial of the Planting and Growth of Presbyterianism in Western Pennsylvania and Parts Adjacent. Pittsburg, 1876. This Book is peculiarly attractive and valuable. It was projected nine years ago, at a convention held in Pittsburg, of representatives from the four Synods of Pittsburg, Allegheny, Wheeling, and Ohio; and completed in the delivery of its contents at another convention of the same sort, held in December last. 1875 was the centennial year of Western Presbyterianism, reckoning from the advent of John McMillan, the first pastor who was settled beyond the Alleghenies. The authors, whose discourses fill the volume, had ample time, and rich resources, and rare abilities for the task assigned, and have done their work exceedingly well. They are the Rev. Drs. D. H. Junkin, Aaron Williams, James I. Brownson, E. E. Swift, S. J. M. Eaton, and S. J. Wilson; Wm. M. Darlington, Esq., and the Hon. James Veech, LL.D. The last mentioned contributed the " Secular History " of that interesting region, so renowned at present for its richness of soil and mineral resources, its coal and iron, and oil, its intelligence also, and high moral culture, not surpassed if equalled by any other country in the world. It is "the backbone of Presbyterianism." And Mr. Veech enlivens the secular portion itself with intimate and vivacious allusions to Presbyterian ministers and institutions. But apart from this, the essay is of the very highest value, as a fragment of history which has never been furnished before. The research of the writer is original and profound, the style is polished and brilliant, and the intelligent reader must marvel that such a pen has been so little used in the literature of which he is master, almost without a rival. His narrative of the "Whisky Insurrection," during the presidency of Washington, is rare and racy, graphic and truthful, and worth more than all the cost of this elegant volume. It is embellished, moreover, with portraits of Dr. John McMillan, Rev. Jos. Patterson, Dr. Elliott, Dr. Beatty, and Dr. Francis Herron, as well as lithographs of numerous buildings, past and present, connected with the various institutions. The only questionable feature of this publication is the extra centennial collection of speeches and documents previously made. For example, the "History of the Western Theological Seminary," given in 1872, by Dr. Brownson, colored with panegyric of living men all around him at the time, though extremely well done for its occasion, hardly belongs in fairness to the calm retrospect of a centenary memorial. The history of that excellent institution is yet to be written. Sacrifices and services both of the dead and the living must be weighed again, if we are to be particular, in turning annals over to impartial history. No one of the gifted authors in this volume could be trusted better than Dr. Brownson himself for the faithfulness of true history, when time shall have done its work, in mellowing tints and bringing shaded figures into fuller view. As a whole, this book is a treasure which our church should keep among her jewels, and the possession of it everywhere would not fail, at such a time as this, to increase the wonder and gratitude with which we exclaim, "what hath God wrought."—A. T. M.

The Old Chapel and the New is the title of two discourses preached by President PORTER of Yale College, on the occasion of the last service held in the Old and the first in the New Chapel, recently erected for the institution. Many interesting and important reminiscences are thus preserved from oblivion, while various important principles are advocated or suggested. We quite concur with him when he says: "But we also contend that faith is as helpful to science as science is useful to faith, and we assert that in a truly Christian university science will be more truly scientific than in one which is atheistic or anti-Christian, simply because faith, when other things are equal, tends to make science more thorough, more liberal, more candid, more comprehensive, more sagacious."

Nelson & Phillips issue *Methodism and its Methods*, by Rev. J. T. CRANE, D. D., one of the leading ministers and authors of the denomination. It is a clear and vigorous exhibition of the peculiarities of that body which will reward careful examination. It is good authority for a large portion of the statements, which form a condensed summary of the leading facts in the case as presented in the opening article of our present number.

The same house also publishes *The Christian Ministry*, a sermon preached before the New York Preachers' Meeting, Feb. 8, 1876, by Bishop E. S. JANES, D.D., LL.D., which is full of wise counsels and fruitful suggestions, in exposition and true application of 1 Peter iv: 11—"If any man speak, let him speak as the oracles of God. If any man minister, let him do it as of the ability which God giveth; that God in all things may be glorified through Jesus Christ." Ministers of all communions may read it with profit.

The American Bible Society publish *Our Treasure and Our Trust; or, The Bible in the Last One Hundred Years. An Historical Discourse for the American Bible Society, in the United States Centennial,* 1776-1876, *Delivered at Its Sixtieth Anniversary.* By WILLIAM J. R. TAYLOR, D.D., a former Secretary of the Society. A discourse worthy of the author, the subject, and the occasion.

A Century in the History of the First Presbyterian Church, Princeton, New Jersey, with Special Reference to its Several Houses of Worship, by JAMES M. MACDONALD, is the last memento, from his own pen, of a greatly honored and lamented minister of our church, and contributor to this RE-VIEW, who died before he was permitted to deliver it; and by it, as in many other ways, he, being dead, yet speaketh.

Centennial. One Hundred Years of Progress in the Business of Banking, is an Address of the Hon. ELDRIDGE GERRY SPAULDING, at the meeting of the Bankers' Association, at the International Exposition, Philadelphia, May 30, 1876, from the press of Baker, Jones & Co., Buffalo. It fills several compact octavo pages, and is an exceedingly thorough, discriminating, and critical history of the development of the banking system of the country, including National and State banks, together with the different fiscal agencies of the Government, such as the successive United States Banks, the State Deposit Banks, the sub-treasury, the legal-tender and National Bank notes of the present time. It is a valuable addition to our financial literature.

Addresses before the Alumni Association of Princeton Theological Seminary at its Annual Meeting in Princeton, April 25, 1876, published at the request of the Association, is a solid pamphlet, with the following contents: The Relation of Princeton Theological Seminary to, 1. the Work of Foreign Missions, by Rev. John C. Lowrie, D.D., New York City; 2. The Growth and Character of the American Church, by Rev. George Norcross. Carlisle, Pa.; 3. The Formation of a Religious Literature, by Prof. Daniel S. Gregory, D.D., Wooster, Ohio; 4. The Work of Education, by Rev. Edward D. Ledyard, Cincinnati, Ohio. These papers have solid value and interest, and will form good material for future history. A tone of occasional exaggeration will be pardoned when it comes of the fervors of Centennial jubilation, and of filial and brotherly devotion, while it was inevitable that some who deserved honorable mention should be overlooked.

We have just received a historical sketch of the *The Second Presbyterian Church of Trenton, New Jersey*, by the pastor, Rev. James B. Kennedy, which illustrates the healthful growth of a Presbyterian church under earnest and efficient pastors and elders, and in the due improvement of the stated ordinances and ministrations of the church of God. It presents an excellent record

The same may be said of the *Manual and Tenth Anniversary Sermon* of the Westminster Presbyterian Church, of Elizabeth, N. J. by the pastor, Rev. WM. C. ROBERTS, D.D., its first and only pastor, a rare instance of constant growth, including the removal of a debt of nearly $40,000, in this year of nethermost financial depression.

Nelson & Phillips issue *Laws Relating to Religious Corporations. A Compilation of the Statutes of the several States in the United States in relation to the Incorporation and Maintenance of Religious Societies and to the Disturbance of Religious Meetings*, by Rev. Sanford Hunt, D.D., *with an address on Laws affecting Religious Corporations in the State of New York*, by Hon. E. L. Fancher, LL.D. Its title shows its character and utility

Centennial Literature. Under this head Nelson & Phillips send to us two substantial volumes, as follows: *Methodism and the Centennial of American Independence; or, the Loyal and Liberal Services of the Methodist Episcopal Church during the First Century of the History of the United States, with a Brief History of the Various Branches of Methodism, and full Statistical Tables*, by Rev. E. M. WOOD, Ph.D. Also, *A Hundred Years of Methodism*, by Bishop SIMPSON. The former of these presents the subject from the points of view set forth in the title-page; the latter is " not designed to be a History of Methodism, but to give the general reader a glance at what Methodism is, and what it has accomplished during the century." This is done in the Bishop's vigorous and glowing style. The value of the book is enhanced by the Appendix, which contains the "Articles of Religion," the " General Rules," and other important facts of the denomination.

The same publishers also bring out, *Past Successes—Future Probabilities; a Centennial Sermon delivered before the New York East Conference of the Methodist Episcopal Church*, By Rev. HENRY WARREN, D.D., in which rapid future triumphs of Christianity are augured from its past successes.

PHILOSOPHY.

Outlines of Lectures on the History of Philosophy, by JOHN J. ELMENDORF, S.T.D., University Professor of Philosophy in Racine College. New York: G. P. Putnam's Sons, pp. 296. A pretty difficult task is attempted in this concise manual, to give an outline of the History of Philosophy from the East Indian Vedas to the latest forms of idealism and materialism. It would have been easier to make a book of twice the size, and we are not sure but that it might have been better. This is almost too compressed. It gives a broad map of the whole field, with commendable fulness and impartiality. The exposition of Aquinas is one of the best points in the book. But the present French Philosophy is not given over to positivism ; there is a strong reaction against it. The account of American Philosophy is rather meagre ; the works of Dr. Hickok, for example, seem to have escaped the author's attention. But such slight defects are outweighed by the general character of the book, which, in the hands of a competent teacher, may be of great use in saving dictation, and for the purposes of a review.

Nelson & Phillips publish *The Modern Genesis ; being an Inquiry into the Credibility of the Nebular Theory, of the Origin of Planetary Bodies, the Structure of the Solar System, and of General Cosmical History*, by Rev. W. B. SLAUGHTER. He opposes the nebular hypothesis on purely scientific grounds. It is quite clear, indeed, that he does not see its full congruity with Scripture. But he does not assail it by arguments from this source. We have long thought that many adherents of this theory have, on very inadequate grounds, assumed its indisputable certainty ; that it is so surely proved as to cast discredit on any utterance, whether of God or man, apparently inconsistent with it. We do not so see it. Whether true or false it is in no necessary conflict with the Bible. But it is by no means so self evident that it ought not to be subjected to the searching criticism of this book. If its advocates can refute the objections to it, their position will only be strengthened. If not, it will and ought to be undermined.

An Address before the Literary Societies of the University of Wooster, by STANLEY MATTHEWS, presents an elevated range of thought, expressed with beauty and force, and delivers some crushing blows at the fashionable materialism and positivism of the day. We need not despair of the Republics or of the church, so long as our laymen furnish them office-bearers of the spirit and power here evinced.

Although in the form of a Baccalaureate sermon to the last graduating class of Wooster University, the address of President A. A. E. TAYLOR gives such a philosophical discussion of the inadequacy of merely secular education to meet the wants of humanity, that we notice it here. All the arguments which prove religion [the most indispensable requisite to man's true well-being and normal development, prove any system of education which ignores or discards Christian teaching and training to be fatally at fault.

The Unseen Universe; or, Physical Speculations on a Future State. By B. STEWART and P. G. TAIT. Fourth edition (revised and enlarged. London: Macmillan & Co., 1876.

This book is one of the products of the reaction against the views of the quasi-scientists, who, for some time past, have managed to maintain almost exclusive control of the ways of access to the ear of the non-scientific public. This reaction is one of the reassuring signs of the times. True science is beginning to speak out against science, "falsely so called." There is not the slightest doubt that the true advanced science of this age owes its origin chiefly to the labors of Christian scientists, and is mainly sustained by their efforts. Witness the glorious line of names from Newton and Boyle to Faraday and Agassiz!

Yet, somehow, the impression has gone abroad, that directly the opposite is the truth. There is a ready explanation of this strange and, at first appearance, almost unaccountable fact. In the first place, the thing is in the atmosphere of the age. In the second place, a class of noisy, shallow, showy men have availed themselves of the investigations and thoughts of the truly great men, and paraded them along with their own most extravagant *a priori* speculations and guesses, assuming the undoubted truth of the whole absurd mass, and arrogating to themselves the leadership in the scientific world. These men have pushed themselves forward in scientific conventions, and wherever opportunity offered, to secure prominence; have enlisted the aid of great and popular publishing houses, and sent out a constant stream of magazines, reviews, and text-books; they have crossed the ocean to give benighted men the benefit of their crude metaphysics, recommended by brilliant experiments, and at the same time to turn a thrifty penny. In their manifold ways they have come up over the world like the locusts of Egypt. In the third place, the vagaries of these men have been so evidently absurd to the minds of the great scientists, that it has seemed to them arrant folly to attempt any answer. Of one of the most popular of these speculations Professor Agassiz is reported to have said, "I will give it five years to run its course and die." So the quasi-scientists have had it pretty much all their own way.

We believe their day is about over. Men are recalling to mind the splendid examples shown by intellectual giants, like Newton and Faraday, and ceasing to stand aghast at the materialistic statements of these *a priori* dogmatists, so often made of late, professedly in the name of science. Ablermen, mostly Christian scientists, are appearing in the exposition and defence of truly scientific views, and combining to show up the brilliant quasi-scientific absurdities. To give an illustration: Professor Tyndall, one of the ablest and most brilliant of his class, published his guesses about dust, under the name of science, and Professor Beale, the great microscopist, straightway appeared to demonstrate his ignorance of the facts. He published his guesses about the stars, in the name of science, and Professor Proctor forthwith demonstrated their absurdity. He sent abroad his imaginative doubts about God and the future existence, in the name of science, and Professors Watts, Stewart, Tait, and others, have already demonstrated that there is neither science nor sense in such views. · The tide is evidently turning.

"The Unseen Universe," we say, is one of the products of this turning tide. It was first published anonymously in Great Britain, and speedily ran through three editions, and it has been reprinted on this side the water. In the fourth edition, the first authors, two of the best-known among foreign scientists, who were scarcely able longer to conceal themselves from the public, came forward, acknowledging their work, and presenting it in a revised and improved form. In general, the writers aim to demonstrate that the presumed incompatibility of science and religion, of which the quasi-scientists have made so much, does not exist. In particular, they contend, from a purely physical point of view, for the possibility of immortality and of a personal God. In their own language (see Preface to the First Edition, p. 10) : "We endeavor to show, in fact, that immortality is strictly in accordance with the principle of continuity (rightly viewed)—that principle which has been the guide of all modern scientific advance. As one result of this inquiry we are led, by strict reasoning on purely scientific grounds, to the probable conclusion, that a life *for* the unseen, *through* the unseen, is to be regarded as the only perfect life."

Want of space precludes us from giving, as we had desired, a pretty full view of the course of the argument, and confines us to the most meagre statement of the main points. The writers frankly state their own position, in opposition to the materialists. They assume that there are two essential requisites to continued, organized, and conscious existence—an organ of memory, connecting the individual with the past, and the possibility of action in the present. Upon this two-fold assumption they build their argument, which is simply an application to this subject of the scientific principle of continuity—a principle of which the quasi-scientists make as much as the scientists. (See, p. 78.)

There are three possible suppositions with reference to individual existence after death. "It may be regarded as the result of a transference from one grade of being to another in the present visible universe ; or, secondly, of a transference from the visible universe to some other order of things intimately connected with it; or, lastly, we may conceive it to represent the result of a transference from the present visible universe to an order of things entirely unconnected with it." The third supposition is set aside as opposed to the principle of continuity, leaving the first two as hypotheses, to be considered in the course of the argument. (See page 96.) Is either of these two hypotheses scientifically tenable ? It is shown, in answering this, that the latest science, holding fast the principle of continuity, as seen in the conservation of energy, assures us that energy, upon which the continuance of life depends, is constantly being transformed, diffused, and degraded, so that the universe must ultimately become a dead universe, and must originally have been such. (See chapter iii.)

The latest investigations concerning the intimate nature of matter and ether, or the stuff of which the universe is made, and which constitutes the vehicle of energy, seem to point to the probable truth of the vortex-atom theory, and to indicate that the ether in which all matter is immersed (so to speak), is not a perfect fluid, but exhibits the action of friction in connection with the movements of light and the other forms of energy, and in the revolutions of the heavenly bodies. If this be so, the material worlds are gradually slowing in their movements, and the physical universe must eventually come to a stand still, and the atoms of matter itself, which was originally formed out of the ether, must be ephemeral, and dissolve in ether again, just as the smoke-rings developed in the air by the strong and sudden puff of the loco-motive, dissolve into the air again, instead of remaining through the ages a huge, useless, inert mass. "Why should not the universe bury its dead out of sight?" (See chapter iv.)

The latest science has established Bio-genesis, or the law that life can origi-nate only from previously existing life. This is another application of the principle of continuity, just as firmly established as the conservation of mat-ter or energy. Admitting, for the sake of the argument, all that is in the least scientifically probable along the line of development, we are brought to the first germ of life in the universe, which must somehow have been devel-oped out of the invisible. The previous argument points to the last life, which, when the universe becomes dead, or dissolves, must go out into the invisible. (See chapter v.)

Immortality is impossible for beings like man in the present physical uni-verse, since the assumed conditions of continued conscious existence will cease to be found in it.

The writers next proceed to show scientifically, that all this power which makes life at present possible in the universe is not derived from superior intelligences who are a part of this visible order of things. There are, doubt-less, other spiritual intelligences, as the angels and God, but they are not of the visible. Science and religion unite in assuring us that man, and beings similar to man, are at the head of the visible universe. We must look beyond it, therefore, for the origin of the mysteries we find in it. (See chapter vi.)

The first hypothesis of immortality having thus been shown to be unten-able, the authors proceed to establish the truth of the remaining supposi-tion, of an immortality through the drifting off of the soul into an unseen uni-verse intimately connected with the visible, somewhat as ether is connected with matter. We cannot here detail the successive steps of an argument of great compactness and exceeding interest. From the small circle of light which we may call the universe of scientific perception, scientists have driven the original mysteries; "but the greater the circle of light (to adopt the words of Dr. Chalmers), the greater the circumference of darkness, and the mystery which has been driven before us looms in the darkness that surrounds this circle, growing more mysterious and more tremendous as the circumfer-ence is increased. In fine, we have already remarked that the position of the scientific man is to clear a space before him, from which all mystery shall be driven away, and in which there shall be nothing but matter and certain definite laws, which he can comprehend. There are, however, three great mysteries (a trinity of mysteries), which elude, and will forever elude, his grasp, and these will persistently hover around the border of this cleared and illuminated circle—they are the mystery of matter and energy; the mystery of life, and the mystery of God—and these three are one " (p. 234). We are thus driven by the mysteries of the visible universe, unexplained by sci-ence, to the idea of a "mysterious, infinitely energetic, intelligent, developing agency, residing *in* the universe, and therefore in some sense conditioned," and yet not strictly belonging to the visible order of things.

It is at this point that science and revelation, the one ascending from below, and the other descending from above, meet and harmonize. In the Trinity the mysteries are explained. "The first person of the Trinity, God, the Father, is represented as the unappr achable Creator—the Being in virtue of whom all things exist." The Scriptures also indicate another subsistence, the second person of the Trinity of the same substance as the Father, "who has agreed to develop the will of the Father, and thus, in some mysterious sense, to submit to conditions and to enter into the universe. The relation of this Being to the Father is expressed in Hebrews (x: 7), in the words of the Psalmist, ' Then said I, Lo, I come ! in the volume of the book it is written of me, I delight to do thy will, O my God ! yea, thy law is within my heart !' In fine, such a being would represent that conditioned, yet infinitely powerful, developing agent, to which the universe, objectively considered, appears to lead up." (See p. 223). The Christian system recognizes a third agent in the universe, the Lord and Giver of life, the third person of the Trinity. "The third person of the Trinity is regarded in this system as working in the universe, and, therefore, in some sense, as conditioned. One of his functions consists in distributing and developing this principle of life, which we are forced to regard as one of the things of the universe, just as the second person of the Trinity is regarded as developing that other phenomenon, the energy of the universe. The one has entered from everlasting into the universe, in order to develop its objective element, energy; the other has also entered from everlasting into the universe, in order to develop its subjective element, life." (See p. 230).

It is through and in this unseen universe, to which true science and religion both point, that the second theory of immortality becomes scientifically possible, nay, probable, and, by divine revelation, certain.

Even this meagre view is sufficient to show that " the unseen universe " is no ordinary work. This judgment is confirmed by the extent and rapidity of its circulation and the verdict of the most competent critics. While not committing ourselves to all the positions and inferences of its learned authors, it seems very clear that they have made their main point certain. The opposing infidel hypotheses are as truly unscientific as they are unscriptural. We have read few things at all comparable with it in breadth and elevation of religious views, in exactness and grasp of scientific principles, in keenness and inexorableness of logic, and in accuracy and clearness of statement. It is one of those rare works which cannot fail to profit the man of intelligence and culture, to whom either a metaphysical turn of mind or perplexing doubts may have rendered the subject discussed one of special interest.

We cannot forbear to add the opinion and wish of the distinguished authors, expressed in some of the closing paragraphs of the book (p. 270) :

"The truth is, that science and religion neither are nor can be two fields of knowledge, with no possible communication between them. Such a hypothesis is simply absurd.

"There is, undoubtedly, an avenue leading from the one to the other, but this avenue is through the unseen universe, and, unfortunately, it has been walled up and ticketed with '*No road this way,*' professedly alike in the name of science at the one end, and in the name of religion at the other.

"We are in hopes that when this region of thought comes to be further examined, it may lead to some common ground on which the followers of science on the one hand, and of revealed religion on the other, may meet together, and recognize each other's claims without any sacrifice of the spirit of independence, or any diminution of self-respect." We notice in parts of the work a Swedenborgian tinge, and, in particular, some views in regard to the supernatural, miracles, and the resurrection, to which we cannot unqualifiedly assent.

Elements of Psychology, by HENRY N. DAY, is issued by G. P. Putnam's Sons, and, as we believe, completes the series of mental science text-books, prepared by the accomplished author, who achieved his first great success in his text-book on rhetoric. His usual acuteness, methodical precision, and sharp definitions and distinctions, even to the extent of sometimes being a little arbitrary and wire drawn, are conspicuous in this volume. It has some characteristics which fit it to be very helpful to teacher and learner.

All this makes us the more sorry that we find ourselves obliged to dissent wholly from what we understand to be its fundamental position, viz.: that the mind can know nothing but its own exercises; he says, "Nothing but idea is object for the mind;" also, "We may define idea, in the words of Locke, to be 'whatever the mind can be employed about.'"—(p. 36.) He then declares, "IDEA, both as of mind and for mind, may be more fully and exactly defined to be *any form of mental activity.*" The capitals and italics are the author's. According to this, the mind can know nothing but "some form of mental activity." It cannot get beyond its own subjective activities. Any real non-ego, or non-egoistic substance or property, is unknowable. We can make nothing of this but idealism—it may be sensuous, it may be spiritualistic. What is more, not only cognitions and thoughts, but volitions and feelings, are thus declared to be ideas. We see not how, on this theory, we can go beyond Locke's doctrine of knowledge, which easily enough developed into the idealism of Berkeley, and the nihilism of Hume and his followers. Locke sometimes defined knowledge as "the perception of the agreement and disagreement of our ideas." But he, himself, points out the apparent impossibility of any real knowledge of objects, upon his theory, that the only immediate knowledge is not of things, but of ideas; and the escape from this impossibility, which he flatters himself he has found, amounts to a contradiction of the doctrine which leads to it. He says:

"It is evident the mind knows not things immediately, but only by the intervention of the ideas it has for them. Our knowledge, therefore, is real, only so far as there is a conformity between our ideas and the reality of things. But what is here the criterion? How shall the mind, when it perceives nothing but its own ideas, know that they agree with the things themselves?" Sure enough. And echo answers, how? This problem must confront every man who adopts the doctrine, that the mind knows immediately only ideas and modes of its own activity.

MacMillan & Co. bring out *Modern Physical Fatalism and the Doctrine of Evolution, including an Examination of Mr. H. Spencer's First Principles.* By THOMAS RAWSON BIRKS, M.A., Professor of Moral Philosophy, Cambridge. In this, Prof. Birks well sustains the reputation he has acquired as a metaphysical writer. He has rendered a valuable service in exposing the flimsy pretensions of the materialistic evolutionism of the day. The fine range of his subjects by no means surpasses the learning and ability with which he handles them. They include the Doctrine of the Unknowable; Ultimate Ideas in Physics; the Relativity of Knowledge, in itself and according to Hamilton and Mill; the Reality of Matter, its Indestructibility; the Continuity of Motion, and the Conservation of Force; the Transformations. of Force and Motion; the Laws of Attraction and Repulsion; Choice and Will in Physical Laws; Evolution, Heterogeneity, Force, and Life; Natural Selection.

The volume contains the substance of a course of lectures delivered during the year 1875-6. Spencer's views he declares "radically unsound, full of logical inconsistency and contradiction, and flatly opposed to the fundamental principles of Christianity, and even the very existence of moral science." In this judgment we fully concur. And, therefore, so far from being alien from the proper sphere of theology and ethics, these sciences must contend against this system for very life. For sale by McGinness & Runyon, Princeton.

BIBLICAL.

MacMillan & Co. publish, as one of the Clarendon Press Series, a second edition, revised and corrected, of *Outlines of Textual Criticism Applied to the New Testament,* by C. E. HAMMOND, M.A.; a neat, compact volume, which brings together in a small compass, a summation of the facts and arguments for and against the retention of the various disputed passages in the *textus receptus* of the original Greek. Those interested in these inquiries—and surely all students and preachers of the Word must be—will find here, accessible and convenient, at small cost, what they could not find with out great difficulty, labor, and probable expense, in any other way. For sale by McGinness & Runyon, Princeton.

Scribner, Armstrong & Co. have imported into this country a special edition of KEIL'S two volumes on the *Prophecies of Ezekiel,* at $3.00 per volume. This constitutes the 49th and 50th volumes of Foreign Theological Library of the Clerks of Edinburgh. Fourth Series. These volumes have the candid, scholarly, and judicious character, which have given value to previous commentaries on other books of Scripture by the same author. They are adapted, not to popular use, but to the needs of students, exegetes, and preachers.

Nelson & Phillips bring out *The Chronology of Bible History, and How to Remember it,* by Rev. C. MINGER, A.M., in which charts are presented tabulating the great facts and personages of the Bible, down to and including Christ, in a form fitted to assist their retention in the memory.

The Name Machabee, by SAMUEL IVES CURTISS, JR., PH.D. Leipzig. Printed by Ackermann & Glaser, 1876. Mr. Curtiss, a graduate of the Union

Theological Seminary in this city, has been pursuing his philological studies in Germany, and this dissertation, appropriately dedicated to Dr. Franz De-litzsch, with whom he studied, gives the first fruits of his researches, and excellent promise for the future.   All that bears upon the origin and meaning of the word *Machabee* seems to have been thoroughly explored, and the different theories are concisely criticised.   Mr. Curtiss rejects the most popular theory, the *Hammer* theory, and prefers with hesitation one which makes it mean the *Extinguisher*.   Dr. Delitzsch, in a letter addressed to the writer, suggests another derivation, which yields the sense—*What is like (comparable to) my Father?*

The Footsteps of St. Peter, by J. R. MACDUFF, D.D. New York: Carter & Bros., pp. 632, with illustrations.   An excellent and popular work, and a fitting companion to the author's *Footsteps of St. Paul*. The descriptions are made impressive by Dr. Macduff's familiarity with the sacred places which were the scenes of Peter's labors.   His character, journeys, and writings are well described.   While Dr. Macduff does not credit the legend that Peter was the first bishop of Rome for twenty-five years, he accepts as sufficient the evidence that he was a martyr there under Nero.

The Carters also publish the third series of DR. DONALD FRASER'S *Synoptical Lectures on the Books of Holy Scripture*, from Romans to Revelation, completing the work, which well deserves the favor it has received, as giving a definite and compressed synopsis of the contents of the Sacred Scriptures. Pastors will find these lectures of great use.

MISCELLANY.

S. C. Griggs & Co., Chicago, publish, and have on sale, at Princeton, through McGinness & Runyon, *Viking Tales of the North ; the Sagas of Thorstein, Viking's Son, and Fridthjof the Bold ;* translated from the Icelandic by RASMUS B. ANDERSON, A. M., Professor of the Scandinavian Languages in the University of Wisconsin, and JON BJARNASON ; also, Tegnier's Fridthjof's Saga, translated into English by GEORGE STEPHENS. These specimens of Icelandic and Scandinavian literature are brought within reach of the English student and reader, in this volume, in admirable style, as might be expected from the past achievements of Prof. Anderson and his collaborators in this department of literature.

Art. XII.—THEOLOGICAL AND LITERARY INTELLIGENCE.
GERMANY.

Journal of Church History. (*Zeitschrift f. Kirchengeschichte.* II. 1876.) The second number of this new and promising quarterly opens with a thoughtful article by Dr. W. Gass on the "Significancy and Working of the Historical Sense"—an appropriate introduction to such a journal ; the need, aim, and limits of historical studies are ably set forth. Dr. Ferd. Piper, the veteran archaeologist of Berlin, follows with a long essay of 60 pages on "the History of the Church Fathers from Epigraphic Sources," showing what services have been rendered to church history by inscriptions and like memorials; these are traced out in the Greek church, in the Latin, and in various libraries with a fulness of special learning, exact and admirable. A. Harnack contributes an interesting essay (part one) on the so-called Second Epistle of Clement in the light of the new edition, as illustrating the characteristics of primitive homilies, especially in the Eastern churches. His own opinion as to this Clementine Homily, however, is that it originated in the Western church—though it is not found "cited by any Roman writer before the seventeenth century." In the East it was for a long time read as a *Clementine* Homily (and Bryennios ascribes it to Clement), though not spoken of as addressed to the Corinthians. Eusebius had heard of it, but had not seen it. Its origin remains obscure; and Harnack promises a further discussion of it. The next article, by Prof. Dr. W. Moeller, is a Critical Review of the Works published in 1875 (chiefly in France and Germany) on the History of the Church between A. D. 325 and 768—an excellent guide to the contents and scope of some fifty works, such as Rothe's Lectures on Church History, Boehringer's Church of Christ and its Witnesses (2d ed.), Werner's Venerable Bede, Hefele's History of Councils, new edition, etc. The *Analecta* in this number are a Criticism on the Text of the new Clementine passages, by O. von Gebhardt: H. Roensch, on the last sentence of the Muratorian Fragment; a Letter of Luther, sent by Fr. Schirrmacher; and a Memoir of the Cardinal of Lothringia, 1563, by A. Fournier.

Jahrbücher f. deutsche Theologie. I. 1876. Dr. C. Weizsäcker, in the opening article on the "Beginnings of Christian Morals," shows from the New Testament, especially the Epistles of Paul, how the new Christian faith manifested itself in a new and higher moral life—the life sprang from and was shaped by the faith: the doctrines about God, and Christ, and the Kingdom of God gave a new character to the daily and social life of Christians. Christian morals are not a mere extension of natural ethics, but have a character of their own, derived from the new revelation, with its higher motives and objects. This general position is illustrated at length, with fine criticism, and in application to a variety of moral duties and ethical questions. Dr. Ferdinand Piper of Berlin, in the second article, writes with great learning on the gain to Church History from the Ancient, especially the Christian, Inscriptions. This is an important essay, by the man best qualified to discuss the subject, he having devoted a large part of his life to these investigations. In his "Monumental Theology" he has written at length on the general question. In the present article (66 pages) he first shows the Posture of the Inquiry, and the use made of these Inscriptions by church historians since the Reformation, as in Baronius, the Magdeburg Centuriators, Bingham, Wald, and others. Then, in the second part of the essay, he runs over the different periods of church history, and shows what light has been thrown upon each of them from these sources. Every careful reader will be surprised to find how much has been gained and garnered up from these monuments, which are dispersed through all the Christian countries, giving indubitable testimony to facts and doctrines. This is followed out through the different epochs, down to the seventh century, taking in all the General Councils. There are two other articles in this number; one by Prof. Schultz of Heidelberg on the last chapters of the epistle to the Romans—(he takes the ground that Rom. xii. to xv., 7, was originally addressed to the Ephesians); and some centennial memorabilia for the year '76—beginning with A. D. 176, and coming down to 1776, "the American War of Independence, and the Conflicts of European Culture." Among the critical notices is a full account by the same writer of the recently discovered **complete** MS. of Clement's two Epistles to the Corinthians, as edited by **Philotheos** Bryennios, metropolitan of Sevrac. The second Heft contains the last literary **work** of the late Dr. Sack, of Bonn, on Psalm 104, verse 4—its correct translation **and in**terpretation, which is thus given : " He lets his angels and servants clothe **them**selves with winds and flames of fire, lets them work in and through these, to **guard** or punish men." Dr. Weizsäcker has a long and able article on "the Oldest Christian Church at Rome," defending the view that it was not made up of **Jews,** but chiefly of heathen converts. The other articles are Geiger on the History of the Study of the Hebrew Language in Germany ; and Wagenmann on the History of the University of Helmstedt.

Philosophische Monatshefte, Bd. XII., 7 Hefte, 1876, Leipzig. Edited **by Dr.** E. Bratuschek, Professor at Giessen, with the co-operation of Dr. F. Ascherson **of** Berlin, and Prof. J. Bergmann of Marburg. Dr. Vaihinger in the first Heft **reviews** "the Three Phases of Czolbe's Naturalism," and it is an interesting contrib**ution** to the history of modern materialism in Germany, exhibiting its various **aspects.** Incidentally the points of agreement and difference between Czolbe and Ueberweg are noted—both of whom, like Lange, denied a personal God and immortality. Articles in the other numbers are by A. Spir of Stuttgart, on the Question **as to** First Principles ; Opitz, the Limits of the Rights and Duties of the State ; **Prof.** Boehm of Budapest, Contributions to the Theory of Consciousness ; J. H. **von** Kirchmann, Berlin, the Significance of Philosophy ; Dr. H. v. Struve, of the University of Warsaw, Psychological and Metaphysical Analysis of the Fundamental Laws of Thinking, etc. Dr. Vaihinger (pp. 84–90) on "The Origin of the Word Erkenntnisstheorie " (Theory of Knowledge), traces it back to the elder Fichte. In the fifth *Heft*, Superintendent Opitz presents a concise and clear exhibition of the general theory of Spinoza, as "a Monist, Determinist, and Realist ;" and Dr. H. Müller sets forth the Doctrine of Plotinus on the Beautiful. The two next parts are chiefly occupied with a discussion by the editor, Dr. Bratuschek, of the charges made by Prof. Mommsen and others against some German universities about conferring degrees in an irregular way—*in absentia*, etc. Kiel and Giessen seem to have been compromised. The dispute in Germany has been a lively one. Dr. Ascherson, custodian of the University Library of Berlin, gives in each number a full and convenient Bibliography of Philosophy, including not only the titles of new books, but also the articles on philosophical subjects in the principal journals, and even newspapers. In connection with these *Monatshefte* are also published, at irregular intervals, " Transactions of the Philosophical Society of Berlin," chiefly of a Hegelian type. The second Heft, 1876, contains an essay by Prof. Michelet on Ideal-Realism, and one by Dr. Lasson on the Problem of Matter.

University Libraries in Germany. The library of the Berlin University contains 115,000 printed volumes and 40,000 charts. The University of Bonn contains 180,000 volumes, several hundred manuscripts and a large collection of maps. The University of Breslau has 340,000 volumes of books and 2,900 manuscripts. The Erlangen University has 110,000 printed volumes and 1,900 manuscripts, besides 50,000 treatises, 10,000 autograph letters, and a collection of designs and engravings. The Freiburg University contains 250,000 printed volumes and 500 manuscripts. The Giessen University has 150,000 printed volumes and 1,268 manuscripts ; that of Göttingen 400,000 printed volumes and 5,000 manuscripts ; that of Greifswald 70,000 volumes ; and that of Halle 100,000 volumes and 1,000 manuscripts. The University of Heidelberg has 300,000 volumes, 70,000 treatises, 3,000 manuscripts, 1,000 charts, a collection of maps and another of engravings. The University of Jena has 100,000 volumes, and that of Kiel 150,000 volumes and several hundred manuscripts. The University of Königsberg has 220,000 volumes, in addition to about 50,000 double copies of books for the purpo se of exchange. The University of Leipsic contains 350,000 printed volumes and 4,000 manuscripts. The University of Marburg has 120,000 printed volumes, but very few manuscripts. The University of Munich contains 283,500 volumes, 17,500 manuscripts, 3,600 portraits and 3,200 medals. The University of Rostock has about 140,000 volumes ; that of Tübingen 280,000 volumes, 60,000 treatises and 2,000 manuscripts ; and that of Würzburg more than 200,000 volumes and 2,000 manuscripts. The library of the Strasburg University is said to contain 300,000 volumes, of which 5.400 relate to the history of Alsace, and about 500 manuscripts. The library of the Vienna University contains 211,220 volumes and 83 manuscripts, and the library of the Basle University contains 100,000 printed volumes, 4,000 manuscripts, and 180 charts.

Theologische Studien und Kritiken, IV : 1876. The first article, by R. Smend, Privatdocent at Halle, is entitled "The Degree of Development of the Israelite Religion presupposed by the Prophets of the Eighth Century" before Christ. It is partly a reply to the recent work of Duhm, on *The Theology of the Prophets.* The object of the discussion, which is successfully accomplished, is to show that there is an organic connection of the prophets of the eighth and following centuries before Christ with the whole of the preceding history—there is unity running through the whole. Amos and Hosea presuppose the main facts of the old Hebrew history as well as Isaiah and Jeremiah. The same spirit pervades the whole prophetic period of over three hundred years to Ezra. Boniface (Winfrid), the apostle of the Germans, has been the subject of renewed investigations in Ebrard's Irish-Scotch Missionary Church, and in the extended life of Boniface by the Roman Catholic divine, Prof. Dr. A. Werner (Lpzg., 1875). Th. Förster ably reviews his character and deeds, and while fully conceding his great qualities, contends that his sanctity and apostolicity have been exaggerated and overlaid with a legendary halo ; this is also the general view of Ebrard in his able work. Prof. Jacobi, of Halle, has a clear and concise account of the new edition of epistles of Clement of Rome, by Bryennios of Macedonia. He fully recognizes the value of the new discoveries. He thinks, however, that the public prayer, which forms so large a part of the new matter in the first epistle, was not contained in the Roman letter, but was added at Corinth (or Alexandria) when the epistle was publicly read in the churches. Seidermann contributes to the History of the Reformation critical editions of three epistles of Melanchthon. Prof. Beyschlag, of Halle, presents a capital review of Hase's History of Jesus, applauding its literary merits, and exposing its doctrinal and historical inconsistencies.

Hilgenfeld's Journal (Zeitschrift f. wiss. Theologie), III.—1876. Alb. Thoma, The Lord's Supper in the New Testament—an essay of 50 pages, critical and exegetical, reducing it to its simplest elements ; in John's Gospel the writer does not find the institution itself, but a meal and a speech. H. Tollin continues his work on Servetus by expounding his doctrine about the devil : he believed in the existence of Satan, as originally an angel, who fell by occasion of the creation. E. Harmsen, on Rom. xi: 36 and I Cor. viii: 6, does not find in these passages that Christ is the mediator in creation ; he excludes it for the verse in Corinthians by substituting the accusative *d'on*, for the genitive *d'ou*, following the Vatican MS. H. Rönsch continues his critical studies on the Itala. Franz Görres shows that

Pope Sixtus V. claimed and proclaimed full papal infallibility in respect to canonization, etc., in a Consistory A.D. 1588, according to the testimony of Galesinius. Dr. Hilgenfeld gives the full Latin version of 4th Ezra, from Bensly's scholarly work (Leod, 1875); the hitherto missing fragment makes a whole by itself, and it is ascribed by Hilgenfeld to Christian authorship. The fourth part contains G. Heinrici on the Christian Church of the Corinth, and the religious societies of the Greeks. F. Görres on the Persecution under the Emperor Maximinus I ; and F. Schürer on Luke and Josephus.

Dr. B. Weiss, formerly of Kiel, who has just been called to Berlin, has published an elaborate critical work on the "Gospel of Matthew, and its Parallels in Luke" (Halle), in continuation of a similar work on Mark issued a few years since. The basis of his criticism is the theory, that the three synoptic gospels have a common "apostolic source," of about A. D. 67, which Mark first made use of, in combination with the narrative he received from Peter. The *Logia* of Papias give the primitive document, which Weiss holds contained not merely the words of Jesus, but also narrations of facts.

The veteran Prof. I. H. Fichte of Bonn, just before his decease, at eighty years of age, addressed to Prof. Zeller of Berlin a letter of "Questions and Doubts about the latest Development of German Speculation," with special reference to Zeller's History of German Philosophy. Fichte claims that Zeller has not done full justice to such writers as Herbart, Fries, Baader, and Krause ; also that he sets aside, with too brief credit, the writings of Weisse, Ulrici, and Carrière, as well as Fichte's own system. The "ethical and religious view of the world" and the personality of God are comparatively ignored by Zeller ; and his general view of German speculation would be no barrier to "the current audacious spirit of negation which is now celebrating its orgies in open market." Fichte says, that "the great idea of a personal author of the world, when once fully grasped, cannot possibly be regarded as a merely plausible hypothesis, or remain idly in the recesses of the soul as an ineffectual article of faith."

The *Neue Evangelische Kirchenzeitung* in noticing the 4th edition of "Lectures on the Mosaic Primeval History and its Relation to the Results of Natural Science," by Dr. F. H. Reusch, Old Catholic Professor of Theology at Bonn, says that it is one of the very best books of its class. It carefully reviews modern astronomy and geology, the Darwinian controversy, etc., and vindicates the Mosaic record in respect to creation, the deluge, the unity of the race, and other questions. "This work, and Hettinger's 'Apology of Christianity' are undoubtedly the ablest apologetic achievements in the recent Catholic theological literature of Germany."

The new work on "the Apostle Barnabas," by a Roman Catholic writer, received a prize from the Munich Theological Faculty. It is especially valuable for its full collection of all the legends about Barnabas.

A new edition of Herzog's Real-Encyclopädie is announced, with a host of contributors ; it is to be in 15 volumes, and completed in seven to eight years. It will be issued in 150 parts, costing 45 cents each, free by mail. Dr. Plitt is to be joint editor.

Of the new edition of the Apostolic Fathers, edited by Gebhardt, Harnack, and Zahn, the second fasciculus is out (pp. lvi., 404), edited by Zahn, and containing the works of Ignatius and Polycarp. A second edition of the first fasciculus contains the additions to the epistles of Clement of Rome, published by Bryennios.

A Text-Book of Symbolics, by the late Dr. G. F. Oehler, is edited by the late

J. Delitzsch, who was engaged upon it at the time of his decease (pp. 653, published in Tübingen).

W. W. Baudissin, in his Studies on the History of Semitic Religions, Part I, 1876, examines, first, the History of Sanchoniathon, in its bearings on the Phœnician religion; then follows an extended critical essay on the Old Testament references to the heathen deities, whether they are regarded as real—which is denied: the third treatise is an enlargement of an article in the Journal of Historical Theology, 1875, on the name of God, *Jao*, refuting the theory that it is the name of a god outside of Israel. A fourth essay is on the Symbolism of the Serpent in the Semitic religions.

A concise memorial of Karl Rudolph Hagenbach, whose works have been so widely used in this country and Great Britain, has been written by Pastor C. F. Eppler (pp. 160, with a likeness of Hagenbach). It gives extracts from his minor works, selections of his poems, and some autobiographical notices. There is said to be a full autobiography among Hagenbach's papers.

Of Dr. Alzog's (Roman Catholic) Handbook of Patrology, a third enlarged edition has appeared (pp. xvi., 572).

FRANCE.

The *Revue des deux Mondes* for the last half year contains several noteworthy articles, bearing on questions of current interest. In the number for July 15, M. Charles Lévêque, of the Institute, reviewing the question about " Instinct and Life, as viewed by Darwinism and Comparative Psychology "—putting at the basis a work by the late Albert Lemoine, *L'Habitude et l'Instinct* (Paris, 1875), which is commended as altogether the best on the subject; he is also the writer of works of good repute on *Body and Soul, Physiognomy and Speech*, etc. M. Lévêque reviews all the noted theories of instinct—the mechanical (automatic), of Descartes, the semirational of Montaigne, the mixed automatism of Buffon (in his *Nature of Animals*), and the reflection which Cordillac ascribes to animals as well as to man, deriving instinct from habit. Following Lemoine, the nature of habit is scrutinized, and it is shown that instinct is presupposed in habit, and that habit does not make instinct : habit is "a second nature," instinct is primitive and irreducible. Lamarck, 1809, first resolved instinct into "*hereditary* habit." It is ingeniously shown, however, against him and Darwin, that Heredity presupposes instinct—viz. all the instincts necessary to the nourishment and reproduction of living beings. Here is the proper domain of Instinct. Plants do not have it, animals live by it. There is desire, and a direction to some end, with feeling, but not reflection. It is simple, necessary, with slight consciousness, and but a pale glimmer of intelligence.

M. E. Vacherot, of the Institute, who is perhaps the most metaphysical of living French philosophers, examines the question of Final Causes in relation to the First Cause, in the *Revue* for Aug. 1, and Sept. 1. He bases his discussion on Janet's recent work on Final Causes, a part of which was translated in our quarterly for April, 1876. He entirely agrees with Janet as to the fact of design, of final causes (as the French say, of *finality*), in the works of nature. This position he cogently defends against the Comtists or positivists, and the materialists. The choice is only between chance and design. Where there is order, where there is law, there is and must be an adaptation of means to ends. The whole Cosmos is an order, a plan, a work of art. In this, all the greatest philosophers of all schools (excepting the purely materialistic) are agreed. Plato and Aristotle, Leibnitz, Kant, and Hegel are all one on the position, that the universe cannot be explained by merely mechanical laws and forces. If this is so, then there is intelligence, wisdom, mind, in nature, working for an end. This, too, is conceded by Vacherot, in agreement with Janet. Vacherot, having strong pantheistic tendencies, hesitates on the point, whether this Intelligence be *immanent* in, or transcendent above, the course of nature ; whether it be conscious, or unconscious—whether it be personal, or above personality. He also objects to the doctrine of pure creation. But though he cannot compend the First Cause, and bind it in a formula, he confesses its " infinite power, goodness, and wisdom." " The Final Cause is the only true cause ; the Efficient Cause is only the instrument of the Final Cause."

Revue Philosophique de la France et de l'Etranger, Mai, Oct., 1876. The chief articles are : F. Bouillier, on the Cause of Pleasure and Pain ; J. Soury, on Lange's History of Materialism ; J. Lachelier, Study upon the Theory of the Syllogism—worthy of careful examination ; A. Horwicz, History of the Development of the Will ; E. von Hartmann, Schopenhauer and his disciple Frauenstaedt, two articles ; Dr. R. Lépine, Cerebral Localizations, two articles ; G. H. Lewes, Spiritualism and Materialism ; P. Regnaud, E. Indian Philosophy, the Vedânta School, two articles on its sources and authorities ; an excellent analysis by Ch. Bénard, of Schasler's History of Aesthetics ; Ernest Naville, on the place of Hypothesis in Science ; Ribot, on Herbert's Psychology ; L. Carran on the Philosophy of G. H. Lewes ; A. Penjon, on the Metaphysics of Ferrier—a good and appreciative account. The October number opens with an article on Art and Psychology, by James Sully : J. Delboeuf continues a discussion on what he calls " Algorithmic Logic," *i. e.*, the representing of logic by symbols, like arithmetic and algebra ; E. Cazelles criticizes the ethical (utilitarian) theory of Grote ; and Luigi Ferry gives an account of the late work of Prof. Berti of Rome on the Trial of Galileo. Among the notices of books is a sharp criticism of Renan's recent Philosophical Dialogues, ending with a *mot* of De la Rochefoucauld : " La plus subtile folie est faite de la plus subtile sagesse."

Revue Théologique, published under the direction of Professors Bois and Bonifas, of the Faculty of Theology at Montauban, Third Year, No. 1, July, 1876. This review is published four times a year, in numbers of about 100 pages, at five francs ; it is proposed to issue it every two months. It contains valuable and instructive papers. The contents of the July number are : P. Vallotton, on the Roman Religion from Augustus to the Antonines ; D. Coussirat, the Principles of Negative Criticism, and the Person of Jesus—discussing the views of Strauss, Renan, and Pécaut ; Jundt, the Precursors of John Huss ; Ch. Bruston, the Hypothesis (of Reuss and others) of Maccabee Psalms ; Doumergue, the Synodal Presbyterian Régime (in France) at the end of the eighteenth century.

We have also received from Montauban an address by Professor Jean Monod, on the object of Dogmatics, delivered at the opening of the public Session of the Faculty of Theology, Nov. 16, 1875. It is a clear and forcible exposition of its theme.

M. Sayons, a conscientious and learned scholar, intimately acquainted with the Hungarian language, has published the first volume of a *Histoire Générale des Hongrois* (Paris, Didier). In the present complications on the Danube, the Hungarians and Turks, it is suggested by French writers, may be forced into some common action against their common foes.

The fifth volume of Pressensé's History of the three first Christian centuries is announced, treating of the organization, worship, and social and domestic life of the Christian church in the third century.

THE

PRESBYTERIAN QUARTERLY

AND

PRINCETON REVIEW.

NEW SERIES, No. 22.—APRIL, 1877.

Art. I. PROBLEMS FOR EDUCATED MINDS IN AMERICA IN THE NEW CENTURY.

By CHARLES E. KNOX, D. D., Bloomfield, N. J.

CERTAINLY the college began the advance one hundred years ago. The six colleges which existed at that time exerted, no doubt, as strong an influence over the nation as our three hundred and thirty colleges now do. Around the sources of opinion the communities of liberty grew. The great questions which were then throbbing in the brain, were profound principles, which needed for their solution the very best order of mind. Neither rustics nor novices could have solved them. The leaders then were men of penetrating vision. They looked far into the century. Their power of analysis, their discrimination, their logical acumen, their resources in learning, their clearness of expression, their broad.comprehension and wise adjustment of difficult and unlike subjects, were largely the result of superior education. From leaders who were accomplished students, bred either in the college or in the local culture which the college created, came those really sublime plans which now, after a hundred years, constitute *our* foundation for the future.

We now stand as they did, looking out upon a new century, with opening vistas which end we know not where. The young men who go out just now from our institutions, go out to problems perhaps even greater than those which invited the courage and the patriotism of our fathers. It is a new and a grand era of life into which they now step. Their standpoint is that of the college—the standpoint of the *educated mind.*

From this source is to come the power which will adjust the complications which confront us. From this standpoint, it will be well for us to look out upon the epoch which now opens, and trace the lines of problem which stretch away from us.

Let us first stand for a moment at the college of a century ago, and note the problems which educated minds then had to meet. Look at the intellectual vigor in those educated and educating councils. Genius often takes shape in art and poetry and polite culture, but the loftier forms of intellectual power are those which discern the principles and laws which affect a race, which penetrate centuries of palpitating life, and which sweep out upon the hopeful progress of mankind. The noble literature of our Revolutionary period belonged to that loftier range. The writings, addresses, speeches, and the great resultant papers of that time, contain those bold comprehensive topics which run, like the established currents of the air, like beams and hues of light, like rocks of geology, above and through and beneath universal society. To these, with the grandest impulse, the eager instincts of the mind then sprang.

1. What a marvelous sifting had gone on, for example, for more than a century before even those strong men knew well their rights, and knowing, dared maintain them. The works of creation are clear after chaos has departed. Along the thin coast of colonies, how much of brooding chaos lay, in respect to the simplest principles of true freedom, from the settlement of Jamestown and Plymouth, until the very hour of seventy-six. Vast numbers of the primitive population were in the mist, thick as an ocean fog, Light was created, but *day* did not dawn till *revolution* began. Adams put forth his solid strength. Hamilton beamed in firm and lucid exposition. Witherspoon glowed in sermon and in speech. Jefferson arrayed his keen philosophical analysis. Washington, in his severe and majestic wisdom, shed light. The whole energy of some of those men, and of others like them, was required to compel the common mind to discern the plain lines along which the *security* of their own rights lay. *Security of personal rights* was the first problem for the educated mind then.

2. Their second problem was *union*. A simple thing it now seems, but debates in the halls of Congress on union have not .

yet ceased; the thunders of the war for a united country have
not yet ceased to echo. Security of civil rights awakened a lively
jealousy of rights between colonies, states, communities, and
individuals. The small and the great colonies looked sharply at
each other all along the coast. Who should harmonize these
interests, and habits, and customs—the verdant conceit of energetic settlements, and the flaring ambition for territory and
power? The wide marches and the common suffering of the
army, the Virginia commander at Boston, the northern troops
in South Carolina and at Yorktown, the increasing acquaintance of cultivated minds from separated states, were knitting
life to life; but to discern the real principle of a lasting union,
to find the central breadth on which all could stand, to persuade resolute communities, to demonstrate that political diversity and political unity might be and should be one, was the
work of masters in penetration, masters in practical sagacity,
masters in the art of address.

3. Then came the third great question of the *Constitution*.
Why did they not drift along into unwritten usage? Simply
because there were men versed in the political literature of
Europe, who knew their exposure to the divisive diplomacy
of foreign powers, and that selfish antagonism and personal
ambition would throw these inexperienced people into a repetition of European factions. Penetrating minds saw the necessity of concentration, consolidation and sovereign power.
How did they ever run the hazard of one written law, with its
hither and thither rocks of over-statement and of under-state-
ment! To form the three-fold checks of legislative, judicial,
and executive powers, to select the single president or the
double or triple consuls proposed, to determine the single or
the double form of legislative bodies, to lay a financial framework bold enough, detailed enough, and not too detailed for a
national scheme—to phrase and frame all these into one short
foundation law of only seven articles within five years after the
war, and in two years more, so to complete the ground-law with
ten additional articles, that it immediately took rank as one of
the great state-papers of history, was the action of comprehensive thought, in the highest, severest, and most exact classifica-
tions of the human mind. It seems like inspiration that they
succeeded. It *was* one of the inspirations of providence.

4. The fourth sublime subject was *education for the whole people*. The colleges which existed before that time were no doubt fully adequate to the limited population. Their systems were planned by graduates of European universities. Measured by the wants of the time, they toned up the cultivated classes to an elevation equal or superior to that now enjoyed. But the people had no system which pervaded the land. The driving necessities of pioneer life left the cultivated settlements behind. When the people turned their eyes from their enemy's departing ships, it was axe in hand against the mighty forests. Then came the great migrations, which with the round century reflow from the Pacific shore. The passion for action, "the ecstacy of energy," as Taine says of the Saxons, the appetite for accepting the challenge of grand obstacles, the absorbing appeal to man's physical and material ambition—these tempted the yeoman away from refinements of knowledge, and might have tempted him from all knowledge. It would have been no new thing in history had cultivated minds retained all the graces of power, and the common mind had gone down to a life of mere sensation. But the college had committed itself to *all men*. Education was not to be simply for the drawing-room and the cabinet. The book was to be a companion to the axe; the school-house as much a necessity as the grist-mill; the art of speech was wedded to the art of industry. Everywhere, therefore, the educated mind was planning a popular education. State after state enacted or revised its laws. Constitution after constitution bound the new state to intelligent citizenship, produced by a system of mental training for all the people. The result was a system of mental training for the whole land, which reached all the people, and which inspired them with universal desire for advancement.

5. The fifth problem was *religious toleration*—a religion of toleration in the presence of the state, and a religion separate from the state. To the far larger part of the population in America religion was the sublimest aim of living. Without it the state was a superficial thing. Towns and churches in New England had been identical; the law, the Biblical code, the commonwealth, a theocracy. A little experience, however, in the use of freedom, had taught them that they could oppress as well as be oppressed. And so they agreed that the intense

conviction of one person, in respect to God and religious obligation, should not override the intense conviction of another. The constitution, therefore, bound itself, by an irrevocable code, to be tolerant of free worship, and intolerant of interference with free worship ; tolerant of free conscience, and intolerant of conscience enslaved ; tolerant of the right of private judgment, and intolerant of the oppression of private judgment ; tolerant of inquiry, and intolerant of dictation ; tolerant of every book, in school or out of it, which exalts the principles of its own republican life, and sensitively intolerant of every attempt to suppress whatever may be its best text-book of liberty ; tolerant of the sacred life of all persons, and sensitively intolerant of that life which thrusts forth the knife or pistol at its OWN life.

6. The sixth subject was the diffusion of *Christianity* through the land. The great heart of the nation beat warmly in unison with the Christian scheme. The people devoted their colleges to the pulpit and to Christian education. There were no colleges which did not spring from the church and the ministry. The college became prolific in multiplying itself for the sake of the church. The church, the ministry, the Sunday-schools, the missionary organization, kept pace with the advancing population. And the organizing mind, which—with a Christian zeal almost outrunning a sound discretion—has erected colleges in every state—was either the educated mind of the original six colleges, or the admiring mind of those who had seen their power.

7. The seventh problem was that of *development*. Territory, population, immigration, state-construction, invention, art, industries, international alliances, internal improvements, the press, universality in education, free scope for the church, commerce, credit, finance, increase of dominion and of power—all these, and all the possible, and sometimes the impossible, activities of the human mind, were the inviting work to which the educating principle introduced the American people.

These were the sublime subjects to which the institutions of education addressed themselves at the beginning of our national life.

Now let us come back to our own day, and from the present

institutions, take an outlook into the future. We can discern
the lines of problems as they run before us,   Rather, we have
already entered into problems which are as broad as those
which our fathers so successfully met.   It is not for any single
person to solve these problems.   They are to be solved only
by the united research and harmonions agreement of many
leading minds.   But a single mind may indicate both the subjects and the elements which may enter into their solution.

1. The first problem, on which we have already entered, is
in respect to the very *life* of the nation—the vital principle of
our republican existence.   That which threatens at once the
breath and blood and nervous centres, is a solid, powerful, antagonistic force.   It is a force which has long since devitalized
free nations, and which now turns its power against our own
robust health.   Already we have entered another " irrepressible contest."   The principles are clearly defined in both the
antagonistic systems.   The opposing forces are broadly and
firmly committed to them : the republic and its lucid propositions, the monarchy and its strongly-drawn definitions, the literature on either side, with authors and advocates.   Since the
Vatican Council of 1870, it has been evident that the energy
of a vast political system, whose organization is interwoven in
subtle forms with the power of the church, has been taking its
line of aggression.   It is not a religious controversy.   It is
not theological.   It is not, on our side, ecclesiastical.   It belongs to the philosophy of civil principles.   It is both political
and philosophical, and challenges the best thought of the best
minds, disciplined with the best education, and informed with
the widest range of international and historic reading.   The
Bible in the public schools is a mere incident in the contest.
Remove the Bible ; place the Constitution of the United
States in its stead ; and the contest would be continued.   If
the contest would not be as strong as it is now, the simple reason would be, that the Bible enforces more strongly than the
Constitution itself the principles of the Constitution.   It is a
contest along the lines of constitutional government—intended
to be from the other side solid shot from needle-guns along
the whole substructure of this republic.   The proof of this is
in the nature of demonstration.   ＊

On the one hand, the American Declaration, precedent to

constitutional law, explicitly asserts, as a truth underlying all government, "that all men are created equal;" in the sense that individual endowments of "life, liberty, and pursuit of happiness," are gifts of the Creator to each person, and "inalienable rights." On the other hand, the encyclical letter of 1864, precedent to the condemnation of the errors of our day, declares it to be "a totally false notion of social government," that the citizens possess the right of being unrestrained in the exercise of every kind of liberty by any law, ecclesiastical or civil:" and this is declared an offshoot of that condition of human society wherein "the government does not submit to the penalties of the Roman Church."

On the one hand, the American Declaration asserts that "governments are instituted among men, deriving their just powers from the consent of the governed." On the other hand, the Syllabus declares that "kings and princes are not only not exempt from the jurisdiction of the church, but are inferior to the church in *litigated questions of jurisdiction*" (error 54); that is, that governments hold their powers from the authorities of the church.

On the one hand, the Constitution declares "the free exercise of conscience in religion shall not be prohibited." On the other hand, the Encyclical declares "an insanity" the opinion "that liberty of conscience and of worship is the right of every man, and that this right is, in every well-governed state, to be proclaimed and asserted by law."

On the one side, the Constitution says, "the freedom of speech, or freedom of the press, shall not be abridged." On the other, the Encyclical, speaking with the most solemn power of the highest authority, declares, "the exercise of every kind of liberty, unrestrained by any law, ecclesiastical or civil, so that they are authorized to publish and put forward openly all their ideas whatsoever, either by speaking, in print, or by any other method," "an erroneous and pernicious opinion," and "a liberty of perdition."

The Constitution on one side declares, that there shall be "no law respecting an establishment of religion, or prohibiting the free exercise thereof;" while the Syllabus itself cites as a *terrible error*, the principles that "the church ought to be separate from the state, and the state separate from the church" (error 55); a terrible *error*, " that the Catholic religion shall no longer be held as the only religion of the state to the exclusion of all other modes of worship" (error 78); a terrible error, " that persons coming to reside in Catholic countries shall enjoy by law the public exercise of their own worship " (error 78) ; a terrible error to say that "civil liberty of every mode of worship, and the full power of overtly and publicly manifesting their opinions and ideas, of all kinds whatsoever, do not conduce to corrupt the morals and minds of the people" (error 79).

The Constitution declares, that " no religious test shall ever be required as a qualification to any office or public trust in the United States." The Syllabus condemns as a grievous error the declaration, " that ministers of the church and the Roman Pontiff (meaning these ministers *as* ministers, and the Pontiff *as* the Pontiff *of the Romish Church*) ought to be absolutely excluded from all charge and dominion over temporal affairs " throughout the world (error 27).

On the one side, the legislative trust of government is charged with power " to promote the progress of science and of the useful arts," with large encouragement and scope to authors and inventors; on the other side, free printing " is a liberty of perdition, and if it is always free to human arguments to discuss, men will never be wanting who will dare to resist and to rely on the loquacity of human wisdom."

On one side, the laws of the states encourage the education of the citizens by the states, inasmuch as intelligence is the foundation of good order and of virtue ; on the other side, the Syllabus denounces the dangerous error, that " the entire direction of public schools, in which the youth of Christian states are educated, may and must appertain to the civil power " (error 45); the dangerous error, that " the best theory of civil society requires that popular schools, open to the children of all classes, . . and for conducting the education of the young, should be freed from all ecclesiastical authority, government, and interference, and should be fully subject to the civil and political power, in conformity with the will of the rulers, and the prevalent opinions of the age" (error 47) ; a dangerous error, that " this system of instructing youth . . may be approved by Catholics "(error 48).

The laws of our states declare matrimony a union by sacred

promises and by a civil sanction, prescribed according to the religious convictions of those entering into it.   On the other hand, the Syllabus denounces the statement, " that a merely civil contract may among Christians constitute a true marriage " (error 73) ; and declares all marriages not undertaken as a sacrament an unholy and unworthy, an unreal and illegal, union " (errors, class viii).   Within the domain of the church this is simply a theological doctrine.   Obtruded into the domain of the state, it is simply a political decree, monarchical and absolute, antagonistic to the family and to all true society.

And to crown all, over against the magnanimous benefits which the American law accords to all strangers who take oath to bear civil allegiance to the government, and who absolve themselves from foreign kings, princes, and rulers, the dogmatic decrees of the Vatican Council require all strangers from Romish countries, on the greatest pains and penalties, to submit to and obey their superiors in the church, to receive "the primacy of the Papal See as a primacy over the wide world," to acknowedge that his decision in *morals*, as well as in faith and discipline and government, is infallible and irrevocable, that he has the power to decide what is moral and what is not moral, and that, when he decides and defines what is moral or not moral in any doctrine concerning morals, his definition is a decree—infallible, irrevocable by any body of opinion or council in the world.

The most important question which underlies all these antagonistic propositions is the question of education ; but the whole contest runs along the arena of philosophical principles, where the broadest rights of mankind are decided.   This is the arena which includes all the principles of republicanism—the freedom of mind and of thought, the freedom of education and of literature, freedom of the press and of debate, the freedom of the school and of the college.   Against these, our familiar rights, stand the dogmatic decree of one person as a decree for all, education under high dictation, education voluminous and free in all that harmonizes with the will of the rulers, education repressive, restrictive and extinguishing in respect to all that disagrees with the rulers, the *index expurgatorius*, the condemnation of Bible societies, the proscription of debate.

Now, the declaration of the recent *political* utterances of the Vatican *may*, many of them, be so interpreted as to refer to the religious life of the church. They are so sophistically wrapped in the concealments of language, that their application to political usages *may* be denied. They are therefore to be interpreted by the historical *consensus*. They are to be read in the light of *results* which now exist where the principles have had expression. They go back to councils and synods and decrees, to courts and cabinets and royal conferences, all along the range of political life in Europe. They sweep in the university life of Europe. They include the consummate learning of masters in the philosophy of mind, the philosophy of state, the philosophy of literature, the philosophy of history. So surely as Italy, with its ignorance, stands opposed to Germany, with its intelligence, as Belgium and Holland are in contrast in productive intelligence, as the masses of France are inferior to the masses of England in ideas of freedom and self-government, as Brazil has never awaked as the United States have done, as Mexico is in contrast with Canada, so certainly is there a contest, inevitable and irrepressible, steadily forcing its way into all the sources of our national life. The issue is likely to be joined before the end of the century, in one of two forms: either a peaceful issue under the amenities of educated reason and the power of religious culture; or a bloody contest, like those which have shaken the continent of Europe. Educational institutions, and the educated mind proceeding from them, are to determine how wisely this antagonism to the principles of our government can be brought to the apprehension of the people, how prudently the dangers may be met which threaten us, without awakening the passion of bitter partisanship; in one word, how clearly and in what simple terms the whole nation may be made to see that a government of the people, by the people, and for the people, is, by the simplest necessity of its structure—as our own republic for a hundred years has been—a *Protestant* republic.

2. The second problem is the problem of *internal structure of civil society*. Freed from outside dictation, have we now, at the end of a hundred years, the qualities *among ourselves* requisite to the state of society supposed to be predicted by our national history? We may take some useful suggestions from

the observations of our enemy. Is there not much serious truth in her representations of free society, when she speaks of "monstrous and portentous opinions" of the present age, "prevailing to the detriment of civil society," "hostile to the everlasting law of nature engraven by God upon the hearts of all men, and to right reason;" of the "loquacity of human wisdom" and its tendencies; of the tendency of such a state of society "to compass its own ends, amass riches, and to follow no other law than the indomitable law" of selfishness; and of the tendency of "the civil liberty of worship and of public opinion to corrupt the morals and minds of the people?" These grave imputations arrest grave minds. These tendencies, and tendencies like these, are certainly as conspicuous as the marvelous advances of the century.

The real question is, simply, does liberty now show a dangerous tendency to license? Does it in wanton wildness, in some things cut itself free from restraint—perhaps from *all* restraint? Does it in narrow wilfulness, in other things, deny to equals the fundamental rights of the constitution? Are the old familiar rights to run wild? Have they no limits? Does liberty of speech, for example, extend so far as to include all malignities of vicious speech in political life, and to give them free scope, even to the verge of blasphemy and obscenity? Does liberty of the press include the liberty to publish every man's private conversation and private letters, to obtrude into his dwelling against his will, to falsify his character and sentiments while he is absorbed with other engagements, to *claim* this liberty on the ground that it has *not* committed legal slander? Does it include the right to create a morbid appetite for morbid news, measured by *civil* morals, and make the morbid news for the morbid appetite; to issue vicious books and journals, to corrupt the people, so that they have no desire to enforce law against them, and so that the young grow fond of immoral literature? Noble as is the power of the virtuous press, confessedly, the daily and the weekly press have revealed within a few years an alarming increase of these morbid symptoms of corruption. In education, are men to have liberty to erect schools of vice? Why not? We have had halls of justice built by robbery. If educated men *will be bad*, why may there not be schools and colleges—the Fisk Institute and the

Tweed College, and the Belknap University—for **instruc-**
tion in affable falsehood and polished deception ; law **schools**
for the evasion of justice by legal methods; medical **schools**
for theoretic demonstration of moral insanity at the **bar of**
justice; and, with the advance of civilization, perhaps, **even**
divinity schools—the Winslow Theological Seminary—to **prove**
that evil and good are indeed like darkness and light, **mere**
necessary complements of each other's existence ?   In **finance,**
are promises to pay borrowed money, made by the government
and by individuals, to *be* paid by a running series of promises
of changing values, till the account is closed at a *post-mortem*
examination ?   Are schools of politics to be simply graded **to**
a permanent Congressional University, in which **governors,**
senators, representatives, and cabinet-officers take a **classic**
course, or a scientific course, in the noble art of advancing **their**
civil station and their emoluments ? And after that, are **grand**
monetary corporations, which constitute a Faculty of the **Arts,**
to teach our legislators how to enact the law ?   Is a reform **of**
the civil service throughout, a reform the necessity of which **is**
universally conceded, to be a genuine growth, or the mere **by-**
play of political schemers ?

The whole realm of political life and of social science **here**
comes into view, with all its lofty relations to truth and justice and honor, with all its tendencies to corruption. We **know**
that the correction must come from another source—from **the**
infusion of virtue and of the religious sentiment ; but is freedom
so swift and so wild already, as to throw off the obligations **of**
virtue, and to refuse conscience this domain ?

So, too, of that narrow willfulness which to equals denies **or**
admits—as convenience may indicate—the inherent rights **of**
the Constitution.   Apparently we had settled the question,
that the black man had no rights which the white man **was**
bound to respect ; but now a new century begins, and this **is**
the opening question, " Have the almond-eyed any **rights**
which the oval-eyed are bound to respect ?"   Have the copper-
colored rights which the whiter-colored are bound to respect ?"

If liberty includes all these extremes, then we can readily **see**
whither we tend.   If it does not include them, then it is **for**
educated minds to find, if possible, the proper limit between

liberty and license, to bind the principle to virtue, and instruct the people in the principle and its elucidation.

What further is to be done in respect to questions which the Constitution never contemplated? Is religion to be protected by the state, when it professes conscientious scruples impelling its votaries to take life, when it demands low vices as religious worship, or when it claims divine inspiration for plain immoralities? If so, why may not bad men organize new religious denominations, and, under the pretext of conscientious scruples, and even of religious worship, commit all enormities? Are Confucianism, and Buddhism, and Tauism, and Mormonism, and Fetichism, and Thugism, religions to be tolerated and protected by the government? If the immigration of a score of millions of Mongolians should set in with the set of the next Pacific tide—an emigration quite small to the Mongolian race—would a majority by universal suffrage be the interpretation of political equality?

If liberty has here exposures which shall prove fraught with peril, as the nation attracts still more powerfully the people of the earth, the college, the seminary, and the educated minds must devise the guards against the exposures. Only after closer thought and more exact and comprehensive investigation, in respect to the whole complication of social laws, will come the happy principle which will form another crystalization in our history.

3. A third problem which educated mind is to decide, lies in the realm of the educational institution. The question has its relation both to the church and to the state. It is the question of the *form* of the college, whether it should be personal, denominational, state, or national. On the predominance of the one form or the other may depend the whole tone of society.

Here the wider relations of the subject to general society compel the decision even of unskilled minds. The comparison of the college and its single faculty, with the university and its group of faculties; the superiority of the atmosphere of culture in the presence of many faculties and many curricula, or of the individual discipline in a single college, with the concentrated faculty and a concentrated curriculum; the high results which growth in a *specialty* often secures in a small institution; the rela-

tions and adjustment of philosophic and scholastic and utilitarian studies to each other, to personal life, and to society; the
practicability of a universal and omniscient university, where
"any man can learn anything" in a limited course of study;
the wisdom or the absurdity of the choice of his life-work by
a raw youth in the presence of a great circle of faculties and
courses; the superficiality of our higher education, in comparison with more healthy and more thorough intellectual methods in Europe; the relation of disciplinary colleges or gymnasia, to professional or technical colleges or universities for
the higher culture; the classification of all our American
colleges in the rank of the German gymnasia; the projec-
tion of a post-graduate national university for the examination of the highest order of subjects, under a universal range
of scientific departments—these subjects and the like, inspir-
ing and important as they are, demanding intimate and exact
research, are all certainly subordinate to one which easily surpasses them all.   The question is not whether there shall be one
or the other form *exclusively* of the institution, for all forms already exist.   Among our three hundred and thirty Protestant
institutions, we have some ten or twelve personal colleges and
personal universities, over two hundred denominational colleges
and denominational universities, and some twenty or more
state colleges and state universities.   Neither is it the question,
whether all these institutions may not co-exist in mutual
healthy inspiration and mutual healthy check.   It is simply
the surpassing question of influence on society—of the quality
of the virtuous sentiment in education—the question in respect
to the decline, or the growth, or the bare feeble existence of
that vital virtue, without which learning and intellectual acumen are simply satanic in tendency—without which great
learning becomes the learning of Jeffries, the art of address,
the brilliant subtleties of Mephistopheles in Goethe's Faust,
the breadth and power of lofty discussion, the sublime debates
of Milton's pandemonium.   Which form shall nurture the best
growth of virtue?   Which form shall assert that pure religious
sentiment, which all men revere, and which is broader and
stronger than all sectarian life?   This is the pre-eminent
question: Which influence shall *rule* the pliable youthful life
of America? the influence of which demands virtue as the

absolute and supreme quality of character, or that which makes intellectual acuteness of more absorbing importance, or that which discourses of philosophical breadth, as above, or beyond, or indifferent to, or inattentive to, personal and universal principles of virtue? Here lies the choice, which is of supreme moment to society in America. It is the choice of placing young men, before the gristle has become bone, *either* in close contact with a positive religious life, *or* in close contact with a purely political life, *or* in close contact with a pure indifferentism. The choicest grapes just ready to ripen take mildew when a damp mist for a few days shuts out the sun.

Jefferson's plan of the University of Virginia gave no place at first to the religious life; afterward, under the compulsion of religious sentiment, a place was devised for religious organizations and religious instructions *in the vicinity*—on the verge of, but not in, the university plan—under the shadow of the shining intellectual edifice. Jefferson's plan no doubt represents substantially the class of purely civil institutions, except only the furthest extreme of Girard College, or of the University of Missouri, the charter of which latter institution prohibits the appointment of a clergyman to the office of president or professor.   .

Three things certainly stand somewhat revealed before our vision, and prompt three short questions on our way to a solution. The first question is: Are we not now proposing to erect on the secular schools for common education, a superior state system of education, and upon the state system a national university, in the whole ascent of which religious life shall hold either a thoroughly subordinate place, or a merely incidental place, or no place? The second question is: Are we not entering, on a colossal scale, upon a new experiment in human history, which may carry us further than we will? When was there before a demand that the supreme interests of society require a system of superior education, dissevered from fundamental religious ideas? Not in ancient Greece and Rome, where the character of the highest education was still pagan. Not in the middle ages, where the rising universities were scholastic and ecclesiastic. Not in modern Germany, where the system is under control of a national church-system and a faculty of theology is one of four faculties required for

the recognition of a true university.   Not in France, notwithstanding a brief atheistic reign of the Academy, where both the
Catholic and the Protestant power are recognized in the system,
and where theology is a marked branch of the academic system.
Not in England, under the Anglican Church, where the universities are state institutions only through the close ties of
rank and of class life.   Not in Scotland, where both the Established Church and the Free Church make their power so directly felt.   In the United States of America only, is it proposed that throughout the rising ranks of educational institutions, the religious life shall be excluded ; and with the proposal is connected the ¦demand, that all denominational
schools, or schools conducted on clearly defined religious
principles, shall give way to the civil scheme of education.

The third question is this : Is it not a grand fact in our national history, that all those institutions which gave birth to
men of noble health and robust power, the founders of our
high estate, were institutions of the most pronounced religious
character?   Was not their virtue derived confessedly from inspiration ?   Was not religion with those institutions the supreme idea and passion ? And in estimating the moral influence
of the present state institutions upon society, up to the end of
this first century, is it not also true, that even in them the religious influence of these grand old institutions is still throbbing and giving firmness to the pulse ?

Whose theodolite, then, shall run the dividing line along
this common ground of education, on which church and state
meet?   Who will show how the basement walls and corner
buttresses lie, on which both edifices rise, in mutual support
and architectural symmetry, one splendid edifice, greeting
earth and sky ?   Who will make plain that the pollution of the
air, political virtue, in the one, will soon infect the wide halls
of the other, and that the exclusion of *light*, spiritual religion,
from one, will drive out the inhabitants in languor and decline,
and leave the crumbling ruin for world-wide visitors to inspect
in astonishment and awe ?   The educated mind of the virtuous college, in alumni and patrons, and sympathizing self-made
minds, is to make possible, a century hence, the utterance of
that robust honesty of the elder day, which Washington ex-

pressed, when he said—an expression so full of significance when we think of the French philosophy then tiding in—" of all dispositions and habits which lead to political prosperity, religion and morality are indispensable supports." " A volume could not trace all their connections with private and public felicity." " And let us with caution indulge the supposition that morality can be maintained without religion. Whatever may be conceded to the influence of refined education on minds of peculiar structure, reason and experience both forbid us to expect that national morality can prevail in exclusion of religious principles."

4. A fourth problem of more agreeable attractions, lies in the subject of *culture*. Culture is a necessity, and not simply a luxury, or a taste. The foundation of it lies, first of all, in the earth and its products. If the soil produced only a bare subsistence for each person on his own labor, then how could there be space for advancement. All that the farmer's land produces more than food for the farmer and for his land, must go either to utter waste, or to physical, or mental, or social improvement. The generous earth yields food for thousands more than they who put in the plow. The hammer and the saw of the carpenter, therefore, create artificial wants in exchange for the farmer's food, on which the carpenter lives. Behind the carpenter follow all mechanism and manufacture. The sail swells away before the wind, and the ship brings back novelties in exchange for the farmer's food, and following the ship goes all commerce. The scales balance the exchanging products, and the store of the merchant brings China, Java, and Brazil to the farmer's door. At the merchant's counter waits all inland commerce. This response promotes thought. Physical comfort once attained, the pioneer mounts up to mental demands for satisfaction. The stir of ideas craves new thoughts and new methods, which is the whole principle of intellectual expansion and of education.

The foundation of culture lies also in purity of moral aspiration. The elevation of an erect mind, the electricity of conscience, the moisture of benevolent motives, these reveal a healthful atmosphere, in which healthy thinking generates virtue, purity, love on earth and in heaven, draw upwards the thoughts as the sun draws upward to itself the vapor.

Now, in our nation, the practical era has gone. The era of culture has come. The soil is in possession. The pioneer stops at the ocean. The grand outlines between the oceans have all been filled with people alert. The vacancies now for first settlements are mere bays and estuaries into which the land-ships may move. Now comes, by necessity, the era of compacting and attrition, the era of scrutiny in every department of life and of action, of penetration into every institution and its principles, of inspection of education and educators, of the revaluation of books and authors and systems of mental nutrition, of storing results in ripened opinion and in measured standards for the next children to take measurement with at their start in life. A high culture is a necessity of our future civilization. The broad continent compels it, as the multitudes outnumber the actual producers. The response between this marvelous domain and its capacities and outlook upon the seas, between the providential productions of the century and the human mind, compels it. If only conscience keep the air charged, and virtue make the atmosphere brisk, and truth be let to form her lines of grace in the mind, as she does in nature, culture can but ripen. If only these moral forces are vigorous, then culture will be robust and broad, and not degenerate into the sentimental, the finical, and the morbid.

The college which would now rank at the head must instruct its alumni as truly as its under-graduates. The under-graduates know much, but the alumni know that themselves know nothing. Never have they craved so much the stimulant of master-minds as since they went out into the world, nor so much desired supplies for their self-known deficiency. From every department in the old ranges of thought, and from all the new departments, the graduates of colleges desire, and will desire, the issue of results of learning which will be a tonic to their weaknesses. The college which *can* not do this, or *will* not, may be a well-appointed institution for the fulfillment of its own conception, but she cannot sit at the fountain-head of culture. Now comes, as never before, the flooding in of science and of art and of literature. Who shall gauge its depth and tell its quality? The quickened mental production of the new century, who shall measure it, and give its value, and adjust it to our needs, but the calm minds at the seats of culture?

We look out upon our land and behold the vision. The best substantial home of all lands is here to grow brighter with American accomplishments and taste. The noblest institutions of the earth are here to find rivals; philosophy open in new and wider generalizations, language attract and absorb the smaller dialects, and science discover new truths. Here, as we look back up the perspective of history, the plan and picture of the ages shall hang in better light, law and legislation resolve into simpler elements, the natural sciences become the healthy delight of the masses, the technical arts explore and bring out the mines and the forests, the rivers and the land, medicine yield new remedies and frame her benignant reliefs, navigation and architecture and engineering yield new security and adornment and comfort, the fine arts multiply their variety, astronomy bring into closer view the remote designs of the material universe, and theology, aided by the true expositor of science, show, in more limpid light, the love and justice of a gracious God.

If we would accomplish this, our leaders must be men of wisdom, learned, thorough, and exact, patient in investigation, skilled in exposition, discerners of the junctures at which popular sources of opinion need knowledge, and ready to supply them—leaders whose power of conscience is large, who are always sending out electricity, and know how to draw it from the skies. There must be institutions for meditation and research, where culture may receive both refinement and strength, taste and health, where sciences and forces, and all forms of life and thought and matter, may be presented in their correlation. And before these leaders must there be a high ideal—not simply of abstract systems of thought; not simply of great and noble men, who shall sway society, nor even of society, harmonious, contented, intelligent, happy, but the ideal of the highest development of every man, of rounding out into reality every plainest, most angular, most deformed unit of a man, in development of his composition, in discipline of his faculties, in personal and social accomplishments and graces, and in dignity and beauty of his moral principles.

5. A fifth problem is that of *science in its relation to religion.* Only a thoroughly scientific mind is competent to discuss the subjects which are *strictly* the subjects of science.

But the strongest and boldest of the relations which have been made so conspicuous do not belong so much to strict science, as they do to that realm of common reason and common judgment which lies between the *results* of science and the principles of religion. A plain mind may know nothing of the *rationale* of the atomic theory, and yet be quite as competent as the scientific mind—perhaps in a healthier state—to judge whether inert atoms can generate life. Plain common-sense may therefore, in child-like innocence, or in Socratean sagacity, ask questions.

To the the casual reader it is almost incredible that the mind of man is asked to pronounce on infinitesimal and invisible changes of matter, myriads of ages away, across stretching periods which have undergone great transformations, and in a condition of the world the most of the elements of which we may not know. It is astounding to a plain, hard mind to be assured that *life*, in that dim antiquity, came into existence from motionless matter, which motion of life the motionless matter itself originated, or that dead matter gave a vital spasm by the deathly energy of its dead self so intense, that in a few ages the energy of death revolved into nebula or star-dust, and that then this nebulous death caught up dead matter and made a universe of life so great and grand that the growing philosophic mind can pierce back through æons of æons to the very instant of the first death spasm itself. It is indeed amazing to be told that *self-consciousness* and the personal *will* are the mere shifting of attitude in the particles of the brain—the play of the organism and its environment. It is wonderful to think that when the mind of man can make communications so grand in distance and degree, it is still impossible for a Great Mind outside our race to communicate with us. It is well-nigh inconceiveable that he who is the Highest Truth of our race is also the highest falsehood; that he who is the Highest Wisdom is the highest self-delusion of mankind. Still, since these things are calmly asserted by men of great intellectual force, who avow themselves sincere, let us respect the declared intention to bring to light only the truth.

At the same time, the contest has vital issues. A great sensitive population of the new century in America feel keenly the life or death here unfolded. They ask the college and the college-bred for calm and clear statement in answer to blunt questions like these :

What is the honest truth in respect to the *uncertainties* of science ?   What does the historic category of sciences show in respect to changing generalizations and alleged facts and palpable fluctuations in systems of scientific-religious thought ? What is the plain bold fact in respect to the *imaginations* of science ?   How far is the charge justified, which characterizes some of these scientific theories, as a mere " agglomeration of fact and fancy ?"   How far is the accusation true, when it is said that we are lead " by the process of abstraction from experience, to form physical theories which lie beyond the pale of experience ?"   How much is due to imagination, when the scientific investigator of facts " prolongs the *vision backward across the boundary of experimental evidence*," and *there, beyond* the boundary of evidence, "*discerns* " " in matter " " the promise and potency of every form and quality of life ?"

What is true in respect to the *inferences* of science ?   Is the logical faculty in the highest exercise, when facts newly discovered, still held by an uncertain grasp, are made the premise of fixed conclusions ; or when the hypotheses propounded in the first essay so grew into the author's very life, that they are used as facts in later essays on the same subject ?   Even supposing that a reptile's claw did develop into a horse's foot, does it follow that the physical vitality of a reptile developed into the moral nature of man ?   What are we to understand in respect to the *assumptions* of science.   Is it or is it not true, after scientific minds have discovered, in a strictly scientific manner, the *facts* of nature, that common sound minds are less qualified to judge of the *application* of the facts to the existence of an immortal mind and of an Infinite Being ? *Why* can not the common mind make as true a logical process from stars to the Creator, as the more subtle mind from star-dust—from the planets and their motions as from atoms and their motions ?   How is the old blunt doctrine of " chance " unlike the more refined doctrine of " a fortuitous concurrence of indivisible atoms ?"

And one blunt question more—What is true in respect to the *aversion* of science toward the strictly scientific evidence which the Christian religion presents ?   This is certainly evidence a thousand times more palpable than the microscopic matter or the probably related fossils, to which our eyes are so constantly turned.   Here also is matter hard as the granite and with the granite's bulk.   Why shut out from the scrutiny of literal science the Man, the Book, the Land, as a correlation of forces—the Christ of history, the text-book of superior civilization, the sacred land with its foot-track of Christ and its bird-track of Noah's dove—a Person, the leading factor in history, a history which has endured the explorations and excavations of Jerusalem and of Moab with sublime steadfastness—a country where every rock and town and ravine is a new table of testimony?   Why shut up these notes of scientific investigators, where Layard and his winged bulls, where Smith with his Chaldaic account of the flood, where surveys of Sinai, and of Moab and of Judea vindicate the record with severe accuracy?   If Rawlinson reverses the estimate of Herodotus, if Schliemann opens the Scæan gate in the great tower of Illium, and leads us

> "to Priam's splendid tower,
> With polished corridors adorned ;"

and so vindicates a history on which Homer's great story lies, who shall ignore the measured walls, discovered implements, and customs, confirmatory inscriptions, exact proportions of land and river and gorge, which bear the eloquent testimony of compass, theodolite, measuring chain and rule, chronometer and barometer, in the hands of Robinson and Paine, and all their scientific contemporaries; who shall say that even Piazzi Smith's theory, founded in strict scientific *data*, in respect to the supernatural origin of the great pyramid, *may* not be true— its mathematical proportions now demonstrating, and still to demonstrate, with scientific accuracy, the truths of revelation ; its statement, from *data* wrought into that structure of massive stone in Egypt's earlier life, that the sun is much less than ninety four millions of miles distant from the earth, confirmed by our present observations on the transit of Venus?

Let the iridescent haze go by—vapor and flame and hue of the laboratory—while its facts remain. Let the must of mouldy parchments which dims the eye to the *holy intention* of the unique Scripture stories be shaken off, and a fairer comparison be made between the divine and the human significance of the sacred and profane histories. Give us educated minds and educating institutions which shall take no exclusive views of science. The Christian mind has much to offer and nothing to evade in science. Individuals may be harmed within the closed doors of laboratories, or entangled in the analogies of legends, but so long as the heavens declare the glory of God, and Christ remains the centre of civilized history, the common mind will make the correct inference.

6. The last and the supreme problem of the new century, is the problem of *Religion*. By the concession of men of science, all other subjects pay respect to this. But this is not sufficient. It is now to appear not simply whether those grand motives which impelled our early American heroes over seas which edged on seas again, and in them faced storms which whistled to approaching storms, and gave them mental courage to master portentous subjects which had blanched the blood of other men, and dilated their life with a spiritual zeal which has now set the cresting of church spires on every successive mountain range, until deep answers unto deep, and ocean floods lift up their voice to Jehovah, were essentially weak and superficial motives, narrowly bound in with mistaken doctrines and a pretended revelation ; but whether these motives are to have a new and grander volume of expression. Now lies immediately before us—who can doubt it—the era when history and poetry, music, art, science, statesmanship, and all social science, are to yield up the religious sentiment because it has touched its height, or are to wed anew with new depth of fondness that transcendent and beautiful passion which leaps up to meet the love and life of God. If we have not all misinterpreted the ages, the grandest era is now before us. If we have applied in America most fully to the individual man the principles of Christianity, a grand era in this land is now to open. If Christian colleges and Christian sons of the college prove leaders for God's great opportunities, the historic march goes on.

Surely the vision is enough to start a prophet's blood. A continent which may prove central in the earth, a people with expanse for health and physical culture, freedom for the mind in every development and every activity, education in all ranges of knowledge, interpretation of the schemes of Scripture which shall enlarge the scope of the past and the future of the sacred book, occultations of Providence which may set the Redemptive Plan of God in majestic outlines like the outlines of the Genesis, illuminations of glory like the spiritual lustre of Jesus' teachings, these seem to be but the natural sequence of history in the next movement of mankind.

Here should not theology be ashamed to re-read her pages in the light of Scripture, or to offer re-adjustments to Scripture on any just knowledge which exploration or history or science may present. Here should she not be ashamed to re-affirm strenously the eternal truths of God in the face of science, falsely so called. Here should the rising churches flame with new zeal to do man good, instinct with liberty for themselves and for all mankind, instinct with intolerance toward slavery, in the church or out of it, in golden voice of God's sweet gospel, lifting up for every soul of man or of self or of Satan, this noble chant, *The soul of liberty is true liberty of soul.* Under leaders who believe in man's immortal mind, themselves generous in culture and deep in tides of conviction, the church of God should kindle that broad love which absorbs petty forms, and which melts and bathes all souls in heavenly constraint to join the elective host. And so should the college fire the young men's heart with truth so broad and strong—like broad masses of burning anthracite—that in their future work, heaven itself shall seem to overtop the earth wherever they may go. Then shall apostles and prophets multiply, beneath whose sway the great majority shall rapidly come over to virtue and to God.

Art. II.—THE PERPETUAL AUTHORITY OF THE OLD TESTAMENT.

By WILLIAM HENRY GREEN, D.D., LL.D., Princeton, N. J.

THE Old Testament has, from the beginning, been assailed by those who deny all supernatural religion. Rightly perceiving that the Old is the basis of the New Testament, and linked indissolubly with it, they have made their thrusts at what they esteemed its vulnerable points, with the view of overturning the entire structure, and burying Christianity beneath the ruins of the former dispensation. It has also been the object of attack from within, as well as from without. It has been assailed professedly in the interests of Christianity itself. By early gnostics, by rationalizing interpreters of later times, by those who assume to speak oracularly as leaders of modern thought, it has been declared to be untenable and indefensible before the march of Christian enlightenment, and its summary abandonment is pronounced essential to the safety of the citadel. It has been claimed that the morality represented or embodied in the Scriptures of the Old Testament is so inferior, and even contrary, to the morality inculcated by our Lord, that the common doctrine of plenary inspiration must be at fault, so far as regards the organs of divine communication prior to Christ himself; that Moses and the prophets cannot in these matters have expressed the mind of God purely and without mistake; their utterances and their writings are not the unadulterated word of God, binding absolutely and unconditionally upon the conscience; but a distinction must be made between that in their teachings which really came from God, and an admixture of human imperfection which arose from their own inadequate conceptions, or their imperfectly sanctified nature.

On the contrary, it was expressly taught by our Lord and his apostles, and it has been from the beginning the common faith of the church, that all the Scriptures of the Old Testament are the Word of God; that they were given by inspiration of God; that the holy men who wrote them spake as they were moved by the Holy Ghost. The Old Testament contains no errors that require correction, no mistakes due to the inadequacy of the organ employed to transmit the divine will.

It precisely represented the mind of God to the people to whom it was given, and for the dispensation under which they lived, as unerringly as the instructions of our blessed Lord expressed the mind of God to those to whom he spake.

At the same time, and upon the same authority, it is maintained that the Old Testament does not contain the ultimate and final form of divine revelation ; it does not make known the truth as fully nor as clearly as it has since been disclosed in the New Testament. It is the infallible word of God, containing the truth and nothing but the truth ; but as compared with the New Testament it is relatively incomplete, for it does not contain the whole truth in that unveiled and developed form in which it has now been made known under the dispensation of the Gospel. This relative imperfection of the Old Testament involves, however, no disparagement of its plenary inspiration; for it is a necessary sequence from the fundamental fact, that the Most High chose to make his revelation to man a gradual one. It being his sovereign pleasure to communicate the truth to men with growing distinctness and completeness, this revelation must of course be incomplete until the last lessons have been given ; and yet this does not impair the certainty or the accuracy of that which, up to any given time, has been actually taught. There must be remaining obscurities which only the latest and fullest instructions will effectually clear up. And as truth and duty are correlative, every obscurity resting on the truth involves a corresponding inadequacy in the presentation of duty. If now it casts no reflection upon the unchangeable nature of God, that he should unfold his revelation gradually, neither is it inconsistent with the immutability of truth and rectitude, that the sphere of faith and duty should be from time to time enlarged, and that they who took their lessons from the mouth of Christ should be required both to believe and to do what was neither known by nor enjoined upon those who were taught by Moses.

And our Lord himself said to his disciples, at the very close of his earthly ministry : " I have yet many things to say unto you, but ye cannot bear them now. Howbeit, when he, the Spirit of Truth is come, he will guide you into all truth." Christ's own personal instructions are here stated by himself to be incomplete, and requiring to be supplemented by what the

Holy Ghost would reveal to his apostles after his departure ; but this argues no imperfection or want of absolute truth in what our Lord did see fit to teach.   And after all the disclosures made by the Spirit of inspiration, every thing is not unfolded to us now which shall be unfolded in the future world. The realm of truth and duty will then have an enlargement beyond anything that we can now conceive.

It may not be possible for us to comprehend all the reasons why the revelation of God has been thus gradual.   But there are some determining considerations which lie upon the surface, and which may be referred to here, because they will help us to a juster view of the relation which the Old Testament sustains to the New.

It would have been premature to bring into full and developed operation God's great plan of saving mercy before the need of it had first been demonstrated in the actual experience of mankind.   If the amazing scheme devised for the recovery of lost man had been set in full operation immediately upon the fall, if the Son of God had at once become incarnate, and wrought his work of expiation, and the gospel had been preached in all its completeness to Adam, and attended with the mighty power of the Spirit sent down from on high, and the whole race had been redeemed from the outset, it would never have been known from what depths of degradation and woe man had been rescued, nor how impossible it was for him ever to have delivered himself.   The dismal experience of many long centuries, during which the nations were left to walk in their own ways, was needed to show that, in spite of all that civilization and philosophy and the refinements of art and the productions of genius could effect, man was hopelessly depraved, and the regeneration, whether of the individual or of the race, could only be effected by a divine interposition.   The development of the fact, that the world was in absolute and perishing need of the gospel, required a protracted period, so that the actual coming in of the gospel must, during all this while, be deferred.

As the work of redemption by the Son of God was to be itself postponed for this long interval, so must any full and adequate disclosure of what this work was to be, not only because the demonstration of the need must precede the statement as

well as the introduction of the only available remedy, but because mere verbal lessons are of small account unless the objects to which they relate are present to the mind. Words are
barren and empty, if there is nothing to suggest the ideas which
they are intended to convey. It were idle to speak to the
blind of colors, or to the deaf of sounds. God does not teach
men in this unmeaning way. When, for example, he would
instruct us respecting his own nature and attributes, he not
merely tells us in words of his almighty power and infinite
wisdom, but he sets before us in the works of his hands that
which lifts us to some conception of what these words signify.
Gospel doctrines are based upon and interwoven with gospel
facts, and the former cannot be intelligibly communicated without a prior knowledge of the latter. In order that the truth
respecting the person and work of Christ should be properly
conveyed to the minds of men, he must first make his appearance among them.

But while the full light of the gospel could not shine upon
men until the advent of the great Redeemer, the world was
not to be left absolutely without light and without hope during all this long and dreary interval. A course of training and
of preparation was instituted from the very beginning, with a
double end in view. One was, by a progressive scheme of instruction, to prepare the minds of men by degrees for the comprehension and the reception of the gospel when the time for
its open promulgation should arrive. The other was, to bless
and save those who should live before the gospel came. The
means necessary to accomplish both these ends were the very
same ; the saving truths of the gospel were to be lodged in
men's minds in advance, and they were to be familiarized with
them by repeated inculcation. In order to this, the identical
truths, which were to have their highest embodiment in Christ
and in his work of grace and salvation, were exhibited before-
hand to men in elementary forms and in outward visible applications. By a comprehensive system of symbolic representation, evangelical truths were shadowed forth by the prominent events in the sacred history, by prominent personages,
and by legal institutions. All was divinely conducted and divinely appointed, and religious ideas found constant embodiment in the most varied forms in the experience of successive

generations, that thus the minds of men might be thoroughly imbued with them, both in order to their own individual salvation and to the preparation of the world for the acceptance of the gospel, when the fulness of time should arrive. And this was, to a certain extent, accomplished, notwithstanding the fact, that all the while a veil necessarily lay over the truth, the conditions not being yet in existence which were requisite to its exhibition with the clearness and amplitude that belongs to it in the gospel.

A further result of this preliminary shading of the truth was its enfeebled power over the heart and the life. The general forms of a landscape may be revealed by the twilight, but its individual features will not stand forth with the same distinctness as when bathed in the searching light of day. So the main outlines of human obligation to God and man are set forth in their true and unchanging reality in the Old Testament; but there are many details which are not specifically announced, nor put into the shape of formal enactments, for the regulation of human conduct. And especially in regard to civil and social usages, much was allowed to shape itself under the guidance of controlling principles, as their application would come to be seen. The correction of existing evils and abuses of a public nature was left to be gradually effected by instilling those sentiments and that sense of obligation which would silently undermine them, instead of the futile attempt being made to effect their instant extirpation by positive enactments. This is what our Saviour means when he says that Moses did not impose certain restrictions upon the people on account of the hardness of their hearts. If right principles are first established, all the rest will follow in healthy development. Life, to be solid and true, should be a growth from within, not constrained into rigid forms from without.

We are now prepared to approach the question of the perpetual obligation of the Old Testament, a question which admits of a ready answer on the basis of the principles now laid down. The Old Testament is the New in undeveloped germ or embryo. Its form is temporary, because it belongs to a preliminary stage of instruction; the truth was not yet unfolded to its own proper dimensions, and was set forth in emblems and elementary applications. But, in its essence and its true intent, it abides and is eternal. It was not abolished and superseded by the New Testament, but merged and perpetuated in it. The animal which has burst the shell that cramped its expanding life, and formed another better adapted to the new stage of being upon which it has entered, is not a different animal from that it was before. The youth grown up to manhood has altered in very many respects, but he is the same identical person, nevertheless. The New Testament is new only in being a larger and freer dispensation of the very same grace which had been revealed only less clearly and fully from the beginning. There is the same God, demanding the same exclusive worship and homage of the heart, the same law of holiness and love, the same Redeemer expected or arrived, the same method of salvation by faith in the divine promise of pardon through expiation. The Apostle Paul declares that he said none other things than those which Moses and the prophets did say should come—Acts xxvi: 22 ; that the gospel doctrine of gratuitous salvation is witnessed by the law and the prophets —Romans iii: 21: that Abraham was justified by faith, and David describes a righteousness without works. It is the ever recurring doctrine of the New Testament, that the Israel of God is perpetuated in those who are his true people, in living union with the Lord Jesus Christ ; that believers in Christ are the children of Abraham and heirs of the promises made to him ; that Christ is the true high-priest and minister of the true tabernacle, which the Lord pitched, and not man ; that all who belong to Christ are priests unto God, and have access through the rent veil to the mercy seat, or throne of grace, and are privileged to draw near with their bodies washed with pure water, and offer incense and the sacrifice of praise to God continually, and to present themselves a living sacrifice unto God. These are not mere figures of speech, borrowed from something wholly different from that to which they are applied, and merely adapted to New Testament objects. But the identical things are continued in their true spirit and intent ; the real heart and substance of all that the ancient people of God possessed and valued is preserved unchanged.

It may hence be seen, that the inspiration of Moses is not discredited by the fact that he affirms, in language repeated from the mouth of the Most High, the perpetuity of the gifts made, and the ordinances enjoined, under the Old Testament. Thus—Gen. xvii: 7—God declares his covenant with Abraham, and with his seed, to be an everlasting covenant, and ver. 8 gives the land of Canaan to him and to his seed for an ever-lasting possession. So Gen. xlviii: 4. So the children of Israel are directed to observe the passover by an ordinance forever—Ex. xii: 14, 17. There is likewise a perpetual in-junction respecting the care of the lamps upon the golden can-dlestick—Ex. xxvii: 21 ; respecting the priest's wearing the sac-. erdotal dress—Ex. xxviii: 43 ; and washing at the laver—Ex. xxx: 21 ; respecting the shew bread—Lev. xxiv: 8, 9 ; the meat offering—Lev. vi: 18 ; and the prohibition of eating either fat or blood—Lev. iii: 17.

This language might, indeed, be abundantly justified, if we were to look no further than the outward form, which is con-fessedly temporary, and was to pass away with that dispensa-tion to which it belonged. For the Hebrew word, which is in-differently rendered in these passages " everlasting," " perpet-ual," and " forever " may, with entire propriety, be employed, and in conformity with constant usage of any protracted period, and particularly one of indefinite duration. Thus, in reference to the past more or less remote, it is often translated " days of old." The Prophet Amos used it—ix : 11—in application to the reign of David, which was but little more than two centuries before his own day. Micah vii: 14, and Isaiah lxiii : 9, use it of the period of the Exodus. Solomon applies it—Prov. xxii : 28 —to the ancient landmarks which the fathers had set up, which must be at least as recent as the time of Joshua ; and David—Ps. xxiv : 7, 9—calls the gates of Jerusalem the everlasting doors. So a man held to service during life is said to be " a servant forever." Hannah vowed that her child should abide at God's sanctuary " forever." The psalmist describes the ungodly—Ps. lxxiii : 12—in terms which the authorized English version trans-lates, " they who prosper in the world," but which strictly de-note " secure forever." If, therefore, Moses had simply meant to say that these ordinances were to continue for a long and indefinite period, the terms he uses would have been the pro-per ones to express it.

But he doubtless meant more than that. These are no transient ordinances, arbitrarily appointed or designed to serve a temporary purpose. Canaan was the gift of Him whose gifts and whose calling are without repentance. It would never be recalled. And so in regard to the ceremonial ordinances. They belonged to the worship of God, and express that homage which the Most High ever requires, and man is ever bound to pay. The shell might drop away, but the kernal, the essence, must forever remain. The truth of the symbol lies not in the outer form, which is the mere husk, but in its inner meaning. There still remaineth a Canaan of rest to the people of God. Christ bids his followers trim their lamps and let their light shine. The apostle exhorts Christians to keep the feast, not with the old leaven of malice and wickedness, but with the unleavened bread of sincerity and truth. These perpetual ordinances are still in force in their true import, and this, the very import in which they were originally given by Moses and accepted by the people. Moses consciously used the language of symbols, which was recognized as such by those to whom it was delivered. The declaration which the Lord makes by the mouth of Moses, respecting their perpetuity, is exactly echoed by the Lord Jesus, that "one jot or one tittle shall in no case pass from the law till all is fulfilled;" fulfilled not only by the vicarious obedience of Christ, and by the types meeting their accomplishment in him, but by all its precepts receiving their complete and final form. The same precepts remain, only they are filled up to their full complement of meaning; they abide in their highest, most spiritual sense, notwithstanding the sloughing off of the outward form.

In thus understanding the language and the institutions of Moses, we are not spiritualizing them away, but simply attributing to them their true import, that which was intended by the Spirit of God, and that which was mainly regarded by Moses himself, and by all those among the people who had any spiritual discernment. The full proof of this could only be adduced by transcribing the whole of the devotional language of the Old Testament, and all that is taught of the spirituality of God and the spirituality of the worship and service that he requires. Doubtless there were numbers then, as now, who did not look beyond the outward forms, and who contented themselves with the external observance of the Mosaic ritual, as men do now with the formalities of Christian service. But this was no more acceptable to God then, than it is at present, and no more in conformity with the spirit and true intent of the Old Testament, than of the New.

It is no mere formal outward service that is demanded when Moses states the requirement of the law to be—Deut. x : 12—"to fear the Lord thy God, to walk in all his ways, and to love him, and to serve the Lord thy God with all thy heart and with all thy soul." It is no mere cleaving to the letter of an external rite when he bids the people—Deut. x: 16—"circumcise the foreskin of your heart." And Moses is so far from regarding or representing himself as the ultimate organ of divine communication, that he expressly points the people to the prophet—Deut. xviii: 18—whom the Lord would raise up, and to whom they will be required to hearken; but he would be a prophet like unto Moses, his counterpart and coadjutor, not his opponent or antagonist; not abolishing and undoing what he had done, but acting in the very same character and spirit, and carrying forward to its completion the work which he had begun.

David's delight in the house of the Lord testifies not his adherence to ritual formalities, but his inward relish for spiritual communion; and how thoroughly the symbolic service was blended in his mind with the devotion of the heart appears from frequent expressions: "Let my prayer be set forth before thee as incense, and the lifting up of my hands as the evening sacrifice;" "The sacrifices of God are a broken spirit;" "Offer the sacrifices of righteousness," etc.

And when the prophets foretell the universal prevalence of true religion in the blissful future, they do it in the terms of the ancient and familiar symbols, but with such accompaniments as forbid the slavish adherence to a literal sense which would be encumbered with obvious physical impossibilities. Thus Isaiah speaks of the nations coming up to the mountain of the Lord, to the house of the God of Jacob; but it is when the mountain of the Lord's house shall cease to be an insignificant eminence, and shall be established in the top of the mountains and exalted above the hills. And the Lord declared by the same prophet—Isa. 66, 23,—"all flesh shall come to worship before me," not merely at the annual feasts, as Israel was required todo, but "from one new moon to another, and from one

Sabbath to another." Now, however contracted a notion of the extent of the earth's surface any may impute to the prophet, the idea of literal pilgrimages from its extremities, month by month and week by week, cannot be relieved of palpable absurdity. Ezekiel describes the temple of the future as set on a very high mountain, and as measuring three thousand cubits on each of its sides, xlii: 17—which is vastly larger than Mt. Moriah could afford a site for; and he sees a stream issuing from the temple, which makes its way to the head of the Dead Sea, notwithstanding the inequalities which would forbid it, if literally understood; and this stream heals the waters of the Dead Sea, and fills them with life.

The prophets also declare the perpetual observance of the legal institutions at the very same time that they incorporate in the picture particulars which are inconsistent with the letter of the requirement, or which imply the abolishing or superseding of the outward form. Thus Isaiah predicts an altar and consecrated pillar in the land of Egypt, and that they should do sacrifice and oblation; whereas, according to the Mosaic law, there could be no altar and no sacrifice but at the one sanctuary in the land of Israel. Malachi predicts that in every place incense shall be offered to the name of the Lord, and a pure offering. And Jeremiah, after foretelling—iii: 16—the loss of the ark of the covenant, and that it shall not be missed, declares—xxxiii: 18—the perpetuity of the Levitical priesthood to be as inviolable as the succession of day and night. What is the Levitical priesthood without the ark? But the real matter at issue was not the prerogatives of the sacerdotal tribe or family, but the blessings which were to be inalienably secured to the people of God in all perpetuity, of the authorized and effectual mediation of a divinely appointed priesthood.

And our Lord himself said to his disciples at the sacred supper—Matt. xxvi: 29—" I will not drink henceforth of this fruit of the vine, until that day when I drink it new with you in my Father's kingdom;" and he promised them—Luke xxii: 30— that they should eat and drink at his table in his kingdom, and sit on thrones, judging the twelve tribes of Israel. Unless t be held to be inconsistent with the perfect inspiration of Jesus that he should speak of heavenly and enduring realities under these material and temporary forms, it is no prejudice to the inspiration of Moses, that he affirmed the perpetuity of divine ordinances, which were emblematic of that which abides forever.

But did not Moses thus create the impression, which he never corrects, and which could not have been corrected without impairing the confidence of the people in the law and their attachment to it, that the old restrictive and ceremonial dispensation was itself to be perpetual? And would not this naturally lead—did it not, in fact, lead—to contempt of and hostile feelings toward other nations? The Jews did indeed come to entertain a contempt and hatred for other nations, accounting and treating them as dogs, so that a heathen historian, with a measure of truth as well as bitterness, calls them "enemies of the human race." But that this was the legitimate tendency of the Mosaic institutions, or was in any degree encouraged, whether by Moses himself, or any of the inspired writers of the Old Testament, we most emphatically deny.

God did enter, it is true, into special covenant with Israel, thus distinguishing them above all other nations; and to prevent their contamination by surrounding idolaters, he laid restrictions upon their intercourse with them. But they are distinctly and repeatedly told, that God's choice of them was due to his sovereign grace, and to no superiority of their own over others. The descent of all mankind is traced from a common ancestry; the other nations of the world are from the same stock with themselves. In the original call of Abraham it was distinctly stated—Gen. xii: 3—that in his seed all the families of the earth (the form of expression bringing into view their common relationship) should be blessed. The same declaration is, on two subsequent occasions, repeated to Abraham— xviii: 18 ; xxii: 18—besides being freshly made to Isaac—xxvi: 4—and then again to Jacob—xxviii: 14. Jacob, on his dying bed, spoke to Judah of the coming Shiloh—xlix: 10—"Unto whom the gathering of the people (Heb. peoples) shall be." This destined blessing of the world is also affirmed by the Lord to Moses—Num. xiv: 21—"As truly as I live, all the earth shall be filled with the glory of the Lord." It was symbolically suggested, too, by the location of the tabernacle, which, while pitched in the centre of the camp of Israel, was invariably set by the points of the compass, thus standing in relation to the whole earth. So Joshua, mindful of this universal destiny of Israel, calls the ark—Josh iii: 11-13—"the ark of the covenant of the Lord of all the earth;" and declares—iv: 23, 24—that the miracle of the Red Sea and that of the Jordan were both wrought in order "that all the peoples of the earth might know the hand of the Lord that it is mighty." It was thus set before the covenant people from the outset, and they were again and again reminded of the fact, that the restriction of the true religion to a single people was but temporary, and was in order to its secure preservation and ultimate diffusion over the whole earth. The same strain was taken up abundantly by the Psalmists, and echoed in varied forms by the prophets of every age, from Jonah and Isaiah to Malachi; so that when the apostle—Col. i: 26; Eph. iii: 5—speaks of it as a " mystery, which in other ages was not made known unto the sons of men as it is now revealed unto his holy apostles and prophets by the Spirit, that the Gentiles shall be fellow-heirs, and of the same body, and partakers of the promise in Christ by the gospel," he cannot possibly mean that this was wholly unknown before. He himself argues the opposite at length in Rom. ch. ix and x. But it was now evidenced with new clearness, both by fuller revelations and by an actual experience, previously unknown of the reality itself.

But besides these statements respecting the future extension of the blessings of salvation to the Gentiles, practical measures were taken from the beginning, to grant them a free and unlimited participation in the blessings covenanted to Israel. In the original institution of circumcision in the family of Abraham, provision was made that the seal of the covenant should be given to any that were born in his house, or bought with money of any stranger who is not of his seed—Gen. xvii: 12-27. And at the institution of the passover it was ordained—Ex. xii: 48, 49—"When a stranger shall sojourn with thee, and will keep the passover to the Lord, let all his males be circumcised, and then let him come near and keep it; and he shall be as one that is born in the land. . . . One law shall be to him that is home-born and unto the stranger that sojourneth among you." The same law was formally repeated at the next anniversary of the passover—Num. ix: 14. So

in the law of sacrifices, foreigners are put on a precise par with
the children of Israel—Num. xv : 14-16—" If a stranger sojourn with you, or whosoever be among you in your generations, and will offer an offering made by fire, of a sweet savour
unto the Lord ; as ye do, so he shall do.   One ordinance shall
be both for you of the congregation, and also for the stranger
that sojourneth with you, an ordinance forever in your generations; as ye are, so shall the stranger be before the Lord.
One law and one manner shall be for you, and for the stranger
that sojourneth with you."   And so in regard to theocratic
offences and penalties—Num. xv : 29, 30—" Ye shall have one
law for him that sinneth through ignorance, both for him
that is born among the children of Israel, and for the stranger
that sojourneth among them.   But the soul that doeth aught
presumptuously, whether he be born in the land, or a stranger,
the same reproacheth the Lord ; and that soul shall be cut
off from among his people."   So in regard to their civil and
criminal matters—Lev. xxiv: 22—" Ye shall have one manner
of law, as well for the stranger, as for one of your own country."
    And these were not inoperative enactments.   The incor-
poration of foreigners with the seed of the patriarchs did take
place in large numbers.   It appears from the record, that
Abraham's servants were actually circumcised; their full
number we do not know, but mention is made on one occasion
of three hundred and eighteen trained servants born in his
house—Gen. xiv: 14.   The retinues and dependents of the several patriarchs were blended with their lineal descendants,
which accounts in part for the immense multiplication of the
children of Israel in Egypt, where they were swelled to six
hundred thousand men—Ex. xii, 37.   And at the Exodus it is
expressly said, that a mixed multitude went out of Egypt with
them—ver. 38—and accompanied them through the desert—
Num. xi : 4.   The mention—Gen. xxxiv : 22-24—of the cir-
cumcising of all the males in the city of Shechem, in the time of
Jacob, shows what was possible in other instances with worthy
motives and better results.   Moses invited the family of his
father-in-law, a Midianite, to accompany Israel with the promise—Num. x : 32—" What goodness the Lord shall do unto us,
the same will we do unto thee."   Solomon, in his prayer at the
dedication of the temple, simply expressed the spirit of the

legislation of Moses and the policy which had been pursued toward other nations from the beginning. I Kings viii: 41–43— " Moreover, concerning a stranger, that is not of thy people, Israel, but cometh out of a far country for thy name's sake, (for they shall hear of thy great name, and of thy strong hand, and of thy stretched-out arm); when he shall come and pray toward this house, hear thou in heaven, thy dwelling-place, and do according to all that the stranger calleth to thee for; that all the peoples of the earth may know thy name to fear thee, as do thy people, Israel." No aggressive movements were made for the conversion of Gentiles, no preachers sent to them, no missions planted among them. The time for this had not yet arrived. In the weakness of her pupilage, the utmost that the church could do was to stand on the defensive, and maintain her own faith and worship in its integrity. But the door ever stood open, and all who were attracted by the holy teachings or the mighty deeds of the God of Israel, were welcomed, from whatever nation. With four signal exceptions, to be considered presently, no hindrance was interposed to the free admission of Gentiles resident in Palestine, or in any country under heaven, to the full privileges of the children of Israel.

And further, so far was the law of Moses from inculcating or encouraging hatred of foreigners, or hostility toward them, that it, in express terms, enjoins the reverse. It not only commands in general terms unselfish love to all—Lev. xix: 18— " Thou shalt love thy neighbor as thyself;" but to guard against the possibility of limiting this to fellow Israelites, it adds—vs. 33, 34—" And if a stranger sojourn with thee in your land, ye shall not vex him. But the stranger that dwelleth with you shall be unto you as one born among you, and thou shalt love him as thyself." Ex. xxiii: 9—" Thou shalt not oppress a stranger; for ye know the heart of a stranger, seeing ye were strangers in the land of Egypt." So Ex. xxii: 21. It is declared to be the attribute of God—Deut. x: 17–19—that " He regardeth not persons; . . . he doth execute the judgment of the fatherless and widow, and loveth the stranger, in giving him food and raiment. Love ye, therefore, the stranger." Special kindness was required to be shown to foreigners, particularly such as were impoverished and needy.

The unreaped corners of their fields and the gleanings of their harvests and vineyards were to be left for the poor and stranger —Lev. xix: 9, 10; xxiii: 22. In their religious festivals the stranger, as well as the fatherless and the widow, were to share their bounty and their joy—Deut. xvi: 11-14. Israel had been grievously oppressed by the Egyptians, and their friendly request for a passage through the territory of Edom had been refused with hostile demonstrations, to their very serious inconvenience, yet they are forbidden to harbor resentment for these injuries—Deut. xxiii: 7—"Thou shalt not abhor an Edomite, for he is thy brother; thou shalt not abhor an Egyptian, because thou wert a stranger in his land."

But it has been a standing objection to the morality of the Old Testament, that the Israelites were commanded to treat the Canaanites with the utmost barbarity and cruelty, utterly destroying all that breathed, men, women, and children; they were likewise commanded to exterminate the Amalekites; and were forbidden to receive Amorites and Moabites into the congregation, even to the tenth generation—Deut. xxiii: 3. Such commands and prohibitions, professing to emanate from the mouth of God, are, it has been urged, simply evidence that Moses could not have been an infallible interpreter of the divine will.

It is sufficiently plain, from what has been already said, that the treatment of these four nations is not the outgrowth of a hostility cherished toward foreigners in general. For these are the solitary exceptions in a system of laws singularly just and humane, and even generous, toward them. It is freely conceded that the treatment of the Canaanites finds no justification in the laws or usages of war. If the Israelites seized upon Canaan by no right but that of conquest, and plundered and massacred the inhabitants without mercy for no crime but that of defending themselves and their homes, then they were a horde of brutal savages, and their conduct was horrible in the extreme; and Moses, in stimulating and sanctioning such atrocities, in the holy name of religion, has outdone the fiercest and darkest fanaticism that the world has ever known. Then the inevitable conclusion would be, not that Moses' inspiration was defective at this point, but that he was inspired from beneath; then the old Manichæans were right in affirming that

the God of the Old Testament was not the same as the God
of the New, but was the original Spirit of Evil. For there
can be no doubt that all this was done under the immediate
direction of Jehovah, whose chosen instrument Moses was.
We here assume the truth of open, notorious facts, recorded in
the books of Moses, the acceptance of which is dependent not
on his inspiration, but on his veracity as a historian. If this be
questioned, it must be settled by an independent line of argument, for which we have no space at present. We only say,
that if the narrative is untrue, then there is nothing to explain ;
the Canaanites may never have been maltreated at all; and
the imputation cast upon the inspiration of Moses on this and
similar grounds is without foundation.

The Lord promised to Abraham the possession of the land
of Canaan, though it is expressly stated that the land was occupied by the Canaanites and Perizzites when he first entered
it. This promise was given to him before he left his father's
house, and afterward repeated in vision and in his waking
moments, by internal suggestion, by a voice from heaven after
the sacrifice of Isaac, and by God appearing to him in human
form, and talking with him as previous to the birth of Isaac
and the destruction of Sodom, these facts being at the same
time foretold to him, and their fulfillment affording indisputable evidence that it was no illusion, but a real divine communication. Abraham's confidence in this promise, as well as in
others which were connected with it, and received in precisely
the same way and on the same authority, is adduced, not only
in the Old Testament, but in the New, as the great proof of
his faith in God, and it earned for him the title of the father of
the faithful and the friend of God. The same promise was
repeated by God himself to the other patriarchs, and formed
the burden of Isaac's blessing to Jacob, and of Jacob's dying
blessing to his sons. When God appeared to Moses in the
flaming bush, announcing himself as the God of Abraham,
Isaac, and Jacob (a fact appealed to and argued from by our
Saviour), it was to announce to him that the time had arrived
for fulfilling these promises, and putting the children of Israel
in possession of the land occupied by the Canaanites, the Hit-
ites, the Amorites, the Perizzites, the Hivites, and the Jebusites. And all the wonders wrought in Egypt, the plagues

sent, the passage of the Red Sea, the miracles and guidance in the wilderness, were but successive steps by which God was conducting them, by his own mighty hand, to the land flowing with milk and honey, which he had sworn to their fathers. The fifth commandment, uttered by God's own voice from Sinai, speaks of " the land which the Lord thy God giveth thee." The sentence that doomed the entire generation which left Egypt to die in the wilderness, and which kept Israel wandering in the desert for forty years, was in consequence of their disobedience when commanded to go in and take immediate possession of the land, notwithstanding the discouraging report of the spies. They are again and again charged to destroy the Canaanites, and severe penalties were threatened if they failed to do so. These nations were mightier than themselves, but immediate divine assistance was promised and granted for their subjugation. The Jordan was dried before them ; the walls of Jericho thrown down ; the sun and moon stood still at Joshua's bidding ; hail-stones fell from heaven upon their foes, and discomfited them. When God deserted them, as upon Achan's trespass, Joshua and the people were in the utmost consternation, and were powerless before their enemies. There is nothing in the divine legation of Moses that is more clearly evidenced, than that it was by God's immediate direction the Israelites marched into Canaan, took forcible possession of the land, and destroyed its inhabitants. There is no room for the assumption that Moses, through defect of inspiration, committed the dreadful mistake of imagining that to have been commanded of God, which he never enjoined, but which was, on the contrary, the most frightful and atrocious offence conceivable against his holy will. Palpable facts made it plain, both to Moses and to Israel, that there could be no misapprehension here. There is no middle ground between denying the truth of these facts and confessing that the whole responsibility, in respect to the treatment of the Canaanites, rests with the Lord himself.

How then can this be reconciled with the divine attributes and with the will of God, as elsewhere revealed ? God is the absolute proprietor of the whole earth, and he had the perfect right to dispose of the land of Canaan as he pleased. If

the Canaanites, who were merely tenants at his will, showed
themselves unworthy occupants, no one can question his righteousness in ejecting them from it, and bestowing it upon
whomsoever else he chose. If he had desolated the region by
pestilence or earthquake, he would merely have done what
the awful catastrophes, which he has sent at other times and
places, abundantly assert his right to do. The chief peculiarity in this case, and the only thing that needs to be accounted for, is that God enjoined it upon the Israelites to do
that which he has elsewhere effected by the unintelligent physical forces of nature.

In explanation of this it may be remarked, that the Canaanites were judicially sentenced to destruction for their detestable crimes and abominations.   This is the reason which is
constantly assigned for their extermination. Thus, in Lev. xviii :
24, 25, after the mention of a number of unnatural crimes, it
is added, " Defile not ye yourselves in any of these things, for
in all these the nations are defiled which I cast out before
you.   And the land is defiled ; therefore I do visit the iniquity
thereof upon it, and the land herself vomiteth out her inhabitants." So Deut. xviii : 12, after another list of criminal practices,
it is added " Because of these abominations the Lord thy God
doth drive them out from before thee." Again, Deut. xviii : 16,
18, " Of the cities of these people, which the Lord thy God doth
give thee for an inheritance, thou shalt save alive nothing that
breatheth ; but thou shalt utterly destroy them, that they teach
you not to do after all their abominations which they have
done unto their gods."

This righteous sentence Israel was charged with executing.
They no more acted on their own responsibility than the executioners of human law in inflicting the penalty of death,
where sentence has been pronounced by the competent tribunal. And they had no more right to overstep the limits
divinely prescribed, than modern executioners have to act irrespective of the decree of the court, and bring to the gibbet
whomsoever they judge to be worthy of death, not to say
whomsoever they may be pleased to sacrifice to their cu-
pidity or malevolence. No discretion was allowed them in
the case. No man or body of men could be either safely or
righteously trusted with so awful an exercise of irresponsible

authority. The Israelites could not sentence any nation or community to extermination which God had not by name expressly sentenced. And others cannot plead the example of the Israelites, unless they are acting with the same indisputable evidence of being under immediate divine orders.

The duty of executing this sentence was imposed upon the children of Israel, not to gratify or encourage a blood-thirsty spirit, but for the sake of the severely solemn lesson which it was designed to teach them. They were warned by Moses, that if they copied the criminality of these nations, a similar retribution should overtake themselves. In executing God's justice upon others, they pronounce their own sentence, if they incur like guilt. This terrible lesson, in which they were required to be actors, followed in the train of others, in which they had been spectators or sufferers during the wanderings in the desert. Every act of rebellion and of murmuring had been followed by instant divine inflictions, plague, and fire, and fiery serpents, and the earth opening her mouth and swallowing down the transgressors, and all that appertained to them. The awfulness of the doom, which God's righteous judgment would inevitably inflict upon the violators of his holy law, was thus doubly inculcated, by penalties inflicted upon Israel and penalties inflicted by them.

And they were required to deal, and did deal out equal severity to apostates of their own number, as to the Canaanites themselves. Thus, after the crime of the golden calf, the sons of Levi were commanded—Ex. xxxii: 27—"Put every man his sword by his side, and go in and out from gate to gate throughout the camp, and slay every man his brother, and every man his companion, and every man his neighbor." And for the pious obedience shown in this summary chastisement, this tribe was rewarded with the priesthood—Deut. xxxiii: 9, 10. And if any, even their dearest relatives or friends, should secretly seek to entice them to serve other gods—"thy brother, the son of thy mother, or thy son, or thy daughter, or the wife of thy bosom, or thy friend, which is as thine own soul" —he was to be unsparingly put to death—Deut. xiii : 6 ; and if one of their own cities should apostatize to idolatry, it was to be utterly destroyed, "with all that were therein, and burned with all the spoil of it, and it should be left an heap forever,

and never be rebuilt"—vs. 15-17. This zeal to put away evil
from the midst of themselves was, in actual fact, shown against
transgressors of their own number, in the case of Achan, in the
formal investigation into the matter of the altar built on the east
of Jordan—Joshua xxii: 11 ; in the assembling of the tribes to
war against Benjamin for the crime committed in Gibeah—
Judges xx. This was no wild and fierce fanaticism, but a
determined spirit of obedience to the divine will. And it
affords no justification to those who, in later ages, have sought
to propagate what they deemed the true religion by fire and
sword, or to extirpate heresy by pains and penalties. Rebellion and disobedience in the face of those immediate manifestations of God's presence and power, with which the age of
Moses and Joshua was filled, betokened an incorrigible contumacy, which merited condign punishment. It may be
likened to the blasphemy of those who attributed the miracles
of Jesus to the agency of evil spirits, and are consequently
said to have committed that crime for which there is no forgiveness, and for which the apostle John forbids even to pray.
But such a crime and such inflictions belong only to an age
wherein there are immediate divine manifestations to be resisted, and special revelations from God himself to authorize
and to prescribe the penalty.

It should further be remarked, that the generation of Israel
which was led by Joshua into Canaan is by no means the
counterpart of that which Moses led out of Egypt, and whose
deep infection with the idolatry and corruption of that land
was shown by its repeated murmurings and acts of rebellion
and apostasy. There would have been a glaring inconsistency
in making the latter the ministers of God's righteousness.
But that old generation was itself completely cut off by divine
judgments in the wilderness. And another generation was
trained up, under the tuition of God's immediate revelations,
and the discipline of immediate divine inflictions, to a prompt
and ready obedience. There were no murmurings against
Joshua, as there had been against Moses, and no overt acts of
disobedience ; on the contrary, the testimony is, that—Josh.
xxiv: 31—" Israel served the Lord all the days of Joshua, and
all the days of the elders that overlived Joshua, and which

had known all the works of the Lord that he had done for Israel."

And the generation of Canaanites, which the Israelites were bidden to extirpate, was not the counterpart of that which Abraham found upon his entrance into the land, nearly seven centuries before. An interval had elapsed equal to that which separates us from the crusades. The degeneracy which might take place in such a period of time cannot be computed. God said to Abraham, that the iniquity of the Amorites was not yet full. Nevertheless, in one corner of the land, even then Sodom had sunk to such a pitch of wickedness that vengeance could be no longer delayed, and it was destroyed by fire from heaven. What a chasm between Melchizedeck, king of Salem, and priest of the Most High God, and Adonibezek, who confessed to the incredible barbarity of having cut off the thumbs and great toes of threescore and ten kings, and obliged them to gather their meat under his table, and who was justly sentenced to be treated as he had treated them—Judges 1 : 7 ; or that degraded race whose worship consisted in sacrificing their own children, and indulging in the impure and beastly rites of the goddess Ashtaroth. Probably, if we knew more of their abandoned wickedness, we should better understand why divine justice decreed that such wretches should be swept from the earth. The fact that none but the Gibeonites sought to make peace with Israel, or to make their submission to Israel's God, notwithstanding the miracles of Egypt and the wilderness, shows that they had reached that pitch of desperate frenzy, that they would consciously fight against a God who wrought such wonders.

The case of the Amalekites need not detain us long. It is evidently governed by the same principles as that of the Canaanites. The Amalekites were the first to attack Israel in the desert, and this just after the mighty wonders God had wrought on their behalf in Egypt, and the miraculous passage opened for them through the Red Sea. Their assault, under such circumstances, upon a people so manifestly under God's immediate protection, was virtually, and in all probability it was consciously, directed against Jehovah himself. The Amalekites were, therefore, by God's decree, made the standing type of the malignant and incorrigible enemies of

God, and the Israelites were directed to effect their extirpation.

So the Ammonites and Moabites, who, instead of taking a
friendly attitude toward a nation so favored and led of God,
hired Balaam against them, to curse them, and, both by in-
cantations and by enticements to the shameful orgies of their
abominable idolatry, sought to compass Israel's ruin. Israel
is accordingly forbidden to enter into peaceful relations with
them, or to admit them to the tenth generation into the congregation of the Lord.

The same principle applies to the imprecations in the Psalms.
It is entirely to mistake the spirit of these inspired writers
to interpret their language as that of personal vindictiveness,
or impotent malice, which, unable to wreak its spite with its
own hand, would engage the Most High to be the minister of
its hate. Thus understood, they could never have been admitted to a place in the Scripture, which is declared to be all
inspired of God, and profitable for doctrine, for reproof, for
correction, and instruction in righteousness; to which our Lord
constantly referred the Jews as the word of God, and which
he declared cannot be broken. Our Lord himself quotes a
Psalm of this character, Ps. xli, as Scripture—John xiii: 18;
and Ps. lxix is quoted by the evangelists in application to
the treatment of our Lord at his crucifixion, and in the book
of Acts in application to Judas.

In relation to psalms of this character generally, it should be
remarked, that imprecations are far fewer than our version
would lead one to suppose. Many verbs translated as imperative are simply declarative; and should be rendered not "let
them be," but "they shall be," so and so. The Psalmist announces what is foreshown to him; the retribution which God
has purposed to inflict. And when the imperative form is used,
it is not expressive of an unauthorized wish of his own, which
seeks the hurt of those who have injured him. It is the
authoritative announcement of God's just displeasure at those
who are not merely personal enemies of the Psalmist, but
enemies of God; and it expresses his approval of the rectitude
of God's righteous sentence of condemnation. Ps. cxxxix:
21, 22—" Do not I hate them, O Lord, that hate thee? And
am not I grieved with those that rise up against thee? I hate·

them with perfect hatred; I count them mine enemies." It is
not the persons of the men, nor their treatment of himself as
an individual, but their character and attitude toward God,
which determines the Psalmist's feelings toward them.

The 41st, 69th, and 109th Psalms, which are among the most
marked instances of imprecation, are, in their titles, attributed
to David, and must in fairness be interpreted by David's known
sentiments, expressed elsewhere, both in his language and his
conduct. He indignantly repels, in repeated passages, the
idea of his indulging malevolence toward his personal enemies,
or taking it upon himself to requite their ill-treatment. He
merely committed his case to the Lord, "who judgeth righteously," and "to whom vengeance belongeth." Thus, Ps.
vii: 4—"If I have rewarded evil unto him that was at peace
with me, and *plundered him that without cause is my enemy*, let
the enemy persecute my soul, and take it; yea, let him tread
down my life upon the earth, and lay mine honor in the dust."
And Ps. xxxv: 12–14—"They rewarded me evil for good, to
the spoiling of my soul; but as for me, when they were sick,
my clothing was sackcloth; I humbled my soul with fasting;
I behaved myself as though he had been my friend and
brother; I bowed down heavily, as one that mourneth for his
mother." And that this was no empty profession, but the
actual rule of his life, appears from the absence of all vindictiveness in his treatment of Saul, whose fierce malignity, when in
the very act of pursuing him, David twice subdued by his noble
generosity; at whose death he sung a touching lament, making
graceful mention of Saul's brave and noble qualities, without
an allusion to his deadly hostility toward himself; and after
David had been fully settled on the throne, he asked, "Is
there yet any that is left of the house of Saul, that I may show
him kindness?—2 Sam. ix: 1-3. The law of his life is expressed by his son, Solomon—Prov. xxiv: 17—"Rejoice not
when thine enemy falleth, and let not thine heart be glad when
he stumbleth." Prov. xxv: 21—"If thine enemy be hungry,
give him bread to eat; and if he be thirsty, give him water to
drink."

It should further be borne in mind, that these Psalms were
not mere individual utterances, but were prepared to be sung
in the temple service and are hence inscribed, "To the chief

musician." The Psalmist expresses, consequently, not his own personal experience and feelings merely, but those which are common to him, with the rest of the true people of God. He speaks in his representative capacity as one of the pious, describes the sufferings to which, as a class, they are subjected from the malignity of wicked men, and the glad deliverance which shall surely be vouchsafed to them by the overthrow and righteous punishment of their foes. It is in virtue of this generic character of these psalms, that they find their highest accomplishment in Christ, the ideal of holy sufferers, and that it is no accommodation of their language to another than their proper subject, but the explication of its true and genuine import, when the evangelists apply it to the treachery of Judas and the barbarity of the murderers of Jesus.

David, as the monarch of Israel, is, further, the head and representative of the entire body of God's people. His cause is theirs, and their foes his, and his language should be interpreted accordingly.

What is said of Babylon, in Ps. cxxxvii, is not the bitter curse of the exasperated patriot. The words are those of a holy seer, foreseeing the terrible retribution which should be meted out to that merciless foe of God's people. She should suffer in her own haughty capital the same ferocious treatment which her brutal soldiery had inflicted on Jerusalem, dashing the very infants against the stones. He celebrates not the barbarous atrocity, but God's righteous vindication of his own cause, and that of his people, with which this atrocity should be connected. Existing relations should be so reversed that he would be accounted happy, and would be saluted with acclamations, who broke the power of this tyrannical oppressor, and in the resulting massacre dashed *her* little ones against the stones.

But while the Psalmists thus display the fearful doom of Babylon, they likewise link its name with a glorious manifestation of grace. Thus, Ps. lxxxvii: 4—"I will make mention of Rahab (*i. e.*, Egypt) and Babylon to them that know me." And the Psalmist goes on to say, that when the spiritual census of the nations shall be taken, this one and that one among hostile powers and distant lands shall be reckoned to have been born in Zion; they shall be her sons, her native-born citizens.   Do such blessings and cursings proceed out of the same mouth ?

And the human sympathies, which are sometimes mingled with these prophetic denunciations, show that these latter are not inconsistent with a tender pity for those whose guilt has involved them in their calamities. Thus Jeremiah, while depicting the overthrow of Moab—xlviii : 31, 32—says, "Therefore, will I howl for Moab, and I will cry out for all Moab ; mine heart shall mourn for the men of Kir-heres ; O vine of Sibmah, I will weep for thee with the weeping of Jazer."

And that such denunciations are not inconsistent with the spirit of the New Testament appears from the language of the loving Apostle John, in the book of Revelation—chap. xviii—respecting the Babylon of the future—ver. 6—"Reward her even as she rewarded you ;" and ver. 20—"Rejoice over her, thou heaven, and ye holy apostles and prophets ; for God hath avenged you on her."   And the Apostle Paul, who could even wish himself accursed from ·Christ for his kinsmen according to the flesh, nevertheless did not hesitate to say—1 Cor. xvi : 22—"If any man love not the Lord Jesus Christ, let him be anathema maran-atha," and of those who do evil that good may come, that their "damnation is just"—Rom. iii : 8.   The same thing appears also from the woes pronounced by our Lord himself upon the scribes and Pharisees, and upon Chorazin and Bethsaida.

Objection has also been sometimes brought from three cases in which the children of criminals were made to suffer the penalty of their father's offense. The provision of the law of Moses is express upon this point—Deut. xxiv : 16—"The fathers shall not be put to death for the children, neither shall the children be put to death for the fathers ; every man shall be put to death for his own sin."   This was the law for human tribunals ; and that it was acted upon in Israel, as everywhere else where a proper sense of justice prevails, appears from the express statement of the fact—2 Kings xiv : 6.   But the Most High is not bound by this law in his own decisions.   He himself declares, that he visits the sins of the fathers upon the children to the third and fourth generation of them that hate him.   There can be no suspicion of error in this statement from the defective inspiration of Moses, since it is in the second commandment which was proclaimed by God's own voice from Sinai, and he perpetually acts upon it in his providence. There is no injustice in this as it occurs in the divine administration, for it is expressly limited to the case of those who hate him ; where the children perpetuate the hostility of their parents, and thus render themselves answerable for their crimes, even though their own criminality may not have taken on precisely the same outward form.   Such visitations are unerringly and righteously made by him who tries the hearts and reins, but cannot be allowed to human tribunals, whose only rule of judgment is the outward conduct.

Now, in each of the cases above referred to, the execution was by immediate divine direction ; it was so with the family of Achan, with the sons of Ahab, and with the sons and grandsons of Saul.   While, however, Jehu acted by God's command in putting to death the entire house of ungodly Ahab, this lends no justification to the atrocities connected with it ; it does not excuse the ghastly spectacle of their heads piled in heaps at the entrance of the gate of the city.

In the case of Saul's family, if the transaction were one of mere superstition, it is detestable.   If, upon the occurrence of a famine, which was due simply to natural causes, David and those whom he consulted imagined that it was sent in consequence of Saul's slaughter of the Gibeonites, and to expiate this crime, which had no real connection with the matter, David executed seven of Saul's unoffending descendants, then it was a cruel, unjustifiable deed.   But if there was a real disclosure of the will of God in the case, and the historian speaks the truth when he says that the famine was designed to mark God's displeasure at a criminal breach of faith, and the whole people were made to suffer in this way for the murderous offense of their king, which they had sanctioned and participated in, who will venture to impugn the rectitude of the Most High in further showing his abhorrence of this cruel treachery by visiting it upon the heads of seven of Saul's descendants? Their hearts and lives he knew, although we do not, and, for all we know, they may have directly participated in the crime itself, which probably was committed near the close of Saul's reign, as the execution certainly took place near the beginning of that of David.   Christ himself said to that generation which filled up the measure of their fathers by shedding his blood, that upon them should come all the righteous blood shed upon the earth from the blood of righteous Abel.

So far the charges of cruelty and injustice often brought against the Old Testament. What has in like manner been said of slavery, polygamy, and divorce, must be discussed in a very few words. Moses regulated and restricted evils which were too deeply rooted in the usages of the time and in the prevailing social system, to admit of immediate and successful extirpation. He ameliorated domestic servitude by various humane regulations, besides limiting its duration to seven years in the case of Hebrew servants. The polygamy of the patriarchs is recorded, but not approved; on the contrary, the domestic dissensions and troubles resulting from it are likewise recorded, and serve to evidence God's providential disapprobation; and Moses positively prohibits marriages like that of Jacob, of two sisters at the same time—Lev. xviii: 18. So far as the evidence goes, it would appear that polygamy never prevailed extensively among the Israelites, notwithstanding the several wives of David and the enormous excesses of Solomon in the face of the explicit prohibition of the law of Moses —Deut. xvii: 17. These evils were not violently and suddenly eradicated, but their correction was left to the gradual influence of those principles of justice and of mutual love which were inculcated, and to the providential disclosure of the unhappy consequences which they entail, together with the setting forth of the true model of marriage in its original institution, to which our Lord appeals as containing its law for all time—Matt. xix: 4ff.

It is not correct to say, that unlimited facility of divorcement was allowed by the law of Moses. Its language is—Deut. xxiv: 1—"When a man hath taken a wife, and married her, and it come to pass that she find no favor in his eyes, *because he hath found some uncleanness in her;* then let him write her a bill of divorcement," etc. There was indeed a lax school among the Jews which affected to interpret this "uncleanness" of the most trivial causes of dissatisfaction; but its genuine meaning was more correctly represented by the opposing school, which held it to denote criminal conduct, which the husband, as in the case of Joseph, did not wish publicly to expose, or something grossly offensive. The word properly means "nakedness," and suggests what is shameful, indecent, or revolting. In so far, however, as divorce was not absolutely limited to the sin of adultery, it came short of the requirement insisted upon by our Lord; a relaxation due, as he declares, not to Moses' imperfect inspiration, but temporarily allowed in consequence of the hardness of the people's hearts.

The wholesale putting away of strange wives in the time of Ezra has sometimes been represented as a case of aggravated wrong. Upon Ezra's arrival in Judea from Babylon, he was informed by the princes of the people that the exiles who had come up in previous migrations, and had now been for years resident in the country, had grossly violated the law of Moses by inter-marriages with the heathen there, and with the predicted result of falling into the idolatry of the people around them, thus annulling the whole effect of the discipline of the exile, and repeating the very transgressions by which it had been incurred. Ezra ix: 1, 2: "The princes came to me, saying, The people of Israel, and the priests, and the Levites, have not separated themselves from the people of the lands, doing according to their abominations, even of the Canaanites, the Hittites, the Perizzites, the Jebusites, the Ammonites, the Moabites, the Egyptians, and the Amorites. For they have taken of their daughters for themselves and for their sons, so that the holy seed have mingled themselves with the people of those lands; yea, the hand of the princes and rulers hath been chief in this trespass." It is not surprising that in such a state of affairs Ezra "rent his garment and his mantle and plucked off the hair of his head and of his beard, and sat down astonied," and that he poured out his heart before God in that prayer of penitent humiliation which occupies the remainder of the chapter; amazed and mortified beyond expression, that the exiles, fresh from captivity, should have already entered upon a course of transgression, which was certain to induce another and a heavier woe. Vs. 13, 14: "After all that is come upon us for our evil deeds and for our great trespass, seeing that thou our God hast punished us less than our iniquities deserve, and hast given us such deliverance as this; should we again break thy commandments and join in affinity with the people of these abominations, wouldst thou not be angry with us till thou hadst consumed us, so that there should be no remnant nor escaping?" Nehemiah, too, gives an account of the same trespass, and speaks—xiii : 23, 24—of " Jews that had married wives of Ashdod, of Ammon, and of Moab; and their children spake half in the speech of Ashdod, and could not speak in the Jews' language, but according to the language of each people."

The prophet Malachi, speaking of the same matter, adds another feature to this iniquity, from which it appears that these lawless transgressors had, in many cases, abandoned their own legitimate wives of native birth, and taken up with these foreign women ; and he depicts the grief thus wantonly inflicted in the most moving terms.   Mal. ii : 13, 14, 16 : "And this have ye done again, covering the altar of the Lord with tears, with weeping, and with crying out, insomuch that he regardeth not the offering any more, nor receiveth it with good will at your hand.   Yet ye say, wherefore?   Because the Lord hath been witness between thee and the wife of thy youth, against whom thou hast dealt treacherously ; yet is she thy companion and the wife of thy covenant.   For the Lord, the God of Israel, saith, that he hateth putting away."

Moreover, the weeping of men, women, and children spoken of in the book of Ezra—x : 1—in connection with this matter of strange wives, must not be misunderstood as though it was the outcries of the strange wives themselves, in consequence of their being repudiated by their husbands.   It was a weeping accompanied by confession of sin, and a weeping, too, in which Ezra himself took part ; the tears were tears of penitence, that this great trespass had been committed against God.   And these strange wives were not hastily thrust out, homeless and shivering, into the cold and rainy street, but a convention of the people called in the interest of reform stood stoutly to their work in the wet and chilly day, and manfully resolved " As thou has said, so must we do."—Ezra x : 12. The actual severance was more deliberately performed, occupying three months, from the first day of the tenth to the first day of the first month, being thus finished on New Year's day.—ver. 16, 17.

It is further added, at the close of the enumeration of all the particular cases—Ezra x : 44—" All these had taken strange wives " (there were 113 out of a population of about 50,000 —Neh. vii : 66, 67) ; " and *some* of them had wives by whom they had children." From this it' may be inferred, that when this misdemeanor was arrested, the offense was in most cases comparatively recent.

The facts then appear to be these: About one hundred foreign women, married in defiance of the law of Moses, and in some cases by the repudiation of broken-hearted native wives, and who had introduced heathen abominations among the people still smarting from the captivity which the like abominations had brought upon their fathers, were separated from those to whom they had been unlawfully married; and this not in a heartless, frivolous manner, driving them out in the rain and the cold, but by a people deeply penitent before God for their fault, and by a solemn judicial process, covering three successive months. It was a painful transaction no doubt to all concerned. But it may be submitted to any candid person, whether the perpetuation of the true worship of God among this feeble band of returned exiles, who were the religious hope of the world, did not warrant the severity of the measure; and whether the entire transaction in itself, or in the manner in which it was conducted, casts the slightest discredit on the inspiration of Ezra as a man of God.

In his sermon on the mount, our Lord takes occasion to set forth, in express terms, the relation in which his teachings stand to the pre-existing Scriptures. A brief consideration of his authoritative statements on this point will conclude the present article. Our Saviour first defines his attitude to the law of Moses, and to the Old Testament generally, in language so explicit, and in such varied forms of statement, that we would think it must preclude the possibility of mistake. Matt. v: 17–19: " Think not that I am come to destroy the law, or the prophets; I am not come to destroy, but to fulfill. For verily I say unto you, till heaven and earth pass, one jot or one tittle shall in no wise pass from the law, till all be fulfilled. Whosoever therefore shall break one of these least commandments, and shall teach men so, he shall be called the least in the kingdom of heaven." . The law is then imperative in all its parts; it is not to be broken, even in its least commandments. Nothing could more flatly contradict the theory, that Moses, through imperfect inspiration, misconceived and misstated the will of God; that many of his supposed revelations were not from God at all, but emanated from his own imperfectly sanctified nature, and are actually shocking to the moral sense. There is not an ordinance in the Old Testament, even the very least, which is not the ordinance of God, or which can be safely broken; and he who teaches that it can, our Saviour declares, is the least in the kingdom of heaven. We do not pretend to define all that our Lord intended by this expression; but it certainly must include this, that such a view of the Old Testament involves a very inadequate apprehension of the New, of that kingdom of heaven, whose foundations Jesus came to lay, and whose laws he was then propounding.

This inviolable, indestructible law Christ came to fulfill, to fulfill not only in other ways, but as a teacher. He came not to abolish or supersede it in the minutest particular, but to complete it in all and every part. He communicates the final lessons, and these final lessons are not something new, freshly introduced into it, engrafted upon it, incorporated with it from some other quarter, but simply the complement, the fulfillment of the Old. And this completing is to reach to every part; not a jot or a tittle is to be lopped off or pared away, but all is to be fulfilled. The full spirit and intent of every particular is to be brought out; its deep meaning and wide applications are to be plainly set forth. In the bud there is no faulty excrescence; when it is developed, its old casing may fall away, but every part of the bud itself enters into that which is unfolded from it; it only comes out in fuller vigor and larger dimensions. The new law of Christ is simply the old law fulfilled; it is not the substitution of the true for the false in even a single item, or the pure for the impure; but it is strictly and simply the genuine expansion of every jot and tittle to that complete and final form, for which it was originally destined.

Our Lord then proceeds to illustrate his treatment of the law by a few examples. He cites the language of the sixth and seventh commandments, and declares that it is not enough to abstain from murder and adultery; causeless anger and the lustful eye are also offenses against God. Here, as is obvious, he simply insists that compliance with the outward letter does not exhaust human obligation. God lays his demand on the heart, as well as on the external conduct. There is nothing in this at variance with the law of Moses; nothing, in fact, which that law does not itself insist upon. It requires no mere formal outward service to be paid to God, but—Deut. vi: 5—"Thou shalt love the Lord, thy God, with all thine heart, and with all thy soul, and with all thy might." So in regard to duties to our fellow men—Lev. xix: 17, 18—"Thou shalt not hate thy brother in thine heart; . . . but thou shalt love thy neighbor as thyself." Deut. xv: 9—"Beware that there be not a thought in thy wicked heart," etc., etc.; compare Gen. vi: 5, which traces corruption to the heart. And the very structure of the second table of the law shows the same thing. The essence of its commands is, "Thou shalt not injure thy neighbor by deed (either in his life, the 6th commandment; his dearest treasure, his wife, the 7th; or his property, the 8th); thou shalt not injure thy neighbor by word, the 9th; and thou shalt not injure thy neighbor in thought, the 10th." The requirements thus range over deed and word and thought, showing that they concern the whole man in his inward and his outward life.

The next case is one in which the spirit of the law was not merely disregarded, but its very letter mutilated in practice by the neglect of a very important particular. "Whosoever shall put away his wife, let him give her a writing of divorcement," those who plead the law in this form quite overlooking the limitation in the express terms of the statute, "because her husband hath found some uncleanness in her." Even with this restriction, however, there was here a temporary tolerance of an evil; not, be it observed, because of Moses' imperfect inspiration, as our Lord in another place expressly explains, but for a very different cause—"the hardness of the people's hearts." Jesus, therefore, as the fulfiller of the law, proceeds to give a full and explicit statement of duty on this subject, limiting the somewhat vague and indefinite term "uncleanness," used in the law, to the specific crime of adultery, and announcing as the true law of marriage what was really involved in its original institution as recorded by Moses, and was but the application to this particular case of the general law of mutual love.

In the next two instances, likewise, our Lord both corrects perversions of the law and elevates the standard of require-

ment. The law forbade false swearing, and enjoined the faithful performance of oaths taken in the name of the Lord. The
perverted inference was hence drawn, that there was no violation of the law if the oath were by anything other than the
name of God, or if the oath by the name of the Lord were
not untrue, however irreverent it might be, or however trivial
the occasion. Christ sweeps these miserable subterfuges
away at a stroke by prohibiting any oaths whatever. Fealty
to God is shown when men make their solemn appeals to him
rather than to false divinities; and when by these solemn appeals they are held to the strict utterance of the truth. But
it is a higher reverence for God, which, even without such
direct appeal, utters only the simple truth, sensible of his all-
pervading presence, While to a superficial view it seems like
a contrariety that Moses should sanction and Jesus should forbid an oath, a deeper insight into the matter will show that
the one proceeds from the very same principles as the other,
only carried to a higher potency, and that the precept of the
New Testament is but the complement, the fulfilment, of the
Old.

So in regard to the penalty judicially prescribed for injuries—
Ex. xxi: 22-24; Deut. xix: 16-21—Eye for eye, tooth for
tooth, which was perverted into a justification of a vindictive
spirit and of private revenge. Jesus applies the needed corrective by enjoining the patient endurance of wrong. It is
not that the sufferer has no rights, or that those charged with
the administration of public justice should inflict no penalties
on evil-doers. But Jesus would lift his followers to a higher
plane of life. The law would inspire such a regard for the
righteous government of God, that men should be strictly just
in all their dealings with their fellow-men. But Jesus would
inspire so high a regard for the divine government, that men
would patiently submit, even to gross and glaring wrongs,
without seeking to right themselves, or appealing to human
tribunals for redress, but confidently entrust their vindication
to God alone. And this surely is not at variance with the
spirit of a law, one of whose requirements is—Lev. xix: 18—
"Thou shalt not avenge nor bear any grudge against the
children of thy people."

The several themes upon which our Lord thus comments are

regularly introduced by the formula, " Ye have heard that it was said to them of old time." And these themes are mostly stated in language taken *verbatim*, or in substance, from the law of Moses, but perverted to a sense foreign from the true meaning and spirit of the law. This perversion is stated in explicit terms in the instance which yet remains: " Ye have *heard* that it was said, Thou shalt love thy neighbor, and hate thine enemy." Thou shalt love thy neighbor " is the language of the law; but " Thou shalt hate thine enemy " is a perverted inference, which those whom the Saviour addressed may often have *heard* drawn, but which assuredly finds no sanction in the law itself. On the contrary, it expressly enjoins acts of kindness to an enemy—Ex. xxiii: 4, 5: " If thou meet thine enemy's ox or his ass going astray, thou shalt surely bring it back to him again. If thou see the ass of him that hateth thee lying under his burden, and wouldst forbear to help him, thou shalt surely help with him." And that our Lord never designed to sanction such an inference from these words of the law is plain, from the fact, that he himself sums up our duty to men in these same words: " Thou shalt love thy neighbor as thyself," and that he spake the parable of the good Samaritan expressly to expound who is meant by " neighbor " in this passage of the law.

One word in conclusion. The best solution of the difficulties which are felt, and the true corrective of the errors which are entertained, in respect to the Old Testament, are to be found in the deeper and more thorough study of this portion of the sacred volume. The prevalent neglect of all that belongs to the former dispensation is avenging itself in other ways than in the resulting misconceptions and consequent skeptical objections which threaten to undermine the authority of the Old Testament, and with it that of the New. It likewise reacts more directly and quite as seriously upon the interpretation of the New Testament, and is the fruitful parent of inaccurate or superficial views. If the New Testament contains the key to the Old, the Old Testament is likewise the guide to the New. It is a divine course of pupilage, by which the people of God were trained for the reception and comprehension of the gospel; and it is one which they cannot, even now, afford to do without. It contains the foundations on which the scheme of gospel truth is built.   If the lesson taught in the Old Testament, of the uncompromising justice of God, had been adequately learned, the divine love could not be so grossly caricatured, as it often is, by those who lose sight of every other attribute, and end by degrading that which it is their professed aim exclusively to exalt.   If the sacrificial system were better understood, the atoning death of Christ would not be so often misconceived.   The divorce of what God has joined together cannot but be fraught with mischief.   If the facts and institutions of the Old Testament, and, not least among these, the very things which are made the ground of flippant or skeptical objection, were more devoutly pondered, more seriously laid to heart, and more faithfully and widely preached, a firmer bulwark would be erected against prevalent and growing errors.

Art. III.—EQUABLE REDUCTION OF THE GENERAL ASSEMBLY.*

By EDWARD P. WOOD, Princeton, N. J.

[The following article was in the printer's hands before the Report of the Committee appointed by the last Assembly on Representation was published.   Without undertaking to discuss it, or expressing assent or dissent with reference to its main position, further than to reiterate our judgment, that the Assembly ought to be reduced, and that some basis ought to be found which will mitigate, or certainly not aggravate, present inequalities in the representation of different parts of the church, we submit a plan which appears to us to meet the essential conditions of the problem.   At all events, the careful and extended numerical tables submitted by our correspondent will, we hope, prove an important help in estimating the bearings of every scheme of representa tion that may be proposed.—EDITOS.]

THE refusal of the Presbyteries to adopt either of the overtures on representation sent down by the General Assembly may be explained by the fact, that one of them was extremely radical, and the other greatly magnified the existing inequalities of representation.   The mind of the church is unmistakably

---

* Report of the Committee on Assembly Representation, appointed by the General Assembly of 1876.

expressed against a radical measure, and also against the exaggeration of present evils. The elimination of such elements as have from time to time been rejected in discussing the problem of representation, has left the question in this condition, viz.: the Presbyterian Church wishes (1) to retain the right of representation where it is in the presbyteries ; (2) to retain such a size for the General Assembly as shall continue its commanding presence ; and (3) to make the reduction to such a manageable size, with the continuance of its commanding presence, in some way, as nearly as may be, similar to our present plan of representation.

The following calculations show that this can be done with the same immediate and prospective fairness to every one concerned which has characterized our method from the first adoption of a ratio of representaton in 1786.

The first General Assembly was organized by a representation* of one minister and one elder for each presbytery of six ministers and less ; and two ministers and two elders for " each presbytery of more than six ministers, and not more than twelve," " and so, in the same proportion, for every six ministers." In 1819 the ratio was changed, " substituting the word nine for six, and the word eighteen for twelve." In 1826 the ratio was again increased, by "changing nine to twelve, and eighteen to twenty-four." " In 1833 the present ratio was adopted," which changes twelve to twenty-four, and twenty-four to forty-eight.

By scanning these figures, it will be seen that the scale, by which this increased ratio has been reached, is by no means uniform. In the first instance, the ratio was raised by adding *three* to the lowest number, six, to make it nine ; and, instead of adding the same to the higher number, by adding its double, *six*, to make it eighteen. In the second instance this plan was continued by adding *three* to nine to make it twelve, and *six* to eighteen to make twenty-four. But in the third instance this graduation was dropped, and a new plan adopted of doubling the numbers which represented the ratio; thus, twelve and twenty-four became twenty-four and forty-eight, as they remain to-day.

This settles one thing in our policy, that we are at liberty to

---

* See *Baird's Digest*, p. 269.

make a new ratio of representation on any practicable and equitable basis whenever the occasion may demand it.   Besides,
we are not restricted to going forward by additions or multi-
plications, but we may go backward, by subtractions or divisions, to a starting point below the present one, and rise from
it by any satisfactory figure.

Having settled the fact, by experimental figures, that we
cannot reduce the General Assembly sufficiently, and at all
equalize the conflicting interests of growing inequality, by
adopting the last plan of increasing the ratio, by making 24 and
48 read 48 and 96, let us try the plan of falling back from 24
to 20, and from 48 to 40, by returning to the plan originally
adopted in the first Constitution of the General Assembly,
merely substituting *four* for *three*, by which the ratio was raised
at one end, and substituting *eight* for *six*, by which the ratio
was raised at the other end.   Observe that these figures of
diminution bear the very same relation to each other that the
figures of increase bore to each other; eight is twice four, as
six is twice three.   Here then we have a representation by
scores ; presbyteries with from 20 ministers downward, from
20 to 40, from 40 to 60, from 60 to 80, from 80 to 100, from 100
to 120, from 120 to 140.

All the attempts at reduction have proved plainly, that there
is no possible reduction to the required Assembly on the
basis of one minister and one elder to *every* presbytery.   This
is the reason why some presbyteries, which have seen the
necessity of such a change, are seeking for a number which will
be a fair minimum to entitle all presbyteries, which fall within
that limit, to *one* commissioner.   Thus, the presbytery of Louisville "adopted a paper, ... for presbyterial representation, on the basis of *thirty-five* members of presbytery for
one commissioner of General Assembly."   But there is no accompanying computation to show that, while this may reduce
the Assembly, it will make the reduction equitably.   And yet,
this growing conviction strengthens the belief, that there is no
way out of our present embarrassment, unless by such an exception to the rule, heretofore adhered to, as shall limit the
smaller presbyteries to a single commissioner.   And while we
must bind the home presbyteries to alternate between a minister and an elder, in order that the Assembly shall consist, as

nearly as possible, "of an equal delegation of bishops and **elders** from each presbytery" (*Form of Government,* chap. **xii : ii)**, the peculiarities of the position of the foreign presbyteries require in equity that they be left at liberty to send, as they **may** be able, a minister or an elder.

Accepting this sentiment as generally prevalent, it is **found** that it is not necessary to bring so many presbyteries into **that** class as the basis of 35 will require. The following figures **show** that the representation by scores, suggested above, will **largely** diminish that class of presbyteries, and, at the same time, **be** entirely equitable to those presbyteries themselves. It will, **also,** establish a better equilibrium between the presbyteries **in the** several classes constituted by this change to scores. And it **will** reduce the Assembly as much as our numbers, wealth, **influence,** and work will allow. We shall find that

THIS REPRESENTATION WILL GIVE A PRACTICABLE GENERAL ASSEMBLY.

This representation by scores, with one commissioner (**one** minister or one elder) for every presbytery of 20 ministers and less ; one minister *and* one elder for every presbytery of more than 20 ministers, and not more than 40 ; two ministers and two elders for every presbytery of more than 40, and not more than 60 ; and so in the same proportion for every additional 20 ministers, will give, in the 173 presbyteries, 72 with one commissioner each, and 67 with two commissioners each, and 28 with four commissioners each, and 5 with six commissioners each, and (there being none with between 80 and 100, and none with between 100 and 120 ministers) 1 presbytery with twelve commissioners.

Putting this in a tabular form, for the convenience of the eye, the commissioners are:

Ratio.	Presbyteries.	Commissioners.
1— 20	72	72× 1 = 72
20— 40	67	67× 2 = 134
40— 60	28	28× 4 = 112
60— 80	5	5× 6 = 30
80—100	0	0× 8 = 00
100—120	0	0×10 = 00
120—140	1	1×12 = 12
	173	360

This estimate reduces the General Assembly to 300 commissioners.   Taking into consideration the usual proportion of vacancies, occasioned by the non-appearance of elected commissioners, these figures make as large a reduction as it is discreet to make, at least at the outset.

In order to clear the way of all embarrassments, let it now be shown that this plan is equally favorable to all, and, therefore, so thoroughly in equity, throughout our bounds, that no objection appears which can bear the test of an impartial examination.

About the only objection may lie in the unwillingness of some presbyteries to fall into any plan which limits them to one commissioner.   And almost the first thought in some minds, searching for equality, will be equality in territory.

The following table will show how these 72 presbyteries are located :

LOCATION OF SEVENTY-TWO PRESBYTERIES, WITH ONE COMMISSIONER EACH.

The Synod of Atlantic includes North and South Carolina, Georgia, and Florida, with its six presbyteries.

The Synod of Tennessee covers the State, with its three.

The Synod of Kentucky covers the State, with its three.

The Synod of Michigan covers the State, and has four.

The Synod of Pacific covers five States, and has four.

The Synod of Minnesota covers the State, and has four.

The Synod of Nebraska covers the State, with its three.

The Synod of Colorado covers the State, and has three.

The Synod of Wisconsin covers the State, and has two.

The Synod of Missouri covers the State, and has two.

The Synod of Kansas covers the State, and has one.

The one in Indiana is in its northern Synod.

The two presbyteries in Iowa, are one in the northern and one in the southern Synod.

The six presbyteries in Ohio, are one in the Synod of Cincinnati, three in the Synod of Columbus, and two in the Synod of Toledo.

The four presbyteries in Pennsylvania, are two in the Synod of Erie, one in that of Harrisburg, and one in the Synod of Pittsburg.

The seven presbyteries in New York, are two in the Synod of Albany, three in that of Geneva, and two in the Synod of Western New York.

The sixteen presbyteries in foreign lands are divided among South America, Africa, India, Persia, Siam, and China.

It will be seen that there is no concentration in any one locality of a large proportion of these 72 presbyteries. Nor are they in undue proportion in the newer synods.   For, by analyzing the above statement, it will be found that Missouri, Wisconsin, and Iowa have together the same number of presbyteries in this class as Florida, Georgia, South and North Carolina have together. Pennsylvania has the same number, four, which Michigan, Tennessee, Minnesota, and the Synod of California have each. Ohio has the same number, six, which runs through Florida, Georgia, South and North Carolina ; and the same which Missouri, Wisconsin, and Iowa have combined ; or the same as Nebraska and Colorado combined ; or as Colorado and Kentucky united. New York has as many, seven, las either Colorado, Nebraska, or Kentucky combined with either Michigan, Tennessee, Minesota, California, or Pennsylvania. So that the weak need not look with envy upon the strong, but should make due account of his own strength.

It will now be shown that so many of these presbyteries are either in foreign countries, or in such remote parts of our own land, or, for some reason sufficient to themselves, are so not disposed to enjoy their full privileges, that this proposed change to one commissioner for each of them is but the continuance, in legal form, of what a large share of them have been doing ; because, substantially,

THEIR AVERAGE PRACTICE IS TO SEND ONE COMMISSIONER.

The minutes of 1875 show that 38 of these presbyteries sent that year 76 commissioners, and 19 sent 19, and 15 sent no commissioners at all. The whole 72 voluntarily limited themselves to 95 commissioners. These 95 being equally distributed among the 72 presbyteries, give a voluntary average representation of a fraction less than 1 1-3 commissioners to each presbytery.

Making the same kind of calculation for the whole period of re-union since the presbyteries were consolidated, we find for the years 1871-2, 3, 4, 5, that this class of presbyteries has sent a voluntary average representation for the five years of 1.35 commissioners to each presbytery. Therefore, for a series of years, the general average practice of the presbyteries, which have twenty ministers and less, is, substantially, to send one commissioner from each presbytery.

So that the relinquishment in law of one commissioner by each of these 72 presbyteries for the adoption of a plan for the general welfare of the church, is a matter of such small practical average consequence to them, that they can heartily adopt this plan to obtain necessary relief from overgrowth.

Let us now see how this gradation will approximate

AN EQUABLE REPRESENTATION OF MINISTERS.

The six presbyteries in the Synod of Atlantic number only 44 ministers. According to the present system, they have a representation in the Assembly of 2 for each presbytery, or, 12, while the same rule, working on a single presbytery, requires it to grow to 49, or five more than their 44, before it can double its commissioners from 2 to 4. So that, while these 44 scattered presbyteries represent in the General Assembly by 12, the presbytery of Alton, Illinois, with the same number, 44, represents by only 4, which is two-thirds less ; and these Atlantic presbyteries of 44 ministers send the very same number, 12, that the presbytery of New York sends for its 125 ministers.

According to this proposed plan of grading for representation by scores, these 44 ministers, divided into six presbyteries of 9, 9, 8, 8, 6 and 4 ministers, will send six commissioners. This will give them one commissioner for every seven and four-twelfths ($7\frac{4}{12}$) ; ministers and New York's 125 will send one commissioner for every ten and five-twelfths ($10\frac{5}{12}$) ministers.

The smaller presbyteries will yet have much the advantage, but since as they now have one commissioner for every three and eight-twelfths (3 8-12) ministers, they will, by the new plan, approximate an equal rate of representation by the difference between their present rate and the proposed one, which is $7\frac{4}{12}-3\frac{8}{12}-3\frac{8}{12}$. The approximation is within the smallest fraction of being one half ($\frac{1}{2}$) nearer an equal representation than it is now.

These six presbyteries of the Synod of Atlantic faithfully represent the class of presbyteries which ranges from 3 to 10 ministers. And we may include two of those presbyteries which number 11, and still have a corresponding ratio. With these latter two there are in the aggregate 240 ministers in 33 presbyteries. This gives an average of one commissioner for between every $7\frac{3}{12}$ and $7\frac{4}{12}$ ministers; which varies less than $\frac{1}{2}$ from the average of the six presbyteries of Atlantic Synod, with which we compared the presbytery of New York. We may add to them the three remaining presbyteries with 11, and then vary from the same ratio by only 3-12, since the 36 presbyteries aggregate 273 ministers, and that gives one commissioner for every $7\frac{1}{2}$ ministers.

But when we take 36 presbyteries, we have made this favorable comparison with full one-half of the 72 presbyteries which range from 20 ministers downward. This is the more satisfactory, because the glaring inequality of the present representation has been most complained of against these smallest presbyteries.

If we canvass the whole class of those with from 20 ministers downward, and inquire for the status of the remaining 36 presbyteries, which rise from 12 to 20, we find that their aggregate number of ministers is 609. This gives them an average representation of one commissioner for every $16\frac{11}{12}$ ministers. This in a measure strikes a fair balance between the advantage which the very smallest presbyteries, from 3 to 11 ministers, have over the largest, and the disadvantage which the other half of the small presbyteries, from 12 to 20 ministers, have beside the largest presbyteries; for while the largest will average $10\frac{5}{12}$ ministers for one commissioner, this upper half of these small presbyteries will require an average of $16\frac{11}{12}$ ministers for one commissioner.

The equilibrium is thus as nearly reached as can ever be maintained in a body, which, from its very nature, must be somewhat variable.

All that is necessary to note in reference to the mutual relations of the higher classes of presbyteries is, that this change continues an equal representation among them for a certain number of ministers. Since the size of the classes is diminished by drawing the lines in from 24 to 20, and from 48 to 40, there will be less space for inequalities, and, of necessity, a general improvement.

HOW EQUABLY IT REPRESENTS THE COMMUNICANTS.

[A.] *In the seventy-two presbyteries, which run from* 20 *ministers downward :*

	Ministers.	Commun'ts.		Ministers.	Commun'ts.
Atlantic	9	2,290	Knox	8	1,016
Catawb	9	1,895	Yadkin	8	2,348
E. Florida	6	147	Portsmouth	20	3,418
Fairfield	4	1,193	Athens	20	1,817

	Ministers	Commun'ts		Ministers.	Commun'ts.
Columbus	19	2,623	Utah	6	91
Marion	14	2,003	Benicia	18	756
Huron	20	2,268	Los Angelos	11	402
Lima	11	1,849	Sacramento	19	909
Butler	18	3,021	San José	17	791
Clarion	17	2,978			
Wellsboro'	13	799	Chippewa	10	744
West Virginia	17	1,697	Lake Superior	8	519
Muncie	15	1,809	Holston	11	863
			Kingston.	9	1,072
Ebenezer	18	2,141	New Orleans	5	134
Louisville	20	2,370	Union	14	1,493
Transylvania	14	1,118	Siam	9	46
Fort Dodge	12	949	Rio de Janeiro	8	543
Council Bluffs	20	1,552	Canton	6	145
Grand Rapids	19	1,303	Japan	5	47
Kalamazoo	16	1,840	Ningpo	14	492
Lansing	19	1,771	Peking	7	20
Monroe	18	2249	Shanghai	8	92
Champlain	19	1,612	Shantung	7	341
Columbia	16	2,031	Ozark	13	895
Chemung	20	1,797	Potosi	7	287
Lyons	17	1,866			
Steuben	17	1,856	Kearney	8	314
Genesee	20	2,303	Nebraska City	15	1,033
Genesee Valley	11	934	Omaha	14	452
Dakota	11	775	Allahabad	8	133
Mankato	17	911	Furrukhabad	7	160
Southern Minnesota	15	707	Kolapoor	5	32
Winona	15	750	Lahore	10	102
Austin	6	414	Lodiana	9	127
			Corisco	6	202
Montana	3	78	Western Africa	6	240
Santa Fe	3	68	Oroomiah	8	767

Before we analyze this table, we must remember that, from
the nature of the case, we cannot form any plan which will show
that for a certain number of ministers there must of necessity
be a fixed number of conversions every year; and then, that
this number must be increased beyond the natural limit in some
localities to compensate for deaths and removals, and also
restrained below its natural limit, where there are no removals,
and death is tardy. There is no such machine movement in
God's grace toward his church. And yet, while God does not
bind himself to such mathematical progression, it is a remarkable fact, which an acquaintance with these tables will illustrate, that while he allows wide range for exceptions, he has so
associated labor with growth as to make the workmen a fair
index of the harvest; or, in other words, the number of work

men and the number of population in one place being about equal to the workmen and population in another place, the number of communicants follows pretty closely on after a similar equality.

Reminding ourselves again that we are not to look for an iron rule of exact conformity, we may be struck with the approximate equality between certain limits which this distribution by scores gives.

Now, analyzing this table, we find that the communicants of the several presbyteries are enclosed by the numbers, one hundred (100), and two thousand six hundred and twenty-three (2,623), with the small exceptions of three cases above and eight below. Then, to reduce the exceptions legitimately, one of the three above needs but one minister to pass the communicants with their presbytery into the higher class, leaving but two; and two of the eight exceptions below need but nine and eight communicants to bring them within the limit of one hundred (100); leaving, beyond a reasonable doubt, within the year, but eight exceptions to 72 presbyteries, including their communicants within a range of twenty-five hundred (2,500); and four of these eight are in India, China, Siam, and Japan.

[B.] *In the sixty-seven presbyteries, with from 20 to 40 ministers :*

	Ministers.	Commun'ts.
Baltimore	40	4,708
Washington	29	3,409
Syracuse	38	4,567
Binghamton	35	3,811
Otsego	30	3,035
St. Lawrence	26	3,535
Cayuga	32	2,817
Geneva	37	4,381
Long Island	21	2 864
Nassau	31	2,345
Niagara	21	2,407
		29,762
Detroit	37	4,012
Saginaw	28	2,002
Chillicothe	28	3,339
Mahoning	30	3,801
St. Clairsville	26	5,287
Steubenville	35	6,067
Wooster	32	4,196
Zanesville	29	3,585
Bellefontaine	21	2,311

	Ministers.	Commun'ts.
Maumee	27	2,444
		31,030
Peoria	37	3,668
Schuyler	40	4,072
Springfield	36	4,108
Freeport	33	2,999
Ottawa	27	1,742
Rock River	34	2,977
Cairo	32	2,285
Mattoon	36	3,124
		24,975
Crawfordsville	38	4,006
Fort Wayne	22	2,393
Logansport	23	2,498
Indianapolis	40	5,415
New Albany	31	4,317
Vincennes	24	2,624
White Water	22	2,732
		23,985

	Ministers.	Commun'ts.		Ministers.	Commun'ts
Emporia	25	1,337	Jersey City	37	3,765
Highland	28	1,424	Monmouth	39	3,932
Neosho	30	1,786	Morris and Orange	40	5,926
Topeka	31	2,170			
					13,623
		6,717	Cedar Rapids	28	2,204
			Dubuque	23	1,962
Oregon	24	1,486	Waterloo	23	1,469
San Francisco	29	2,490	Des Moines	29	2,653
			Iowa	30	3,502
Saint Paul	35	2,371	Iowa City	29	2,899
Colorado	23	1,128			
					14,689
Alleghany	36	4,770			
Kittaning	29	5,550	Milwaukee	31	2,048
Shenango	25	4,161	Winnebago	21	1,384
Northumberland	34	5,097	Wisconsin River	26	2,027
Westminster	28	4,222			
Blairsville	28	4,212			5,459
Redstone	24	3,476	Osage	26	1,732
Washington	32	6,054	Palmyra	24	1,694
			Platte	24	1,659
		37,532			
					5,085

There is more encroachment here on the class below and on the class above, than in any other place. By allowing this class to lap over the class below by 600, we shall find that only 12 presbyteries fall under 2,000 communicants. Making 4,500 the higher extreme, which gives a range equal to the first class of 2,500, there are but 8 presbyteries whose communicants exceed it. Of those below, one requires but 38 communicants to make the 2,000. Of those above, two require but one minister each to raise them with their communicants into the next class, leaving 17 which encroach both ways.

But there is another standard of measure which is worth applying here as an index of equilibrium. Take the population into account, and we will then see there is a remarkable nearness of communicants in the States of the same size and density. Thus, New York and Ohio have respectively 29,762 and 31,030 communicants in this class, a difference of only 1,268; and Pennsylvania has 37,532. Indiana and Illinois, which have grown up together, have 23,985 and 24,975; the difference is less than 1,000 communicants. Iowa and New Jersey have 14,689 and 13,623. So Kansas and Michigan have 6,717 and 6,014. Again, Missouri and Wisconsin have 5,085 and 5,459; while the Pacific wants but 24 communicants to reach the 4,000.

The lowest in the scale is Colorado. But the Synod of
Colorado was not organized until October, 1874.

[C.] *In the twenty-eight presbyteries, with from* 40 *to* 60
ministers :

	Ministers.	Commun'ts.		Ministers.	Commun'ts.
Albany	51	7,530	Huntingdon	48	8,728
Troy	51	5,860	Chester	43	4,766
Utica	57	5,430	Lehigh	45	4,352
Brooklyn	49	9,509	Philadelphia	59	10,601
Boston	43	3,138	Phila., Central	58	9,636
Hudson	45	5,648	Philadelphia, North	42	5,193
North River	47	4,580	Bloomington	45	4,186
Westchester	55	5,010	Alton	44	4,008
Buffalo	48	4,928	St. Louis	43	3,857
Rochester	60	7,659	Elizabeth	50	5,678
Dayton	42	5,889	Newark	43	5,603
Cleveland	47	4,223	Newton	41	4,661
New Castle	48	5,188	West Jersey	44	4,290
Carlisle	52	5,696	New Brunswick	59	6,036

Letting this class lap over the one below by only 500, there
are here but two presbyteries which fall below 4,000 communicants ; and one of these wants but 143 communicants to bring
it within that number.

Making 6,000 the higher extreme, there are seven varying
numbers beyond it. Of these, one lacks but one minister in its
presbytery to raise it into the class above; and to make the
same transfer, two of these exceptions need only two ministers
each ; leaving but four which may remain long outside the
the lines; and, indeed, one of these, being in Philadelphia, may
very soon make up its three, and pass above with the mother
presbytery, with which it keeps such an even pace, both in
ministers and communicants.

If, however, we rise by 2,500, as we have done in the preceding classes, there will be but *four* which vary from 4,000 to
6,500; and these figures give more of a margin for these communicants in company with the usual growth of the ministry.

[D]. *In the five presbyteries, with from* 60 *to* 80 *ministers:*

	Ministers.	Commun'ts.		Ministers.	Commun'ts.
Cincinnati	64	6,256	Lackawana	75	6,727
Erie	65	6,949	Pittsburgh	61	8,118
		Chicago	74	6,926	

If, with these communicants, we take the limits of 6,000 and
8,500—the same rise of 2,500—there is no encroachment above
and but one from below. Yet, since we may allow 500 for a

margin of rise to the class below, and still very much increase the higher limit without any collision, and avoid the single encroachment below, we may take as the boundaries, 6,500 and 12,000, to accommodate the presbyteries of Philadelphia and Philadelphia Central, so soon as they obtain their increase of two and three ministers, to entitle them to the transfer. This rise of boundary line will require one of this class to make the accession of only 244 communicants to conform it to the line; and the density and rapid increase of its population will very soon yield them.

It may be said here, that the presbyteries of Philadelphia are an anomaly in any general scheme, since they are not one body to cover a city. If, like that of New York, they were one, they would form a class by themselves, beyond New York, both in ministers and communicants, having 159 ministers and 25,430 communicants, with 14 commissioners to the General Assembly. And as that class has its ministry run 140–160, united Philadelphia lacks by this plan of scores but two ministers to give them the same number of commissioners (16) which they send now as three presbyteries.

Referring once more to the above table, it is worthy of notice how this class, which is represented by increased commissioners, is evenly distributed through the church territorially. Three of these presbyteries lie in what may be called the East, and two in the West.

[E]. *In the one presbytery, with from 120 to 140 ministers :*

	Ministers.	Communicants.
New York	125	15,886

There are no presbyteries with from 80 to 100 ministers. There are none with from 100 to 120 ministers. When we reach the presbytery of New York, we have these two intermediate scores to represent for—and the highest score will have for its class a representation of five ministers and five elders. Hence New York's commissioners by this scheme of scores will be six ministers and six elders, or twelve; the same number which that presbytery has under the present arrangement.

The result shows how singularly equitable this plan of distribution by scores is. The ministers in the presbytery of New York are almost exactly double those of each of the presby-

teries [D] which have half as many commissioners, excepting
two nearly in the higher class, and the communicants of the
presbytery of New York are but a little more than double the
communicants of each of these presbyteries but one, and only
350 less than double that one. So that there appears to be a
very even average growth of both ministers and communicants by scores.

Let us now see how this plan secures

FREEDOM FROM EARLY RE-ADJUSTMENT.

The probabilities are, that the church will grow with less rapidity in the more densely populated parts of the country,
because if the maximum of population is not nearly reached,
the excess of development within their power beyond their
present census will come more slowly than what they have
hitherto gained, and the growth in the newer States, it may
properly be supposed, will continue to follow the same slow-
ness of increase by which it has been marked, aside from exceptional cases, for which allowance must always be made.

This statement will prove advantageous to any plan of gradation on which a system of representation may be based.
But it may be of greater advantage in some one system of
gradation than in any other. And, so far as any proposed
plan has shown, this plan of scores contains that greater advantage, because

1. It starts from the reasonable figures of 360 for a General
Assembly; and

2. These five different classes of ministers, from which the
commissioners are drawn, so generally lie well defined that
there will be no rapid transition of large numbers into higher
classes.

Hence the increase of commissioners to the General Assembly will be so gradual as to restrain it from rapid increase. And
it is a matter of the same prime importance to keep the numbers of the Assembly within reasonable bounds, as it is to reduce it now.

By an analysis of these several tables, we find that in the first
class of 72 presbyteries there are seven which have 20 ministers each, and hence want but one minister each to give each
presbytery an additional commissioner; and five which have
19 ministers each, and want two ministers each to increase

their commissioners ; and four presbyteries will have 18 minis-ters each, the scale descending rapidly and low. From these 72 presbyteries we can look for but seven commissioners as an early addition, and a further addition of five in the remote future.

In the second class of 67 presbyteries, there are four which have 40 ministers each, and want but one minister each to give each presbytery two additional commissioners; and but one presbytery with 39 ministers, which lacks two ministers to increase its commissioners; and there are only two presby-teries as near the line as 38 ministers. From these 67 presby-teries we can look for but eight commissioners as an early ad-dition, and a further addition of two in the remote future.

In the third class of 28 presbyteries, there is one which has 60 ministers, and wants but one minister to give it two ad-ditional commissioners ; and but two presbyteries with 59 min-isters each, which lack two ministers each to increase their commissioners ; and only one presbytery as near the line as 58. From these 28 presbyteries we can look for but two commis-sioners as an early addition, and a further addition of four in the remote future.

In the fourth class of five presbyteries, the largest presby-tery must add six ministers to warrant any increase of its com-missioners ; while in the fifth class of one presbytery, there is the lack of 16 ministers to entitle it to any increase in its commissioners.

Collecting these figures representing the increase of com-missioners, which we must calculate on, we have by this plan of scores

```
General Assembly (reduced to)..........................360
Probable near increase from first class.................... 7
    "        "        "    second class ................ 8
    "        "        "    third class .................. 2
                                                        ____
                                                        377
```

Or, looking further ahead, we have

```
General Assembly (reduced to).........................360
Probable remote increase from first class................. 12
    "        "        "    second class .............. 10
    '        "        "    third class................ 6
                                                        ____
                                                        388
```

It is thus apparent that this plan allows ample ground for growth before that growth will become burdensome. And further, all things considered, it appears to be the most desirable plan of reduction which has been developed for the consideration of the church, for the following reasons :

1. It gives a moderate figure for the General Assembly at the outset—360.

The last General Assembly sent down an overture to start beyond 380; and the committee on church polity recommended an overture which would begin a General Assembly with 392. It is only that fitness of things commending itself to every one which thus gives expression to the general belief, that the dignity of the Assembly will not permit it to fall numerically below a Synod; the last minutes of the Synod of New Jersey report members present, 316.

2. It gives a system which continues the distribution of commissioners, with but a single exception, as they are now distributed; and hence lies so nearly in the old paths that but a portion of the presbyteries are thrown out of their accustomed mode of reckoning, by a minister and an elder.

3. It does not strain the system of representation to create that exception, but discovers an existing and average working exception, which it desires to secure against the possibilities of a variable quantity, and fix as a certainly constant quantity by a legal form,

4. It finds such a large portion of the exception in the older and stronger States, that the younger and weaker States have the excepted presbyteries generously shared with them.

5. It so classifies the presbyteries, that those which have an appearance to the casual observer of excessive representation are so far behind the extreme limit which would entitle them to more, that the future increase will mainly come from the gradual development of the smaller presbyteries.

6. It makes a just distinction between the smaller presbyteries on our own soil, and those on foreign soil. In order that the General Assembly shall continue to " consist as nearly as possible of an equal number of bishops and elders," it requires the smaller home presbyteries to alternate their commissioners between a minister and an elder. In order to avoid binding them up to an impossibility, it excepts the smaller foreign presbyteries from rigid alternation. The equity of this liberty will be seen by looking over the min-

utes for successive years, to find that when our foreign presbyteries send commissioners they always send a minister,
and to require them to alternate between a minister and an
elder would practically exclude them from one-half their representation ; because, in foreign fields they have not the
proper English-speaking material for eldership to send.

7. It makes the present approximate equality of representation very much more nearly equable, and hence fulfills Paul's
injunction to the Philippians—ii : 4 : " Look not every man on
his own things, but every man also on the things of others."

8. It associates an equable relation of communicants with
this equable representation of ministers, so that communicants
and their presbyteries, taken together, exhibit a common relation to the presbyterial representation. This is strikingly evident in the class of presbyteries and communicants marked
[D.] While our method of representation has never been based
on any reference to this, it is nevertheless desirable to consider it an advantage where it naturally accompanies a distribution which is consonant with established usage.

9. It secures the General Assembly from a sudden expansion, and holds it to such a gradual growth, that this system is
not likely to require a change for a long time to come.

We have been working on our present grade of 24 and 48
since 1833, which is 44 years. There are but 23 years to the
close of this century—and if this plan will carry us there, it
will have done a good work. But if any one has such an insight into the future development of the church as to enable
him to say positively that his plan will not last so long, we can
still say that we need a good system of reduction immediately,
and that this is not only shown to be an excellent plan, but it
gives a good prospect of continuing effective for at least a
reasonable time.

Moreover, by reference to the dates of the changes of the
ratio of representation, the earlier changes were made more
frequently. The first change was made in 1819, and the next
in 1826, running only seven years ; the next change in 1833,
another seven years. So that heretofore it has been found expedient to change so soon as there was an imperative call
for it.

If the suggestion is made, that an expected union with the

Presbyterian Church South should defer a new basis of representation, it is yet true that the present emergency requires an immediate reduction of numbers, which should not be uncomfortably carried under a constant protest up to the point of union, when, humanly speaking, the union is so largely prospective. If that union is ever consummated—which we·sincerely desire at the right time—no present change can possibly interfere with a free and full consideration of that new state of things which will then call for a new adjustment.

Therefore, let the General Assembly be overtured, " Shall the Form of Government, chapter xii, section ii, be changed to read thus : ʻThe General Assembly shall consist, as nearly as possible, of an equal number of bishops and elders, chosen by the presbyteries in the following manner, viz. : Each presbytery consisting of not more than twenty ministers shall send one representative, who must be alternately a minister and an elder, from the first half of these presbyteries in alphabetical order, and alternately an elder and a minister from the second half in alphabetical order—except that each such foreign presbytery may send a minister or an elder ; and each presbytery consisting of more than twenty ministers shall send one minister and one elder ; and each presbytery consisting of more than forty ministers shall send two ministers and two elders ; and in the like proportion of one minister and one elder for every additional twenty ministers in any presbytery, and these delegates so appointed shall be styled, Commissioners to the General Assembly.'"

NOTE.

The Minutes of 1875 have been used throughout, because this paper was written before the Minutes for 1876 were published. The relation of the presbyteries in the meanwhile has changed to the following extent, viz. : Pp. 75 and 76 of the last Minutes show that the General Assembly granted the request of the presbytery of Oregon, as indicated by Overture No. 6, and erected a new synod, under the name of the Synod of Columbia, with three presbyteries, Oregon, Puget Sound, and South Oregon. There will now seem to be three more presbyteries to call for representation. But since these three will fall within the exception of the present plan, they will each send one commissioner, and increase the Assembly by three. However, instead of this case of expansion bringing three new presbyteries, it divides the original presbytery of Oregon into these three ; therefore it makes only two new ones. Moreover, it does not even increase the General Assembly by two commissioners, because, by our plan, the old presbytery was entitled to two, and in this divided state to but one; which leaves them three against their former two, an united increase of only one.

But p. 77 of the same Minutes states, that "The presbytery of Southern Minnesota has been disbanded." This counterbalances the increase of the Assembly by the one commissioner from Oregon, and leaves the number as it stands in our calculation from the Minutes of 1875.

Art. IV.—PROFESSOR HENRY BOYNTON SMITH.

By Marvin R. Vincent, New York.

THE lesson of consecrated intellect is one which needs to be emphasized in the hearing of this age. The current sentiment of our time tends altogether too strongly to regard the possession of great mental endowments and broad culture, as the best of reasons for *despising* faith, and for withholding consecration from all but selfish ends. When, therefore, a representative scholar and thinker gives faith the first place in his life, and holds that knowledge

"Is the second, not the first;"

that

"A higher hand must make her mild,
 If all be not in vain; and guide
 Her footsteps, moving side by side
 With wisdom, like the younger child ; "

when faith is the light of his learning and the master-key of his logic, it is well to tell the story to those who habitually group faith with weakness, and consecration with fanaticism. It is well for such to know that thought so vigorous and far-reaching, culture so finely toned, and energy so effectively guided, have taken their mightiest impulse and their warmest glow from the gospel of Jesus Christ.

Such a lesson is the life of him in whom our church has been so lately called to mourn the loss of her foremost scholar—HENRY BOYNTON SMITH.

Professor Smith was born in Portland, Maine, on the 21st

of November, 1815. He completed his collegiate studies at Bowdoin College in 1834, and was appointed tutor almost immediately upon his graduation. His theological studies were begun at Bangor and Andover. While at Bangor, his first article appeared in the *Maine Monthly Magazine*, for August, 1836, in the shape of a review of a shallow pamphlet, by one Lieutenant Roswell Park, entitled *Outline of Philosophy*. The "Outline" was an ambitious attempt at a scientific classification of human knowledge; and the title-page was adorned with the picture of a tree, in which this classification was embodied under the figure of branches labeled Periphysics, Geotics, Prostheotics, Perichronics, etc. In the same year appeared an article from his pen in the *Literary and Theological Review*, edited by Dr. Leonard Woods, Jr., on Moral Reform Societies. In the student's vigorous handling of these themes, it is not difficult to detect the germinal characteristics of the riper scholar. In the impatience of false method, the ready detection of fallacy, the facility of dissection, and the fine, genial humor, are foreshadowed the reviewer of Strauss. The latter of the two articles is noticeable for its exposure of the subtle error which lurks in so many later schemes of reform—the assumption of the insufficiency of the gospel for its own peculiar work.

The studies begun at Andover and Bangor were continued at Berlin and Halle. His intellect, naturally large of grasp and broad in its ideal of culture, found its true and congenial place in the atmosphere of German scholarship; and those later studies confirmed and developed that breadth of scope, that critical accuracy, that laborious patience in study, which made him the admiration of even German thinkers, and which marked him the more strongly from their comparative rarity among the American students of that day.

His estimate of German theology, formed from his personal contact with its best exponents, was singularly discriminating. Not blind to its defects, his whole generous nature went out in sympathy with the struggle through which it was taking shape in the minds of " the most philosophical and the most Christian scholars of Germany." His appreciation and his sympathy alike found expression in his address before the Porter Rhetorical Society of Andover, in 1849: " In the name of the repub-

lic of letters, in the name of all generous scholarship, in the
very name of Christian charity, I dare not refrain from testifying, that the indiscriminate censure of all that is German, or
that may so be called, is a sign rather of the power of prejudice than of a rational love for all truth.   A criticism which
describes a circumference of which one's ignorance is the gen-
erating radius, can only stretch far beyond the confines of
justice and of wisdom.   A criticism which begins by saying,
that a system is absolutely unintelligible ; which, secondly, asserts that this unintelligible system teaches the most frightful
dogmas, definitely drawn out ; and which concludes by holding it responsible for all the consequences that a perverse
ingenuity can deduce from these definite dogmas of the unintelligible system, is, indeed, a source of unintelligent and anxious wonder to the ignorant, but it is a profounder wonder
to every thoughtful mind.   A criticism which includes the
Christian Neander and the pantheistic Strauss in one and the
same condemnation is truly deplorable.   Let us at least learn
to adopt the humane rules of civilized warfare, and not, like
the brutal soldiery of a ruder age, involve friends and foes in
one indiscriminate massacre.   *Germany cannot give us faith ;*
and he who goes there to have his doubts resolved, goes into
the very thick of the conflict *in a fruitless search for its results ;* but even Germany may teach us what is the real ' state
of the controversy ' in our age ; *what are the principles now at
work more unconsciously among ourselves.*   And can we, in our
inglorious intellectual ease, find it in our hearts only to condemn the men who have overcome trials and doubts to which
our simple or iron faith has never been exposed ; who have
stood in the very front rank of the fiercest battle that Christianity has ever fought, and there contended hand to hand
with its most inveterate and wary foes, and who are leading
on our faith—as we trust in Christ so will we believe it !—to the
sublimest triumph it has ever celebrated ?"

His relations with the leaders of German philosophy and theology were those of an associate rather than of a student. The German language was thoroughly at his command; not only in its
colloquialisms, but throughout its enormous literary and philosophic vocabulary, and he communed with the giants as one of
themselves.   At Halle, Tholuck and Ulrici, in whose family he

resided, were his intimate friends.   Both regarded him with the utmost affection and admiration; and with both he maintained a correspondence for many years after his return to America. At Berlin he won the high esteem of Neander and Hengstenberg.   One who studied with him says: "Probably but few young Americans have ever adapted themselves more readily to German ways, been so generally popular, or gone deeper into German thought and German theology."

In 1842 he became the pastor of the Congregational Church of West Amesbury, Massachusetts, where he continued for five years in the most happy and affectionate relations with his people.   During two years of this time, in addition to his pastoral work, he discharged the duties of Hebrew professor at Andover Seminary, besides furnishing a number of articles for the reviews, most of which were translations from the German.   Among these were Harless on the Structure of Matthew's Gospel; Lasaulx on the Expiatory Sacrifices of the Greeks and Romans; Twesten on the Doctrine of Angels; A Sketch of German Philosophy; Twesten on the Trinity; and a review of Hagenbach's History of Doctrines.   But though greatly beloved by his people, and faithful to the work of feeding the flock of God, his destiny was evidently not the pastorate.   His pre-eminent qualifications for the work of an instructor, and his own strong predilection for literary work and Christian research, pointed him another way, and in 1847 he accepted the appointment of Professor of Mental and Moral Philosophy in Amherst College, remaining there until, at the end of three years, the Union Theological Seminary of New York, under protest from the college, called him to its chair of Church History.

Here he may be said to have entered upon the great work of his life.   In his later days he said, "My life has been given to the Seminary;" and it is with Union Seminary that his name will be permanently identified.   He commenced his duties with an inaugural address on "The Nature and Worth of the Science of Church History," which commanded the admiration of Christian scholars throughout the land, by its rare breadth, power, and brilliancy.   It revealed, distinctly confessed, indeed, the influence of Neander in shaping his conception of church history, besides betraying his clear discernment of the lack of the true historic spirit in America, and of the consequent misconception and depreciation of church history in particular, by American students. Under the spur of this error, he set himself to bring up church history from the rear into the first rank of historical study. The key-note of his lectures was, "church history is the true philosophy of human history," or, as he eloquently put it in his inaugural address: "He who would reach forth his hand to grasp the solemn urn that holds the oracles of human fate, can find it only in the Christian church." Such a 'conception was in itself magnetic, and when urged by his profound enthusiasm, delineated with his wonderful power of crystalline statement, and illustrated by his copious learning, it is no wonder that it evoked a corresponding enthusiasm in his students. Much of the work of his pen was expended in this direction, notably upon his "History of the Church of Christ in Chronological Tables," issued in 1859, a marvel of condensed knowledge and accurate classification. His lecture on "The Problem of the Philosophy of History" was delivered before the Phi Beta Kappa Society, at Yale College, in 1853, and his address on "The Reformed Churches of Europe and America, in relation to General Church History," before the General Assembly at St. Louis, in 1855; while for some years before his death he had been engaged upon the translation and revision of Gieseler's Church History.

So closely intertwined in his studies was church history with theology, that his transfer, in 1855, to the chair of systematic theology, could scarcely be called a change. In both chairs he taught theology, and in both church history. In his view, neither could be successfully studied without the other. The cross was the key to both sciences. Christ was the focal point of human history, and "the mediatorial principle the centre of unity, by the light of which all parts of theology could be best arranged." The theologian was to be "an interpreter of history, and of revelation in the light of history." "The most diligent investigation of Christian history," he says, on assuming the chair of theology, "is one of the best incentives to the wisest study of Christian theology. The plan of God is the substance of both; for all historic time is but a divine theodicy; God's providence is its

law, God's glory is its end.   Theology divorced from history
runs out into bare abstractions; history separated from theology becomes naturalistic or humanitarian merely.   The
marriage of the two makes theology more real and history to
be sacred   .   .   .   All history and all theology meet in the
person of the God-man, our Saviour.   The life of history and
the light of theology should ever go together; as an early
Christian apologist said : 'Life is not real without knowledge,
nor is knowledge safe without life; they must be planted together, like the trees of paradise.' "

That he should be an enthusiastic vindicator of *systematic*
theology was to be expected from the very structure of his
mind, which, though speculative, was intensely and severely
methodical.   Systematizing theology he regarded as the inevitable consequence of having anything to say consistently
and definitely in defence of Christianity.   His love and ven-
eration for Christian truth made him impatient of any feeble
or vague drawing of its lines, yet system in theology was, to
him, not the ingenious articulation of dead bones.   It was the
marshalling of living forces under the breath of the Spirit of
God.   He believed in formulas, but he insisted that no truth
should be held as a mere formula.

Hence his theology glowed with life and practical power.
His system, as we have already seen, was historic in its basis
and method; historic as against "the resolution of revelation
into intuitions," the attempt "to find the kingdom of God in
psychology."   A dogma was valuable to him, solely as the expression of " a fact of faith."   In his eye, "the historic reality
of Christianity was the basis of Christian theology, as the
valid being of nature is pre-supposed by the naturalist."

The living thrill of historic development, therefore, pervaded
his theology.   Far from slighting the past, he saw that the
roots of a true theology must be in the past; but he also saw
that the life of the roots must develop new forms in the branches : that all that is *essentially* true in the past, is *eternally*
true, and enters into the religious thought and life of the
present; but under conditions as different as those of the
root in the dark mould, and those of the swaying branches
and rustling leaves, and tinted blossoms, in the flooding sunlight of summer.

Christ, therefore, as the master motive of this *historic* progress, the under-lying theme of all its variations, necessarily held the central position in his *theological* system; and that not merely as a hero, a teacher, an example, a martyr, but as a *living mediator*. The-key note of the Christian dispensation was "God in Christ, *reconciling* the world unto himself." He laid the true Pauline emphasis on the—"*and him crucified*." He somewhere said—"*All* religion is *union* between man and God. The *Christian* religion is a *re-union*, a *re-instated* fellowship." As he saw in the repulsion between a sinful man and a holy God, "the highest moral antagonism of the universe," so he saw its final reconciliation only in the sacrificial death of Jesus Christ. "He is the centre of God's revelation and of man's redemption; of Christian doctrine and of Christian history; of conflicting sects and of each believer's faith; yea, of the very history of this our earth, Jesus Christ is the full, the radiant, the only centre, fitted to be such because he is the God-man and the Redeemer; Christ—Christ. He is the centre of the Christian system; and the doctrine respecting Christ is the heart of Christian theology."—(*Relations of Faith and Philosophy*).

The central position of this truth impressed him early in his career, and was itself an important force in directing his studies and in shaping his methods and ultimate statements. His review, in the Bibliotheca Sacra of 1849, of Dorner's "*Lehre von der Person Christi*," develops his profound sympathy with the author in his setting up of the historic manifestation of God in Jesus Christ, as the sole and sufficient antidote to the mythicism of Strauss, the pantheism of Hegel, and the gnostic idealism of Baur. He discerned no less clearly than Dorner himself, the inevitable convergence of the theologic conflict toward the person of Jesus; that "the whole Christian faith lives or dies, as ever of old, in all its other conflicts, with the doctrine of an incarnate Redeemer." Nay, more he saw that the negation of this truth could not stop, logically, short of pantheism. There is a terrible inflexibility in that utterance near the close of his review of Hagenbach's "History of Doctrines:" "The time is sweeping on when he who will not be a Christian, *must be a pantheist;* when he who does not find God in Christ, will find him only in the human race; when he

who does not love the human race for the sake of Christ, will
have no higher love than love to humanity."

It was the clear recognition of this truth which called out
his affectionate admiration of Schleiermacher, " the man much
misunderstood, who led the German theology in its returning
course to our Lord." While he disclaimed sympathy with his
numerous errors, he vindicated the sincerity and ardor of his
love to Christ, and his " invaluable service to the Christian
science of his native land in the time of its greatest need, by
making Christ and his redemption the centre of Christian theology."

The large historic element in his theology made it strongly
objective, yet not to the neglect of its subjective side.   While
he deprecated all attempts to commit Christianity to the cultivation of mere frames of feeling, to the definition of faith
" by its internal traits rather than by its objects," to the emphasizing of "trust rather than of God," to the defense of the
atonement " by its relations to us, and not by its relations to
God," he yet insisted that " this Christianity, so sublime as
an objective fact, becomes subjectively a renovating power—
the life of God in the soul of man—the mysterious consciousness of an unearthly presence in the soul." All theology translated itself ultimately into experience ; and he claimed this experimental character for New England theology pre-eminently,
asserting that it had always been held by the heart quite as
much as by the head. " We have not only *discussed*, we have
also *experienced*, almost everything."

His theology united philosophy and faith in beautiful proportion. He refused to admit the dilemma, " faith *or* philosophy." He substituted for it " faith *and* philosophy." He maintained that "philosophy and faith are set at variance only by
sin, and kept in discord only from not seeing Christ as he is.
Philosophy and faith"—(I continue the quotation from his
Inaugural of 1855)—"both are from God ; the one may descry
the end, and the other gives us the means ; the one states the
problems which the other solves ; philosophy shows us the
labyrinth, and Christ gives us the clue ; the former recognizes
the necessity of redemption, the latter gives us the redemption
itself. The two at variance ! . . . Only when philosophy
goes 'sounding on its dim and perilous way,' averting the

heart from him who of God is made unto us wisdom, as well
as, and because, righteousness and redemption. At variance!
Only as the light of the sun is at variance with the heat of the
sun, or as the light and heat of the great ruler of the day are
at variance with the lesser lights that rule the night. At variance! Only as redemption is at variance with sin, eternity with
time, the incarnation with the creation, and the God of grace
with the God of justice. At variance! Even and only as a true
answer is at variance with a solemn question, as the solution
of a problem is at variance with the problem itself; since all
that Christ proposes and does is to solve, in a practical, living
method, the absorbing problem of the relation of man to God,
and of sin to redemption." He himself was a remarkable illustration of the breadth of range which an intellect of the highest philosophic type can find within the realm of faith. Far
from being impatient of mysteries, he was "content with
miracles, and ready to accept mysteries." He was even foremost in asserting that "the Christian system has its ultimate
grounds beyond which thought cannot penetrate." There
were Horebs, far up in the thin atmosphere of his pure reason,
where he stood with unshod feet, "resting in that mysterious
awe which is essential to religion and inseparable from our
finite capacities."

To his students he was always interesting and stimulating,
by his breadth, his freshness, his vigor, and his clearness of
statement. He was a good illustration of the words of one
of his colleagues, that "power of statement is power of argument." He aimed to make them form their own views,
rather than passively to accept his. His object was to inaugurate a growth, and not to leave the mere impress of a
mould. He was a power through his personal character, no
less than through his knowledge and culture. He was not
magnetic to a stranger. Men grew rather than flashed into
personal sympathy with him; but they came to know, in no
long time, that his clear and vigorous brain was joined with
a most tender heart and a most helpful hand. His time, his
aid, his counsel were never grudged to his students, and not
a few have cause to remember, besides the help bestowed out
of his richly stored mind, other help out of resources in which
he was far from being as rich.

Amid the duties of his chair, his pen was busy with sermons, reviews, addresses on the themes of his special studies, the general interests of religious education, and the great questions of polity which were agitating the Presbyterian Church. He early revealed the qualities of a great reviewer. Rapidly but firmly he grasped the main positions of a book, stated them with the nicest precision, discerned at a glance their relations to other discussions of the same subject, as well as to the principles of the subject itself, and so fixed the true relative place and value of the volume. He knew *books* well, but he 'knew *subjects* even better; and it was his knowledge of subjects which imparted the chief value to his estimate of books. He knew, as few others did, whether a book was a real contribution to human thought, or a mere brilliant revamping of old rubbish. He was not imposed upon nor confused by the new dress of an old error, or of an old truth, but penetrated straight to the kernel through all the husks of verbiage or new terminology. His skill in detecting fallacy was only equaled by his felicity in exposing it. His exhaustive analysis made short work with defects of method. His sarcasm was like a Damascus blade, yet he was far removed from the littleness of the empirical critic, whose ideal of criticism exhausts itself in picking flaws. He was just and kindly to books as to men. If he could censure severely, he could also praise ; and he praised as one who delighted to find merit and truth, even in an antagonist's work.

His pen was not suffered to remain idle in the important controversies of the church, and his presence and counsel were in earnest request in the higher church judicatories. It was not that he swayed church assemblies with his eloquence, though he was at no loss for pithy, pungent speech on occasion ; not that he won the notoriety which so often attaches to inferior men of ready utterance. It was rather that he was behind so much of the formative sentiment of those bodies, with his clear, broad comprehension of issues, his readiness in detecting latent tendencies, and his unrivaled power of lucid statement. In such scenes he developed the statesmanlike qualities of his mind. He lighted as by an instinct on the real cleavage lines of parties. He detected latent divergence under apparent coherence. He read men accurately, and weighed them justly. He never moved forward until he knew his ground. As Moderator of the New School Assembly of 1864, in his ringing utterance on " Christian Union and Ecclesiastical Reunion;" by his vigorous vindication of the fidelity of the New School Church to the standards, after the presentation of the Re-union Plan of 1867; as delegate to the Philadelphia Convention of 1867, from which his modest little amendment of two lines to the second article of the Basis, went up into the Assembly of 1868, and became one of the strong strands of the bond of union; by his liberal, conciliatory, frank spirit, and his delicate Christian tact, he has associated his name indissolubly with that great crisis in the history of the American Presybterian Church. It is always true in the evolution of such great movements, that the masses of men do not know the points of power from which their thought is directed ; and only to the clearer seeing of another state shall there fully appear the equal honor due to him who lays the foundations in the silence of the deep trenches, with him who brings to its place the capstone with shoutings of " grace, grace unto it."

An attempt to describe the peculiar fibre and flavor of his character cannot get far beyond these words themselves. They express something too subtle for analysis, but none the less appreciable to those who were favored with his friendship. The whole man was most delicately and harmoniously strung. His atmosphere was that of truth and purity, no less than of culture. Culture was not a *veneering*, overlaying a shrunken and shriveled manhood. His manhood, in its moral robustness and compactness, was larger than his culture. Some men get all their quality from their culture. His culture took its finest quality from him. He reminded one of Goethe's words about Niebuhr: " *Niebuhr* war es eigentlich, und nicht die römische Geschichte was mich beschäftigte."

One would not naturally associate his slight frame, his delicate features, and his reserved, almost shy, bearing, with aggressive courage, yet there never was a braver man, nor a more positive man, in the best sense. He was indeed deliberate in reaching his conclusions, but his deliberation was that of a man who saw in a question more elements and wider relations than others. His caution was in the interest of truth, not of self. And what he thus illustrated in his own character, he heartily admired in others. Nothing called out his enthusiasm more than courage, wherever it showed itself. The very last time the writer saw him in conscious life, he dwelt admiringly upon the *pluck* of the Turk in facing Europe alone. He did not like compromises. He had little sympathy with the proverb, " In medio *tutissimus* ibis." His object was *truth*, not *safety*, and he believed that truth was always safer than half truth.

The strong traits of his intellect and character were illumined by the most exquisite sense of humor. No man was quicker to catch the fine flavor of the purest wit and of the most delicate satire; yet none more heartily enjoyed broad and genial humor. Fun which was thoroughly human, which appealed to his own nicely poised mind with quaint out-croppings of character, and odd groupings and disproportions of untutored speech; mirth which sprang spontaneously from simple, child-like happiness, were as welcome to him as fresh springs by the wayside, and evoked a quick response in the sparkle of his own kindly and delicate wit. Even toward the last, when his brain had yielded to disease, the quaint conceits of his partial delirium, and the exquisite oddity of some of his wandering utterances, would provoke a smile, even from those whose hearts were breaking at his bedside.

It has already appeared, from what has been written, that his native powers were of the highest order, and his culture of the broadest. His mind was severely analytical, seizing promptly the key to every intellectual position, holding it with a grasp which no sophistry could loosen, driving his thought, like a ploughshare, straight through the field of inquiry, and never swerving from the right line through fear of what the share might turn up. This is a dangerous quality in men whose strict logic moves in a narrow range of knowledge or of sympathy, but it was balanced in him by a grade of attainment and a breadth of outlook such as marked very few of his contemporaries. The range of his reading was immense, both in extent and variety. His great specialties, church history, theology, and philosophy, represented only a part of the field which his eager intellect traversed. He

talked on most subjects as though they were his specialties.
The whole range of religious thought, on its practical no less
than on its philosophic side, all the struggles of the human
intellect after God, their points of departure and their bearing, the labyrinthine windings of German thought, the last
developments of materialism, as related to man's origin and
destiny,'these, with the whole array of apolegetic lines, lay in
his mind like a map.   Added to these, taken in the swing of
larger studies, were the treasures of the classics, of poet, es-
sayist, and historian, to the lighter play of whose fancy, and
the picturesqueness of whose portraiture, he was no less
keenly alive than to the grim grapple of Kant or Hegel.   He
kept abreast with all great topics of popular interest, with
questions of education, politics, and religion, throughout
the world, as well as with the discussions of literature and
science.   A letter dated the day after his death, from Professor Park of Andover, contains the following words : " I do so
heartily regret that I failed to see him when I was in New
York twenty months ago.   I desired to ask him many questions, some of which he was the only man capable of answering.   I have this winter desired to propose some other questions to him ; and I do not know any man who can answer
them as well as he could.   In certain departments of study he
had traversed ground which few persons in this country had
ventured upon."

On these deep wells of his learning all might freely draw. If
one were really in want of information he would spare no
pains to give it.   If he did not, as was most usual, tell you
out of hand what you wanted to know, or where to find it, the
old common-place book would come down, literally crammed
and burdened with references ; and then, as he mentioned
book after book, and his memory began to kindle along the
old lines, he would pour forth a stream of talk, until one
scarcely knew whether to admire more the riches of his
thought and knowledge, or his charm in imparting them.   He
might have sat for Casaubon's portrait of Scaliger—"A man
who . . . had gathered up vast stores of uncommon lore.
And his memory had such a happy readiness, that, whenever
the occasion called for it, whether it were in conversation, or
whether he were consulted by letter, he was ready to bestow,

with lavish hand, what had been gathered by him in the sweat of his brow." Yet, withal, he was one of the most unassuming of men. He never betrayed the consciousness of his intellectual superiority ; vanity seemed to have been omitted from his composition. He was neither supercilious nor condescending. Generous as he was in imparting knowledge, he never brandished his learning to dazzle or to humiliate.

> "Not being less, but more than all
> The gentleness he seemed to be,
> Best seemed the thing he was, and joined
> Each office of the social hour
> To noble manners, as the flower
> And native growth of noble mind."

His generosity extended to some things in which most scholars assert their right to be parsimonious. His cheerful readiness in loaning the rich treasures of his library reminded one of the motto on Grollier's book-plate—"*Joannis Grollierii et amicorum.*" He was as generous of time as of books. Though he must have been often tempted to echo the Genevan scholar's cry against the "*amici quam parum amici,*" who came between him and his books, too often to no purpose, the only consideration which seemed to weigh with him was that he might be able to serve those who wished to see him. About the severest thing he was ever known by his family to say on the subject was once, when some one had frittered away a good part of his morning, and he came down to dinner saying, in his dry way, " May the Lord forgive him for taking so much of my time."

Ah ! those hours in that library ! Who that has enjoyed them can ever lose their fragrance ? Who can forget that room, walled and double walled with books, the baize-covered desk in the corner by the window, loaded with the fresh philosophic and theologic treasures of the European press, and the little figure in the long gray wrapper seated there, the figure so frail and slight that, as one of his friends remarked, it seemed as though it would not be much of a change for him to take on a spiritual body ; the beautifully moulded brow, crowned with its thick, wavy, sharply-parted, iron-grey hair, the strong aquiline profile, the restless shifting in his chair, the nervous pulling of the hand at the moustache, as the stream of talk widened and deepened, the occasional start from his seat to pull down a book or to search for a pamphlet, how inseparably these memories twine themselves with those of high debate and golden speech and converse on the themes of Christian philosophy and Christian experience!

In 1868 came the first decisive reminder of overtaxed energy. Under a complete nervous prostration he sailed for Europe, spent some months in travel there and in the East, and returned, to begin a terrible fight for life. Possessed by his work, burdened with the interests of truth, watching with the intensity of a master in Israel the movements of the leaders of infidel thought, stirred through his whole being with the joy of meeting them upon their own ground and with their own weapons, he was constantly reminded that his strength would no longer answer the enormous exactions of his brain. Day after day, in lassitude and pain, his overworked brain clamoring for rest, often discouraged and lonely, he forced himself to his desk when he might better have been upon his bed. Gradually his work outreached him, until in January, 1874, with a pang of which only his nearest friends knew the bitterness, he signed his letter of resignation of the chair of theology.

And it was just at this stage that the pure gold of his faith and Christian character shone out in full lustre. In a letter to Dr. Prentiss, his life-long companion and intimate friend, he said, speaking of his resignation, " I think I see everything more and more clearly; and I feel better and stronger for it. I am looking away more and more from the incidents and accidents, and trying to read God's purpose in it; and that seems to me clear. I needed the chastisement; I pray it may do me good, and cause me to live wholly and only to my Master. . . . I have no special fear about the future; the Lord will provide. I humbly hope that he who has spared me will not forsake me; that he will in very deed deliver my life from destruction, and let me yet see his goodness in the land of the living."

His last public utterance was in the prayer-meeting at the Church of the Covenant, on the evening of November 1st, 1876:

The subject for the evening was one of the Pilgrim Psalms, the 122d: " Jerusalem is builded as a city that is compact together. Pray for the peace of Jerusalem." He rose, and taking up the thought of what Jerusalem had been to the church of all ages since its foundation, he dwelt upon the love and longing which had gone out to it from the hearts of the pilgrims in its palmy days, from beneath the willows of Babylon, from prince and devotee and crusader, touching here and there upon salient points in its history, until, with the warmer glow of emotion stealing into his tremulous voice, he led our thoughts to the Jerusalem above, the Christian pilgrim's goal, and the rest and perfect joy of the weary. The talk was like the gem in Thalaba's mystic ring—a cut crystal full of fire. Perhaps something of his own weariness and struggle crept unconsciously into his words, and gave them their peculiar depth and tenderness. Be that as it may, we never heard his voice in the sanctuary again.

Not even to the dear ones of his own household did he tell the violence of the wrestle with suffering, unless it were, now and then, when the struggle was for the moment too mighty for him to bear alone, and then it was with a half apology for having spoken: "*I don't know why I spoke of that to you.*" Once, when the 12th chapter of Hebrews was being read to him, he referred with special emphasis to the verse, " If ye endure chastisement, God dealeth with you as with sons; for what son is he whom the father chasteneth not?" and said "Yes. How often have I said that over to myself." His courage was indomitable in his fight with pain. To see him at work at his desk, to sit with him and hear him discuss questions of current interest, one would not have thought that often, at these very moments, he was being racked with sharp torture, and his brain struggling with the lassitude engendered by sleepless nights of thought.

During the early part of the present season, he lectured a few times at the Seminary, temporarily borne above his weakness by his zeal for his work. In the hope that he might yet rally, the directors and faculty of the Seminary had appointed him to deliver the next course of the Ely Lectures. It was a task which he heartily welcomed. The field of Christian Apologetics no man knew better than he. His plan was drawn up, and had he been permitted to carry it out, our Christian literature would have been enriched by a powerful answer to the later utterances of the materialistic school. His interest in this task was most touching. He said, almost plaintively, "I want to deliver those lectures; and if I can only complete that course, I think I shall be ready to go." But it was not to be. His work was drawing to its close. He began to yield to the conviction that he must leave the battlefield, and turn his face homeward. He said one day to an old friend, "I have ceased to cumber myself about the things of time and sense, and I have had some precious thoughts about death." On the evening of the 16th of December he was present at the house of Dr. Henry M. Field, with that circle of brethren where he was always found on the Saturday evening, when his health would permit. The night was intensely cold, and he imprudently walked to his home, nearly a mile distant, and never left it again until he left it for his Father's house above. He lay quietly week after week, not as hopeful for himself as his friends were tempted to be, willing to stay by the flesh if God so willed, yet knowing that to depart was to be with Christ. He said, one day, "I have trusted in the Lord Jesus Christ, and have tried to serve him in spite of everything." "And you do *now?*" was asked. "Yes," was the emphatic reply, "*with all my heart.*"

Just before the last sad days when he entered the dark ante-chamber of death, and unconsciousness drew the veil between him and earth, while so feeble that it was doubtful if he could understand the question, some one asked, "Are you able to pray?" The reply came very feebly, "Verbally, no. Actually, yes. I can't talk of much of these things."

On Sabbath afternoon, the 4th of February, it seemed as if the hour of release was near. The tidings came as the church which he loved was gathering at the Lord's table, and the thought added deep solemnity to the heightened feeling of the hour, that while the church was drawing nigh to her Lord through symbols, he was passing to the open vision of the King in his beauty. Yet the day waned and the night passed, and still another and another day and night, and yet he lingered. It seemed to those who stood by his bedside, as though a spent swimmer, with distressful breath, were oaring his way over a restless sea, pausing at intervals to look for shore, and then renewing the struggle. And at last, as the morning broke, the beloved son who watched him suddenly saw a great peace come into his face; the lines of struggle faded out, and he knew that land was near. The panting breast was still, the tired child was in his Father's arms.

He lay in his last, peaceful sleep, where he had most loved to be in his life, among his books, in the chamber where his active brain had wrought so vigorously for God's truth, and where he had held such high and earnest communion with the mighty dead of the ages.

So he has passed unto the general assembly and church of the first-born, which are written in heaven. He is with the Christ whom he loved forever. He sees no more through a glass darkly, but face to face. Being dead, he yet speaketh: speaketh through the lips of the scores of Gospel ministers who have gone from under his hand to their work; speaketh in the written thoughts which will none the less go on with their work of moulding minds and hearts in knowledge and love of the truth, now that the hand which penned them is still; speaketh in the ever-loudening voice of the church, to whose service his life was given, and to heal the divisions of which his calm wisdom contributed so much; speaketh in the impress of his character, so sweet, so true, so strong, so tender, upon those who knew him best, and therefore loved him best.

> "For safe with right and truth he is!
> As God lives, he must live alway;
> There is no end for souls like his,
> No night for children of the day."

To him, as to Jacob, the vision of the angels has come. The sleeper has gone away. The ladder and the angels are not for our grosser sense, and the stones are black and bare; but there is still the pillar, the monument of consecrated character, and so it is bright sunshine on the spot where the pilgrim "tarried for a night," and we say, as we draw near, "This is the gate of heaven."

Art. V—EVANGELISTS AND LAY-EXHORTERS.*

By Rev. J. M. P. Otts, D. D., Wilmington, Del.

PART FIRST—EVANGELISTS.

THERE is no reason to suppose that the four evangelists have given an exhaustive account of all that Jesus said and did in that last interview with his disciples on the Mount of Ascension. But, as some of them record facts omitted by others, we may safely infer that many things were said and done on that memorable occasion, not recorded by any one of them. They all have chronicled the great commission given by the Master to his church, as the enlarged charter for the new dispensation, in which it was then made the duty of the church to go into the world, to preach the gospel in every nation, and to teach every creature to observe and do all things whatsoever he had spoken unto them. But they are all silent as to what offices Christ instituted by which this great commission was to be carried into effect. It is, however, the economy of the Holy Scriptures, that one inspired penman should supply the omissions of others, where this is necessary to complete this revelation; and, as this is done incidentally, it furnishes a strong internal evidence of the truthfulness of the sacred records.

We have an instance of this in the case before us. The evangelists tell us that Christ, on the ascension-day, gave a new and enlarged commission to the church, and then the apostle Paul, in one of his epistles, incidentally supplies what seems to be lacking, by telling us that among his ascension gifts was the appointment of certain offices by which the gospel commission was to be put into execution. When he ascended on high he gave gifts unto men, and among these gifts were apostles, prophets, evangelists, pastors, and teachers. Two of these, apostles and prophets, in the very nature of their offices, were intended to be temporary, and when they had served their specific purposes they ceased to exist, leaving evangelists, pastors, and teachers as the permanent officers, who are to go into all the world, to preach the gospel in every nation, and to teach every nation to know and do the will of

---

Evangelists in the Church. By Rev. P. C. Headly. Henry Hoyt, Boston.

Christ unto salvation.   Collating Eph. iv. with Rom. xii. and
1 Cor. xii., we find that the permanent officers in the Christian
dispensation are evangelists, pastors and teachers, ruling elders
and deacons, by whose official labors, as supplemented by the
prayers, exhortations, and services in various ways of the general brotherhood, the gospel is to be spread over the world,
until the knowledge of Christ shall fill the whole earth as the
waters do the great deep.   But it is not our purpose in this
essay to give a dissertation on ecclesiastical polity in general,
but to select from among our Saviour's ascension gifts the office
of the Evangelist, and inquire into its import and importance.

We begin by inquiring, what is the nature and import of the
evangelistic office ?   This question can be best answered by a
careful consideration of the public duties and labors of those
who, in apostolic times, filled this office.   It is, therefore,
necessary for us to know, at the outset, who, of those mentioned in the New Testament, held this position.   We may
enumerate as evangelists, Luke, Mark, Titus, Timothy, Philip,
Epaphras, Epaphroditus, Tychichus, Trophimus, Demas, Apol-
los, and, on Calvin's authority, " perhaps, also, the seventy
disciples, whom Christ ordained to occupy the second station
of the apostles."* From among these we will select Timothy,
and prove that he was an evangelist ; and then, from the
official instructions imparted to him by the apostle Paul about
his labors, and from his official acts, deduce the nature and
functions of the office he filled.

Well, then, was Timothy an evangelist ?   He was a pastor,
an apostle, a diocesan bishop, or an evangelist.   It is quite
evident that he was not a pastor, because he was all his ministerial life an itinerating preacher.   He never had a settled
flock over which he could have been the pastor.   He could not
have been an apostle, because he was destitute of the prime
qualifications requisite to that office.   He never saw the Lord
Jesus Christ, either before his crucifixion or after his resurrection.   The apostle was a witness on personal knowledge of
the fact of the resurrection.   In order to give this qualification
for the apostolic office to Paul, Christ appeared unto him by
miracle, as to one born out of due season.†   There is no inti-

---

* *Vide Inst.*, book iv, chap. iii, sec. 4.
† Acts i : 21, 22 ; xxii : 14, 15 ; and 2 Cor. xii : 12.

mation to be found in Scripture that Timothy was an apostle. On the contrary, Paul, in writing to him, is careful to style himself an apostle, but equally careful not to give this appellation to Timothy. Paul always addressed Timothy as being inferior to himself in office. His style of address is inexplicable on the hypothesis that Timothy was an apostle. Hence, the argument is narrowed down to the alternative—Timothy was either a diocesan bishop or an evangelist. This brings us into the great battle-field between Prelacy and Presbytery. We might summarily dismiss this point by saying that we have already shown that Timothy was not, and could not have been, an apostle, because he never saw the risen Lord; and, inasmuch as it is claimed that diocesan bishops are successors to the apostles, therefore, he could not have been a bishop in the prelatic sense of the term. This would be simply denying that there is, or can be, in the church any such office as that of diocesan bishops and successors to the apostles. This is what we believe to be the fact; but allowing as a conceit what we cannot concede as a fact, we hold that Timothy could not have been a diocesan bishop, for the following reasons:

1. He could not have been a diocesan bishop in the modern sense of the office, because he was ordained to his office " by the laying on of the hands of the presbytery." Of the particular session of the presbytery which ordained him, Paul was a member—very probably the moderator. In either case, he would have, conjointly with the other presbyters, imposed his hands on Timothy in the act of ordination.* Presbytery, according to the prelatic theory, could not have ordained a diocesan bishop.

2. Timothy could not have been the bishop of Ephesus—of which he was bishop, if bishop at all—because he remained there only at the earnest entreaty of Paul, and that, too, for a specific reason assigned.† It would have been a very curious thing for Paul to have exhorted the bishop of Ephesus to remain at home and discharge his diocesan duties. If Timothy was the bishop of Ephesus, he must have been a very delinquent bishop, to have given occasion for such a charge. Such a bishop deserved to be ignored, as, indeed, Paul did subse-

---

* 1 Tim. iv: 14; and 2 Tim. i: 6.   † 1 Tim. i: 3.

quently, on two very important occasions, ignore the existence of any such office at Ephesus ; first, when he met the presbytery of Ephesus, and delivered to it a solemn charge, without recognizing the bishopric of Timothy, or any body else ; and secondly, when he wrote an epistle to the Ephesians, in which he gave a catalogue of the offices of the Christian church, without giving the slightest intimation of the existence of any such office as that of the diocesan bishop.* These are facts absolutely inexplicable on the hypothesis that Timothy, or any body else, was the prelatic bishop of Ephesus. Furthermore, if Timothy was the bishop of Ephesus in the episcopal sense of the word, he was put in ecclesiastical authority over the apostle John, for Polycrates, who lived in the second century, relates that John lived and died at Ephesus. Irenæus, Clement of Alexandria, Origen, Eusebius, and Jerome, all testify to the same fact. In Fulgentius we read of " *Cathædra Johannis Evangelistæ, Ephesi.*" Did John the evangelist have a parish under Timothy the bishop? Well, then, it was a cathedral church, and in that, perhaps, he found some comfort when Timothy was promoted over him. "The legend," says Dr. Killen, "that Timothy aud Titus were the bishops, respectively, of Ephesus and Crete, appears to have been invented about the beginning of the fourth century, and at a time when the original constitution of the church had been completely, though silently, revolutionized."† It is, therefore, evident that Timothy was not a diocesan bishop, but an evangelist. So was Titus, as can be proved in the same line of argument. We conclude this part of our essay in the words of Bishop Stillingfleet, who, after a most careful examination of the whole subject, was constrained to admit, that "both Timothy and Titus were evangelists, notwithstanding all the opposition made against it, as will appear to any one that will take an impartial survey of the evidence on both sides."

As Timothy was ordained to his office by the presbytery, we are to infer that the evangelist was a presbyter, and nothing more. In the ecclesiastical courts he had equal authority with pastors, and no more. Hence, the evangelistic office is not incompatible with the purity of the ministry. In the

---

*Acts xx: 17–38 ; and Eph. iv: 11.   † *The Ancient Church*, sec. iii, chap. 2.

presbytery the evangelist is an equal among equals; but he goes out of presbytery into the sphere of his peculiar labors invested with somewhat superior, or rather, additional, powers to those of the pastor, because his duties require them. He is an itinerating preacher of the Word, invested with authority to preach the gospel, and to plant churches in the unevangelized parts of the earth. He goes forth as the pioneer of Christianity and the missionary of the church. Hence, he must be invested with authority to originate and organize new churches, and, to this end, to receive members into the communion, *in the first instance without the concurrence of a session;* and, thereupon, to ordain ruling elders, and thus constitute a session in and over the newly organized congregations; and even in foreign lands, where the concurrence of a presbytery is impossible, he may license and ordain ministers of the gospel, and of them originate and constitute a presbytery. But all this he is to do only by the authority and under the supervision of the presbytery or synod to which he belongs.* We are happy in having the authority of the immortal John Calvin to fall back upon in support of this view of the nature and dignity of the evangelistic office. "The evangelists," says he, "ranked as assistants next to the apostles. It is more likely that Timothy, whom Paul has associated with himself as his closest companion in all things, surpassed ordinary pastors in rank and dignity of office, than that he was only one of them."† And in another place he says, "The evangelists, in my judgment, were in the midst between apostles and doctors. For it was a function next to the apostles to preach the gospel in all places, and not to have any certain place of abode; only in degree of honor were they inferior to the apostles. For when Paul describeth the order of the church (Eph. iv : 11.), he doth so put them after the apostles, that he showeth that they have more room given them than the pastors, who were tied to certain places."‡ To this we add the opinion of Bishop Stillingfleet, which has the peculiar value of being the concession of a bishop of the Church of England. He says, in the same chapter of his Irenicum, which has been already quoted, "Evangelists were those who were sent sometimes into this country to put

---

*1 Tim. i : 3; iii : 1, 15; 2 Tim. ii : 2; Titus i : 5.
†*Vide Calvin's Com. on 2 Tim. iv; 5. ‡Com. on Acts xxi : 7.*

the churches in order here, and sometimes into another; but wherever they were, they acted as evangelists, and not as fixed officers."

The important question now arises, Is the evangelistic office permanent in the church? We answer in the affirmative, and think that the following facts and considerations will prove that it was designed to stand as a permanent office of the gospel ministry along side of the pastoral office, and as being of equal importance with it.

It continued to exist long after the apostolic age. Eusebius, who lived toward the close of the second century, informs us that there were many evangelists in his day, and describes their labors as follows : "After laying the foundation of the faith in foreign parts, as the particular object of their mission, and appointing others as the shepherds of the flocks, and committing to these the care of those that had recently been introduced, they went," says, he, " again to other regions and nations with the grace and coöperation of God."[*]   And, again, speaking of Pantænus, the philosopher, who flourished about 180 A. D., he says that he went as an evangelist of the Word to India, and adds, that " there were there many evangelists of the Word who were ardently striving to spend their inspired zeal after the apostolic example."[†]   Since the office did not cease with the days of inspiration, we conclude that Christ designed it to stand as one of the permanent offices in his church.

The evangelistic office is the aggressive arm of the church's power, and the settled pastorate is her conservative force; and while there are unevangelized regions, there will always exist the necessity for the work of evangelists. There will always exist the cause and the call for this office till all the world shall be gathered into settled pastorates and each congregation shall have its own regular pastor. This will never be the case till the millennial glory shall burst upon the face of the world. There have always been evangelists in the church under some name. Our domestic and foreign missionaries are scriptural evangelists. They are neither apostles, nor prophets, nor pastors ; but evangelists.

---

[*] *Eusebius' Hist.*, Lib. iii: c. 37.   [†] Lib. v, c. 10.

The importance of this office cannot be over-estimated. In point of usefulness it is in no degree inferior to the settled pastorate. These two offices stand on a parallel in authority and importance. The additional authority, of which we have spoken as belonging to the evangelists, is only accidental to the nature of his work. No church can attain unto the highest degree of prosperity which does not include both these offices in its polity and practice. As we have already said, one is the aggressive and the other the conservative arm of the church's power. If the church neglects to use her aggressive power, it will soon come to pass that she will have nothing left to conserve ; and if it only uses its aggressive arm, it will lose ground in old places about as fast as it gains in new ones. The true policy of the church is to neglect neither the one nor the other, and not to give undue preponderance to either over the other. The weakness of the Presbyterian Church, heretofore, has consisted in the neglect of the office and work of itinerating evangelists ; and the weakness of the Methodist Church has consisted in giving undue importance to this office to the neglect of the settled pastorate. The conseqence is, the Methodists run fast, and the Presbyterians hold fast. The Methodists gather more and lose more than the Presbyterians. These two offices are to the church, what the two side-wheels are to the steamer : both must be kept in simultaneous motion in order to safe, certain, and secure progress. If one stops and the other moves, the church will only gyrate in a vicious circle. There will be motion without progress.

There are many in these modern days called evangelists, who are not evangelists in any scriptural or true sense of the word. They are merely peripatetic and irregular preachers, who oftentimes run before they are sent, and come before they are wanted. They have no constitutional place in the church. They are like wandering stars, with no certain orbits to move in, and, crossing frequently the lawful orbits of others, they come into collision with them. In such cases there is always a shock and a check to the real prosperity of pastoral work, and, not infrequently, a rupture between the pastor and the people of his charge. The sphere of the evangelist is as clearly defined as that of the pastor. He is appointed to labor in the destitute regions and for the unevangelized masses.

The evangelist is just as much an officer of the church as the pastor, and it is just as essential for him to labor under the supervision and control of the presbytery as it is for the pastor. Timothy and Titus and the primitive evangelists were men ordained of the church, as well as called of God to their office and work. The example—which has the force of a law to the church for all time to come, because it was divinely ordered— was set in the case of Paul and Barnabas.* They were inducted into the evangelistic office at the order of the Holy Ghost, by the solemn act of ordination by prayer and laying on of hands. Previous to this ordination to the evangelistic office and work, Paul had preached and served the church as an apostle for the space of ten or twelve years; but for the apostolic office there was not and could not be any ordination by the laying on of human hands. In the case of Matthias, who was chosen of the Lord to "take part in this ministry and apostleship, from which Judas by transgression fell," there was no election by the congregation of the church, nor ordination by the school of the apostles. He was chosen by lot, and when the Lord had thus indicated his will, he was, without any human ceremony, "numbered with the eleven apostles."† And afterward Paul was chosen and made "an apostle, not of men, neither by man, but by Jesus Christ, and God the Father, who raised him from the dead."‡ In this office there can be no successors to the apostles, unless they should be chosen and appointed by miracle. Barnabas, also, for ten or twelve years previous to his ordination to the evangelistic office, had served the church in the extraordinary office of a prophet, for which there was no ordination, and in which there is no succession. For these extraordinary offices there was required a miraculous call and the investment by the Holy Ghost of miraculous powers and knowledge. With the cessation of miracles in the church, these extraordinary offices ceased to exist, because the miraculous qualifications requisite to them were withdrawn. By ordination, Paul and Barnabas were inducted into and invested with the ecclesiastical authority and powers of the ordinary and permanent office of evangelists, without being deprived of the miraculous investment of their extraordinary offices. Paul continued to be an apostle, and Barnabas a prophet, while

---

*Acts xiii: 2, 3.   †Acts i: 23-26.   ‡Gal. i: 1; xi: 12.

they went forth everywhere invested, as evangelists, with the ordinary ecclesiastical authority and powers, still and permanently remaining in the church, to organize new congregations, and to ordain over them elders and deacons, and to set things in proper order in vacant churches.

From this view of the evangelistic office, which seems to us to be the scriptural and only true view of it, it follows that there can be no more room or authority in the church for lay-evangelists than for lay-pastors. ' Both are divinely appointed and permanent officers in the church, and ordination is required for the one just as much as for the other.

In the book mentioned at the head of this essay—"The Evangelists in the Church, from Philip of Samaria, A. D. 35, to Moody and Sankey of America, A. D. 1875," by Rev. P. C. Headly—there is a confusion of ecclesiastical ideas from beginning to end. The book is very interesting to read, because it is made up of personal biographies, which cannot fail to interest all classes of readers, especially those who read to be interested rather than instructed; but it is not a safe book to be put into the hands of young men as an authority on points of ecclesiastical law and order. It brings together all classes of independent, irregular, and peripatetic preachers and laborers, men and women, the ordained and the unordained, under the common name of evangelists. With Mr. Headly, any independent and itinerating preacher, no matter how irregular and disorderly his ministry may be, is an evangelist. No wonder that Mr. Headly, with this indefinite, undefined, and indefinable idea of the evangelistic office, could say, "we reverently affirm that Jesus, in his earthly ministry, occupied the place of the evangelist." And this because "he was not a pastor, nor, in the popular sense of the term, was he a missionary." Of course he was not; neither was the Lord and Master a prophet, nor an apostle, nor an evangelist, "not even in the popular sense of the term," for he was the true Messiah, the eternal Son of God; not merely a divinely inspired teacher, but the Divine Teacher, the Divine Head of the church, from whom all authority to preach and teach is derived, and in whom all offices, functions, powers, gifts, and authorities of the church reside, and from whom alone they can emanate.

PART SECOND—LAY-EXHORTERS.

The question here arises, does this view of the evangelistic office, demanding ordination for it as much as for the pastoral office, shut the mouths of all laymen? We think not. Of course it excludes all laymen from assuming the attitude and functions of the preacher, either as evangelists or pastors, and it puts the church in the alternative of either prohibiting all such preaching, or, by recognition, of investing it with the ecclesiastical authority of ordination. But all public addresses on the part of laymen in open assemblies cannot be held as preaching in the technical and ecclesiastical sense of the word; nor do such lay exercises invade the office and functions of the ordained ministry. Exhortation is one thing, and preaching, in the ecclesiastical sense of the term, is quite another thing. The ordained preacher, whether as evangelist or pastor, delivers his sermon under the endorsement, and by the authority, of the whole church that conferred upon him his ordination. He is the authorized mouth-piece of the whole church, and as the church is held responsible for what he says, so the church holds him responsible for all his authoritative utterances. It is on this principle alone that the right of trial for heresy is founded. The ordained preacher is the authorized and authoritative teacher and expounder of the doctrines of the church from which he received his ordination. Now the laymen, receiving the doctrines at the lips of the ordained ministry, may thereupon exhort, beseech, and encourage one another to the faithful discharge of the practical duties enjoined and implied in the doctrines thus received, and may also exhort and entreat sinners to the exercise of faith and repentance. Here is a wide and orderly field for the legitimate labors of laymen. By way of exhortation they may speak to one, two, a hundred, a thousand, or ten thousand at a time. Whether to many or few, in the private house or on the street, in the public hall or in the church, the principle is the same. If it is lawful for laymen to speak at all, there can be no "let or hindrance" in the place or number of hearers. Some would call this public exercise on the part of laymen "lay preaching," and we must admit that the word "preaching" has such a variable and india-rubber-like meaning in popular use, that it can be stretched out over this exercise without any abuse of the term. But we prefer to call it lay exhortation, because that is the name given to it in Scripture, and because by holding to this name we can always keep clear and distinct the proper discrimination between the legitimate spheres and labors of laymen and of ordained ministers. When we hear so much talk about lay-preachers and lay-preaching, we are reminded of the riddle, which has come down to us from the ancients, to show us how nearly a thing may be what the name given to it indicates, and yet be wanting in the essential element to constitute it the very thing designated by the name. This is the riddle : " A man that was not a man, threw a stone that was not a stone, at a bird that was not a bird, that was perched and yet not perched, on a tree that was not a tree ;" the meaning of which is: A eunuch threw a piece of pumice-stone at a bat, suspended by its claws from the top of a reed, that had grown to the dimensions of a tree. Now, when a lay-preacher preaches, we have a preacher that is not a preacher, preaching and yet not preaching, a sermon that is not a sermon. Is it not better, therefore, to say, he is an exhorter making an exhortation ? Only pride and ambition can object to the use of these terms, and aspire to more high-sounding titles.

For lay exhortation, for the active and abounding services of laymen, there is the most abundant scriptural authority to be found in the precepts of the apostles, and in the common practice of the church in the apostolic days. St. John saith, "Let him that heareth say, come." Is not this not merely permissive authority, but an authoritative injunction, to every individual, who himself has heard the gospel, to invite and exhort all other sinners to come to Christ and be saved ? St. Paul saith : " Let him that exhorteth wait on exhortation." He specifies the work of exhortation as distinct from that of preaching and teaching. In Heb. x : 25, he enjoins this duty upon the brethren : " Not forsaking the assembling of yourselves together as the manner of some is, but *exhorting one another*." This certainly was instruction given to laymen how they were to do when no minister was present to hold public assemblies for them. It is the generally received opinion that the infant congregations in the primitive times, before they received settled pastors, met together on the Lord's day to

read the Scriptures and exhort one another.   On this point we
have the testimony of the safe and conservative Dr. Killen,
who, while holding that all the primitive elders were not
preachers, says, "it was necessary that at least some of the session or eldership connected with each flock should be competent to conduct the congregational worship. As spiritual gifts
were more abundant in the apostolic times than afterward, it
is probable that at first several of the elders were found ready
to take part in its celebration."* It appears that in the
Church of Corinth several speakers were in the habit of addressing the same meeting, and it does not appear that all the
speakers were necessarily elders, as Dr. Killen seems to hold ;
but as women, and only women, are forbidden to speak in
the public meetings, it would seem to be implied that
permission was given to all the male members of the congregation to speak the word of exhortation, if any one of them
had a word to say unto edification.† It is too well known
that lay-exhortation was a common practice in the synagogues,
to leave any necessity for us to cite authorities to prove that
fact.   But as a recent and competent authority on this point,
we quote the words of Dr. Farrar, who says ; " As there were
no ordained ministers to conduct the services of the synagogue, the lessons from the parashah and hophtarah, the law
and the prophets might not only be read by any competent
person who received permission from the rósh hak-keneséth,
but he was even at liberty to add his own midrash, or comment."‡ It was in accordance with this custom that Paul and
his company were called upon to speak the word of èxhorta-
tion in the synagogue of Antioch-in Pisidia.§ It is generally
agreed that the early Christian churches, in worship and
government, were founded upon and fashioned after the model
of the synagogues.   Bishop Whatley says, "the primitive
Christian churches were converted synagogues."

From all this it appears that there was in the church,
in the apostolic days, the ministry of lay-exhortation. This
ministry of lay-service without office has always existed in
the church in some form, and has at all times been more
or less clearly recognized as, at least, a permissible ministry.
At certain periods, always in times of revival, it has been

Ancient Church, sec. iii., ch. 2.   †1 Cor. xiv : 26, 31.
‡*Life of Christ,* ch. xvi.   §Acts xiii : 14, 15.

more active than under ordinary circumstances, and has come more clearly under ecclesiastical recognition. In the days of John Knox, and under his authority and approbation, there were appointed in the Church of Scotland lay-readers and lay-exhorters, who relieved ministers of a part of their public services, and who, when there were no ministers, read the Scriptures and delivered exhortations to assemblies of the people.* These lay-readers and exhorters filled very much the same place that our modern Bible-readers and so-called lay-evangelists fill, only—and this is a very important difference—they were appointed by the ministers, and labored under the supervision of responsible ecclesiastical authority. This same thing exists to-day in the Southern Presbyterian Church. The General Assembly of that church, in 1869, authorized its presbyteries to give "permission" to qualified laymen to exercise their gifts here and there, as the Lord may furnish opportunity. The Southern Church is filling up with these lay-exhorters, who labor under the authoritative permission of the presbytery. In this way, possibly, a solution to the perplexing problem of lay-preaching may be reached. These men do not abandon their secular pursuits, nor are they regarded as in ecclesiastical office. They are simply laymen. They are not self-called and self-appointed preachers. They do not call themselves lay-evangelists, nor do other people call them lay-preachers. They go under the name of lay-exhorters. If any choose to call their exhortations lay-preaching, then it is lay-preaching, kept within proper limitations and under proper authority.

Here the important question for the Presbyterians arises, Is the appointment of lay-exhorters by presbytery constitutional? The very most that can be said against it can only hold it to be extra-constitutional. It is not contra-constitutional, because it does not run contrary to any existing constitutional provision or prohibition. It only puts under rule and regulation what has always existed in some form in the church. There have always been lay-talkers, and there always will be, and ought to be; and because their legitimate sphere has not been clearly defined, and their labors brought under

---

* *McCries' Life of John Knox*, Period vii.

ecclesiastical recognition, they have sometimes transgressed all due limitations, and invaded the sacred functions of the ordained ministry, and thus given offence and made trouble. It may be said that the appointment of lay-exhorters has the effect of creating a sub-ministry in the church, the ministry of unordained men. Let it be so, then. It would be simply the ministry of lay-exhortation, for which there is the most abundant scriptural authority. It would not be creating a new ministry, but only giving ecclesiastical recognition to what is already in existence by divine appointment. Thus, that vast reserved power in all our churches, which has hitherto been largely running to waste for the want of having proper recognition and direction given to it—the labors of laymen—will be brought under control; and being thus regulated. it may be utilized to the best and very highest advantage. We have seen that the two divinely-appointed offices for preaching the gospel, in the churchly and official sense of preaching, are those of the evangelist and pastor, the one thing the aggressive and the other the conservative arm of churchly power; and that it is divinely ordered that those admitted into these offices should be inducted into them by ordination. By ordination we understand nothing more nor less than the investiture by the church of a man, who is supposed to be divinely called, with all needed ecclesiastical authority for the work of his office. It does not give the call to the holy office, nor does it confer any grace, or mental or spiritual qualifications for its work. It presupposes all this, and thereupon proceeds to invest the man with ecclesiastical authority to exercise the functions of the office to which he seems to have a divine call, and for the work of which he is supposed, on reasonable evidence given to the church, to be endowed with all needed natural and supernatural qualifications. The investiture of ordination in the Presbyterian Church is usually made by "the laying on of the hands of the presbytery," for which form of ordination there is abundant scriptural authority. But the formal act of "the laying on of the hands" is not essential to the fact and validity of ordination itself. Ordinations may take place, and hold as valid, without the formality of laying on of hands. Neither John Calvin, nor John Knox, was ordained by the "laying on of hands." Presbyterians cannot afford to be over nice and particular on this point. In the case of Calvin, there was not even a prior papal ordination to fall back upon, to make up for any supposed deficiency in this presbyterial ordination. Paul Henry says: "No trace of his ordination can be found in the records of his life." * In the case of John Knox, there was no formality of laying on of hands, nor any other ceremony, save the solemn call of the congregation of the Castle of St. Andrews, delivered to Knox in a most solemn and impressive charge, by John Rough, at the conclusion of a sermon appropriate to the occasion. Knox did not set the least value upon his prior ordination by the popish bishop; for McCrie informs us, "In common with all the original reformers, he rejected the orders of episcopal ordination, as totally unauthorized by the laws of Christ; nor did he even regard the imposition of the hands of presbyters as a rite essential to the validity of orders." † If the formal act of laying on of hands is essential to the validity of ordination, then the two foremost and most honored men in the Presbyterian Church were never anything more than laymen.

We have brought out these facts in order to apply them to the case of Mr. Moody, and all others who stand in the attitude he occupies in the church. We believe that Mr. Moody, whether he recognizes the fact or not, is constructively ordained to the work of an evangelist by the general consent and approval of the ordained ministry of the holy Catholic Church. All necessary ecclesiastical endorsement and authority have been imparted to him in the hearty co-operation of ministers and people of all evangelical branches of Christ's church. In this way there is just as truly the authority of ordination in his ministry as ever there was in the ministry of John Calvin and John Knox. Without the laying on of the hands of bishop or presbytery, by the manifest call and approval of the divine Head of the church in heaven, and by the manifest call and approval of the people of the church on earth, he is constructively and most truly ordained to the work in which he is engaged. Not being formally ordained by any one

---

* *Henry's Life of Calvin.* Part i. ch. ii—"Calvin was never ordained priest, and did not enter the ecclesiastical state." Bayle. art. Calvin, Beza.

† *Life of Knox.* Period iii.

denomination, but constructively ordained in the united endorsement and approval of all, as shown in their hearty co-
operation with him, he goes forth in his labors, not as the
minister of this or that branch of the church, but as the undenominational, or rather, as the inter-denominational evangelist of pure Christianity to the great mass of non-church-goers,
who fill up the wide and waste places intervening between the
churches and their ordinary congregations.   In this field, which
is in the strictest sense an evangelistic field, he has the authority of ordination in his preaching just as thoroughly and truly
as John Calvin and John Knox ever had the authority of ordination in their ministry in the fields to which the Lord called
them, and in which the church has always recognized them as
princes and leaders in the great work of reformation.   With
this kind of ordination for their work, Presbyterians ought to
be very well satisfied with Messrs. Moody and Sankey.   They
are more than satisfied ; they rejoice in their work, and thank
and praise God for giving such workmen to the church and the
world.

If Mr. Moody should be unwilling to recognize himself as
placed in the way we have explained above, under constructive
ordination by the universal acceptance and approval of all the
denominations of evangelical Christianity, then, still, we would
bid him God-speed in his labors as simply a layman ; only, if he
persists in holding himself as a layman, we cannot recognize in
him competent ecclesiastical authority to administer the sacrament, to govern in the courts of the church, and to do such
other things as can only be orderly done by the ordained ministers of the Word.   But it does not require a formal and pronounced acceptance on the part of Mr. Moody, any more than
a formal and ceremonial act of laying on of hands on the part
of the church, to complete his ordination, and to establish its
validity.   It is only needed that he silently and unceremo-
niously adjust himself to the peculiar position in which he finds
himself placed by the providence of God, and in which he is
recognized as " the right man in the right place," by the universal consent and approbation of all evangelical denominations.

There is, as we think we have conclusively shown, a divinely
appointed place in the church for the private and public labors

of laymen—a ministry without an office. A man may be a patriotic politician without holding or seeking a political office. In this way, in private and public, though unofficial labors, he may serve his party, or, what is far better, his whole country, to the great advantage of the highest interests of the nation. There is such a thing, in both state and church, as a ministry and service without office. When, therefore, such men as Messrs. Wanamaker and Stuart of Philadelphia, and Dodge and Cree of New York, and many others whom we might mention, engage in active and public efforts for Christ and humanity, without abandoning their secular employments, they are not to be looked upon as eccleciastical outlaws, to be condemned and silenced, but they should be recognized by the church and her ministry, and encouraged in their labors, as doing an orderly work, for which there is divine authority. It is not their fault if the church fails to recognize and to bring under rule and regulation their lay ministry, and to utilize its results for its own highest interests. If they have imparted to them a divine message, and the gift of uttering it, then it is their privilege to speak in the way of lay-exhortation, and they dare not keep silent. But being unordained men, only laymen, they cannot assume to themselves the ecclesiastical authority and functions of the ordained ministry without a breach of constitutional order. Like these men, Mr. Moody at first began to labor for Christ and humanity as a layman ; but when he gave up all secular employment, and devoted himself exclusively and entirely to preaching and the work of evangelization, then he ceased to be a layman, and become, in the eyes and estimation of all the world, a preacher of the gospel ; and the church, by her recognition of him in this attitude, and by her endorsèment, in thus receiving and co-operating with him in his labors, has, by common consent, invested him with all needed ecclesiastical authority for his ministry and work.

There are, we think, three classes of laborers in the vineyard of the Gospel-ministry. First and foremost, the regularly and formally ordained pastors and evangelists ; and then the unordained ministry of laymen who, without abandoning their secular employment, and without coming into ecclesiastical office, speak the word of exhortation from place to place and from time to time, as the Lord gives them ability and opportunity ;.

and then, between the regular ministry of formally ordained clergymen, and the regular ministry of laymen, there comes in a third class of men, who, having begun their labors as laymen, have gradually grown into the ministry of the Word as their exclusive employment, and have thereupon abandoned all secular engagements, and consecrated themselves to the sacred avocation ; and being recognized in the holy office by the common consent and general approval of the churches, and their labors being endorsed by general co-operation with them, they are thus constructively ordained and invested with all needed ecclesiastical recognition and authority for their work.

We observe, in conclusion, that another class of so-called lay-preachers is coming forward, upon whom we cannot look but with disapprobation and alarm, because they neither re. cognize the church, nor desire to be recognized by it. They not only ignore all constitutional ecclesiastical authority, but go so far as to place themselves in an attitude of antagonism to the church and her ordained ministry. We have met, and have come into collision with such men, who claimed to be followers of Mr. Moody, but who, evidently, neither knew him nor were known of him. They are the counterfeit Moodyites; the bare and base imitators of some of his external manners, without having entered, or being able to enter, into the inner spirit of the man and his work. They are like Mr. Moody only in the one point, that each one of them runs around with a Bagster Bible in hand. Money can buy the Bible at the book-store, but only the Holy Ghost can baptize a man into the spirit of the Bible, and endow him with the requisite gifts to do a real Bible-work for Christ and for souls. The Bible will do these men no harm, and there can be no possible objection to their having Bibles; but the fear is, having Bibles in their hands, and setting themselves up as Bible-teachers, without having the spirit of the Bible in their hearts, they may do the cause and the true people of the Bible a very serious damage. These men, of whom we now speak, have not been baptized into the spirit of humility and modesty ; and, therefore, manifestly, they are neither called of God nor wanted of man. They have neither office nor gifts for unofficial work, and should, we think, be severely discountenanced. To all such let it be said, a Bagster Bible cannot make a Moody of any man, though it may help a presumptuous man to ape a Heaven-sent evangelist. And where that evangelist himself has not been seen in his work, such crude and weak imitations may tend to bring him and his holy work into disrepute. Imitation is never genuine work; and when it is prompted by vanity and pride, it can only end in mischief and harm. We have known some of these peripatetic Bible-carriers, who go about calling themselves Bible-readers and lay-evangelists, to make themselves ridiculous in vain attempts to imitate the marvelous rapidity of utterance, the peculiar stammering and stutter, the angular and jerky gestures, and even the mispronunciations, of Mr. Moody. And when we have seen weaklings thus imitating the mere external habits, and even the defects and faults, in the manner of the good man's preaching, we have been reminded of the lines of Coleridge on imitation, especially the following words:

> "On folly every fool his talent tries;
> It asks some toil to imitate the wise;
> Though few like Fox can speak—like Pitt can think—
> Yet all like Fox can game—like Pitt can drink."

Our best policy is to let these mere imitators alone—severely alone—and they will soon die out; for imitation is the mere shadow of a passing man, and can last but for a day. When God wants another Moody, he will call him into existence, and call him into his ministry, and then call upon and constrain his church and people to recognize him and to co-operate with him in his labors. But when God sends another man to stir up his spiritual Israel from Dan to Beersheba, and to move the world, most surely he will be like Mr. Moody in spirit, but most likely he will be unlike him in manners and means. The Haldanes—those genuine and godly laborers in Christ's vineyard in the first quarter of this century—were men of great wealth and high literary tastes and attainments, and were very different in modes of operation from Moody and Sankey of this last quarter, but were like them in spirit, zeal, self-sacrifice, and earnestness. All the God-appointed evangelists, from Philip to Moody, have always been alike in spirit, but generally very unlike in external habits and modes of work. God is fertile in resources, and seldom repeats himself.

Art. VI.—THE POWER AND IMPORTANCE OF UNCTION IN PREACHING.

By Rev. Arthur T. Pierson, D.D., Detroit, Mich.

How the pulpit may be made more attractive and effective, is a question which absorbs much of the best thought of our day. Men of big brain and great heart, who possess the graphic power of the painter's pencil, are at work, drawing the profile of an ideal ministry. Hence the able essays on " Pulpit Talent," and kindred themes, which lift up so high a standard of fitness for the sacred office.

The one great need of the pulpit is *power*. With all the confessedly high qualifications of the ministry as a class, there is yet a nameless deficiency in much modern preaching. Trace the lack to what you will, there is a lack of power. Even where the pulpit is attractive, how seldom is it effective to the great end—the saving of souls! Many sermons interest and instruct, please and profit, which do not win men to Christ. They gratify the mind, but do not satisfy the soul; they convince and persuade, but do not convict and convert. Men speak, week after week, in a full house, to an attentive audience, on vital gospel themes, and after studious preparation, and yet their preaching is attended with but little *power*. And a more important question can scarcely be asked than this: *Wherein consists, and whereby may we secure, the true Power of the Pulpit ?*

The lack of power is not to be attributed to a lack of scholarship. In the ministry, as in other callings, there are examples of incompetency and superficiality, yet the average culture is high. Nor can this lack of power be traced to a lack of intellectuality; for the modern pulpit lays just claim to some of the mightiest efforts of human genius. Nor can the lack of power be accounted for by a lack of spirituality, in the general sense of the deeper Christian experience and the ampler Christian furnishing ; for the ministry deservedly rank as spiritual leaders.

Shall we find the lack of power in the lack of truth, the substitution of something else for the pure and simple gospel message ? That there is a great evil here, none can deny. Without the truth of God, there will not be the power of God. But is there always power, even where there is truth? Truth and power are not synonyms in this wicked world; would to God they were!

We have carelessly adopted the old pagan maxim: "*Magna est veritas, et prævalebit ;*" forgetting that the whole history of mankind shows its fallacy and falsity. To a large extent, truth has always been known. Yet look at the annals of our race. At the beginning, our first parents heard the truth of God from the lips of God himself; yet, even in an Eden of innocence, it did not prevail. A satanic lie there proved mighty to the ruin of the race. Look at the antediluvian world. Noah, a preacher of righteousness, proclaimed the truth for a century, and made not a convert. Greece and Rome knew enough truth to save them ; yet, to day, we read the records of the rise and ruin of the most refined and of the most martial of ancient nations. France has known the truth, yet has been perpetually rocked in the crater of ruin, and, instead of the truth prevailing, we see a whole people, in a revolutionary crisis, arraying falsehood in truth's white robes, and crowning vice with the diadem of virtue.

Were the truth spoken in a sinless world, it might prove great and prevail. But in fallen natures the wrong is mightier than the right, and error keeps the mastery. The Gospel is not unto salvation, until it is not only the truth of God, but the power of God.

The parting words of our Lord, as recorded by St. Luke, in Acts i: 8, promise to supply this great lack. They contain a prophecy of power. The grand word of this prophecy is δυναμις. It bids us study the science of spiritual dynamics; to inquire what that is which makes preaching a dynamic force in the church and in the world.

The power promised is of the Holy Ghost: " Ye shall receive power after that the Holy Ghost is come upon you." Here, then, is unveiled the secret, both of the lack of power and of the source of power, in preaching.

That these valedictory words of our ascended Lord refer to spiritual power in preaching is scarce open to a doubt. Here, indirectly, Christ himself defines the office and work of his

ministers : " Ye shall be witnesses unto me." So said Ana
nias to Saul: " Thou shalt be His witness unto all men, of
what thou hast seen and heard" (Acts xxii: 15). Preaching
is pre-eminently a *witness*, which any one is competent to give,
independent of any special spiritual gift. But power to witness—power to make this witness effective, effectual—is only of
the Holy Ghost.

It will be seen, then, that the words of Christ suggest the
theme of this paper, which will present some thoughts upon
" The Power and Importance of Unction in Preaching.".

As applied to preaching, unction is not a scriptural term.
Only once does the word occur in our New Testament—1 Jno.
ii : 20 : " Ye have an unction (Χρισμα) from the Holy One."
where it means an anointing, or chrism, applied to Christians
generally, in the gifts and graces imparted by the Holy Spirit.
Applied to the ministry, it is understood to express the anointing of the preacher with a divine gift and grace of preaching;
that chrism of spiritual authority whereby he reaches, touches,
moves, and moulds the inmost being of his hearer—the power
of the Holy Ghost.

" Unction " implies " power." and this constitutes its " importance." Taking these words of Christ as the germ of our
thought, let us consider the *power of the Holy Ghost in preaching.* In developing this germinal thought, all that is vital to
the theme will receive due attention. The word unction,
though it means anointing, must not be understood to imply
only smoothness, lustre, fragrance, or even consecration. It
means power to open the eyes of men, " turn them from darkness to light, and from the power of Satan unto God."

In asking for the causes of a lack of power in preaching, it
would sometimes seem that the error is fundamental. It is
common in these days to look upon the ministry as a mere
trade, business, or, at best, profession ; and hence we are prone
to measure our qualification for it by human standards. Let
us start aright, and, at the outset, fix firmly in our minds this
truth, that the ministry is not a human profession, but a divine
vocation. God, calling us to it, must fit us for it.

One great practical mistake of the preacher is, that he in-
wardly conceives of power as human. Perhaps he really depends upon intellectual might, cogent argument, vigorous

thought, happy illustration, poetic imagination, to move the mind ; upon fervent feeling, earnest emotion, persuasive appeal, to move the heart. Even where we feel that to all powerful preaching, there must be a certain glow, how often do we, depend upon intellectual effort—the march of thought—to warm us, so that the glow is not spiritual, but intellectual, magnetic, sympathetic.

Eloquence is not unction, though unction confers the truest and highest eloquence. The power to move men in spiritual things is a power purely of God, and to be carefully distinguished from all those channels through which it flows, and all means by which it works, as the lightning is distinct from the cloud it charges, or the wind from the wave it heaves and rolls.

This anointing of the Holy Ghost, this enduing with power from on high, is a process which defies all analysis. The secret seems to lie now in the preacher's glowing ardor and fervor, and then in tearful tenderness; now in flaming earnestness, and then in omnipotent argument. But whether in the logic of reason, or in the logic of love, in warning or in invitation, there is a power not of man.

So also does unction defy description. You can no more define it than you can the savor of salt, or the flavor of fruit, or the fragrance of a flower. But you may be profoundly sensible of its presence or absence. Who has not felt the lack of it! We sometimes hear preaching full of learning, but empty of life. It is the mummy of divinity. The form is there; the spirit is gone. The cerements of a venerable antiquity wrap it round, but it has the scent of the grave, the odor of decay. And we have a quaint but expressive popular phrase which just describes such preaching—"dead orthodoxy." How well that portrays a tame, stale, lifeless statement of those grand truths of the Word of God, which should rather prove so living and life-giving as to wake the dead.

I. The Importance, to the Preacher, of Unction or Power from the Holy Ghost appears, first, in *its necessity to a proper apprehension of divine truth*. This is especially true of certain themes. Light takes color from the imperfection of the media through which it passes. Beautiful as are its hues and shades, tones and tints, they all imply discoloration, imperfect reflection and refraction of a colorless ray.

So the light of truth is discolored by passing through the human media of its representation. To speak in a paradox, we need unction to modify our very conceptions of God and truth. Our mental and emotional states and habits, our dispositions and tempers, doubtless affect our notions of divine things. If the preacher have a tyrannical temper, may not God's law, passing through such medium, take a false tinge, and appear as the arbitrary code of an infinite Will? If his disposition be vindictive, will he not be prone to conceive of divine wrath as a revengeful rage, with elements of malice, malignity, malevolence, wholly at variance with His character, so that the holy anger of God, from the medium of its transmission, shall assume a lurid glare? Nor is it incredible that a melancholic temper may impart, even to divine promises, a sombre tint. And so if the preacher have that type of amiability which lacks force and will, he will be prone to form unregenerate notions of divine benevolence, and conceive God as a ruler whose mercy is laxity, whose indulgence verges upon indifference.

Thus it is that men not endued and imbued with the Spirit of God, misconceive, and so misrepresent, the divine character, and, in effect, hold up to view a God whose image is colored and qualified by a yet unsanctified, perhaps unrenewed, disposition. No man can declare God's truth as it is, until he is brought, by the power of the Holy Ghost, into real, vital, personal sympathy with God. The power to teach and preach rightly and truly implies an antecedent power rightly and truly to *think*—to conceive the truth. " For what man knoweth the things of a man, save the spirit of man, which is in him? Even so the things of God knoweth no man, but the Spirit of God "—(1 Cor. ii : 11).

How manifestly essential is the Holy Ghost to all vivid conceptions of the sinner's condition! It is only now and then that we realize the actual peril—the lost state—of impenitent souls; that we see the sinner doomed and damned. Only now and then that we feel how glorious is heaven ; how awful is hell; how certain the danger ; how perfect the deliverance.

This realization, or sense of the reality, of divine things, only God can give. And when the Spirit unveils our eyes, uncovers to our spiritual vision the real woe of lost souls, the real bliss of souls saved, then all the thoughts and feelings, powers and purposes of the preacher become like combustible material set aflame with divine earnestness.

II. If the Holy Ghost must thus lead us to right apprehensions of the truth, all *true power, in its presentation,* must be also of God. The office of the preacher is that of an interpreter, not of words only, but of the spirit which they embody. He is to speak " the truth in love ;" not only to represent God's message as a messenger, but to represent God as an ambassador. The nearer he gets, therefore, to a divine point of view, the closer he comes into spiritual sympathy with God, the more complete his identity with Him, the mightier he is as a representative. Here, again, then, appears the importance of divine unction, in its necessity to real power in the presentation of gospel themes. This also will most clearly appear as to a certain class of truths.

The ill-success of our attempts to bring the severer attributes of God near to the consciousness of man, may be owing not wholly to the moods of the hearer, but partly to the modes of the preacher. During the writer's seminary life, a sermon was preached before the class upon the wrath of God. So violent and vindictive was its whole tone, that it drew from a boy of six summers, who was present, the remark, that " the man preached about a *wicked God.*" We shall never forget how DR. SKINNER, in reviewing the sermon, cautioned us against misconceiving and misrepresenting the holy anger of God. " This brother," said he, " seems to find pleasure in excoriating people, and talks with apparent satisfaction, if not delight, of their guilt and exposure to hell. I fear he has still unregenerated notions of God's anger, which he conceives as malevolent, while it is infinitely benevolent." Then, with great unction, he proceeded to show us how love and hate are equally perfections in God—in fact, only opposite poles of the same great attribute of holiness. And we went from that class exercise with such views of divine wrath as made God seem only the more lovable, because he hates sin with infinite hatred.

Whitefield's preaching, which so gently and softly echoed the messages of grace, sometimes thundered with the stern voice of the law. But his tearful tenderness, his affluent emotion, made Sinai seem almost as sweet and subduing as Calvary. That famous sermon of Edwards,' on "Sinners in the hands of an angry God," would, without unction, have been almost an assault upon God, an apology for infidelity. What marvel, if the great Scotch preacher, on hearing that one of his brethren had preached upon "The terrors of God," asked, "Did he do it with unction? without that he has wrought only harm."

III. Unction imparts power in the *interpretation of truth.* The prime quality of an actor is the power, not of affecting emotion or passion, but of assuming a character not his own— of throwing himself, by a subtle sympathy, into the characters, scenes, and times which he represents. Somewhat so in the pulpit. The prime requisite of the preacher is the power of real, vital, spiritual sympathy with God, divine themes, and spiritual truths.

Musicians singularly differ in their renderings of vocal and instrumental compositions. Thousands have a merely mechanical power. There is, in their musical performances, a flexibility, rapidity, accuracy, which astonish you. They seem to have acquired a perfect mastery over the tones of the voice, or the keys of the instrument. Others have what may be called an original power. There is, in their performances, a striking originality, a startling brilliancy, which proves a native, creative, genius for music. Yet a third class, and they are but few, possess a spiritual power. They may have neither the rapid and skillful mechanical execution of some, nor the brilliantly original style of others, but they have a marvelous, almost miraculous, power of entering into the secret life of the composer, and interpreting to the hearer his musical idea or thought. For in every true musical composition there is an *idea* wrought into its very structure, and he is the finest musician who can, by instinct or study, discover that musical thought, and give it expression in the language of melody and harmony—who can sing out with the voice, or play out upon an instrument, the original conception of the composer. He becomes an interpreter.

In the pulpit, among our foremost preachers, will be found three great classes. First, those whose power is, in a sense, mechanical. There is a rapidity of thought, a fluency of utterance, a flexibility of voice, an accuracy of diction, a grace of gesture, which proclaim the finished orator. Others possess an original power. They, perhaps, transgress not a few rules of oratorical propriety, but they reveal a genius for public address. The brilliance of their conceptions, the sublimity of their imaginations, their wild, weird, startling suggestions, amaze and overwhelm you. The intellectual firmament seems to be flashing with auroras and raining meteors.

There is a third class, who have acquired in preaching a true spiritual power. They may or may not possess the mechanical graces of the finished, polished speaker, or the original genius of the natural orator. What matters that! What if they cannot, with graceful fluency, produce what is rhetorically faultless. What if they cannot throw into their public address the originality, versatility, and force which charm and chain you. They have a mysterious, spiritual power to render God's truth clear and cogent, to enter with intellectual, emotional, spiritual appreciation into the spiritual mind of the Divine Author. Imbued with his spirit, endued with his power, they catch *his* thought and give it expression. They are *God's interpreters*. Their exegesis or exposition has no aim and works no end but the bringing forth of the hidden spiritual sense and meaning, and through them the Spirit of God feeds you with the " hidden manna."

IV. If unction—this enduing with divine power—be thus essential to the true apprehension, presentation, and interpretation of truth, it must find its *importance*, also, in its *necessity to all real success*.

Fidelity in the work of preaching is not to be gauged by seeming success; but we cannot help feeling that the infrequency of conversions is mainly traceable to the lack of unction in preaching. DR. SKINNER used to say that " God may give to a church and to a pastor every type of piety but that which is found in a *sense of the powers of the world to come*, and the impenitent will remain unconverted. But when the preacher, in any way, gets this consciousness of eternal realities, he is prepared to become, under Christ, a saviour to souls." This sense of eternal things in the preacher, awakening a similar consciousness in the hearer—this is unction, this is the power of the Holy Spirit in actual exercise.

When this power endues the preacher, it is manifest in a
mighty logic of argument, and a mightier logic of feeling. His
words are now like drawn swords, keen at the edge and keener
at the point; now like the hammer, whose heavy blows
break in pieces even the flinty rock; and again like the fire,
that burns, melts, and subdues all things. It is manifest in the
hearer, in the consciousness that "a spiritual power is grap-
pling with him," laying hold upon his convictions, emotions,
conscience, will; compelling him either to yield or fight. And
while no preacher is responsible if he do not command success,
he is responsible if he do not command power. The final decisions of destiny he cannot control; but he may compel a
soul to make a decision.

Theremin was right: " Eloquence *is* a virtue," and pre-eminently, sacred eloquence. No human gifts, or combination of
gifts, can constitute a man a true preacher. Whether or not
he have the graces of oratory, he must have the graces of the
Spirit. His power must be that of a renewed soul, endued with
divine authority, imbued with holy unction, transmitting to
others the glow of his own earnestness and enthusiasm.

This spiritual power is, perhaps, the only thing in a preacher
which cannot be feigned. He who never tasted of the grace
of God may build discourses of faultless homiletical proportion and theological symmetry. A hypocrite may play the
part of an actor, assuming an ardor, a fervor, an earnestness, a
tenderness, a pathos, a passion, which he does not feel. But
only he who waits before God till endued with power from on
high, can so wield the sword of the Spirit as that he shall pierce
"even to the dividing asunder of the soul and spirit, and of
the joints and marrow," and prove "a discerner of the thoughts
and intents of the heart."

So important to the preacher is unction, that, without it, the
right and privilege of the man to preach is, at least, questionable. For what is it which constitutes the commission by
virtue of which we occupy the sacred office? First, the divine
call to teach in this school of souls. Next, the possession of
gifts fitted to edify. And, third, the unction which gives power
to testimony. The first, the divine call, none but the man
himself can decide. As to the second requisite, the edifying
gift, the church must judge. The last, the divine anointing, only

the actual fruits can prove. Without *this*, the last and greatest requisite, all else is vain. For as a Christian without the
savor of godliness is worthless *as a Christian;* so the preacher
without unction is worthless *as a preacher.*

V. Unction gives character, not only to the truth preached,
but to *the man preaching.* The word "unction" means anointing, and suggests fragrance. The ancients used to say that
the purest forms of virtue were aromatic to the senses ; so that
persons of distinguished purity and beauty of character were
encompassed with an atmosphere of fragrance. Who that has
moved in the companionship and enjoyed the ministrations of
a man of God, peculiarly and habitually anointed with this
divine chrism, has not observed how his whole utterance and
bearing are fragrant with gospel aroma ! Unction imparts
savor to his sermons, power to his testimony, soul to his voice,
and a nameless charm, even to his presence. You think of
what was said of Lord Chatham : "There was something in
the *man* finer than he ever said ;" or of Aaron, at whose
anointing for the priestly office, the precious ointment "ran
down upon his beard, and went down to the skirts," or fringes,
"of his garments."   Of the truly anointed preacher, it may be
said : "All thy garments smell of myrrh and aloes and cassia,
out of the ivory palaces of the heavenly King.—Ps. xlv : 8.

We are beautifully told that our risen Redeemer was made
known to his disciples "in the breaking of bread."   It was not
in his general appearance, blooming with resurrection glories,
nor in his celestial converse only, that Jesus shewed himself
to his disciples.   But when he went in to tarry with them, and
sat down to meat, took bread, and blessed it, and brake it, and
gave to them, the reverent simplicity, the holy devoutness, the
childlike gratitude, with which that evening grace was said,
that simple act performed, left no doubt who it was.

It is said that the wood of the violin becomes changed in
structure by being played upon, and is reconstructed upon a
finer principle. For this reason, a very old instrument, thus
refined in texture by long service in the hands of some master
of melody, can scarce be bought at any price, having yielded
up its original coarseness and harshness in obedience to this
strange law. When the great Norwegian violinist wished to
repair his favorite instrument, he waited till an accident in the

orchestra shivered the grand bass viol, and secured a portion of the wood, to incorporate with his own violin.

We have often thought that somewhat so *the whole man*, upon whom the Spirit rests, and through whom, as by some subtle instrument, God chooses to breathe into human ears and hearts the melodies and harmonies of a divine gospel, must become refined in spiritual texture, lose his original coarseness and harshness, and, throughout, feel the pervasive influence of the enduing, imbuing power.

Hume said that " he who would teach eloquence, must teach it chiefly by examples." And we may, perhaps, get no little help in forming a true conception of sacred eloquence, by citing examples." What a power was Peter on the day of Pentecost, when that vast multitude were " pricked in their heart, and cried out, ' Men and brethren, what shall we do ?' " and when three thousand that same day received his word with repentance and faith, and were baptized into the fellowship of the church. What power unction gave to Stephen before his stoners, so that, filled as they were with murderous hate, they were " not able to resist the wisdom and the spirit with which he spake."

· One of the most remarkable examples of this spiritual power in modern days was, perhaps, Whitefield, who has been called the most successful preacher since apostolic times. What ardent, fervent, pungent logic ! What flaming evangelism ! What glowing enthusiasm ! What a divine earnestness ! His mingled simplicity and sincerity, tenderness and directness, quelled the rabble at Moorfields, the rough colliers at Kingswood, and the murderous miners at Cornwall ; and enchanted the versatile Garrick and the elegant Chesterfield, the philosophical Franklin and the skeptical Hume, as well as the ignorant, degraded, brutalized outcasts of society.

Where lay the secret of this power? Not in native genius, not in transcendent powers. John Angell James says his elements of success were " solemnity, tenderness, earnestness, courage ;" and his biographers agree that his were not very extraordinary abilities. His voice, indeed, was wonderful, having a strange power to charm and thrill, persuade and subdue. Yet even that voice would have been but the soulless sound of a brazen trumpet, the empty clangor of a silver cymbal, without the emotion—unction—that gave expression, life, power to his whole elocution. God endued him with power. This alone accounts for that soulful earnestness, habitual un-selfishness, fondness for his work, tearful tenderness, impas-sioned appeal, passion for souls, which made this modern evan-gelist the Elias of the eighteenth century, and enabled him, with almost divine authority, to insist on instant, visible, decisive action in those who heard him.

So the great Northampton pastor, calmly repeating the words, "Their feet shall slide in due time," so alarmed his audience that they shrieked and groaned aloud, till their cries actually drowned the preacher's voice and compelled him to pause, while they seized the pillars of the meeting-house as if they felt their feet sliding into ruin.

So Nettleton, violating all rhetorical rules and homiletic standards, in his simple sermon on the words, "I thought on my ways, and turned my feet unto thy testimonies," neverthe-less, wrote those words on every heart as with a pen of iron and the point of a diamond, till every hearer seemed ready and resolved to turn his feet unto God.

It only remains to add a few words upon *the conditions upon which we may expect this divine enduement.* The promise is: "Ye shall receive power after that the Holy Ghost is come upon you." To whom is it addressed? Is this glori-ous assurance limited to the great and gifted? No! One may possess only the most ordinary abilities, and yet be endued with power from on high. As William Arthur says: "The tongue of fire may be combined with any form of talent and with any style of composition:" through unimpassioned tran-quility or calm argument, instructive exposition or doctrinal teaching, imaginative description or fervid exhortation, the divine fire may burn and glow. The preaching gift, like the gospel message, knows no aristocracy of intellect, no monop-oly of genius.

1. And yet it ought to be borne in mind, that one condition of our reception of the supernatural power is, that we make diligent use of the *natural.* Because God is glorified by the foolishness of preaching, it by no means follows that we are justified in preaching foolishness. We are not to be content with weakness because God can use it for his glory. Surely

we are not to imagine weakness a virtue, because it is not by might, nor by power, that souls are saved. That is the wrong kind of simplicity that makes men almost simpletons. Away with the notion that even prayer is to displace *studious preparation*. Grace never sets a premium on idleness or laziness. The beaten oil befits the sanctuary. There is a natural basis even for supernatural power; and the natural basis for unction in preaching is a mind and heart by devout study filled with the Word. A man who thus habitually comes to his pulpit, after diligent research into the Bible in the original tongues, with his whole being infused and suffused with biblical themes, will most likely to be filled with the Holy Ghost. We are to do our very best, and then, with deep consciousness that all our strength is but weakness, ask God's blessing, not on our laziness, but on our labor.

2. There is also a *spiritual* basis for the heavenly enduing with power, to be found in a spiritual mind, and heart, and life; in general goodness of character. Can you imagine a man wielding this power who is not filled with the Holy Ghost? The *anointing* process implies a previous *cleansing* process. The holy oil refuses to be poured upon that which is unclean, or to mingle its precious perfume with the scent of an unwashed, defiled person and garments. If ever one wants to come with clean hands and a pure heart, it is when about to take up the golden vessels of the sanctuary.

This natural basis of diligent study, this spiritual basis of a godly character, being secured, what remains in order to realize the blessing of the divine enduing?

3. There must be, first of all, a *consciousness of our need*. We do not deeply feel our impotence in handling sacred subjects. We often mistake intellectual enthusiasm, passional force, or emotional fervor, for spiritual power, and practically lean upon ourselves.

Socrates defined his work in the garden city of the east as a negative one: "To bring men from ignorance, unconscious, to ignorance, conscious." So we may say that the first work of the Spirit in preparing us to preach is a negative one, to bring us from *impotence, unconscious, to impotence, conscious*. Then our conscious need draws or drives us to God. Out of a longing soul we breathe the earnest prayer for power, such as only he can give. We begin to *feel* that clear views of truth, warm emotions, studied discourse, eloquent appeal alone, cannot save a soul or move a will; that it is not by might, nor by power, but by the spirit of the Lord.

4. This securing of unction must be not only a distinct subject and object of prayer, but an honest, specific, *supreme aim.* No man ever attains spiritual power so long as he is satisfied without it; so long as, whatever be his formal petitions, the real desire of his heart is to originate brilliant and startling thoughts, or clothe them with the golden and silver tissues of ornate speech; or, so long as the supreme desire is set upon any human type of power. While our aim is after excellency of speech, and enticing words of man's wisdom, let us not expect the demonstration of the Spirit. And let us remember, that the same prayer which earnestly begs for preaching-power, brings down that consciousness of eternal realities which comes only from God; and which renders "the groan of one wounded" soul more grateful to our ears, than the shouts of a thousand voices, "praising the skill of the archer."

We have already referred to Whitefield as an example of power in preaching. Where did he get power? He tarried at the throne of grace till he was divinely endued. He came from closest closet communion with God; and, like Moses issuing from the canopy of cloud, he came with a face shining with reflected glory, a soul overflowing with holy emotion, so that a simple look at his audience would sometimes open the fountains of his tears, and, for a time, close the gates of speech. Then, overcoming his emotion, he would hurl his heart at his hearers in hot words, all aglow with love and grace, until, under this sacred bombardment, the citadel of unbelief hauled down its hostile flag, and ran up the blessed banner of the cross.

Would that we all might come to feel that we need not the iron tongue of impassioned denunciation, nor the silver tongue of musical and persuasive oratory, nor the golden tongue of brilliant and gorgeous rhetoric; but the divine tongue of fire, lit from the altars of God!

When the ministry come to recognize and realize this need, breathe this prayer, and cherish this aim, then will begin a new era of pentecostal power. While we feel sufficient in ourselves, God withholds the divine anointing. But when we feel that our sufficiency is of God, then we look for higher help ; we go to the closet to be warmed with a heavenly fire and fervor. Then we receive the chrism from the Holy One, whose worth the alabaster box of ointment but faintly symbolizes; and whose fragrance, even that pervasive perfume which filled the house with its odor cannot express.

All important as is this heavenly anointing with power, it is yet without price. God waits and wills to give it simply for the asking. A dying world lies about us ; the quickening Word is in our hands. But we are powerless successfully to apply the remedy. The gospel, falling on listless ears, becomes only a savor of death unto death. But let the Holy Ghost come upon us and we receive power. Lo, our unworthy utterance is attended with the demonstration of the Holy Ghost ! The dry bones in the valley of indecision show signs of life ; bone cleaves to bone ; the skeleton of cold and dead intellectual belief begins to be clothed with the warm flesh of spiritual faith, and where once lay the slain of Satan, gather the hosts of God. That thus our preaching may become to sinners a quickening power, our every breath may well become a prayer.

Art. VII.—THE NEW MANUSCRIPT OF CLEMENT OF ROME.

By C. J. H. ROPES, Res. Lic., Union Seminary.

AMONG all the writings ascribed to the Apostolic Fathers, the Epistle of Clement to the Corinthians occupies the foremost place. Unquestionably the oldest of them,[1] it is also the one which offers the smallest field for criticism. Thus, the genuineness of Clement's Epistle is generally conceded, while opinions differ widely about the letters of Ignatius. Its style is dignified and sober, in marked contrast to the Epistle of Barnabas; and its theology has a catholic breadth very different from the Judaizing tendencies of the Shepherd of Hermas. Clement is, moreover, free from peculiar and, to us, distasteful elements, like the allegorical exegesis of Barnabas, the fantastic vagaries of Hermas, or the constant enforcement of episcopal authority which characterizes Ignatius. Connecting, as it does, the principal church in Greece with that of Rome, the Epistle of Clement to the Corinthians may be regarded as the faithful mirror of primitive Christianity.

By some freak of history, there has been linked with this genuine letter, the so-called Second Epistle of Clement of Rome to the Corinthians.

Until the present time, these Epistles have been known only from the last few leaves of the Alexandrine Bible manuscript. The text throughout is very faulty—in many places entirely obliterated—and three leaves are lost, containing five chapters of the First Epistle and eight of the Second.

The Latin Church, from the fifth to the sixteenth century, was so ignorant of the whole epistles, that Thomas Aquinas could speak of "Pope Clement's Epistle to the *Athenians.*"[2] But till within two years those thirteen chapters have been deemed entirely lost.

In 1875, however, a book appeared, which tells its own story:

The Two Epistles of our Father among the Saints, Clement, Bishop of Rome, to the Corinthians, now for the first time published complete, from a manuscript of the Library of the Most Holy Sepulchre

---

1. Some place Hermas and Barnabas almost as early, but their dates are very uncertain.

2. Pat. Apost., opp. edd. Gebhardt, Harnack, Zahn, Lips. 1876. Fasc. I. Pars I., ed. 2; pp. xxxvi, xxxviii, note.

in the Fanar of Constantinople ; with Prologemena and Notes, by Philotheus Bryennius, Metropolitan of Serrhæ ; at the cost of Mr. George Zarifé, a gentleman distinguished by his liberality and zeal for Christian and ancient literature. 8vo. Constantinople, 1875.[3]

The manuscript here mentioned, is a small 8vo parchment codex, of 120 leaves:

"Finished in the month of June, in the 11th century, the 3d day, the 9th (year) of the Indiction, the year 6564, by the hand of Leo, notary and sinner."[4]

It contains Chrysostom's Summary of the Old Testament— as far as Malachi (leaves 1–32), the Epistle of Barnabas (33— 51 b), Clement's First and Second Epistles to the Corinthians (51 b—70a—76 a), the Doctrine of the 12 Apostles (76 a—80), the 12 Epistles of Ignatius in the longer Greek Recension, preceded by that of Mary Castabalensis to the Martyr (81–120).

The manuscript is a cursive, neatly and distinctly written ; words, accents, aspiration, and interpunctuation being clearly indicated. Itacisms are very rare, excepting the interchange of $\dot{\eta}\mu\epsilon\hat{\imath}s$ and $\dot{\nu}\mu\epsilon\hat{\imath}s$. If the fac-simile given by Bryennius is a fair example, there can have been no difficulty in reading the text, though it is not free from abbreviations, and iota subscript seems to be written only in a single instance. The mistakes, indeed are so few as to suggest that the scribe revised his original. Peculiarities of spelling appear to have been removed, moods and tenses corrected, order of words improved, and Scripture quotations abbreviated or conformed to the Septuagint.[5] Even the theology has not wholly escaped.

We have already three editions of Clement in which the new manuscript is used. It is gratifying to meet in the Greek Church with such a proof of acquaintance and sympathy with occidental patristic study, as is afforded by the learned and elaborate edition in which Bryennius has made known his discovery. The minute and careful survey of the subject contained in the prolegomena shows a comprehensive knowledge

---

3. Trans. in *Academy*, May 6, 1876, p. 436. The *Fanar* is the Greek quarter ; Serrhæ (Heraclea) is an ancient See in Macedonia (Stud. u. Krit., 1876, p. 708., Bleek, Einl. ins A. T., 2 ed. (1865), p. 111, note.)

4. *l. c.*, June 3d, A. D. 1056. 1056 is the year 6564 of the 'Byzantine era· whose year 5509 coincides with A. D. 1. The Indiction is a cycle of 15 years, beginning with B. C. 3. So 1056 (*strictly* Sept. 1, 1055—Aug. 31, 1056) is the 9th, year of the 71st Indiction.

5. Cf. Pat. Apost. opp. l. c., p. xiv, and notes.

of even the more recent literature relating to Clement in several different languages.[6]   While such a wide range of reading for the preface shows that no external source of information has been neglected, an equal care for the text of the epistles is shown in the punctiliousness with which every possible allusion to Scripture has been noted.[7]   In view of these merits, we can readily pardon the editor's allusions to "some Protestants who are afflicted with episcophobia," and to "the lofty criticism" of certain Germans.[8]   We must, however, regret that Bryennius did not have access to Tischendorf's text of Clement (1873), or to Lightfoot's admirable edition (1869).   The result of this deprivation and of a natural partiality for his own discovery, is seen in the text, which leans too much to the new readings, though the older codex should have the greater weight.[9]   The greatest fault, indeed, of this edition is that it can scarcely be called critical in any sense. This may be illustrated by the fact that Bryennius finds no difficulty in supposing the so-called Second Epistle to be a genuine work of the Roman Clement.[10]

The same fault cannot be attributed to Hilgenfeld's new edition of Clement,[11] yet he falls into some similar errors The prolegomena will repay perusal, and there are a few good notes under the text and at the end of the volume.[12]   The editor has also done well in relinquishing a large number of the conjectures he hazarded in his former edition (1866).   But

---

6. It is amusing to read familiar names in the references of Bryennius: *e. g.* Κονσταντῖνος ὁ Τισενδόρφιος, Ἀγευμφέλδος, θείρσιος, Σουέγλερος, Οὐλχόρνιος (Thiersch, Schwegler, Uhlhorn).

7. The supposed parallels to John's Gospel and 2 Peter have no strength.   On the other hand, the quotations from 1 Peter may be held to refute Hilgenfeld's theory, that 1 Peter was written as late as the reign of Trajan. (Zeitschr. für. Wissensch. Theol., 1876, p. 58.)

8. Οἱ ἐπισκοφοβίαν πάσχοντες τῶν Διαμαρτυρομένων κ. τ. λ. p. ξστ.· Ὑψηλὴ δὲ κριτικὴ καλεῖται κ. τ. λ. p. ξζ´.

9 Cf. Theol. Literaturzeitung, Feb. 19, 1876, p. 99; Stud. u. Krit., 1876, p. 708; Hilgenfeld's ed. of Clement, p. xxi, sq.

10. P. σξζ´.

11. Clementis Romani Epistulæ: edidit, commentario critico et adnotationibus instruxit, Mosis Assumptionis quæ supersunt collecta et illustrata addidit, omnia emendata iterum edidit Adolphus Hilgenfeld. Lipsiæ, 1876.

12. *E. g.* p. 7, on the gender of ζῆλος; p. 68, on the use of καί with a preposition (σὺν καὶ Φορτυνάτῳ); and especially p. 98, on "worlds beyond the ocean."

both text and notes are open to serious criticism, and the whole book is hastily put together and ill arranged. The notes are a confusion of text criticism, Scripture references, and patristic parallels, much space being unnecessarily used in quoting at full length illustrative passages from Clement of Alexandria and others. Several notes, which should be under the text, are at the end, and *vice versa*. While containing much that might profitably have been condensed, the notes often leave us scantily informed on interesting topics. The volume, moreover, does not contain an index of any kind, and this defect, with the confused form in which the notes are printed, greatly hinders the usefulness of the work. But while the notes leave much undone, the text has had too much done for it. The editor has not abandoned his taste for arbitrary conjectures. Not content with a very decided and indefensible preference throughout for the new codex over the old, he even amends the text against both manuscripts on the authority of Clement of Alexandria, or on that of his own opinion.[13] Where, however, we have only the new manuscript, the editor's reverence for it seems to abate. In the five new chapters of the first epistle he makes ten changes in the text, of which five or six are unnecessary, and two others infelicitous conjectures.[14] But it is in the treatment of the fragments, of which we shall speak later, that this editor's arbitrary construction of the text culminates.

---

13. With Clement, e. g. c. 48, p. 53, l. 9, ἥτω γοργὸς ἐν ἔργοις κ.τ.λ. Cf. Lightfoot's note (p. 146, sq.) against trusting Clement's citations. Another instance c. 18, p. 23, l. 3. On his own judgment, e. g., c. 19, p. 24, l. 17, τοὺς γέ; c. 44, p. 48, l. 4, ἐπὶ δοχιμῆ. c. 45, p. 50, l. 2, ἐξηρέθισαν. l. 3, παραβαλεῖν.

14. c. 59, p. 64, l. 18, ἄνοιξον; c. 59, p. 65, l. 10, adds δέ; c. 60, p. 65, l. 23, ἐρωμένοις; c. 60, p. 66, l. 3, add (ἡμῶν); c. 60, p. 66, l, 3, ὑποχόων γινομένων; c. 60, p. 66, l. 4, παντοχρατοχινῷ; c. 61, p. 66, l. 5, δέ; c. 61 p. 66, l. 22, γενεάς; c. 62, p. 66, l. 24, a lacuna is assumed; c. 62, p. 67, l. 3, εἰ ἀρεστεῖν. This last emendation is good and needed; ἄνοιξον also is justifiable; but we have yet to hear of any usage of ἐρωμένοις, *the beloved of God*, instead of the usual ἀγαπητοῖς (cf. Rom. i : 7.), which Clement uses, c. 8, p. 12, l. 13; Ὑποχόων γινομένων is put instead of ὑποχόους γινομένους; Gebhardt's emendation (Zeitschr. fur Kirchengeschichte, 1876, p. 305) ὑποχόοις γ᾽νομένοις makes equally good sense, with less violence to the text. Παντοχράτορι (for which Hilgenfeld substitutes παντροχατορικῷ) is found in similar use, Hermas, Vis. iii : 3. (in Pat. Apost. opp., l. c., p. 102, the reference is incorrectly given *Sim.* iii : 3.) τοῦ παντοχράτορος καὶ ἐνδόξου ὀνόματος. This peculiar use of παντοχράτωρ may have originated in an indefinite remembrance of Jer. l : 34 (lxx), κύριος παντοχρύτωρ ὄνομα αὐτῷ.

The best work on Clement's epistles is, undoubtedly, that of Gebhardt and Harnack in the new Leipzig edition of the Apostolic Fathers.[15] This is worthy of almost unqualified praise.

The arrangement is systematic and perspicuous. The text criticism is printed by itself. The text is conservative, and based on true principles, without being slavishly bound to mistakes of the manuscripts. The notes show great erudition and patient research, but are carefully condensed and modestly stated. The prolegomena are full, yet concise, and convey the impression, that very few works in the immense list of literature there given,[16] have been unconsulted by the editor. The indices, though not so full as those of Jacobson's fourth edition (1863), yet contain enough for most purposes of reference.

We hazard a few suggestions, which might tend to make the work still more complete. It would have been well to include in the Prolegomena a concise statement of the theology of the First Epistle, and a rather more extended survey of the Second in its proper character of a homily. Among the references to the Phœnix (I. c. 25), those in the classics ought to find a place.[17] The liturgical parallels to I. cc. 59–61 might, as we shall see, have been largely supplemented, had sources other than the Apostolic Constitutions been consulted. We conclude with two minor criticisms.

The note on ἀρχέγονον (p. 98) is very defective. The word is not so uncommon as seems to be implied. The lexicons give several instances of its use in profane writers, and Irenæus uses it four times at the beginning of his work, in stating the doctrines of the Gnostics.[18]

---

15. Patrum Apostolicorum opera textum ad fidem codicum et græcorum et latinorum adhibitis præstantissimis editionibus, recensuerunt commentario exegetico et historico illustraverunt, apparatu critico versione latina passim correcta prolegomenis indicibus instruxerunt, Oscar de Gebhardt, Adolphus Harnack, Theodorus Zahn. Editio post Dressellianam alteram tertia, fasciculi primi, partis prioris editio altera. Lipsiæ. 1876.

16. Very few, and those unimportant, omissions are noticeable in this list, on a careful comparison with those of Jacobson, (Apostolic Fathers, 1863, vol. I, p. lxiv) and Lipsius (de Clem. Ep. priore disquisitio, Lips., 1855, p. 3, sq.)

17. In Herodotus, Ovid, Seneca, Pliny, Tacitus, etc.

18. I. i, §§ 1, 2; 5, § 2; 9, § 3.

The least justifiable thing in the edition is Gebhardt's substitution of (*C*) for (I), (adopted by Bryennius and Hilgenfeld) to designate the new codex. There is no apparent reason for the change; and two names for one manuscript are always a source of confusion.

Having thus sketched the history of the new manuscript, let us see what we have gained by it for the correction of the old text, and from the new fragments which complete the Epistles.[19] The defaced condition of the Codex Alexandrinus has always afforded a wide field for conjecture, in which, as no one has had the opportunities, so no one has equaled the success of the first editor, Patrick Young. Among recent editors, Lightfoot (1869), Tischendorf (1873), and Gebhardt (1875), have given the best texts. Many of these conjectures have been confirmed, and many rendered superfluous by the new manuscript.[20] But in other cases, where the reading is undisputed, the sense is so doubtful that various emendations have been proposed.

Such are the references to *the sufferings of God* (c. 2), to Peter and Paul (c. 5), to the Danaids and Dirce (c. 7), to prayer to the Saints (c. 56); also the strange word ἐπινομήν (c. 44). In most of these cases the reading of the Codex Alexandrinus is confirmed by the new MS. It reads ἐπιδομήν, but this seems to be a mere corruption, as the word is unknown. In the references to Peter and Paul, the conjectural reading Πέτρος[21] is confirmed; so that Zeller's hypothesis, Ἰακωβός,[22] is no longer possible; and the whole connection of the passage is strengthened in a way that makes it a better argument than before for the presence and martyrdom of Peter at Rome.

In the well-known passage (c. 2):

"Being satisfied with the provision of *God*, and diligently giving heed to *his* words, ye had laid them up in your hearts, and *his* sufferings were before your eyes;"

---

19. For the completeness of the Epistles, cf. Theol. Literaturzeitung, Feb. 19 1876, p. 101; Pat. Apost., opp. l. c., p. xv. Contra, Hilgenfeld's ed. of Clement (1876), p. xix.

20. A list of conjectures illustrating these statements may be found, Theol. Literaturzeitung, l. c., p. 100.

21. The new MS. reads Πέτρον, ὅς.

22. Zeitschr. für wissensch. theol., 1876, p. 47; cf. also Hilgenfeld, ibid. 1872, p. 349; 1876, p. 57. In the Protestant. Kirchenzeitung, 1876, No. 3, Hilgenfeld announced that the new MS. "throws new light on the character of the controversy carried on between Peter and Paul." Harnack (Theol. Literaturzeitung, l. c., p. 100) puzzles himself to account for this statement, but as Hilgenfeld seems never to have recurred to the subject since, it may be inferred that the "new light" has proved an *ignis fatuus*.

recently discussed by Dr. Abbot,[23] the new MS. reads *Christ* for *God.* But *God*, as the more difficult reading, and that of the older MS. by six centuries, is to be preferred.[24] *Christ* seems to have been substituted to correct the christology, as the new MS. does in one other case.[25] But the ancient reading does not necessarily involve Patripassianism.

"We have only to suppose a somewhat negligent use of αὐτοῦ (of which we have an example near the end of the same chapter, and others in cc. 32, 34, 36, 50), referring to Christ *in the mind of the writer*, though not named. . . . . .
Observing, then, that Clement had just borrowed a saying introduced, in Acts xx: 35. by the phrase '*remembering the words* of the Lord Jesus,' how natural that he should go on to say, ' and diligently giving heed to his words, ye had laid them up in your hearts, and his sufferings were before your eyes.'"[26]

This explanation seems very satisfactory, and closes the internal evidence in the case. But the testimony of Photius is used[27] against the reading *God*, because he complains (Bibl. Cod. 126) that Clement does not give the higher—the divine—titles to Christ.[28] Dr. Lightfoot rejoins:

"As the reference to Christ's divinity lurks under the reference of the pronoun αὐτοῦ, it might very easily have escaped the notice of Photius. who, in the course of this single embassy, read as large a number of books as would have sufficed many a man not ill-informed for a life-time."[29]

This is a plausible explanation, but the words of Photius seems to show, that he made a careful and critical examination of Clement's First Epistle, with the object of discovering Arianism in it; and it may be that he took the view of αὐτοῦ adopted above.

Photius first mentions Clement's Epistles, apparently from hearsay, after reviewing the Apostolic Constitutions and the Clementine Recognitions (Bibl. Cod. 112–113). He praises the Recognitions especially for their style. To several criticisms on the Constitutions, he adds two on the Recognitions—that "they contain many absurdities, and are full of blasphemy against the Son according to the doctrine of Arius."

23. Bib. Sac., 1876, April, p. 342, sq.   I use Dr. Abbot's translation.

24. Conjectures like μαθήματα for παθήματα are excluded by the concurrence of both MSS.

25. Ep. ii : c. 9. A. reads Χριστός . . ὧν μὲν τὸ πρῶτον πνεῦμα. I. reads in place of the last word, λόγος, evidently a correction of the christology. For a similar instance see Ignat. ad Ephes., c. i, where the shorter Greek, with Severus, and Cureton's Syriac, reads ἐν αἴματι Θεοῦ the old Latin, *in sanguine* Christi *Dei*, the longer Greek, ἐναίματι Χριστοῦ. The notes of Petermann and Bunsen, quoted by Dr. Abbot (l. c. p. 338), are refuted by the strength of the MS. evidence.

26. Dr. Abbot, in Bib. Sac., l. c. See the entire page (343), strengthening by weighty arguments and authorities the position taken. It may be added, that a similar indefinite use of αὐτός is found in Hebrews, to which Clement owed so much; *e. g.*, Heb. iii: 2, 5, 6.

27. By Hilgenfeld, Zeitschr. für wissensch, theol., 1876, p. 441; ed. of Clement (1876), p. 5, sq.

28. It is possible that Photius found the reading *Christ* in the 9th century, since our new MS. had it in the 11th.

29. Ed. of Clement, pp. 385, sq., note.

When Photius comes (Bibl. Cod. 126) to read Clement's First Epistle, he evidently has in mind these criticisms on a work which he seems to attribute to the same author.   Thus he remarks, that " it is simple, clear, and suited to the ecclesiastical and inelaborate style."   He objects, that " it locates worlds beyond the ocean, and uses the Phœnix as a trustworthy argument."   He complains that, " while it calls Christ our High-priest and Patron," it does not give Him the higher—the divine—titles, although He is nowhere openly blasphemed in it. "

The parallel between the estimate of the Recognitions and of the Epistle is salient.   There is, indeed, a difference of style, but that is explained by the object in view.   Absurdities find a place in the Epistle, and its Arianism is only not positively, openly expressed.   We see that Photius came from the Recognitions with the expectation of finding Arianism in the Epistle, and it would have needed some *explicit* assertion of Christ's deity to refute that presumption.

It may be objected, that immediately afterwards Photius (Bibl. Cod. 126) contrasts with the First Epistle of Clement, the Second, "which at the very beginning proclaims Christ as God."   The reply is easy.

1. This reference is of the most explicit kind—" Brethren, we ought to think of Christ as of God, as of the judge of quick and dead."

2. Photius rightly regarded the Second Epistle as not by Clement (Bibl. Cod. 113), and therefore did not expect to find Arianism in it.

3. Though the Arians frequently speak of Christ as $\theta\epsilon\delta s$, they could hardly accept the expression just quoted.

We conclude, therefore, that the bias visible in the testimony of Photius very much weakens its force against the reading, *God*. On the other side, Hippolytus, six centuries before Photius, knowing only the first epistle as Clement's, and therefore not prejudiced against it by the Recognitions, includes Clement among those who speak of Christ as God ; and there is even reason to believe that he had in his mind this very passage.[31]

The assertion of Hippolytus is sufficient to balance that of Photius, and the probabilities of the case thus favor the ancient reading.

Of the many fragments attributed to these epistles, only three are confirmed by the new manuscript.

The quotation made by Basil (De Spir. Sanct. c. xxix), is found I. c. 58; the passage cited by John of Damascus (Sacra Par. p. 783 *Le Quien*) occurs II. c. 20, and the reference in the Questiones ad Orthodoxos (Resp. 74). is probably to II. c. 17.[32]

Hilgenfeld long ago expressed great doubt of the genuineness of the only fragment now proved to belong to Clement.

---

30. Three times, cc. 36, 61, 64.

31. Lightfoot, l. c., gives almost conclusive reasons for supposing Clement of Rome (not of Alexandria) is referred to here (Euseb. H. E., v. 28).   Hilgenfeld (ed. of Clement, 1876, p. 5, note) meets them with a bare denial, unsupported by a single argument.

32 Apost. Vaeter, p. 74, note.   He afterwards, however, admitted the fragment into the text of his edition (1866).

From this, one might perhaps have expected more caution in his new edition. It is, therefore, by no means a pleasant surprise to find a lacuna *assumed* in II. c. 10, and two fragments there *interpolated* in the text, one of which, as stated, belongs to c. 17, if at all to the epistle.

One statement generally attributed to the lost chapters of the First Epistle, merits examination.

The reference in Irenæus to "fire prepared for the devil and his angels," finds no explanation in the new MS. I think, however, that it is not necessary to assume a quotation, and that Dr. Lightfoot (ed. of Clement, p. 166, note) speaks a little too strongly—"*preparaverit* . . shows that the narrative is oblique, and that Irenæus is speaking in the words of another." The same moods and tenses prevail throughout :

"Annuntiantem unum Deum omnipotentem, factorem cœli et terræ, plasmatorem hominis, qui induxerit cataclysmum, et advocaverit Abraham, qui eduxerit populum de terra Ægypti, qui collocutus sit Moysi, qui legem disposuerit, et prophetas miserit, qui ignem preparaverit diabolo et angelis ejus."

Some of these statements are directly made by Clement, *e. g.*, "who conversed with Moses" in c. 17 ; but Clement nowhere insists on *one God;* nowhere speaks of God as having *brought on the flood, led the people out of Egypt, ordained the law, sent the prophets.* The unity of God may be inferred, because no second God is spoken of, such as some Gnostics held. The flood is never mentioned by Clement, but may be inferred from c. 7.

"Noah preached repentance, and those who harkened were saved." (c. 9) "Noah being found faithful, preached regeneration to the world through his ministry ; and the Lord saved, through him, the animals, which, with one accord, went into the ark."

That God brought on the flood is nowhere hinted. In c. 53, Exod. xxxii : 7, is quoted, where God said to Moses :

"*Thy* people, which *thou* broughtest out of the land of Egypt."

God's action here also, must be inferred.

The Mosaic law is, I think, never mentioned in Clement, except in the next quotation we make, though the commandments and ordinances of God, among which it may be included in a general way, are referred to—cc. 2, 50, 58.

The sending of the prophets by God may be inferred from c. 43.

"When the blessed Moses, also, ' a faithful servant in all his (God's) house,' noted down in the sacred books all the injunctions which were given him, and when the other prophets also followed him," etc.

The judgment by fire of the devil and his angels may also be inferred from c. 11.

"Lot was saved out of Sodom when all the country round was punished by means of fire and brimstone ; the Lord thus making it manifest, that He does not forsake those that hope in Him, but gives up such as depart from Him to punishment and torture."

The punishment and torture (fire is suggested) of all the wicked is evidently contained in this passage ; and the inference, transferring it to fallen angels, is only a little more distant than some of the other inferences of Irenæus in this place. But there is another reason for

the form which this inference from Clement assumes in Irenæus:
" Who prepared fire for the devil and his angels." It is taken from
Matt. xxv: 41, and is the common phrase used by Irenæus in describing the punishment of the wicked.

Irenæus uses the whole phrase at least eight times besides this place
(i: 10, §1; ii: 7, §3; iii: 23, §3; iv: 33, §11; 40, §1, 2; v: 26, §2; 27,
§1). In three other instances Irenæus uses only part of the phrase,
of the punishment of sinners (ii: 28, §6; 32, §1; iv: 28, §2); and
iii: 23, §3, he explains that there is but one punishment, originally
prepared for the devil and his angels, yet which is also to include all
the wicked.

It appears then, to me, that the frequent use of the phrase in Irenæus,
and the meaning he attached to it, justify its use here as equivalent to
the punishment of the wicked; and the inference that Clement held this
doctrine might be justified to a more minutely critical mind than that
of Irenæus by Ep. i: c. 11.

The references of Irenæus to the doctrine of the Epistle are so indefinitely connected with its *words*, and so evidently put into the form
in which they would be most effective against the Gnostics, that there
is not sufficient reason for singling out the one phrase, *qui ignem præ-
paraverit diabolo et angelis ejus,* and ascribing it to some lost fragment of the Epistle. Of course, however, we argue to-day on the basis
of the complete Epistle, while Dr. Lightfoot had only a mutilated copy;
and reasons which might warrant the insertion of a fragment in a
lacuna, do not warrant the *assumption* of a lacuna for that purpose.

We now turn to the missing chapters of Epistle I., and present them in a literal translation.

Codex A leaves a long quotation from Proverbs unfinished.
The new MS. completes this, and continues:

LVIII.—Let us, therefore, be obedient to his most holy and glorious
name, shunning the threatenings which were spoken before by wisdom[33]
to the disobedient, in order that we may rest, trusting in the most holy
name of his majesty. Receive our counsel and it shall not repent you.
For as God liveth, and the Lord Jesus Christ liveth, and the Holy
Spirit, the faith and the hope of the elect; he that in humbleness of mind
with unfailing gentleness, doeth cheerfully the commandments and ordinances given of God, the same shall be reckoned and counted into
the number of the saved through Jesus Christ, through whom is glory
to him forever and ever. Amen.

LIX.—But if any are disobedient to the words spoken by him through
us, let them know that they shall involve themselves in transgression
and no small danger. But we shall be blameless of this sin, and shall pray
with unceasing prayer and supplication, that the maker of all things may
preserve unbroken the determined number of his elect in all the world
through his beloved Son, Jesus Christ, through whom he hath called us
from darkness into light,[34] from ignorance to the knowledge of the glory

---

33 Referring to the quotation from Proverbs, (ἡ πανάρετος σοφία), which immediately precedes.

34 1 Pet. ii: 9. (The scripture references are furnished by Bryennius).

of his name, to hope in thy name, the author of every creature, having opened the eyes of our hearts that we may know thee, who only art most high among the highest, holy resting among the holy,[35] who humblest the arrogance of the proud,[36] who bringest to naught the desires of the nations,[37] who settest the humble on high, and humblest the lofty,[38] who enrichest and makest poor, who killest and makest alive,[39] the only benefactor of spirits and God of all flesh,[40] who lookest upon the depths,[41] beholder of the works of men,[42] helper of those in peril, saviour of those without hope,[43] creator and guardian of every spirit,[44] who increasest the nations on earth, and from them all hast chosen out them that love thee, through Jesus Christ, thy beloved Son, through whom thou hast taught us, sanctified us, honored us. We beseech thee, O, Lord, to be our helper and protector.[45] Save those of us who are in tribulation, have mercy on the humble, lift up the fallen, appear to those in want, heal the ungodly,[46] turn those of thy people who have gone astray; feed the hungering, deliver those of us who are in bonds, raise up the weak, comfort the faint-hearted;[47] let all the nations know that thou alone art God,[48] and Jesus Christ, thy Son, and we, thy people, and the sheep of thy pasture.[49]

LX.—Thou hast made manifest the perpetual constitution of the world through thy workings;[50] thou, Lord, hast created the earth,[51] who art faithful in all generations,[52] just in judgments, marvelous in might and majesty, wise in creating, and prudent in establishing that which is created, good in the things which are seen,[53] and faithful to them that trust in thee; O, thou, who art full of mercy and pity, forgive us our transgressions of thy law and our iniquities, and our trespasses and our faults.[54] Impute not any sin of thy servants and handmaidens, but purify us with the purification[55] of thy truth, and order our steps,[56] that we may walk in holiness of heart,[57] and do that which is g od and well pleasing in thy sight,[58] and in the sight of our rulers. Yea, Lord, make thy face to shine upon us for good[59] in peace, that we may be covered with thy mighty hand, and delivered from every sin by thine uplifted arm,[60] and deliver us from them that hate us unjustly. Give harmony and peace to us, and to all that dwell on the earth, as thou gavest to our fathers, when they called upon thee

---

35 Isa. lvii: 15 (lxx).   36 Isa. xiii: 11.   37 Ps. xxxiii (xxxii): 10.
38 Job v: 11; cf. Ezek. xv: 11, 24.   39 1 Samuel ii: 7; cf. Deut. xxxii: 39.
40 Numb. xxvii: 16; cf. xvi: 22.   41 Sirach xvii: 18 sq.
42 Esther v: 1 (lxx).   43 Judith ix: 11.   44 Job x: 12.   45 Judith ix: 11.

46 ἀσεβεῖς. Gebhardt conjectures ἀσθενεῖς because all the rest of these prayers are for Christians.

47 1 Thess. v: 14.   48 1 Kings viii: 60.   49 Ps. lxxix (lxxviii): 13.
50 Wisdom vii: 17.   51 Ps. lxxxix (lxxviii): 12.   52 Deut. vii: 9.

53 (cf. Ro. i: 20) δρωμένοις, Harnack conjectures σωζομένοις, Gebhardt ὡρισμένοις, Hilgenfeld ἐρωμένοις.

54 Sirach ii: 10sq.   55 Numb. xiv: 18 (lxx).   56 Ps. cxix: (cxviii) 133.
57 1 Kings ix: 4.   58 Deut. xii: 25.   59 Ps. lxvii lxvi): 1.
60 Ps. cxxxv: 12 (lxx); cxxxvi: 12.

in faith and truth, becoming obedient to thine omnipotent and most excellent name.

LXI.—"To our rulers and governors upon the earth, thou, Lord, hast given the power of their kingdom, through thine excellent and unspeakable might, in order that we, recognizing the glory and honor given them by thee, may be subject unto them, in nothing withstanding thy will. Give to them, Lord, health, peace, harmony, well-being, in order that they may exercise the authority given them by thee without offence, for thou, heavenly Lord, eternal King,⁰² givest to the sons of men glory, and honor, and power, over that which is upon the earth. Order their counsels, Lord, according to that which is good and well-pleasing in thy sight,⁰³ so that they, in peace and clemency, devoutly exercising the power given them by thee, may find thee gracious. Thou who alone art able to do these and yet more abundant good things among us,⁰⁴ we confess to thee, through the high priest and patron of our souls, Jesus Christ, through whom to thee be glory and majesty, both now and from generation to generation, and for ever and ever. Amen.

LXII.—Now, respecting those things which pertain to our religion, and are most useful for a virtuous life to those who wish to order (it) righteously and godly, we have written suitably to you, brethren. For, concerning faith and repentance, and sincere love and temperance, and sobriety and patience, we have touched upon every topic,⁰⁵ putting you in remembrance, that by righteousness and truth and patience, ye ought in holiness to please⁰⁶ God, being of one mind, forgetful of injuries, in love and peace, with unfailing gentleness, as also our fathers, of whom we have spoken, pleased (him), walking humbly before their Father and God and Creator, and all men. And the more gladly have we put you in remembrance of these things, since we knew certainly that we write to men faithful and most worthy,⁰⁷ and who have looked deeply into the oracles of the instruction of God.

LXIII.—Therefore, it is right for those succeeding to such and so great examples, to bow the neck, and to occupy again the place of obedience; in order that, ceasing from vain sedition, free from all blame, we may reach the goal set before us in truth. For ye shall cause joy and gladness to us, if, becoming obedient to those things which have been written by us, ye cast out through the Holy Spirit the lawless violence of your strife, according to the exhortation which we have made concerning peace and harmony in this epistle. But we have sent faithful and prudent men, who have lived blamelessly among us from youth to old age, who shall be witnesses between you and us. And this we have done, that ye may know that all our care has been and is that ye may speedily be at peace.

---

61 For the general subject of this chapter, cf. Ro. xiii: 1 sq; 1 Pet. ii: 13 sq. 17; 1 Tim. ii: 1 sq; Tit. iii: 1.

62 1 Tim. i: 17.   63 Deut. xii: 25 (lxx).   64 Eph. iii: 21.

65 πάντα τόπον (sc. Bibliorum, Harnack, Bryennius).

66 MS. εὐχαριστεῖν. Gebhardt, Harnack, Hilgenfeld, εναρεστεῖν, an evident and necessary correction.

67 Literally *most elect*, ἐλλογιμωτάτοις.

This fragment adds little that is essential to the Epistle, since it contains only the prayer, renewed exhortations to obedience, a general summary, and a commendation of the bearers of the letter. These messengers are called "men who have lived blamelessly among us from youth to old age," which indicates, if further proof be needed,[68] that the Epistle belongs to the time of Domitian, not to the reign of Nero. It may be noted that Christ is called "Beloved Son" twice in the prayer (c. 59), and no where else in the Epistle; and that the doctrine of the Trinity is found in c. 58, where "God and the Lord Jesus Christ, and the Holy Spirit," are designated "the faith and hope of the elect."

But these chapters are chiefly remarkable, as showing the attitude and spirit of the Roman Church. It must be remembered, that the advice of Rome was wholly unasked and unsought by the Corinthians. The Epistle owes its existence simply to tidings, which, in some way, had reached the metropolis (c. 47), of a sedition in Corinth against the officers of the church, joined to the solicitude which those tidings awakened. We may find the Roman ideal of a Christian church sketched (c. 2) in speaking of the former condition of the church at Corinth.

"Ye wrestled night and day (in prayer) in behalf of the whole brotherhood. . . . Every faction and every schism was abominable to you. Ye grieved over the transgressions of your neighbors; their faults ye deemed your own."

So we find the Roman Church here,[69] assuming responsibility for the schism at Corinth, and sending men to be "witnesses between us and you," because "all our care has been, and is, that ye may speedily be at peace." Not only does the Roman Church consider its interference abundantly warranted, but it even urges its plea with divine authority.

"Receive our counsel, and it shall not repent you, for he that humbly doeth God's commands shall be saved" (c. 58). "Ye shall cause joy to us if, becoming obedient to what we have written, ye cast out through the Holy Spirit the lawless violence of your strife."[70]

---

68 Cf. the list of authorities for the later date, Patr. Apost. opp., l. c., p. lix sq.

69 C. 59. But if any be disobedient, ... we shall be blameless, implying that the Roman church would have sinned had it not reminded the Corinthians of their duty.

70 C. 63. ὑπήκοοι γενόμενοι τοῖς ὑφ ἡμῶν γεγραμμένοις διὰ τοῦ ἁγίου πνεύματος ἐκκόψητε κ. τ. λ. Jacobi suggests (Stud. und Krit.

Here the Roman Church plainly regards its advice **as virtually** embodying God's commands to the Corinthians, **and** invokes the help of the Holy Spirit to assist them in **obeying** that advice.

And this divine authority is explicitly asserted, c. 59:

"But if any are disobedient to the words *spoken by him* (*God*) *through us*, let them know that they shall involve themselves in transgression and no small danger."

This earnest sympathy and help in the difficulties of other churches; this Christian love, which never failed either in the "faithful wounds" of rebuke for spiritual failings, or in the liberal supply of temporal wants, seems to have been from the first peculiarly characteristic of the church at Rome. Already Rome has assumed a part in "the care of all the churches," and writes to Corinth in terms of the severest reproof, yet with rare wisdom and warm Christian love, such as Paul himself had exemplified. From its position in the world's capital the Roman Church early acquired a great importance and influence in the West, and the orderly, law-abiding Roman spirit soon made it powerful as an organization. Whatever the Roman Christians saw, they saw clearly; whatever they held, they held firmly; and their claims to divine guidance in their actions as a church are not, in those early times at least, more conspicuous, than the sagacity, liberality, and piety by which those claims were supported. It is this early maturity of development, this keen eye, warm heart, and ready hand, which put Rome so soon into the first place among the Christian churches.[71] It is this Catholic spirit which accounts for such utterances as that of Dionysius from this same church of Corinth, about seventy years after receiving the Epistle of Clement.

"For this practice has prevailed with you from the very beginning, to do good to all the brethren in every city, and to send contributions to many churches in every city; thus refreshing the needy in their want,

---

1876, p. 715.) that the above may be read "becoming obedient to what has been written by us through the Holy Spirit, ye cast out," etc. But it is more natural to translate as we have done (cf. Harnack's note ad loc., Patr. Apost. opp. l. c.), and we can hardly imagine the Roman Church here using a formula like that in Acts xv: 28.

71 cf. Harnack, Theol. Literaturzeitung, 19 Feb., 1876, p. 102 sq.; Jacobi, Stud. und Krit., 1876, p. 715, from which are borrowed some of the thoughts here expressed.

and furnishing to the brethren condemned to the mines what was necessary; by these contributions which ye have been accustomed to send
from the beginning, you preserve as Romans the practices of your ancestors." . . . . "To-day we have passed the Lord's holy-day,
in which we read Soter's Epistle, in reading which we shall always
have our mind stored with admonition, as we shall, also, from that written to us before by Clement. "[72]

We may infer that Clement's Epistle was received in a
Christian spirit like that which dictated it, since it was read
in the church on Sunday for many years. Soon after
Dionysius, Irenæus, and especially Cyprian in the third century, emphasize the pre-eminence of the church at Rome.[73]

But we must carefully notice that there is no assumption of
authority in Clement's Epistle on the part of the church which
sent it. The Roman Christians appeal to the reason of men
whom they recognize as worthy of such an appeal (c. 62).
They exhort the Corinthians on the ground of general truths:
the unity of the church (c. 37, *sq.*), the apostolic institutions
(c. 42), the ordinances of God (c. 40, *sq.*), the example of
Christ (c. 16). They distinctly define their own office, as that
of reminding, admonition (c. 42), and they urge their brethren
in Corinth to submit, "*not to them*, but to the will of God"
(c. 56).

They appeal to Peter and Paul (c. 5), but it is as examples,
not as authorities; they adduce the Jewish priesthood (c. 40),
but only to prove that all things should be done decently and
in order; they uphold the officers of the church throughout,
but only the presbyters of the local church in Corinth are referred to. There is here not a trace of any hierarchical aim;
not the sign of any attempt to exercise authority over the
other church. Irenæus and Cyprian are witnesses that the pre-
eminence of the Roman church was due only to its representative position and character. While both these bishops conceded
Rome's dignity and superiority, yet they both sharply remon-
strated against the usurpation by a Roman bishop of power
over other churches.[74]

---

72 Euseb., H. E. iv: 23. Eng. Tr., vol. ii, p. 176, of Bagster's Ed. of the Greek
Ecclesiastical Historians.

73 Irenæus (iii: 3, § 2.). Cyprian (passages collected in Rothe, Anfænge der
Christlichen Kirche, p. 655 sq.) regards the Roman Church as the centre, and
as representing the unity of the Catholic Church.

74 Cf. Irenæus, Ep. to Victor, and Cyprian, Epp. to Stephen and to Pompeius.

I have dwelt on this feature of the Epistle, because we often need to be reminded that Rome held a high place in Christian honor and Christian love long before the Isidorean decretals and the fabled gift of Constantine; and that, without the true influence of her Christian history and position, forged documents had availed her little.

Let us now look at the prayer, which forms the principal part of the new fragment. It is evidently liturgical, and its slender connection with the objects of the Epistle shows that it was not composed expressly for its place here. Indeed, Jacobi has recently made use of this want of continuity to set up a theory, that the prayer is of Corinthian origin, and was interpolated in the Epistle from being used when the latter was read in the church service.[75] But this hypothesis is untenable for three reasons: 1. The phrases of the prayer are in many cases found repeated in other parts of the Epistle, where they must be regarded as reminiscences of the liturgy. ·2. This prayer does not stand wholly alone in the Epistle, for a comparison of c. 20 with part of c. 12 of the liturgy (book viii.) in the Apostolic Constitutions, reveals a similarity which suggests that c. 20 also is liturgical. 3. The extended prayer for rulers (c. 61) is much more probable as a part of the church service in the metropolis of the empire than in Corinth.

But the liturgical origin and place of this, the oldest church prayer we know, can be shown only by comparing it with the oldest extant liturgies—those, namely, of James, of Mark, of the Apostolic Constitutions, of "the Apostles" (Nestorian), of Chrysostom, and of Basil.[76]

LIX.—ὅπως τὸν ἀριθμὸν τὸν κατηριθμημένον τῶν ἐκλεκτῶν αὐτοῦ ἐν ὅλῳ τῷ κόσμῳ διαφυλάξῃ ἄθραυστον.

Cf. Const. App., viii: 22.—τὸν ἀριθμὸν τῶν ἐκλεκτῶν σου διαφυλάττων—Chrys. pp. 116, 45.

LIX.—εἰς ἐπίγνωσιν δόξης νόματος αὐτοῦ (i. e., Χριστοῦ).

Cf. Const. App., viii: 11.—εἰς ἐπίγνωσιν τῆς σῆς (i.e., Θεοῦ) δόξης καὶ τοῦ ὀνόματός σου.

---

75 Stud. und Krit., 1876, p. 715.

76 The liturgies of James, Mark, Chrysostom, and Basil are cited by the pages of Neale's Primitive Liturgies (Second Ed., London, 1868). The prayers and the liturgy in the Apostolic Constitutions are cited by book and chapter. The liturgy of the Apostles and the Blessed Apostles, with some other references, are cited from Daniel's Codex Liturgicus. 4 vols. Leipzig, 1847-53.

LIX.—τὸν μόνον ὕψιστον ἐν ὑψίστοις, ἅγιον ἐν ἁγίοις ἀναπαυόμενον.

Cf. Const. App. viii : 11. ὕψιστε ὁ ἐν ὑψηλοῖς κατοικῶν, ἅγιε ἐν ἁγίοις ἀναπαυόμενε—Chrys., p. 118; Mark, pp. 13, 27. Liturgia Apostolorum, Codex Lit. iv., p. 173. "Gloria in excelsis" (Hilary of Poictiers, 5th cent.).

All these liturgical formulæ may be traced to Isa. lvii: 15 (lxx) as their source, but they agree in their deviations from it.

LIX.—μόνον εὐεργέτην πνευμάτων καὶ θεὸν πάσης σαρκός.

Cf. Const. App. viii: 38.—ὁ θεός, ὁ τῶν πνευμάτων καὶ πάσης σαρκός.

LIX.—τὸν ἐπιβλέποντα ἐν ταῖς ἀβύσσοις.

Cf. Const. App. xiii: 7.—οὗ τὸ βλέμμα ξηραίνει ἀβύσσους.

LIX.—τὸν τῶν ἀπηλπισμένων σωτῆρα.

Cf. Mark, p. 17.—ἡ ἐλπὶς τῶν ἀπηλπισμένων.

LIX.—βοηθὸν γενέσθαι καὶ ἀντιλήπτορα ἡμῶν.

Cf. Const. App. viii: 12.—πάντων βοηθὸς καὶ ἀντιλήπτωρ—viii: 13.

LIX.—τοὺς ἐν θλίψει ἡμῶν σῶσον, τοὺς ταπεινοὺς ἐλέησον, τοὺς πεπτωκότας ἔγειρον, τοῖς δεομένοις ἐπιφάνηθι, τοὺς ἀσεβεῖς ἴασαι, τοὺς πλανωμένους τοῦ λαοῦ σου ἐπίστρεφον. χόρτασον τοὺς πεινῶντας, λύτρωσαι τοὺς δεσμίους ἡμῶν, ἐξανάστησον τοὺς ἀσθενοῦντας, παρακάλεσον τοὺς ὀλιγοψυχοῦντας.

Cf. Mark, p. 21.—Λύτρωσαι δεσμίους, ἐξέλου τοὺς ἐν ἀνάγκαις, πεινῶντας χόρτασον, ὀλιγοψυχοῦντας παρακάλεσον, πεπλανημένους ἐπίστρεφον, ἐσκοτισμένους φωταγώγησον, πεπτωκότας ἔγειρον, σαλευομένους στήριξον, νενοσηκότας ἴασαι.

For similar prayers—Cf. Const. App. viii: 10; viii: 15; Mark, pp. 17, 20; James, pp. 52, 63, 70; Chrys., p. 114; Basil, pp. 165–6; Liturgia Beatorum Apostolorum, Codex, Lit. iv., p. 182.

For an analysis of this prayer in its oldest forms, see Codex Lit. iv., p. 115 sq.

LX.—Σὺ τὴν ἀένναον τοῦ κόσμου σύστασιν διὰ τῶν ἐνεργουμένων ἐφανεροποίησας.

Cf. Const. App. viii: 22.—ὁ τὴν τοῦ κόσμου σύστασιν διὰ τῶν ἐνεργουμένων φανεροποιήσας.

LX.—ἐλεῆμον καὶ οἰκτίρμον.

Cf. Const. App. vii: 33.—ὁ ἐλεήμων καὶ οἰκτίρμων.—James, p.43.

LX.—δὸς ὁμόνοιαν καὶ εἰρήνην ἡμῖν τε καὶ πᾶσι τοῖς κατοικοῦσι τὴν γῆν.

Cf. Mark, p. 16.—τὴν σὴν εἰρήνην δὸς ἡμῖν ἐν ὁμονοίᾳ καὶ ἀγάπῃ. Prayers for all men are mentioned—1 Tim. ii: 1; Polycarp, ad Phil., 12; Justin Martyr Apol. i: 65; Dial. cum Tryphone, 133.

LXI.—*Τοῖς τε ἄρχουσι καὶ ἡγουμένοις ἡμῶν ἐπὶ τῆς γῆς
.   .   .   .   οἷς δός, κύριε, ὑγίειαν, εἰρήνην, ὁμόνοιαν,
εὐστάϑειαν.*

Cf. Codex Lit. i., p. 156.—Ut Imperatori nostro Regibus et Principibus Christianis pacem et veram concordiam largiri digneris. (From a monastery liturgy for Good Friday; date 1712.)

For the absence of prayers for rulers from Roman liturgies—cf. Daniel, l. c., p. 137, sq.

For prayers for peace and for rulers—Cf. Const. App. viii: 10, 12, 15 ; Mark, pp. 16, 18; Basil, pp. 165, 171.

For mention of, and exhortation to, prayers for rulers—Cf. Ro. xiii: 1–6 ; 1 Pet. ii: 13–17 ; 1 Tim. ii: 1, sq. ; Tit. iii : 1 ; Polycarp, ad Phil. 12; Martyrium Polycarpi, 10 ; Justin Martyr, Apol. i: 17 ; Tertullian, Apologeticus, 30, 31, 32, 39; Ad Scapulam, 2; Cyprian, ad Demetrianum, 20 ; Origen, contra Celsum, viii: 73 ; Arnobius, contra gentes, 4 ; Dionysius Alexandrinus, in Eusebius, H. E. vii: 11; Const. App., vii: 10.—(Cf. Patr. Apost. opp., edd. Gebhardt, Harnack, Zahn, fasc. 1, pars. 1, ed. 2, 1876, p. 103, sq.)

LXI.—*δέσποτα ἐπουράνιε, βασιλεῦ τῶν αἰώνων.*

Cf. Const. App. vii: 47.—*βασιλεῦ ἐπουράνιε;* vii: 34—*βασιλεῦ τῶν αἰώνων.*

Some of these parallels are, doubtless, purely accidental; some may arise from a common source in Scripture; some of them do not prove more than that certain formulæ were early used in church prayers. But the very existence of this prayer is much earlier and more definite evidence of liturgical worship than has hitherto been discovered.[77] I do not contend that the liturgies were necessarily *written* at this early date. But this prayer does, I think, clearly show the use of a fixed form of worship in the Church of Rome at the close of the first century. The prayer evidently consists of three main parts; the glorification of the Father (c. 59), the petitions for the church (cc. 59, 60), and the supplication in behalf of rulers (c. 61). All these are found, as the parallels show, in the eucharistic liturgies of the early church. The prayer for rulers, though so frequently enjoined by the apostles and early fathers, is much less prominent in the liturgies than in Clem-

---

77 Ignatius, ad Magnes, c. 7, where he exhorts them to have *one* prayer and *one* supplication, and the *common* prayers (κοιναὶς εὐχαίς) mentioned by Justin, Apol. , 65, are adduced by Trollope (Greek Liturgy of S. James, Edinburgh, 1858, p. 3 sq.), but they are too indefinite to prove the use of liturgies,

ent's epistle.   The temporal supremacy of the Pope excluded it from the later Roman liturgies.   But no such cause could operate in the days of Clement, and the frequent collisions of the Christians with the authorities at Rome render very natural an extended reference to them in the church prayers. The sublimity of this prayer gains a peculiar significance when we remember that it was Domitian in whose behalf it was offered. The prayer for rulers is, however, not omitted in the ancient liturgies, as the references show.   The concurrence then of these three prayers, in Clement's epistle and in the oldest eucharistic liturgies, seems to show that this ancient letter contains a part of the service of the Lord's Supper in the Roman church.

Besides this, the striking verbal resemblance observable in many parts suggests that the Christian church possessed from a very early period a common treasury of liturgical formulæ. The importance of this new fragment for the history of Christian liturgies must be estimated by those who are specially versed in the subject, but I have deemed it necessary to call particular attention to these leading features, because they do not seem to have attracted the attention they merit.

The new manuscript thus not only corrects and completes the text of the Epistles, but also gives interesting hints respecting the position and character of the Roman church near the end of the first century, and preserves to us the mother of liturgies, a prayer used in the service of the Roman church when the Apostle John had not yet passed away.

The Second Epistle will be considered by itself, and we may hope for additional light on the whole subject from a new-found Syriac manuscript of the twelfth century, and from an appendix to Dr. Lightfoot's edition of Clement. Both of these will be published shortly.

Art. VIII.--CURRENT NOTES.

PROF. HENRY B. SMITH AS EDITOR, AND HIS SUCCESSOR.

THE decease of HENRY BOYNTON SMITH, D.D., LL.D., one of the associate editors of this journal, has been fitly signalized in the just and beautiful tribute to him, already set before our readers, from the pen of his late pastor, Dr. MARVIN R. VINCENT. We are glad to have been able to procure so suitable a memorial from so competent a source, and to give it a permanent place upon the pages of a periodical, with which, and some of its principal predecessors, he has been so long and so honorably connected. Many of the finest leading articles, which gave those Reviews character and influence, were from his pen. Since they had become merged in this journal, he has, with the undersigned, had the responsibility of conducting it. Much of its interest and value have been due to his editorial counsels and contributions. These would have been far more frequent, had not the frail and capricious state of his health prevented. Greatly as our readers must have felt this loss, none felt it so severely as his associate-editor; and none can feel, more deeply, his entire withdrawal from this service to the nobler service above. It is not necessary to repeat the eulogy, or any part of it, already spread out upon our pages, in which we most heartily concur. It is proper, however, for us to say, that he had peculiar endowments for editorship, especially of a Quarterly Review. He had an assemblage of requisites for this work, some of which may be common in one individual and some in another, but all of which are rarely found blended in any one. He had earnest convictions, strength and tenacity of principle, depth and breadth of learning and scholarship, unusual mastery of the great questions of philosophy and theology, theoretical and applied; a keen eye both for the speculative and the practical side of great religious, moral, philanthropic, ecclesiastical, and sociological questions, coupled with unusual versatility, tact, judgment, and taste. As he had for some time retired from his professorate, the main service of which he was capable was devoted to this REVIEW. And it, aside from his own household, most of all suffers from that loss, which is his everlasting gain.

In this emergency, it is cause for devout gratitude that his former associate in the editorship of the *American Presbyterian Review* has consented to step into his place. The country contains no one more experienced in the editorship of quarterlies and monthlies than the Rev. J. M. SHERWOOD. As editor of the *Biblical Repository,* *National Preacher, Hours at Home, Eclectic Magazine, American Presbyterian Review,* and other periodicals, his experience, added to his judgment and culture, is invaluable. He is also widely known to the Presbyterian, and general religious public. With the aid of his practical judgment, and of other helpers, it is our hope and purpose to add important improvements and attractions to this REVIEW in the near future.

LYMAN H. ATWATER.

CONTRIBUTIONS OF PROF. HENRY B. SMITH.

IT seems fitting that brief mention should be made in this connection of the leading articles contributed to this REVIEW by our former associate. While his name was appended to most of them as they appeared, yet they may have passed out of the recollection of many, who read them at the time with profound admiration and interest.

It will only be necessary to give the *titles* of these contributions to show the extraordinary breadth and comprehensiveness of his studies and scholarship ; for he conscientiously abstained from writing, even in the pages under his immediate control, on any question or topic that he had not prepared himself, by patient study and original investigation, to discuss intelligently and profitably to his readers. In this respect, his example, as in many other matters, was worthy of warm commendation. No pressure brought to bear upon him could ever induce him to swerve from this purpose. We often suggested to him subjects in the line of his studies, and on which we knew his mind was at work, which would be timely, and none could handle better, and which we desired to have discussed in the QUARTERLY, but the uniform reply was, "I am not yet ready. I am thinking about it. Some of these days I hope to feel competent to make the attempt." For several years past he had contemplated a paper on a subject of vital moment to religion and true science, in relation to which a fierce conflict of opinion is raging. He was anxious to write upon it. He was master of the literature of it. He had pondered and studied it in all its phases, conditions, and relations, near and remote, and yet he died without giving to the world the contribution we had so long and eagerly coveted. The brethren who listened to his remarks on "Evolution," the last time he met with them, are prepared to appreciate the eminent service he would have rendered to Christian science, had he been spared to make his "powerful answer to the later utterances of the materialistic school." And it was not indolence, or lack of courage or definite convictions, that held him back, but a high sense of responsibility in making the attempt, and a due estimate of the qualities and conditions requisite to a proper and profitable discharge of the self-assumed task. He felt deeply—and would that the feeling were common—that it is better not to discuss a grave subject of this character at all, than to discuss it in a flippant and crude, superficial and incompetent manner.

Before we proceed to the pleasant task of recalling to the reader's memory the contributions of one with whom we were associated for nine years, in editorial labors, we submit a brief historical statement.

In the year 1859, an association of gentlemen, in Boston and vicinity, originated the *The American Theological Review*, with Dr. Joseph Tracy as editor. "It was designed to meet the wants of those churches that accept the Westminster Assembly's Shorter Catechism as an expression of their theological views." After the issue of the first number, it was deemed expedient to secure an editor from this city. Dr. Smith was offered, and accepted, the position, and remained its chief editor till it was united with the *Presbyterian Quarterly*, at the close of 1862. The death of Dr. Wallace, the founder and editor of that journal, and the choice of the writer as his successor, having prepared the way for this union, under their joint editorship, with the title of *The American Presbyterian and Theological Review*. It was a remarkable compliment that Boston and Congregationalism thereby paid to the New York Presbyterian professor. The position did seem a little anomalous, and gave rise to more or less criticism. And yet, there was a real sympathy and vital doctrinal harmony between tne founders of that Review and the school of theology of which Dr. Smith was a fitting and distinguished representative.

Several of his most noteworthy contributions are scattered through the four volumes of the *American Theological Review* (1859–1862).

In January, 1869, the title of the Review was modified; the original Boston name ("Theological") being dropped, and thereafter it bore the name simply of the *American Presbyterian Review*, until its union with the *Princeton Review*, in January, 1872. This change in the name was significant, and indicated the fact, that the Review had come to be more distinctively Presbyterian. Not a few of his ablest contributions are contained in the volumes covering the years 1863–1871. Owing to the failure of his health in the latter part 1868, he was able thereafter to use his pen in consecutive effort only at long intervals, and then not always to his own satisfaction. We find but five papers from his pen after his break-down in 1868, and in but one of these—that on Strauss—do we recognize the vigor and masterly ability of his former self. So that a period of *ten years*—from 1859–1869—embraces the main life-work of our brother, as it will live and speak to posterity from the printed page. How precious seem those pages in the light of this fact! In common with the Church at large, we mourn over the fact, that his Lectures on Theology cannot be given to the world, and that he died before executing his purpose and desire, which he expressed to us with flashing eye and radiant brow, to embody his matured views and convictions in a course of Lectures on the Ely Foundation. But there is cause for devout gratitude, that, amidst his other pressing and important duties, he found time to devote himself so largely to the *Review*, which he considered a sacred trust, and through whose pages he has so wonderfully enriched our Christian literature. These contributions—so characteristic of the man and the scholar, the philosopher and the theologian, the student of the divine mysteries and the true-hearted Christian—will constitute no mean memorial of HENRY B. SMITH. That the more valuable of them will be gathered into a volume we have no reason to doubt; and in that form will attract even more attention than they did when fresh from his pen; and will add new laurels to a crown, won by incessant application and the combination and entire consecration of rare powers and gifts, and worn with singular meekness and modesty.

The following list, we believe, contains the titles of all his contributions to the above-named Reviews, and the date of their appearance.

" Christ : Prophet, Priest, and King" May, 1859 ; "The American Theological Review " (showing its objects and the state of things out of which it grew) May, 1859 ; " The Limits of Religious Thought," Feb., 1860 ; " Unitarian Tendencies," May, 1860 ; " Hamilton's Theory of Knowledge," Jan., 1861 ; " The New Latitudinarians of England," 1861 ; " The Theological System of Emmons," Jan., 1862 ; " Dr. Gardner Spring and the Brick Church," Jan., 1862 ; " British Sympathy with America," July, 1862 ; " The General Assemblies," Old and New, July, 1862 ; " Laboulaye on the United States of America," Jan., 1863 ; " Archbishop Whately's Letter to Mrs. Stowe," April, 1863 ; "Draper's Intellectual Development of Europe," Oct., 1863 ; " Renan's Life of Jesus," Jan., 1864 ; " Theories of the Inspiration of the Scriptures," April, 1864 ; " The General Assembly," July, 1864 ; " Wheedon on the Will," July, 1865 ; " Julius Müller's System of Theology," July and Oct., 1865 ; Mill's Examination of Hamilton's Philosophy," Jan., 1866 ; " Report to the Evangelical Alliance " at Amsterdam, Oct., 1867 ; " Presbyterian Reunion," Jan., 1868 ; " The Philadelphia Convention," Jan., 1868 ; " Roman Letters on the Vatican Council," Oct., 1870 ; Bishop Hefele on Pope Honorius," April, 1872 ; "Allibone's Dictionary of English Literature," July, 1872 ; " The New Faith of Strauss," April, 1874 ; "Christian Apologetics," July, 1876.

In addition to these, nearly every number of the REVIEW contained Criticisms on Books from his pen, some of them elaborate and highly valuable ; and a condensed summary of theological and literary Intelligence, gleaned from the whole field of current literature, domestic and foreign. No one, not familiar with this kind of literary work, can form any adequate idea of the labor expended on this department of a. Review. The reading necessary, the discrimination and sound judgment and independence demanded in a reviewer ; and then to be compelled to compress one's criticism, on fifty or sixty different works, into a dozen or twenty pages, is a task few are competent to perform. In no part of his work was Prof. Smith more conscientious, pains-taking, and proficient, than in his criticisms on the current issues of the press. Sometimes in a single sentence he would lay bare the essential defects of a book, however ingeniously and elaborately they were concealed, or point out its real merits.

It is not our purpose to pass in review the several contributions which we have grouped above. Our space will only admit a passing reference to a few of them. Not the least remarkable of them all is the article, covering about seventy pages, and written in the dark hour of our civil strife (July, 1862), entitled, " British Sympathy in America." It is specially a review of the utterances of *The North British Review*, —the organ of the Free Church of Scotland—in regard to the North. Where, if any where on the face of the earth, we had a claim for sympathy, and fair and friendly treatment in *such* a controversy, we got only reproach, bitter denunciation, and a grossly unjust presentation and arguing of the case against us. Stung to the quick by what he regarded as almost unparalleled perfidy and injustice, Prof. Smith took up the gauntlet thus thrown down, and made the most eloquent and logical, exhaustive and triumphant vindication of the policy and jus'ice of our cause that has fallen under our notice. To say that, when the clangor of arms had ceased, the enemy was no where visible—routed, driven from the field in dishonor and irretrievable defeat—would be to use very mild language. We know not which to admire most in this sharp conflict—the persistent and irresistible logic of the writer, assailing and driving his antagonist from point to point, until not a solitary defence remains to him ; or his impassioned eloquence and patriotic enthusiasm, which, rising to the majesty of his subject and the occasion, swept on and on with gathering force to the end, raining red-hot shot on the discomfited foe. We have reason to know that this labor was not in vain. It reached and influenced many leading minds on the other side of the water; notably such men as John Stuart Mill, the reflecting political economist; and John Bright, the noble Quaker. The former makes honoring mention of this article in one of his works.

The review of " Draper's Intellectual Development of Europe," is highly characteristic of the writer. The reader may recall with what a flourish of trumpets this work was introduced to the public, and with what apparent ease and self-complacency the distinguished author solved by it one of the profoundest problems of human destiny. Ignoring, either by design or through ignorance, the elaborate researches and speculations of Schelling and Hegel, of Comte and Buckle, of Condorcet and Guizot, and of many others, who had striven to grasp and exhibit the "rationale and the end of human progress," the reviewer proceeds to demonstrate the falsity of every important proposition of the author, the utter lack of originality in his theories, and the amazing superficiality and audacity exhibited in the pretentious book. Almost in disdain he says : "A man who can write a history of the 'Intellectual Development of Europe,' and say nothing of the systems of Descartes, Malebranche, and Spinoza ; pass over Leibneitz and Kant with a word or two ; utterly neglect Fitche, Schelling and Hegel; not to refer to Cousin, and pass by in silence Reid, Stewart, Mill, and Hamilton, must have a very singular notion of the task he has set before himself."

"The Limits of Religious Thought," a review of Mansel's Lectures delivered before the University of Oxford, furnishes a fine illustration of the reverent spirit and wonderful acumen with which he discussed "the ultimate problems of theological and philosophical speculation." While approving and emphasizing all that is tenable and sound in this very able work, when considered as an argument upon the high question between Christianity and Rationalism, he yet detects and points out in a masterly way its " fatal defects in its exposition of the relation of reason to revelation, or of revelation to rationalism."

His contributions on Sir William "Hamilton's Theory of Knowledge," and on John Stuart "Mill's Examination of Hamilton's Philosophy," are worthy of those ablest representatives of the Scottish school of philosophy. They will compare favorably, by any standard of fair judgment, with the productions of these authors, or of their most celebrated disciples. The latter felt that he had a powerful logical antagonist in Prof. Smith.

In "Wheedon on the Will," the Calvinistic system seldom found an abler expounder, or the Arminian an acuter or more effective opponent. "The Theological System of Emmons" will help the reader to a better understanding and appreciation of that wonderful man.

The Criticisms on " Renan," and on "Strauss " are not surpassed by any of the multitudinous replies which their subtle and audacious attacks on the true Faith called forth, both in this country and abroad; while his remarkable paper on " Presbyterian Reunion," probably contributed more to bring about that consummation than any other single agency.

But we must forbear. How often was it our high privilege to enjoy his converse in our office. And when he and the late Dr. Gillett met there—as not unfrequently they did—it was, indeed, a feast of good things. But both are gone! So ripe for usefulness; so full of holy resolves; so intent on high ends; and gone in the maturity of their powers! On whom shall their mantles fall?

J. M. SHERWOOD.

AMERICAN ECLESIASTICAL LAW.

UNDER this title *The British Quarterly Review*, Oct., 1876, contains an instructive article as to the relation of church and state in this country, based largely on Justice Strong's admirable *Lectures* before the Union Theological Seminary, delivered last year, and on Wallace's Reports of Cases Argued and Adjudged in the Supreme Court of the United States. We give a summary of the leading points, as they are clearly set forth in this article:

1. "American law acknowledges a jurisdiction in the church; leaves all church questions (questions of worship, doctrine, discipline, and membership) to the decision of the church itself; and refuses to review these decisions."

2. "American law claims for itself complete and exclusive control, not only over the life, liberty, and goods of all churchmen, but over all church property and church funds."

3. But in order to decide purely civil questions of person, goods, and estate, the law necessarily deals with innumerable religious questions and church relations." "The law has to do—at least, may have to do—with the whole working of a Christian church, as well as with its whole property, and this even in its native state of non-establishment." It does this, however, not directly, 'but indirectly,' as a means to the determination of a question of property or money."

4. "Where such civil question (of property or money) turns upon an express trust, American law inquires for itself into the fulfilment of the conditions of that trust, whether these be religious or ecclesiastical, to the uttermost; and it enforces the trust to the effect of settling the question of property, but to that effect only." "This is, as Judge Strong rightly puts it, 'an apparent, though not a real, exception' to the general rule, that the civil law will not interfere with church organization or with questions of religious faith." Here comes up all cases where property is *expressly* conveyed to a Presbyterian or Episcopal Church, as such. In case of litigation, the court must inquire which of the parties conforms to the conditions. Where a trust is "unequivocally expressed," there will generally be little difficulty.

" The case which all jurisprudences are beginning to find more difficult. is that which immediately follows."

5. Where property is held by a church generally, or for church purposes unspecified, and *not on an express trust* for the maintenance of certain doctrines or government, *American law presumes, in questions as to that property, that the decision of the church is right.*" The chief difficulty here comes up in cases where the church may have changed its order, or even doctrines. Here the decisions of the New York and Philadelphia courts are different, the latter leaning to the side of greater freedom.

6. "But the Supreme Court of the United States has also decided, that *where there is no express trust* as to the property, the law will not only presume that the decision of the church (by its majorities or judicatories) is right, but *will hold that decision as conclusive between the parties,* and will regulate the civil question of property accordingly." The *Review* says, that this is "by far the most important decision in the whole ecclesiastical law of America." It was given by the Supreme Court of the United States in the case of Walton vs. Ives, decided in the year 1872 (*Wallace's Reports,* vol. xiii, p. 679). It had to do with the action of the Presbyterian churches in Kentucky and Missouri. The decision was of the whole bench, two declining to express agreement, chiefly on the ground that the case had come before them informally. The judgment of the court is in these broad terms :

" That whenever the questions of discipline, or of faith, or ecclesiastical rule, custom, or law, have been decided by the highest of the church judicatories to which the matter has been carried, the legal tribunals must accept such decisions as final, and as binding on them in their application to the case before them."

7. " *The principle* on which the Supreme Court in such cases regulates questions, even of property, according to the decisions of the church, is that the church is not only *the best judge, but the only proper judge,* of church matters, and that there is a separate *ecclesiastical jurisdiction.* " This recognition of a real and binding "ecclesiastical jurisdiction " is the main point.

8. "*The two jurisdictions work together on the quasi-international principle of comity.*" This is particularly applied to cases of church membership and church offices. The decisions of the church (see Judge Strong's work) are held to be final. This matter is thus summed up by the *Review:*

1. " The courts will never on any pretext review *directly,* or reverse a church decision as to membership or office."

2. "The courts will not review it, even *indirectly* (*i. e.*, as a means of deciding a civil question which turns upon it), where it is only alleged that it is a false or wrong decision. That was a matter for the church court, and there is no appeal from it to the civil court, which, on the contrary, enforces the purely civil results of such a decision."

3. "Neither, thirdly, will the courts review the church decision, even for their own purposes; nor *indirectly*, where it is merely alleged that the decision was irregularly or informally arrived at. Questions of church form have been repeatedly held to be questions for the church, and if its decisions are final, even when their substantial justice is questioned, much more ought they to be conclusive on mere points of procedure."

Judge Strong, in his lectures, lays down this general proposition: "Whenever questions of discipline, of faith, and of church rule, of membership, or of office, have been decided by the church as its own modes of decision, civil law tribunals accept the decisions as final, and apply them as made." He says that there still remains the question, "at present pending:" Can a civil court inquire and determine for itself whether a church judicatory was properly constituted in accordance with the established order of the church organization, and can it disregard its decisions, if, in its opinion, the judicatory appears not to have been thus constituted?" This raises difficult and delicate questions, which cannot yet be said to have been finally adjudicated; though the above decision of the Supreme Court is thought by the reviewer to favor the view that the church action is final; as also the decision in the Illinois case, Chase vs. Cheney (in Thompson's "*American Reports*," xi, p. 95, Albany). " The civil court will ordinarily not question the jurisdiction, even for civil purposes."

The *British Quarterly* then refers to "the marvelous rarity of the seeming collisions which have been recorded, between the energetic church life of the states and the civil law. Seeming collisions we call them, for real collision can scarcely exist, where the church concedes all civil questions to the state, and where the state refuses to interfere internally with the church.

" We see no reason to doubt that this hundred years of transatlantic jurisprudence has solved the problem which lies before Europe. In the United States the state has been, during the century, separate from the church and independent of it; and yet the legal position of the church, as disclosed in the records of the law, is one of extraordinary energy, dignity, and independence. And recent events

of all kinds have conspired to direct attention to the great precedent."

The latest case, involving some of the above principles, is that of
the Third Reformed (Dutch) Church of Philadelphia, on which
Presiding Judge Allison read an elaborate opinion, in the Court
of Common Pleas, Philadelphia, Oct. 28, 1876—which opinion is
published in full in the *Legal Intelligencer*, Philadelphia, Nov. 9, 1876.
The Dutch Reformed Church, by a large majority of elders, trustees,
and members of the church and congregation, united with the Western Presbyterian Church of Philadelphia, under the title of the Im-
manuel Presbyterian Church, extinguishing the two previous corporations, and carrying all the property to the new organization.   The report of the master on the case thus raised took the following ground,
which was fully confirmed by the judgment of the court :

"Whenever a church or a religious society has been duly constituted, as in connection with, or in subordination to, some ecclesiastical organization or form of church government, and as a church
so connected and subordinated, has acquired property by subscriptions, donations, or otherwise, it cannot break off this connection, and unite with some other religious organization, or become independent, save at the expense of impairing its title to the property
so acquired.

" The property of a religious society is held upon a trust, the terms
of which are declared in the doctrines of religious belief upheld by
the society, and in case of a congregation constituted as above described, its connection with the larger organization, of which it is a
part, is one of these fundamental doctrines.   An illegal severance of
this connection is a violation of these fundamental doctrines, and,
therefore, constitutes a diversion of the property to a wrongful use, to
prevent which, a court of equity will interpose on application of a
party in interest."

Art. IX.—A GRAMMAR OF THE HINDI ·LANGUAGE.

A Grammar of the Hindi Language, in which are treated the Standard Hindi, Braj, and the Eastern Hindi of the Rámáyan of Tulsi Das, also the Colloquial Dialects of Marwar, Kumaon, Avadh, Baghelkhand, Bhojpur, etc., with Copious Philological Notes. By the Rev. S. H. KELLOGG, M. A., American Presbyterian Mission, North India ; Corresponding Member of the American Oriental Society. Printed at the American Presbyterian Mission Press, Allahabad, and sold by Thacker, Spink & Co., Calcutta, Trübner & Co., 57 and 59 Ludgate Hill, London, 1876.

The volume whose title is thus given in full is a royal octavo, of 433 pages, about 50 of which are strictly philological. It adds another to the already abundant illustrations of what our missionaries are doing for the advancement of the scholarship of the world, especially along the line of linguistic science. It is an undoubted truth, as Müller admits, that modern philology in its application to the languages of the heathen nations, would have had but the slenderest possible basis without the contributions of Christian missionaries. The work before us is one of the most valuable of these contributions.

The Hindi language is by far the most important and extensively used of the Sanskrit-derived languages of India, which, beginning in the East, are usually reckoned thus: Oriya, Bengali, Hindi, Punjabi, Sindhi, Gujarati, and (to the south, toward Bombay and Goa) Marathi. These languages all stand in precisely the same relation to Sanskrit that the Romance or Italic languages of Europe (the Italian, French, etc.) sustain to the Latin. Like them, while closely related to the classic language of the country, they are more immediately related to the various currupt dialects of the Sanskrit speech, known as the Prakrit, which, from the earliest ages, co-existed with the Sanskrit of the educated Brahmans, as the language of the uneducated masses of the people. Until recently these languages, together with the Sanskrit, which constitute the Indic class of the southern division of the Aryan or Indo-European family, were regarded as the only representatives of that family in Hindostan. It is still certain that the numerous aboriginal dialects spoken in the Deccan have no such connection with the Sanskrit, but belong to a different family, the Turanian. But the latest researches seem to indicate that the Dravidian languages of South India (the Tamil, Telugu, Malayalim, etc.), placed by Max Müller, in his lectures of fifteen years ago, under the Tamulic class of the southern division of the Turanian family, may possibly belong also to the Aryan tongues, although they have no such close connection with the Sanskrit as have the languages of North India, but must be classified as a different sub-family of the Aryan speech.

The importance of the Hindi language, in itself considered, appears from the opening paragraph of the author's preface : " Of the two hundred and fifty million inhabitants of India, speaking a score or more of different languages, fully one-fourth, or between sixty and seventy millions, own the Hindi as their vernacular. In all the great centres of Hindú faith in North India, alike in populous Benares, Allahabad, and Mathurá, and in the mountains about the sacred shrines of Gangotrí, Kedárnáth, and Badrínáth, among the Himalayas; in many of the most powerful independent native states of India, as in the dominions of the Mahárájá Sindhia, and the extensive territories under the Mahárájá of Jaipúr and other Rájpút chiefs; in short, throughout an area of more than 248,000 square miles, Hindi is the language of the great mass of the population. Only where Mohammedan influence has long prevailed, as in the large cities, and on account of the almost exclusive currency of Mohammedian speech in government offices, have many Hindús learned to contemn their native tongue and affect the Persianized Hindi, known as 'Urdú.'"

The Hindi exists in a large number of (perhaps fifteen or twenty) dialects, which differ very much one from another in grammatical forms, and to a limited extent in vocabulary, so much so, that a native villager, for example, of Ajmere in the West would understand with difficulty a Hindoo of Tirhoot in the East.

The chief difficulty which the author had to encounter, however, was found in the fact, that the entire region of his investigation was comparatively unexplored. There have been for many years grammars and dictionaries of the Hindustani or Urdú, which, by one of the great anti-Christian blunders (of which there have been not a few) of the English in India, is the court language of the Northwestern Provinces of the Punjab. But when the author began his work a few years ago, there was no grammar of Hindi in English, except a brief syllabus of the Braj dialect only, by the late Dr. Ballantyne, of Benares. Professor De Tassy, of Paris, had also written, in French, a very meagre syllabus of the same dialect. A meagre grammar of the Braj, and that dialect of Hindi which is grammatically identical with Urdú, had once been published by government in Calcutta; but this never was worth much, and had long been out of print. After the work was begun, Mr. Etherington, of the Baptist Mission, Benares, put out a small Hindi grammar; again, however, ignoring, like his predecessors, the most important classic dialect of Hindi, called the Púrbí, or Eastern, as well as all the colloquial dialects, and confining himself to that form of Hindi which agrees with Urdú. Dr. Fitz Edward Hall, a native of the United States, who was successively Superintenden of Education in the Northwestern Provinces in India, Professor of Sanskrit in the Queen's College, Benares, and Professor of Sanskrit and Indian Jurisprudence in King's College, London, and who is at present a member of the Board of Examiners for the Indian Service, a man acknowledged by all competent judges to hold a front rank among living Hindi scholars, has long been promising a Hindi grammar, but of the Braj dialect only; but it has never appeared. All writers on this subject hitherto have alike dealt only with one or two western forms of the speech, ignoring entirely all eastern types, and many important western dialects. No one has ever before attempted to deal with the Hindi as a whole, nor have any even attempted to show philologically the unity of these dialects, and their précise relation to each other and to the ancient Sanskrit and Prakrit dialects.

Mr Kellogg has attempted to supply this deficiency. He has set forth fully every dialect of the Hindi which has a literature, besides giving many colloquial dialects with less fulness, so as to cover all the Hindi speaking territory. For practical reasons, the Standard Hindi, or high Hindi (to name it after the analogy of the German), which agrees in grammatical form with the Urdu, and which has been adopted by the educational authorities as the medium of vernacular instruction in all Hindi schools, has been taken as the basis of the grammar. At the same time the author has endeavored to treat with equal thoroughness the two great dialects of classic Hindi literature, the Braj representing the Western, and the old Purbí representing the Eastern type of Hindi. In treating of the nine or ten colloquial dialects, the declension and conjugation are fully set forth, so as to give a fairly complete view of the actual living speech of the Hindi-speaking population of North India.

Attention is called in the preface to the special features of the work. The principles of literary Hindi are amply illustrated, not by newly-coined examples, nor examples drawn from European writers of Hindi, which always bear the marks of their foreign origin, but by examples drawn chiefly from the two great works, the *Prem Ságar,* and the *Rámáyan* of Tulsí Dás, which are most widely and popularly known among the Hindú masses, and which have been chosen by the government for the examination of candidates in connection with the civil and military services of India. Another peculiar feature is found in the philological notes, occupying in all about fifty pages, in which the author has "attempted to indicate the probable origin and derivation of the forms of the Hindi language, and the relation of various dialectic forms to one another, and to the Sanskrit and old Prákrit dialects of India."

But besides the above, the author modestly suggests that "much else will be found in the grammar which is strictly new, both in matter and arrangement." He has not been content to limit himself to the dead forms—some of them a thousand years and a thousand times dead—which are the bane of the mere grammar mongers. The higher principles established and developed by the German grammarians, and the more definite laws of language revealed by modern philology, are constantly and freely applied. This appears especially in the nomenclature of the tenses, in the treatment of the derivation and composition of words, in the discussion of compound sentences, and in the complete and accurate unfolding of the prosody which is so essential to the interpretation and comprehension of the literature. There is, indeed, much that is new, and, chief of all, the everywhere manifest mastery of a philosophic mind over the hitherto chaotic mass of material. This mastery may be illustrated once for all by a single example. The application of the common idea, that tense in the verb is primarily a distinction of *time,* has resulted in the Hindi, as in so many western languages, in "confusion worse confounded." Laying hold of the principle, that the "participles, with their dependent tenses, *represent action in different stages of progress,* not necessarily at different points of time," the author at once brings perfect order out of the chaotic mass of fifteen Hindi tenses and three participles. "Every action or state, whether actual or contingent, may be conceived of under three different aspects, relatively to its own progress, *i. e.*, as not yet begun; as begun, but not completed; or as completed. It is believed that these are the essential ideas which pervade these three groups of tenses." This principle at once removes all difficulties.

Of the points thus far noticed—the scope and general features of the work—one unacquainted with the language may fairly judge; of the special Hindi features, only competent Hindi scholars can give an opinion which will be of any value. We, therefore, make brief extracts from the criticism of four or five men, who take rank among the best living Hindi scholars.

Mr. Beams, author of a "Comparative Grammar of the Aryan Languages of India" (not yet finished), Collector of Cuttack in Orissa, writes, that he thinks the author has "selected his dialects so that no more are really needed," as every important type is noted and tabulated. Dr. Fitz Edward Hall, a scholar equally distinguished in Sanskrit and Hindi, in acknowledging a copy, writes: "In a single day I have been able to examine the work only cursorily. However, I have seen enough of it to satisfy myself that it is an immense advance on any kindred work that has as yet been published." Mr. Pincott, editor of a critical, annotated edition of *Sakuntala* (a Hindi translation of the Sanskrit drama), and one of the Board of Examiners for the India Service, gives an equally favorable judgment in Trübner's *Oriental Record*, of the etymological portion of the work, which was all that had then reached him: "It is a grammar of the Hindi language, dealing with the subject in a thorough and masterly manner. The portion of the work which has reached our hands is eminently satisfactory, as it discusses the language in the only sound way, that is, in connection with its many dialects. The Hindi, though hitherto shamefully neglected by scholars and despised by officials, is by far the most important language in the whole peninsula of India. The absence of a literary standard has allowed it to exist in the form of a mass of closely related dialects, some one or two of which have recently been brought to notice by the industry and patriotism of native scholars. The prominence which these dialects have acquired is thus due to accidental causes; it is, therefore, apparent, that no scholarly knowledge of the language can be gained until the principal dialects have been examined, and the light which each is able to shed upon the literary forms of speech is made commonly available. Considerations such as these, which can be only in this way alluded to, give to the work upon which Mr. Kellogg is engaged a high interest. If this work, in treating of the syntax, maintains the high character of the etymological portion, a Hindi grammar will be provided for students of the greatest value and importance."

In a review of the work, by an eminent Hindi Scholar in her Majesty's Civil Service, published in the *Pioneer*, a daily paper in Allahabad, we read: "We look upon this work as the most important contribution to oriental philology that has been made by any scholar writing in India for many years past. It, in fact, opens out a line of country of immense interest and extent that has hitherto been almost absolutely untrodden by the general European student. Yet, though Mr. Kellogg has had no predecessor on whose foundations to build, and has had himself to collect all the materials for the work, his design is so admirably carried out, so well-based on sound research, and so finished in all its details, that it is not likely to require any additions or corrections of the slightest importance, but will remain a permanent monument of its compiler's scholarship, and the one standing authority on the subject of which it treats."

To the commendatory notices of these distinguished Hindi scholars may be added that of Dr. Monier Williams, the distinguished Sanskrit Professor at Oxford, author of a Sanskrit Grammar (in many respects the best produced), of a Sanskrit-English and an English-Sanskrit Dictionary, and editor of the Sanskrit story of Nala, or *Nalopákhyánam*, and of the Sanskrit Drama of *Sakuntala*. He says of Mr. Kellogg's grammar: "It is a most valuable work, and one for which all engaged in Indian studies will be grateful. I consider that it rises to a higher level than any grammar of the same kind yet produced."

Such is the tenor of all the criticisms thus far offered upon the work. Coming, as they do, from both sides of the globe, and from the men best of all qualified to judge the work, they establish beyond dispute its great merit, and bespeak for its author an international reputation.

It is now twelve years since Mr. Kellogg, having completed his collegiate and theological course at Princeton, went out to India to engage in the mission work. Had he in these years done nothing but master the language and complete his grammar, it would justly have been esteemed a great task; but it must be borne in mind, before the real extent of his labors can be appreciated, that he has been, in every way, one of our most earnest and active missionaries, preaching the gospel to the heathen until the Hindi has become as natural to him, in preaching, as his native speech, and that for several years he has been engaged in the Seminary at Allahabad for training a native Hindú ministry. What he has accomplished proves him capable of accomplishing much in any field of labor, but, more than all, it proves him pre-eminently fitted for prosecuting still further the work in which he has been engaged. In short, we cannot resist the conviction, that he is just the kind of man to do a grand work in that most difficult of fields, among a people that has shown itself possessed of enough of genuine intellectual power to mould the religion of half the inhabitants of the globe, in India and China, and which will, perhaps, some day be looked upon as having given to the Germany of our age, along with its Sanskrit learning, the systems of Pantheism which have long held so many of her strong men bound in spiritual fetters.

Art. X.—MACDONALD'S LIFE AND WRITINGS OF ST. JOHN.

SCRIBNER, ARMSTRONG & CO. publish a noble octavo bearing this title, by the late James M. Macdonald, D.D., pastor of the First Presbyterian Church, Princeton. It has the great advantage of having been edited by and honored with an extended introduction from the pen of Dean Howson, known as one of the authors of that great and, in many respects, not dissimilar work, Conybeare and Howson's Life of St. Paul. Dean Howson was enabled to bestow this editorial supervision upon it, because it was first published in London, where it has been before the public some weeks, and has received warm and discriminating commendation from many religious journals in Great Britain. Although as to date posthumous, it is not so in substance, or in any sense which detracts from its value. The entire manuscript was in the hands of the publisher six months before the lamented author's death. By it he yet speaketh. Through it he hath left a worthy monument to himself, and benefaction to the church.

One of the British journals puts it at the very head of those Johannean works which have recently been so numerous, and of which we elsewhere mention two, both of high mark. We think in some important respects it deserves this encomium. It is altogether *sui generis* among them. Like Conybeare and Howson's Life of Paul, it aims not merely to give the biography, or exegesis, or doctrines of the subject of it, but these as severally and mutually illustrating each other; especially to throw light upon John's writings, by a precise and accurate survey of the antecedents and surroundings which drew them forth, and so far forth explain them. This is the more valuable and interesting, because the author brings to the illustration of his subject whatever can be gathered from the latest researches, as well as from older authorities. He lays under tribute, so far as is necessary to his purpose, the treasures of ancient and modern Johannean, Christological, and New Testament literature. The indications are abundant, that during his entire ministry his mind has been like a magnet, seizing and laying hold of whatever, in all his readings and experience, could help him to elucidate the life and writings of John. We find here the concentrated essence of many an elevated pulpit discourse, re-appearing in an animated page or suggestive paragraph. For, after the blessed Saviour, John and his writings furnish his most frequent and favorite topics of discourse. This volume is the ripe product.

It consists of Dean Howson's introduction, of the elaborate biographical and historical sketch, divided into chapters, some of which run largely into those discussions into which history ever runs, when it fulfils its high function of being philosophy teaching by example. The biography is followed by the writings of the apostle: the Apocalypse, his gospel, and his three epistles, accompanied by terse and valuable notes—exegetical, doctrinal, and homiletical. The volume in its several parts is at once scholarly and popular—suited alike to the pastor's study and the devotional library of the private Christian. It is such as none but a genuine scholar and devoted pastor could produce. Its attractiveness is greatly increased by the scope it affords for that species of descriptive composition in which the author greatly excelled. In sketching the geographical, historical, social, and religious features of the places, communities, and persons which were connected with the lives, teachings, and labors of our Lord, of John, and the other apostles; in describing the characteristics, sayings, and doings of these greatest personages in the world's history, as well as those of the Roman emperors and their subordinate rulers, under whose dominion they taught, labored, made converts, planted churches, or suffered persecution and martyrdom, we see the pen-sketches of a master in graphic delineation. Passages are not wanting which, in style, remind us of the great English classics.

The volume is much increased in value and interest by maps and pictorial illustrations—mostly taken from photographs of places and scenes, or from copies of busts of persons—remarkable for their fine execution, which serve admirably to illustrate the subjects treated. The outline figures of the Roman emperors, Julius Cæsar, Augustus, Caligula, Nero, as well as others, are well worth study, and highly suggestive of traits which history ascribes to them.

We have observed that this volume interprets the teachings of John by the incidents of his life. But more than this, it aims, and with good success, to show how the apostles generally, and John pre-eminently, were themselves prepared and trained by their constant intimacy with Christ, and under his direct, special instruction, for the teaching and other ministerial functions of the apostolate, but, especially, for work of inspired authorship. The following passage presents this in a striking light:

At night he [Christ] sought retirement; he went out into a mountain near Capernaum, and spent a whole night in prayer. That night of prayer had some reference, there can be no doubt, to what was to occur the following day. In the morning "He called unto him his disciples, and of them he chose twelve, whom he also named apostles." In this honored list occurs the name of John, who, together with his brother, the first apostolic martyr, received the surname *Boanerges*, sons of thunder. It was a great office, the greatest to which man was ever called. In virtue of it, he was to be endowed with miraculous power, and the gift of inspiration; he was to receive the keys at the kingdom of heaven, and to be entrusted with the organization of the church, and the dissemination of the religion of Christ among men. He had been already more than a year with Christ before he received solemn appointment to this high office. His tuition and discipline were to be continued during the whole period of the Lord's ministry, and after his ascension he was to receive those supernatural gifts which would qualify him to perform the high functions he would be called to exercise. The founder of Christianity did not send forth uninstructed, untrained, undisciplined men to do his work. The apostles have been so often described as rude, untaught fisherman, that it is the more important to notice their contact and close association with the greatest of teachers for a period of more than three years.—p. 72.

In the chapter immediately following this, the author very powerfully exhibits St. John's "preparation for his work, from intercourse and instruction in private, in the last days of Christ, especially as a witness of the crucifixion." We should be glad, if we had space, to cull some extracts from this, but must forbear.

Dr. Macdonald in early life published a volume on the Apocalypse, which attracted much attention, and was highly commended as one of the very foremost works on that subject by such high critics as the late Dr. J. Addison Alexander. His power in descriptive composition greatly aids his successful handling of this wonderful book, which, in many aspects, is so confounding to exegetes, that Calvin himself is said to have shrunk from making a commentary upon it, because he could not understand it. The weight of critical opinion is against Dr. Macdonald's view of the early date of this composition, which he nevertheless supports with great ability. But we think the following a very judicious account of its aim and scope :

"The great theme of the Apocalypse is the coming of Jesus Christ to this world in compassion to his people and judgment on his foes, and, after the destruction of all the anti-Christian powers that may arise in different ages of the world, and the church has enjoyed a long season of unexampled prosperity, his final coming to raise the dead and judge the righteous and the wicked ; so that this book might be entitled, not inappropriately, THE BOOK OF THE COMING OF JESUS CHRIST. The New Testament informs us of a two-fold appearance or coming of Christ. One, his appearing in the flesh, was visible. The other, or second, relates to the preservation, propagation, and consummation of his kingdom. The second coming is partly *invisible*, as in the instance of the destruction of Jerusalem, or when he interposes for his sincere followers, and grants them the light and comfort of his presence. And it is partly *visible ;* that is, Christ at the end of the world will thus appear to raise the dead, and pass the irreversible sentence of judgment on every man. Now, it is the second, partly visible and partly invisible, coming of Christ which this book reveals, and which should never be lost sight of if we would have the blessedness it promises : ' Blessed is he that readeth, and they that hear the words of this prophecy, and keep those things that are written in this book.' "—Pp. 173.

We notice an occasional slip, which would probably have been avoided had the author lived to revise the proofs. A marked instance of this is observable in the apparently conflicting accounts given on pages 138 and 225, with regard to the continuance of the literal as distinguished from the figurative or mystical Babylon. But such mistakes are rare. It deserves mention that the table of contents, references, and the index of topics are remarkably complete, and add much to the value of the book.

One of the most *noteworthy* chapters is that entitled, " St. John as a disciple of John the Baptist," and we should be glad to transfer to our pages the fine portraitures drawn of the characters of both these great leaders, in the introduction of Christianity and founding of the church. We cannot do this; but we make room for the following passage, in regard to one prevalent conception, or rather misconception, of the main subject of the volumes, pp. 28, 29, 30.

"From his honored position at the Last Supper, and his peculiar designation as 'the disciple whom Jesus loved,' and because, in his epistles and gospel, he dwells so much on love, John has been frequently described as being all mildness, distinguished by a feminine softness, and destitute of strong, positive elements. But to imagine that he was a merely contemplative being, tame, and of a weak, sentimental nature, is, unquestionably, to do serious injustice to his character. His natural traits appear rather to have been those of decision and energy; traits which it is not the province of divine grace to eradicate, but to regenerate and sanctify. He possessed a temperament, indeed, which, if it had not been subjected to the influence of this grace, might have made him fiery and fierce, if not cruel and unforgiving. The love which dwelt in him in so eminent a degree, might easily, under adverse influences, have been changed into its opposite—violent hatred. It was the strong, manly quali- ties of John which so commended him to the regard of the Redeemer of the world, and led to his selection for the great share he had in the work of laying the founda- tion of the Christian faith, amid opposition, confusion, and blood. In him the searching eye of the Redeemer recognized faculties which, diverted from the low ends of worldly ambition and contact, might be exalted to the great works of divine benevolence. He could see how the impulses, which, misdirected or left uncon- trolled, must tend only to evil, ' could be made the guide of truth and love,' and in his " fiery ardor, the disguised germ of a holy zeal," which, under his careful tuition, " would become a tree of life, bringing forth fruits of good for nations." It was in perfect keeping with these characteristics which Josephus ascribes to the whole Galilean race, ' ardent and fierce,' that when the inhabitants of a certain Samaritan village refused to show Jesus hospitality, the two brothers, James and John, the more ready doubtless to take fire on account of the old national grudge, desired permission to call down fire from heaven for their destruction. It was a delicate susceptibility to impression which led John to respond so readily—and some- times in a way not so amiable—to the events and disclosures, which were ever multiplying around him, as he followed his Master. To refuse hospitality to such a being as he knew his Master to be, seemed to him unpardonable. This same quick susceptibility appears on another occasion, when he came and told the Saviour that he had rebuked a man for casting out devils, because he did not follow Christ in his company.

" The character of John, even when more matured, showed itself strongly colored by the same constitutional peculiarity. ' Had this native quality been left to itself, unchecked by harmful influence, and unchastened by the grace of God, that John, whose soul, pouring itself forth in inspired writings, one delights to observe, so yielding to the slightest touch of heavenly truth, would have been known, if at all, only as the dissolute prey of contending passions. His susceptibility would have been like the perturbations of angry waters, which surrender themselves to every coming gust. But in the confirmed Christian and apostle, this trait appears like the rapid and transparent picturing of past succeeding beauties and glories of the opening heavens on the bosom of some stream, charmed by the presence of an unseen pre- siding spirit. If this responsive picturing in his soul was sometimes overcast with a shade from untimely objects, such a disfiguring shadow was but transient.' He used no softened, honeyed terms, when he described evil-doers. With him a false pro- fessor was a ' liar;' a hater of his brother, ' a murderer;' a denier of fundamental doctrines, ' anti-Christ.' "

Art. XI.—CONTEMPORARY LITERATURE.

THEOLOGICAL AND RELIGIOUS.

Peter, the Apostle. By the REV. WILLIAM M. TAYLOR, D.D., Minister of the Broadway Tabernacle, New York City. Harper & Brothers. This volume contains no less than twenty-three chapters, which are evidently the substance of as many discourses preached upon the most notable and instructive events in the life of the Apostle Peter, beginning with his conversion, and ending with a survey of his character and career as a servant and apostle of Christ. It is on the same general plan, and has originated in the same way, as the author's previous volumes on David and Elijah. Although Dr. Taylor's sermons owe much of their electric power over audiences to a commanding and impassioned delivery, which, no less than the words spoken, voices his very soul to his hearers, yet it is only necessary to read them to perceive that there is an electricity in the matter of them, without which the most vehement vociferation would be comparatively *vox et preterea nihil.* They carry along the reader by an inherent force and attraction which come from the unfailing light and power, freshness and vivacity, with which "truths, of all others the most awful and interesting," are so sent home to the understanding, heart, and conscience, that they can no longer "lie bed-ridden in the dormitory of the soul side by side with the most despised and exploded errors."

These sermons, we judge from frequent allusions in them, and from their special application to revivals of religion, to have been preached in close connection with and reference to the great awakening in New York in the winter of 1875–6, which centered in the Hippodrome meetings under the preaching and conduct of Mr. Moody. While there is much in them to instruct and inspire, as concerns the ordinary Christian life, they are still more special in respect to the methods and motives which relate to Christian work for promoting the growth of the church by conversions and revivals. And such are the justness and importance of the truths set forth, and the fertility and appositeness of the illustration and imagery which vivify them to our apprehension, that they keep up an unflagging interest in the reader, as they previously did in the hearer.

These discourses are replete with scriptural truth, uttered with the authority which is backed by a "Thus saith the Lord," challenging assent and obedience as such, and as spoken by the ambassador of God. And here lies the open secret of their power. Much has been written and said in regard to the occasional calling of foreign clergymen to our pulpits, and the pre-eminent success which a few of them have achieved. We once heard a young man, not a professor of religion, who had, during a season's residence in New York, taken the opportunity to hear the most distinguished metropolitan preachers, ascribe the remarkable success of those ministers from abroad, whose names our readers will readily recognize, to the superior Scripturalness of their preaching. We believe that this explains the secret, in part, at least; and that, if not true in every sense, it is in one particular, to which our young American preachers and their homiletical teachers will find it worth their while to take heed. And we advert to it just here, because it is strongly illustrated in this and the previous volumes of Dr. Taylor. We think the great body of our evangelical preachers are just as Scriptural in the sense of conforming their discourses to, building them upon, and fortifying them in all their positions by, the Bible, as these leading foreign preachers, of whom Dr. Taylor is a distinguished specimen. But their peculiar excellence, in which they may profitably be held up for study and imitation in our view, is, that they set forth the truth of Scripture less in the abstract, and more in the concrete forms of life, experience, and example, in which it is held forth in the Bible; only adapting and applying it to the analogous cases of our own time, and to the circumstances of the men and women of the passing day and hour. Thus, they are constantly holding up the Bible as a glass through which men see their own experiences, actions, habits, characteristics, whether good or evil, photographed, and then reflected back in their own consciousness for comparison with Scriptural standards. "As in water face answer to face, so the heart of man to man." Thus it is, that the same essential Scriptural truth penetrates and stirs all the faculties of the soul, because so presented as to find its counterpart and verification in the living consciousness of that soul. It then grapples the man, so that he becomes not a hearer only, but a doer of the Word, and is blessed in his deed.

It is just in this region that we think our American preachers may learn something to their advantage by the study of these and like discourses of the best foreign preachers. Not the mere taking a text, or logically unfolding and applying, or raising important doctrines from it, and duly confirming them by other Scriptural testimonies; not the delivering of an elegant essay or cogent argument about them; but the bringing truth out in the concrete, living forms in which the Bible presents it, causing it thus to permeate the whole discourse, so that in all its parts it takes on a Scriptural hue, and speaks with a divine authority—a pungency sharper than any two-edged sword.

Dr. Taylor, repeatedly in this volume, gives forth his own ideas on this subject in his portraitures of the preaching of Peter and others. Of Peter's pentecostal sermon he says:

"This discourse was eminently biblical. He brought the Bible to the front, and by its simple exposition he proved that Jesus of Nazareth was indeed the Messiah. Now-a-days we have a great deal said in the pulpit that might be just as appropriate in the hall of the layman, or in a class-room of a professor of philosophy. But Peter began and ended with the Word of God. And when our preachers will give over apologizing for the Bible, or criticising it, and will let it simply speak for itself, then we, too, may look back for a new day of Pentecost. What mean the crowds that everywhere throng to hear those evangelists whom God has so signally honored? They are the proof, if men only are to be convinced, that no book is so interesting to the common people as the Word of God, and that no magnet is so potent as the attraction of the cross."—Pp. 182-3.

Again he says of John the Baptist:

"He had the grand old Tishbite's peculiar power. He knew neither fear nor favor. He called things by their right names; and though he had dwelt so long in the desert, he let his hearers feel that he had not forgotten the evils which he had seen practised in the cities. He aimed right at their consciences, and spoke in plain and unmistakable terms of the sins with which they were chargeable. He knew nothing of that simpering propriety, all be-gloved and sleek, which has chloroformed so many modern preachers; but he exposed, in words as unadorned as his own camlet robe, the iniquities of his hearers, and called upon them there and then to repent."—Pp. 8, 9.

The Presbyterian Board issue *Christian Love as Manifested in the Heart and Life.* By JONATHAN EDWARDS, *sometime Pastor of the Church in Northampton, Mass., and President of the College of New Jersey.* Edited, from the original manuscript, by the REV. TRYON EDWARDS, D.D. This is a comparatively recent addition to the published works of Edwards, although it was selected, and in part prepared, for publication by Hopkins and Bellamy, which for some unknown reason they failed to accomplish. It is fortunate that the original manuscripts fell into the hands of his accomplished descendant, Dr. Tryon Edwards. Nothing need be said to show the value of an extended treatise on such a subject by such an author. We can quite understand why John Angell James once said to an American clergyman: "Had I seen this noble work ot Edwards before I published on the same subject, I should hardly have allowed my work (Christian Charity Explained) to go to the press. It is admirable, every word of it."

The same Board have published a very neat and beautiful edition, illustrated, of *Pilgrim's Progress;* a book that has lost none of its marvelous power to fascinate and instruct, alike the old and the young, the saint in near view of his celestial home, and the pilgrim who has just left the city of Destruction.

Scribner, Armstrong & Co. have issued two more of the uniform edition of Bushnell's Sermons, the one being that on *Living Subjects;* the other on *Christ and his Salvation.* It is hardly necessary to call attention to the originality, freshness, and the generally devout and edifying character of these discourses, which also here and there show traces of the gifted author's eccentric tendencies in doctrine and speculation.

The Clarks, of Edinburgh, have issued, and have for sale in this country, through Scribner, Welford & Armstrong, in New York, and McGinness & Runyon, of Princeton, at $3.00, *Sermons for the Christian Year;* translated from the German of the late Richard Rothe, D.D. They run from Advent to Trinity; and are profitable not only to the general reader as aids to Christian knowledge, practice, and devotion, but they deserve the study of preachers, as showing how sermons, remarkable for their brevity and condensation, may nevertheless be the vehicles of much precious truth and kindling warmth to the heart. They have in them a quiet power and earnestness, a strong Scriptural coloring, and a constant mingling of application with principles, which give them that indescribable something called unction, more easily felt than defined, and which imparts to the evangelical pulpit its grandest power.

" In the Days of thy Youth." *Sermons on Practical Subjects, Preached at Marlborough College*, from 1871 to 1876. By F. W. FARRAR, D.D., F.R.S. Published by Macmillan & Co., New York. Those who have read and enjoyed Farrar's Life of Christ will, we feel sure, welcome this volume of sermons from the same writer's pen. Though addressed in the first place to the youth of Marlborough College, all classes may also derive pleasure and profit from their perusal.

Scholar's Hand-Book (Part VII.) on the International Lessons, from January to July, 1877. Studies about the Kingdom of Israel. By REV. EDWIN W. RICE. Philadelphia : American Sunday-School Union.

The Clarks of Edinburgh, and Scribner, Welford & Armstrong in this country, publish, at $3.75, *The Christian Commonwealth*, by HENRY W. J. THIERSCH, translated into English under the direction of the author. It did not reach us in time to admit of more than a cursory examination. This, however, has convinced us that it is a work of high value on a great subject, which is constantly coming to the forefront of discussion, and forced there by the progress of speculative inquiry, no less than the urgency of imminent practical problems. It is none the less valuable, even though it calls in question many principles which have long been admitted to the rank of virtual axioms among ourselves. If the author disputes the propriety of universal suffrage, it is only what many of our wisest and best men are coming to do, as the late admirable Report of the Committee on the Government of Cities, appointed by Governor Tilden, composed of the choicest representatives of both political parties, abundantly proves. We take occasion here to call attention to that document, as deserving the attentive consideration of all interested in good municipal government.

This volume of Thiersch treats many fundamental topics from a Christian standpoint ; and while we can now barely indicate these, and sometimes differ with the author, we hope to have some future opportunity of returning to fuller consideration of it. It treats of the Definition of a Christian Commonwealth, Christianity, Christianity in its Relations to Existing Authority, and the Various Forms of Government, Christianity and Absolute Monarchy, Christianity and Modern Liberal Tendencies, the Temporal and Spiritual Power, their Common Ground, Education, and Matrimony, the State Church, Freedom of Commerce, Christian and Unchristian Toleration, the Emancipation of the Jews, Separation of Church and State., the Lawfulness of Taking an Oath in a Christian Commonwealth, the Position of a Christian State Toward the Pretensions of the Papacy, the Duty of a Christian Commonwealth with Regard to the Working Classes, Criminal Law, War and International Law, the Duties of Subjects, the Duties of Rulers.

The same houses bring out, at $3.00, the Anti-Pelagian works of St. Augustine, being the 15th of DR. MARCUS DOD'S edition of the works of this great divine, and the third and last volume of his Anti-Pelagian productions. It is translated by Drs. Peter Holmes and Robert Ernest Wallis. It contains the great treatises on Grace and Free-will, Rebuke and Grace, Predestination and Perseverance; also his answer to Two Letters of the Pelagians. It is needless to speak of the importance of these great productions, which no progress of speculation or inquiry can ever render obsolete. This volume finishes the series of fifteen, originally planned for this edition of Augustine's works. His life, by Dr. Rainey, is yet to appear, and will be eagerly awaited. We are glad to see that the enterprising publishers now propose to begin the publication of Chrysostom's works.

W. F. Draper, of Andover, has reprinted from the *Bibliotheca Sacra* six articles from the pen of Dr. THOMAS HILL, former President of Harvard College, in a thick pamphlet, entitled, *A Statement of the Natural Sources of Theology, with a Discussion of their Validity, and of Modern Skeptical Objections; to which is added an Article on the First Chapter of Genesis.* We think these articles well worthy to be thus collected in a form available for those who wish to study them in connection, or who have not access to the scattered numbers of the Quarterly in which they first appeared. They deal with the most important positions, strongholds, and authors of recent skepticism, while they expose some of the weak positions taken by some philosophers and theologians in refutation of it. Especially does Dr. Hill take in hand the system which remands religion to the sphere and category of the Unknowable, whether taken by adversaries like Spencer, or by friends like Hamilton and Mansel.

The chapters on the Natural Foundations of Theology and on the Testimony of Organic Life are especially able. He makes an impregnable argument against atheism and materialism from "our intellectual intuitions, our natural affections and sentiments, our ethical judgments, the manifestation of intellect in the *cosmos*, the manifestation of purpose, the universe as a work of art, the true doctrine of the Unknowable, the testimony of the church, and revealed religion."

A Tract by C. R. ROBERT, a prominent layman of New York City, entitled the *Mixed Multitude, Ancient and Modern*, has just been published for special circulation among church members and ministers. Its great theme is, the several particulars in which the church has become "conformed to the world" during the last twenty years. It is a serious and powerful arraignment of the people and the clergy, charging declension in many respects. Without saying that there is no overdoing or exaggeration in any part of this tract, we unhesitatingly say, that it will repay earnest attention and thought. And, with due allowance for all over-statements, it unquestionably indicates truly the growing religious tendency and danger of the times, against which all need to keep double guard.

Sheldon & Co., of New York, have brought out, *Why Four Gospels? or, the Gospel for all the World. A manual designed to aid Christians in*

the study of the Scriptures, and to a better understanding of the Gospels.
By PROF. D. S. GREGORY, D.D., of Worcester University, author of
"Christian Ethics." We regret that this book only reached us at the last
moment, too late to admit of a searching examination. This is the less
necessary, however, inasmuch as the substance of large portions of it has
already been before us and many of our readers, in articles published a few
years ago in the *Princeton Review*. These commanded favorable attention
and brought to the author many requests to complete and embody them in
a volume. In yielding to these, he has given us a volume highly creditable
to his industry, learning, and judgment, which cannot fail to promote the
right understandtng of the four Gospels, their several aims, and their
mutual relations; and to increase the interest and profit with which they
may be read and studied.

His theory is, that, as the Gospel was designed for the world, so it could
best reach the world by being prepared for and specially adapted and
addressed to each of the four great peoples of the world—the Jewish, Roman,
Greek, and the Church, or Christian people gathered out of all these. The
four authors of the respective Gospels were selected each with reference to their special fitness to commend it to the particular people for whom
his narrative was written—Matthew for the Jews, Mark for the Romans
Luke for the Greeks, John for the Christian Church. The previous condition and characteristics of these several peoples, the preparatory religious
training and culture of the Jews; the conquering and organizing power, the
might and laws of the Romans; the literary culture and philosophic subtlety
of the Greeks; the evangelical and spiritual experience superinduced upon
each of these in the members of the Christian Church, required precisely
the qualifications which we find in the author of each Gospel, This lets in
a flood of light upon their respective peculiarities, which explains why one
relates what another omits, or, *vice versa* ; why one brings forward the same
acts and deeds of our Lord in one connection, another with different surroundings. It does away with most of the seeming discrepancies which
have so troubled the harmonistic interpreters and commentators. Nor are
its advantages negative merely, in solving perplexities and removing difficulties; but it gives a weight of meaning to many parts, and to the whole
scope of each gospel not otherwise discernible.

In following out this view, the author of course discards and demolishes
the allegorizing and fanciful harmonistic attempts to interpret the Gospel;
as if each had no distinct and separate aim peculiar to itself. Still more
decisively he sweeps away the rationalism, which is the rebound from these
extravagances to a far worse extreme; whether it be, as with Strauss, the
outcome of that transcendental pantheism which overflies human nature ; or,
as with Renan, of that reptile positivism or materialism which sinks below
it. We think the book will prove a welcome addition to our evangelical
literature among all engaged in the study of the Gospels, or the Scriptures
generally.

Salvation, Here and Hereafter; Sermons and Essays. By JOHN SER-
VICE, Minister of Inch, London.   Macmillan & Co., 1877, pp. 267.   These
twelve sermons and essays are mainly on subjects of special current interest,
and are handled with great vigor and freshness, and with no little critical
skill.   We should dissent from some of the views of the author as being
decidedly Broad-Church ; still, in the main, the book is healthy in tone,
catholic and evangelical in spirit, and well worth reading.   We give a specimen or two from the work, to show the author's style.   The first extract is
certainly "liberal in sentiment," to borrow the language of the London
Spectator, and is taken from the sermon on "The Rich Man and Lazarus."

"But still, beggarly as was his soul, he was not without a heart.   He was earnest
with Abraham about his five brethren.   Now, for my part, if I were going to argue
anything upon this ground, I should not argue that sinners in the next world are past
all hope and all feeling of what is good, but rather, that even the prayer of a lost
soul must find some response with God.   Will any man tell me that a man can be
represented as praying, in the place of torment, that his brethren may not be allowed
to come into it, and that God, who is the Father of all men, can be supposed to have
so much less humanity than a man, as not to heed, whether the suppliant himself is to
remain forever in that place ?   Will you make man more humane than God ?   Will
you represent men as concerned about their kinsmen, lest they should go to hell, and
then will you represent Him as not caring if as many as are once there stay there?"

Another excerpt is as just in sentiment as beautiful in expression :

"There is one city of the East, of biblical and historical renown, which is surrounded
on all sides by deserts; but which, to the astonishment of the traveler, who has
been toiling for days over burning sands to reach its gates, presents to the eye, as he
enters, a wonderful succession of gardens, gay with the richest verdure and the most
gorgeous blooms.   Above that city—the most ancient, perhaps, in the world—above
that desert-girdled city, Damascus—towers the lofty Lebanon, with its snow-clad head
piercing the fleecy clouds of a summer sky.   It is in its lofty summits that the secret
of this wonderful verdure lies.   There, in those snows that mingle with the clouds,
are the inexhaustible fountains of the innumerable rills of water by which, in Damascus, the desert has been turned into a garden, and the wilderness made to blossom as
the rose.   All history proves that it is only from the foundation of a religion which,
like Lebanon, lifts its head above the ground, and represents the aspirations of the
soul after the unseen and eternal, that the sustenance which is needed for the
purest and heavenliest virtues of humanity, the truest and noblest morality, can ever
flow."

The following needs to be taken with much allowance :

"To identify or associate it [Christianity] with any sort of antagonism to science
is necessarily, however unwittingly, to associate or identify it with vulgar ignorance,
imbecility of mind, cant, credulity—with the effect, of course, of weakening its hold
upon all but the most unintelligent and unthinking.   Hence, for one man who is
shaken in his belief of this or that religious doctrine by arguments advanced by men
of science, a hundred might, perhaps, be counted who owe a suspicion of all religious
teaching, or a contempt for it, to apologists for Christianity, who undertake to defend
it against science, and succeed only in showing with what bad arguments a good
cause may come to be supported.   .   .   .   .   Ignorance, not science, is the arch-
enemy of the simplicity of the Gospel, the purity of the faith, or whatever you choose
to call the spirit as distinguished from the letter of the Christian revelation.   Our

controversy on this score is not with the few who have learned from science to believe little, but with the many, who, from ignorance, doubt nothing. Whatever may be the case, then, with regard to ecclesiastical and doctrinal systems, calling themselves Christian, it is at the expense of the purity, and therefore at the expense of the life and power, of the Christian faith, that science is in any way opposed or depreciated in the name of Christianity. No greater gain to ' pure religion and undefiled ' could be wished, than what it would be for Christian churches to take friendly account of science, as having much to say in favor of the simplification of their creeds. No greater loss, perhaps, could be incurred by Christian churches than what they do incur by maintaining, as against an arch-enemy in science, and with fresh ardor and incensed dignity, ancient doctrines and traditions, which, whether true or false, are at any rate at once antiquated and trivial."

BIBLICAL LITERATURE.

Scribner, Armstrong & Co. have brought out Volumes VII. and XIII. of the great *Commentary of Lange* on the Old Testament. The former is made up of the Books of Chronicles by Dr. OTTO ZÖCKLER, Professor of ·Theology in the University of Greisswald, Prussia ; translated, enlarged, and edited by JAMES G. MURPHY, LL.D., Professor in the General Assembly and the Queen's College, Belfast; also of the Book of Ezra, by F. W. SCHULTZ, Professor in the University of Breslau, Prussia; translated, enlarged, and edited by REV. CHARLES A. BRIGGS, D.D., Professor of O. T. Exegesis in Union Seminary, New York; also Nehemiah, critically and theologically expounded, by Rev. HOWARD CROSBY, D.D., LL.D., Chancellor of the University of New York. Finally, the Book of Esther, also by Professor SCHULTZ; translated, enlarged, and edited by JAMES STRONG, S.T.D., Professor of Exegetical Theology in Drew Theological Seminary.

Volume XIII. consists of the Prophet Ezekiel, by FR. WILHELM JULIUS SCHRODER, and having for its English translator and editors the late Dr. PATRICK FAIRBAIRN and Rev. WM. FINDLAY, aided by Rev. THOMAS CRERAR and Rev. SINCLAIR MUNSON. To this is added that on Daniel, also by Dr. OTTO ZÖCKLER, having Prof. STRONG, of Drew Seminary, for its translator and American editor.

These massive volumes fully maintain the high character thus far kept up by the previous volumes of this great Commentary. They constitute an exigetical thesaurus which no expounder of the Word can afford to be without. The remarkable compactness and directness of that by Dr. Crosby, shows how English and American commentators can so work up the matter furnished by the wondrous German exegetes, as to adapt it still better to the wants of English and American students. For sale by McGinness & Runyon, Princeton.

T. & T. Clark, of Edinburgh, have published, and Scribner, Welford & Armstrong have imported, a special edition for use in this country, of the first volume of *St. John's Gospel, Described and Explained According to its Peculiar Character*, by CHRISTOPH ERNEST LUTHARDT, Professor of Theology at Leipzig, and translated by CASPAR RENE GREGORY, Doctor of Philosophy, Leipzig. Students of Scripture have had their appetites already sharpened for this great work by the author's previous volume proving

John to be the author of the Fourth Gospel. The present volume is almost wholly occupied with the introduction to the main exposition. The latter barely enters upon the beginning of the first chapter, and opens out its teachings concerning the Person, the Godhead, the Sonship, the Incarnation of the Logos. The introduction is very learned, profound, and suggestive. It takes a comprehensive and well-considered view of the chief matters prominent in this gospel, and the positions of different schools and writers concerning them. Among these topics are the integrity, the language, the narration, the design, the arrangement and construction, the authorship of the gospel. We are glad to see that our friend, the translator, has not buried his talent since he has gone to dwell in a foreign land. He is doing important service by making such works accessible to English readers and students. We are happy to add, that few can do it better. It is seldom that a profound, or even shallow, German work is translated into such pure and idiomatic English.

From the same houses we also receive the first volume of a *Commentary on the Gospel of St. John,* with a Critical Introduction, translated from the Second French Edition of F. Godet, D.D., Professor of Theology, Neuchatel, by FRANCIS CROMBIE and M. D. CUSIN. Like the volume of Luthardt, it is almost wholly occupied with the introduction, and barely enters upon the exposition of chapter I. We have before called the attention of our readers to the excellent qualities of his exposition of Luke. First, is a valuable biographical sketch and characterization of the Apostle John. Then follow the analysis and the characteristics of the Fourth Gospel. After this, the origin of the Fourth Gospel, time and place of its composition, its occasion and aim. If there is a great increase of Johannean exegesis and apologetics, it is fully demanded by the destructive skepticism and unbelief now fashionable. No book of Scripture more completely lifts us above the level of materialism and rationalism, now current, into the plane of the spiritual, supernatural, and divine. The above volumes of John are also on sale by McGinness & Runyon, Princeton, at $3.00 each.

The same houses in, Edinburgh, New York, and Princeton, bring out, at $7.50, *A Treatise on the Grammar of New Testament Greek, Regarded as a Sure Basis for New Testament Exegesis.* By Dr. G. B. WINER. *Translated from the German, with large additions and full indices,* second edition, by Rev. W. F. MOULTON, D.D., being the eighth English edition of this great work in different translations. The present translator has, in deference to a demand from high sources, abridged somewhat two or three cumbrous chapters on less important subjects, such as that in relation to the disputes between the Purists and Hebraists. He has verified the almost countless references contained in the book. The translator's additions to the German constitute about one-sixth of the massive volume. In these he aims (1) to supplement Winer's statements, and bring them into accordance with the present state of our knowledge, it having been a score of years since his last edition, and more than a half century since his original edition of it was published. Great light has been shed on the subject by the labors of more recent commentators, of which Dr. Moulton has availed himself. (2) He has undertaken to show, under each head of the subject, how much may be considered as settled, and how much remains border-land; (3.) He has sought, by means of continuous references to English writers on Greek Grammar, and on New Testament Greek, to place the English reader in the position occupied by one who uses the original; (4.) To call further attention to the many striking coincidences between modern Greek and the language in which the New Testament is written. This is in many respects the best English edition of this great work, which underlies modern New Testament exegesis, and has done so much to purify it from arbitrary and baseless assumption and hermeneutical traditions, that had before so stubbornly held their ground. It cannot be spared from the working apparatus of any thorough exegete.

Warren F. Draper, of Andover, Mass., has published, from the third London edition, and has on sale by Hurd & Houghton, New York, *The Book of Psalms; a New Translation, with Introduction and Notes, Explanatory and Critical*, by J. J. STEWART PEROWNE, D.D., in two solid 8vo volumes. The work is an important addition to our means of understanding the Psalms in their true grammatical and exegetical sense, and their doctrinal and devotional characteristics. It is enriched from the best sources of ancient and modern learning on the subject, and gathers all available light from the very latest commentaries and treatises, not only on the whole Psalter, but on particular Psalms, and groups of Psalms. The doctrinal interpretation of the Psalms is with some marked exceptions sound and judicious ; equi-distant from a frigid, anti-Christian rationalism, which finds no Christ predicted, and no supernatural or evangelical element in the Psalms; and from that constrained allegorizing which finds him alluded to in every Psalm, and even verse. The work seems to us one of the most serviceable within reach for consultation on this precious portion of the Scriptures.

Biblical students will find a useful auxiliary to their studies in the following publication, by Nelson & Philips, to be followed, we understand, by a similar one, to include the entire New Testament. The title-page explains the work, and is as follows : " The Epistle to the Romans in Greek, in which the text of Robert Stephens, third edition, is compared with the text of the Elzeirrs, Lachmann, Alford, Tregelles, Tischendorf, and Westcott, and with the chief uncial and cursive manuscripts; together with references to the New Testament Grammars of Winer andButtman." By HENRY A. BUTTZ. Professor of New Testament Exegesis in Drew Theological Seminary.

PHILOSOPHY.

Chase & Hull, of Cincinnati, publish *The Problem of Problems; or, Atheism, Darwinism, and Theism.* By CLARK BRADEB, President of Abington College, Illinois. Although this is our first introduction to the author, so far as his name and publications are concerned, whether or not it be his first experiment in authorship, we expect to hear from him again.

The quantity of matter packed in these nearly five hundred pages is immense. And we take pleasure in saying, that its quality is generally equal to its quantity. No one book within our knowledge treats the evolution of the atheistic and infidel school so thoroughly and exhaustively, or deals it such many-sided, sledge-hammer blows. It is strange that such a work should be necessary, or that such vast labor should require to be expended to prove that no blind, unconscious, unknowing, and unknowable force affords any proper solution of the phenomena of the universe; and that a Personal, All-wise, and Almighty God affords the only and the edequate solution of the problem. If we grant that the author is sometimes a little wanting in breadth and calmness of view, this does not detract from the substantial truth, ability, and conclusiveness of his reasonings. We repeat, without endorsing every position or paragraph of this powerful volume, it is in the main a most vigorous defence of fundamental truth; and contains more that is fitted to meet the wants of minds inquiring or unsettled on this great subject, than any single volume within our knowledge. Works of this kind generally treat the subject in single or partial aspects. This looks at it from all important stand-points; and effectually explodes that materialism which, as our author says, through Holyoke, its leading English apostle, declares, "science has shown that we are under the dominion of general laws—inexorable laws of unyielding necessity—evolved by irrational matter and force. There is no special providence; prayers are useless; propitiation is in vain. Whether there be a deity, or nature be deity, it is still the god of the iron foot, that passes on without heeding, without feeling, without resting. Nature acts with fearful uniformity; stern as fate, absolute as tyranny, relentless as destiny, merciless as death; too vast to praise; too inexplicable to worship; too inexorable to propitiate, it has no ear for prayer, no heart for sympathy or pity, no arm to save."—P. 474. We have no heart to argue or hold parley with such blasphemy. It speaks its own sentence, and must become its own executioner. That it, or any approach to it, of which it could be even a conceivable caricature, should have won the assent of real or professed scientists, claiming a monopoly of the reasoning faculty, is among the portents of the age and prodigies of human credulity.

Rev. James W. Hanna, Pastor of Presbyterian Church, Mt. Vernon, Iowa, has written and published *Celestial Dynamics; a New Theory, with Discoveries in Astronomy.* It may be that it is reserved for a minister in a rural congregation, far away toward the frontier, to become a second Kepler or Newton, either by the extent of his discoveries of the hitherto unknown, or by reconstructing the very basis and ground-principle of astronomy. Such a claim is not forthwith to be rejected on the ground of *à priori* impossibility. It must be confessed that it is not very probable. The scientific zeal and enterprise manifest in this pamphlet are creditable to its author, even if it should turn out that its "new things are not true, and its true things are not new." Whether this be so in the present case, it would be presumptuous in us to say. We can only relegate it to the astronomical experts and savants, to whose decision we shall readily bow.

Economical Science. Scribner, Armstrong & Co. publish an *Introduction to Political Economy*, by ARTHUR LATHAM PERRY, LL.D., Professor of this department in Williams College. This is not a new edition of the former work of Prof. Perry, which has been so largely used as a text-book, and has enjoyed a success which has carried it through numerous editions. It is designed rather to unfold some of the elementary principles of the science in a form which will simplify them to the apprehension not merely of students, but of the great body of thinking and intelligent people. In this attempt he is very successful. He generally places the science on its right elementary foundations, although we do not think every point is worked out in the most perfect manner.

The Harpers have issued the *Logical Method of Political Economy*. By J. E. CAIRNES, LL.D., late Professor of this Science in the University of London. This, with the other volume by the same author, entitled " Some Principles of Political Economy Newly Expounded," establish his reputation as an authority in economic science. We quite agree with him in his opposition to Jevons' doctrine, that this and ethical science can be reduced to a mathematical basis, so as to make its problems soluble by a mathematical calculus, and reducible to mathematical formulæ. This doctrine has its origin in materialism, and supposes that the motives which determine the human will are as capable of being put in determinate mathematical ratios, as those of matter and the heavenly bodies, whereby astronomy becomes so largely a mathematical science. It supposes not only the Hedonistic system of ethics, but that the intensity and duration of pleasurable sensations can be quantitatively ascertained and expressed in numerical ratios. All this is an illusion.

The great principle urged by Prof. Cairnes, profusely illustrated and carried out to its results, is, that in the long run free competition proves the best regulator and equalizer of all the mal-adjustments that arise between different branches of industry, and between labor and capital; and that, unless in exceptional cases, if left to themselves, they come to a right adjustment, even as the daily supplies for the tables of the millions of people in London will surely come in right measure, place, and time, if left to the unimpeded operation of the laws of supply and demand.

HISTORY AND BIOGRAPHY.

The Clarks, of Edinburgh, have published, and Scribner, Welford & Armstrong have imported, a special edition for use in this country (price $4.00), which is also on sale by McGinness & Runyon, Princeton, *Hippolytus and Callistus; or, the Church of Rome in the First Half of the Third Century, with Special Reference to the Writings of Bunsen, Wordsworth, and Gieseler*, by JOHN J. IGN. VON DÖLLINGER. Translated, with Introduction, Notes, and Appendices, by Alfred Plummer.

Whatever Dr. Döllinger may publish on questions of historical ecclesiasticism or theology will command deserved attention. This volume on the

Philosophumena, discovered within recent years, and then traced to the authorship of Hippolytus, one of the very earliest of the patristic theologians, sheds much light upon the state of doctrine and life at that primitive period, so near the apostolic age. It overflows with invective against Callistus, the then primate of the Roman See, and his predecessor, Zephyrinus, on account of abuses and laxness which they tolerated in the church. The invective is so bitter, that Dr. Newman, who assigns Hippolytus pre-eminent rank as a primitive theologian, cannot believe that the lately discovered book containing it can be his, for he cannot believe that so great a divine could have been so anti-Romish and anti-Popish. Dr. Döllinger, however, shows by irrefragable internal and other evidence that Hippolytus was their real author. In this he is supported by some principal authorities in church history: Duncker, Schneidewin, Jacobi, Gieseler, Bunsen, Bernays, Milman, Robertson, and Wordsworth. Dr. Döllinger says, that Hippolytus, and not Novatian, "must be considered the first forerunner of that long line of anti-Popes, which begins with Felix II. and ends with Felix V. Callistus, the victim of his bitter invective, may, on the other hand, be regarded as the forerunner of those liberal-minded and reforming Popes who have ever met with opposition, and have generally been thwarted. There is no long line of *them.* It would be hard to point to one in a century, or, perhaps, even one in the alternate centuries; and, so far as the present prospect reveals the chances of the future to us, there is no probability of any such Pope in the present century. He would be a bold prophet who ventured to point to a future reformer in the present College of Cardinals "—p. 15. Protestants and Old Catholics are agreed here.

Amid much to which we should like to call attention, we can barely note the apparent view of Hippolytus on some important doctrines. One of his principal assaults on Callistus was directed against his doctrine of the Trinity. Neither were wholly free from some of the confusion and error quite natural in the then imperfectly developed and formulated state of the doctrine. But Hippolytus, with a strong Sabellian learning, was furthest astray. It appears that the title, presbyter, was freely applied by him to the bishops, apparently as honorary, showing that he recognized no superiority of rank in the letter; that he recognized the sacrifice of Christ's body in the Eucharist, showing it to have been held thus early, by some at least, in the primitive church; while along with it the universal priesthood of believers was also, more or less, in vogue. Asceticism had already shown itself. Hippolytus was a Chiliast. His doctrine of Hades was, that it was the abode of departed souls; that Christ's descent into it was preceded by that of John the Baptist, heralding his advent thither, as before on earth; that Christ went thither and preached to those souls 'the good tidings of his incarnation and redemption; "that it was the human soul of Christ which descended into Hades to the souls confined there, while his body lay in the grave; while the Godhead, at one and the same time, in its essence, was with the father, but also remained in the body, and descended with the soul into Hades."—Pp. 328-9.

Scribner, Armstrong & Co · publish, and have on sale by McGinness, at Princeton, one of the most important biographies of recent date. It is *The Life and Correspondence of Thomas Arnold, D.D., Head Master of Rugby School, and Professor of Modern History in the University of Oxford,* by DEAN STANLEY. It is not often that so worthy a subject finds so worthy a biographer, so sympathetic, appreciative, and on the same general plane of opinions, gifts, culture. That author and subject, while so earnestly religious and Christian, should be so lax in their views of inspiration, and so decidedly Broad-Church in their general views, is greatly to be deplored. But it is a relief that they are among the noblest specimens and types of this tendency.

The Head Master of Rugby is even more famous as a prince among educators, than on account of any doctrinal or ecclesiastical bias. All who have to do with the teaching and training of youth, especially in the sphere of classical or liberal culture, may learn much to their own advantage, and that of their pupils, by a close study of the chapters on his school life at Rugby.

Rowland Hill; His Life, Anecdotes, and Pulpit Sayings. By VERNON I. CHARLESWORTH. With an Introduction by C. H. SPURGEON. New York: American Tract Society. Rowland Hill's name is associated with humor in the pulpit, and a multitude of anecdotes are current illustrative of it. But he was downright earnest as a preacher. "Take him for all in all," says Mr. Spurgeon, "we shall not soon look upon his like again. In him was no guile. He loved his Lord and the souls of men, and he threw all his might into the pursuit of doing good. Surely no man was ever more unselfish or less self-conscious. Men called him eccentric because they themselves were out of centre ; he, with his great heart, calm soul, wise mind, and loving nature, had learned to wait upon his Lord, and so had found the right centre and true orbit for his being."

The biographies of this remarkable man are scarcely known to the present generation, and are only to be met with occasionally on second-hand book stalls. The author of the present volume had access to several volumes of Mr. Hill's MS. sermons, still preserved in the library of Surrey Chapel, and for many years past has enjoyed the friendship of the old members of the church, who delight to recall the memories of their early days. The materials at his command were ample, and he has used them judiciously and with effect, omitting "nothing necessary to enable the reader to form a just estimate of Rowland Hill and his life-work—a gentleman by birth and education, a man of noble carriage, and a Christian minister of a type which may be said to be apostolic."

The Memorial of Morris C. Sutphen, D.D., is published by the Carters, and is a fit delineation of the life and character of one of the rising and gifted ministers of the church; remarkable for his purity and loveliness, while prematurely consumed by the fires of his own self-sacrificing zeal and devotion.

The Carters publish *Bernardino Ochino, of Siena. A Contribution Toward the History of the Reformation.* By KARL BENRATH. Translated from the German by HELEN ZIMMERN. With an Introductory Preface by WILLIAM ARTHUR, A.M., New York. This book is an interesting history of one of the Italian Reformers, all the more so because his very name has been comparatively unknown. The writer has had a somewhat difficult task to perform, the reason of which we give in his own words: "The Inquisition has branded the names of those men who unfurled the banner of the Reformation in Italy; she has effaced or calumniated their memory; and has endeavored, but too successfully, to hinder the diffusion of their writings. The consequences of this are still felt by those who seek a closer acquaintance with the history of Italian reforms."

Not the least interesting part of the work is the chapter embracing the Reformer's sojourn in England, whither, a fugitive from his own country by reason of his religious opinions, he came at the invitation of Cranmer, and spent six peaceful years. The whole makes a valuable contribution to ecclesiastical history, and illustrates afresh the terrors of Papal despotism and the cost of our deliverance from it.

Dr. GEO. S. MOTT, of Flemington, N. J., and Rev. GARNET CLARK, of Rondout, N. Y., have published well-prepared historical discourses pertaining to the churches of which they are pastors.

The History of Liberty ; a Paper read before the New York Historical Society, Feb. 6th, 1866, by JOHN F. AIKEN, with selected Notes, is published by A. S. Barnes & Co., New York.

We have received a well-written *Historical Sketch and Manual of the Shady Side Presbyterian Church,* Pittsburgh, Pa., prepared by the pastor, Rev. WM. T. BEATTY.

GENERAL LITERATURE.

The Rev. DR. BURR, author of "Ecce Cœlum," etc., has prepared a new book of a practical character. *In the Vineyard* ; *a Plea for Christian Work,* New York, published by T. Y. Crowell; pp. 454 ; which will be found to be both an incentive and an aid in Christian work.

The American Tract Society publishes a compact and useful volume ($1.50), entitled *Bible Student's Companion,* containing a Bible, Text Book, Concordance, Table of Proper Names, Twelve Maps, Indexes, etc. ; also a convenient *Pocket Concordance to the Scriptures,* much condensed, yet referring "*to one word at least in every verse of the Bible,*" with few exceptions; a *Home Garden,* compiled by Mrs. M. W. LAWRENCE, an excellent collection of short poems, of and for children. It is a gem of a book.

The Presbyterian Board of Publication issues an excellent tale, entitled *Grace Westervelt*; *or, the Children of the Covenant,* designed to illustrate the subject of infant baptism. The same Board publishes two new works, which are to be cordially recommended for Sunday-school libraries : *Watt*

Adams, the Young Machinist, and his Proverbs, by Mrs. MARY D, R. BOYD, and *Leaves and Fruit,* by M. E. GRIFFITH.

Besides the works already noticed, Carter & Bros also publish, in handsome editions: *My Old Letters,* by HORATIUS BONAR, D. D., pp. 352, being a narrative poem in twelve books. *Oliver of the Mill,* by MARIA LOUISA CHARLESWORTH, pp. 380, the favorite author of "Ministering Children," etc. *Rays from the Sun of Righteousness,* by Rev. RICHARD NEWTON, D.D.

Memoir of Norman Macleod, D. D., Minister of Barony Parish, Glasgow, one of Her Majesty's Chaplains, etc., by his brother, Rev. DONALD MACLEOD. New York: R. Worthington, 1876. We have already noticed the original edition of this most interesting and instructive memoir, published in two volumes. The present more compact and cheap ($2) edition will insure an increased circle of readers. Some of Dr. Macleod's curious pen-and-ink sketches are omitted.

Public Libraries in the United States of America ; their History, Condition, and Management. Special Report. Department of the Interior, Bureau of Education. Washington. Government Printing-office. Pt. I., pp. xxxv, 1187; Pt. II., pp. 89. S. R. WARREN and S. N. CLARK, editors. The second part is by S. N. CUTTER, on the rules for a Printed Dictionary Catalogue, full and minute. The whole report is the best account yet given of the public libraries in this country. The statistics are ample, and have been collected with great care. There is also a large variety of special reports by competent hands. The theological libraries are described in pp. 127–159. They number forty-four. The two largest are Union Seminary, N. Y., and Andover—each credited with 34,000 vols. Princeton, 26,779 ; New Brunswick, 26,000; Columbia, S. C. (Presb.) 18,884; Cambridge, Divinity School, 17,000; Middletown (Epis.), 16,000; New York (Epis.), 15,400; Woodstock, Md., 18,000; 18,000; Chicago (Bapt.), 15,000; Bangor (Cong.), 15,000; Baltimore (St. Mary's), 15,000; Rochester (Bapt.), 10.000; Lane (Presb.), 12,000; Mt. St. Mary's (Cincinnati), 15,000; Allegheny (Presb.), 15,000; Lutheran at Gettysburgh, 11,000: Reformed Church, Lancaster, 10,000; Meadville, 12,000; Alexandria (Epis.), 10,000; Hampden Library, Union Presb., 10,000.

The Religious Principles in American Politics is the title of an able and patriotic discourse, by Rev. NEWMAN SMYTH, Pastor of the First Presbyterian Church, Quincy, Illinois. It is a sound and philosophical examination of several questions recently revived, as to the relation of religion to the State, the Bible in public schools, etc. The right ground is strongly advocated.

The Carters, of New York, publish *Pine Needles.* By the author of "The Wide, Wide World." Also, *Little and Wise; or, Sermons to Children.* By WILLIAM WILBERFORCE NEWTON, Rector of St. Paul's Church, Boston. The gift and spirit of the father, Dr. Newton, of Philadelphia, in preparing wholesome instruction and incitement to the young, appear to have been transmitted to the son, who shows himself in this little volume to be, in this behalf, a workman that need not be ashamed.

A Tractate of undoubted value, received too late for analysis in this number, and to which we hope to recur in our next, is entitled *The Second Coming of the Lord, Considered in Relation to the Views Promulgated by the Plymouth Brethren and So-called Evangelists.* By JOHN LAING, M.A., Minister of Knox Church, Dundas, Ont.

Thoroughly Furnished. A Sermon to Show the Bearing of the Doctrines, Polity, and Usages of the Reformed Church upon the Formation of Character and Fitness for Citizenship; by REV. CORNELIUS H. EDGAR, D.D., Pastor of the American Reformed Church, Easton, Pa; prepared by appointment of General Synod; preached May 14th, 1876; well exhibits the power in life and manners of that Calvinism which is common alike to the Reformed and Presbyterian Churches.

The Mikado's Empire. By WILLIAM E. GRIFFIS, A. M. Harper & Brothers. This interesting and instructive volume contains, first, the history of Japan, from 660 B. C., to A. D. 1872; and second, the personal experiences and observations of the author, during a residence from 1870–1874. In the first division of the work, a great amount of information has been condensed respecting the aboriginal inhabitants, the mythology, the ancient religion, the introduction of the continental civilization, the rise of the dual system of government, the incoming of Buddhism, the introduction of Roman Catholicism, and, finally, the recent revolution in the government, and the present condition of the empire. Few books impart more knowledge within the same number of pages.

Mr. Griffis has gone to the native annalists for his information—his knowledge of the language giving him uncommon facilities. In deriving from them the early history of the nation, the author has studied their accounts with a critical spirit. National annals can, of course, be trusted in respect to the mythology of a people, since the more imaginative the record, perhaps the more trustworthy is the picture of the mythological ideas and systems. In respect to history, more skepticism is required; and this Mr. Griffis has employed. While not claiming for his conclusions absolute certainty in every particular, he appears to give good reasons for believing that the Japanese are to be traced rather to India than to China. His essay upon the connection between the Japanese and the North American Indians, contains much that is striking, going to prove that the Western hemisphere received its population from the Eastern, by the way of Japan, the furthest out-lying portion of that Asiatic continent, which is the birth-place and cradle of the human race. The bearings of such facts upon the Biblical accounts are apparent. The movement of population eastward from the Caucasus into India and China, and ultimately across the narrow strait between Asia and America, is easily seen to be continuous, and consequently probable. The reader will also find a careful examination of Buddhism, and a fair estimate of its influence upon the people. In respect to the subject of religions, Mr. Griffis, while claiming for Christianity what its founder claimed for it—absolute and paramount authority—yet recognizes with candor whatever elements of truth and morality are to be found in the native religions of Asia.

Our limits do not permit us to enter into detail respecting the matter contained in the second portion of the volume. For the general reader it is extremely interesting. The writer's experiences in Japanese life, and his observations upon manners and customs, are related with uncommon freshness and vivacity. No one of the several works upon Japan, of which a considerable number have been written within a few years past, brings the reader into closer intimacy with the every-day life of the people than this. On the whole, Mr. Griffis' book must be recommended as thus far the best single treatise upon the whole subject of Japan.

Voluntaryism in Higher Education is a pamphlet by President M. B. ANDERSON, of Rochester University, which is as able as, it is timely. It shows conclusively, that it is impossible to sever the higher education from the religious element, and from more or less positive religious dogma; that for this, as well as for other reasons, the whole people ought not to be taxed to confer it on a few; that the purest and richest culture is bestowed in our religious and denominational colleges, which teach the broad doctrine of Christianity, without any exactions or imposition of narrow dogma, or interference with the truest religious freedom ; that the proper support of these colleges should come from the voluntary benefactions of their friends; and that the late outcry against denominational colleges, and in favor of Christless and godless State colleges, is alike senseless and groundless.

A Confession of Faith in Peace Principles, by Prof. EDWARD A. LAWRENCE, read before the Christian Conference, held in Franklin Institute, Philadelphia, October, 1876, ought to be in every house in the land. It is but four pages long—*multum in parvo.*

The Boston University Year-Book, for 1876, edited by the University Council, contains a very able and thorough paper, by the President, WM. F. WARREN, S.T.D., LL.D., exposing the fallacies which underlie the movement for the taxation of hospitals, churches, and colleges. We deem it very seasonable. The battle on this subject is not yet fought out. It is only begun. We are also glad to see the substance of an address on the same subject, before a Meeting of Ministers and Church Officers, in Washington, D. C., by Rev. A. W. PITZER, D.D., author of ECCE DEUS HOMO, which takes vigorous ground against this attempt to "reverse the general sentiment of the race since its creation." The usual fallacy in all attempts to refute the argument in favor of their exemption from taxation, founded on their being the gifts of benevolence for the good of society, by alleging that manufactories and hotels also further the public welfare, lies in ignoring the fact, that the latter differ from the former in not being gratuities for the public weal, but investments for private material profit.

The American Colonization Society have published an important paper, entitled *The Color Question in the United States; a Paper Prepared for the*

Sixtieth Annual Meeting of the American Colonization Society (Jan., 1877.)
By EDWARD P. HUMPHREY, D.D., LL.D.   This question, so far from being
settled by the emancipation of the colored race, is only lifted into new prominence by it. It is now the most complicated question which our philanthropists,
sociologists, and statesmen have to meet.   Dr. Humphrey discusses it, and
shows the fatuity of attempting to separate the blacks from the whites by con-
centrating the former in the Gulf States, and removing the latter from them—
of amalgamation—of abiding by the present posture of affairs, with all the collisions and antagonisms it breeds ; and which, whatever else it may do for the
blacks, will never give them that social standing which, as they advance in dignity and culture under the elevating influences of freedom, they will be sure to
crave, and to chafe under the deprivation of it.   Dr. Humphrey sees in emigration to Africa, especially the vast stretches of habitable and salubrious
territory lately brought to view by explorers, the possible and not improbable solution of this problem during the second century of our national existence.   This gives a vaster scope to the principle of the Colonization Society
than its founders or supporters have heretofore dreamed of.   Yet it involves
no larger emigration than came from Europe to the single port of New
York in the quarter of a century ending in 1873.   We agree with Dr. H.
The color question must be met and the sooner the better.   Perhaps colonization may yet solve the question, and prove an unspeakable blessing to two
races and two continents.

Dodd, Mead & Company publish *Silenci;* a Poem, by S. MILLER HAGE-
MAN, which has received commendation from the venerable poet, Whittier.

Mr. Wallingford's Mistake. By Mrs. A. K. DUNNING.   Presbyterian
Board.   An admirable temperance tale, illustrating the danger of even the
moderate use of wine in the home circle, where the taste for strong drink is
so often acquired, which in after-life conquers and destroys the most promising.   Alas! that at the present moment there should be so much need,
that warnings like those here uttered, should fall upon thousands of the
families of wealth, culture, and even piety.   How many fathers repeat " Mr.
Wallingford's Mistake," and find it out only when it is too late to prevent
the fearful mischief it has wrought !

The Board also publish *Eyes and Ears; or, How I See and Hear.*   By
AUNT YEWROWNCKIE.   The object of this book is good, and the execution
is fairly done ; yet there is too much baby slang in it like the following :
'Well, then, Nanty dear, here comes Sis. I've fuddled her good ; and she
wants you to read the whole of it over aloud, so that she can be as wise as
I. Didn't I make her stare just ? She don't believe in retinas at all, nor
images. You see, she's awful mad to think I know more about such things
than she." But aside from this, we fail to see the wisdom of our Board in
publishing books of this class.   Surely, its legitimate scope is broad enough
without going into the publication of semi-scientific books.   Far better works
of this class are found by the score in the catalogues of our publishing firms.

Standard Facts and Figures. Revised and enlarged edition. **New York**, Morton & Dumont, 1877. It is seldom that such a vast amount of information, interesting to all, but specially valuable to business men, is compressed into 148 pages of moderate size. There is scarcely any subject pertaining to commerce, banking, or general business, that this book will not supply just the "facts and figures" desired relating to it. It is not strange that it is highly valued and extensively used by our most eminent business men. It is printed in very superior style, from the press of Rogers & Sherwood, who are fast acquiring the reputation of executing some of the finest printing done in this city.

Art. XII.—THEOLOGICAL AND LITERARY INTELLIGENCE.

[This "Intelligence" was prepared by our lamented associate, Dr. HENRY B. SMITH, and is probably among the very last fruits of his pen.—EDITORS.]

GERMANY.

Year-Book of Protestant Theology, IV.—1876 (*Jahrbücher f. Protest. Theologie*). The last *heft* of the second volume of this journal opens with an article of more than eighty pages by Dr. R. A. Lipsius, in continuation of his thesis—that "Peter was not in Rome." In our REVIEW for last July, a full summary was given of his positions and arguments, derived in part from his published works, and in part from a manuscript furnished to Mr. Jackson, the writer of that article, by Dr. Lipsius, and which had not then been published in Germany. The substance of these additions is contained in the above article of the *Year-Book*, together with an extended reply to the objections made to his views by Dr. Hilgenfeld in the Tübingen *Zeitschrift.* All the points raised are here minutely re-argued, with reference to the whole of the recent literature. The silence of the Acts of the Apostles, and especially of Paul in his Epistles, is brought forward with new force. If Peter had been in Rome before Paul went there, or while he was there, it is incredible that there should be no allusion to it in any of the Pauline writings. The alleged testimony of Clement of Rome to Peter's martyrdom at Rome is subjected to a new investigation, and it certainly seems improbable that Clement's allusion should be so doubtful and obscure if Peter had really been his predecessor in the Roman See. The most difficult point in Dr. Lipsius' argument is his identification of Paul with Simon Magus in the legendary tradition of the church—Simon being " a caricature of Paul." This requires further elucidation, ingeniously as it is argued by Dr. Lipsius. The other articles in this number are, Dr. Otto Pfleiderer, "Two Faith-Philosophers," Havana (spoken of in the previous number) and Jacobi, whose views are here expounded and combated, as giving too much authority to sentiment, and too little to reason ; Herman Schultz on " The Protestant Dogma of the Invincible Church," in review of Krauss' recent full and able work on that subject; a good summary of the morals (*ethos*) of the Germans, as portrayed by Tacitus, from the pen of Gustav Roskoff; and Paul Mehlhorn on the Idea of Reward in the Teachings of Jesus.

Year-Books of Protestant Theology (*Jahrbücher f. d. Protestant Theologie*)—1877. No. I. This is the third year of this new theological quarterly, which has been kept up with learning and ability. The first article, by Allard Pierson, is the beginning of a review of the Dogmatics (second edition) of Dr. Kahniz, of Leipzig, and is severe in its criticisms and exposure of apparent contradictions ; it is, in fact, hyper-critical, and has little sympathy with the evangelical and orthodox system of faith, even in its milder forms. The second article, by Pünjer, is a popular lecture on Darwinism in its relations to religion and ethics, showing that no religious or moral system can be built up on such a basis. At the close, there is a short account of Häckel's latest theory as to the germs of living beings, in what he calls the "plastidules," or the primitive germ or form of life, proving that after all something beside chemical and mechanical forces must be assumed in order to account for the exists ence of life. August Baur, on the Idea and Outline of a Theory of the Universe, takes, and ably maintains, the position, that such a theory (*Weltauschaung*) must be essentially religious, and that the general Christian theory alone fully meets and answers the questions and problems which are involved. The discussion is rather prolix, but clear, and, in its general view, correct, that "the Christian theory of the world is neither the deification of the world, nor yet the giving it over to the devil, neither its exaltation nor its denial, but rather the transfiguration of the world by the victory over it." Carl Alfred Hase contributes an excellent account of the Italian martyr, Pietro Carnesecchi—the first authentic publication of all the main documents. (Professor Gibbing, of Dublin, gave a part of them in a memoir published in 1856.) It is one of the most interesting and instructive narratives of the Reformation times in Italy, and exhibits clearly the principles and aims of the Roman See. Carnesecchi was one of the ablest and most honored men of his times. He was of noble descent, born in Florence, highly educated, renowned for his classic learning, and as a poet and orator, the friend of the Medici, and such a special friend of Pope Clement VII., that it was commonly said that the church was ruled by him, rather than by the Pope. He was Apostolic Prothonotary and State Secretary of this pontiff. In 1536, at Naples, where he held an abbey, he came into connection with the Spaniard, Juan Valdez, Donna Giulia Gonzago, Duchess of Camerini, Bernardino Ochino, and Cardinal Pole, and also read and approved the famous book on *The Benefit of Christ's Death* (by Avnio Paleario, at the time ascribed by some writers to Pole—reprinted in an English version, Boston, Gould & Lincoln, 1860). Thus he fell under the suspicions of the Italian authorities, and was subjected to various trials, the last of them, before the Inquisition, prosecuted from July 8, 1566, to April 7, 1567. He was condemned for alleged doctrinal errors, all centering in the doctrine of justification by faith, and, under Pius V., executed and burnt up, October 3, 1567. His tragic story is admirably told, with all the official documents, in this instructive memoir. The last article of this number is by H. Holtzman, of Strasburg, on the origin of the traditional images of Christ, based on the recent works of Kraus, Glueckselig, Grimm, Keim, and others.

Historische Zeitschrift. Herausgegeben von H. von. Sybel, 1876—III. The first article is a concise and valuable account of the Children's Crusade, A.D. 1212, by Reinhold Röhricht. The second is on the History of the Council of Trent, on the basis of the "*Acta Genuina*," as edited by Theiner, in two 4to volumes, which, though far from complete, adds many new incidents and points of view for judging of the real character and results of this counsel. The next article, by H. Baumgarten, of Strassburg, contains contributions to the History of the Smalcald War, 1546, in part derived from the English State Papers. It exposes the selfish policy of the leaders in this critical contest, and the way in which the hitherto victorious progress of the Reformation began to be stayed. The fourth article, by H. Delbrück, is on the Political Character of the English Ecclesiastical Decisions in the seventeenth century. C. Grünhagen's " Frederick the Great on the Rubicon " (as the king himself spoke of it, Dec. 15, 1740), gives a full account of the momentous consequences involved in this decisive step. In the sixth and last article, Dr. F. Gregorovius, the well-known author of the History of the City of Rome, describes the present condition of the Roman archives, as newly gathered from the old libraries and convents by the present Italian government, and collected for public use. From the papal manuscript diaries many interesting memoranda are culled as to the daily expenses of the papal palaces and tables, etc.

Theologische Studien und Kritiken. 1877. I. Professor Riehm, of Halle, in an elaborate essay of nearly one hundred pages, investigates the Idea of Expiation in the Old Testament Sacrifices, on exegetical and theological grounds, in reply in part to the one-sided view of them advocated by Ritschl, in his work on Justification and Reconciliation (Atonement). The discussion is a very able one, learned and scholarly, and shows Prof. Riehm's accustomed acuteness and comprehensiveness. He shows that the Old Testament system of sacrifices is unintelligible except as it includes a distinct relation of them to the maintenance of the divine holiness in connection with the forgiveness of sins. The Second Article, by Dr. Koestlin, is on the State and Church, and their Rights in the Light of Christian Ethics, the first part of a general investigation, examining the Biblical statements, and giving an exposition of the Lutheran doctrine and of recent theories, such as those of Rothe, Wuttke, Stahl, Vinet, and others. Prof. Kleinert, of Berlin, on Isaiah, xx–xxii, and 2 Kings, xviii–xx, examines the date of the expedition of Sennacherib against Jerusalem and Egypt, B. C. 701. C. E. Caspari, on the Historical Sabbatic Years, finds four of them in the period after the Exile : 1. The year 150 of the era of the Seleucidæ; 2. The year after the murder of the High Priest, Simon ; 3. The year of the taking of Jerusalem by Herod ; 4. The year of the destruction of the Temple by Titus. He notes the fact, that after the Exile the Jews had no national era.

ENGLAND.

British and Foreign Evangelical Review. Oct., 1876. The first article, by Rev. DANIEL EDWARD, of Breslau, on " Schleiermacher Interpreted by Himself and the Men of his School," gives a one-sided view of Schleiermacher's system, exaggerating its defects, and not seeming to appreciate its real sources of influence. It is intended in part to counteract "the partial and tender treatment of Schleiermacher's errors," by such writers as Tholuck and Dr. Hodge. Dr. Bruce, of Glasgow, contributes an excellent lecture on " The Apologetic Function of the Church in the Present Time." Professor Croskery describes " Romanism in the United States," with a full and fair estimate of the facts, which he has thoroughly investigated. He shows a better acquaintance than most English writers have with our exact position—its dangers and difficulties, and also its signs of promise. Dr. Forbes, professor in Aberdeen, in an ingenious and able philological discussion on Gal. iii : 20, and Heb. ix : 16–17, advocates a literal translation of both passages as the best one. Thus, Gal. iii : 20: *The* mediator [*i. e.*, of the law] is not [a mediator] of one " [" seed "], including Jew and Gentile; " but God is one," God of Jew, and Gentile. In the passage in Hebrews, Dr. Forbes retains the literal rendering of *diatheke* as covenant, and renders verse 16 : " For where a covenant is, there must of necessity be brought in the death of the covenanter. Ver. 17 : "For a covenant is valid over the dead; whereas, it is never of force while the covenanter liveth." Ver. 18: "Wherefore, neither was the first [covenant] dedicated without blood." It all refers to covenants ratified by sacrifices. Both discussions will reward close study. Professor Mitchell, of Aberdeen, reviews Dr.

Killen's Ecclesiastical History of Ireland in a thoroughly competent way. The best "original article," by Prof. Leebody, in "the Scientific Doctrine of Contin. uity," is, on the whole, favorable to it, making exceptions in three points: 1. The eternity of matter. 2. The origin of life. 3. The origin of man; which exceptions plainly show that physical continuity has got to be supplemented by a higher power in order to explain things. The accounts of current literature and notices of books are as usual very well done. This is a remarkably able number of the best English Theological Review.

The Theological Review. July and October, 1876. A. Kuenen, D.D., Yahveh and the "Other Gods;" Hon. Roden Noel, Free Will and Responsibility; H. S. Solly, Schopenhaur; P. Magnus, The Jews in England. Oct.—E. R. Russell, The Religion of Shakspeare; W. Sandy, The Nature and Development of Monotheism in Israel—in part, a reply to Kuenen; G. W. Cox, The Range of Christian Fellowship; C. B. Upton, Lord Amberley's Analysis of Religious Belief; Alx. Gordon, Bernardino Ochino, etc.

Dickinson's Theological Quarterly, Oct., 1876, is wholly from American periodicals and works. Among these articles (with no indication of the reviews in which they first appeared) are Prof. G. P. Fisher, on Rationalism; Dr. Thos. Hill, on the First Chapter of Genesis; Dr. Hurst, on Seneca; and Prof. Harrington, on Lucretius; Dr. Woolsey, The Religion of the Future; Dr. H. A. Nelson, "God in Human Thought" [from our own REVIEW]; Dr. D. R. Goodwin, The Reciprocal Influence of Christianity and Liberty, etc.

Mind: a Quarterly Review of Psychology and Philosophy. Williams & Norgate. Nos. III., IV., 1876. No. III. contains: H. Helmholtz, The Origin and Meaning of Geometrical Axioms; R. Flint, Associationism and the Origin of Moral Ideas; Fred. Pollock, Evolution and Ethics; Max Müller, The Original Intention of Collective and Abstract Terms; Shadworth H. Hodgson, Philosophy and Science (III. conclusion); T. M. Lindsay, on Herman Lotze; W. H. S. Monck, Philosophy at Dublin. No. IV.: J. A. Stewart, Psychology—a Science or a Method; James Ward, An Attempt to Interpret Fechner's Law; James Sully, Art and Psychology; J. Vena, Bode's Logical System; R. Adamson, Schopenhauer's Philosophy—an able criticism; A. Bain, Life of James Mill; II., Philosophy in London (not much of it), by the editor, G. C. Robertson, Prof. in University College, London. Each number also contains good analyses and reviews of new French and German books, and gives the contents of all the leading philosophical journals of England and the Continent. It is very well conducted, and admits discussions from various philosophical quarters. The price is 12s. a year.

Edward Wm. Lane, the orientalist, died August 10th. He was born at Hereford, September 17, 1801. He lived in Egypt, 1825 to 1828; and again, 1833 to 1835. In 1835 he published his *Manners and Customs of the Modern Egyptians;* sixth edition lately issued. His translation of the *Thousand and One Nights* appeared 1838-40. The first volume of his great *Arabic Lexicon* appeared in 1863; five vols. have been published; the sixth is nearly printed; two more vols. will complete the work, from Mr. Lane's manuscripts. The Duke of Northumberland bore the main cost of this work. His sister, Mrs. Poole, wrote the *Englishwoman in Egypt.* Mr. Lane's Lexicon is derived from native sources.

Bagster has published *A Concordance of the Hebrew and Chaldee Scriptures,* prepared by B. Davidson; price, three guineas.

The Psalms, with Introduction and Notes, by Rev. A. C. Jennings and Rev. W. H. Lowe, is now completed, in five books, and published by Macmillan. The Rabbinical learning of the editors is praised.

James Maclaren, a Dublin barrister, in an acute work, entitled *A Critical Examination of some of the Principal Arguments For and Against Darwinism* (London, 1876), admits the probability that some so-called species may have originated in some kind of evolution, but denies that Darwin's natural selection is a sufficient theory or explanation.

In consequence of the Union Conference at Bonn, the doctrinal differences of the Eastern and Western Churches are receiving new attention in England. Dr. Pusey has published, "A letter to the Rev. H. P. Liddon, on the clause, 'and the Son,' in regard to the Eastern Church and the Bonn Conference" (pp. 188), and H. B. Swete has written "On the History of the Doctrine of the Procession of the Holy Spirit, from the Apostolic Age to the death of Charlemagne." (Pp. 240.)

The four Scotch universities had 4,338 students in 1874-5, against 3,369 in 1864-5, showing an increase of 1,000, while the population increased from 3,250,000 to about 3,500,000. There was one student to 964 inhabitants in 1864-5, and one to 806 in 1874-5. In the latter period St. Andrew's had 143 students; Aberdeen, 635; Glasgow, 1,484; and Edinburgh, 2,076.

Mr. Bentley announces Capt. Charles Warren's "Underground Jerusalem," an account of his well-known investigations, with a narrative of an expedition to the Jordan valley, and a visit to the Samaritans; a translation of Duncker's "History of Antiquity," translated by Evelyn Abbott; and the twelfth volume of "Lives of the Archbishops of Canterbury," consisting of the Index. Macmillan & Co. announce Prof. T. R. Birks on "Modern Physical Fatalism and the Doctrine of Evolution."

R. C. Bensly, of Cambridge, reports in *The Academy,* June 17th, that their library has received a Syriac manuscript, bought at the sale of the books of Julius Mohl, at Paris, containing the Heracleian translation of the New Testament, and also a Syriac translation of the epistles of Clement of Rome. The manuscript is dated A.D. 1170. Mr. Bensly is preparing this Syriac version for the press. He considers it so accurate, that, in doubtful cases, it may well decide between the only two manuscripts of the Greek text—the Alexandrian (A) and the Jerusalem (I), which last is the one recently published by Bryennius.

A new edition of Finlay's History of Greece under Foreign Domination, is to be published by Macmillan & Co., for the University of Cambridge, edited by Rev. H. F. Tozer, and continued from 1843 to 1864—the year after the present king ascended the throne. Parts of it will be enlarged, especially the fourth volume, on Mediæval Greece and Trebizond, which will be almost a new work.

L. Tyermann, the biographer of Wesley, is writing a Life of George Whitfield. A Life of Servetus, by R. Willis, is announced. The materials for this work have been much enlarged by the recent German researches of Tollin and others. A translation of Benrath's Life of Bernardino Ochina, by Miss Zimmerman, is announced. It is a valuable monograph.

The death is announced of Mr. George Smith, the English orientalist, at the age of fifty-one, while still engaged upon his uncompleted studies. In 1866, while examining the collection of Assyrian remains in the British Museum, he discovered an inscription which gave some account of the war against Hazael, and with the hope that other inscriptions might be found to throw light upon the world's earliest history, he began at once the study of "Cuneiform inscriptions with great diligence and zeal. The first of his publications in this direction was a volume of " Cuneiform Inscriptions of Western Asia," prepared for the British Museum. His discoveries were recorded from time to time in the " Transactions of the Society of Biblical Archæology," and among the earlier ones was a tablet recording the eclipse of June 16, 763 B. C.; an Assyrian religious calendar; an account of the conquest of Babylon by the Elamites in the year 2280 B. C., and the tablet on which an account of the flood is given, which he afterward found to be one of the series of twelve tablets, some of them badly mutilated, that he described fully in his latest work. In the year 1871 he published an important work concerning the history of Asshur-bani-pal, which gave a new direction to the study of oriental antiquities. Since the year 1873 he has been engaged pretty constantly in explorations of Nineveh and the Euphrates Valley, undertaken at the expense of the London *Daily Telegraph*, and prosecuted with extremely valuable results. His later works have included accounts of his explorations and discoveries—" Ancient History from the Monuments " and " The Chaldean Account of Genesis." This, his latest published work, was founded upon Chaldean legends concerning the early history of the world, the value and interest of which were greatly enhanced by the fact, that in many respects they coincide with the Mosaic account, or run closely parallel with it. This work was put forth as provisional, and the author explained, that while it was necessary thus to put upon record the results already reached, he had reason to believe that further discoveries and further study of the inscriptions would enable him to make a later and much more complete treatise on the subject, in which the significance of the newly-found historical material could be more accurately determined than was possible at the time. What results have been attained by the work he has done since the Chaldean account of Genesis was written the public have as yet no means of knowing, but it is pretty certain that so careful a recorder of facts as this enthusiastic scholar has not neglected to put whatever materials he has gathered into such shape that they may be used by other scholars in finishing the work which he did not live to complete. We suffer loss in his death before his work was done, but the work is not lost, incomplete as he has left it.—*Post.*

Mr. Matthew Arnold is preparing for the press, to be published by Macmillan & Co., a new edition of his poetry, including his later compositions; together with some of his recent papers on questions of the day, which have appeared in *Macmillan's Magazine* and the *Contemporary Review.* The same publishing firm announce a small work by Mr. Edward A. Freeman, on the *Ottoman Power in Europe: Its Nature, Growth, and Decline,* uniform with his *History of the Saracens;* also a new theological treatise, written by the Rev. Dr. Abbot, entitled *Through Nature to Christ,* founded on his Hulsean Lectures, lately delivered at Cambridge.

Mr. Edward Fitzgerald, who a few years since achieved such great success, tardily recognized, by his admirable translation of the *Rabaiyat* of the Persian poet, Omar Khayyam, has recently published an equally remarkable version of the Agamemnon of Æschylus. The following is his spirited translation of the " Signal from Troy: "

Hephaistos, the lame God,
And spriteliest of mortal messengers;
Who, springing from the bed of burning Troy,

Hither by fore devis'd Intelligence
Agreed upon between my Lord and me,
Posted from dedicated Height to Height,
The reach of land and sea that lies between,
And first to catch him and begin the game
Did Ida fire her forest pine, and waving,
Handed him on to the Hermæan steep
Of Lemnos, Lemnos to the summit of
Zeus consecrated, Atkos lifted; whence,
As by the giant taken, so dispatched
The torch of Conquest, traversing the wide
Ægean with a sunbeam stretching stride,
Struck up the drowsy watchers on Makistos,
Who, flashing back the challenge, flash'd it on
To those who watched on the Mersapian height,
With whose quick-kindling heather heaped and fired
The meteor-bearded messenger refresh'd,
Clearing Asophus at a bound, struck fire
From old Kithæron; and, so little tired
As waxing even wanton with the sport,
Over the sleeping water of Gorgopis
Sprung to the Rock of Corinth, thence to the cliffs
Which stare down the Saronic Gulf, that now
Began to shiver in the creeping Dawn;
Whence for a moment on the neighboring top
Of Arachnæum lighting, one last bound
Brought him to Agamemnon's battlements.
By such gigantic strides in such a Race,
Where First and Last alike are Conquerors,
Posted the traveling Fire whose Father-light
Ida conceived of burning Troy To-night!

One of the most admired choruses is thus rendered:

Some think the Godhead couching at his ease
Deep in the purple Heav'ns serenely sees
Insult the altar of Eternal Right.
Fools! For though Fortune seem to misrequite,
And Retribution for a while forget,
Sooner or later she reclaims the debt
With usury that triples the amount
Of Nemesis with running Time's account.
For soon or late Sardonic Fate
With man against himself conspires,
Puts on the mask of his desires;
Up the steps of Time elate,
Leads him blinded with his pride,
And gathering, as he goes along,
The fuel of his suicide,
Until, having topt the pyre
Which destiny permits no higher,
Ambition sets himself on fire;
In conflagration like the crime,
Conspicuous through the world and time,
Down amidst his Brazen walls,
The accumulated Idol falls
To shapeless ashes; Demigod
Under the vulgar hoof down-trod,
Whose neck he trod on; not an eye
To weep his fall or lip to sigh
For him a prayer; or, if there were,
No God to listen or reply.

THE

PRESBYTERIAN QUARTERLY

AND

PRINCETON REVIEW.

NEW SERIES, No. 22—JULY, 1877.

Art. 1.—THE HIGHER LIFE AND CHRISTIAN PERFECTION.[*]

By Lyman H. Atwater.

THAT the prevalent tone of Christian experience and holy living is quite below the level of scriptural standards and privileges; that there is an urgent call for the great body of Christians to rise to a much higher plane of inward piety and its visible fruits; that none are so high that they should not make it their supreme endeavor to rise higher; that to struggle onward and upward through the strength, holiness and grace already attained to yet higher measures of them, so that receiving grace for grace, they may go from strength to strength toward the goal of sinless perfection whenever and wheresoever attainable; that so there is required the ceaseless effort to get free from sin and overcome indwelling corruption, are propositions which few will be found to dispute, unless, indeed, some Perfectionists dispute the last of them, claiming to have reached

---

[*] *The Higher Christian Life*, by Rev. W. E. Boardman.

Pioneer Experiences; or, the Gift of Power Received by Faith. Illustrated and Confirmed by the Testimony of Eighty Living Witnesses of Various Denominations. By the author of "Way of Holiness," &c. Introduction by Rev. Bishop Janes.

The Rest of Faith, by Rev. Isaac M. See.

Autobiography of Rev. Charles G. Finney. Chapter xxvii.

Holiness the Birthright of God's Children, by the Rev. J. T. Crane, D. D.

The Old Paths; a Treatise on Sanctification. Scripture the Only Authority. By Rev. Thomas Mitchell.

Purity and Maturity, by Rev. J. A. Wood.

A Plain Account of Christian Perfection, by Rev. John Wesley.

entire sinlessness in this life. They are to the eye of true
Christian insight their own evidence.

To emphasize and magnify the "Higher Life" in this sense
is simply to recognize and strive to give effect to the principles of our common Christianity ; and in this all will or ought
heartily to join. It is worth while to mark this distinctly at
the outset. For this term "higher life" is constantly used
now to denote something quite different, as if it were the
peculiarity of a small select circle who make it their watchword,
a badge of the chosen few who have reached summits of Christian experience quite above the great mass of the commonwealth of Israel. Theirs are the gifts and endowments to
which Christians generally are strangers, and theirs the joys
with which a stranger intermeddleth not. The distinctive
views of the class we refer to, amid many minor and circum-
stantial variations, are for substance:

1. That sinless perfection is attainable, and by those who
attain the higher life in question, actually attained in this
life.

2. That it is gained instantaneously by an act of faith in
Christ, which appropriates him for immediate and entire sanctification, in the same manner as for immediate and full justification ; and that each is equally, with the other, immediate,
equally complete, equally conferred co-instantaneously with
the act of faith which receives it ; and in equal independence
of works, as in any sense either the procuring, instrumental,
efficient or meritorious cause.

3. Therefore, that this perfect sanctification is not through
any process of gradual growth, striving, or advancement toward sinless perfection, whether in this life or the life to
come ; but is at once grasped by faith, and held by it till let go
by backsliding or apostasy—the latter being regarded by the
Higher Life Arminians as liable, by those that are Calvinists
as not liable, to occur.

4. This attainment is attended with the constant or ordinary presence of unclouded peace, joy and hope, such as the
Bible connects with the highest grades of Christian experience.

5. Some, perhaps most, of this Higher Life school, so far especially as it has appeared in Calvinistic communions, maintain

that this act of faith which instantaneously grasps perfect sanctity is preceded by an act of entire consecration to God in Christ. In other words, it is preceded by itself—for entire consecration is perfect holiness.

In regard to all these points we think the position taken in our standards scriptural and impregnable, and that no more correct and adequate enunciation of Christian truth in the premises can be found. *

We may remark, before going further, that with some the doctrine of Higher Life means merely the habitual possession and enjoyment of Christian assurance, in which they erroneously conceive themselves exceptional or superior to any recognized standards of Christian experience in evangelical churches. This, however, as our standards affirm, belongs to the normal development of Christian experience; not, however, so that it usually becomes firm and enduring, even if it appear at all, in the early stages of the regenerate life. It rather belongs normally, though not exclusively, to the maturer stages of Christian experience; it is confirmed by the culture and consequent evidence of the graces, which are also the fruits of the Spirit, and evidences of his saving work. These, however, are so wrought in us by the Spirit as to depend at the same time upon our "giving all diligence unto the full assurance of hope unto the end"; all "diligence to make our calling and election sure," the Holy Spirit herein and hereby witnessing with our spirits that we are the children of God.

It is too true that far fewer attain this blessed estate than might be looked for in a normal condition of the church; far fewer than those to whom the privileges of the gospel estate and Christian vocation open it, who might and should work up to and reach it. It is no less true that those who attain a sound assurance sustained by good Christian fruits, reach a higher than average Christian life, and generally higher than their own previous Christian life. In this sense a higher life than the average among Christians may be maintained. But this is not, or is only in part, the kind of higher life intended. This latter involves not only assurance, which rests on perfect justification duly proving itself by holiness of life, but perfect

---

*See *Larger Catechism*, answers to questions 77 8-9-80. *Shorter Catechism*, questions 35-82.

sanctification; and this sanctification received by some single act of faith as an accomplished fact, which keeps the soul in a continuous state of freedom from sin, and from all conscience of sin, and so of abiding peace and joy, by a sort of quietistic resting in Christ, not only for justification, but for sanctification. This peace and assurance, too, come not mainly from the sense of pardon through Christ's imputed righteousness, but of sinlessness through the perfect inherent righteousness or holiness wrought by him within us, and received by us, like his justifying righteousness, by faith, without personal works or strivings on our part to effect or to promote it.

As we shall see more fully further on, this perfectionism is defined and vindicated in different and often inconsistent ways by its advocates. It is apt to run into some form of Quietism or Mysticism, or Antinomianism, or licentiousness, while a large proportion of those embracing some forms of it give every sign of leading holy lives.

The Reformed and Calvinistic doctrine, as expressed in our standards, and as held by nearly all evangelical Protestants, the Methodists and Lutherans excepted, differs from the foregoing by asserting that sin, although subdued and growing weaker, is never entirely eradicated in this life; while the renewed spirit, ever struggling against it, is, notwithstanding possible occasional vicissitudes and backslidings, on the whole gaining the mastery over it, till the grand consummation of complete deliverance from sin is reached at death, which itself with sin—its cause—there dies. Hence it maintains that sanctification is a gradual work, growing with the growth, and promoted by the efforts, struggles and prayers of the Christian; who, while in his predominating character holy, is yet never free in this life from the remains of sin, which, though ever dying, is not dead, but still maintains its dying struggle. till the soul, freed at death, passes to be one of the spirits of the just made perfect.

In further clearing the issue before us, it is expedient to dispose of a number of inconclusive arguments, often and confidently advanced by the advocates of the theory in question.

1. Those passages of Scripture which attribute sanctification, holiness, or purity to believers, or which exhort them to seek, pursue or practise the same, or which promise deliver-

ance from sin in its guilt, pollution and dominion, or which covenant full and complete salvation—all these prove nothing in behalf of sinless perfection in this life. They prove nothing because they are applied to all Christians and saints as such in the Scripture, and not merely to a few select ones of a higher grade of Christian life than the mass. But it is admitted by this school that the mass of Christians have not yet attained, and in this life most of them never will attain, sinless perfection. Therefore, if they are actually addressed to those who are Christians, but yet not sinlessly perfect, then this demonstrates that they give no evidence of the perfect sinlessness of those to whom they are addressed, or for whom they are designed.

Not only so, but the Christian to whom all pretensions of sinless perfection are alien and offensive, interprets these passages as applicable to himself and suiting his own case, without the least consciousness or suspicion of distorting, perverting, or overstraining their proper import. Full salvation is indeed promised and secured to all the faithful in Christ Jesus. But it is only in part or in its beginnings here; in its seed first implanted and quickened in regeneration, herein having the pledge of onward growth in holiness, and increasing christian fruitage upon earth. The soul is to be made perfect therein at death; then immediately passing into glory to await reunion with the body at the resurrection of the just, when Christ shall raise it again, and make it like unto his glorious body. So we receive a full salvation in Christ when we receive him by faith; but a salvation begun here, and completed only with respect to the soul when we pass by the gate of death to the realms of glory; and with respect to the body when it shall also be raised in glory. All these things are included in salvation, a part at once finished and perfect upon the first act of faith, as justification and a title to the heavenly inheritance; a part inchoate and germinant, to have a future development and growth, as sanctification and Christian maturity and fruitfulness; or part in promise and foretaste, as the resurrection of the body and the life everlasting. He who receives Christ indeed, receives "all things pertaining to life and godliness." "Whom he did predestinate, them he also called; whom he called, them he also justified; whom he justified, them he also glorified."—Rom. viii. 30. Is not glorification here declared to have been conferred on the elect, concurrently with **justifi-**cation, and in terms as completely implying what is already, in some sense, as really done or effected as justification, **and as** surely indicative of its full accomplishment, as are **ever used** with reference to our full salvation, or any part of it, **even** personal holiness or sanctification itself? But no **one not** fanatically blinded will pretend that heavenly glory is **our por-**tion in this life, or is ours on earth otherwise than in the per-fect title to it secured by justification, and the preparation for it begun in regeneration and conversion, and carried forward in our progressive sanctification.

No passage of Scripture can *prove* sinless perfection in this life, which is indisputably addressed and applied to those who are confessedly imperfect or defiled with any remainder of sin. But the great majority of professing Christians, whom perfec-tionists allow to be real Christians according to the judgment of charity on the one hand, and to be imperfect in holiness on the other, are addressed or referred in nearly if not quite all the passages habitually quoted as proving sinless perfection in this life. Thus, the passage 1 John iii: 9: "Whosoever is born of God doth not commit sin, for his seed remaineth in him, and he cannot sin because he is born of God," and other less emphatic declarations in the context, must be so interpret-ed as to be true, whatever else they may signify, of all Christian people—all who are "born of God." But confessedly the most of these come short of the sinless perfection claimed for a few. The sense in which such cannot sin, because the seed of grace and holiness remaineth in them, is that they cannot sin prevailingly, persistently, with full purpose, allowance, or without resistance and repentance. They cannot sin in such wise that "sin shall have dominion over them," or that holi-ness shall not be the ascendant, and increasingly ascendant principle within them, until at death its victory over sin is ab-solutely complete and exterminating. It is all solved by the nature of the Christian conflict between the flesh and spirit, so graphically depicted, Gal. v: 17, and Rom. vii: 14–25, which, however we may find it hard to harmonize with the psychol-ogy or metaphysics any may have engrafted on their theology, finds its response and counterpart in normal Christian experi-ence. All Christians know what it means to have the flesh lusting against the spirit, so that in a sense they "cannot do the things they would." While they "delight in the law of God after the inward man," still they do what they allow not, and yet, amazing paradox! in a sense, it is no more they "that do it, but sin that dwelleth in them," and then, whether we can explain it or not, it is the man himself who with the mind serves the law of God, and with the flesh the law of sin. It is the same Ego, or self, that is tainted with the sin, against which it strives, going on from conquering yet to conquer it, and at last, through grace, utterly extinguishing it.

Another climacteric text adduced by perfectionists is Eph. v: 25, 26, 27: "Husbands, love your wives, even as Christ also loved the church, and gave himself for it; that he might cleanse it with the washing of water by the Word; that he might present to himself a glorious church, not having spot or wrinkle or any such thing, but that it should be holy and without blemish." It is undeniable that this applies to the church of the saved and redeemed, militant and triumphant; to all real Christians, as representing their state already attained or to be attained. But inasmuch as confessedly in the militant state the great body of Christians are not yet without spot, wrinkle or blemish, it follows that this passage does not prove any present sinless perfection in this world, but only in the future life.

If perfectionism derives no support from texts of this tenor, much less does it derive any from passages ascribing, promising or enjoining holiness or sanctification upon the people of God. Yet passages of this scope and tenor are constantly and freely quoted in behalf of sinless perfection. Its advocates speak and argue as if holiness and sanctification belonged to them alone, and were distinctive of them in contrast to the whole church besides; and generally as if it became theirs, not at their original, but at some second conversion. This notion of a second conversion, which introduces to the "higher life" of sinless purity, is maintained expressly by such writers as Boardman in "Higher Christian Life," and in substance by all the Higher Life and Perfectionist school. And they are very apt to represent it as simply an entrance upon, or attainment, or beginning, of sanctification or holiness. They even use these terms as the very titles of their books and treatises in advocacy of the attainableness of sinless perfection.   Thus, the title of one of the best of these books, by a leading Methodist divine, Rev. J. T. Crane, D.D., is " Holiness the Birthright of God's Children." Rev. J. A. Wood, author of a work on " Perfect Love," in his volume on "Purity and Maturity," says : " Purity or holiness, significant of quality, implies entirety. It does not mean a mixture of purity and pollution, partly clean and partly defiled " (p. 25).   Binney, in his " Theological Compend Improved," under the head entitled " Holiness — Sanctification," says : " This state . . . is called holiness, sanctification, purity, perfection, fulness of God and of Christ and of the Holy Ghost, and full assurance of faith.   What is meant by these expressions is that participation of the divine nature which excludes all original depravity or inbred sin from the heart, and fills it with perfect love to God and man—perfect love, the unction of the Holy One, and the baptism of the Holy Ghost " (p. 128).

According to this, none can be holy or sanctified who have any remains of " *original* depravity or inbred sin," or less than " perfect love to God and man." At this rate all Christians, all who have experienced the new birth, must be in this elevated state. So he proceeds to tell us, " Holiness begins when the principle of purity—namely, love to God—is shed abroad in the heart in the new birth." And yet he immediately adds : " But entire sanctification is that act of the Holy Ghost whereby the justified soul is made holy. This instantaneous work of the sanctifier is usually preceded and followed by a gradual growth in grace. The Spirit certifies this purification."—1 Cor. 11, 12. Can there be greater confusion and self contradiction than this? Holiness and sanctification are defined to be " perfect love "; yet holiness—*i.e.*, perfect love—begins at the new birth ; while " entire sanctification " comes later by an instantaneous work of the sanctifier, " usually preceded and followed by a gradual growth in grace." How does " perfect love " differ from " entire sanctification ? " And what room remains for growth in grace beyond " entire sanctification ? " This, by the way, is one specimen of the enormous inconsistencies into which perfectionists and higher life advocates run, of which we shall see many more as we go on.

Among all the adherents of this doctrine since the Quietists and Mystics of a former age, we rarely find any more refined, cultured, disciplined, endowed with natural and acquired strength of mind, delicacy of taste, and vigor of spiritual graces, than the late T. C. Upham, Professor of Mental Science in Bowdoin College, and author of popular text-books on that subject, as well as of publications on this peculiar type of what he styled the "Interior Life." He, if any who catch the magnetism of the converts to this theory, should have been superior, not only to all shams and impostures, all cant, hypocrisy and affectation, but to all loose bandying of the catch-words and watchwords which form the shibboleths of sects, parties and self-exalting coteries. He speaks of "the true idea of Christian perfection or holiness" as if such perfection were the only holiness," also of being "sanctified unto the Lord," as being identical with the "blessing of perfect love" (*Pioneer Experiences*, pp. 96, 97); also of coming "ultimately to the undoubting conclusion that God required me to be holy, that he had made provision for it, and that it was both my duty and my privilege to be so. The establishment of my belief in this great doctrine was followed by a number of pleasing and important results."—*Id.* p. 91. It could not be otherwise—if, indeed, it was a discovery for the first time that God requires and makes provision for holiness in his people. Of course the only holiness which could have been the subject of such discovery is that which is sinless. Whence it appears that a large part of the arguments and pretensions of this school fall to the ground, unless the holiness and sanctification of the Bible always mean sinless perfection; and hence, that all true Christians are sinless, which these same people do not even claim to be true of more than a small part of them.

Closely connected with all this is the constant confounding of sanctification with justification; of inherent with imputed or forensic righteousness; of the cleansing from the guilt, or condemnation to the punishment of sin, with the cleansing from its power and pollution. Justification is instantaneous and complete upon the first act of faith in Christ or vital union to Him. In its nature, justification is entire, or not at all. "He that believeth shall no more come into condemnation, but hath passed from death unto life." There is indeed "no more condemnation to those that are in Christ Jesus, who walk not after the flesh, but after the Spirit." Sanctification, on the other hand, is begun in infantile yet prevailing strength at conversion, and advances by a gradual and progressive growth, in which the new-born soul goes forward, " having these promises, to cleanse itself from all filthiness of the flesh and spirit, perfecting holiness in the fear of God "; so always cleansing stains which, although thus growing less, yet still remain in this decreasing form to be contended against till they are wholly expunged.

Now, how often is this declaration, and others the like, that Jesus, " by one offering hath perfected forever them that are sanctified," quoted in favor of perfect and sinless sanctification in this life? Yet, to this construction it is a fatal objection, that it applies to all the sanctified, all who are saved through Christ's offering. But of these it is allowed that the vast majority have not become thus sinless. The perfecting, therefore, must relate to that which is at once made perfect by the offering of Christ, viz., justification. This is conceded on all hands to be perfect from first to last, whatever may or may not be the sense of it in the believer's consciousness. So the declarations, 1 John i: 7-9, " That the blood of Jesus Christ his Son cleanseth us from all sin," and that " if we confess our sins, he is faithful and just to forgive us our sins, and to cleanse us from all unrighteousness," obviously refer to justification as the immediate and finished result of the application of this blood, and only indirectly to sanctification which accompanies justification, at first initial and germinant, but gradually carried forward to perfect sinlessness in heaven ; for the 8th verse declares, to the utter discomfiture of any perfectionism founded in this passage, " If we say we have no sin, we deceive ourselves, and the truth is not in us." So all promises of cleansing refer to that washing away of sins in the blood of the Lamb which consists in perfect justification, or to progressive cleansing of the pollution of sin by gradual sanctification. To this latter the command to cleanse ourselves refers; charging us to " purify ourselves in obeying the truth through the Spirit," not as a thing yet finished, but always progressing ; so that whatever be our assurance of hope, he that hath this hope must be ever purifying himself, " even as God is pure." One source of obscurity and confusion on this subject, therefore, is the tendency of many of the Higher Life persuasion more or less to confound justification with sanctification.

Perhaps the strongest pleas are those founded on the Biblical use of the words " perfect," " blameless," or their equivalents, in reference to the people of God. But that these words are used in various senses, some of them not implying absolute sinlessness, is too plain to admit of plausible denial. Even the injunction so often quoted by the perfectionists, that " having these promises we cleanse ourselves from all filthiness of the flesh and spirit, perfecting holiness in the fear of God," implies that this process of perfecting is to go on, and is therefore not yet finished. It implies that the normal Christian life here consists in having the ideal of perfect holiness before the eye of faith, and constantly working toward it, ever approaching, but not reaching it this side of heaven. And this is the only way in which we can consistently interpret Phil. iii : 12, 15, in the former of which the Apostle explicitly says : " Not as though I had already attained, or were already perfect; but I follow after, if that I may apprehend that for which I am apprehended of Christ Jesus'; " while in the latter, his words are : "Let us, therefore, as many as be perfect, be thus minded." Here it is clear that " perfect " means truly apprehending and struggling toward the standard of perfection in holiness, which, in the former, he represents himself as not having yet attained. Not different is the meaning of the word, Eph. iv : 12, where he represents the ministry as given *inter alia* " for the perfecting of the saints." What else does this mean but that they are instruments employed to constantly advance the saints toward that holiness which befits the atmosphere of heaven?

Perfection is also applied to Christian character to denote, not sinlessness, but the elements and constituent parts of Christian character in due proportion and symmetry. So James, i : 4: " That ye may be perfect and entire, wanting nothing." Then it is often used like the word blameless, to mean inward sincerity and a life outwardly irreproachable in the sight of men, as when it is said of Noah, that " he was perfect; " of Job, that " he was perfect and upright ; one that feared God and eschewed evil "—Job i. This is precisely the equivalent of the description given of Zacharias and Elizabeth—Luke i : 6: " That they were both righteous before God, walking in all the

commandments and ordinances of the Lord blameless."
Here the inward righteousness before God was evinced by the
visible blameless walk in the ways of God, without any breach
or deviation obnoxious to human censure.   It is precisely the
equivalent of the phraseology applied to Christians as such—
Phil. ii: 14, 15: "Do all things without murmuring and dis-
puting, that ye may be blameless and harmless—the sons of
God, without rebuke in the midst of a crooked and perverse
nation, among whom ye shine as lights in the world, holding
forth the word of life."   Surely this points to a kind of excellence which, while bringing honor to Christ and his religion,
implies no sinless perfection.   While these terms, as employed
thus, denote a relative perfection in the sense of uprightness,
integrity, a conscientious and exemplary life, or of wholeness
and symmetry of the Christian virtues, or of mature growth,
as when it is said the stony ground hearers bring forth no fruit
unto perfection, they do not mean to assert sinless perfection
of any saints on earth.   Indeed, it is so demonstrable that the
term "perfect" is often used in various senses in the Bible
that perfectionists themselves are constrained to confess it,
and thus virtually to acknowledge that it does not of itself import present sinlessness unless the surrounding context and
the analogy of faith require it.   Thus, Mr. See says (*Rest of
Faith*, p. 72): "We merely say of another term, which is *Christian perfection*, that if the candid reader will refer to the Epistle to the Philippians, third chapter, he will find the word
"perfect" used in two senses.   The one referring to our resurrection perfection (verse 12), and the other (verse 15) referring to the Christian perfection, which we must conclude was
preached, professed, and lived in Apostolic times.   But how
does it appear that the latter was sinless?

Two passages are constantly quoted in behalf of the doctrine
we combat, which show the impossibility of always attaching
the literal or any other one sense to words used in Scripture.
This arises from the poverty and ambiguity of language which
compel us to use words in varied senses, to be determined in
each case by its proper exegetic law.   We refer to the use of
"fear" in the passages, "perfect love casteth out fear," and the
injunction that we "perfect holiness in the fear of God."

The latter fear belongs to those who are perfecting holiness

at every stage of their progress, and belongs to the very essence of religion in both worlds. It is mingled with filial love
and trust, takes the form of reverence, and comes of that
grace whereby we serve God acceptably with reverence and
godly fear—terms which are equivalent. The former is described in the context as that slavish "fear which hath torment;" which is none other than that spirit of bondage which
is unto fear—*i. e.*, servile fear, which is a repelling dread, instead of a confiding, revering, attracting love. Love in proportion to its perfection exorcises this fell spirit in all its forms
and remnants; but it is not asserted that this love becomes
perfect in this life, or if so, that sinless perfection is meant.

Much is said of "entire sanctification," and I Thess. v:
23, is constantly quoted as proving it in the sense of sinless
perfection in this life: "And the very God of peace sanctify
you wholly; and may your whole spirit, soul, and body be preserved blameless unto the coming of our Lord Jesus Christ."
The wholeness of our sanctification refers to all the parts of
our being, body, soul, and spirit, as the context shows, and
may signify its future progressive as well as its immediate accomplishment. Enough has already been said in regard to
the Biblical import of the word "blameless" in the final
clause.

If there are no scriptural proofs of sinless perfection in this
life, there are abundant and decisive scriptural proofs against
it, not so much in isolated texts—though these are not wanting—as in the whole tone and drift of the inspired portraitures
of Christian experience. "If we say we have no sin, we deceive ourselves, and the truth is not in us"—I John i: 8. "If
I justify myself, mine own mouth shall condemn me: If I say
I am perfect, it shall prove me perverse." This could not be
true of the claims to any but sinless perfection, as other kinds
of perfection are freely ascribed to the faithful servants of
God. The Lord's prayer is for all Christians of every age and
nation. It is therefore their duty always to pray, "forgive our
trespasses, even as we forgive those who trespass against us."
It has been the comfort and support of the most eminent
saints that this prayer is always acceptable to God and becoming in his children. Baxter is said to have rejoiced on his dying
bed that the publican's prayer, "God be merciful to me a sin-

ner," is never unacceptable to God. Christians are always laying aside every weight (the *impedimenta* coming upon them from the world, the flesh, and the devil), and the " sin which so easily besets them "—(Heb. xii) ; and " striving against sin," if need be, " resisting it even unto blood."—ver. 4.

Moreover, that chastisement which is the indispensable badge of sonship, without which all pretended sons are but bastards, is for sin—not for sins long past, repented of, and given up, but for present sins; not indeed for vengeance and destruction, but in fatherly love and faithfulness for our salvation—" for our profit, that we may be partakers of his holiness." This shows that sin still cleaves to all the sons of God, for which they need divine discipline and chastisement in order to its correction and removal ; a chastening which they must not despise on the one hand, nor faint or despair under on the other, unless they would miss its saving benefits. But what less than remaining sin in all the sons of God does all this imply? And how does perfectionism consist with that chastisement of which all but bastards are partakers?

The Christian conflict so vividly depicted—Gal. v: 17, and Rom. vii: 14, 25—is proof incontestible of the remains of the σὰρξ still warring against the spiritual man, producing all manner of paradoxical antagonisms in the soul ; but involving also phenomena impossible in the unregenerate soul. For in what unregenerate soul does the spirit lust against the flesh? At all events, was it not to the experience of the churches of Galatia, consisting of professed Christian converts, that he was writing?

And after all the efforts to torture Rom. vii. into a mere picture of the phenomena of an unregenerate soul, has it ever been plausibly shown how such can truly say, " I love the law of God after the inward man ; " " with the mind *I myself* serve the law of God, but with the flesh the law of sin." " O wretched man that I am ! who shall deliver me from the body of this death ? I thank God through Jesus Christ our Lord." If this is the language of impenitent unbelievers, where shall we find what is distinctive of the new-born soul? Do we need more evidence that the flesh, and sin in itself, as well as the outside world, are among the foes with which the Church militant must ever contend?

If we do, it is furnished abundantly in the statements, un-foldings, and defences of sinless perfection given by its advo-cates, whether they reach it from the Pelagian, Arminian, An-tinomian, Romish, or Mystic sides. Some of these frequently run or develop from and into each other.

One and all, they are, or come to be, essentially Antinomian. This is a grave charge. It suffices to overthrow the whole of them, not only as in absolute antagonism to Christ's teaching and standard, who came not to destroy the law, but to fulfill and establish it in every jot and tittle thereof, but as in and of itself, however it may often be counteracted by other influences, tending to foster looseness and apostasy in life. When we say that they are essentially Antinomian, we do not mean that their abettors call them such. Some of them, like John Wes-ley, even warn its adherents against Antinomianism. And many of them have no suspicion that the scheme logically or practically involves such a taint. What we maintain, how-ever, is, that its advocates really take Antinomian ground; that they in one form or another lower the standard of perfect holiness below the only perfect and immutable standard of goodness—*i. e.*, the divine law—to some vague and indetermi-nate level, depending on and varying with the subjective states of each person who supposes himself to be perfect. With many—we believe with most—each one's assertion of his own Christian perfection is to be taken and treated as proof of it, unless contradicted by unmistakable impieties or immoralities. The essential thing is, that the perfection claimed and insisted on is not in conformity to the original, true, and only law of God, but to some lower, yet undefined, standard level to the infirmities and incapacities of our present fallen and debased state. This is enough; but it is much worse to leave us with-out any tangible and clear definition of the infirmities that do and do not involve sin.

1. The Romish theory of perfection lowers the original strictness of the law of God not only as it pronounces evil concupiscence to be no longer of the nature of sin, as the law declares in forbidding it (Rom. vii: 7), but as it allows for the tolerance of minor or venial, in distinction from mortal sins. Thus it provides for an easy perfection among the "mass and file" of its average members, whose lives show a very imper-

fect perfection in holiness, while it makes room for an extra-
legal perfection in the select classes of its saints, who by monastic vows and discipline, or other volunteer penances and self-
inflictions, strive thus to mortify the inclinations and remove
the temptations to sin.   This they rank as an extra-legal perfection, which consists of works of supererogation and surplus
merit, out of which such enormous mischiefs to morals and religion have arisen.   This was a process originally devised to
mortify the flesh and subdue or extirpate its evil concupiscence,
so as to make an end of its antagonism to the law.   But when
they adopted the dogma that concupiscence had not the nature
of sin, thus reducing the demands of the law to this level, they
raised the monastic and other equivalent discipline and volunteer
self-inflictions to the rank of extra-perfect living and surplus
merit.   They denominated the super-legal rules prescribing this
discipline " evangelical counsels." in contradistinction to the
mere requirements of the law, thus reduced from its oiiginal
strictness, conformity to which constituted ordinary Christian
perfection.   This perfection pervades the good acts of the
faithful, so that they, each and all, are entirely holy, but is
compatible at the same time with venial sins intervening between them, which appear to be acts forbidden by the original
law of God, and therefore requiring pardon, and making the
petition in the Lord's prayer always appropriate ; but nevertheless not bringing under condemnation according to the law
as reduced to the present level of human infirmity, and so not
bringing the soul into jeopardy.   That they hold good works
of Christians to be sinless, the following utterance of the Council of Trent evinces :   " Si quis in quolibet bono opere justum
saltem venaliter peccare dixerit   .   .   .   anathema sit."   The
reason of this is, that while perfect love constitutes the extra-
perfection of select saints to which we have referred, a mere
defect of such perfection of love in ordinary saints is not held
to be of the nature of sin, or to impart any taint of sin to works
destitute of it.   Bellarmin, as quoted by Dr. Hodge, says:
" Defectus charitatis, quod videlicet non faciemus opera nostra tanto fervore dilectionis, quanto faciemus in patria defectus
quidem est, sed culpa et peccatum non est. Unde etiam charitas
nostra, quamvis comparata ad charitatem beatorum sit imper-
fecta, tamen absolute perfecta dici potest."   Perfectionism,

therefore, as maintained by the Romanists, lowers the law of God to the infirmities and defects of our present state, and thus destroys its authority. The perfection it advocates is not even a pretence of sinless conformity to that law. Nor does it lay down any clear line of demarcation between what is or what is not now obligatory in that law ; or show us the precise level of the requirements of the law they now recognize as our binding rule of action. They gain perfect holiness not by lifting men up to the law, but by bringing the law down to them. See Article *Perfectionism*, in Hodge's Theology, vol. III., p. 245, *et seq.* ; also, Article on *The Protestant Doctrine of Evangelical Perfection*, in " British and Evangelical Review" for January, 1876. Another article on the *Means and Measure of Holiness*, in which, *inter alia*, the higher life views of Mr. and Mrs. Pearsall Smith are sifted, is worthy of attention. The sum of the whole is, that the difference between the Reformed and Romanists about perfection has its root in a difference as to what is sin, and how far the divine law is now in force. Had the latter our views of these things, the claim of perfection would sink in the outcry, " Lord, if thou wert strict to mark iniquities, who could stand ? " And we see in this, as we shall in other schemes to be noticed, the amazing incongruity of a theory demanding forgiveness and atonement for sinless and faultless conduct. Its supporters establish and annul the divine law in the same breath.

2. We find the same Antinomian element in the Arminian type of perfectionism which we take up before the Pelagian, because, though not first in original historical development, it has been more prominent in the Protestant churches, chiefly as being a prime article of Wesleyan Methodism. Wesley says : "The best of men still need Christ in his priestly office to atone for their omissions, their shortcomings (as some not improperly speak), their mistakes in judgment and practice, and their defects of various kinds. For these are all deviations from the perfect law, and consequently need an atonement. Yet, that they are not properly sins, we apprehend may appear from the words of St. Paul: ' He that loveth hath fulfilled the law, for love is the fulfilling of the law.'—Rom. xiii: 10. Now, mistakes and whatever infirmities naturally flow from the corruptible state of the body are no way contrary to

love, nor, therefore, in the Scriptural sense, *sin*." It would seem from this that the doctrine is, that love is so the fulfilling of the law that where it exists, in whatever degree, perfection exists, and there can be no infirmities or faults which are properly "*sin*."

Yet he cannot abide by this, and goes on : "To explain myself a little further on this head : 1. Not only *sin properly so called*—that is, voluntary transgression of a known law ; but sin improperly so-called—that is, involuntary transgression of a divine law, known or unknown, needs the atoning blood. 2. I believe there is no such perfection in this life as excludes these involuntary transgressions, which I apprehend to be naturally consequent on the ignorance and mistakes inseparable from mortality. 3. Therefore, *sinless perfection* is a phrase I never use lest I should seem to contradict myself. 4. I believe a person filled with the love of God is still liable to these involuntary transgressions. 5. Such involuntary transgressions you may call sins if you please ; I do not, for the reasons above mentioned."—*Plain Account of Christian Perfection*, Wesley's works, vol. I., pp. 28–9 ; Harper's edition, 1834.

The confusing and groundless distinctions here set forth in support of this scheme are enough to throw suspicion upon it, even if they could be sustained, as they cannot be in any degree which will make them serve their purpose. What is undeniable is, that the perfection maintained is below some requirements of the divine law known or unknown to its possessor ; that his transgressions of, or want of conformity to, the same require to be atoned for by Christ's blood ; that he will neither venture to call these sins, nor the normal state to which they belong one of *sinless perfection ;* that all sins arising from ignorance are of this innocent character, which does not mar the Christian perfection contended for ; that in these are included those arising " from the corruptible state of the body," which, when we consider the mysterious union of soul and body, and the implication of the moral states and actings of the former with those of the latter, have a vast, undefined reach, excluding, who can tell what, actions from the category of sin? What of the acts arising from a drunkard's appetite, the "eyes full of adultery," the " feet swift to shed blood," the " poison of asps under the lips," of the very flesh itself, which, though not meaning the body simply, mean the whole man as implicated with, affecting, and affected by the body, lusting against the spirit, so that no less a saint than Paul, therewith, to some extent at least, still "served the law of sin?"

Then, as to faults and wrongs committed, or duties omitted, through ignorance. Some of our most dangerous sins are sins of ignorance. Nay, the very ignorance of moral and Christian duty is itself often most culpable, and incurs the divine condemnation, even the woe upon those who call good evil and evil good; who put light for darkness and darkness for light. It is the very essence of sin to be deceitful, to disguise itself, to hate the light, and refuse to come to the light which would unveil it—and is not this declared by the Light of the world to be eminently its condemnation? What! do men become innocent by blinding themselves to their guilt, and sinless by ignoring their sin? Paul "verily thought that he ought to do many things contrary to the name of Jesus of Nazareth." Can a man be innocent and perfect in persecuting the Church, whatever his ignorance or sincerity therein? Out upon such casuistry, no matter how plausible and acceptable it may be to a worldly and backslidden church, or those who think they are something when they are nothing, or who "say they are perfect," by whatsoever names sanctioned!

And as to the distinction of voluntary and involuntary transgressions or shortcomings, who can know where this will lead us until we have a clear definition of the terms to show whether it and its corresponding adjectives are used, as was common down to the days of Edwards and Reid, for all the non-cognitive powers of the soul, including moral habits and states, or in the more restricted later meaning of many, in which it excludes not merely the cognitive, but the sensitive, affectional, appetitive, or orectic—all the optative powers of the soul, even in regard to moral and spiritual duties, but that of deliberate choice? If so, there is no end to the deformities and sins which may consist with this sort of perfection, and which even the Romanists would find it hard to pass over as venial sins.

In all this, Wesley simply goes in the track of the leading Arminian divines. Limborch, as quoted by Dr. Hodge, in the chapter already referred to, styles this obedience "perfect as being, correspondent to the stipulation contained in the divine covenant." "It is not a sinless or absolutely perfect obedi-ence, but such as consists in a sincere love and habit of piety, which excludes all habits of sin, with all enormous and deliber-ate actions." But it does not, according to this, exclude all sins. So Fletcher and others are quoted to the same effect. "With respect to the Christless law of paradisaic obedience, we utterly disclaim sinless perfection." "We shall not be judged by that law, but by a law adapted to our present state and circumstances, called the law of Christ." What! is this law of Christ laxer than the original law of God, and who will de-fine it so that imperfect conformity to it may be certainly known and tested?

Recent Arminian and Wesleyan writers take a similar posi-tion. Thus, Binney's *Improved Theological Compend* teaches: "Errors of judgment, infirmities of body, fears occasioned by surprise, unpleasant dreams, wandering thoughts in prayer, times when there is no joy, a sense of insufficiency in Christian labor, and strong temptation, are by no means inconsistent with perfect *love*. Yet errors need the atonement" (p. 132). So the late Bishop Janes, in his introduction to the book enti-tled *Pioneer Experiences*, says that "while entire sanctification makes us perfect Christians, it does not make us perfect men. Our bodies have been greatly impaired by the fall. We are encompassed with infirmities. Our knowledge is imperfect; our judgment fallible. We shall need the reconstruction of the judgment day to make us perfect men. But, thank God, His grace can make us perfect Christians, now and here" (p. 9). The distinction between perfect Christians and perfect men, in a moral sense, we understand to be that between those who keep the original and perfect law of God, and those who keep some supposed and undefined relaxation of it, called the law of Christ or the Gospel. Conformity to this relaxed standard is the perfection claimed.

Dr. Crane, in the little volume already referred to, so appre-hends the difficulties of thus holding to a perfection that is not perfect, that he sets himself to discover and remove the cause of Wesley and others of this school being thrown into an atti-tude so weak and vacillating. He finds it in Wesley's still retaining in his creed that clause of the Anglican articles which asserts that " this infection of nature doth remain, yea, in them that are regenerated." He thinks it essential to any consistent holding of the doctrine of perfection that this be abandoned. He is not far wrong. It is difficult to maintain the co-existence of a corrupt *im*perfection of nature with sinless *per*fection, without lowering the divine requirements so as to take this " infection" and its fruits out of the category of sin, or sinful imperfections, while yet conceding that they are contrary to the original and perfect law of God. But notwithstanding the protestation of Dr. Crane, the evidence is painfully abundant that this " infection" does remain in the best of men. And those know it most who know themselves best. On the other hand, if no such infection remains in the regenerate, it is difficult to see how their sanctification is not entire, and why each and every regenerate person is not perfectly sinless. This contradicts his doctrine, that a large proportion of Christians are yet imperfect, and that entire sanctification is rarely attained at the beginning of the Christian life. This book of Dr. Crane is mainly a critique on Wesley's modes of stating and defending perfection. He is successful in exposing their weakness and fallacy; but we do not see that his own position is any stronger. This is not his fault. The fault lies in the nature of the doctrine itself. It runs so counter to Scripture and normal Christian experience that it admits of no strong and consistent statement and defense. Hence we are not surprised when Dr. Crane tells us that—

"Hardly one in twenty of our ministers professes it, either publicly or privately, so far as I can learn. We preach it occasionally; but among our people its confessors are still fewer, in proportion to members, than in the ministry. Even among our bishops, from 1784 to the present day, confessors are as hard to find as in any other class of our people. The very princes of our Israel have been silent in regard to their own experience of it. The apostolic Wesley never professed it. In the sixty-fourth year of his age and the forty-second of his ministry he published in one of the leading journals of London a letter containing these words : ' I have told all the world *I am not perfect;* I have not attained the character I draw.' Bishop Asbury, who, if possible, exceeded Wesley in the toils and sufferings of his fruitful ministry, did not profess it. The saintly Hedding, approaching the grave by lingering disease, always calm, and often joyous in view of death, was importuned to profess it, and declined. Myriads of men and women among us, whose lives were bright with a holy light, saints *of whom the world was not worthy*, never professed it".—Pp. 14, 15.

Even so; and this no way to their detriment, however it may be to the doctrine of sinless perfection here below.

3. If we examine the Pelagian or semi-Pelagian doctrine of Perfection we shall find it equally in derogation of the continued authority of the divine law. The essential difference between this and the Arminian is, that the latter asserts that the ability, be it natural or moral, to render such obedience as is required by the law of Christ and constitutes Christian Perfection, is itself largely the result of a gracious assistance given to reinforce the weakness induced by the fall. The law is lowered and our weakness strengthened, until our increased ability and God's reduced requirements meet and become commensurate. The Pelagian theory, however, maintains that our natural powers in their native moral state are, *per se*, adequate to fulfill the demands of the law; that no law can be binding, *i.e.*, be a law, which surpasses our full ability without divine aid to keep it. Pelagius himself accordingly held that the fall did not debilitate our moral powers, and that they still remain, equal to keeping the law in its original, unabated strictness. The evident opposition between this view of the present condition of human nature and the representations of Scripture, reinforced by both the natural and Christian consciousness, has rendered it difficult for any but the lowest of Socinian and Rationalistic divines to entertain or adhere to it. Hence the fundamental thesis that no binding law can exceed our ability, whether natural or moral, is brought to bear in a semi-Pelagian or Arminian way, to lower the demands of the law to the moral state and ability of a race lapsed into such weakness. Men are in some degree corrupted and debilitated by the fall, to be sure; but the requirements of the law are accommodated to their weakness, and they are fully adequate to keep it perfectly; nor can they be under obligation to obey any law which they are not fully able perfectly to keep. It is in this line that perfectionism has been developed in this country by those whose metaphysical or philosophical views in theology made this the most obvious route to sinless perfection. When we were students in theology, a little coterie, becoming wiser than their teachers or fellow-students, strained the doctrine of ability beyond the scope contended for or admitted by its most eminent champions, to the length of maintaining, not only that

all men can, but that some do, reach sinless perfection in this life, of which, so far as the students there were concerned, a trio or so were the principal confessors.   The net result of the whole was that the leader, instead of going forward into the ministry, ran into various socialistic and free-love heresies, on the basis of which he founded the Putney and Oneida communities, over the latter of which he now presides.⏋ Other sporadic outbreaks of the distemper appeared here and there in the Presbyterian and Congregational communions, or among separatists and come-outers from them, these often uniting with the radicals or advanced reformers of other communions.

But the only strong and serious development in this line had for its centre Oberlin, and for its great expositors and defenders Professor Finney and President Mahan.   The *Oberlin Evangelist* and *Quarterly Review* were the organs for propagating and defending this scheme.   These are not now within our reach, and we are obliged to depend on the undisputed quotations from them in the controversial papers of the time.   The *Princeton Review*, for April, 1841, p. 241, quotes, from the *Oberlin Evangelist*, vol. 2, p. 50, Mr. Finney as saying:

"It is objected that this doctrine (of perfect sanctification) lowers the standard of holiness to our own experience.   It is not denied that in some instances this may have been true.   Nor can it be denied that the standard of Christian perfection has been elevated much above the demands of the law in its application to human beings in our present state of existence.   It seems to have been forgotten that the inquiry is, What does the law demand?—not of angels, and what would be entire sanctification in them; nor of Adam previously to the fall, when his powers of body and mind were all in a state of perfect health; nor what will the law demand of us in a future state of existence; not what the law may demand of the church in some future periods of its history on earth, when the human constitution, by the universal prevalence of thorough temperance principles, may have acquired its pristine health and powers; but the question is, What does the law of God require of Christians in the present generation, of Christians in all respects in our circumstances, with all the ignorance and debility of body and mind which have resulted from the intemperance and abuse of the human constitution through so many generations?

"The law levels its claims to us as we are, and a just exposition of it, as I have already said, under all the present circumstances of our being, is indispensable to a right apprehension of what constitutes entire sanctification."

Unmistakably this asserts that the law lowers its claims to our strength as debilitated by sin and corruption.   But when is this process of deterioration to stop, which, it has been well said, makes sin "its own remedy and apology"? It is easy enough to be perfectly sanctified, according to such a standard. Can any one tell how far men, by sinning, may become enslaved to sin, without making this very servitude, the very invincibleness and obduracy of sin, their own apology, whether in this world or the realms of outer darkness? Or is there any lower deep beneath this lowest deep in which this ceases to be? It is obvious on the face of the foregoing presentation why this form of Antinomianism may, like that of the Romanists, lead to a certain outward ascetic as well as inward looseness in its regimen and cultus.

But another strange result was logically reached by overstraining what was formerly known as the "Exercise Scheme" to extreme consequences wholly unlooked for, and repudiated by many of its supporters. Said Mr. Finney, *Ob. Evan.*, vol I., p. 42., *et passim :*

"It seems to be a very general opinion that there is such a thing as imperfect obedience to God, *i. e.*, as respects one and the same act, but I cannot see how an imperfect obedience relating to one and the same act can be possible. *Imperfect obedience!* What can be meant by this but *disobedient obedience! A sinful holiness* Now, to decide the character of any act, we must bring it into the light of the law of God; if agreeable to the law, it is obedience—it is right—*wholly right.* If it is in *any respect* different from what the law of God requires, it is wrong—*wholly wrong.*"

According to this there is no medium between a state of perfect sinlessness on the one hand, and perfect impenitence on the other. The soul is liable to alternations from one to the other each successive moment, and with each transient instantaneous volition. No enduring moral bias deeper than such momentary volitions is recognized. And as each of these follows each, he may soar one moment to the summit of absolute perfection, to plunge the next moment to the abyss of carnal obduracy. This is no unfair interpretation of this system by an adversary. It is precisely that given by a leader in Higher Life teaching, when comparing and endeavoring to harmonize into substantial unity the theoretical grounds adopted by different classes of its advocates. Says Boardman, *Higher Life*, pp. 61–2 :

"For the Oberlinian idea that the experience brings the soul into a state of sinless perfection or entire sanctification the grounds must be sought in three things: first, their philosophy of the will, according to which each volition or choice is in itself absolutely holy, or absolutely unholy and altogether so. So that when God is chosen, while that choice is predominant, the soul is perfectly holy; and when the world is chosen, then while that choice is uppermost, then the soul is perfectly sinful. This, with their view of the law of God as graduated to the sinner's condition, whatever it is, not requiring of all alike the same entire conformity to the absolute and unchangeable standard of heavenly holiness, but claiming no more than the sinner's earthly blindness permits him to see, and no more than his earthly weakness permits him to do. And to these two a third must be added: viz., their definition of sanctification, according to which it is consecration only— or setting apart to God—and so is man's own work, instead of God's. Whereas, according to the popular acceptation, sanctification is the work of God in the soul after it is set apart to God by voluntary consecration. These three things taken together, and taken together with the experience, may serve to show us why and how the Oberlinians adopt the terms and accept the idea of ' entire sanctification' as attained in the experience."

If the Antinomian character of this system, in its different forms and potencies, has been proved, then it makes out sinless perfection by lowering the divine law to men. It is also certain that not only can its advocates take and hold no uniform and consistent position on the subject, or draw any clear line between the perfectly and the imperfectly sanctified, but much of their reasoning is to the effect that all Christians are entirely sanctified. This is the necessary consequence of the Oberlinian dogmatic which acknowledges no holy act which is not perfectly holy, but of all arguments in its favor based on Scriptural passages that apply indiscriminately to all the saints. This is so inevitable that one of the recent treatises on this subject is written for the express purpose of proving that there is no conversion from sin save to spotless purity; that" sanctification admits of no degrees, and is never used in a limited sense designating degrees of cleanness or purity. If a thing or being has the least degree of uncleanness or defilement, it is unsanctified."*

Dr. Crane says: " The ablest writers who have discussed this subject, on the residue theory of infection of nature still remaining in the regenerate, have not been able in their descriptions of the Christian life to maintain a clear, practical distinction between those who are supposed to be simply regenerate and

*The *Old Paths, a Treatise on Sanctification*, by Rev. Thomas Mitchell.

those who are accounted to be freed from all depravity." [We have seen what those are capable of who ignore or fritter away this infection.] He proves by quotations from Wesley that he sometimes puts the " religious state of the sanctified man below that of one who is simply born of God." That he now represents the perfect man as liable to " something wrong, in tempers, words and actions," and now as exceeding the imperfect Christian in being " freed from evil thoughts and evil tempers." Dr. Wakefield is quoted by Dr. Crane as saying that " entire sanctification does not differ in essence from regeneration."—See *Holiness the Birthright of God's Children*, pp. 83–86.

But it may be asked, however wrong theoretically and doctrinally, must not the effects of such a standard of life as entire sanctification be benign and purifying? We do not believe that error can promote holiness. God sanctifies by his truth, and his word is truth. Important life-giving truths may accidentally become associated in the view of many with baneful errors, and may exert their proper purifying influence, and serve as an antidote to the errors which accidentally contributed to give them prominence. We believe that the Millerite delusion prevalent about the year 1843, that the second advent of Christ was to occur in that year, and on some certain day of it, was overruled of God to the awakening of many callous persons from their soul-destroying slumbers to prepare to meet their God by embracing his salvation. Yet it was a fatal delusion to those who hung their faith upon its truth, while it served to harden the sceptical and worldly in their inclination to regard Christianity as mere fanaticism or imposture.

There is no question that, in the minds of many good people, the higher life movement has a grasp on their consciences and hearts, owing to its arousing them to recognize and feel the duty of rising to higher grades of sanctity and consecration, greater elevation above self and the world. Furthermore, it is often confounded with that assurance of hope which is the common privilege of justified persons, who, though imperfectly sanctified, evince the genuineness of their faith to themselves and others by their Christian works ; who thus assure their hearts before God, and know that they know Christ because they keep his commandments ; who also receive in and through all this the witness of the Spirit with their spirits that they are the children of God. But all these truths, duties and privileges are better gaindd and conserved without this pretension of higher life, and perfect holiness, and assumed superiority to the great brotherhood of the redeemed, than when burdened with these fungus parasites. In themselves considered, and in their own proper influence and tendencies, we regard them as evil only, and that continually. It is propef to add, moreover, that not all who join in these higher life movements embrace the perfectionism which so largely underlies and permeates them. They are conscious only of arriving simply and purely at a higher Christian life, and deeper experience. These constitute the only truth and good accompanying such movements that are likely to give them power.

1. We deem it a great evil for those to think themselves perfectly holy who are not so, or at best only imperfectly so. It is an evil which makes a dangerous approach to thinking themselves something when they are nothing. It fosters spiritual pride, and is destructive of humility. It checks or stops struggles to overcome indwelling sin, and to advance to a nearer conformity to the divine law. Instead of stimulating us to forget the things which are behind and press forward to those which are before, it makes us easy with our present attainments in holiness, "as though we had already attained or were already perfect." We are quite aware, and do not mean to question, that these people hold to a continual growth in the Christian life ; but it is such a growth as takes place in heaven —a growth in general capacity, but not in moral purity or freedom from sin. This is already perfect, and cannot be more than perfect. So they no longer need to die unto sin. It is already extinct within them. It is as if in our investigations of truth we should take remaining ignorance for perfect, and infallible knowledge.

2. Closely connected with this is the denial and stoppage of growth in sanctification by struggling toward its entireness and perfection and ever making closer approximations to it, till all sin disappears in the spirits of the just made perfect. The favorite doctrine of these people is, that as perfect justification is received at the new birth by the initial act of faith, so, at some later period, perfect sanctification is received instanta-

neously by a single act of faith. And this is variously styled the rest of faith, the rest of the soul, &c., &c., implying that the soul rests at peace in its reliance on Christ for sanctification as well as justification, and this in such a sense as to be freed from the necessity of working to promote holiness, and subdue sin within us, in the same way and measure as in our justification, which is wholly by faith to the exclusion of all works of our own. " Thus," says one of these writers, " sanctification, like regeneration, is a supernatural, instantaneous work; and not a human, gradual work. Both are God's work. Both are instantaneous."—*Purity and Maturity*, p. 223. " There is no gradual growing out of sin."—*Id*. p. 145. This is very unsafe teaching. The constant teaching of Scripture, confirmed by sound Christian experience, is that we " work out our own salvation with fear and trembling, while God works in us to will and to do"; that this is a continuous process, and that we never cease, not merely works of holy living and service according to the measure of our present attainment, but in striving against sin in heart and life, laying aside the sin which easily besets us.

And we have observed that even those who come to perfectionism by the Pelagian or semi-Pelagian method of plenary ability without divine grace to perfectly keep the divine law, no sooner conceive themselves to have attained perfection in the exercise of this ability than they reverse their attitude into one of almost passive receptivity—of simply receiving by one act of faith the gift from the fulness of Christ—of waiting, resting in Christ, to the discarding of all works or efforts of our own, or in our own strength as subservient thereto. A notable case of some remarkable and elevated phases of this experience is found in the 27th chapter of Mr. Finney's Autobiography. Those who read it will find how he " seemed to be in a state of perfect rest," even to the point of a super-scriptural, if not anti-scriptural, Hopkinsian submission, in respect to " the salvation or damnation of his own soul, as the will of God might decide" ; his mind " too full of the subject to preach anything but a full and present salvation in the Lord Jesus Christ." " What I had been praying for, for myself, I had received in a way that I least expected. Holiness to the Lord seemed to be inscribed on all the exercises of my mind. I had such strong faith that God would accomplish all his perfect will, that

I could not be careful about anything." . . . " I then realized what is meant by the saying, that he is able to do exceeding abundantly above all that we ask or think.   He did at that time teach me, indefinitely, above all that I had ever asked or thought.   I had had no conception of the length and breadth, and height and depth, and efficiency of his grace.   It seemed then to me that that passage, ' My grace is sufficient for thee,' meant so much, that it was wonderful I had never understood it before," etc., etc.   Much in this chapter verges upon an elevated tone of hyper-Calvinism, Mysticism, and Quietism.   So Dr. Mahan (*Pioneer Experiences*, p. 14) says: " For sanctification, on the other hand, to overcome the world, the flesh and the devil, I had depended mainly upon my own resolutions. Here was my grand mistake, and the source of all my bondage under sin." . . . " If my propensities which lead to sin are crucified, I know that it must be done by an indwelling Christ " (p. 17).   He proceeds to state his belief " that the Lord Jesus Christ has provided special grace for the entire sanctification of every individual. . . . The first inquiry with me is, in what respect do I need the grace of Christ? . . . Thus having discovered my special necessities in any one of the particulars above referred to, my next object is to take some promise applicable to the particular necessity before me, and to go directly to Christ for the supply of that particular necessity."   This is all right on two suppositions: 1—that in these approaches to Christ for sanctifying grace, the sufficient grace be expected according to the measure of the present dispensation, but not in the measure of sinless perfection ; and 2—that it be in such wise that Christ's working in us to will and to do the things pleasing in his sight will be evinced by our working out our own salvation, even if with (holy) fear and trembling.   But all will recognize in this the complete swinging from the extreme of self-sufficient reliance on native powers to that of a life consisting in a comparatively passive recipiency of divine grace.

3. In perfect consonance with the scheme, and as its logical outcome, all that implies imperfection, the conflict between the flesh and spirit, penitential confession and humiliation for present spiritual faults and shortcomings, are unwelcome to these people.   Mr. See, in his *Rest of Faith*, gives vent to these feel-

ings in an introductory chapter, in which he maintains that the
"church is not a hospital," *i.e.*, for the cure of enfeebled or
the strengthening of imperfect Christians.   He represents, in a
condemnatory tone, that "the churches through the land are
only infirmaries where people come to be treated by the Great
Physician, who proceeds to cure people by a slow process, in
the meantime leaving them to the oversight of these sick ministering nurses."   He warns (p. 179) against being entangled in a
"seventh of Romans difficulty 'and a Galatian snare,' which in
our journey we do well to keep in the distance by simple
faith."   He would banish from the worship of the church
"hymns that hurt," among which he classes those that voice
the Christian's penitential confession ; specifying explicitly
those beginning :

> "Come, Holy Spirit, heavenly Dove."
> "O for a closer walk with God."
> "Come, thou fount of every blessing."
> "Thus far my God hath led me on."

Comment is needless.

4. It cannot be denied that while many persons of sweet and
unpretending spirit are allured into these Higher Life circles
for reasons already stated, the system tends to nourish a spirit
of Pharisaism and uncharitableness.   It does so, as its professors assume a superiority to ordinary Christians; they are perfect, while the church as a whole is imperfect, or if not this,
they are leading a higher christian life than the average.
Many of their adherents assume, what most of their arguments
imply, that those not entirely sanctified are not regenerated,
and, therefore, if professing Christians, are hypocrites.   The
very gathering into separate meetings, called "holiness meetings," or "higher life meetings," is an assumption of superiority—nay, it implies that the ordinary meetings and services of
the church are not thus in the interest of holiness, which is to
impeach their Christian character.   This spirit says literally,
"Stand by, for I am holier than thou."   It cannot, as a whole,
and exceptions aside, be otherwise than divisive, denunciatory
and censorious.   What the ultimate issue of all this must be,
that on the whole it must be disastrous to religion, all history
and reason prove.

5. It cannot be denied that the Antinomian feature of this
system has strong logical and practical affinities for licentious-

ness: men who esteem themselves perfect are apt to make themselves, their own subjective exercises, experiences, judgments, desires, and appetites, the measure and standard of perfection; to make these the rule and measure of rectitude, rather than God's word; or rather to construe them as God's voice and word, speaking in and through them. They have often · maintained that as Christ was living within them, their desires, and words and deeds were Christ's. This, of course, is the extreme of fanatical and blasphemous Antinomian pride and licentiousness. It goes to seed in Onedia communities. Mr. Finney says (Autobiography, p. 341) that about the time he commenced preaching on perfection, it came to be agitated, in the Antinomian sense of the term, a good deal at New Haven, at Albany, and somewhat in New York City, and that he could not accept these views. History shows their melancholy course and results. But there are other and higher forms of making our subjective feeling the standard of truth and holiness besides the gross and low form above noted. It often develops in simple mysticism, in which the feeling of the subject, devout and elevated though it be, still becomes a law unto itself, and sets its own impulses and bewilderments above the law and the testimony. Against all this we cannot too sedulously guard. Nor do we think it wrong or uncharitable in this connection to refer to the career of Mr. Pearsall Smith, who has been so conspicuous in Higher Life leadership.

Art. II.—THE GREAT MESSIANIC PROPHECY.

By Wolcott Calkins, D. D., Buffalo, N. Y.

"OF whom speaketh the prophet?" was the pertinent question of the Ethiopian Treasurer concerning the most remarkable prediction ever recorded. Never was the question more urgent than now. We get disquieted by doubts about the Bible and the certainty of our Christian hopes, because we permit ourselves to be diverted by trivial and irrelevant objections from resolute investigation of truths which are decisive. Such a truth is before us, and it demands thorough and dispassionate research.

In the sublime description of the sufferings and triumphs of Jehovah's Servant, which the Ethiopian was reading, three portions are distinguished by the form of the address. In the first, the speaker is Jehovah himself, who discloses in outline the exaltation of his servant, after unexampled humiliation. In the second, the prophet enumerates these sufferings in detail, and closes with assurances of his final triumph. In the third, Jehovah confirms these assurances and closes the prediction as it began, with the sure word of God, that through sorrow and death his Servant shall prosper, and be exalted above all majesty and power.

I. Behold, my Servant shall prosper,
He shall rise up, and be extolled, and stand triumphantly exalted.
Even as many were shocked at him
(His countenance was so marred as to be no more that of a man,
His form no more that of sons of men !)
So also shall he sprinkle many nations.
The kings shall shut their mouths before him;
For what had not been told them they shall see,
And what they had never heard they shall consider.*

II. Who hath believed our report ?
And to whom is Jehovah's arm revealed?
For he shall grow up before Him as a tender plant,
And as a sprout out of dry ground.
He hath no form nor comeliness that we should look up to him,
No beauty that we should take pleasure in him.
He is despised and rejected of men,
A man of sorrows, well acquainted with sickness ;

---

*Isa lii :13-15.

And like one hiding his face before us,
He was despised and we esteemed him not.
And yet it was our own sickness that he bore,
And our sorrows that he loaded upon himself.
But we supposed he was punished,
Smitten of God, and tormented !
O, no ! He was wounded for our transgressions,
Bruised for our iniquities.
Chastisement for our peace was upon him,
And with his stripes we are made whole.
All we like sheep have gone astray,
We have turned every one to his own way,
And Jehovah made the guilt of us all to meet upon him.
He was oppressed, and yet he humbled himself;
And he opened not his mouth like a lamb that is brought to the slaughter,
And as a sheep is dumb before her shearers,
So he opened not his mouth.
He was dragged to punishment by violence, and yet by process of law ;
And who of the men of his generation took it to heart
That he was cut off from the land of the living,
That the stroke for my people's transgressions fell upon him !
They appointed him his grave with criminals
(Still he was with a rich man in his death !)
Although he had done no wrong,
Neither was any deceit in his mouth.
And yet it pleased Jehovah to bruise him.
He laid sickness upon him.
But when he has made over his soul as a sin-offering,
He shall see offspring; he shall prolong his days,
And the pleasure of Jehovah shall prosper in his hands !*

III.—Free from the travail of his soul,
He shall see and be satisfied.
By his knowledge shall my righteous servant make many righteous,
Because he shall bear their iniquities.
Therefore will I give him the great as a portion,
And he shall distribute the strong as spoil.
For he hath poured out his soul unto death,
And he was numbered with transgressors,
While he was bearing the sin of many
And was making intercession for the transgressors !†

Of whom speaketh the Prophet thus? Only one answer has
ever been derived from the simple reading of the words, without a previous theory.   Jewish writers were almost unanimous
that this was a Messianic prophecy until the Christian apolo-

---

* Isa. liii: 1-10.   † Isa. liii: 11-12.

gists made the admission fatal to them. And modern rationalism did not discover, until late in the last century, that if this
prediction refers to a person who appeared in history hundreds
of years after it was made, it is a miracle which makes all the
miracles of the New Testament credible. What answer, then,
have Jews and rationalists made to this question which they
cannot evade—Of whom speaketh the prophet?

"Of the whole Jewish people. In the first part Jehovah
applies to his chosen people the well-known name—my servant,
and contrasts their present misery with their future glory.
In the second part the heathen confess their sins, and look to
Israel as their Saviour. In the third part the Lord assures
them that their sins have been pardoned through the intercessions of his anointed people."

This was the first attempt of Jewish writers to escape the
Messianic interpretation.* The theory has been embraced by
many of the ablest modern rationalists,† some of whom seek
to evade its gravest difficulties by applying the description to
the ideal Israel whom God called out of Egypt and purposed
to establish in the Holy Land, not to the actual Israel of the
exile.‡ The latter hypothesis encounters more embarrassment
than it escapes, for it leaves no place for the sufferings of the
exile, which are said to inspire the whole description.

It is unnecessary to dwell upon the contradictions involved
in this conjecture. Our prophet carefully distinguishes the
people from the servant of the Lord: "Ye are my witnesses,
and my servant whom I have chosen."§ The two are wholly
different in character. Israel is blind, deaf, stiff-necked,
treacherous;‖ the servant innocent and guileless.¶ Israel is
never described as the redeemer of the heathen. On the contrary, Egypt, Ethiopia, and Seba are given for a ransom of
Israel.** The servant of the Lord is afflicted, not for his own
sins, but for transgressors. But who gave Jacob for a spoil,
and Israel to the robbers? The Lord, for they would not walk
in his ways, neither were they obedient to His law.†† Of this
rebellious people it could never have been said—

---

* Abenezra, Kimchi, Abarbanel.
† Rosenmüller, Hitzig, Köster.
‡ Ewald, Beck.
§ Is. xliii: 10.

‖ xliii: 8; xlviii: 4-8.
¶ liii: 11.
** xliii: 3.
†† xlii: 24; lxiii: 10.

> "It pleased the Lord to bruise him,
> Although he had done no wrong,
> Neither was guile found in his mouth."

Of whom speaketh the prophet? " Of the obedient portion of the people in contrast with the idolatrous; the collective body of the prophets;[*] the faithful exiles;[†] those only of the faithful whose true piety made them zealous to return to their homes, especially patriotic elders, priests, Levites and prophets.[‡] Some class of the Jewish people, more or less extended, is described as suffering oppression, and often martyrdom itself; the disobedient at length confess that their own sins have involved their innocent brethren in calamity; and restored to repentance and fidelity by this means, they are pardoned by their God for the sake of His servant."

In some form this is the theory of the ablest scholars who now reject the Messianic interpretation. But they all fail to find a class of men who bear any resemblance to the description. There is no such exceptional class among the people. "We are all as an unclean thing; all our righteousnesses are as filthy rags; there is none that calleth upon thy name."[§] The grammatical construction forces these writers themselves to make the prophet the speaker in the second part. He confesses his own sins, and at the same time belongs to the class who are suffering innocently for the sins of others!

These sufferings are also wholly voluntary. " He bore our sickness; he loaded our sorrows upon himself."[‖] " He made over his own soul as a sin-offering."[¶] But the faithful exiles endured only what they could not escape. He was patient. "He opened not his mouth." The mouths of the exiles were always open—" By the rivers of Babylon, there we sat down; yea, we wept when we remembered Zion."[**] The sweetest lyrics of the most poetic nation in history are elegies of sorrow, and dirges of bereavement. And why does this immortal song of the exiles glide so naturally into bloodthirsty cursings of enemies?

> " O daughter of Babylon!
> Blessed shall be he that taketh and dasheth
> Thy little ones against the stones !"

---

* De Wette, Gesenius, Winer.
† Thenius, Paulus, Maurer.
‡ Knobel.
§ Isa. lxiv: 6.
‖ liii : 4.
¶ liii : 10. Both lost in the authorized version.
** Ps. 137: 1.

What mean the fearful execrations of many of the Psalms?

> " Let his days be few, and let another take his office ;
> Let his children be fatherless, and his wife a widow ;
> Let his children be continually vagabonds, and beg ! "*

What mean the eulogies of treachery, and of hospitality desecrated by perjury and assassination ?

> " Blessed be Jael above women !
> She stretched out her hand to the tent pin,
> And her right hand to the hammer of the workmen.
> She hammered Sisera, she smote his head ;
> She beat him, she struck through his temples ;
> Between her feet he bowed, he fell, he lay ;
> Where he bowed, there he fell down slaughtered !
> So perish all thine enemies, O Jehovah ! "†

It is no part of our purpose to propose any theory of these frightful utterances of vindictive passion which abound in Jewish prophecy and poetry. All theories admit this one fact, that they are true and imperishable records of human opinion. Like the pillar of salt overlooking the plains of Sodom and Gomorrah, these bleak, rugged shafts of vengeance stand sentinels by the shores of the buried past, defending from doubt the deep resentment of the human mind, and pre-eminently of the Jewish mind, for oppression.   From this natural infirmity no Israelite was exempt.   David, the sweet Psalmist of Zion, was the most fervent curser of them all.   Jeremiah never suppresses his sobs but to breathe out vengeance.   Isaiah exhausts ridicule and malediction upon his idolatrous foes.   Where in all the wide wanderings of these kinsmen of the fierce Bedouin, who never forgives; where in the eventful history of this strange people, whom hatred for others has held together when love for one another had lost its cohesive power, are we to look for a class of men who humble themselves when they are oppressed, who open not the mouth when they are led like sheep to the shearers, like lambs to the slaughter?   This theory of a righteous and submissive class of sufferers in Israel is one of the perversions of history which nothing but the credulity of modern rationalism can tolerate.

But, after all, we might have dismissed both these theories summarily, by remarking what is evident to the Ethiopian,

---

* Ps. 109: 8–10.   † Judges v : 24-27.

and to every candid reader who has no *à priori* theory, that the prophet is not speaking of a collective class at all, but of an individual. He has the countenance and form of a man. His growth, his life, his death, his burial, are described circumstantially. It is within the range of poetic license to portray the vicissitudes of national calamity under the figure of an injured person; and possibly to speak of their destruction as the grave of the buried nation. But such precise and vivid representations as these, applied to so vague a subject, would be offensive in any poet, intolerable in any prophet. Of whom speaketh the prophet? Of himself or of some other man? The question has been evaded, not answered, by nearly all who have written in the interests of unbelief.

Some, however, have dared to answer: "He is speaking of himself,[*] of King Josiah,[†] of Jeremiah,[‡] of King Uzziah,[§] of King Hezekiah,[||] of an unknown prophet slain by the Jews in exile, of Cyrus, of the Maccabees, of some unnamed king of Israel."[¶]

It is a remarkable fact that no one of these candidates for canonization in the calendar of unbelief has had more than one advocate at a time. Knobel says of them all that they scarcely deserve mention, much less refutation.[**] But there is one remark to be made on this theory, which will also apply to the others, that is too important to be omitted: On this or any other theory of modern Jews and skeptics, our prophet teaches the doctrine of expiation by the vicarious suffering of a human victim.

From the fortieth chapter to the close of the book, a twofold deliverance is incessantly proclaimed. And, like the predictions of the destruction of Jerusalem, and of the judgment day in Matthew, the two are not always clearly distinguished, although the first nine chapters refer chiefly to the deliverance from Babylon, the rest of the book to the redemption from sin and misery. Each of these great blessings shall be accomplished by a servant of Jehovah; the former by Cyrus, the latter by the servant in this chapter. Cyrus shall save Israel by

---

[*] Ständlin.   [†] Aberbanel, as an alternative.   [‡] Rabbi Saadias Haggaon.
[§] Augusti.   [||] Konynenburg and Bahrdt.
[¶] Anonymous writers in rationalistic periodicals.
[**] Kurzgefasstes Exegetisches Handbuch, Jesaia, p. 387.

his courage, by his power, by his military supremacy ; but this servant by his meekness, his submission, his suffering, his death and burial.   Nor are his sufferings merely preliminary to his work.   They do the work.   This is disclosed, *chiaro oscuro* after the usual prophetic manner, in the opening announce-ment: "He shall sprinkle many nations."   The well-known word, with the technical meaning of sacrificial worship, to sanc-tify the unclean by sprinkling on them the blood of innocence, is boldly and deliberately chosen.   But even if this meaning is rejected,* the following descriptions are so precise that ration-alism has made no attempt to evade them.†

These words can bear but one meaning.   Guilt, and suffering for guilt, were taken off from transgressors and borne by their innocent substitute.   He expiated their sins by his atoning death.   Men may say that this is only figuratively true, and describes no real transaction.   They make no attempt to deny that the prophet believes and affirms that sinners are saved by the sacrifice of this victim.

Now, what if this servant of the Lord is Isaiah, or Jeremiah, or any other martyr of Israel—or, for that matter, any collect-ive class of good men?   Then human guilt is expiated by the death of a human victim! And no trace of such a doctrine can be found elsewhere in the Bible.   When it is said that God will give Seba, Egypt and Ethiopia as a ransom,‡ or that the evil-doer is a ransom for the righteous, and the ungodly for the pious,§ this figurative sense of ransom has nothing in common with the expiation of guilt by the substitution of an innocent victim.   Prophecy knows nothing of the atonement of guilt by human suffering.

Or rather the Scriptures know and reject with horror this refuge of guilty despair. It prevailed in every nation surround-ing Israel.   It prevailed in Greece, and Rome, and ancient Mexico.   It prevails still in savage Africa.   And once God did tempt Abraham, for this among other purposes, to fix in the minds of all his descendants a horror of human immolation, and make it forever impossible for them to believe that he could command them to make their children pass through the fire

---

* Gesenius, De Wette, Knobel.   ‡ Is. xliii: 3.
† See our version of liii: 4, 5, 6,10-12   § Prov. xxi : 18.

as did the Moabites; or to bleed on the altars in high places, as in the cruel rites of the Canaanites and Philistines. It is the gloomy and venal prophet of the fire-god of the far East who puts the startling question: "Wherewith shall I come before Jehovah? Shall I give my first-born for my transgression—the fruit of my body for the sin of my soul?"[*] The horrid conjecture makes the prophet of Israel shudder. It was the one indestructible conviction of the national mind, engendered by the selection of the kid, the most insignificant of their spotless victims, for their sin-offering, that Jehovah reserved in his own hands the provision of atonement for sin; that man could not furnish the victim; and, above all, that the intrusion of a human victim was something immeasurably worse than murder; it was sacrilege and blasphemy against the author and defender of human life.

And here we have reached at a bound a momentous conclusion concerning our prophecy. That this servant of Jehovah could be any martyr, or any class of righteous sufferers, is a conception which no true Israelite could entertain. Nothing marks so painfully the degradation of modern Israel as the admission of this heathenish idea. But this is not all. This sprinkler of the nations; this sin-bearer for all the people; this mysterious being who takes away sin by making his own life a sin-offering, cannot be a man at all! That is, he cannot belong to the sinful race he redeems. The prophet must have in his mind a servant of Jehovah who comes down from heaven, not up from sinful earth. This is the thought which links the present indissolubly with the former description:

> "They shall call his name God-with-us!"[†]
> "The government shall be upon his shoulders,
> And his name shall be called
> Wonderful, Counsellor, the mighty God,
> The everlasting Father, the Prince of Peace."[‡]

Of whom speaketh the prophet this? Of the Messiah of God. Of the divine Redeemer provided from heaven to sprinkle the sinful nations of the earth. Of the Lamb of God that taketh away the sins of the world. All other theories involve hopeless contradictions. This alone leaves the impress of truth.

---

[*] Mic. vi: 6.   [†] Is. vii: 14.   [‡] Is. ix: 6.

But the Ethiopian meant more than this by his question. Has this prediction been fulfilled? All attempts to find in any possible development from our sinful race the original of this clearly defined and heavenly portrait have been self-contradictory and vain. But has one come down from heaven, stood upon the earth, and been recognized as the substance of this photographic shadow thrown forward upon the sensitive page of prophecy?

It is a relief to observe that Döderlein's theory of the later composition of this part of Isaiah, from the fortieth chapter to the close, is no embarrassment to the discussion of this question. It is admitted by all that if the prediction be Messianic, it was not fulfilled until hundreds of years after the exile. The few Jewish scholars who hold it to be Messianic are looking for its fulfillment still. It was absolutely necessary for those who denied the possibility of miracles to invent this theory, that an unknown prophet of the exile added to Isaiah's work the marvelous disclosures of Israel's two-fold deliverance from Babylon and from the guilt of sin, after the former had been accomplished. But the latter was not accomplished by the return from captivity. Nothing at all resembling these descriptions occurred for many centuries after the latest date assigned by destructive criticism to their publication. To our argument it is a matter of complete indifference whether Isaiah or some other prophet wrote this chapter; whether it was written eight hundred or only six hundred years before its fulfilment.

For it has been fulfilled to the letter! This is the startling fact which we have still to point out. On any hypothesis of the date of the work before us, we are in the presence of an incontestable miracle. Let us try to get some adequate impression of it. Go back in the centuries, not eight hundred years, as we might, but the six hundred years conceded to this prophecy by unbelievers themselves. Six hundred years ago England was beginning the struggle for civil liberty; the Magna Charta had just vindicated the great principle of Anglo-Saxon legislation—no taxation without representation; the first regular parliament had just assembled. Now, what if in that germinal period of liberty and equality before the law, more than two hundred years before the discovery of America, some renowned reformer had made and recorded the prediction of a terrible struggle to extend these rights of man, not alone to baron and freeholder, but to workingmen and slaves; the leader on the side of emancipation is depicted as a tall, awkward, ungainly man, destitute of culture or refinement; he is misunderstood, suspected, and bitterly opposed; against all this hostility he steadfastly persists in his purpose, and publishes a proclamation of freedom to milli ons of the oppressed ; at last he is put to death by the hand of an assassin ; the weapon employed is described as one entirely unknown at the time of the prediction ; and after his death, the cause for which he sheds his blood attains the most signal triumph.

Would it be possible for us to mistake the verification of such a prophecy? Would it be possible to doubt that these words were inspired by the omniscient God, to whom the future is ever present? Would it be difficult for us to convince an intelligent stranger from the interior of China, whom we might find reading it with wonder, that it certainly referred to Abraham Lincoln? Precisely this was the miracle of prophecy, just fulfilled to the letter, which gave to the apostles of the first century their irresistible arguments. The Ethiopian is reading a prediction in every respect as exact and detailed as the one supposed.   And Philip began at the same Scripture and preached unto him Jesus.   He compared unquestionable facts, of which the stranger had full knowledge, with the prophecy. He demanded the surrender of reason and conscience to the certain conclusion from this coincidence that this was the work of God for the salvation of men. The same facts are before us. Let us make the same comparison, and yield the same homage to divine truth.

The descriptions of the Messiah's origin among men and personal appearance deserve our first consideration. The marring of his form and countenance so that men were shocked at him and despised him, refer to his violent death.   But it appears that he grew up from childhood in a family that had fallen into utter obscurity, like a sprout out of dry ground, and that he had no form nor comeliness that men should look up to him; no beauty that they should take pleasure in him. These words must refer to his humble origin, and insignificant appearance among men. And such a picture could never have been drawn at random by human ingenuity. It is true the Jews were the most democratic people on earth. They loved to think of their first victorious king, coming to his encounter with the uncircumcised giant, armed with nothing but the shepherd's sling. But the lowly origin of the peasant boy was fully compensated by his manly beauty, his magnificent strength, and his impetuous courage. The descendants of Samson, of Saul, of David and of Judas Maccabaeus, could never conceive of a king of Israel with neither form nor comeliness.

The prophet foresees that this description will be incredible —Who hath believed our report? Nor is it incredible to Jews alone. The history of its fulfilment has proved incredible to the Christian world. We have in Christian art an undesigned but marvelous verification of this prophecy. Whence have painters and sculptors derived that form of majesty and face combining the tenderness of woman, the strength of manhood, and the divinity of the Son of God, which rises before us in such masterpieces as the Ecce Homo? They are pure fancies. They are the fancies which artistic minds must form of God incarnate. But they are certainly false. In pictures of the transfiguration, or of the ascension, they may be possible conjectures. As representations of Christ in his humiliation, they are exactly contradictory to the facts. We know nothing of what his appearance was; we know it was not what art represents. Such a man could not appear anywhere, in any period of history, without attracting general attention. But there was nothing in Jesus' form or features to cause any one to turn and look at him a second time. John was on the lookout for the Messiah, but had never heard of this cousin of his as a remarkable man, and "knew him not" until the miraculous sign was given him. It took a miracle to call the apostles to follow him. His brothers could not be convinced by any miracle but the last. The great multitude, led by imagination more than by reason, were fascinated by the miracles, but soon offended by his humble appearance. Few will believe it even now; our readers will probably be shocked that their Saviour is described in such commonplace language. But the fact is incontestable. The Servant of Jehovah had no form nor comeliness that men should look up to him, no beauty that they should desire him.

The Messiah was also to be the greatest sufferer in the world. He is a man of sorrows and acquainted with grief. He is despised, rejected, bruised, smitten with stripes and put to a cruel death. Who hath believed our report? For this is not the prediction of one prophet alone. Centuries before, David had described these sufferings of the Messiah in no less startling language. He was to become a worm, and no longer a man; he was to be surrounded by gaping multitudes scoffing at his anguish; he was to cry out in momentary despair, "My God, my God, why hast thou forsaken me!* The prophet exclaims, in behalf of himself and of all who had foretold these sufferings—Who hath believed our report! Through the captivity, after the expiration of prophecy, during the dark ages of Syrian, Macedonian and Roman oppression, under the Maccabees, under Hillel, to the final destruction of Jerusalem and dismemberment of the nation, the Jews preserved faith and hope in their Messiah, but they never expected a suffering Messiah. With the insignificant exception of the old prophets, of John the Baptist, who was looking for the Lamb of God to take away the sins of the world, and of a few other men and women of exceptional penetration, these unequivocal predictions of the Messiah's extreme sufferings were completely forgotten or else resolutely rejected. Their fulfillment to the letter failed to bring them back to recollection and to faith. Masters of Israel, readers and teachers of Psalms and prophets, stood by the cross and proposed this test of his Messiahship: "If he be the King of Israel, let him now come down from the cross and we will believe on him. He trusted in God; let him deliver him now if he will save him."†   He was not only enduring the very sufferings foretold of the Messiah, but these exact words of theirs are unwittingly repeated from the twenty-second Psalm, and yet they never take it to heart. To the last they reason against the Scriptures they profess to revere.

The apostles were no less blind and slow of heart to believe. They kept echoing the one immovable conviction of the national mind: "We have heard out of the law that the Messiah abideth forever; how sayest thou that the Son of Man must be lifted up?"‡ Near the close of his life, he told them

---

* Psalm xxii.   † Mt. xxvii : 42.   ‡ John xii : 34.

plainly of his impending sufferings, of the manner of his death, and how long he would lie in the grave. They understood none of these things. Peter took him and rebuked him. This complete ignorance and confirmed unbelief in his own times is a miraculous fulfillment of one portion of our prophecy which is wholly lost in the English version.

> " Who of the men of his generation took it to heart
> That he was cut off from the land of the living,
> That the stroke for my people's transgressions fell upon him!"[*]

It is no wonder that such predictions are discredited when they are made. But even when they are fulfilled to the letter, and the blow falls which cuts off from life the Redeemer, and saves the redeemed from death, the eye-witnesses of the event fail to take it to heart.

To the thoughtful mind these disclosures of the public opinion of ages far in the future, and the exact verification of them in history, are proofs that prophecy is miraculous and Jesus is the Messiah, more decisive than coincidences of facts in detail, with their prediction. And yet the latter are convincing enough. Some of these may be briefly enumerated:

The prophets foresee a form of suffering which is absolutely unknown to Jewish law and custom. All the nations of antiquity except the Jews were accustomed to put condemned persons to death by torture. A morbid ingenuity was exhausted to prolong human suffering. The Philistines burned their prisoners alive.[†] The awful picture of the mother compelled to see her seven sons dismembered and burned piecemeal by their heathen tyrant, is undoubtedly painted from the life.[‡] The Greeks reserved for the execution of their own citizens a painless but fatal narcotic. But barbarians and slaves were tortured. Socrates is described by Plato as defending a man for binding one of his slaves in chains, and leaving him to die of hunger and thirst. Demosthenes boasts that he once caused a wretch to be flayed alive. There is no improbability in these stories. The most cultivated men of those times instinctively felt that torture was a necessary ingredient of punishment. The instinct survives in the barbarous execution still practiced in England and America. Christianity is not yet powerful enough to substitute instant death by painless an-

---

[*] Isa. liii: 8.   [†] Judges xv: 5.   [‡] Mac.: vii.

æsthetics for slow strangulation, as the penalty for the worst crimes.

But of all the tortures ever sanctioned by law, nothing can compare with the excruciating punishment employed rarely by Persians, Egyptians, Carthagenians and Macedonians, but never in common use among the Orientals, until Rome extended her conquests to the Euphrates. We have come to venerate the cross. Delicate woman wears its emblem without a shudder. We must divest ourselves of this feeling. We must ask ourselves what it would be for a French lady to fondle among her jewels a model of the guillotine on which her husband died, or for us to erect the scaffold of death as the most conspicuous monument of our cities. We can thus form some idea of the horror which the cross excited in the days of the apostles. It was one of the most familiar objects in their country. In their many journeys, they had often come upon the executioners at their savage work. They had heard the despairing cries of sufferers, lingering all night long in their anguish. This was something worse than heartless cruelty—it was a gratuitous outrage to the merciful institutions in which they were educated. The death penalty under the law of Moses, inflicted alike on citizen and alien, bond and free, was rude but humane. The first stone cast, often destroyed sensibility. Hanging was only employed after death, as additional disgrace. Suffering by torture was more repugnant to their feelings than it is to ours. But the shameful, inhuman torture of the Roman crucifixion, the torture that made Cæsar, the man of blood, faint away the first time he beheld it; the torture that prolonged life and intensified anguish in extreme cases for twenty-four hours—no words can express the revulsion it excited in the soul of an Israelite.

And yet Israelites foretold this punishment centuries before the nation that brought it into general use had grown to threatening power. Nay, centuries before the traditional date of the founding of Rome, Jewish prophecy exclaimed: "They pierced my hands and my feet."* The details of our present prophecy are less precise than this, and the words of Zechariah: "The inhabitants of Jerusalem shall look upon him

---

* Psalms xxii : 16.

whom they have pierced, and shall mourn."* But the scourging by stripes, the laceration of the brow with thorns, and the shocking abuse of his suffering body, as if he were a beast and no more a man, are fearful descriptions of barbarities unknown and unsuspected until the period of Roman tyranny.

But there are three combinations peculiar to this prediction, which serve to fix the date of its fulfilment with absolute certainty. The English version renders the eighth verse : " He was taken from prison and from judgment" ; that is, a mob snatched him out of prison and put him to death without a regular trial. Nothing of the kind occurred in the death of Jesus, and the prophet says nothing of the kind. All authorities are now agreed in giving this as the exact meaning of the original: " He was dragged to punishment by violence, and yet under due process of law." Now how could such a combination of things be possible? Men were killed by mob violence in Isaiah's time. The innocent suffered under process of law. But both forces meeting—the turbulence of a lawless conspiracy, the stern requisitions of that august authority which always defies such anarchy—what human sagacity forecasting all probabilities or possibilities could have stumbled upon such a conjecture? It was no conjecture. It was a divine revelation of the one tragic period in the national history, when unprecedented freedom reigned in strange alliance with despotism. The Messiah was dragged to punishment by violence. The infuriated mob exhausted their cruelty upon the unresisting victim, as if the old times had come back again when every man did that which was right in his own eyes. But all was done under due process of law. The Roman legion stood by, to see that every requirement of criminal law was rigidly executed.

Another combination of two things apparently conflicting is still more remarkable. It appears that others were to be executed with him : " he was numbered with transgressors." It would naturally follow that he would also be buried with them. And this was the intention of his enemies: " They appointed his grave with criminals."† The loathsome receptacle of the dead in the valley of Hinnom would naturally receive

---

* Zechariah xii: 10.

† Isaiah 53: 8. The English version is certainly at fault here. The subject of the verb is indefinite. "Man gab bei Frevlern sein Grab." Knobel. De Wette.

the remains of him who in life was despised and rejected of men. "They gave him his grave with criminals, although he had done no wrong, neither was guile found in his mouth." This is what the writer is going to say. The spirit of God will not let him say it. A strange parenthesis breaks the continuity of his mournful thoughts with one bright beam of light: "They gave him his grave with criminals (still he was with a rich man in his death!), although he had done no wrong!" Could anything but Omniscience have foreseen that in the appalling hour, when the dearest disciples had forsaken him, a rich man, who had hitherto been afraid to avow his allegiance to him, would have had the faith and the moral courage to rescue from nameless sepulture the bruised and lifeless remains of the Messiah of God!

But the third combination is positively unanswerable. And it is disclosed, not in casual remarks, but throughout the whole prediction. He is a suffering and a triumphant Messiah. His death is not the end, but the beginning of his victorious career. In other Messianic prophecies his sufferings are reserved for separate and guarded descriptions, and the impression they made at the time was like that which we all receive now from the unfulfilled prophecies in the Apocalypse, of woes and disasters in the last times. We do not discredit them, neither do we understand them. But on the whole we are sure that our Lord Christ will finally triumph. So the Jews were disquieted by these strange predictions of humiliation and sorrow, but they kept the eye fixed on the assurances in Moses and all the prophets, that the anointed king of Israel would overcome all his enemies and reign in majesty.*

The number and affluence of these promises of his glory were mercifully designed to keep out of sight in times of despondency the most crushing woe that was ever to befall them, their own betrayal and murder of their Messiah. The few shadows thrown upon the canvass by his sufferings were seldom observed, as they served to heighten the brilliant colors in which their everlasting and omnipotent king was portrayed to their ardent hopes.

But here the light and shade are wonderfully blended. The

---

* Gen. iii: 15; xlix: 10; Num. xxiv: 17; Deut. xviii: 18–19; Ps. ii; Ps. xlv; Ps. lxxii; Ps. cx; Mal. iii: 1; Mic. v: 2: Is. ix: 6, 7.

foreground and background are brilliant. The description begins and ends in triumph. There is radiant glory lining the
darkest clouds. Even death and burial do not interrupt his
redeeming work. He makes over his soul as a sin-offering, he
is entombed in the grave of a rich man, and then he prolongs
his days, he beholds offspring, the pleasure of Jehovah prospers
in his hand, he makes many righteous, he secures the great as
his portion and the strong as his spoil! Of whom speaketh the
prophet this? Tragic poetry lingers with fond melancholy
over the untimely death of heroes, who conquer and die with
only distant visions of victory. And history makes grateful
record of the inheritance which posterity receives from the
blood of martyrs.* But here, he whose soul travails in sorrow
beholds the fruit of his suffering and is satisfied. This song of
triumph seems to be inspired by the grave itself. It is precisely when he is dead and buried that the glorious redemption
for which he has poured out his soul begins to attain decisive
victory. Of whom speaketh the prophet this? Has this combination of two contradictory things also been exactly verified
in history?

A few weeks after the crucifixion and burial of Jesus, his
apostles stood before a vast multitude of his murderers, trans-
figured with a new faith and hope. There was a strange reserve of power in their quietness and unhesitating courage to
meet the present emergency, which hushed the turbulent assembly to silence. One of their number, who on the night of
the arrest had become confused by the disappointment of
all his hopes, and swore that he knew nothing about this
Jesus of Nazareth, now steps forth, unrolls the prophecy
we have in hand, and others of the same import, which
he could never be made to understand before, and by just such
a comparison of prediction with fact as we are now making,
without the slightest appeal to passion, convinces every man
of them, who will use his reason at all, that God has made this
Jesus, whom they crucified, to be both Lord and Messiah.

What has made this marvellous change? What has suddenly opened this mysterious page of prophecy? What has mar-

* Knobel begs the question, by adducing this peculiarity of our prophecy as a
proof that it refers to a collective class, so that when one dies others continue the
work.

shalled in their true place all those magnificent descriptions of the Messiah's power and majesty? And that repulsive instrument of torture, from which every instinct of nature and every feeling engendered by their education made them shrink with a shudder ; the cross, the hideous emblem of Jewish submission to Roman supremacy ; the cross, where their beloved lingered in anguish and expired—what has tranformed it all at once into a standard of glory and victory?

For it was not on the day of Pentecost, but on the third day, and in Jerusalem, by the very grave of their lost Messiah, that this sudden revulsion of thought and feeling transpired. To this fact we have the testimony of a historical document whose genuineness no skeptic ventures to question.* Here is a stupendous miracle. The apostles did not expect a suffering Messiah. They could not be made to believe their own prophecies. The very night before he suffered Jesus tried in vain to make them understand that the last things written in our chapter and in the twenty-second Psalm were just coming to an end.† But they could not believe. They buried in his grave their last hopes. And three days later they did believe in a suffering Messiah ! In a few weeks they made thousands of the conspirators against him believe, by an hour's reasoning on the very prophecies that had always been sealed books to them. They have made millions in every age believe on Him. They have revolutionized the religious thought of the world.

One fact only can make such a miracle as this credible—the fact of the resurrection of the crucified Messiah from the dead. This sudden, complete, and enduring change of opinion could never have taken place without this intervening fact. Jesus the Messiah rose from the dead, was exalted by the right hand of God, received and shed forth the promised Spirit, and then convinced his disciples that the true Messiah ought to have suffered all these things, planted in their hearts hopes, never to be shattered again, that he would reign in all the majesty foretold in the prophets.

For this was a literal prolonging of his days. The Holy One was not suffered to see corruption. As soon as he was free from the travail of his soul he welcomed one redeemed soul to Paradise, and began to behold with satisfaction the accession of

---

* 1 Cor. xv : 4.   † Luke xxii : 37.

innumerable offspring to the redeemed family of God. Among them are the great. The mightiest of the earth have been gathered for his spoil. And it is by his knowledge that this righteous servant of Jehovah is making many righteous. The fierce followers of the false prophet extended their conquests with the fury of the iconoclast and the devotion of the mono-theist. But this strange zeal, the offspring of sensuality and of fatalism, has destroyed, never regenerated nor assimilated the ignorant nations of the earth. And Christianity sinks gradually to the level of Judaism and Mohammedism when its central truth, of justification through faith in the crucified Messiah of God, is outraged by bloody conquests, obscured by superstitious displays, or confused by false philosophy. The only trace of Romish missions surviving in many portions of China and Japan, is the suspicion of political conspiracy that clings to the Christian name.

Mere intellectual culture, without this divine knowledge, is no more effective in sprinkling the nations. During the life-time of pastor Harms, his church of farmers and mechanics sent more missionaries to the heathen than all the wealthy congregations in New England, who deny the atonement and divinity of Christ, have commissioned during their whole history. The religion of unbelief is necessarily a religion of self-development, not of self-sacrifice for lost souls. These are not the religions of Prophecy. This Servant of Jehovah is neither the good man of rationalism, nor the awful Judge who cannot be approached without the mediation of saints. He is the sprinkler of nations. He is the bearer of infirmities and sins. He is the conqueror of the great by the omnipotent sway of divine love alone. He is spreading his bloodless and beneficent conquests wherever burdened souls feel their guilt before God, and find peace in the chastisement that was laid upon him. He has taken upon himself the sins of the world; he is making intercessions for transgressors; and in due time he shall see and be satisfied.

Art. III.—THE LAW PASSING AWAY, NOT BY DESTRUC- TION, BUT BY FULFILLMENT.

BY ADDISON BALLARD, Lafayette College.

Two entirely opposite ideas of liberty and progress are in- dicated in the assertion of Christ, that he came not to destroy, but to fulfill the law; coupled, as it is, with that other declar- ation, that " not one jot or tittle shall in any wise pass from the law till all be fulfilled."

These asseverations of Christ were necessary as guides and correctives to both the radical and the conservative thinking of his time. For while it is implied in them that the prog- ress of his kingdom will be marked by the passing away of the law, the important distinction is made between a passing away of it by destruction, and a passing away by fulfillment. This distinction cannot be too clearly seen, nor too strongly emphasized. But in this we shall be helped by first consider- ing how much is embraced in that law which Christ came to fulfill, but not to destroy.

It includes the Decalogue. He did not come to destroy one of those commandments, the whole of which he summed as su- preme love to God and equal love to our neighbor. He did not come to paralyze or perplex the conscience, loosen the bond of virtue, or give new license to sin. Instead of destroying, he aimed to reconsecrate and to establish the law, by paying to it such honor and devotion as, in the nature of things, it could not receive from men or angels. Coming to save sinners, he under- took their rescue only on the condition that justice should re- main uncompromised, and holiness untarnished. Thus did he who was above the law give to it its mightiest sanction by his voluntary obedience and atoning death.

Nor, again, did Christ come to destroy the ritualistic or ceremonial law. He did not destroy the Passover, nor Pente- cost, nor the daily sacrifices of slain victims. He did not say to the Jews, " Leviticus is an antiquated, worthless book. Cut it out of your parchment rolls, and from new copies of the Scriptures see that it be rigorously excluded." Never did he disturb the temple worship, upbraid or ridicule the priests for the too exact performance of their duties, nor turn back any who were going to God's house with either money for its treasury or lambs and turtle-doves for its altar. The temple he purified, but did not destroy. He drove out the men who defiled its sacred precincts by fraud and avarice, but molested none who resorted thither for instruction and worship.

Nor, again, did Jesus come to destroy the civil law. He expressed no purpose or wish to free his countrymen from their political obligations. Never did he pander to the plotting discontent of party faction. Not by act or word did he stimulate or encourage revolutionary zeal. Never did he seek to intensify the uneasy spirit of his time, or rally it to the support of any ambitious scheme of his own. Rather he strove to allay the fever of insurrectionary turbulence by directing the thoughts of his fellow-citizens to that prevailing corruption which was the true cause of their national humiliation. He had no quarrel with government. He did not complain of taxation. He spoke no rebellious words against Cæsar. On an attempt to inveigle him with some disloyal utterance, asking the loan of an imperial penny, with exquisite adroitness he inquired who was represented by the image and superscription stamped upon the coin ; and when it was answered " Cæsar," " Render then," he said, " unto Cæsar the things that are Cæsar's." As much as to say, " Do not expect that I shall justify your impatient bitterness under the restraints of civil order. Do not hope for my aid in dissolving the bands of political authority. I am not come to destroy the civil, any more than to destroy the moral, or the ceremonial, law."

This earnest declaration was an admonition to the progressive thought of those who imagined that the Messiah was to inaugurate a freer and easier system of both religion and government ; that he would discard the old for one entirely new, with precepts less strict, and duties less onerous; who were weary of incessant painstaking in matters of religion ; who were tired of restrictions, tired of exhausting performances, tired of monotonous and never-ending routine ; who chafed under the triple yoke of restraint, service and penalty. For them the law was too severe in its exactions, the prophets were too harsh in their denunciations. They wished that both might be overthrown and pass away. At least, they longed that both might be disarmed : the law of its rigor, the prophets of their maledictions.

There was, however, another class which did not desire this, but desired the contrary; the class which dreaded any disturbance of the old and settled order, deprecated innovation, viewed with indignation any attempt to invalidate transmitted requirements, or modify established usages; the class which insisted that the letter of the law must be punctiliously kept, that the mint, anise and cummin must be scrupulously tithed, that the last gnat must be strained out from every Abrahamic wine-jar.

Now, both these classes of persons were correct in part; in part both were wrong. Both misjudged the nature of that liberty which Christ was to introduce, and the characteristics of that better future which he was to usher in. Yet a good and true idea lay under the expectations of each. What was right and true Jesus interpreted and retained; what was false and injurious he exposed and rejected.

Jesus did indeed come to give freedom. It had been foretold of him that he would open prison-doors and give liberty to them that are bound. Yet not an absolute freedom was this to be, not a breaking of all bands asunder, not a casting away of all cords. His coming was to be, indeed, the signal for the passing away of both the law and the prophets, but this passing away was not by any means to be a *destruction*. They were to pass away only by being exactly and perfectly *fulfilled*. Not the smallest particle was to pass away by subversion, by abrogation, nor even by relaxation. The law was to bind in the letter until fully accomplished in spirit.

This leads us to illustrate more fully the difference between these two modes of disappearance or passing away.

When plaster is thrown over hills of corn, or scattered over wheat-fields, the white patches are visible for a few days, after which they disappear, and the ground is a uniform brown or black as before. The plaster is not, however, destroyed, because its end is fulfilled. It is not lost; it is simply transformed. It reappears in blade, stalk, ear and grain. It passes away, but only by absorption into new and more valuable forms. The leaves that strew the forest do not perish. They fall, but it is only to rise again, mounting in the stems they nourish to loftier heights, and spread out in wider amplitudes of growth. The mould cast about our fruit-trees is heavy, inert, cumbrous; but, sought out and vitalized by the roots, it acquires power and motion and upward impulse, and takes on shapes of glad and living beauty, and wealth of fruitfulness. The great river does not dry up in its course, but pouring on with increasing volume and momentum, instead of failing at its delta, just there where it ceases to be a river, it finds enlargement in the expanding lake or estuary. While as affluent and prophecy the river passes away, as a fulfillment it abides, only with freer scope and larger room. Examples, all these, of passing away by passing into higher and more enduring forms.

Thus it is—to take a single example—that the Passover passed away by passing *into* the Lord's Supper. Thus it is that we still have a propriety and a living interest in all the typical worship of the Old Dispensation, fulfilled and glorified as it is in the spiritual worship of the New. Were the import of these words of our Lord more deeply pondered, there would be fewer of those who "aim to depreciate Christianity by discovering in it as many marks as possible of Jewish weakness and bigotry." It were much better if they would instead turn their thoughts to the nobler object of elevating that older worship by tracing in it the rudiments and promise of Christianity. Was it a day of shadows? Yet shadows are resemblances, and wherein shall the resemblance be found but in the common truths and relations pervading both? By means of an earthly sanctuary and the carnal ordinances growing out of and continually encircling around it, God manifested on his part the same character and government toward his people, and required on their part the same exercises of principle toward himself which he now does under the spiritual dispensation of the gospel. In both alike we see a pure and holy God enshrined in the recesses of a glorious sanctuary, unapproachable by guilty, polluted flesh, except through a medium of powerful intercession and cleansing efficacy; yet to those who thus approach, most merciful and gracious, full of loving-kindness and plenteous in redemption, while in every act of sincere approach on their part are brought into exercise the same feelings of contrition and abasement, of self-renunciation and realizing faith, of child-like dependence and adoring gratitude.*

---

* Fairbairn (Typology.)

The distinction we have illustrated indicates further the methods to be employed, if moral requirements, in their aspect of penal severity, are to pass away from those who are under bondage to them by reason of transgression. That method is not to take part with the criminal against the requirement. It is not to tell him that the law is inhuman and merciless. It is not to sympathize morbidly with him, as if he were the victim of circumstances and a martyr to civil order. It will not do to say to the inmates of our prisons, " The law displays a retaliatory, vindictive spirit to immure you in these dreadful walls, separating you from your friends and affixing to your person the badges of dishonor." To say that would but make the matter a thousand times worse; worse for the criminal, as well as worse for society. It would encourage him in crime, and so complete his ruin. What we desire is, that the law may pass away from the transgressor as an object of dread and of antipathy. And this is to be effected, *not by our destroying the law, but by his fulfilling it.* Offenders must be made to see the wisdom, reasonableness, safety, and greater satisfaction of virtuous citizenship, and to surrender their lawless propensities intelligently and freely. They must be led to see that the attitude of society toward them is not that of gratuitous and hostile menace, but of calm justice and necessary self-defence. Something wonderful is it to see how completely the law, as an object of aversion and terror, passes away from the violator of it so soon as he comes into relations with it of right and willing obedience.

This same distinction leads us on to the true idea of both political and religious enlightenment and freedom, and points out how that idea is to be realized. It instructs us that the millennium of political freedom is not to be brought in through the destruction of government; not by communism nor agrarianism ; not by the burning of decrees, codes and statutes ; not by the tearing down of senate houses and thrones. Political abuses, oppressions, inequalities are surely to pass away, but not through the iconoclasm of mobs. "All the overthrows of all the tyrannies of ancient or modern times were never able to make corruption free. Let changes (of policy or administration) be as specious as they may, the political suffering will only deepen until the personal reform come to redeem the

land." True, abiding freedom can be attained only as men
are instructed into the knowledge of that wherein true freedom
lies; only as they are roused to the intelligent, hearty adoption
of those maxims of industry, frugality and integrity through
which alone law ceases to be compulsion by passing into self-
control.

And, lastly, this far-reaching declaration of Christ gives us
the true conception and method of religious freedom. Everywhere we see men chafing against restraint; against just limitations of human reason and human pride. Everywhere we
see restless desire and determined effort to break bands and
cast away cords. "Are we slaves," demand many, "that we
must be chained down forever by menacing prohibitions, under
which the generations have groaned from the beginning? Are
we never to outgrow the narrow dogmas, hampering superstitions and craven fears of ignorance and childishness? Never
to be done with the rusty, antiquated creeds of our forefathers?
Must we ever gasp in the atmosphere of old and smothering
bigotry? Is it not time that we assert our majority and break
loose from the tyranny of the past?"

There is to be progress. There is to be enlargement of
privilege. There is to be increase of spiritual liberty. But
this is not to come in the manner which many conceive. There
is to be a passing away of prohibition, restraint, dogmas; but
this is not to be by annihilation of any just obligation, nor of
any truth. Christ, the animating, guiding spirit of all true
enlightenment and progress, has purposed that better future
when men shall be free from galling yokes. But he it is who
"verily" assures us that the ends of law are not to be secured
through mere destruction of its outward forms; he is not
deceived, and will not be mocked by that pretended superiority
to the letter which only veils a lack of its spirit. That independence of restraint for which many sigh, is not born of radical resolutions, free-love conventions, nor of hackneyed wholesale denunciations of Calvinism and Puritanism. It comes, and
can come, only as the great underlying, ever-abiding *principles*
of civil order, moral precept and spiritual worship are incorporated into the soul; only as men become free in the love of
right and of order, in perfected love towards God and man.

"In all its sacred constitution," says Huntingdon,* " society

---

*Aspects of Human Society.

preaches the sacredness of law, and so points with reverent finger from human law to the divine, and to Him in whose breast both have their seat at last. By being servants we become children and heirs. By law we gain liberty. By waiting at the foot of Sinai we are taken up into Olivet and Tabor. The tables of stone lean against the cross. Moses is followed by the Messiah. Beyond the valleys of subjection rise the eternal hills of peace. The years of unquestioning and obedient toil ended, there is proclaimed the great Sabbatic festival, where law is love, and order is choice, and government is Fatherhood, and the Ruler's will is the impulse of every heart."

Art. IV.—PRESBYTERIANISM ON THE FRONTIERS.*

By Rev. Joseph F. Tuttle, President of Wabash College.

THE Presbytery of Philadelphia, formed "about the beginning of the year 1705," "consisted of seven ministers" and a score of churches. This germ in half a century had grown into two Synods, which included ninety-four ministers, and a still greater number of churches. From that time "to the commencement of the Revolutionary War the growth of the church had been rapid and almost uninterrupted."

When the differences between the Colonies and the mother country were "submitted to the arbitrament of war," the Presbyterian Church had become a commanding power in the Middle and Southern States. Although Mr. Jefferson, in his autobiography, did not name the Presbyterian clergy in his account of the means adopted "to fire the heart of the country," we know from other sources that they were prominent in the movement. He says: "We were under the conviction of the necessity of arousing our people from the lethargy into which they had fallen, as to passing events, and thought that the appointment of a day of general fasting and prayer would be most likely to call up and alarm their attention. * * *

---

*The Synod of Indiana was formally organized on the 18th of October, 1826. On the fiftieth anniversary of that event the Synods of Indiana South, and Indiana North, met in the First Presbyterian Church of Indianapolis, which occasioned the preparation of this historical sketch.

* * We cooked up a resolution somewhat modernizing the phrases—of the Puritans—for appointing the 1st day of June, 1774, on which the Port bill was to commence, for a day of fasting, humiliation and prayer, to implore Heaven to avert from us the evils of civil war, to inspire us with firmness in support of our rights, and to turn the hearts of the King and Parliament to moderation and justice. * * * This was in May, 1774. * * * We returned home, and in our several counties invited the clergy to meet assemblies of the people on the 1st of June, to perform the ceremonies of the day, and to address to them discourses suited to the occasion."—(Jefferson's Works, I., 7.)

It is sufficient to remark that none responded with greater zeal to this invitation than the Presbyterian ministers of the Middle and Southern States. Until the war began our church had shown great vigor, and was rapidly spreading in all the States south of New England; but with the war came disastrous changes. The ministers were scattered, churches enfeebled, some houses of worship were burned, others desecrated by the enemy, and the community at large seemed unusually afflicted with an extraordinary increase of impiety and infidelity. And hence it was not strange that when the war closed, our church was much weaker than when it began.

From the beginning it had been a missionary church. Its early preachers had been famous for their extensive journeys to preach the gospel in destitute regions. They were not content to visit the regions that could be safely and easily reached, but many of them, with rare courage, went to the very frontiers, which were often rendered dangerous by the incursions of the Indians.

As already intimated, the immediate effect of the war on the church was disastrous, but no sooner was it ended than new life began to show itself. Decayed churches were resuscitated, new ones planted, pastors installed, missionaries sent out, young men of promise educated for the ministry; in a word, the church once more became aggressive.

All this was preparing the way for the more perfect organization of the church in 1788, with the General Assembly as its highest judicatory. And now we reach a period of the greatest interest, both from the positive opposition encountered, and the positive encroachments which our missionaries made on the world.   In the older States the French infidelity had obtained a powerful hold on the minds of multitudes who did not hesitate to denounce " religion as mere priestcraft."   It was commonly reported that Mr. Jefferson himself had said, "that in fifty years the Bible would be no more consulted than an old almanac !"

After the war was over infidel clubs were formed, which included large numbers of wealthy and intelligent men.   These were formed in different States.   The late Mr. Israel Crane of Bloomfield, N. J., once named the societies of this sort, which formed a cordon from Paulus Hook through New Jersey, to Newburg on the Hudson, and many of their prominent members.   He stated that they were violent in their opposition to religion ; and also the remarkable fact that many of these men came ·to a violent death.   The late Rev. Peter Kanouse, of Sussex County, N. J., a very intelligent witness, also made the same statement.   The purpose seemed to be to uproot Christianity.

Nor was this hostility confined to words and sneers, but in some cases showed itself in such sports as horse-races on the Sabbath, and even in defiling the hated meeting-houses outside, and covering the walls within with obscene and blasphemous caricatures.   At least one of the Presbyterian churches in Morris County, N. J., in the immediate neighborhood of one of the most violent of these infidel clubs, was so daubed over with filth and caricatures as to be unfit for use, the desecration not having been discovered until Sabbath morning. Nor was this the only case.   Besides this the ministers were sometimes subjected to violence, and often were treated in the rudest manner by these drunken and bitter opposers.

It would be easy to multiply statements of this sort, showing the condition of the country when our church, beginning to recover itself from the distressing demoralization of the war, renewed its consecration to the great work of preaching the gospel, not merely in the older regions, but in the new and distant sections, both at the South and West.   It is not meant to assert that the difficulty was one entirely arising from the widespread infidelity.   It originated in other causes also, as in the illiteracy of vast numbers in the remote regions, where schools were few and usually poor, and also in the alarming lack of the English Scriptures—a lack so remarkable that the New England clergy were impelled to call the attention of the Presbyterians to it.   There were whole counties in Virginia, North Carolina and Tennessee in which there was not a church of any sort, and it was alleged that there were multitudes of American people who had never attended a religious service or heard a religious discourse.   In some cases, where a traveling minister had preached and then gone away, persons convicted of sin by this means absolutely did not know of a Christian man or woman anywhere within many miles, of whom they could go and ask the question, "What shall we do to be saved ?"

If now we recur to the year 1788, when our General Assembly was formed, we shall find the beginning of great changes.   The printing of the Holy Scriptures in English had been started only six years before ; although against the law of England, two editions of the English Bible had been previously printed in this country, and the circulation of the Scriptures was carried forward to some extent in the destitute regions.

The condition of things in the "Old Redstone Country"—as Western Pennsylvania was called—had become very interesting, as also in Western New York.   Soon after the Revolutionary War the pioneers began to push westward up the Mohawk, toward the valley of the Genesee and the shores of Lake Erie. In like manner the bold frontiermen left the valleys of the Susquehanna and Juniata, and, crossing the Alleghenies, settled in the valleys of the Monongahela and the Allegheny. Of the most thoroughly Presbyterian stock, these last made the " Old Redstone Country" scarcely less famous than Scotland itself for its devotion to Presbyterianism.

It is affecting to note the alarm of the General Assembly near the close of the last century, in view of " the profligacy and corruption of public morals, profaneness, pride, luxury, injustice, intemperance, lewdness, and every species of debauchery and loose indulgence," which prevailed in the older sections of the country, as also " the formality and deadness" of the churches.   And yet the church was getting ready for those glorious revivals which make up so marked a part of her history, during the latter part of the last century and the first third of the present.

If the churches seemed dead in the older regions, the power of God was wonderfully displayed in some portions of the newer, at the West and South. Beginning with " Morris" Reading House"—1740—it seemed as if some irresistible influence were pressing God's people to wrestle with him for Virginia. And if we consider the origin of the movement, its progress and its instruments, we are struck with astonishment. That most extraordinary man, President Davies, although the greatest among them, was the type of the minister who heralded the great revival in Virginia. Throngs followed him . As an orator, even with his manuscripts before him, his friends in Virginia regarded him a greater preacher even than Whitefield. But it was not mere eloquence that enabled him to do what he did. He opened the secret of his power as a pulpit orator to a friend, and we see what was the lock of his strength. When he preached the terrors of the Lord, he himself shuddered; or the love of Jesus, he himself melted into unutterable tenderness. Sometimes more than at others, yet habitually in some degree, when he preached, he felt that he might not preach again, and as if he might step from the pulpit to the judgment-bar.

The war dealt harshly with these churches in Virginia; but about the time our General Assembly was organized there came another season of extraordinary revival power to that region. Although Davies had been away for years, there were on that field such men as William Graham of Liberty Hall Academy, the trainer of Archibald Alexander, and John Blair Smith. If we may credit Dr. Alexander, the American church has had few greater men than these. There was also James Waddell, "the blind preacher," whose eloquence was said to be beyond even the lofty eulogium of Wirt. Nash Le Grand was also a rising luminary, and William Hill, afterward " the patriarch of Winchester," was just coming on the stage. In some respects not one of them was greater than Moses Hoge, whom John Randolph believed to be the greatest divine of his day. Drury Lacy, Vice-President of Hampden Sidney College for a time, was another very remarkable man, who appeared in what was called by Dr. Alexander " the great revival."

And while this work was sweeping over Virginia, young Archibald Alexander wrote that they had " heard of a revival

of the same kind in Western Pennsylvania, under the labors of
the Rev. Joseph Smith, the Rev. John McMillan, and others."
He adds a remark concerning the Scotch Presbyterians of the
Valley of the Virginia, which no doubt expressed a similar
feeling among the Scotch Presbyterians in " the Redstone
country."   The remark was this, "the general impression was
that these religious commotions would pass away like the
morning cloud."   The fear was proved to be groundless, as
applying to Western Pennsylvania.   The religious history of
this region has been very remarkable., There is no part of the
history of Presbyterianism on the frontier more so.   In November, 1758, the Rev. Charles Beatty preached the first
Protestant sermon west of the Alleghenies within the walls of
Fort Pitt.   The mission of Beatty and Brainard in 1763 to the
"distressed frontier inhabitants" in that region, had been prevented by the renewal of savage hostilities on such a scale
that west of Shippensburg every building was burned, many
people were murdered, and many perished in the flight.   Dr.
Wing speaks of the panic among the people as "one of extraordinary extent and intensity."   The people "fled almost
in a body over the mountains toward Lancaster."   (Wing's
Discourse on Presbyteries of Donegal and Carlisle 16, Cen.
Mem., West Penn., 209.)   The author of "Old Redstone"
describes the pitiable condition of those who found refuge at
Shippensburg.

Although a Mr. Anderson, soon after Mr. Beatty's visit—
probably in 1767—was directed to preach to the people in this
region, and the Presbytery of Donegal was ordered by the
Synod " to supply the western frontier with ten Sabbaths of
ministerial labor," yet Dr. Eaton asserts that "the first of the
pioneer ministers who visited this region," to prepare the way
for a permanent settlement, " was the Rev. James Finley, in
1771.   The Rev. James Powers made his first visit in 1774, and
in 1776 removed his family. (Cen. Mem., West Penn., 209,
Sprague III, 327.)

In 1775 the Rev. John McMillan, one of the most remarkable of our pioneer preachers, made his first visit to the Redstone country.   In 1776 he was ordained at Chambersburg, but
on account of the hostility of the Indians did not remove his
family until 1778; but during the intervening period he him-

self visited his selected field of labor to perform ministerial duties among the people in that truly distressed region. He is described by Dr. Eaton as "not attractive in personal appearance; six feet in height, rough-hewn in features, brusque in manner, and with a voice that was like the rumbling of thunder."

The Rev. Thaddeus Dodd, of New Jersey, reached the Redstone country in 1777 the first time, and in 1779, having been ordained, returned for permanent settlement. For a time his labor was within blockhouses and forts, which the people had built for protection against the savages. It is an interesting fact that in these unfavorable circumstances his preaching resulted in a revival, which added forty converts to the church, or rather they professed their faith before the church was organized in 1781. It was an affecting sign of the distresses of the times, that this pioneer preacher, who had seen "converts multiplied" under his ministry, is said to have been on his field four years before he administered the Lord's Supper. In 1783 he held his first sacramental meeting in a barn.[*]

In 1779 a fourth man, the Rev. Joseph Smith, came to the Redstone country who was the worthy co-worker of the three already named, and who was also to exert a powerful influence in that region as a preacher and as one of the founders of Jefferson College. The descriptions given of him show how it was that he should exert such a powerful influence as a pioneer preacher. Winning in manner, imposing in person, powerful in thought, devoted in piety, impassioned in voice and action, he was at times overpowering in his discourses. His work as a preacher was only exceeded in results by his relations to the founding of Jefferson College. McMillan, Dodd and Smith, like Tennent at Neshaminy, taught schools in their own houses, chiefly for the purpose of training young men for the ministry. And it surely was not the smallest of the results they achieved that two colleges—now happily one—grew out of these schools in the wilderness.

In May 1781 the Synod of New York and Philadelphia organized the Presbytery of Redstone, the first west of the Alleghenies. Powers, McMillan, Dodd and Smith—all just

---

[*]*Sprague* iii: 358; *Gillett* i: 262.

described—were its first members. Although its first meeting was appointed to be held at the Laurel Hill Church, on the third Wednesday of the following September, Dr. McMillan says the "first Presbytery that met on this side of the mountains was held at Mount Pleasant on the third week of October, 1783."

Although the church edifices were few and rude for several years, religion greatly flourished in this region. It is true that at times the people were compelled to flee to their blockhouses and forts, and that even in the most favorable times their circumstances were by no means inviting; yet, whether in the grove, the log meeting-house, or the fort, they were favored with some great religious awakenings.

In 1778 the exhortations of Joseph Patterson, in "Vance's Fort," were the means of leading a score to Christ, the germ of the Cross Creek church, of which one of the converts, the Rev. Thomas Marquis, was the pastor for many years. (Cen. Mem., 41.) Dr. Sprague says: "Mr. Dodd's labors throughout his whole ministry seem to have been attended with much more than an ordinary blessing. Besides the regular increase of his church from year to year, there were several seasons of special religious interest which brought in large numbers." He died in 1793, while his church was still feeling the power of a great revival.

Dr. McMillan says that from 1781 to 1794 his churches were experiencing powerful refreshings, and that during those thirteen years numbers were added at every sacramental occasion. Indeed, it may be said that this remarkable man lived in almost a perpetual revival during his ministry of more than half a century. Some of these awakenings were very extensive and wonderful in their power. They spread through Western Pennsylvania, and reached the frontier settlements in Kentucky and Tennessee.

Dr. Carnahan describes Mr. Powers also as not only an effective preacher, but a truly successful one. The Rev. Joseph Smith was one of the most remarkable men that ever preached on any of the frontiers, not only in his piety and gifts as a preacher, but in the truly astonishing effects which often attended his ministry.

If now we add to the names of the original members of the

Redstone Presbytery, such as Joseph Patterson, Elijah Mc-
.Curdy, David Smith and others, who belonged to it or to Presbyteries springing from it—"able, devoted and self-denying
men, whose influence is felt at the present day"—we shall see
why Presbyterianism obtained such an overmastering influence
in Western Pennsylvania. It began with a remarkable population, had remarkable pioneer ministers, and truly remarkable
revivals of religion. The history of it abounds in incidents
that seem like romance. Indeed, if we consider them, the revivals and the results, we have no more thrilling chapter in the
history of our Church than this.

Such were the beginnings of Presbyterianism on the frontiers
of Western Pennsylvania. They were not less remarkable in
Western New York and Northern Ohio, but as the Synod of
Indiana was descended from the Presbyterianism of Western
Pennsylvania, Virginia and Kentucky, we may omit extended
descriptions of that which has exerted so great an influence
in the northern half of Ohio, and in all the States west of
Indiana.

Our sketch will not be complete, as related to the organization of the Synod of Indiana, without referring briefly to the
introduction and history of Presbyterianism in Kentucky.

In 1783 the Rev. David Rice began his labors in Kentucky.
In 1784 the Rev. Adam Rankin and Rev. James Crawford
came to the same field; and in 1786 the Rev. Andrew Mc-
Clure and Rev. Thomas B. Craighead. That year these men,
with an evangelist, the Rev. Zerah Templin, were organized
into the first Presbytery in that State. Not long afterward
came Robert Marshall, a remarkable man, a convert of Dr. Mc-
Millan, and Carey H. Allen. Their journey to Kentucky was
perilous, but its results were great in extensive revivals. The
history of Presbyterianism in Kentucky is full of romantic interest, and is connected with remarkable men. The church
grew in spite of the fanatical scenes connected with the revivals which swept over the State during the earlier years of
the present century, and which occupy a prominent place in
the religious history of that period.

In Tennessee Presbyterianism began about 1785, and its history is not very unlike that in Kentucky. Some of the offen-

sive extravagances of the great revival in the latter State were said to have been imported from Tennessee.

Without proposing to name all the men who were influential in these States, it is sufficient to remark that in both there were men of very great ability, and that they gave to Presbyterianism a hold there which it still retains. And further, the extravagant outbreaks of religious fanaticism seemed to have spent themselves, or to have been corrected, before the pi‹ neers from that region came to this State. In other wor‹ the very best force of these religious movements had be‹ preserved for use in our own State. The wisdom, piety ar. preaching power of Doak and Blackburn, in Tennessee, and Craighead, Marshall, Allen, Blythe, Cleland, Campbell, Cameron, and others, in Kentucky, did much to prepare the way for the introduction of Presbyterianism into the new regions north of the Ohio.

The influence of the Old Redstone Presbytery is at once seen, even before the close of the last century, in the pioneer work in Ohio in 1799, when the Rev. James Hughes began his labor in Eastern Ohio, at Mt. Pleasant. In 1802 the Rev. James Snodgrass began his pastorate at Steubenville. Meanwhile "Father Rice," in 1790, had organized the first Presbyterian church in Cincinnati, but it was not able to build for itself a house of worship until 1792. The Presbytery of Washington—the first north of the Ohio—was organized in 1799, but in 1802 it included only five pastors and thirty-two congregations. If now we trace the history of Presbyterianism in Ohio down to the date of our own Synod in 1826, we shall find that to a large extent its ministers were either directly from Kentucky, or the Redstone. To this general statement there are many exceptions, especially in the northern part of Ohio, where the New England element expressed itself in its relations to our church in "the Plan of Union." The sterner type of Presbyterianism which Dr. Joshua L. Wilson of Cincinnati, Dr. Robert G. Nelson of Chillicothe, and Dr. James Hoge of Columbus represented, fairly embodied the views of the great body of our church in the south half of the State and the eastern counties, of which Steubenville was a center. The church had made great progress in numbers and material strength. It held protracted meetings, sacramental meetings, and even camp-meetings, quite similar to those which occurred in the ministry of McMillan of Western Pennsylvania, and Cleland of Kentucky. Our church in that State then had possession of the two State Universities at Athens and Oxford, at both of which places many were educated for her ministry. It, in a word, was a great power in Ohio.

We have thus sketched in a very general outline the several religious antecedents of the Synod of Indiana. In the eastern portions of the country there was the extraordinary outpouring of God's Spirit as the last century closed, and repeatedly during the first quarter of the present century. The same was true of Virginia, Western Pennsylvania, Kentucky, Tennessee, and Ohio. It might be rash to assert that in these new regions our church grew faster and more vigorously than other churches. It is enough to say that in spite of the sparseness and the poverty of the people, and the occasional outbreak of fanaticism, as in Tennessee and Kentucky, the Presbyterian Church had a vigorous growth, as the Assembly's minutes and other authorities prove. These regions were invested from the very first with all the interest of romance, and attracted to themselves multitudes of people who easily adopted our faith and polity. But whatever we may say of these regions in this respect, we find the antecedents of our Indiana Presbyterianism to have been of the type of the original Synod of New York and Philadelphia, of Virginia, the Old Redstone, and Kentucky. Northern Ohio was powerfully affected by the direct emigration of New Englanders, and also that of Central and Western New York. About the time the Connecticut Missionary Society, and then the American Home Missionary Society, began to send out in large numbers the graduates of New England colleges and seminaries, many of the churches in the western half of Ohio, as well as on the Reserve, were modified into a type that did not harmonize at once with the other type just named. But in either case it was strongly imbued with the revival spirit that frequently shook with Pentecostal power the churches of our order, East and West and South, during the half-century 1780–1830. It is a record of antecedents of which our Synod has no reason to be ashamed.

We now reach the part of our narrative that pertains to the planting and growth of our church to the communities north of the Ohio. In 1787 Dr. Manasseh Cutler had negotiated with Congress for the purchase of several millions of acres, including the tract of the "Ohio Company," in the region of Marietta, and that of Judge Symmes in the Miami country. On the 7th of April, 1788, Gen. Rufus Putnam, with forty-seven men, most of whom were Revolutionary soldiers, landed at Marietta; on the 13th of July Governor St. Clair, by proclamation, defined the boundaries of Washington county, the first in territory of the Northwest; "on the 20th of July the Rev. William Breck, a New England man, and one of the Ohio Company, delivered on the banks of the Muskingum the first sermon ever preached to white men in the present State of Ohio"; and on the 2d of September, with religious and civic ceremonies of an imposing character, the first Court of Common Pleas was opened at Marietta. On this occasion Dr. Cutter officiated as chaplain.

As this eminent clergyman and scientist was on his way to the Muskingum in August, 1788, he had met Judge John Cleves Symmes, at Bedford, Pa., on his way with his family and some colonists to the Miami. The advance guard, under Matthias Denman, of New Jersey, reached Cincinnati in December of this year, Symmes himself not getting there until the following February.

While the New Englanders, under the lead of Putnam, attacked the wilderness of the Northwest at Marietta, and the New Jersey colonists, under Symmes, attacked it at Cincinnati, other brigades of colonists were subduing the Genesee country. From 1761 to 1788 the Moravians, on the Muskingum and on the Cuyahoga, were striving to introduce Christian institutions among the savages. While several sales of lands on the Western Reserve were effected by Connecticut as early as 1788, and to the Connecticut Land Company in 1795, the first permanent settlement in Northern Ohio was not effected until 1796. How difficult of access all these regions north of the Ohio were may be inferred from the length of time consumed by the various bands of colonists to Marietta, Cincinnati, and Cleveland. Whittlesey says that "for thirty years before 1788 rude highways had been in existence over the ridges of the Allegheny Mountains, made by Braddock and Forbes, to the forks of the Ohio at Pittsburgh. From thence they could float onward with the stream"; but in 1798 Edwards and Doane were ninety-two days on their journey from Connecticut to Cleveland. James Kingsbury reached Conneaut in the fall of 1796, by a journey very tedious and even perilous, and such were the straits of his family that during the following winter, the snow being too deep for the oxen, " he was obliged to drag a hand-sled to Erie—thirty miles—and obtaining a bushel of wheat to draw it himself to Conneaut." Atwater says that " Kingsbury and his hired man drew a barrel of beef the whole distance at a single load."*

To reach the new country under the most favorable circumstances during the first twenty-five years after the military colonists landed at Marietta, in 1788, was a tedious and sometimes dangerous undertaking. Dr. Cutter, in the summer of 1788, took about six weeks to travel by sulky and canoe from Massachusetts to Marietta, and the late Mrs. Judge Burnet, as did many other ladies, repeatedly made the journey from New York to Cincinnati on horseback. To reach the great valley in those days was no child's play, and even at a later day, during the existence of the first bank in Chillicothe, so slow were the public conveyances and so bad the roads, that a man who was offered a large reward to get to Philadelphia in time to stop the payment of a draft fraudulently obtained, preferred to make the journey on foot, and actually did so, obtaining the reward!

According to Judge Law, the French had effected settlements, as trading and military posts, both at Kaskaskia and Vincennes, " as early as the year 1710 or '11—probably the former."—(Law's Vincennes, p. 12.) In 1796 Volney found not only the French people at the latter place, but " new settlers from the neighboring States." In 1798 there were twelve families of these new settlers in the place, and in 1799 Col. Henry Vanderburgh, an old army officer, and a citizen of Vincennes, was a member of the Legislative Council, which constituted the upper house of the first Territorial Legislature that met north of the Ohio. The following year the territory of Indiana was organized, including all that now constitutes the States of Indiana, Michigan and Illinois. In 1804 an im-

---

* Whittlesey's Cleveland, p. 264; Howe's Ohio, p. 39.

mense portion of the Louisiana purchase west of the Mississippi was added to it. Dillon says the entire Territory in 1800 was estimated to have a civilized population of 4,875. In 1808 this immense region had about 28,000, of whom some 11,000 were within the present State of Indiana. In 1807, according to Dillon, there were in Indiana "2,524 free white males, of twenty-one years and upward." Of these 2,516 were in the south quarter of the State, or south of a line connecting Lawrenceburg and Vincennes.

The General Assembly of Virginia had granted Gen. Geo. Rogers Clarke, and the men who assisted him in the capture of Vincennes and other French posts, 450,000 acres of land, which are chiefly in Clarke County, Indiana, and in 1783 passed an act establishing Clarksville at the Falls of the Ohio, a few miles above New Albany. In 1801 Clarke County was established. In a private letter the indefatigable historian of Indiana, John B. Dillon, states that "the earlier civilized settlements within the original boundaries of Clarke County were, without an exception, founded on the borders of the Ohio river. A few soldiers were stationed at a small fort that was erected at the site of Jeffersonville before the year 1789, and a block-house, which bore the name of 'Armstrong's Station,' was built in 1795 on the right bank of the Ohio, about seventeen miles above the Falls. Clarksville was a small village in 1808, and in the year 1810 the only *villages* on the Indiana side of the river, between the Miami and the Wabash, were Lawrenceburg, Madison, Jeffersonville, and Clarksville. Charlestown, in Clarke County, and Corydon in Harrison, were both founded about 1808. Very few of the founders of these villages were from New England. The most of them came from Virginia, Kentucky and North Carolina, and a few from Pennsylvania."

In 1791 eight men, bearing the name of Hayes, and two named Miller, settled in the Miami bottom, near Lawrenceburg. In 1796, and again in 1798, other families came to Dearborn County, so that in 1800 the settlements there were quite strong. At Rising Sun, in Ohio County, adjoining Dearborn, we learn from a discourse by the Rev. B. F. Morris, that in 1798 emigrants began to find homes at that pleasant spot on the Ohio. From a remark of Perret Dufour, in his history of the " Early Times in Switzerland County," it may be inferred that the earliest date of settlement there was 1797, although John James Dufour did not begin at Vevay until 1798.

It is very probable that emigrants had settled at other points on the river than those mentioned before 1808, where Madison was located. *The Indiana Gazetteer* of 1849 says: " The first settlements of any consequence were made from 1790 to 1800 in the towns along the river, so that the inhabitants, on the first notice of the approach of the Indians, might escape into Kentucky."—(*Ind. Gaz.*, for 1849, p. 192.)

We have the following dates, which belong to this sketch : The first settlement at Vincennes was about 1710 or '11, and American settlers at the same place about 1795 ; in 1789 there was a small military post at Jeffersonville, and from 1791 to 1800 settlements were made at Lawrenceburg, Rising Sun, Vevay, " Armstrong's Station," and probably at some other points on the Ohio. In 1808 such points as Madison, Corydon, and Charlestown were settled. In 1800 the Territory was organized. The first county—Knox—was organized in 1790, the second—Clarke—1801, Dearborn County in 1802, and Harrison in 1808. " A court of civil and criminal jurisdiction was organized at Vincennes, June, 1779 "—the first after the conquest by Clarke, and on the 4th of November, 1790, " the judges of the Superior Court of the Northwest Territory" appointed regular times for holding courts at Vincennes.— (Dillon 169–297.) " The first school-teacher in Indiana, of whom we have any account, was M. Rivet, a Romish priest at Vincennes, who opened a school at that place in 1793. The second school was near Charlestown, in Clarke County, in 1803. —(Daniel Hough. in Schools of Indiana, pp. 53–4.) And on the 4th of July, 1804, Elihu Stout published at Vincennes *The Indiana Gazette*, the first newspaper within the present bounds of Indiana, Michigan, and Illinois.—(Law's Vincennes, p. 138.)

It is said that in 1804 the Rev. Peter Cartwright preached the first discourse ever delivered by a Protestant minister in Indiana. In the spring of 1805 the Rev. Thomas Cleland preached the first Presbyterian sermon at Vincennes. So far as we know, this was the first delivered in Indiana.

The Territory of Indiana had been organized six years when the Rev. Samuel B. Robertson formed the first Presbyterian church within the present bounds of this State. This was the "Indiana Church," not far from Vincennes. In 1807 a second church was formed, which did not live long. If this weakling, that long since died, be excepted, the second church formed was at Charlestown in 1812. From this time until the formation of the Synod of Indiana, in the autumn of 1826, the growth of our church was not very rapid, but it was healthy. The new Synod included forty churches, among which may be named that at Washington, 1814, Madison, 1815, Salem, New Albany, Livonia, Blue River and Pisgah, 1816, Bloomington, 1819, Hanover, 1820, Evansville, 1821, Indianapolis, 1823, Crawfordsville, Franklin and Columbia, 1824, and several others. Among the ministers who had preached statedly or occasionally we find the names of Samuel B. Robertson, Samuel T. Scott, Joseph B. Lapsley, John Todd, John M. Dickey, William Robinson, Thomas C. Searle, James McGrady, James H. Johnston, William W. Martin, Daniel C. Banks, James Balch, John F. Crowe, Isaac Reed, Baynard R. Hall, Charles C. Beatty, David C. Proctor, George Bush, Samuel G. Lowry, and quite a large number besides.

Until 1824 the Transylvania Presbytery of Kentucky included Indiana. On the first of April of that year the Presbytery of Salem was formed, the first in Indiana, and was attached to the Synod of Kentucky. According to the Salem *Presbytery Reporter*, there were seven ministers in it, and Gillett adds, "most of the churches in the State." In 1825 the original Presbytery was divided into the three Presbyteries of Salem, Madison and Wabash, the aggregate strength of which amounted to fourteen ministers and forty-three churches. (Dickey's Brief History, 21). The Assembly's minutes for 1826 illustrate the weakness of the churches at that time. The eleven churches of Salem Presbytery had a total of 478 communicants; the thirteen churches of Madison Presbytery had 536 communicants; and there was no report from the churches of Wabash Presbytery. From what we know of these churches, we shall do no injustice in saying that the entire membership of all the Presbyterian churches in Indiana did not exceed 1,500.

By the time the Synod was formed, October 18, 1826, some changes had been effected. Our first church had been formed in 1806, and after that such towns as Madison, Charlestown, Corydon, Evansville, New Albany, Princeton, Terre Haute, Crawfordsville, Lafayette, Indianapolis, Columbus, Franklin, and some others had been settled. The Territorial capital had been removed from Vincennes to Corydon in 1813. In 1816 Indiana was admitted into the Union. In 1820 Indianapolis was located, and in 1825 became the capital of the State. The population, from about 11,000 in 1807, had increased to about 250,000 in 1826.

And yet this new country was not very attractive in many respects. The author of the *Indiana Gazetteer* for 1849, referring to the transfer of the State capital from Corydon to Indianapolis in 1825, says it required ten days to perform the journey of only one hundred and twenty-five miles; and, moreover, that " on two occasions, after hours of weary travel, the writer had found himself very unwillingly at his starting-place of the morning; and his good friends, the present Postmaster at Indianapolis, and the Auditor of State, after a day's travel, as they thought, toward Cincinnati, were back at their own town, which they took for some unknown settlement in the wilderness. And another traveler from Ohio, when asked if he had been through Indiana, replied that he could not tell with certainty, but he thought he had been pretty nearly *through* it in some places! "

Although emigration was making inroads into the northern half of the State, the most of the population was thinly scattered over the southern half, and, according to Dillon, the most of it was from the slave States; and in spite of the ordinance of 1787, there were in Indiana nearly 200 slaves in 1826. As for the condition of the country, we may learn it from the statements of those who visited it in early times.

In 1822 the Rev. John Ross made a missionary tour from the Miami valley to Fort Wayne, and he describes the journey. One night the wolves howled about their little encampment, and when not far from their destination they were met by a terrible snow storm; their wagon wheels were frozen fast in the mud; they sought in vain to light a fire, and at last, leaving their wagon with its contents in the care of a dog, they made their way to Fort Wayne, reaching it late at night. And yet, the brave man, the next day being the Sabbath, preached twice in the Fort. Between 1822 and 1826 he made five such missionary tours to Fort Wayne.—(*Williams' Fort Wayne,* 13).

This venerable patriarch passed away at Tipton, Indiana, March 11, 1876, aged ninety-two years, having spent more than half a century in the ministry in this State and Ohio. His history is one of singular interest, and his ministerial life was crowned with unusual success.

When Dr. Post reached Logansport, Christmas day, 1829, it was "a town of thirty or forty families—a community number-ing between two and three hundred. Dispersed in the coun-try were eight or ten log cabins, holding the entire residue of Cass county. We were literally on the confines where civil-ized man had overtaken the savage, and they had stopped for a day and struck hands. . . . Wild forest and prairie, un-occupied by the white man, stretched away westward over Il-linois to 'the Father of Waters,' and in the direction of the Great Lakes to an almost indefinite expanse; toward the rising sun, and the remote southeast and south were spread out 'the solemn woods.' Some rude fixtures of the French trader were found at long intervals on the large water-courses. On nearly every side lay a wide extent of unorganized terri-tory, and all around was a dark, massy solitude. Out of Fort Wayne and Logansport there were not in Indiana, north of the Wabash, 300 inhabitants. From several points of the com-pass a traveler, day after day, might have taken his course in a direct line to this place without his eye being cheered with even the roughest quarters of the backwoodsman." He de-scribes his journey in December, 1829, from Madison to Logansport on horseback, requiring nine days of hard rid-ing, "with roads which were almost a continuous morass—long, weary miles of a deep, half-liquid compound of earth, water, snow, and ice—roads without bridges, high waters, impassable fords, and with 'swimming horse,' and sometimes his rider, too, through full angry currents."—(*Post's Retro-spect,* 9, 10.)

If we had time to cull hints and more positive statements from various sources within reach, we should find that Indiana, although ten years a State in 1826, was a vast wilderness that was only just beginning to tremble before the axe of the pioneer. In 1822 that truly able man, the late Mr. John Beard, found only one cabin between Indianapolis and the cabin or two built at Crawfordsville. And that very year Mr. Charles Beatty, now our venerable patriarch at Steubenville, riding from Terre Haute to Crawfordsville, to preach the first sermon there, and to perform the first marriage in the county, encountered several wolves near where the village of Warrland now is, and performed both the religious services referred to in an unfloored cabin which had not even a door. The bridegroom of that Sabbath, hearing that a minister was to be there, had gone the week before to Indianapolis to get his license—the eleventh issued in Marion county—and the journey required nearly four days' hard riding, although the distance was only a little more than forty miles.

As late as 1829, Dr. Thomson, our missionary in Syria, took three hard days' riding to make that same journey one way. And even as late as 1834, a member of one of the Wabash College families was two days in the stage-coach going from Crawfordsville to Lafayette, and thence made the journey by steamers down the Wabash and up the Ohio, and thence by stage-coach to New Hampshire. Chicago was a trading post, to which farmers in Central Indiana hauled their wheat, exchanging a load of it for a barrel or two of salt. The hogs of Indiana were driven to Louisville and Cincinnati for market at ruinously small prices; and the cattle and horses were driven over the mountains to Eastern markets by journeys so long and expensive that the producers had but little left them when the expenses were paid.

As an illustration of the times, it may be added that Maj. Ambrose Whitelock, for several years land receiver at Crawfordsville, was accustomed to put in kegs the specie he received for lands, and to send large sums of money in this shape by a teamster without guard to Louisville, a distance of nearly two hundred miles. In one case the wagon was upset and one or more of the kegs burst. The man gathered up the shining treasures and delivered the whole safely to the Government office at Louisville.

While the local history of Indiana has received no very

general attention, there are a few historical discourses which abound in sketches of the State as it was fifty years ago.*

Dr. Beatty, in 1822, missionated from Vincennes to Crawfordsville, but he found only here and there a settlement. That indefatigable itinerant and organizer of churches, the Rev. Isaac Reed, everywhere found himself in the wilderness, except as occasionally he emerged into the small settlements that were indeed "few and far between." The pioneer was raising his axe against the forest, but as yet he had made little impression. It was still a "massy solitude."

In his fine paper on the history of the first Presbyterian Church in Franklin, Judge Banta presents to us the picture of the first party that settled at that point in 1823, " wearied and foot-sore," and forced to camp out for the night ; and such were the trials from deep mud, undrained swamps and dense forests, that "we may well imagine that it was in many instances a very struggle for life."—(Pres. Ch., Franklin, 122-5.) In 1824 Rev. Baynard R. Hall, in describing Bloomington, says that "east of it was an uninhabited wilderness for forty miles." And as early as 1829, when the Rev. David Montfort went with his family from Oxford, Ohio, to Terre Haute, the journey of 160 miles was "through an almost unbroken forest."

Mr. Reed, in 1827, describes some of the largest towns in the State. Madison and Charleston had about 1,200 people each; Jeffersonville, 800 ; Vincennes, 1,000 ; Terre Haute—"a handsome little village of white buildings"—300 ; Bloomington, 400 ; Indianapolis, 800. It has " a well-finished meeting-house and settled minister," and "the attention to good order and to religion is favorable." Mr. Reed did not see much in the common schools to praise, and the State has "many men and women who cannot read at all." But there was much " true hospitality. There is much equality among the people. * * A man is an idle and lazy fellow if he does not soon get a farm of his own. Money is scarce and provisions low. It is very easy to lay out money, but very hard to get it back again."

---

*The sketch of Fort Wayne by Jesse L. Williams, Dr. Post's Retrospect, Williamson Wright's Pioneer of Cass County, Judge Banta's Franklin, Father Johnston's Forty Years' Ministry in Indiana, are charming specimens of our local historical literature. There are books and documents of a similar kind and walue.

And this very year that the Synod was formed Mr. Reed describes his journey out of Indiana in the month of May. He speaks of leaving Indianapolis and "entering the woods on the road to Centerville." It is difficult to realize, as we are now whirled so easily over the railway between the two points named, the sorrows of our pioneer on his way to happier regions at the East. One day he only traveled thirteen miles. At some places he found the high waters had made great confusion among the log causeways, floating the logs in every direction. Often the mud was so deep that his wife had to get out and make her way on foot, while he "led the horse by the check rein, walking before him, and frequently with the mud and water as deep and deeper than his boots!" On the fourth day he passed through Centerville, sixty miles from Indianapolis.

To go from Owen county, in this State, to Essex county, in New York, had taken Mr. Reed "eight weeks and a day."—(Reed's Christian Traveler, 222–233, etc.)

These facts are mentioned as affording glimpses of Indiana as it was fifty years ago. It was on the frontier, or nearly so, and it was famous for the obstacles which hindered rapid locomotion. Goods were wagoned from the Ohio, or brought up the White or the Wabash, with great labor and cost. The produce of the country was worth little on account of the distance of the markets and the difficulty of reaching them. We can hardly do honor to the pioneer work of those who organized our first Synod without thus recalling the Indiana of half a century ago, so different from the Indiana of to-day.

The small numbers and strength of our church have already been referred to, and it will be readily seen how small the figures are in comparison with the present ; but Father Johnston, in his delightful "Forty Years' Ministry in Indiana," says that the Salem Presbytery in 1825, within eight months, "held no less than eight distinct meetings at points remote from each other. * * * In performing these laborious and self-denying duties, so important in their bearing on the spiritual interests of our State, these fathers and brethren spent weeks of precious time and traveled many hundred miles. * * * At that time traveling was for the most part on horseback, and often with no little difficulty even in that way. But labor and toil and difficulty did not deter those indefatigable pioneers from the full discharge of the duties, which the circumstances in which they were placed required at their hands."

The Rev. Isaac Reed says—"My travels in Indiana in 1824 were 2,480 miles." Now he is at Salem, or Charlestown in the far south, and then at Indianapolis or Crawfordsville, and anon at Terre Haute, or across the river at Paris in Illinois. The first licensure was at Charlestown in 1824, and the first ordination at Bloomington in 1825. In this last year—1825—Reed says " there were six ordinations in the Presbyterian Church in Indiana." He attended four of them himself. It is really wonderful to note this man's journeys on horseback through this great wilderness, but it was only more wonderful than the tours of other "preachers of the Word" in that we have his record of what he did, while we have little record of what they did. Such men as Proctor, and Dickey, and Crowe, and Martin, and Johnston, and others, accomplished numerous long journeys. Proctor rode regularly for a time between Bloomington and Indianapolis. Johnston made frequent missionary tours; Dickey was constantly in the saddle, riding from " The Pocket" to " Mouth of Eel"; as was also Crowe, who made at least one extended journey through Indiana and Illinois, to explore the country with reference to the planting of churches. And this was only a specimen of his missionary tours.

These missionary scouts were soon joined by others as brave— James Thomson of Crawfordsville, James N. Carnahan of Dayton, Martin M. Post of Logansport, Edward O. Hovey and Caleb Mills, of Wabash College, David Montfort of Franklin, and many others. Montfort was a marvel of heroic power and enthusiasm, who on account of his crippled condition had to be lifted on and off his horse, and yet made long missionary journeys, not only among his own people, but in the State. Jesse L. Williams, of Fort Wayne, then a young surveyor, who had stopped over Sabbath at Knightstown, heard this resolute and able man preach twice. It was no uncommon thing, as related by Dr. Cleland and others, for these missionaries to lose their way in the woods, or to be overtaken by night far from any habitation. So far from esteeming the hardship as great, they felt themselves happy if they had flint and tinder with which to kindle a fire both for warmth and protection.

Dr. Post, in his "Retrospect," speaks of "the long rides several times every year to Presbyteries and Synods, often distant from sixty to two hundred miles," and of "the missionary excursions," even as far as the Lake, "organizing churches, preaching and exploring."

And did space permit it would not be difficult to cull from many sources other incidents, which show how great were the embarrassments and hardships of our pioneer ministers in this State. And yet Dickey, and Martin, and Crowe, and Johnston, and Carnahan, and their worthy peers, could have adopted as their own the eloquent words of Dr. Post, who has just gone to his rest. In his "Retrospect" he said: "Nor have I regretted my choice of a place. Unworthy to serve Christ anywhere, I have found here reasons for attachment, and *have made no sacrifices, none which can be mentioned, when the eye is fixed on Gethsemane and Calvary.*"

Father Johnston, in his "Forty Years' Ministry," describes the organization of the Synod, as one who took part in the act, and I quote his words. After showing that the Presbytery of Salem had been divided into three, as already referred to, he says that "by an act of the General Assembly of the Presbyterian Church, adopted May 29th, 1826, these three Presbyteries, together with the Presbytery of Missouri, were constituted into a synod denominated the Synod of Indiana. Agreeably to the appointment of the General Assembly, this Synod held its first meeting at Vincennes on the 18th day of October, 1826. There were present at that meeting eight ministers and twelve ruling elders. Other brethren would have attended had they not been detained at their homes by sickness. The following are the names of the ministers who were permitted to be present at that first synodical meeting ever held west of the State of Ohio and north of Mason and Dixon's line: From Salem Presbytery but one minister attended, Tilly H. Brown; from Wabash Presbytery there were three, Samuel T. Scott, George Bush and Baynard R. Hall; Madison Presbytery furnished the same number, John M. Dickey, John F. Crowe and James H. Johnston; from Missouri Presbytery, which included the whole State of Missouri, the only minister present was Salmon Giddings of St. Louis; while from Illinois, whose entire territory constituted the great central portion of the Synod, not a solitary representative appeared."

And such were the small but grand beginnings of the synodical organization, which included nearly all there was of Presbyterianism in Indiana, Illinois and Missouri, not to speak of Michigan, with all the West and Northwest. On the territory defined as belonging to the Synod of Indiana, as it was fifty years ago, with its four feeble presbyteries, there are now six synods and twenty-four presbyteries, including seven hundred and fifty-eight ministers, nine hundred and ninety-four churches, and seventy-eight thousand seven hundred and eighty members. In all other respects the growth has been as marked.

It is not necessary to carry this investigation farther, nor to enter into details at any great length. Indiana, fifty years ago, was described in the Assembly's narrative as having " an immense territory lying waste without laborers to cultivate it. Now and then a traveling missionary scatters the seed of the kingdom." And yet the churches in these vast wastes were not only few, but in one year five became extinct for want of ministers. The General Assembly speaks of these destitutions in Indiana, and the feeble churches dying for lack of ministers. And was it so strange that with our highest judicature saying officially, " *they are our brethren, and they cry to us for help,*" that such a want should have pressed from the agonized and beseeching churches in the wilderness its *two Christian colleges?*

Of what has occurred since the 18th of October, 1826, be it bright or dark, be it sweet or bitter, be it of the nature of aggressive warfare or unfraternal strife, it is not necessary here to speak. In the reminiscences of those times there is much both to gladden and to sadden us; many things we could wish were undone; but, on the whole, we shall find that the Presbyterian Church has made progress in all respects, in the number of its churches and their strength, in its financial and moral power, in its educational institutions, and in most other respects. There are now single churches in this State that have more wealth than all our churches in 1826. There are men, not a few, who commune at our altars, who singly can endow either of our colleges, or build institutions for the unfortunate. We are not poor, and if we will, we can overshadow the State itself by the magnitude of our endowments and the magnificence of our churches. The Synod of 1826 was weak in its wealth and its constituency, but it was glorious in its missionary zeal and self-denial. The Synod of 1876, inspired with the spirit of the men of '26, have numbers, intelligence, organization, wealth, force to make our church " fair as the moon, clear as the sun, and terrible as an army with banners." With not an exception, the ministers who met in Vincennes just fifty years ago, are gone. A year ago our venerable Johnston was the sole survivor, but he, too, has fallen asleep, full of years and glory. Brown, Scott, Bush, Hall, Dickey, Crowe and Giddings had all been summoned away, and Johnston alone lingered. And now he, too, has taken his departure to join the fellowship of the saints in heaven. And if we add another decade, bringing our church down to that period when she was about to be met by divisions, we find that the fathers who belonged to that pioneer period, with only here and there an exception, have joined the great church on the other side of the flood. A few men remain, crowned with the glories of long service in this field, like Carnahan, and Hovey, and Mills, and Chase, and Henry Little, and Hawley, and Kent, and Stewart, and Scott. But, one by one, they are passing away. We have just laid in his own new tomb the remains of our St. John, our dear and venerable Post, and also our patriarchal Ross. And thus they pass away into the heavens, but as the fathers of our church—the pioneers—leave to us the work they so well begun ; and we shall prove our admiration of them by carrying forward with great zeal and power the work they loved and ennobled, to a glory they never dreamed of.

Art. V.—TOTAL DEPRAVITY.

By Henry A. Nelson, D. D., Geneva, N. Y.

Assuming that human nature, as found in every individual specimen of it, is depraved, the degree or the intensity of this depravation becomes a subject of serious inquiry. If all mankind are morally and spiritually depraved, to what extent, or in what degree, are they so? If we must confess that our human depravity is universal, must we couple with this the confession that it is total? As God's ambassadors to men, must we not only affirm the universal depravity of mankind, but must we also insist that it is a total depravity?

In the very beginning of such an inquiry it behooves us to remember that what is true on this subject is likely to be offensive to those of whom it is true—to men generally—to ourselves. There can be no reasonable doubt that mankind are much more depraved than it is pleasant to them to believe or to be told. We certainly have a natural pride which repels the imputation of depravity, of perverseness, of sin. We ought not to think it strange if the natural pride of our hearts renders it difficult to accept the view of ourselves which our understandings may find to be actually given in the Bible. This liability is well stated by Dr. McCosh:* "We are afraid to examine ourselves, lest humbling disclosures should be made. And when we have the courage to examine our hearts, prejudice dims the eyes, vanity distorts the objects seen, the treacherous memory brings up only the fair and flattering side of the picture, and the deceived judgment denies the sinful action, explains away the motives, or excuses the deed in the circumstances."

In all human jurisprudence this liability to too favorable judgment of ourselves is recognized and guarded against. Nothing could be proposed which would universally be pronounced more absurd than to allow any man a place on a jury whose verdict would involve a judgment upon his own character. All literature, and all conversation, are pervaded by the sentiment that no power has gifted us, or is likely to gift us, with the ability "to see ourselves as others see us," or to see

---

*Divine Government, p. 362.

ourselves altogether as we are. It clearly is our duty to be carefully on our guard against prejudice in favor of ourselves, while we study the question now proposed.

The teachers of religion must also be faithful to the doctrine of the Bible as they find it, however distasteful it may be to those to whom they are sent. The surgeon must acquire fortitude to cut steadily and firmly, undeterred by the writhings or the cries of his patient. True kindness requires this of him. On the other hand, no doubt, this is a subject on which the truth may be spoken with unnecessary harshness; may be presented in a manner and in language needlessly offensive. Thus may hearers or readers be prevented from attending to truth, which it is necessary for them to receive in order to that conviction of sin without which they will not seek the Saviour.

It is our duty to understand this truth so thoroughly, and to learn to state it so justly and so well, that, on the one hand, we shall not needlessly repel men from the consideration of it ; nor, on the other hand, shall we explain it away, take all its own proper pungency out of it, and reduce it to a soul-destroying opiate. With such care, and in such a spirit, let us proceed with the inquiry, Are all mankind by nature *totally depraved?*

1. It is not true that all mankind are depraved in the highest degree that is possible. In other words, it is not true that all are as bad as they can be. This is not true, indeed, of any one of the race. On the contrary, the Scriptures themselves affirm of some very bad men, that they are still growing worse. "But evil men and seducers shall wax worse and worse, deceiving and being deceived."—2 Tim. iii : 13. This would clearly be impossible if they were already as bad as they are capable of becoming.

2. It is not true that all mankind are equally bad. Many passages of Scripture indicate various degrees of sinfulness or ill-desert in different persons and classes of persons. Particularly the scriptural representations of God's judgment show that it will be a discriminating judgment; that in the day of judgment it will be " more tolerable " for some than for others. —Matt.: xi : 20, 24, x : 15. xii : 41, 42.

3. It is not true that every movement of unregenerate human nature is, *per se*, sinful. We have the record of our Saviour being much pleased with a man of whom, neverthe-

less, He said that he "lacked one thing"; and the sequel con-
strains us to think that it was a fatal defect in his character.
Mark : x : 21.

Says Dr. McCosh: " Does any man stand up and say, I was
in a virtuous State at such and such a time, when I was defending the helpless and relieving the distressed ? We admit at
once that these actions are becoming.   .   .   If we could
judge these actions apart from the agent, we should unhesitatingly approve of them."*

Some one may say that if we cannot judge the actions apart
from the agent, we have no right to judge the agent except by
his actions, and that even God will judge every man " according to his deeds." This is true, for it is Scripture. But, doubtless, it is the whole of a man's deeds by which God will judge
him, and we ourselves may find reason to question, in many
particular cases, whether a man's doing a particular virtuous
deed proves him to be, even at that time, in a soundly virtuous
state.

4. It is true of every unrenewed man that the ruling principle of his life is wrong. In the last analysis this ruling
principle has ascendency over the whole man, over all the powers and susceptibilities of his being, and penetrates with its
pernicious influence his entire character. The tendency of one
in such a condition obviously is to grow worse. The natural
proclivity is to evil. We are held back from this, or lifted out
of it, only by some gracious power coming upon us from without ourselves; coming down upon us from above. The most
amiable of young men, the most lovely of young women, the
sweetest babe that smiles back its mother's smile, if left forever
to the purely natural development of what is in it by nature,
will (we have scriptural reason to believe) become as bad as
Satan. The leprosy may yet have appeared only in one small,
faint spot; nay, to human eyes it may yet be quite invisible,
but being in the system, its malign power is equal to the fearful
work of corrupting every member and organ, and reducing the
whole body to a mass of loathsomeness. It possesses the
whole body, and in due time will assert its possession. So does
sin reign over the whole man. So does it possess and corrupt

---

*Divine Government, p. 360.

man's entire nature.   Gen. vi : 5 ; Prov. xxi : 4 ; Eccl. viii : 2 ;
Rom. vii : 18, viii : 7 ; 1 Cor. ii : 14.

We have spoken of the ruling principle of the unregenerate
man's life being wrong, and vitiating his whole character.
It is not unreasonable to ask us what that wrong ruling principle is.   It may not be possible to give any simple and brief
answer which is not liable to convey an erroneous impression.
If required to answer in one word, the word shall be *selfishness.*
We would define this as supreme regard for self.   Yet it is not
a regard for one's own true welfare.   It often involves reckless
disregard of this, or mad shutting of the eyes to it, and rushing
on destruction, giving one's self up to present gratification,
however destructive that gratification may be known to be.   It
is doubtful whether there has ever lived a more unselfish man,
save the man Christ Jesus, than he who wrote as the foremost
of his seventy famous resolutions, "Resolved, that I will do
whatsoever I think to be most to God's glory, and *my own good,
profit and pleasure,* ON THE WHOLE ; without any consideration
of the time, whether now, or never so many millions of ages.
hence ; to do whatever I think to be my *duty,* and most for the
good and advantage of mankind in general, whatever *difficulties*
I meet with, how many and how great soever."*   No selfish
man ever had such a wise regard for *his own welfare,* ON THE
WHOLE.

Perhaps we should be viewing our subject more advan-
tageously from the opposite direction, viz. : if we should consider the want of any right governing principle in the natural
man.   Such a system of powers as the human soul is, working
on evermore without a right governing principle, is as fearful
an example of organized disorder as can be imagined.

We may not all agree in our statements of what should be
the governing principle of the human soul.   The difficulty of
agreement, however, will be found with reference to the ultimate ground of obligation, and not in respect to the rule for
man's practical guidance.   That the will of God is right in
every case, none will question, whether they think that right
is constituted by his will, or is determined by his nature, or is
the eternal principle to which his will and his nature eternally
conform, and *therefore* deserve the supreme regard which he

---

*Life of Pres. Edwards.

claims. In either view of that question, the known will of God is man's rule, and God himself ought to be the supreme object of man's regard and affection.

Dr. McCosh, and his great instructor, Chalmers, have impressively exhibited the lack of " Godliness" as the preëminent feature of universal human depravity. They have shown how radically defective that virtue must be which concerns itself never so scrupulously, equitably, or tenderly with the obligations which exist toward one's fellow-creatures, but is indifferent, or negligent, or obdurate toward God. Are they not right in this? Is there not some radical defect in a morality which finds all its applications earth-ward, and none heaven-ward ; all man-ward and none God-ward ; which renders its possessor scrupulous in his dealings with men, generous and kind to them, but content to live in confessed neglect of his obligations to God?

Dr. McCosh affirms these general principles : (1.) " That in judging of a responsible agent, at any given time, we ought to take into view the whole state of his mind. (2.) That the mental state of the agent cannot be truly good, provided he is in the meantime neglecting a known obligation."* He illustrates these principles by applying them to several supposed cases. (1.) " A boy arrived at the age of responsibility, running away from his parents without provocation of any kind." All the generous and chivalrous behavior of such a lad among his fellows cannot put him into a sound and good moral condition while he persists in his truancy. " All his kindness will not draw a single smile of complacency from the rightly constituted mind till he return to his father's house and to his proper allegiance."

(2.) A person who has unjustly got possession of a neighbor's property, and is then "very benevolent in the use which he makes of his wealth." We may instructively extend this illustration to men who grow rich in public offices, in which they handle the public revenues, and are then admired by the unthinking for the liberality of their expenditure, and their gifts to the poor. The silly sheep bleat their admiration and gratitude for the corn lavishly fed to them, not careful to reckon with how small a part of the price of their own fleeces it has been purchased.

---

*Divine Government, pp. 357-358.

But surely no thoughtful and intelligent citizen approves " the whole state of mind" of a man whose liberality is shown in the use of money which he dishonestly stopped on its way to the public treasury.

Dr. McCosh adduces several other illustrations, showing very clearly " how the moral faculty cannot approve of an agent, even when doing an act good in itself, provided he is in a bad moral state, and living, meanwhile, in neglect of a clear and bounden duty."

Perhaps those principles may be brought home more impressively to us by an illustration drawn from our national experience. There were men, a few years ago. in rebellion against the Government of our country, whose private lives were unstained by vice, and were adorned with social and domestic virtues and graces. They were chivalrous in their intercourse with companions in arms, merciful to prisoners of war, chaste, temperate, truthful. Were all these private virtues of any account to the Government so long as they were in arms against it? In dealing with them as rebels, could the Government abate anything of its severity on account of any good deeds done in rebellion? Doubtless we must feel a less degree of abhorrence toward such men than toward any who to rebellion superadded cruelty to helpless captives, or wanton outrages upon loyal households, or indulgence in low and degrading vices. Yet toward the Government against which they were in rebellion their character *as citizens* was utterly lost. The forfeiture was complete, entire, total.

Now let us recollect that in this earthly relation of citizenship a man's entire character is not involved. His whole duty is not included in loyalty to the Government of his country. But loyalty to God does include all his duty, and does involve his whole character.* Disloyalty toward the Divine government is universal moral failure. Wrong there, at the centre, a man is wrong throughout. He may not actually do wrong in every case, but he is totally destitute of any principle which would insure his acting right in any case where the inducement to wrong is great enough.

These observations show a just sense in which the depravity of mankind is indeed a total depravity. They fitly illustrate

---

*Eccl. xii. 13.

the sense in which that affirmation is made by Calvinists. We are not to be understood as affirming that all mankind are equally wicked ; nor that any one man is as wicked as he can be ; nor that there is no difference in moral character between men and devils. All such statements are uncandid caricatures of Calvinism, or ignorant exaggerations, or unfortunate misapprehensions of it.

Nevertheless, we ought candidly to recognize the liability to occasion such misapprehensions by harsh or unguarded statements. In preaching and in writing, we are bound to consider what impressions our words are likely to make upon our actual hearers or readers, in their actual circumstances, and with their actual culture, antecedents and prejudices. It is not enough to consider only what impressions they are entitled to receive, or would receive, if they were all capable of estimating our words with grammatical and logical precision. We ought to do all in our power, with the most patient care and painstaking, to ensure true impressions, even to ignorant, or weak, or prejudiced hearers.

This may depend upon the state of our hearts, even more than on the accuracy of our thinking, or the rhetorical faultlessness of our statements. Are we chiefly desirous of confounding and silencing opponents, or of winning and saving souls— winning them unto acceptance of the truth, that they may be saved by its power, begotten through it into sonship to God?

If we believe in total depravity as a matter of our own experience, the awful burden of which we share with our hearers; if we solemnly, and humbly, and thankfully feel that from such utter ruin and helplessness Christ has redeemed us, and the patient love of the Holy Spirit is delivering us, this view and this feeling will not probably be misunderstood. If we address our hearers, not with harsh and imperious objurgation, but with respectful, sorrowful, tender sympathy—not as if we forgot that the human nature is our own nature, but confessing that we, as well as they, need deliverance from its guilt and misery —if we speak to men thus humbled, awed, burdened, they will be apt to get our true meaning. The painful but necessary truth will be apt to reach them, however rhetorically imperfect our utterance of it may be. They will be apt to feel themselves as depraved as we honestly confess ourselves to be.

Neither they nor we will dicker and chaffer about the adjectives with which we shall define our depravity, and try to express our sense of its intensity.

The question may still arise, " Shall we use the terms *total depravity* in describing the actual moral condition of unregenerate man ?" We have no categorical answer to this question. The obligation to do our best to make the truth understood, to give truthful impressions to the minds actually addressed, may forbid giving one and the same answer to that question for all times and places. The use of that phrase would not make the same impression on all classes of hearers; it would not convey the same idea to all classes of minds. We cannot acquit ourselves of the responsibilities which rest upon us in the pastoral care of souls in any so summary and easy way as would be implied by a categorical answer to such a question.

There have been ministers who accounted the frequent affirmation of *total depravity*, in those very terms, necessary to fidelity in preaching. They could not see any variation from this usage in any other light than that of an attempt to soothe and flatter those who need to be humbled and alarmed. The omission of those terms from any discourse relating to the natural man's spiritual condition would make them suspicious of its orthodoxy. Yet those terms are not found in the Westminster Confession of Faith, nor in the Shorter Catechism, nor in the Larger Catechism, nor in the Bible. Doubtless we do find in the Bible, and in those admirable summaries of its doctrines, all which is intended to be expressed by those terms, as orthodox writers and preachers have used them. This justifies the use of them wherever they are likely best to convey the truth they are intended to convey, or with such explanation as will guard them against making a false impression, injurious to souls that need faithful and careful leading. But it does not justify requiring any man to use them on pain of having his orthodoxy impeached or suspected, if he believes that he can more successfully convey that truth to the minds of his hearers by the use of any other terms. Every one of us has the same liberty, which our brethren of the Westminster Assembly took, of judging for himself, before God, by what terms he can most surely and most effectually convey the truth into the minds for the instruction of which he is responsible.

The necessity of explaining these terms, which experience has made apparent—the tendency of almost all explanations to begin by declaring that the terms do not mean what experience shows that many persons take them to mean—goes far to justify any preacher in the endeavor to find other terms to express the truth which these terms are intended to express, without the erroneous impression which they have been found liable to make. If such terms can be found, they are likely to send the truth home the more convincingly because they can be uttered by the preacher without any misgiving, and without explanations which may seem to explain them away.

There is another and opposite class of minds, inclined to repudiate the phrase " total depravity," and even to discard it with some tokens of contempt. To such persons we would say, Beware, lest you make not only an erroneous but a fatal impression on many persons who are glad to hear your scornful rejection of a phrase which they have associated with orthodox teaching, and who desire to escape from the pressure of such teaching. You also ought carefully to study the laws of impression as well as the laws of language. Beware, lest you dispel from your hearers' minds the conviction of that solemn truth which those terms have been used to express. Beware, lest you soothe into fatal apathy consciences which need to be roused. Beware, lest you let yourselves be understood to cry, " Peace, peace," to them to whom God has said, " There is no peace." Nay, beware lest you yourselves fail to see and to understand the awful, the fathomless depth of guilt and misery from which you yourselves, as well as those to whom God sends you, must needs be delivered.

There is not much danger, after all, of men feeling their own sinfulness to be greater than it really is.

Art. VI.—THE MALAY ARCHIPELAGO.*

By Rev. J. K. Wight, New Hamburg, N. Y.

RENEWED attention will doubtless be drawn to this book because of the more recent and elaborate work by the same distinguished author, the title of which we give in full below, † and which is an attempt to collect and summarize the existing information on the distribution of land animals, and to explain the more remarkable and interesting of the facts, by means of established laws of physical and organic change ; in other words, to show the important bearing of researches into the natural history of every part of the world upon the study of its past history. The main idea, which is here worked out in such fulness of detail for the whole earth, was embodied some years since in a paper on the "Zoölogical Geography of the Malay Archipelago," which appeared in the *Journal of Proceedings of the Linnean Society* for 1860; and again in a paper read before the Royal Geographical Society in 1863. (Preface.)

We shall have occasion to refer again to this more recent work, which in its department, and for those specially interested in geology or natural history, must prove an exceedingly valuable addition to our stores of knowledge. Yet, as better suited to the general reader, and because of the special interest attaching to a portion of the globe so little known, and because of some questions not touched upon in the larger and more elaborate work, we turn to this former publication of Mr. Wallace, which, though given to the world some years ago, remains the best authority upon the natural history of those islands, giving at the same time many pleasant pictures of life and travel in scenes so unlike our temperate zone and our civilized habits.

Mr. Wallace dedicates his book on the Malay Archipelago

---

* The Malay Archipelago : The Land of the Orang-utan and the Bird of Paradise. A Narrative of Travel, with Studies of Man and Nature. By Alfred Russell Wallace. Illustrated, pp. 638. New York : Harper & Brothers, 1869.

† *The Geographical Distribution of Animals.* With a study of the Relations of Living and Extinct Fauna, as Elucidating the Past Changes of the Earth's Surface. By Alfred Russell Wallace. author of the " Malay Archipelago," etc. In two Volumes. With Maps and Illustrations, pp. 503, 607. New York : Harper & Brothers, 1876.

to Mr. Darwin, and in his more recent work he says that they were undertaken through his and Prof. Newton's encouragement, so that though he does not often place himself in direct antagonism to Scripture statement, he yet pursues a line of investigation which he doubtless thinks is opposed to traditional forms of belief. We welcome, however, thorough investigation in all lines of study, believing, as Dr. Wm. M. Taylor has well said, that the workers in Revelation and Science, as on each side of the Mount Cenis Tunnel, will not meet in opposition but to remove barriers in the inquirer's way. Light will shine through what now appears darkness.

There are two points which we assume will be of special interest to the readers of this REVIEW in connection with the Malay Archipelago. First, the bearing of researches into their natural history upon revealed truth; and, secondly, the condition of man, morally, in those islands, which are so rich in material resources.

Doubtless few whose attention has not been especially directed to this region, realize the extent of these islands. The Archipelgao is 4,000 miles in length from east to west, and 13,000 in breadth from north to south. In Borneo the whole of the British Isles might be set down and have a margin for one or two islands of the size of Ireland. New Guinea is still larger, being 1,400 miles long, and in the widest part 400 broad, or, if we except Australia, the largest island in the world. The whole amount of land in this Archipelago is supposed to be about the same as in Western Europe, or Germany, Holland, France, Italy, Switzerland, Spain and Portugal. The variety in size and formation is almost endless, from the small coral lagoon to the high volcanic summit, with its extinct fires, or as, in many cases, smoking and heaving at intervals still. Situated within the tropics, the vegetation on most of these islands is luxuriant—extending from the water's edge high up the craggy sides of its mountains, and including most of the famed woods and fruits of tropical climes—sandal-wood, bamboo, rattan, palms of all descriptions, fruits and spices. Borneo is the home of the orang-utan, which is only equaled by the gorilla, and, next to that monster of the West-African forests, is the largest of the monkey tribe. Du Chaillu found gorillas five feet nine inches in height, while the largest orang is only four feet two inches high. Monkeys of all kinds, and nearly all of the larger animals, disappear as you go east. But New Guinea and the adjacent islands can lay claim to being the home of that most beautiful of all birds—the bird of Paradise.

The products of these islands are so valuable and peculiar that there is no little reason for supposing that Solomon's ships touched at some of them in their three years' voyage to Ophir. Gold and diamonds are to be had in Borneo. Apes and elephants' teeth are there, or on the Malay Peninsula, while the peacocks we fancy were this more rare, and most beautiful bird of the world.*

Without following Mr. Wallace in detail as he traveled from island to island, now living in European towns, now in native huts, now traveling in a steamer, and then in a native prau, we wish to state some of the results of his researches ; and—

---

* The word translated peacocks in 1 Kings x: 22 and 2 Chron. ix: 21 is, תֻּכִּיִּים —*toucayim*, which Gesenius fancies to have been the domestic name of the peacock in India, of which country it is a native. A bird very similar to the peacock of India is found in Java, and it is easily domesticated in almost any country. That India was not the Ophir or Tarshish of Solomon's three years' voyages seems likely, not merely because it was so near, but also because it was in all probability reached by an overland trade, of which we have an indication in the building of Tadmor, 120 miles N.E. of Damascus, and more than half the distance to the Euphrates. While the peacock can be easily domesticated, and thus introduced without difficulty into neighboring countries, it is almost impossible to tame the Bird of Paradise or make it live in confinement, and thus transport it to other countries. Mr. Wallace tried caging several varieties, but though feeding well, and lively for a day or two, they all died by the third or fourth day. He finally found a pair alive at Singapore, and purchased them for £100, and brought them to England, where they lived for a year or two. It is doubtful whether any light can be thrown upon the question of the right interpretation of *toucayim* from the present names of these birds. Gesenius says the Sanscrit name for peacock is *sikhi.* Mr. Wallace says one variety of the birds of Paradise (for there are eighteen different kinds) is called by the natives "goby goby," and its cry is wawk-wawk-wawk, wok-wok-wok, which resounds in early morning through the woods. The nearest resemblance that we know in sound is the Toucan of South America. But neither the beauty of the bird, nor the direction from Ezion-geber, would point to South America as the Ophir. Besides beauty of plumage, another idea may possibly have been the attraction when apes were brought in those ships, and that is the power of imitation which belongs to the parrot tribe. The distance across oceans is not such an obstacle as we might suppose. The Asiatics of Solomon's time, and a few centuries later, when Babylon was built, and when Lautoz, the Chinese philosopher, visited Greece, and Brahminism spread to Java, where its solid brick and stone ruins are now seen among bamboo huts, and Buddhism sent its missionaries to Ceylon, Siam and Japan, and across the Himalayas to Thibet and China, were a race whose intellectual activity and enterprise are in striking contrast with the apathy and sluggishness of their descendants.

1. As to the distribution of animal life. The impression with most would be that in islands located as these are, within the tropics, and in near proximity, and with a flora very similar, that the fauna should be very much alike. But instead of that, the variations are distinct and marked. The larger animals, as the elephant, the rhinoceros, wild cattle, and also monkeys, are to a great extent the same in Sumatra, Borneo and Java, as in the Malay Peninsula. But eastward all the larger animals disappear. In New Guinea none are to be found ; and instead are pigs, bats, opossums and kangaroos. The birds differ as widely as the animals. Thus, out of three hundred and fifty varieties of land birds inhabiting Java, not more than ten have passed eastward into Celebes. Of the one hundred and eight land birds of New Guinea and adjacent islands, twenty-nine are exclusively characteristic of it. Thirty-five belong to that limited area which includes the Moluccas and North Australia. One-half of the New Guinea genera are found also in Australia and about one-third in India and the Indo-Malay Islands (p. 578). It is in New Guinea and adjacent islands alone that the different varieties of the Paradise bird are found.

According to our author, the different races of men vary almost as much as the lower orders of the animal creation. In the west, or in Sumatra, Borneo, Java, Celebes, etc., the islanders belong to a race allied to the Malay. In the coast regions of Borneo and Sumatra are what may be called the true Malay race, who are Mohammedans in religion, speak the Malay, and use the Arabic character in writing. Besides these Mohammedans there are the savage Dyaks of Borneo, who are not Mohammedans. In Java a similar race exists, though their language differs from the Malay. Their religion is, however, Mohammedan. The Malays are smaller than Europeans, their complexion brown, hair straight and black, and no beard.

The race which is strongly contrasted to this is the Papuan or New Guinean. Between the two there has, however, been more or less of mixture, and in many places a commingling of other races, especially the Chinese, who are found among these islands as on the Malay Peninsula, wherever there is any opening for trade. The Malays are so nearly allied to the East Asiatic population, that in Bali the Chinese who had adopted the native costume could hardly be distinguished from the Malay. The typical Papuan, however, is unlike the Malay. The color of the body is a deep sooty-brown or black, approaching in color the true negro. The hair is peculiar, being harsh, dry and frizzly, and standing up from the head like a mop. The nose is large, arched and high, the lips thick and protuberant, and the face covered with beard. In stature they nearly equal the average European. In character the Papuan is bold, impetuous, excitable and noisy. The Malay is bashful, cold, undemonstrative and quiet. From this description it will be seen that the Papuan bears a close resemblance to the negro of Africa, and also to the inhabitants of Polynesia.

We come now to the question, How is this peculiar distribution of animal life to be accounted for? So far as man is concerned, he has the means of passing from island to island. But here are two strongly marked races in close proximity, and what is the cause of the wide divergence? This question with respect to man we will take up after looking at the lower order of animal life.

Two facts are to be considered—one of similarity to the productions of the main-land, and the other of divergence. How, first, are we to account for the similarity, or how did the products of the animal and vegetable kingdoms cross these seas and straits, and propagate themselves in their island homes? Mr. Wallace adopts the theory, first suggested by Mr. Earle in a paper read before the Royal Geographical Society in 1845, that these islands, in some former geologic period, were connected with two great continents—Asia on the one hand, and Australia on the other. And that as evidence of this a shallow sea, less than forty fathoms deep, now connects them with these continents, while a sea of over one hundred fathoms in depth to the eastward of Celebes separates them from one another. That there have been great geological changes in this region, and not necessarily at a very remote period, is evident from the existence of so many extinct and active volcanoes, some of which are elevated six to eight thousand feet. A corresponding subsidence in the same general region would be expected after any great elevation of land.

It might be thought that the seeds of plants could be borne by winds and currents to neighboring islands; and that birds and animals could pass from one to the other. While this is true of the vegetable creation to some extent, and is also true of some birds, yet to many land animals and many varieties of birds, even a narrow channel of the sea forms an impassable barrier. To illustrate what would be the case, supposing the causes which are now in existence only to operate, let us take Celebes, the strange-shaped island near the center of the Archipelago. From its position, separated only by a narrow intervening strait from Borneo, and surounded by other islands, and with large indentations of the sea, and having comparatively only a narrow breadth of land, it is admirably fitted to receive the forms of life which exist in at least the neighboring islands. But Mr. Wallace says it is the poorest of them all in the number of its species, and the most isolated in the character of its productions (p. 277). Of the land birds there are one hundred and twenty-eight different species. Of these twenty roam over the whole Archipelago, leaving one hundred and eight species more especially characteristic of the island. Of these only nine extend to the islands westward, and nineteen to the islands eastward, while no less than eighty are confined to Celebes. Of these there are many which have no affinity with birds on the nearer islands, but bear a close resemblance to those in such distant regions as New Guinea, Australia, India or Africa.

The peculiar isolation of the fauna of this island Mr. Wallace is disposed to account for by supposing that it is older land, or was elevated above the surrounding ocean before the other islands.

Whether this theory of subsidence of sea and elevation of land, will answer all the necessities of the case, seems doubtful. It might, if the types of animal and vegetable life were in all respects similar to the mainland; but as they differ so radically in many particulars, there is the necessity of accounting for the isolated and peculiar forms of life.

In glancing at the questions here involved, we cannot adopt the statements and conclusions of our author. As, for instance, Mr. Wallace says: " Naturalists have now arrived at the conclusion that by some slow process of development or transmutation, all animals have been produced from those which preceded them ; and the old notion that every species was specially created as they now exist, at a particular time, and in a particular spot, is abandoned as opposed to many striking facts, and unsupported by any evidence."*

* Geographical Distribution of Animals, Vol. I., p. 6

This modification of animal life, he acknowledges, has taken place very slowly, so that the historic period of three or four thousand years has hardly produced a perceptible change in a single species.   Even to the last glacial epoch, 50,000 or 100,000 years, modification has taken place only in a " few of the higher animals into very slightly different species."* It will be seen that this theory takes for granted what even Mr. Wallace admits has never taken place in historic times, a single clear instance of transmutation of species. 2. If there has been transmutation, it does not do away with the necessity of creation.   Modification, development, evolution, from lower to higher forms, which all recognize, is not creation or calling things that are out of those that are not.* 3. All the facts adduced by Mr. Wallace point to an entirely different conclusion than that of transmutation.   No one has demonstrated better than he that the habitat of very many animals is exceedingly limited.   There are a few that are somewhat cosmopolitan, but every continent, and almost every island, especially in this Malay Archipelago, has its distinct fauna.   Even those continents which are connected, as Europe, Asia and Africa, have, in different parts, their own special forms of animal life.   These differences are more marked when wide seas intervene.   In Australia there are no elephants or tigers, no apes or monkeys, no deer or oxen, none of the familiar types of quadrupeds existing in other parts of the globe, but kangaroos and opossums. So, also, its birds differ from those of other regions.

The present distribution of animal life, therefore, would indicate not a transmutation of species from one common centre or origin, but a creation of many species in their particular locality.   The distinction between man and the other animals in this respect is quite plain in the record.   According to the Bible, all mankind were descended from one pair, and were spread abroad over the face of the whole earth.   But with both animals and vegetables, the method was different.   The waters, not in one place, but everywhere and in all directions, were to bring forth moving creatures, and the earth living creatures.   For the locality, for the food provided, for all the circumstances in which the creature was to be placed, the crea-

---

* Geographical Distribution of Animals, Vol. I., p. 7

ture made was adapted—opossums and kangaroos in Australia, elephants, tigers, and the domestic animals on the larger continents, and beautiful and strange birds on nearly every island of the sea.

But the objection will readily occur, If this distribution of animals agrees with the Mosaic account of creation, how about the deluge? Were all the animals gathered into the ark, and if so, whence the wide difference of species from those at present existing in Asia, and how did the animals cross barriers which they are never known to cross now? Transmutation of species, if we believed in it, would be a convenient theory to help us out of this difficulty, or the subsidence and elevation of continents, or the survival of the fittest. We must concede that in the present state of our knowledge it is not easy to reconcile the geographical distribution of animals with the theory of a universal deluge. Theologians must look at all the difficulties of the case, and in due time the solution will come. Hugh Miller thought he had found a solution in a limited deluge, brought about in part by the subsidence of the earth in that locality where man existed, and which by its depression would bring in the fountains of the great deep. Another solution which Prichard advocates, is the recreation on those distant lands and islands of forms of life that had previously existed. But it might be asked, (1) why not recreate all the forms of life, and not attempt to preserve some of them in the ark? And (2), the account of creation seems to imply that when God finished it, he rested not to take it up again. With man, the last and highest type, the work was complete, and its completion was emphasized by the Sabbath or period of rest. When man sinned, God did not destroy them all and recreate a new human race, but preserved one family. And so with the animals. There is no record of recreation. Is the only conclusion, then, that the deluge was limited? To this we must say, that from the side of natural history there are facts on both sides which render the question, for the present at least, not easy of solution. On the one hand there are all the physical difficulties of collecting birds, insects and animals over seas which they never cross, and supplying this vast concourse with appropriate food. And on the other, we find this equally remarkable fact, which Mr. Wallace emphasizes, " of the recent and almost universal change that has taken place in the character of the fauna over the entire globe.* In Europe, in North America, and in South America, we have evidence that a very similar change occurred about the same time." The remains of mastodons, huge armadillos, large horses and tapirs, cave-lions, etc., are found in peat-bogs, gravels and cave-earths, and since the deposition of the most recent of the fossil-bearing strata, we can certify to the correctness of this, so far as the mastodons of this country are concerned. Again, in Australia there is a similar appearance of extinct fauna, some of gigantic size, belonging to the same geologic period—kangaroos as large as an elephant.† His theory of accounting for this simultaneous change over large portions of the earth's surface, is the great change wrought at the time of the glacial epoch, some 50,000 or 100,000 years ago. "We live," he says, "in a zoölogically impoverished world, from which all the largest and fairest and strongest forms have recently disappeared, and it is no doubt a much better world for us now they have gone."‡ How, then, are remains found in the very last of the tertiary deposits in the pliocene and post-pliocene periods ? Mr. Wallace would say, We are to weigh the evidence whether this recent disappearance of strange fauna is not more likely to have been caused by the deluge than by the glacial epoch. The fact that it was the deluge is strengthened in our minds by the remains of human bones found in the same cave-earths with those of the ancient fossils of the Old World, though this is not mentioned by our author, as he leaves man out of his geographical distribution of animals. We would not be too positive in our assertions, where as yet the data have not been perhaps sufficiently examined, but the acknowledged change requires a recent cause, and this recent and sufficient cause seems to be met by the deluge. Mr. Wallace is justly severe on " those who would create a continent to account for the migrations of a beetle;" so we question the propriety of dodging an adequate cause of three or four thousand years ago, for a questionable solution of 50,000 or 100,000 years previous. To those who look for a wise and kind Providence, even in the midst of judgment, we have it in the sweeping away of so many fierce

---

* Distribution of Animals, vol. i., p. 149., *et seq.*
† Ibid., p. 157.   ‡ Vol. I, p. 150.

and strange animals, which made the world after the flood a
better habitation for man. As we said, however, we put this
fact of the recent disappearance of strange and huge fauna,
which favors the belief in a universal deluge, over against the
other of the isolated distribution of different forms of animal
life, which seems to make it impossible; and wait for further
investigation and research to tunnel through this difficulty.

We pass now to the question about the two races, so dissimilar, which occupy different portions of this Archipelago. Our
author considers them so entirely different, that they belong
to two distinct races, rather than modifications of one and the
same race.* To this we may assent so far as they present distinct peculiarities, and show an origin which for centuries has
been separate, but not if he means, as we suppose he does, that
they did not descend from one common pair. If man was only
an animal, there would have been a chance for transmutation
of species; but as he is man, he must forsooth have come from
another race. However, we accept the fact of difference in
many peculiarities. The Papuan or New Guinean resembles
first the Polynesian ; and second, has certain clearly marked affinities which connect him with the negro of Africa, rather
than with any of the nations of Asia. Supposing the ancestors of the Papuan to have come from Africa rather than Asia,
the difficult question is, how did they get across the Indian
Ocean to Polynesia? It seems a big distance to pass by sea
for any methods of navigation now known to these races. Possibly there has been a decadence in knowledge, as exhibited by
the native races on our own continent and in other parts of
the world, when the descendants of former generations could
not rebuild the cities and temples among the ruins of which
they dwell. Europeans and Americans are always thinking of
the progress of the race ; Asiatics of its decadence. When we
find the savage, we hope our idea is true of his future, that of
the Asiatic may be correct of his past history, rather than that
he has always stood in the same position. Mr. Wallace himself states that in Java there are ruins of elaborate and well
constructed temples, where solid mason-work has in a measure
resisted the ravages of time in a tropical climate, which are

* *Malay Archipelago*, p. 532.

surrounded by bamboo huts—the highest style of architecture of the descendants of these old temple builders. It may be that, as nations, which in Solomon's time could make long voyages, and the descendants of which could not make them now, so the Africans may have had the enterprise then to leave their native shores and find homes in Polynesia.

Still another conjecture is open without being obliged to resort to any such theory as that Polynesia and Africa have been peopled by more than one race. There are some animals allied to apes, which go on all fours, called lemurs, which are common to some of these islands, and also to Madagascar. The baribossa of Celebes and Bouru resembles the wart-hog of Africa, and there are other striking resemblances in birds. Dr. Sclater has suggested that a continent even existed in the Indian Ocean which formed a link between Africa and Polynesia, and has given to this hypothetical land the name of Lemuria, from the animal which first suggested the connection of those now widely separated regions (p. 290).

This subsidence of continents is a convenient escape from many difficulties. And of the fact in the general there is no doubt, just as there are rocks all about us which have been elevated from their ocean beds; but yet subsidence may be assumed in directions where it never existed, and may be placed at periods which cannot be definitely determined by any indications which we now have. Mr. Wallace, rightly we think, hopes for light in the study of extinct fauna and flora in connection with living types; but there is need of great caution in the way of inferences. In his later work he seems to think the line of connection between continents has been north and south, rather than east and west, and so is inclined to give up the hypothetical continent of Lemuria.

Leaving these questions of physical and scientific interest, let us look briefly at the present condition of these Islanders, and see what has been done toward their moral and spiritual elevation.

The Papuans are heathen, and have been left more undisturbed in their heathenism than any other large island on the face of the globe. Until recently, though long the resort of traders, and constantly passed by vessels going to Australia, and frequently by those going to China, yet the only attempts at evangelization, so far as we know, are those to which we will presently refer. The inhabitants of this island have had a character for violence to which they do not seem entitled. They are fierce looking, and cut up into hostile tribes: but Mr. Wallace lived among them without difficulty. They are noisy, boisterous, but no worse than other savages, and assimilating in many respects to the natives of Madagascar; there may be as great triumphs of the Gospel in store for them as have been shown on that island. Under a tropical sun they have but few wants, and those easily supplied. They have but little occasion to resort even to agriculture. A sago palm cut down, and the whole inside of the tree washed and dried and made .into cakes, will produce something like 600 pounds of sago, or enough to last a year, and requiring only about ten days' labor of one man, or more usually woman, to get it ready (p. 385). The easier the means of subsistence and the plenty which might be had, results, in the savage state, in the greatest poverty and scarcity. Where the sago tree abounds the Papuans live almost entirely on that, and a little fish, raising scarcely any vegetables or fruit. In one of his excursions Mr. Wallace lived for a time on the Aru Islands, a little south of New Guinea, and acknowledges that the monotony and uniformity of every-day savage life revealed a more miserable kind of existence than when it had the charm of novelty. Their food, when they had no fish, was mostly vegetable, imperfectly cooked, and these in varying and often insufficient quantities. To this did he attribute the prevalence of skin diseases, and ulcers on the legs and joints.

" The chief luxury of these Aru people is arrack (Java rum), which the traders bring in great quantities and sell cheap. A day's fishing or rattan cutting will purchase at least a half gallon bottle, and when the trepang or birds' nests collected during a season are sold, they get whole boxes containing fifteen such bottles, which the inmates of a house will sit round day and night till they have finished. They themselves tell me that at such bouts they often tear to pieces the houses they are in, break and destroy everything they can lay their hands on, and make such a riot as is alarming to behold " (p. 453).

He says they seem to enjoy pure idleness, often sitting for days in their houses, their women bringing the vegetables or sago which form their food.   •

On these islands there were three or four villages on the

coast where schoolmasters from Amboyna reside, and the people were nominally Christian, and to some extent educated and civilized. Their intercourse with Mohammedan traders had also some effect, as they would often bury their dead, though their national custom was to expose the body on a raised stage until it decomposed.

On New Guinea itself there was no Dutch colony at the time of Mr. Wallace's visit, though explorations were going on for the purpose of planting one. Trading vessels pass along the coast, and at the fine harbor of Dorey, which was the only point where Mr. Wallace made any tarry, he found two German missionaries. At that time they were the only ones on the island; one of them had been there for two years and had learned something of the language, and was attempting to translate portions of the Bible, and had also started a small school. These missionaries were accustomed to labor and trade, and were obliged to eke out the small salary granted from Europe by trading with the natives—buying their rice when it was cheap, and selling it back when they were in need, at an advanced price. The effect of this on the natives was the impression that the missionaries, like other traders, came among them for their own personal advantage, and not for the good of those among whom they labored.

From a recent work* we learn that these two German missionaries are dead, and that their places have not been supplied. "The London Missionary Society" directed Mr. Murray to commence a mission on New Guinea. This he did in 1871, on the southeastern extremity of the island, opposite to Australia, landing some native missionaries from the Loyalty Islands at two different points. One party of these was murdered by the natives; what was the reason for the act Mr. Murray could not discover. He testifies, however, that he found no difficulty in going among them unarmed at all points where he landed. At the other point the mission was successfully established, and to the native missionaries was added a missionary from England.

The islands to the westward, where the Malay race predomi-

---

*Forty Years' Missionary Work in Polynesia and New Guinea, 1835 to 1875, published by the Carters.

nates, have been brought more under the influence of civilization than those to the east. Amboyna, Java, and some other points have been visited, and occupied for the purposes of trade for three hundred years. On the large island of Aram, near Amboyna, there are schools and native school-masters, and many of the inhabitants are nominal Christians. In the larger villages are European missionaries. Mr. Wallace's estimate of the so-called Christians on this island was not very favorable. He says they were spoken of as thieves, liars, drunkards and incorrigibly lazy (p. 357). One cause of this, he thinks, is that with Mohammedanism, temperance is a part of their religion, and has become such a habit that practically the rule is never transgressed. One fertile source of want and crime is thus present to one class which is not to another.* Doubtless, in coming out of one system, which is made up of ceremonies and particular observances and with greater freedom from restraint, and yet imperfectly comprehending the doctrines of Christianity, and imperfectly brought under its morality, there is some cause for this statement. Christianity, with a race naturally indolent and in a low state of civilization, has a struggle which it is not to be expected will transform at once such a people into the high standard toward which civilized nations have been struggling for hundreds of years.

Partly as an offset to the above unfavorable view, and also as giving more fully the Dutch method of colonization and christianization, we will abridge his favorable report of the change wrought within fifty years on the northeast extremity of Celebes. Before 1822 this was a savage community, cut up into small, isolated tribes and villages, with houses built on lofty posts to defend themselves from their enemies. Strips of bark were their only dress ; and human skulls were the chief ornaments of the houses of their chiefs. The country was a pathless wilderness, with small, cultivated patches of rice and vegetables. In the year 1822 the coffee plant was introduced

---

*Notwithstanding what he says here about the temperance principles of Mohammedanism, we find that on another island he was asked by Mohammedans for spirits, "the people," he says, "being merely nominal Mohammedans, who confine their religion almost entirely to a disgust at pork and a few other forbidden articles of food."

into this region, and it was found to be admirably adapted to its cultivation. . The country rises quite rapidly from the sea into a high, volcanic region with a rich soil. Arrangements were made with the village chiefs, who were to receive a certain per cent. of the produce. The country was divided into districts, and a " controlleur" appointed, who was the general superintendent of the cultivation of the district. He was obliged to visit every village in succession once a month, and send in a report of their condition to the resident. Under the direction of the Dutch, roads were made, houses built, missionaries were settled in the more populous districts, and schools were opened. Mr. Wallace describes one of the villages in this region through which he passed. The main road, he says, along which the coffee is brought from the interior in carts drawn by buffaloes, is turned aside at the entrance of the village and passes behind it, and so allows the village street to be kept neat and clean. In this village the street was bordered by a neat hedge formed of rose trees, which were perpetually in bloom. There was a broad central path kept clean, and a border of fine turf, which was neatly cut. The houses were all of wood, raised on posts about six feet from the ground, with a broad veranda and balustrade, and the walls neatly whitewashed and surrounded by orange trees and flowering shrubs. He stopped with a native chief, now a major under the Dutch. His house was large, airy, substantially built, and furnished in European style, with chairs, tables and lamps. Meals were served on good china, while his host sat at the head of the table, dressed in black, with patent leather shoes. This man's father was one of those whose dress was a strip of bark, and whose house was ornamented with human heads. In this village there was a school-house, its teacher a native, who had been educated by the missionary at one of the larger places. School was held every morning for about three hours, and twice a week there was catechising and preaching. There was also a service Sunday morning. The language used was the Malay.

Near the villages were the coffee plantations. The trees are planted in rows, and kept topped to about seven feet high. Each tree produced from 10 to 20 pounds of cleaned coffee annually. The plantations are formed by Government, and cultivated by the villagers under the direction of the chief. Certain days are appointed for weeding and gathering, and the whole working population are summoned by the sound of a gong. An account is kept of the day's work of each family, and the produce is divided accordingly. The price is fixed by Government. This system has been called a "paternal despotism," and has features which seem strict, and wanting in that freedom which we imagine is essential. But for a people just emerging from a savage state, it has its advantages. The people were well cared for, better fed, housed, educated, and apparently making more progress than in any other place in the Archipelago. There seems to have been a combination of causes—the natives falling in with the system, and the officers of Government and the missionaries doing their work well— which made this place one of the most favorable examples of the Dutch system. It is worth studying in seeking to provide a system which shall reach the wants and elevate the condition of savage races.

These islands—even those forming the west portion of the Archipelago—though largely occupied by the Dutch, are not all held by them. Part of Borneo was for a time governed by an Englishman, Sir James Brooke. Other portions are held by native chiefs. There are also Dutch settlements on the island. Sumatra, until within a few years, was governed almost entirely by native chiefs. Some European government would be favorable to missionary work, but it undoubtedly might be pushed into regions not yet occupied by the Dutch Government, or by German missionaries. Without attempting at all to interfere with their work, some contact with other methods of evangelization would, we are assured, lead to healthier results.

Because two men were killed on Sumatra years ago, and because the mission among the Dyaks of Borneo was attended with difficulty and little success, or even because China offers a larger field for missionary labor, we see no reason why islands, some of which are the largest in the world, and which are capable of sustaining a dense population, and which produce almost spontaneously every variety of tropical fruit and vegetation, should be left without any effort to evangelize them except by the missionaries from Holland, or the few who may go from Germany. The Chinese are there with opium, and the Dutch, Portuguese, English and Malay with rum, seeking spices, beautiful birds, gold dust, diamonds. Why not hasten with the glad tidings, and elevate regions where savages roam, and where the wilderness is tangled, and seek to make it the garden of the Lord?

Art. VII.—A JEWISH PRAYER BOOK.

By REV. D. W. FISHER, D.D., Wheeling, West Virginia.

עלת תמיר—*Book of Prayers for Israelitish Congregations.**

THE Hebrew words (*Olath Tamid*) which constitute the title of this volume, are those with which the sixth verse of the twenty-eighth chapter of Numbers begins. They are translated, both by the compiler and in our English Bible, *a continual burnt-offering*. As they stand in the Scriptures, they relate to the daily sacrifice which was required by the Mosaic ritual. The lamb which was offered every morning and evening, together with a tenth part of an ephah of flour, and a fourth part of a hira of beaten oil, was to be " a continual burnt-offering, which was ordained in Mount Sinai for a sweet savour, a sacrifice made by fire unto the Lord." This whole verse is placed in both Hebrew and English on the title-page of this volume. The appropriation of these words, and especially the care which is taken to let it be known that they are a part of this verse in the Pentateuch, are significant of the wide departure of the phase of modern Judaism, represented in this book, from that type which formerly prevailed almost universally among the Israelitish people. They are here applied, not to the daily sacrifices of the tabernacle and the temple at Jerusalem, but to a ritual in which such offerings are assumed to be things which are gone forever, and which there should be no desire to restore.

This is a book which is well worth the study of Christians. It is true that there are some purposes for which it would be vain to search it. It does not, like the Targums, throw any

---

* Prepared by Dr. D. Einhorn.

light upon the sense in which the Jews ages ago interpreted the Old Testament. Scripture, for the most part, is quoted literally. Paraphrase is not formally attempted ; and when incidentally introduced, it has no special value. There are here no stores of quaint Rabbinical learning, such as the lamented Deutsch delighted to exhume from the Talmud. The He-brew of this volume is no help to the student of that language, for it is either literally quoted from the Scriptures, or it is carefully modeled after the pattern of the sacred writers. He-brew, as a language, died long before Christ was born. Subse-quently it was carefully embalmed by means of the vowel points and the accents. No mummy ever has been more completely preserved in the condition in which it was left when the process of preparing it for burial was concluded. And it would be about as reasonable to expect the mummy to awake and perform the functions of life as to look now for, any manifestation of present vitality on the part of the Hebrew language. The use which is here made of it is no more a natural, living outgrowth, than are the exercises which the student writes in Latin or Greek composition the spontaneous product of the classic tongues. The Hebrew of this book, so far as it is not quota-tion from the Scriptures, though it may be free enough from grammatical fault, is no better than an imitation of a petrifac-tion, and throws no light on the difficult problems pertaining to that tongue.

But for other reasons we have been interested and profited by the perusal of the *Olath Tamid.* It joins itself to the re-mote past, and both conducts our thoughts in that direction, and, at the same time, casts light upon the pathway. Hence, provision is made for the religious commemoration of such events as the destruction of Jerusalem by the Romans, deliv-erance by the Maccabees in the time of Antiochus, and the overthrow of Haman in the days of Esther and Mordecai. We are here conducted still further back, beyond the era of Saky-amuni, the founder of Buddhism ; beyond the era of Zoroaster and the fire-worshipers; beyond the probable era of the old-est of the sacred books of the Hindus, to the exodus of Israel, under Moses, fifteen hundred years previous to the birth of Christ. Provision is made for the celebration of the Passover which was originally kept at that remote date. True, the ceremonies are not the same which were of old employed, but the change is explicitly declared to be made because of a change in the circumstances and relations of Israel. The real existence of the ancient rites is freely conceded, and the fact of the Exodus is received without question as the reason of the modern observance. Here, then, is a ceremony which dates back its origin nearly thirty-four centuries. It is the latest link in a historical chain which is fastened, as to its other end, in Egypt in that remote period. Through this long interval, the Passover has been, with slight intermissions, constantly observed. And it is, as at present kept among the Jews, a monument to the reality of the event which it commemorates, just as the Lord's Supper among Christians, having been celebrated ever since the death of Christ, is a witness to the reality of the event which it commemorates. In the nature of the case there is no probability that either of them would or could have been invented and successfully imposed upon the people without a real historical origin, for they both point distinctly to·truths which are not welcome to human self-esteem—to bondage on the part of Israel, and to the need of redemption on the part of Christians. And there is no time which can be fixed when such an imposition could first have been successfully introduced among Jews or Christians, even if, in the nature of the case, there was no insuperable obstacle. We can account for the existence of the Lord's Supper only by the reality of Christ's death, and of the Passover only by the reality of the Exodus under Moses.·

But it is not for this historical aspect in which this book of prayers may be viewed that it is most worthy of the study of Christians. It is chiefly to be valued on account of the light which it throws upon the religious doctrines and practices of a part of the Jewish people of the present day. Everything which concerns the spiritual condition of the scattered remnants of Jacob's descendants ought profoundly to interest us. And we believe that, as a rule, intelligent Christians both desire to know their views and are anxious for their welfare. To them the Jew is not an object to be despised or hated. We cannot forget the past of this peculiar people. It has not merely been more romantic, more tragic, more wonderful, than that of any other branch of the human family, or even than that which fiction could invent when taxing the imagination to the utmost. Over and above this, we remember that they were the chosen of God for ages. To them we are indebted for the perpetuation of the church, the writing and preservation of the Old Testament, and the maintenance of true religion when it everywhere else was extinct. Of them Christ was born, and from them the apostles were called. And they still have a great future before them. Of this, the fact that amid all their wanderings and persecutions they have been preserved, so that their distinct existence as a people, though without a country or national organization, is everywhere maintained, is a convincing, presumptive indication. And the testimony of the New Testament is absolutely conclusive on this point. It does not foretell their restoration to Palestine, or the re-erection of their nationality, but it does assure us that into the Christian commonwealth the whole of the remnant of ancient Israel will be brought. And this will be inseparably associated with the coming of the fullness of the Gentiles. The latter event will be the signal for and harbinger of the former. Millennial glory will be inaugurated by the conversion of this wonderful people.

. This volume is a ritual for divine worship, public, social and domestic. It is safe to assume, therefore, that in it we have an expression of the very heart of the religion of the part of the Jewish people who use it. For those who prepare a ritual of worship would not be likely to put into it anything which they do not regard as belonging to the vitals of piety. And its effect upon those who use it is to conform them to the type of religion which it embodies. It is true that this volume does not profess to come with the weight of any ecclesiastical authority. It does not assume to bind the conscience. But for the very reason that it is voluntarily received by the people, it is all the more to be regarded as an expression of the genuine religious sentiments of those who employ it.

The Jews of the present day are divided as to their religious doctrines and practices into three great general classes. One class is known as the *stationary*, or *extreme orthodox*. They are mainly found in Poland, Russia, Palestine, and in some other Asiatic and African countries. They have a profound reverence for the Talmud, and for the forms which the ecclesiastical authorities prescribe for them. They still look to Palestine as their country, and covet to be buried within its limits. Even a handful of earth brought from that land to be scattered in the grave, is regarded as a most precious treasure. They long for the restoration of Jewish nationality, and compare their present state to that of their forefathers, when they sat down by the rivers of Babylon and wept. One article of their creed, as compiled by Moses Maimonides, in the eleventh century, is: "I believe, with a perfect faith, that the Messiah is yet to come; and although he retard his coming, yet I will wait for him till he come." They expect that the Messiah will bestow the sceptre of universal dominion on the house of Judah.

The other two classes both owe their origin to the influence more immediately of Moses Mendelsshon, who lived in the last century, but more remotely to Moses Maimonides. Both have largely thrown off the narrow notions of the *extreme orthodox*. But they have separated into two schools. One is known as the *conservative*, or *moderate orthodox*. It prevails especially in the countries of Western Europe. This school, while characterized by emancipation from Talmudic and Rabbinical authority, yet shows a tendency to subordination to a regularly constituted ecclesiastical head, such as chief Rabbi in each country. They have an intense love for their ancient land and forms of religion. But they do not look for a return of the Jews to Palestine, or for the restoration of their nationality in any sense which is incompatible with citizenship of the world. The degree of rigidness with which such religious duties as are prescribed are enforced, varies in different countries.

The other of these Jewish schools is variously known as the *reformed, liberal, progressive*, or *modern*. It prevails most extensively in Germany, Austria, and the United States. Dr. Einhorn, who prepared the *Olath Tamid*, and who was formerly of Germany, but is now of the United States, is of this way of thinking, although in his radicalism he is scarcely in the front of his party at the present time. Most of the Israelitish congregations in this country are of this school. So wide has been the demand for this book, that several successive editions have been published. Let us now proceed to a more

minute examination of the religious doctrines which it embodies. We will thus be able to learn what are some of the
most prominent peculiarities of the type of Judaism which it
represents.

Of these the most notable relate to the peculiar office and
work ascribed to the Jewish people. First, the doctrine of the
Messiah. The idea of a personal Christ is renounced. At the
same time a doctrine of the Messiah is taught in the most unequivocal manner. What is to be understood by that name is
not treated as an open question. THE JEWISH PEOPLE ARE
THE MESSIAH. The expression, "Israel, thy Messiah," is one
of the most common in the book. One of the questions to be
asked of the candidate at confirmation is, whether he believes
that Israel is destined to fulfill this high mission as the Messiah of all mankind. It is the race at large to which this
name is given. And as a part of this doctrine, a universal priesthood is ascribed to this people. The sacerdotal
office is assumed to have passed from the one family, on which
it was conferred by the law of Moses, over to the whole nation.

In the afternoon service for the Day of Atonement the reader
is to say—"The priestly dignity has not vanished from our
midst, but it has passed from the house of Aaron to the whole
community." And again, as a priest, Israel is represented as
performing a double work. One part of it is to suffer. His
sufferings are not understood to be a real satisfaction to the
offended law and justice of God; but in his work as a world-
redeeming people, suffering is a consequence, and so becomes a
necessity to the removal of human guilt. We quote again
from the afternoon service for the Day of Atonement : " Not as
a penitent sinner, but as a suffering Messiah, Israel had to go
forth into the world—abandoning his ancient home, with
its temple, its sacrifices, and its priest-pageants, with all its typical and preparatory institutions, [in order to found everywhere seats of the true worship, and by self-sacrificing devotion *to lead the nations to atonement.* At once priest and tool
of atonement, he was sent, like the sacrificial goat of old, into
the wilderness, to take the guilt of mankind upon his shoulders,
and *carry it off.** The other part of his priestly work is to be a

---

* The *Italics* are from the book.

spiritual 'teacher and guide for the nations of the earth. At Confirmation, the candidate is to be asked whether he believes " that God has chosen Israel to be his priest-people, to propagate by his character, his wonderful fate, and his unwearied struggle, the doctrine of sanctification all over the earth, and unite all men in the true knowledge and worship of God."

Second, The redemption of the world. This doctrine is inseparably associated with the other which has just been considered. By virtue of the Messiahship of the Jewish people and of their priestly office, all the nations of the earth are to be brought to the knowledge and practice of the truth, as it is committed to the charge of Israel, and thus the brotherhood of all men is to be re-established. They are taught here, in the prayers, to speak of themselves as " a world-redeeming race." A proselyte, at his reception in the synagogue, is required to profess his belief that " God has chosen Israel to be his priest-people, and ordained him to propagate the doctrine of the Only-One, and of his holy will among all the inhabitants of the earth ; that through the mediation of Israel, the true knowledge and worship of God will one day become the common good of mankind ; and that the time of such brotherly union of all nations in God will be the true kingdom of the Messiah."

It must be conceded that these two doctrines relating to the peculiar office and work of the Jewish people are calculated to arrest attention. In Judaism the reception of them as a part of a creed constitutes a new departure. For ages it was universal among Jews to believe in a personal Messiah. Attempts in the past were made to fix the time of His appearance, until, on account of repeated disappointments, the Rabbinical edict was issued, " Cursed is he who calculates the time of the Messiah's coming." Some still look for a personal Christ to appear. Others leave it an open question whether the Messiah is a person, a time, or an event. But those who hold with this book, turn their backs alike upon the traditions of the past and the uncertainties of the present, and say that the Jews themselves are the Messiah. The departure which is thus taken, also has the merit of boldness. It is a daring thing for a party, claiming to be liberal beyond others, to assert for their race an office and work which renders their place among the nations as unique in the present and future as it ever was, according to the most conservative, in the past. And if the scrutiny is not too close, these doctrines may seem to satisfy some existing facts, and some Scriptural testimonies. They may appear to explain why, ever since the destruction of Jerusalem and the dispersion of the Jews, that people, although so widely scattered, and exposed to so many persecutions, has been so wonderfully preserved and kept distinct. There are Messianic prophecies also which might be forced into a semblance of harmony with these ideas, although they cannot be said positively to teach them. For example: " Judah, thou art he whom thy brothers praise. . . . The sceptre shall not depart from Judah, nor a law-giver from between his feet, until Shiloh come ; and unto him shall the gathering of the people be."—(Gen. xlix : 8, 10.)

But a little more careful scrutiny of facts and Scripture shows these doctrines to be without a solid foundation. Space will not here permit the full statement of the arguments against them. Nor is this necessary, for the most part, for those who shall read this article. But it is to be remarked that existing facts do not point to the Messiahship of the Jewish people. They are not leading the nations to God. Proselytism to Judaism is a rare occurrence anywhere. And outside of the pale of Judaism, so far as progress is making by the nations toward a higher religious condition, it is mainly through the instrumentality of Christians. If we turn from existing facts to the Scriptures, we notice that in all the thirty-nine times in which the Hebrew word מָשִׁיחַ (*Mashiach*) occurs in the Old Testament, it is not once applied distinctly to the Jewish people. And the same is true in regard to the other titles of the Messiah which are there employed. This of itself is presumptive evidence against such an application as that which this book makes of the name. The Scriptures also plainly point to a person as the Messiah. The circle within which he is to appear, according to the first promise, is wide as the race. But in all the subsequent predictions there is a gradual limitation, until eventually the circle is narrower even than a tribe in Israel. The house of David is to have the honor of his lineage. It must be a person, therefore, that is meant. Indeed, he is so designated by the use of pronouns, just as unequivocally as it is possible. It is worthy of note, too, that this doctrine of the Messiah leaves the ritual of the Levitical law without any adequate meaning. The sacrifices and the washings then were not clearly the types of better things to come. And what becomes of the reign of the Messiah, which is so abundantly foretold? The idea held out is that the time of "brotherly union of all nations in God will be the true kingdom of the Messiah." But if the Jewish people are the Messiah, this is not his reign. All nations will have an equal part in it.

The truth is that it is manifest that this whole doctrine of the Messiah is a theory to which an exigency has driven its propagators. It is not here meant that they are not honest in its adoption. We concede the fullest measure of sincerity. But the swelling floods of modern progress have borne this Jewish party away from the old moorings. It has to them become necessary to find a new ground upon which to cast anchor, or be carried entirely away from Judaism. This doctrine has been accepted as furnishing the best refuge which is available. How unsatisfactory it is when compared with the Christian doctrine of the Messiah! The character of Jesus harmonizes with all of the Messianic prophecies of the Old Testament. He fulfills the types of the ancient ritual. He, by his word and his works, proved himself to be the Christ. In him all the nations of the earth are being blessed, and shall be still more in the future. He has already suffered, and here on earth in some form he shall yet reign from sea to sea.

Some of the other doctrines and practices inculcated in this book it will be sufficient briefly to mention. Upon the subject of divine revelation, the most explicit statement is the following, from the questions for Confirmation: "Do you believe that God, the purest and most perfect spirit, reveals himself to man in the spirit, according to his essence and will, in order that man may walk in his ways and sanctify himself in thought, word, and deed, after the sublime model of Divine holiness; and that the doctrine revealed on Sinai to Moses, the greatest of all the prophets, is truly Divine, and destined and apt to lead to such sanctification?" Here it is noteworthy that "the doctrine revealed on Sinai to Moses" is alone specified as Divine. God also is declared to reveal himself "to man in the spirit." The language seems to look decidedly in the direction of rationalism. And yet it cannot be said that rationalism is anywhere taught unequivocally in the book.

Original sin is explicitly denied. Nothing is affirmed in regard to the fall of man. But it is frequently declared that the moral nature with which we enter the world is holy. The proselyte, at his reception in the synagogue, is required to profess before God that "man, like all other beings, has come pure and good from thy hand, being born free from the stain of sin, and is naturally capable to conquer sin completely."

There is no vicarious sacrifice for sin, according to this book. The sacrifices of the ancient ritual were more or less typical. The Messiah suffers, but his sufferings are in no sense a satisfaction to the law and justice of God. They are the consequence merely of the relation of the Jewish people to the other nations. And no satisfaction for guilt is required in order to reconciliation with God. Repentance and holy living are sufficient. In the afternoon service for the Day of Atonement, the reader says: "The sacrifices and the altar thou hast taken from us, but not their essence, not the atonement, not the power of sanctifying our heart-blood for thy holy service—which he who is conscious of guilt can execute but in his spirit, and everywhere, as ever; not thy forgiving love which is always ready to receive him who repents and desires to return to the paternal lap, and for which there is no limit of time or space." The proselyte, in his profession, says, before God : " The intimate communion between thee, O most holy, and man, is brought about by no other mediation than that of the imperishable spirit dwelling in us, and is chiefly promoted by strict obedience to the revealed word, and even the sinner can find atonement and redemption if he returns to thee in sincere repentance."

The following question in the formula for the reception of proselytes, although general in the wording, seems to be aimed especially at the Christian faith as to the incarnation of God in Christ Jesus : " Do you believe that he, the inscrutable spirit of all spirits, can never assume the form of any being that is in heaven or on earth ? "

Prayers for the dead are provided. After the interment the Reader says at the grave: " May the Lord place under his almighty protection the returning soul, that it may behold his loveliness, and dwell in his sanctuary ; that peace may follow it and sooth its resting-place. May God be thy guardian, O slumbering friend ; thy shadow on thy right side. May God preserve thee from all evil, and guard thy soul ; may he protect thy going in and going out, now and through eternity." A similar .prayer is to be said subsequently in the house of mourning. Indeed, the rabbinical influence is more apparent in the burial ceremonies than anywhere else in the book. It is natural that it should here last lose its hold. People are always slow to cast off customs which are by long usage associated with proper respect for the dead. We have here in its peculiar Hebrew form the KADDISH which is to be said by the reader, mourners, and friends at the grave.

We rise from the examination of this volume with mingled feelings. There is in some of the forms a pathos which touches the heart. This is especially true in regard to certain of the utterances in regard to the past history of the Jewish people. The voice is not that of wailing, but it has an undertone of sadness which sounds like mournful music. But the dominant spirit of the book is of a different character. It is meant to kindle the feeling that the Jewish people have a sublime mission in the present and the future. And as we read we cannot avoid sympathy with the general object, although we cannot accept the particular form in which it is presented. And we wonder what will be the influence of such religious forms upon the Jewish people. In one direction it looks toward the perpetuation of a feeling of separation from other nations. They are taught to regard themselves as the Messiah. But in another direction it looks toward a breaking down of the barriers by which hitherto they have preserved their isolation. Much that is distinctly Jewish in the services of religion is abandoned. There is a longing for a close fellowship with the whole race of mankind. The ultimate aim presented is the accomplishment of universal brotherhood in God. Is this form of Judaism a mere episode? Is it a slight temporary departure from the general course of the stream? Or is it a new channel which is begun to be opened, and into which the waters will more and more pour themselves, until the whole volume empties itself at length by this way into the sea? We are confident at least of one thing. It is that this modern form of Judaism is one of the methods by which God is preparing his ancient people, in the fullness of time, to receive Jesus of Nazareth as the promised Messiah and the Redeemer of men.

> "Come then, thou great Deliverer, come ;
> The veil from Jacob's heart remove ;
> O bring thine ancient people home,
> And let them know thy dying love. "

Art. VIII.—WHAT IS TRUTH?

BY PROF. JACOB COOPER, D.C.L., Rutgers College.

THIS is a question of prime importance, since it underlies all moral and metaphysical speculation. Moreover, all progress in knowledge assumes not only the existence of Truth, but that it can in part be discovered. This question is, at the same time, a crucial test by which to determine the character of the inquirer; for it is easy or difficult to answer according to the temper of mind in which it is approached. He who desires to know, and is willing to receive with becoming humility the response to this momentous inquiry, will invariably find a solution to his immediate difficulties, which is all that can reasonably be demanded. For if light be given at each successive step, the conditions of life are met; since this exists only in the present, and each moment is a stepping stone to that which is beyond.

But, if we will receive an answer to any question, it must be propounded according to the conditions under which the subject of inquiry presents itself to us. Neither Nature* nor Revelation will be forced to testify and yield their secrets except to those who come into full sympathy with them.

The question concerning the nature of Truth is as old as speculative philosophy, and the responses given have been most diverse. Frequently it has been asked contemptuously,

----

* Bacon, *Nov. Organum*, Lib. I., Aph. III. Natura enim non nisi parendo vincitur.

under the belief that it could not be answered; and this rendered the questioner both averse to the labor necessary to find a solution, and unwilling to accept it if offered. Besides, a fruitless search in the wrong way begets doubt, since the mind is prone to conclude that what it does not find after laborious effort, cannot be discovered. For men readily adopt the doctrine of Protagoras,* and make themselves the measure of all things; and hence believe that what does not submit to this standard does not exist, or is not worth the discovery.

Truth, in its essential nature, is one of those primary notions which are so simple that they cannot be explained; since any of the terms employed in the definition are more obscure than the thing to be defined. For a necessary condition of a definition is that it makes something clear, which before was dark. The labored efforts to explain this notion in words have, therefore, been misspent; and the results, assuming the protean shape of the terms employed to elucidate, have diverted attention from the real object of pursuit. This has led Pyrrho, Democritus, and their many followers, to doubt the existence of Truth; and, as a necessary consequence, to believe nothing. For if there be not this foundation to build upon, of course there cannot be knowledge, and this unbelief is a magician's serpent, which does not merely swallow up all others, but, if consistent, swallows itself. The trouble, however, in such definitions, arises because that has been attempted which is impossible from the nature of the case to be done, save by a superior intelligence. It cannot be doubted that he who gave understanding to men, can, if he choses, make primary notions more clear than they now are to us, either by strengthening the intellectual powers, or by presenting the idea in a different view. This might be done by resolving that which is to us, with our present powers, a primary notion, into something more elementary; or by elucidating the idea through its relations. The latter was done by our Lord, when on trial before the Roman governor, through the explanation of an abstract primary conception by means of a concrete example. This is, indeed, the most satisfactory sort of elucidation; for nothing

---

* Plato Theaet., 152 A. Πρωταγόρας φησί γὰρ πού πάντων χρημάτων μέτρον ἄνθρωπον εἶναι, τῶν μὲν οντων, ὡς ἐστι, τῶν δέ μὴ ὄντων, ὡς οὐκ ἔστιν.

can be clearer than the exhibition of a principle in its actual working. Accordingly, the definition by which Christ declared himself to be the embodiment of the Truth, becomes clearly intelligible through its relations. Guided, then, by this authoritative utterance, we may adequately define Truth to be: CONFORMITY TO THE WILL OF GOD.* This may be described further as: The relations of things established by the Divine Will, and which are expressed in the creation and government of the universe.

A moment's reflection will satisfy any professed Theist that the relations of things, both physical and moral, are not fortuitous, but exist in the modes we find them because the Creator fixed them so. Whether he could, consistently with the Divine character, have arranged all things in different relations toward each other, is no question of ours; for we have to deal with them as they are, not as they might be conceived to have been made. Yet we know it must be the will of a perfectly independent originator to dispose those things which he has created in that way which seems good to himself. For before the act of creation, the choice to form a universe of matter and spirit must depend on himself alone; and out of all the possibilities within the reach of infinite resource, that must be selected which conforms to his will. "He spake and it was done; he commanded and it stood fast." Thus the simple reason why we find the relations of moral and physical nature to be what they are, is because God willed them to be in this way rather than any other. Hence, the idea of morality or physical law existing independently, or being antecedent to the will of God expressed in their constitution, is an absurdity. The question indeed, mooted by Kant, "whether it is conceivable that the universe could have been created on any other principle, as, for example, that the truths of geometry, physics, or morals, would have been diametrically opposite to what we, as now constituted, apprehend them to be," has no relevancy to our subject. It *is* conceivable, we think, because we are not limited by our experience in making postulates.

---

* The "Will of God" is not employed to denote a *single* one of the Divine attributes, but the result and expression of all in harmonious action. The distinction between the ethical and voluntary character of the Divine Nature is not well taken, and shows confusion of thought in those who contrast these attributes.

Hence, any supposition contrary to fact may be entertained, even contradictory to the senses, and may be thought of apart from all its relations, without involving absurdity merely by its conception. But the instant we connect it with the order of thought, such conception falls to the ground.

Truth, then, being the conformity to the will of God, as made known to us by its expression in creation and the Divine government, it follows:

1. This Truth is one and indivisible, save in thought, wherever it is found. It would be impossible, without writing a history of speculative philosophy, to discuss all the theories which have been held respecting the essence and relations of Truth. For every inquiry after new facts, every investigation of unexplained phenomena, is only a question about Truth in its applications. A search after its essence embodies the substance of Realism ; while the substitution of a name instead of the essence in each case where truth exists, is Nominalism. Both these conflicting systems, however, are only species embraced under a higher genus, and are coördinate in our conception of Truth. Plato, and those who follow him, hold that names, whether general or particular terms, represent actually existing things, and these are ideas or images which have had a being from all eternity, and were the patterns after which God created the world.* Hence, the embodiment of these ideas in creation are the manifestations of *Noῦs* as *Δημιουργὸs*, a Divine Intelligence.† This is Realism, and so far presents no objectionable features, because we are compelled to believe that God created the universe according to his pleasure, and that each thing made was fashioned in conformity to an act of his will. Those, again, who follow Aristotle and reject Realism, discern in the name of a thing no actual existence, but merely a sign by which it is signified. Yet these have in mind some energy, blind or intelligent, according to their attitude toward Theism, which, while known to us only by name, because it cannot be apprehended by the senses, produces a

---

* Timaeus, 38 C. *Καὶ κατὰ τὸ παράδειγμα τῆς αἰωνιάς φύσεως, ἵν' ὡς ὁμοιότατος αὐτῶ κατὰ δύναμιν ᾖ· τό μὲν γὰρ δὴ παράδειγμα πάντα αἰῶνά ἐστιν ὄν, ὁ δ' αὖ διὰ τέλους τὸν ἅπαντα χρόνον γεγονώς τέ καὶ ὧν καὶ ἐσόμενους.*

† Parmenides, 132 D. *Τά μὲν εἴδη ταῦϑ ὥσπερ παραδείγματα ἑστάναι ἐν τῇ φύσει, τα δ' αλλα τούτοις ἐοικέναι καὶ εἶναι ὁμοιώματα.*

world from nothing, or develops it from matter eternally existing.   Truth, according to this view, is the correspondence with things as they are ;* and the existence of all things must be conformed to the Supreme will, whether that be conceived of as a personal God, or as the laws of Nature.   So we see that the earliest schools into which all metaphysical speculation has been divided, agree in this, that Truth is conformity to the supreme directing power.   Indeed, according to the deep utterance of Coleridge, all men must be either Platonists or Aristotelians ; that is, must accept one or the other view of the relation of mind to matter.   Hence, if the universe be a creation, Truth is the conformity of the thing made to the will of the Maker ; and if it be a development, this is conformity to the law of growth.   Undoubtedly the Platonic idea is more agreeable to Christian modes of thought ; and, accordingly, his whole philosophic system readily adapted itself to the doctrines of Revelation.   For if the Greek thought of the world being made after the ideas which were taken by the Divine mind as models, the Jews believed that not only all the articles of ceremonial worship were fashioned after the pattern shown to Moses in the Mount,† but also the entire earthly system was a transcript of the heavenly.‡   The Christian notion that Jesus was the instrument by which the universe was made, and is the Divine energy pervading all things, agrees well with the Platonic conception of preëxistent types. For as the Idea was in the *Noũs* or Divine Mind from all eternity, so the Only Begotten was in the bosom of the Father. And as the embodiment of the Idea produced a visible world,§ so the Eternal Father was declared in the person and work of the Son.‖   The Christian Church was perfectly justified in holding that Christ was the Truth itself, for he distinctly declared this fact.   And as he was the Truth, both personified and embodied, so he knew no will but God's, and did no work but his.   Through him was the will of God actualized ; since without him was not anything made that was made.¶   Thus

---

* Aristot. Met., 993 Bekk. Ὡσ᾽ ἕκαστον ὡς ἔχει του εἶναι, οὕτω καὶ τῆς ἀληθείς.

† Numb. xxv : 40.   ‡ Ezekiel xl–xlvii.

§ Plato Timaeus, 37, C. D.   ‖ John i : 14, 18.   ¶ John i : 3.

the Divine purpose was revealed through him to the comprehension of men; and as he acted in perfect conformity to the Divine will, his whole life was a continued exhibition of the Truth, not merely as a mental abstraction, but realized in a concrete example. The pious believer views Christ as the expression of the will of God, who sums up in himself all that we can know of Deity or his works. And so, in Christian logic, he is the middle term of comparison through which alone the creature can know the Creator. Hence, when the saintly and acute Malebranche would see all things in God, this means that nothing can be known in its absolute verity, except when viewed in its relations to the Divine nature.

Now, if Truth be conformity to the Divine Will, it must be one and indivisible, except in thought. Plato got a glimpse of this oneness, and struggled hard to develop the doctrine, but was forced to admit that it transcends finite intelligence.[*] There cannot be two wills about the same thing, without being either identical, which is absurd; or at variance, which would involve a contradiction inconsistent with the Divine character. This conformity is seen perfectly in the order of the natural world. There is no such thing as error or conflict here. Nature is everywhere constant to herself, and exhibits unity of plan and ultimate design. Every process of scientific investigation proceeds upon the constancy maintained by the laws of Nature, whether they be themselves a directing power, or merely the expression of God's will. However much a scientist may question the dicta of morals, or doubt the existence of a higher Intelligence which directs the movements of matter, still he is positive in his belief in the constancy of those laws which govern the material world. He experiments with the view of obtaining a particular result; he interrogates matter by his crucibles, his scales or his glass, in the full assurance that if he asks aright, the correct answer will be given. Moreover, he is equally sure that the answer is correct whether it establish or demolish his theory; and hence, no matter how many times he fail to attain his object, the interrogation is renewed again with as much confidence in the constancy of Nature's laws as though he had not failed a single time. Thus far he is consistent, because he rests on the firm basis that

---

* Plato Republic, 511, A. B.

whatever nature responds is true. But when he pushes his theory so far as to substitute the process by which force acts on matter, or the laws which regulate this movement for that Intelligence which directs and gives efficacy to those laws, then he forsakes his own method. For he attempts to put the mode by which Intelligence acts in place of that Intelligence, the result of force for force itself. With jealous incredulity he guards the process up to the chasm between mind and matter, then makes the leap from the natural, and, as he acknowledges no spiritual, lands nowhere. Even when he is aware by the highest of all knowledge, distinct consciousness, that his determination to try an experiment is wholly distinct from the bodily act, still he assumes, in the face of his own rigid method, a generative force in those materials which his senses teach him act only as they are acted upon. Here is the greatest absurdity of all the ages. Cicero well said there is no tenet so absurd that it has not found some philosopher to advocate it.* And surely there is none comparable to this, that while all the operations of Nature are invariable, that they are so fortuitously because nothing has made them constant. But when we listen to the voice of reason speaking within us, or the word of Revelation without us, we recognize a univ erse which is not the result of chance. The stones and minerals beneath our feet did not create themselves out of star dust (which, like Topsy, " growed "), nor, by fortuitous jumble, arranged themselves with mathematical accuracy. The forces of Nature did not correlate themselves; since these are, *per se*, repellant, and do not spontaneously combine for concerted action. As well might a conflagration collect and arrange the materials so as to build up a Chicago in a night. It would be absurd indeed to expect that an explosion of nitro-glycerine would build a ship, and direct it successfully through a long voyage. But what shall we say of the theory, that Titanic forces, without an intelligent master, elaborated this world of marvellous symmetry and beauty, then directed it on its voyage, not for a day or a year, but from age to age, impelling it on its course without stop or collision? Yet this is only one of an infinite number of similar spheres sailing through space, in a system of connected orbits so intricate that no calculus of

---

*Cicero, De. Div., II., 119: Nescio quomodo nihil tam absurde dici potest quod non dicatur ab aliquo philosophorum.

earth can grasp its movements. To believe that this is all effected by fortuitous impulse, does violence to common sense, and proves the mind which clings to such a theory unfit for rational speculation. For no person, not wilfully blind, can fail to see that undirected force segregates rather than aggregates, and destroys instead of creating. Thus the mind instinctively recognizes that all harmony and beauty in the visible world, all symmetry of atomic structure in organized matter, all obedience to law and constancy of action, result from the command of a Being possessed of infinite intelligence and power. Again, Truth is shown to us by answering the end for which a thing was made. Hence, accident or uncertainty in the result to be reached is inconsistent with its conditions as fixed by a superintending governor. In any scheme of intelligent providence, every part must have its purpose and fulfill the mission assigned to it. For in this way it conforms to that will which foresaw all the possibilities of things before they were created and willed their arrangement and issue. The members of this vast creation were written in the Divine book of universal Providence when as yet there was none of them.* And when in continuance they were fashioned, they grew up into that wondrous Cosmos whose parts are so fitted to each other that they have one common end in view,† and work, both matter and mind, like soul and body, together.

But while Truth is one and indivisible, save in thought, we may speak of physical and metaphysical, or moral and political Truth ; but these are only different names for parts of one and the same thing—that is, conformity of the agent to the creating and governing purpose of the Supreme will. There can, therefore, be no conflict between these coördinate parts of one idea which rests for its authority upon the determination of God. Yet we hear so much said about the conflict between Religion and Science that many are prone to think they are irreconcilable, and therefore the utterances of one or the other must be false. And as those facts which appeal immediately to the senses offer a readier and simpler criterion of proof, it is taken for granted that they are true ; while the utterances of Revelation which do not, from the

---

*Ps. cxxxix: 16 (Hebrew).   †Cleanthes' Hymn to Zeus, 12–13.

nature of the subject matter, submit to the test of the senses;. must be false whenever the latter appear to be in conflict with the former. It is forgotten that, before we can say there is such a conflict, we must fully comprehend the testimony of both these witnesses. Without this we may think we have convicted one or the other of falsehood, while in reality we have only exposed our own ignorance. Hence, we cannot say that either is false according to the testimony of the other;. unless we master and classify all the facts of physical nature, and fathom the depths of Divine intelligence. For, however glaring a contradiction there may be apparently between them, yet a single one of the innumerable facts which never entered our minds might, if known, resolve every difficulty, and show, instead of hopeless discord, a most beautiful harmony, when the coördinate utterances of verbal and material revelation are viewed in their complete generalization. Hence, we assert that *it is impossible for any intelligence, short of omniscience, to convict Revelation of falsehood by the testimony of Nature.*

The conditions of all knowledge are groping through the darkness of ignorance, and fighting errors of our own creation. The absurdities of the Ptolemaic system of astronomy subjected it to the taunt of Alphonso, King of Castile: "If this. be the plan on which God made the universe, had I been consulted I could have suggested a simpler working scheme." But this false structure of the cosmical system was really no charge against the true one. Men of shallow brains and deep prejudice against religion said, in this generation, that the Bible could not be true because it sanctioned human slavery. Men of still shallower brains endeavored to prove its lawfulness by appeals to the usages of those who were the channels through which Revelation was delivered; as though the truth could be blamed with all their personal failures in duty. Advance in science and morals has swept away both errors. We may now laugh at the mazes of the Ptolemaic Cycles; but we do not believe the truths of astronomy have been changed. We rejoice that a higher plane of religious life enables all men to see that the spirit of the gospel forbids every condition that rendered slavery possible; how much soever Moses may, for the hardness of the Jewish heart, have suffered these things.. Still the Bible is no more true and pure,. now that we are able to receive its doctrines, than when men charged God foolishly. Yet the bitter controversy between scientists or nature-worshipers and those who reverence a spiritual God, continues unabated. Both have often erred through lack of knowledge, and made themselves ridiculous by assertions which a better understanding of their respective subjects enabled them to disavow. Each, for a time, thought that he alone possessed all the truth. Many are the bulls which Popes have hurled at comets or other scientific meteors which crossed their ignorant horizon. Theologians have, through a great preponderance of zeal over knowledge, compromised their cause by asserting that certain results of scientific research were false because in conflict with the Bible. But the mistake was that they made the Bible assert what it does not, and substituting their own interpretations, have been put to shame because their theories have been falsified by the undoubted facts of science. Yet the persecution of Galileo is not due to any error or intolerance of revelation, but to a false interpretation of what it really says. Such mistakes have made theologians more cautious and humble—cautious in not jeopardizing the cause of religion by asserting a conflict between it and science where there is none ; more humble, because they find that the Bible does not reveal all its meaning at once, but from age to age, as the world becomes prepared to receive its teachings. But any number of mistakes of a similar sort fails to teach scientists modesty when bitten by the rabies of hostility to Divine Revelation. For they are bent on discovering, not identity, but contrariety of teaching betwen the two witnesses. And as no person ever desired, strongly and persistently, to believe anything without setting out to obtain facts to sustain his pet idea, or else distort those already known, so as to make them subservient to his purpose, such discrepancy is sure to be found. One part of human nature is enmity against God ; a fact undeniable, whether we look at the world in general, or interrogate the individual conscience. The revelation from heaven increases this enmity by exposing and reproving sin ; and so men are bent on destroying the light lest it may disclose their hidden works of darkness. No other theory will account for the inveterate hatred which is exhibited against revealed Truth, since it comes laden with joy and blessings to a world full of misery.

Repeated failures in discovering the secrets of nature have made scientists humbler in their own sphere, so that when they come to an apparent contradiction in natural phenomena, they do not, for an instant, suppose this discrepancy is real, but rather that it results from their imperfect deductions. Hence, they seek some higher law by which the seemingly discordant results can be harmonized, or struggle with patient experiment to discover whether nature will verify their facts. However the issue may be, they always think the fault lies with themselves, or arises from the necessary limitations of human knowledge. They may well remember the multitude of theories that have been paraded before the world in all the pride of confident ignorance, yet had soon to be buried out of sight as an untimely birth. Each of the sciences is the record of a struggle up through false theories, many of them now so ridiculous that it looks like a caricature of the human intellect to believe they were ever advocated. These facts ought to make scientists respectful in their attitude toward revealed religion, and cause them for shame to stifle their exultation at the *pretended* periodical collapse of that revelation towhich the world owes all its liberty and material progress—at least until their own bantlings cease " mewling and puking in their nurse's arms."

The greatest achievements in scientific research have been made by those who admitted no conflict with revealed Truth. The pioneers in every department of investigation have been those who recognized the universe to be the handiwork of God, and who explored every part of nature with the feeling of true children disporting themselves in their Father's house. His revealed Truth becomes more clear because it is mirrored in the material world. For since the Divine countenance is visible in all the works of creation, and there is but one kind of truth, its different parts testify to each other. Cleanthes says, in his Hymn to Zeus,* " There is but one reason which pervades all things, and by which all are governed." And Virgil embodies this doctrine when he says :

> "Spiritus intus alit ; totamque infusa per artus
> Mens agitat molem, et magno se corpore miscit."†

Common sense must teach any unprejudiced mind that if

---

* Line 20.   † Æn. VI., 726-7.

Truth manifests itself through significant signs, there is every reason to believe its utterances, though rational speech will be still more clear. If a Supreme intelligence must precede to establish order, this will communicate with those possessed of intelligence by unmistakeable utterances. And hence, while the declarations of Truth are equally veracious, however they are seen or heard, when the God of Truth speaks directly, his voice must be obeyed first, because its authority cannot be misunderstood. Every candid mind must therefore believe, with Bacon, the revealed word of God, no matter what contradicts; and rather consider his own reasonings at fault than the divine oracles. The great pioneer in modern scientific research, and the author of the only method of inquiry recognized as valid, is pleased to say:* " Atque illud insupee supplices rogamus ne humana divinis officiant; neve ex reseratione viarum sensus, et accensione majore laminis naturalis, aliquid incredulitatis et noctis, animis nostris erga divina mysteria oborietur; sed potius, ut ab intellecta puro a phantasiis et vanitate repurgato, et divinis oraculis nihilominus subdito et prorsus dediditio, fidei dentur quæ fidei sunt. Postremo, ut scientiæ veneus, a serpente infuso quo animus humanus tu-·met et inflatur, deposito, nec altum sapiamus, nec ultra solinem, sed veritatem in charitate colamus." If scientists would imitate this reverential spirit of their acknowledged pathfinder, we would have no more of the conflict between religion and the laws of nature.

II. Truth is unchangeable because it is the embodiment of the Divine attributes.

A glance at the visible world reveals constant changes going on about us. These are not confined to the narrow sphere of our lives, where everything is mutable to such a degree that our mortal existence is compared to whatever is most transitory. Even the solid earth undergoes transformations from age to age, so that the grotesque fauna and gigantic flora of a former period look as though they belonged to an entirely different world. The winds toss the sands in deserts where once the sea thundered against its shores. Portions of the earth's surface have sunk, and the sites of cities are covered by the ocean; or by the lake, where the mountains flowing down have

---

* Pref. ad Instan. Mag.

raised the level of the waters. But the laws producing these results abide unchanged amid all the revolutions they make, for the everlasting God directs each movement. The same mysterious vapor goes up to water the earth now as when creation was but just finished. The plant produces seed after its kind, varying within specific limits, but constant to its established order as the pendulum to its arc. The fish swims, the bird flies, the ravenous animal tears its prey, the ruminant quietly chews its cud. Man walks erect, and the troglodyte goes on all fours, just as at the first. All is regularity and order. The same laws sway the material world, and therefore the phenomena are constant. This gives confidence in all the offices of life. The cultivator of the soil goes forth to his work in the full assurance that seed time and harvest will never fail. The investigator of Nature's secrets pursues his studies relying on the same recurrence of phenomena, without possibility of failure, provided the like conditions be observed. On any other supposition all his efforts would be made at random, and new discoveries could not be classified, because no one could tell to what department of science they belonged. This constancy, however, is corroborated afresh by each new induction, no matter where it be made. For even those physical phenomena which up to our own day were considered so entirely accidental that their fickleness passed into a proverb, have, when better understood, been found to be equally certain with the rest. Hence, the expression, "As uncertain as the wind," can no longer be used, because the course of the wind and the state of the atmosphere are now predicted with nearly the same accuracy that other physical phenomena are anticipated.

The same fact may be seen amid the varying and seemingly contradictory modes of mental action. It is true, that when we look at a multitude of the conflicting metaphysical systems, instead of presenting the clearness and constancy of truth, they "come like shadows, and so depart." Many problems which are as old as speculative thought, and whose solutions have often been claimed by self-appointed leaders, are still unsolved; and some of the laws which regulate the mental processes are not yet explained so clearly as to leave no doubt. But the reason for this is obvious. The facts are not sought first, and the law educed by a patient and unbiased classification; but the theory is predetermined, and then the facts distorted to fit it.   Yet despite this confusion of systems, there are certain leading principles running through all; and speculative thinkers, like scientists, however unreasonable in other respects, have never been absurd enough to charge their own mistakes and incomplete deductions upon the unerring Truth after which they were searching.   Still the establishment of law, the offer of rewards and threat of punishment, proceed on the assumption that there is constancy of mental action under given circumstances.   All theories of morals, all systems of art and criteria of beauty, the canons of criticism and science of persuasion, must rest upon such assumption.   If the mind of man acted without any uniformity, there could be no logical or mathematical formula.   Nay more, words would convey different significations to each man; and any common sign of communication could not be found.   The progress of knowledge depends upon this certitude of mental action.   Otherwise there could be no acquisition of theoretical knowledge in the aggregate of mankind, nor experience in the individual. Though natural phenomena were invariable, and the actions of moral agents the same under given conditions, yet, if the modes by which each man viewed them were diverse, there could be no matured experience.   The individual would know no more in ripe age than the child when it first opened its eyes upon the world.   Hence, he would have no legacy of collected and verified information to bequeath to his successor; and each age of the world must remain equally ignorant, because the sport of intellectual uncertainty.   But because mental phenomena, under fixed conditions, are invariably sure, the historian gives us results which have been arrived at after a careful review of human conduct in the past, and these serve as a lamp to guide us in the future.   Euclid's Geometry has remained for more than two thousand years as the basis for mechanical mathematics; and the Organon of Aristotle still supplies the mode in which men must reason, if they do so correctly. Sophocles forces our tears at the miseries of the unfortunate; Aristophanes provokes our laughter at the absurdities of mankind, by appealing to precisely the same feelings and presenting the same motives that Shakespeare and Rabelais did in

their day.   While individual phenomena of mind may be unaccountable, and the actions of men occasionally abnormal,
still there is constancy within limitations.   Nature must have
room for play in her operations, else they cease.   So metaphysical phenomena; while subject to law, must have freedom
of action, even more because a new factor, the self-determining
power of the will, is necessary to its production.   Even the
doctrine of chances, in its relations to human conduct, is subject to a higher law of certainty by which any event, however
variable in its production, has its inconstancy confined within
fixed bounds, and, therefore, can be predicted with perfect
confidence.   Life, when considered in the individual, is subject
to so many fortuitous circumstances, that no person can have
the assurance of an hour's existence, yet in the aggregate of a
large multitude can be predicted with mathematical precision.
Perhaps there is no business which, if carried out with perfect
accuracy and integrity, is more sure to enrich than life assurance ; yet the duration of life depends on an innumerable multitude of contingencies, which mostly arise from each man's
own course of action in conforming to, or disagreeing with,
the laws of health.   His action may be good or bad, according to his own voluntary choice.   And this choice is swayed
by so many motives, apparent, it may be, but often hidden
even from himself, that nothing but Infinite wisdom could
determine the special result of each act.   Yet they are all
amenable to a governing principle which·can be discovered.
And such is the case with all intellectual and moral actions.   Were it not so, we repeat, progress would be impossible, and men more helpless than the brute.   For the
latter is taught by instinct, and so contains within itself
all the knowledge necessary to enable it to fulfill its destiny—
blindly, it is true, to itself, but still certainly.   Men, however,
having no guide but reason, and this having no fixed data
from which to draw inferences, each would be made subject to
every chance, and perish because he could never accumulate
knowledge.

This conformity to the will of God is evidently complete in
all his works save in human volition.   Here, however, is an
element of disorder, which cannot be accounted for save on the
principle that man can act in opposition to his Maker's com-

mandment. This freedom is a primary truth, incapable of explanation, yet necessary to be assumed unless the distinctions between right and wrong be obliterated. The presence of sin in a world created and governed by a holy God is also unaccountable, but yet testified to by consciousness, our highest appeal. Indeed, this truth, and the assurance that our guilt arises from our own wrong-doing, is certified to as emphatically by the individual consciousness as by direct revelation. It introduces a new element in the calculation of human motive, but no uncertainty in the result. For while this manifests lack of conformity to the Divine will, the discord is confined within determinate limits. Pharaoh acted as freely, as wickedly, when, deaf to oft-repeated warnings, and while he saw more than the sword of Damocles hanging over his head, he persisted in opposition to the command of God. Still for this very cause was he raised up, that he might exhibit the power and glory of the Divine government in the punishment of wicked men. The obdurate Jews acted freely in putting to death a man declared to be innocent after the most searching examination which stern Roman law could enforce. Yet this was effected by the determinate counsel and foreknowledge of God. The hot passions of men rage in fury like the waves of the sea. But it is written of both : Thus far shalt thou go, and no farther. Both in the moral and physical world, the influences act either separately or in combination to produce the determinate result. The heathen poet saw this when he said : "The counsel of Jove was fulfilled all the time."* God commissions his prophet to declare: "My counsel shall stand, and I will do all my pleasure." † Hence, each particle of matter, each natural force, each voluntary action, is subjected to this all-controlling principle, and is perfectly obedient to its mission. Were it not so, everything would fall into confusion. For if one portion of this world could act contrary to its duty, then each other part, being connected with it, must be influenced by its error. A mistake of a single figure in the largest calculation vitiates all the process subsequent to its occurrence. The smallest wheel in a complicated machinery can mar the action of the whole. Hence, failure in the least of Nature's processes leads to failure in all. But since every part alike is

---

* Iliad, I., 5.   Διὸς δ' ἐτελείετο βουλή.   † Is. xlv : 10.

impressed with this conformity to the Divine will, and accomplishes the end for which it was created, the whole moves on from age to age in perfect harmony. No confusion mars the perfect movement; no flaw in the mechanism causes a stop; but the universe marks out its unending years on the dial of time.

III.— This truth is capable of demonstration in exact proportion as we come into harmony with it and it falls within our range of possible vision. Much is said about the clearness of proof which some of the sciences afford. Their methods of demonstration are lauded as though they cannot lead astray; and are themselves attractive since they give the student a tangible reward for his labor. The mathematical sciences, as they deal with abstract number and discrete quantity, are supposed to yield a sort of proof unique in kind, and possessed of a certainty which belongs to no others to the same degree.

Next to these, those sciences which deal with matter directly, which can therefore be subjected to sensible tests, offer almost or quite equal certainty. Their certitude is often contrasted with the working in other departments of knowledge, especially with those which employ metaphysical or moral reasoning. The one kind is claimed to offer infallible demonstration ; the other probable, or, from the nature of the subjects about which it is conversant, moral proof. And this is said to range all the way from possibility to moral certainty.

What this may mean, it is the business of those who use the terms to explain. One thing, however, is beyond, question : that the certitude in the one case or the doubtfulness in the other does not arise from the nature of the objects investigated, but from the methods of inquiry or the persons who institute them.[*] For when we examine closely we see that the accuracy of results in geometry, for example, arise from the character of the terms used and the data agreed upon. There is no reason, in the nature of the thing, why a definition should not be as clear touching one department of knowledge as another. For unless Truth lies at the basis of each of them, it is impossible that the

---

[*] Aristol. Met. 993, Bekk. Οὐχ ἐν τοῖς πράγμασιν, αλλ' ἐν ἡμῖν τὸ αἴτιόν ἐστιν αὐτῆς. Ὥσπερ γὰρ καὶ τα τῶν νυκτερίδων ὄμματα πρὸς τὸ φέγγος ἔχει τὸ μεθ' ἡμέραν, οὕτω καὶ τῆς ἡμετέρας ψυχῆς ὁ νοῦς πρὸς τὰ τῇ φανερώτατα πάντων.

responses given to such as investigate them should be worthy of acceptation. For, however clear the method and cogent the application, the answer can be no more true than the subject which furnishes it; as the stream can never rise higher than the fountain. Each science, then, rests ultimately on the Divine will as manifested in the nature of its subject matter.

In those cases where infallible responses have been given, if any there be, the reason is that the conditions under which Nature submits herself to be questioned have been complied with implicitly. For God speaks distinctly, in his works and in his word, to those who are willing to ask aright. Seek and ye shall find; knock and it shall be opened unto you, is written over every door of knowledge fit for the use of men. But in no other way can an answer be expected. Had Pythagoras entertained some conceit as to the relation between the square of the longest side of a right angled triangle to the sum of the squares of the other two sides, he would never have completed the demonstration. But by using adequate terms always in the same sense, and divesting them of all irrelevant meaning, he arrived after the result which was true to Nature. Had he pursued any other course, the truth of the proposition, though not attained by him, would still have existed in Nature all the same, awaiting some discoverer who would seek according to the conditions of geometry. The whole body of scientific truth, as now known, and all that lies in the fertile womb of the future, existed *in esse* in the beginning of time; and only awaited compliance with the proper laws of investigation suited to each case, to be *in posse* for the good of the world. Those in the pursuit of truth have often had an inward assurance that they had arrived near where their prize lay concealed, yet failed to reach it. This fact is seen in any of those sciences which are thought to yield the most satisfactory proof. In the application of geometry to the measurement of angles, heights, or distances, the approach to perfect accuracy is indicated precisely by the degree of compliance with the conditions imposed by Nature.

A near approximation is obtained, so that we may confidently say, the sum is greater than A and less than B. Mount Everest is more than 28,000 and less than 30,000 ft. high. Is there any uncertainty about its height in reality? No sane man can think this; and when by instruments of greater accu-

racy, and through the use of methods more precise the altitude
is established for all practical purposes, it is still not absolutely
correct. This process is like the asymptotes, where there is a perpetual approach of the two lines without ever meeting.　Still it
is all the time plain that the facts in the case are not changed
by our ignorance or knowledge. Take an example more nearly
concerning practical life. Let it be proposed to establish the
latitude or longitude of a given place. It is determined approx-
imately, so that geodesy can fix upon one point in a certain locality, and another at a short distance from the first, and assert
with full assurance that the desired meridian is between them,
without being able, however, to say precisely where. By a better compass and more accurate trigonometrical calculations,
the point may possibly be found and the absolute meridian
is fixed. So, in the early survey of a territory, the lines may
not, either through haste in the survey, or employment
of unskillful men, be correctly laid off, and prove fruitful
sources of dispute between contiguous owners. A strip of land
may be in litigation, while each proprietor willingly admits that
his neighbor rightfully possesses the greater part of what is
considered his estate. The boundary is somewhere between
the two lines claimed by the respective parties. The point is
to determine where, so that the true amount of land may be
adjudged to each. In all these cases the matter in dispute is
not uncertain in itself, and is made plain provided the proper
appliances be employed for determining the facts.

It may be said that these are examples taken from concrete
mathematics, and that the uncertainty of the result arises from
the elements of imperfection introduced by instruments or their
manual application. But the like failures to obtain absolute accuracy is shown when the calculations are made from numerical data. For in the integral calculus there are multitudes
of cases where more than one answer will satisfy the requirements of the problem. Many equations again are interminate;
and there is as much room for ingenuity in fencing with the cabal-
istic signs of quaternions as there was with Barbara, Celarent,
etc, of the schoolmen. Besides, pure mathematics, like every
subject of investigation whose terms are, *ex necessitate*, postulates, must, as an independent science without applications, be
a nullity. For, if you dissever numbers from objects, you di-

vest them of their significance, and they become purely arbitrary signs. They can be made to signify anything at the caprice of him who employs them; and consequently they carry with them no more certitude than words dissociated from ideas. For a term, whether it be angle, number or logical postulate, becomes a variable when applied to any concrete quantity, and ceases to be a factor in demonstrative reasoning, in the strict application of that term. While in the region of pure abstractions, the results deduced from them may be ever so true, they are meaningless to us, and therefore of no practical value.

The claim that moral truths can be established with undoubted certitude by a process of demonstration, even as the facts of material science, has been scouted as chimerical. The few who have attempted the purely scientific method in metaphysics or morals, have been derided as on a par with those who sought the philosopher's stone—mere visionaries, who pursued an *ignus fatus*. The comparative ease of demonstration in physics, the extreme difficulty of reasoning in morals, being assumed, have given speciousness to the notion that the difference between the processes in these two subjects results either from a necessary diversity in the methods employed, or the facts lying at the basis of the inquiries. Let it be granted however, that there is truth in spiritual things, and that the phenomena of mind range themselves under laws; then, assuredly, if the proper methods of investigation be adopted and pursued with sufficient patience, vigor, and energy, these laws may be—nay *must be*—disclosed with as much certainty as those concerning any other class of subjects. Let the true issue be kept clearly in view. If it be asserted that there is no Truth, or that it is unknown to us as Democritus held,[*] then there can be no controversy. For what does not exist or is not knowable, of course cannot be discovered. But if it exists, then, wherever it leaves vestiges of its presence, there it can be traced while these are kept in view. And if as Goethe says, [†]"there be in man a desire for Truth, and aptitude for discerning it when found,"

---

[*] As quoted by Aristotle, Met. 1009, Bekk, ἤτοι οὐδέν εἶναι ἀληθές ἢ ἡμῖν ἄδηλον.

[†] Wahrheitsliebe zeigt sich darin, dass man überall das Gute zu finden und zu schatzen weiss.

then a pursuit which looks steadfastly upon its vestiges without being turned aside by individual bias, must end in its discovery. For whether the Truth be called by this or that name is
immaterial, provided the mind has an appetency for it. In considering the dual nature of man, if we assume, as is rational,
that provision is made for both parts in proportion to their
wants, we must admit that moral truth fills a larger sphere in
his requirements than physical. For the chief difference which
discloses itself at first sight between man and the lower animals is that the former have spiritual powers in predominance,
while the latter are nearly all corporeal. If pabulum be furnished according to the need of each part of man, the sum of
spiritual truth must greatly exceed physical. Why, then,
should it not be as easily attainable? The reason is, that men's
minds are darkened by error, their opinions colored by prejudice; and so choose falsehood because it is in harmony with
their nature. In pure science the result is a matter of perfect
indifference. The powers of numbers take no hold upon the
passions of men. It matters nothing to our inclinations whether
two angles be equal to each other or not. The composition
of water appealed to no man's predilections so as to sway his
judgment in the analysis. Hence there is no trouble from
this source in defining terms and fixing a nomenclature of science which shall be invariable. And when this is done, the
reasoning process will bring the conclusion with equal precision everywhere. But the diversity lies in settling upon the
data employed. These pass out of the sphere of indifference
where pure abstractions remain, and come under the influence
of our feelings, our prejudices, or our desires. Each man,
then, defining an idea according to his subjective condition,
even when he hears the same word that another does, may
not think of precisely the same thing. So the quantities employed in the metaphysical calculation being different, the answers must be diverse. Yet in each case there is an approximation to agreement, else men could not understand each
other. If vocal sounds and written characters had not something more than casual agreement, there could be no such thing
as communication between man and man. Babel would be
enacted all the time. Language grows out of the roots of
mutual understanding by symbols, and is the concrete expres-

sion of identity in thought. Its laws are as certain as those of the anatomical structure of the body. The fragmentary roots of languages, whose peoples have long since been buried with them, when accidentally exhumed by the comparative grammarian, enable him to reconstruct the framework of the ancient speech; even as the single bone in Cuvier's hands would be sufficient for him to build again the skeleton of the animal which had perished from the earth.

This partial agreement in the use of words shows that there is identity at the bottom after which all are striving; and the approximation will be proportionate in every case to the clearness of each man's idea and his freedom from prejudice. Given two shades of meaning, one of which conveys less than the reality, and the other more ; then the Truth must be somewhere between them, as surely as the proper line is between the disputed boundaries of two proprietors, or the different determinations of the meridian in geodesy. If the mind could be cleared sufficiently from individual bias to give each term its exact meaning, every man who is equally free from prejudice would accept this term as an adequate expression of an idea understood between them. If, next, a vocabulary were invented for each special department of reasoning with fixed meanings, like the nomenclature of chemistry or botany, the logical process employing these terms must deduce as trustworthy responses as geometry. While demonstration in mental phenomena is more difficult to most persons than in material, yet this arises, as we have seen, not from the inherent obstacles of the subject, but from those thrown around it by our methods. Besides, when we look at the subject with candor, we see that there are many truths in mental and moral action quite as well established as any facts in physics. Certain acts are pronounced good or bad, according to some inherent quality, by every person possessing a given amount of moral training, with as much confidence as the mind passes judgment on any facts in nature. That it is wicked to remove landmarks ; that it is inhuman to oppress the orphan, to rob the widow, to withhold the wages of the hireling, were facts as clear to the mind of Job as that the Pleiades always rose in their season, or that silver ore was found in its proper veins. There can be no doubt that it is sinful to lie and steal ; for parents to abandon their infant

children; to injure the helpless or abuse those who have not
provoked us.   If we look about us we will discover an im
mense stock of moral truths attested by everybody of given
intelligence and culture, and which are no more likely to be
disputed than the postulates of science.   Conventional regulations may declare certain acts to be right on the other side of
the Alps which are held wrong on this side; but such enactments do not affect our consciousness of immutable morality:
and, of course, do not change the nature of the acts themselves.
Besides, the first truths in one department of knowledge rest
on precisely the same basis as those of another.   They are
self-evident facts which are accepted as soon as they are presented to that mind which is capable of taking in their full
meaning.   It is vain to say that many, perhaps all, these fundamental truths in morals have been disputed in some age or
nation, and that there is no agreement now among men as to
the exact number of these which are to be accepted.   For the
same objection could be as legitimately urged against the first
truths in physics, provided the words be employed in the same
sense in both departments of speculation.   For we must bear
in mind that first truths depend for their reception on a given
amount of intelligence.   As soon as a man has a full comprehension of the terms employed, he accepts as true, beyond dispute,
that the whole is greater than any one of its parts; that two
things which are equal to one and the same third are equal to
each other; or that two plus two are four.   But there was a
time in the history of many nations, just as in the life of the
individual, when these facts could not be considered first truths
or necessary conditions of thought, because they were not
comprehended.   The decimal notation clearly points to a
period when no person using it could reckon beyond the number of his fingers.   For him all the superstructure of concrete
arithmetic had no meaning; while the abstract number, in its
most elementary conceptions, never entered into his thoughts.
Not one of the axioms of geometry could be accepted by him
as a primary truth, for his mind was not sufficiently advanced
for its comprehension, and nothing can be accepted as such
unless it present itself under the two conditions—full understanding, and the immediately consequent assurance of its
verity.   When the moral perceptions are blunted by continu-

ance in sin, or where they have never been educated up to any standard of intelligent virtue, its most rudimentary notions might be denied or questioned. And this might be done by persons of the highest intellectual culture, as in the case of Rousseau, Macchiavelli, and the most refined voluptuaries among the later Romans, or such as are sunk in the lowest depths of barbarism. The conscience which is dead cannot perceive first truths in morals; the intellect utterly uncultivated fails to discern, and therefore may deny as well as affirm, the axioms of science indifferently. No legitimate argument in proof of a radical difference between the clearness of scientific and moral truth can therefore be drawn from the nature of their respective first truths, or the treatment they have received among men.

There is no subject in speculation about which we hear more loose talk than this of first truths. It is impossible to fix an infallible criterion for their determination, because they differ in number according to the natural capacity or special culture of the individual. Euclid's Geometry contains no truth, first or of any order, to the majority of mankind. But when this book, after being carefully withheld for a long time by Paschal's father, accidentally fell into the hands of the wonderful twelve-year-old boy, the young genius turned over page after page, from the first to the last, with the remark, "All this is plain!" So to Mrs. Somerville, whose friends wished to preserve her girlhood unharmed by such dangerous things as Algebra, when the forbidden work was obtained by stealth, it was all first truths, because it found a capacity just suited to its acceptance. It is plain, therefore, that first truths depend on culture; as we may see illustrated continually in young children, or persons at any age who are mastering a particular branch of knowledge. As they rise to a higher level, new facts present themselves under such conditions that they are at once understood and accepted. The mind then appropriates them as ideas so clear that they need no proof; nay, rather their proof is involved in the general growth of the mind, for they are as evident and as true to it as the consciousness of its own actions. This is the method of advancement in culture; and first truths multiply in exact proportion to the expansion of the mind, and the strength which experience gives it through the sloughing off of old errors. Like the change of night into day in the material world. At first all is darkness, and nothing is seen. There is no knowledge; because while there are objects innumerable close by, and the sense of sight is present and vigorous, there is no medium through which they can be discerned. The benighted traveler is lost, and gropes around in vain to find where he is. He may feel something touching him ; but even this he cannot recognize. Yet, as the few faint rays of light reveal the outlines, he sees the distorted shapes, but cannot comprehend anything around him. Gradually, however. the eye of day opens, and his intelligence expands with the increasing light. He determines the larger objects with accuracy, and traces the more minute. And when the full flood of light is spread by the risen sun, all is so clear that he takes in at a glance the entire panorama which was around him before, but of which he had no conception. This capacity for first truths is not confined to any one department of knowledge, and is everywhere amenable to precisely the same laws of growth. It must, however, be borne in mind, that the growth will be in the department in which the knowledge is gained. Hence the culture of pure intellect will not necessarily enable the moral sense to gain new truths; neither will the development of this attribute insure mastery by the reasoning power. These may, and often do, act and react on each other; but they may also be cultivated in isolation, or at one another's expense. But in precisely the degree that they are respectively cultured will be their capacity in their several spheres to receive new truths, and these in time become primary and fundamental to further growth. It may be asked, What, then, constitutes a first truth, and wherein does this differ from other information clearly apprehended by the mind ? As soon as an idea becomes so clear that it is spontaneously accepted, and requires no explanation or proof—nay, rather, is obscured thereby—it is a first truth to that order of capacity and culture which so receives it. And those conceptions which so commend themselves to the universal acceptation of cultured people, are, by common consent, classified by themselves. But it is evident that their subjective nature, as well as their number, is regulated by a sliding scale. For if the power of the mind were greatly enlarged, not only would their number be increased, but their clearness also. And even the most fundamental and primary of them all, while incapable of explanation in terms, may still be elucidated by concrete examples. And hererein was the power of Jesus Christ as a teacher pre-eminent above all others, by raising from the dead and rehabilitating the ideas of virtue, which before were thoroughly comprehended and possessed by all, but had lost their vital power. This he did constantly, illustrating abstract truth by parables, and actualizing it in his life.

It is further claimed that there must be a radical difference in the nature of proof which the moral and physical sciences furnish, because of the opposite fortunes which they exhibit. It is said that not only the first principles of scientific truth are unquestioned, but that a grand system of matured results have for ages defied doubt; while, on the other hand, all questions of moral and intellectual philosophy are still open and subject to frequent controversy. It is astonishing to hear it maintained that the first principles of science are so well settled and clear that there can be no question about them, when this assertion is in the face of undoubted history. For example: The constituents of many metals which have been long known are each, *sui generis*, and have the same structure, hardness, weight, and other properties. They can be mixed, separated, changed in form, but the identity of each ultimate particle remains the same in all these mutations. It was conceded that no one of these substances could be made without uniting their constituent parts in their due proportions. Yet, in defiance of all established laws of chemistry, the foremost scientific men of the middle ages, and almost to our own time, wearied themselves in the fruitless search after some substance, which, by its mere touch, would transmute the base metals into gold. So again: No physical truth seems more obvious than that no power can be generated by the multiplication of machinery, and that action and reaction are equal. But the world still abounds in visionaries, the lineal descendants of those who gave their lives to the attempt to invent perpetual motion. It is further accepted as a fundamental maxim that, *ex nihilo nihil fit*, or that every effect must have an adequate cause. But, to escape from the necessity of admitting a Creator, such as common sense, as well as revelation, declares to be a necessary condition of the existence of a

world, this axiom is quietly ignored or sneered at as absurd.
Scientific men will reason with perfect clearness and cogency,
proceeding upon the principle of causation up to a certain
point, and then, because they cannot trace it any further without admitting a personal Creator as an indispensable factor, will
stop short and say that the world created itself; that the law
of development first enacted and next executed itself. True,
we are left in doubt as to the method. And equally in the
face of experience—an experience as certain and satisfactory
as demonstration can be—it is asserted that mind cannot
influence the action of matter, or that there cannot be a physical effect without a physical cause; that my will does not
determine whether my pen write this word rather than that.
In this way, to carry out a favorite theory, the plainest and
most common facts of consciousness are belied, and skeptics
forsake all consistency in a futile attempt to show that Revelation is a myth.

It is indisputable that men can attain scientific truth in no
other way than by putting themselves *en rapport* with the processes of nature. Conformably to this process, those modes of
action by which the natural world accomplishes its work are
discovered through the generalization of a great number of
facts by observation and experiment. They are called laws,
because they are, to the extent we comprehend physical phenomena, the methods by which the world is governed according to the notions of a Theist, or governs itself in the view of
the naturalist. But, in either case, these laws mean nothing
more than the mode by which the world is controlled; and are
more or less adequate expressions for this government in the
proportion that men, by submitting their intellectual powers to
the course of nature, come into harmony with its motions. So
the laws of thought, whether framed in logic or pure mathematics, signify no more than the mastery which the mind
gets over its own processes, by submitting to the necessary
conditions of thought as applied to itself, or to numbers in
their abstract relations. In moral ideas the case is the same.
Whence arise the notions of Civil Law or of the government of
men in their social relations? It is not, certainly, a matter of
chance or indifference that some things are deemed virtuous
and others vicious; and, as a consequence, the former de-

serve protection and encouragement, while the latter call for repression. If we consider law as the expression of the moral sense touching what is required between man and man, we can discern that this arises spontaneously from sympathy with those relations which the Creator established between himself and his creatures. Hence, that greatest of all discoveries, the discovery of law, is nothing else, so far as it is of human origin, than the gradual assimilation of man's ideas to the will of God. The growth of a code is a clear illustration. At first, among savage tribes, the notions of justice are crude and variable; so changeable, indeed, that nothing but the most rudimentary principles can be considered fixed. Force, directed by individual passion or caprice, is so powerful, and the general conceptions of right so weak, that club law usually prevails. Still, at this stage, we see that even the names of right and wrong, force and law, show a struggle after the realization of a more perfect system; and this felt want in time triumphs over the chaos, and reduces it to order. The ideal of right and justice as the principles by which men should be controlled, seen dimly at first, just as all abstract conceptions must be by the uncultivated, become clearer during the weary struggle between right and might, until at last the divine will expresses itself in a code claiming to provide for all the relations of man in civil society. Nor is this code inferior, in point of distinctness, to any system of scientific truth ever discovered. The *Corpus Juris Civilis* may well take its place by the side of Euclid's *Elements*, Aristotle's *Organon*, or Newton's *Principia*. For, though the methods of proof be different, they are as convincing in the one class of ideas as the other. Demonstration, as we have seen, in the most rigidly exact of all sciences, may produce more than one answer, which will satisfy the conditions of the problem. Yet, if the terms be constant, but one answer can be correct. Thus the processes of Nature escape our notice* when we are looking on, and mature their results, which we must accept, though unable to account for their production. This shows, not the imperfection of the truth itself, or its manifestations, but the infirmity of the understanding whose powers

---

*Bacon, Nov. Org. Aph. IV.   Reliqua intus transegit; Aph. X. Subtilitas naturæ subtilitatem sensus et intellectus multis partibus superat.

are hedged in by boundaries on all sides which it cannot pass. Hence, the distinction between demonstrative and what is called moral reasoning has no foundation in reality, and should be abandoned as futile. For all that is purely demonstrative consists in postulating terms, which are either first truths, or assumed as such, and therefore incapable of proof, and, by reducing them to the syllogistic form, compel a conclusion. But this is, in fact, a begging of the question, as has often been said of Aristotle's _Dictum;_ an assertion which is undoubtedly true, if considered apart from the matter of the argument. For, as you must assume a first truth for a major premise, and then compare the extremes with this in order to discover their agreement or disagreement with it, this process rests in its last analysis upon a _petitio principii._ The whole reasoning starts out from a truth assumed but not capable of proof—assumed because believed, not believed because proved. For if it were capable of further proof, logic forbids its assumption 'until its claims to credibility be established. This dealing with assumptions, however, effects no progress ; for it is reasoning in a circle, as every process must be which employs only pure abstractions. This was the field cultivated so assiduously by the logicians of the Middle Ages, yet nothing grew there but bristling subtleties and endless war of words. But in the so-called probable reasoning, which is the only kind that can have any relation to us, if we take the labor sufficient to possess ourselves of the facts, and have culture enough to comprehend them in their special application, we accept the response they give with as implicit faith as the mind has in its own processes. If uncertainty linger anywhere, it is because some of the facts bearing on the subject are still hidden or not comprehended. But by increasing information—that is, by bringing ourselves more into harmony with the subject—we narrow down the uncertainty to us, while confirmed all the time that we are near the truth, and believe it as strongly as though already in possession. Belief bridges over the chasm which separates us from absolute knowledge,* and does this equally for the Christian and the naturalist,

---

* Montaigne, Essais; Livre, II, Chap. XII. La participation que nous avons à la cognoissance de la Verité, quelle qu'elle soit, ce n'est point par nos propres forces que nous l'avons acquise ; Dieu nous a assez apprins cela par les tesmoigns qu'il a choisis du vulgaire, simples et ignorants, pour nous instruire de ses admirabiles secrets.

by bringing them into harmony with that Infinite Wisdom who formed the relations which hold throughout the universe of mind and matter. For it is the prerogative of God, who created all things, to see them just as they are; and hence the nearer we are conformed to his character, the closer we will approach to that standard of knowledge. Consequently, the sum of all knowledge is, to know God in the person of Jesus Christ, who is the embodiment of his will, and therefore of the Truth.

The conclusion to which we arrive then, is, that all Truth is one; that it is unchanging; that it can be known with as much certainty in one department of knowledge as another, provided the like methods be employed in its investigation, and these methods consist in bringing ourselves into harmony with its subject matter. Hence, no man who is a skeptic can be a safe guide in scientific inquiries, much less in morals; for his method is radically vicious. "*Falsus in uno, falsus in omnibus,*" is an incontrovertible maxim of human nature. However much progress he may make in his special researches, he cherishes so much error of method by habitual unbelief that all is thereby vitiated. For, just as in spiritual things, he who clings to one violation of God's law will sap all his own moral character, and make shipwreck of faith; so he who admits one false principle in his scientific investigation will tincture the whole with error, and convict himself of folly.

Art. IX.—THE GENERAL ASSEMBLY.

THE General Assembly of the Presbyterian Church of the United States of America met in Farwell Hall, Chicago, Ill.. on the 17th of May, 1877. It was organized by the election of the Rev. James Eells, D.D., of Oakland, California, as Modera-tor, whose prompt and wise rulings, firm and courteous bearing, greatly facilitated the dispatch of business and promoted the order of the body.

The time required for the judicious selection of committees and preparation of business is represented to have left the body with little to do the first three days of the session. The evils of such a state of things are so many and obvious that none will dispute the importance of devising a remedy. For this we have not far to seek. It can be had in two ways: 1. Arrangements may be made for proceeding forthwith with the reports from the boards of the church, although these must usu-ally go to their appropriate committees, whose reports must come in, before the Assembly becomes ready finally to dispose of the questions that may arise. Still,we think arrangements might be made by which all matters pertaining to them, not involving debatable questions of policy, might be at once disposed of, such as hearing the reports, with the general statements and speeches of the secretaries and others. 2. Another way of occupying the first days of the meeting is to hear, discuss and dispose of reports of committees appointed by previous Assem-blies to report to the next. There are always some such re-ports to be made, often on important subjects. In the Assembly at St. Louis, in 1874, the majority and minority reports of a committee on the consolidation of the boards were made at the very beginning of the session, and the time of the Assembly from the very first was fully occupied with the discussion and disposal of this subject, when not occupied with other matters. Thus full justice was done to this great question of that ses-sion, while other matters received their usual, but, in too many cases, inadequate attention ; we say inadequate, because some crude deliverances, abstract and concrete, were hastily rushed through the body near its close. Many such would die before coming to their birth, if they could be properly discussed.   Fortunately most of these lie dead upon the records, and are never heard of afterward.   But some live to cause a sad amount of needless irritation and discord.   We shall proceed to notice a few of the topics which engaged the attention of the Assembly.

REDUCED REPRESENTATION.

Both overtures sent down by the previous Assembly to the Presbyteries, for such a change in the basis of representation as will sufficiently reduce the size of the Assembly, were rejected by decisive majorities.   This result disappointed no one.   The report of the committee appointed by the last Assembly on the subject was also presented.   Although this virtually advised acquiescence in the present basis for a time, with an enlargement of the minimum number of ministers requisite to institute a Presbytery, in order to mitigate the growing inequality in the basis of representation, and slightly check the increase of the Assembly, yet the sense of the evils of the present system is too keen and wide-spread to admit of any quietus not provided in their removal or abatement.   It was forced upon the Assembly by the utter absence of invitations from any place for the next Assembly.   No place wanted, or felt itself equal to, the task of entertaining so vast a body for two weeks.   It has been quite a fashion to decry reference to the burden upon hospitality as a petty thing, very unworthy to come into the argument on this subject.   This will do for romance and sentiment ; and if these were the only elements in the case, it might safely be ignored.   But excessive demands upon hospitality have their own way of compelling consideration.   When no place can be found willing to undertake the burthen, it being too grievous to be borne, then it will have weight in the argument and policy adopted.   The case of the annual conventions of the American Board, so often alleged for the purpose of showing that the entertainment of vast numbers of people may be easily accomplished, is not parallel.   That is a meeting for only two or three days.   Let it extend itself for a fortnight, and how many places would be found to welcome the convocation ?   The churches in the cities in which the Assembly has met since the reunion have, after exhausting the possibilities of private hospitality, been put to an expense of thousands of dollars for the entertainment of the body.   What conceivable justice is there in the whole church imposing such an assessment on the Presby. terians of a single city?

The subject, therefore, has not been and cannot be laid to rest.   The Assembly referred the whole subject to a new committee, of which Dr. Van Dyke was Chairman.   They renewed the recommendation of Synodical representation on the basis of two delegates, one Minister and one Elder for every fifty ministers or fractions thereof.   The result was that after recommitment and amendment, following the most searching discussion, it was agreed by a nearly unanimous vote to send down the following alternative overtures to the Presbyteries:

Shall Chap. XII, Sec. 2, of the Form of Government, be so amended as to read: "The General Assembly shall consist of an equal delega- tion of Bishops and Elders from each Synod in the following propor- tions, viz.: Each Synod consisting of not more than fifty ministers shall send one minister and one elder; and each Synod consisting of more than fifty ministers shall send two ministers and two elders; and in the like proportion for any fifty ministers in any Synod; and these delegates so appointed shall be styled Commissioners to the General Assembly.

" The Commissioners shall be chosen by the Synod with due regard to the rights of its Presbyteries. If the Synod send three or more ministers or three or more Elders to the General Assembly, not more than one-third of its Commissioners, and if it send two ministers and two elders, not more than one-half of its Commissioners, in any year, shall be taken from the Presbytery, and in a series of years equal to the number of Presbyteries in any Synod.   At each stated meeting of the Synod it shall be determined and announced which of the Presby- teries composing it are entitled to furnish Commissioners to the General Assembly to be held next to the one ensuing, and to how many Com- missioners, ministers, or elders, or both, such Presbyteries are re- spectively entitled.   And prior to each election of Commissioners by the Synod, the list of the Presbyteries entitled to furnish Commission- ers at that time shall be read, and each such Presbytery shall be called on to nominate, through its representative or representatives, who shall have been designated by it for the purpose, as many Commissioners as it is entitled to furnish, and an equal number of alternates.   If such nominations are not made, the Synod shall, nevertheless, proceed with the election; every Presbytery shall be represented by at least one minister and one elder."

Also, shall Chap. XXII., Sec. 1, be so amended as to read: " The Commissioners to the General Assembly shall always be appointed by the Synod from which they came at the meeting next preceding the meeting of the General Assembly, and as much as possible to prevent all failure in the representation of the Synods arising from unforeseen accidents to those first appointed, it may be expedient for each Synod to appoint an alternate to each Commissioner to supply his place in case of his necessary absence " ?

And in Art. II. shall the word " Presbytery," wherever it occurs, be changed to "Synod " ?

Your Committee recommend that the foregoing overture be transmitted by the Assembly to the Presbyteries for their action.

Your Committee also recommend that the following alternative overture be transmitted to the Presbyteries :

Shall Chap. XII., Sec. 2, of the Form of Government be amended so as to read: " The General Assembly shall consist of an equal delegation of Bishops and elders from each Presbytery in the following proportion, viz.: Each Presbytery consisting of not more than forty ministers actually engaged in ministerial work as pastors, co-pastors, pastors-elect, stated supplies, evangelists, missionaries, professors in theological seminaries, or those assigned to the work of the Church by the General Assembly, shall send one minister and one elder; each Presbytery consisting of more than forty and less than eighty ministers, employed as above specified, shall send two ministers and two elders ; each Presbytery consisting of more than eighty and less than 120 ministers, employed as above specified, shall send three ministers and three elders in like proportion for each additional forty ministers actually engaged in ministerial work ; and these delegates so appointed shall be styled Commissioners to the General Assembly" ?

It was also ordered that meanwhile, until a decided reduction of the Assembly can be accomplished, an assessment be made upon the churches of two cents per member, in addition to that now made for the mileage fund, to be paid to the Committee on Entertainment for each Assembly, so as to aid them in making provision for it. This is simply just. It lays upon the whole church, and not the Presbyterians of some single city, the burden of paying for that portion of the entertainment of Assemblies to which private hospitality is inadequate.

In regard to the overtures themselves, it is not unlikely that one will defeat the other. But together they voice and evince the almost unanimous judgment of our church that the Assembly ought to be reduced, and its readiness to work at the problem till some satisfactory solution is reached. In regard to the comparative merits of these overtures we have only to say that the Synodical method affords the easy and natural basis for a reduction of representation, which can be carried to any extent as the future growth of our church may require, and always preserve the nearest possible approach to a substantial equality of representation of the different portions of the church. We see no conceivable objection to it on principle. The Book, chap. xi: 1., defines the Synod thus: "As the Presbytery is a convention of the Bishops and Elders within a certain district, so a Synod is a convention of the bishops and elders within a larger district." It is only a larger Presbytery. But for reasons so well understood that they need not here be specified, there is a widely prevalent and deeply-rooted aversion to taking the power of election out of the hands of the Presbyteries. We and, so far as we know, all the advocates of reduction are desirous of still conserving this Presbyterial privilege so far as is possible without sacrificing other essential principles. Although we have favored the two previous overtures in favor of Synodical representation, yet in the failure of these we ourselves have also in committee recommended one much less to our taste, in the hope it might prove more acceptable. It counted as the basis mainly pastors and missionaries, and retained the present number, 24, as the unitary basis of representation of Presbyteries by one pastor and elder. It was rejected summarily, to say nothing more. The same has been true of every attempt at thorough reduction thus far made, by retaining Presbyterial and evading Synodical representation. In the overture now made for Synodical representation, provision is made to secure to each Presbytery of the Synod the nomination of its due proportion of delegates, in the hope of thus meeting the demand for Presbyterial, while adopting the method of Synodical representation. It remains to be seen whether it will be accepted and ratified as an adequate concession to that demand.

The alternative overture still retains the representation exclusively by Presbyteries. It makes 40 the unitary basis instead of 50, the number adopted in the overture of last year, which was objected to by an overwhelming majority. It makes the disproportion between the representation of small and large Presbyteries less thari that just rejected, but still, in our opinion, altogether too great. We can conceive of measures of the most vital importance under that system being carried or defeated by the representatives of a very decided minority of the church. We do not believe this to be right or salutary. It is to no purpose to adduce the case of the U. S. Senate, in which the smallest and largest States are equally represented. The House of Representatives, which is apportioned upon the basis of the population of the States, together with the Presidential veto, offsets the Senate and completely neutralizes the danger referred to. This, therefore, affords no parallel. Aside of this aspect and tendency of the overture, we would not complain of another feature, which rules out ourselves from any place in the basis of representation along with other editors of Presbyterian journals, and professors in Presbyterian colleges. We once ourselves, for the sake of accomplishing reduction, took part in preparing an overture having this feature. But who are those "assigned to the work of the church by the General Assembly"? Do they include the members and secretaries of the boards who are otherwise without ecclesiastical charge? We think the line thus attempted to be drawn somewhat arbitrary and undefined. But we do not object. It must be arbitrary, if drawn at all. For better or for worse, this plan is only a temporary palliative, not a permanent remedy for the evils under which we now labor. But this would be far better than nothing, were it not that it makes it possible for one group of 40 ministers to be the basis for several times as many votes in the Assembly as another 40 of equal capacity and fidelity to the true church. But whether either of these plans is sanctioned by the Presbyteries or not, we are sure that a way will soon be found for accomplishing what is so generally felt to be a necessity—a large reduction of the Assembly. The question of entertainment aside, so large a gathering is unfavorable to the proper maturing and due dispatch of business. The analogy sometimes claimed to exist between the present Assembly and the British House of Commons in this respect fails, simply because six hundred men sitting for prolonged periods of months and years may overcome difficulties arising from its own magnitude which are insurmountable by a body of the same size, composed mostly of new and inexperienced members sitting only two weeks. Closely connected with this is the subject of a

FINAL COURT OF APPEALS,

brought up in a report from a committee appointed by the last Assembly, of which Dr. Musgrave was chairman. It was referred to another committee, who reported it back, somewhat amended, in the form of an overture to be sent down to the Presbyteries for sanction, as an amendment to the constitution. It was, however, referred to the next Assembly, being deemed as yet too crude and imperfect in form to be submitted to the Presbyteries. Some were for strangling it at once, denouncing the whole project as needless, and tending to a sort of star-chamber inquisition or despotism. The majority of the Assembly, however, appear to have been impressed with the necessity of seeking some plan of accomplishing the objects for which this tribunal is designed. It is quite clear that a body of six hundred men, crowded with more non-judicial business than it can well handle, is unfitted for any judicial business beyond the decision of questions of doctrine and order, pure and simple, to which, if reduced to half the number, it would be less unsuited ; still it would remain seriously unfitted for the work, incapable of fairly digesting and issuing half the appeals and complaints that must inevitably reach it from the various parts of a communion so widely extended. This was felt and urged by Dr. Hodge and others thirty years ago, when the churches and assemblies were less than half the present size. The exigency is met partially at present by judicial committees and temporary judicial commissions, appointed by each Assembly *pro re nata.* The only question is, whether it shall be provided for in future by such temporary and casual expedients, or by a permanent tribunal, one-third of whose members shall have their terms of office expire each year, the vacancies thus arising to be filled by the General Assembly? We confess that this question seems to us not altogether one-sided. The advantages of a permanent tribunal. with its records, precedents, by-laws and growing experience in ecclesiastical litigation, are obvious. But then the possible tendency toward a set of rigid, cast-iron precedents, whereby technicalities become petrified, so as to constrain the free actings of that eternal justice they were invented to support, is not to be overlooked or ignored.

THE SEWICKLEY CHURCH CASE—PUBLICATION OF SUNDAY NEWSPAPERS BY CHURCH MEMBERS.

The editor and publisher of the Pittsburgh *Leader*, which issues a Sunday edition, is a member of the church in Sewickley, which quick railroad connections make a virtual suburb of Pittsburgh. The session of that church has taken no steps to discipline him, although often urged to do so. The Presbytery of Allegheny, to which the Sewickley church belongs, enjoined the session to proceed to take action upon the case, and investigate the charges so loudly made by the tongue of common fame. The session appears to have been in doubt as to their duty, or for some reason determined to take no step until they could obtain a deliverance from the General Assembly touching the present interpretation and application to such cases of the law of the Sabbath as laid down in our standards. They accordingly referred the order of Presbyetery to the Synod of Erie, which reaffirmed it in a very emphatic and decisive manner, and finally referred this action of Synod to the Assembly. for its decision in the premises. The Assembly, after earnest and thorough discussion, with only three votes in the negative, adopted the following paper, reported from the Commitee of Bills and Overtures:

First—This Assembly reaffirms the resolutions adopted by the Synod and Presbytery setting forth the binding obligation of the Fourth Commandment as expounded in the standards of the Presbyterian Church and in the repeated deliverances of the General Assembly; and also the declarations of Synod and Presbytery: That any voluntary and responsible participation in the publication and sale of a Sunday newspaper is inconsistent alike with the decree of the law of God and with membership in the Presbyterian Church.

Second—That it is entirely within the constitutional authority of a Presbytery to direct the sessions of a church under its care to proceed according to the Book of Discipline, and that it is competent for a Synod to reaffirm such instructions upon a reference of a case asking for its advice. That the session of the church of Sewickley were bound to carry out the plain meaning of the instructions of the **Presbytery of** Allegheny, and that their reasons for declining to do so are **insufficient.**

Third—That the proper remedy for the Presbytery to apply **to that** session, if they continue to disobey the instructions of the **Presbytery.** is to put the session under discipline for contumacy.

The protest signed by Dr. Bettinger, Pastor of the **Sewickley** Church, and two others, in its fifth article brings to view **the** main issues on which the discussion turned, and is as follows:

5. We protest because the exception seems invidious, since, **if its** application is correct, it singles out one class of offenders—the **pub-** lishers of Sunday papers—a very small class, while it passes over **to** the respective Sessions of our churches the thousands, if not **tens of** thousands, of similar offenders against the Fourth Commandment— all those violators of the Sabbath—who voluntarily continue **employ-** ers or stockholders in the various Sabbath-breaking commercial **and** manufacturing agencies and establishments which a modern **civilization** has brought with it.

This is a leading case, and bids fair to be the precursor of others through which the mind of our Church will gradually unfold and define itself, not with reference to the sanctity of the Sabbath or the general law of its observance, but with ref- erence to its judicial interpretation and application to parties implicated in what the protest calls "the various Sabbath-break- ing commercial and manufacturing agencies which a modern civilization has brought with it." The great question, indeed, is, which of them is or is not "Sabbath-breaking"? Nor is it possible to formulate the law of the Sabbath more than any other law, human or divine, so that all the varying cases and circumstances that may arise can be foreseen, or its application to them determined in advance. We deem the law of the Sabbath, as expressed in our standards and summarized in the *Shorter Catechism*, to be as accurately expressed as is possible in our language, and, as such, to be of perpetual obligation. "The Sabbath is to be sanctified by a holy resting on that day, even from such worldly employments and recreations as are lawful on other days; and spending the whole time in the public and private exercises of God's worship, except so much as is to be taken up in the works of necessity and mercy." It is obvious, however, that the words "worship," "necessity" and "mercy" in this statement must be understood somewhat broadly, in order to acquit vast numbers of Christians, who are of un-challenged piety, from the charge of Sabbath desecration. And it is no less obvious that, in its application to new cases and circumstances, everything depends upon the breadth or nar-rowness of construction we give to the terms "necessity and mercy." Is the "necessity" intended absolute, the contrary of which cannot be in the nature of things, or without the most palpable and demonstrable injury to the soul or body, the individual or society, the Church or the world, God or man? Or is it a relative necessity, a necessity only as it is judged to be beneficial in the slightest degree, to the health, the comfort, the welfare of ourselves or others? And of the things supposed to be, in this sense, necessary to man's highest good, who is the judge, or how far is it to be left to the judg-ment and conscience of the individual Christian; or the Church courts, or each for each, within its due sphere, and what are the bounds of that sphere? The same, too, of mercy. Mercy re-quires those services on our part which mitigate or prevent suffering, or danger to the life and health of man, and often of beast. But who shall undertake to say how much of the labor done on the Sabbath without scruple by most Christian people might be avoided without loss or harm of any sort to man or beast? Such queries show how much remains to be done be-fore unmistakable lines of clear and sharp definition can be drawn in reference to the law of the Sabbath, in its applications.

By this, however, we do not mean that there is ordinarily any difficulty for the candid mind in determining what is, and what is not, a desecration of the Sabbath in any concrete case. But there is great difficulty in formulating definitions and phrasing detailed rules so that they will precisely include all actual cases of Sabbath desecration and exclude all others. It is commonly supposed that accurate definition is in fact, as it is logically, the first step in any science. But with respect to all but the formal sciences, all the sciences of actual being, accurate definition has been shown to be the last achievement. Nevertheless, people know objects from each other, though they cannot specify the marks of the difference. The most untutored know a man from an animal, and humanity from brutality, though they cannot ac-curately define the differentia, just as all can distinguish differ-ent faces and chirographies, although, on the witness-stand, a lawyer might puzzle them out of their wits in trying to worm out of them the differential marks   So, by a sort of holy intuition, the great mass of God's people clearly discern whether given actions have or have not in them the Sabbath-breaking element, although they cannot give anything more than a confused or inadequate definition of this element in them.   The larger part of the knowledge of men does not get beyond the first of three stages, severally noted by philosophers as Clear, Distinct and Adequate. Education, Science, Philosophy are ever struggling onward from the first toward the last stage of adequate, or relatively perfect knowledge.   Now, in this light, we should think few would have any difficulty in adjudging the publication of a Sabbath newspaper, in ordinary times and circumstances, a violation of the Sabbath.   It is a piece of secular work wrought on the Sabbath, not only demanded by neither "necessity," nor "mercy," but diverting the minds of vast numbers from the sanctities of divine worship to the secularities of this world.   While the publication of bulletins of news in times of war, revolutions, or great public catastrophes, may fall under the category of works of necessity and mercy, as well as a thousand things done by the best of people without censure or question, this does not excuse the publication of a Sunday newspaper in ordinary times, whose only influence must be to divert and distract multitudes of people from the proper observance of the Sabbath.

Indeed, we do not understand the defenders of the Sewickley Session to dispute this.   The protest of Dr. Bittinger, as above quoted, distinctly classes the Sunday newspaper with "Sabbath-breaking" agencies, and its owners and publishers among the "offenders against the Fourth Commandment," "violators of the Sabbath."   But Dr. Bittinger raises the point that the definitions laid down by the Assembly do not clearly distinguish it from other "Sabbath-breaking agencies," which no one thinks of interfering with by church discipline, or otherwise than by leaving them to the discretion of church sessions.   He said in the debate:

"Now, why was this case made an exception? That was what he complained of—if he had any ground for complaint at all. And why was it insisted that the church in question should not have further time? But, it would seem, it must be brought up step by step until the Assembly was supposed to stand against the recalcitrant session of the little church nestled among the hills. That church stood by the theoretical doctrine of the Sabbath, but did the Presbyterian Church, as a Church, consistently live up to that doctrine? What, then, would become of the great railroad corporations? Did Presbyterians hold any stock in them? What became of the Sabbath when street-cars were run in Chicago and all other great cities? Was this a work of necessity? Must the Fourth Commandment be broken in order that God's people might be religious? Why were the Sunday trains run, and why did ministers travel on them to preach the Gospel?"

We confess that, while it is no good reason for failing in the proper use of church discipline in this case, that it is omitted in others to which consistency would require its application, it is none the less true that the church should seek consistency in her action, and try so to enunciate her principles and laws that they will cohere and harmonize, not only with each other, but with her practice, and that her exercise of discipline also shall be self-consistent. And we do not quite see that she has reached a deliverance on the subject that squarely meets the queries above propounded. The minute adopted makes only that participation in the ownership and publication of a Sunday newspaper which is " voluntary and responsible" amenable to Church censure. But what participation, in the case of any who have control over their own property and faculties, can be otherwise than " voluntary and responsible"? And does, or does not, the same question apply equally to the ownership of stock in horse or steam railways, or steamers, or the use of cars and trains run on the Sabbath, even if they be Sunday or church trains? We confess that we were never more surprised than when spending a Sabbath in Pittsburg, at the consummation of the Reunion, to read and hear of " church trains" run to that Presbyterian centre from the neighboring villages. We remembered how a delegate from the General Association of Connecticut, at an Assembly meeting in that city before the disruption in 1837, told us, on his return, that it and the region around it were beginning to surpass New England in the all-pervasive hold which Christianity, with its institutions and manners, had of the people. He said that New England would soon be compelled to confess that the glory is departed to the West, which was coming to eclipse the East. Certainly we have heard of no church trains on the railways of New England or the East. But we have seen a great decline in the standard of Sabbath-keeping in New England. We recently attended one of the leading orthodox churches in Massachusetts, famous for its long line of pastors of national fame, who had been among the foremost promoters of strict, puritanical Sabbath observance, and opposers of Sunday mails, *et id genus omne.* We saw the leading members of that congregation go directly from the morning service to get their mails at the post-office across the street. This appeared to be deemed as much a matter of course and beyond exception as walking or riding to church. And we fear that this is an index of the general relaxation of Sabbath observance which has stealthily overspread that land, until lately, beyond all countries except Scotland, celebrated for the strictness of its Sabbath observance. Nor is New England alone in this degeneracy, as the facts, not so much brought to view as recognized beyond dispute, in this Assembly discussion about the Sewickley case abundantly prove.

But, after all, are the "church trains" necessarily in violation of the Sabbath? Circumstances, it seems to us, must determine in each case. It may be. The presumption, where they are freely used by the Christian public, till the contrary is made to appear, is that they come under the condition of necessity and mercy, *i. e.,* that they enable more people to attend public worship with far less labor for man and beast than would otherwise be required. We suppose it must be for this reason that the ministers to whom Dr. Bittinger refers use them. Otherwise we are sure we must have heard some protest in the *Presbyterian Banner*, which is not apt to utter an uncertain sound. We judge that it is due to the same principle that in the large cities the running of street horse-cars on the Sabbath so largely prevails and continues, and that they are patronized by great multitudes of Christian people without scruple in going to public worship on the Sabbath, notwithstanding the earnest and persistent opposition which for a time they met from the Christian community—an opposition always justified, and often effective, where no such necessity prevails. In the immense growth of cities, largely due to steam and electricity, all the arrangements of life, and especially of residence and business, are determined at once by the necessities created and the conveniences afforded by the modern modes of cheap and expeditious public conveyance. Thus, homes are pushed more and more away from the seats of business, either in urban or suburban localities, these new means of recent and quick conveyance virtually bridging over the distance. The same is often true with reference to schools and churches, and other necessities of civilized and Christian life. And hence, while all ordinary transportation should cease on that day, the movement of some cars may be demanded by necessity and mercy, as involving far less of labor to discharge the necessary offices of life and religion than would result from their stoppage. They are in the methods of modern life, in such places as New York and its suburbs, much in the position of the East and North river ferries. They are in place of streets, roads and bridges, because by them alone can multitudes of people now use these roads in which these tracks are for purposes of necessary travel. To this it is due that, notwithstanding all protests to the contrary from ecclesiastical bodies in the earliest days of the practice, milk-trains continue to be run, as the only means of supplying the cities with that indispensable necessity of life, pure milk. Presbyterian communicants and elders of unquestioned repute for piety, after church on Sabbath, carry the milk of their dairies to these trains, often for delivery to and consumption by those other Presbyterian people who will use no other, because thus alone they judge that they get a pure article. All this neither justifies nor palliates any movement of railroad trains for business purely secular, for excursions of pleasure, or for any purposes not fairly within the domain of necessity or mercy. While much that is done on many railroads is clearly not within this description, there is undoubtedly a considerable border-land in which opinions of persons, equally pure and intelligent, might honestly differ, as almost always happens in casuistry, or the application of undisputed principles, to *cases* of disputed facts, or facts dubious in their inferential relations, if not *per se*. But still, a large residuum is left of Sunday work done by many railroads, which can be justified on no plausible plea of necessity or mercy, and must, therefore, go to the account of Sabbath desecration, pure and simple. We do not, then, regard all the cases of Sunday railway travel referred to by Dr. Bittinger as in point, because some are not necessarily "Sabbath-breaking" in their nature. But take the case of those that are such beyond question. Their stock is owned by thousands of Christians, including elders and ministers, and held without scruple and without question. And inasmuch as it may be readily sold or transferred, can their participation in it be deemed less than "voluntary and responsible"? How, then, is Dr. Bittinger and those who agree with him, to be met when they allege this fact, as *pro tanto*, of the same moral quality as issuing Sunday newspapers?

The venerable Dr. McKinney, a member of the Sewickley congregation, a veteran ever "valiant for the truth," said:

If the gentleman came before the Session and said, " Though I am a stockholder of this concern, I don't approve of the Sunday paper ; but I cannot control it," that was enough to satisfy the Session, be believed. He had heard members of it say so. That would be enough to satisfy the brethren. He knew that, because he was one of them. All that was asked was for the brother to say he did not do what he could prevent—the issue of the paper on Sunday. Just as men did who owned railroad shares, or stock in a gas company ; when they had an opportunity to vote against working on Sunday they did so ; and when they could elect officers they elected men who were opposed to running cars on the Sabbath—all that in them lay to prevent desecration ; but they didn't feel bound to sell their stock ; they were not personally engaged in it, or engaged in promoting it in any way, but in such a way that they yielded to it, and submitted to it, as they did to the Government, and the Sabbath mail. He put his letters in Saturday and took them out Monday. He was not concerned in the way they were carried. He had written against Sunday mails, and voted against them, and done everything in his power to prevent the opening of the Post-Office on Sunday, but he paid his taxes and was a good citizen. All they could ask, in the publication of a newspaper, was, " Hold your stock if you so please, but, as far as your influence is concerned, prevent its being published on the Sabbath day."

In some cases, undoubtedly, the conscience would be sufficiently cleared by such a protest without further steps to get rid of all participation in forbidden, anti-Scriptural occupations. But would it be so in reference to the gains of a gambling or betting association, or of a railway making its chief gains from conveying multitudes to places of drunkenness and prostitution on the Sabbath? We trow not. And here, as in so many other cases, it is often hard to draw the line within which protest and opposition without withdrawal are sufficient, beyond which they are not. The cases also are innumerable in which we are to use the food and the conveniences of life provided for us without troubling ourselves with questions as to what Sabbath-breaking or other immoralities may have been implicated in their production or procurement, "asking no questions for conscience' sake," since, if we did, the ongoings of life would be impossible. We once knew a bright youth of morbidly scrupulous conscience who, for a time, became afraid to eat any but a few domestic esculents, in the production of which he felt sure that Sabbath desecration and slavery had no part. His friends became anxious lest he should be, in a similar way, set against eating the few articles which yet sustained life. It is plain that such scrupulosity would render life intolerable, if not impossible. But, on the other hand, can one well patronize a Sunday newspaper without knowing, encouraging and participating in whatever infraction of the Sabbath its publication has involved? Again, supposing all this settled, we are not yet free from questions of perplexing casuistry in the premises. Dr. Edson of Indianapolis said during the debate, by way of showing the necessity of a caution and parsimony in the Assembly's deliverances that would keep them from being a network of future entanglements:

"It would be impossible for any one to turn the General Assembly into a house that favored, in any sort of way, the desecration of the Sabbath. [Applause.] They were unanimous about that. But this was a most intricate and delicate question; and the statement of it needed to be so careful, with so little verbiage, and so little rhetoric, and so much of Scripture, and so much of formal deliverances of the Assembly, that they could stand upon it anywhere. . . . He had not heard that most interesting "personal explanation," but it appeared from that explanation that a gentleman quite distinguished upon the floor must either have borrowed or purchased a newspaper, which he (the speaker) supposed had no special reputation for piety, and possibly might be called a Sunday newspaper; and any voluntary participation in the publishing or reading of such a paper, he supposed, ought not to be encouraged there. [Applause.] He wished to know if they were going to discipline a member of the Presbyterian Church who worked all day Saturday and sold his newspaper on Sunday, and let that brother go scot free who worked all day Sunday and sold his paper on Monday? [Applause.] He believed in putting the Sunday question squarely and fairly—opposing all desecration of the day—so that it would accord with the standards, the deliverances of the Assembly and the Scriptures."

Dr. Briggs of Union Seminary believed

" That the publication of a Sabbath newspaper was unscriptural, but he was opposed to such an extreme measure as that contemplated by the resolutions, even as amended by the insertion of the word " responsible." There were numerous questions of casuistry which must be left to the churches themselves, and which the Presbyteries, Synods and General Assemblies should not have brought before them, for if so, the work would be endless."

If the case of those who labor through the Sabbath to prepare a Monday morning's newspaper, which church-members take without scruple, become none the less perplexing in view of the present action of the Assembly, what ought to be done with those who, in order to give their employés the rest of the Sabbath, issue their daily paper on Sunday but not on Monday mornings? Such a paper, a friend informs us, is published at Montgomery, Ga. It is evident that the strongest stand possible should be taken in arrest of the increasing desecration and relaxed observance of the Sabbath. But much close thinking is required in order to formulate deliverances which will stand so that they can be carried out in every exigency to which the principles of law they lay down will apply. And to enunciate such as, through incautious or inadequate statement, are in the end self-destroying, hurts more than it helps the cause they are designed to promote. We do not intend to intimate that the Assembly's deliverance could be improved, but we think it wise to look clearly at the possible cases to which it may apply, and see whether it requires any additions.

FRATERNAL RELATIONS WITH THE CHURCH, SOUTH.

The following communication was received from the General Assembly of the Presbyterian Church in the United States, now in session at New Orleans, La.:

New Orleans, May 22, 1877.—The Committee of Correspondence recommend to the General Assembly the following as our Church's reply to the communication received at this session from the General Assembly of the Presbyterian Church in the United States of America:

Whereas, The General Assembly of this Church, in session at St. Louis in 1875, adopted a paper rendering "special thanks, in the name of the whole church, to our Committee of Conference at Baltimore for their diligence, fidelity and Christian prudence," and in particular approving and indorsing "as satisfactory to the Southern Church the condition precedent to fraternal relations suggested by our Committee," viz.: "If your Assembly could see its way clear to say in a few brief words to this effect, that these obnoxious things were said and done in times of great excitement, and are to be regretted, and that now, on a calm review, the imputations cast upon the Southern Church [of schism, heresy and blasphemy] are disapproved, that would end the difficulty at once"; and,

Whereas, Our General Assembly, in session at Savannah in 1876, in response to a paper from the General Assembly of the Presbyterian Church in the United States of America, which met in Brooklyn, adopted the following paper, viz.:

"We are ready most cordially to enter on fraternal relations with your body on any terms honorable to both parties. This Assembly has already, in answer to an overture from our Presbytery of St. Louis spontaneously taken the following action:

"*Resolved*, That the action of the Baltimore Conference, approved by the Assembly at St. Louis, explains with sufficient clearness the position of your Church. But inasmuch as it is represented by the overture that misapprehension exists in the minds of some of our people as to the spirit of this action, in order to show our disposition to remove on our part all real or seeming hindrance to friendly feeling, the Assembly explicitly declares that, while condemning certain acts and deliverances of the Northern General Assembly, no acts or deliverances of the Southern General Assemblies are to be construed or admitted as impugning in any way the Christian character of the Northern General Assembly, or of the historical bodies of which it is the successor"; and,

Whereas, The said General Assembly at Brooklyn, in response to the foregoing paper of our Assembly at Savannah, adopted the following, which has been communicated to us at our present meeting, viz.:

"The overture of this Assembly having been received by the General Assembly in the South with such a cordial expression of gratification, the Committee recommend that the same resolution, declarative of the spirit in which this action is taken, be adopted by this Assembly, **viz.**: 'In order to show our disposition to remove on our part all real or seem'ng hindrance to friendly feeling, the Assembly explicitly declares that, while condemning certain acts and deliverances of the Southern General Assembly, no acts or deliverances of the Northern Assembly, or of the historic bodies of which the present Assembly is the successor, are to be construed or admitted as impugning in any way the Christian character of the Southern General Assembly, or of the historic body or bodies of which it is the successor,'"; now, therefore, be it

Resolved, By this Assembly, that we cannot regard this communication as satisfactory, because we can discover in it no reference whatever to the first and main part of the paper adopted by our Assembly at Savannah and communicated to the Brooklyn Assembly. This Assembly can add nothing on this subject to the action of the Assembly at St. Louis adopting the basis proposed by our Committee of Conference at Baltimore and reaffirmed by the Assembly at Savannah.

If our brethren of the Northern Church can meet us on these terms, which truth and righteousness seem to us to require, then we are ready to establish such relations with them during the present sessions of the Assemblies.

Adopted in General Assembly of the Presbyterian Church in the United States, in session at New Orleans, La., May 22, 1877.

C. A. STILLMAN, Moderator.
JOSEPH R. WILSON, Stated Clerk.
WILLIAM BROWN, Permanent Clerk.

To the General Assembly of the Presbyterian Church in the United States of America, in session at Chicago, Ill.

This was referred to the Committee on Correspondence, which reported through its chairman, Dr. Marquis, in favor of the Assembly's passing resolutions expressing regret that the terms " heresy," " schism" and "blasphemy" had ever been applied to any proceedings or declarations of the Southern Church or Assembly by any body to which this Assembly is the successor. After long debate, this recommendation was rejected by the Assembly, which, by a large majority, adopted the following substitute:

Whereas, The General Assemblies of 1870 and 1873 have solemnly decreed that all the deliverances of the General Assemblies during the late war, so far as they impeach the Christian character and doctrinal soundness of the body known as the Southern Presbyterian Church, are null and void ; and

Whereas, Our last General Assembly, reiterating the action of former Assemblies, declared our confidence in the Christian character and doctrinal soundness of the Southern Presbyterian Church, and our desire to enter into fraternal correspondence with them upon terms of perfect equality and reciprocity, and cordially invited the Southern Assembly to send a corresponding delegate to this Assembly; therefore,

Resolved, That while we are sincerely desirous to be reunited in closer relations with the brethren from whom we have been separated, we do not deem it expedient at present to take any further action upon the subject except to repeat the declaration of the last Assembly, that we are ready cordially to receive a representative from the Southern Church, and to send a delegate to their Assembly whenever they may intimate a willingness to enter into fraternal relations upon such terms. But while this General Assembly is ready at any time to enter into fraternal relations with the General Assembly of the Presbyterian Church in the United States, no further action in this matter on the part of this Assembly is called for at present.

The arguments which prevailed to lead the Assembly to this issue, forcibly presented by Drs. Van Dyke, Edson and others, were substantially that, having already declared the action complained of by the Southern Assembly null and void, it was going quite beyond our legitimate province to express regret or repentance for the doings of former Assemblies of churches now having no distinct, continued existence, and most of whose actors were no longer on the stage to speak for themselves; that fraternal relations would come much sooner by quietly waiting till things ripen for it than by attempting prematurely to force it while it yet remains unwelcome to our Southern brethren; and, above all, that to establish fraternal relations by humiliating confessions on our side, with no corresponding concessions on the other, was to betray moral and historical truth; to proclaim to the world by the most solemn acts possible that while we were at fault in the utterances of former Assemblies with respect to the Church South, they were no way at fault when they declared it the "mission of the Church to conserve slavery," and thus provoked the severe denunciation of which they complain; when they pronounced our Assembly a "prevaricating witness"; when they met our first courteous advances to them proposing fraternal correspondence with the following salutation, containing charges about as grave as could well be brought against any body pretending to be a Christian Church:

"1. Both the wings of the now united Assembly, during their separate existence before the fusion, did fatally complicate themselves with the State in political utterances deliberately uttered year after year; and which in our judgment were a sad betrayal of the cause and kingdom of our common Lord and Head. We believe it to be solely incumbent upon the Northern Presbyterian Church, not with reference to us, but before the Christian world, and before our Divine Master and King, to purge itself of this error, and by public proclamation of the truth to place the crown once more upon the head of Jesus Christ as the alone King of Zion. In default of which the Southern Presbyterian Church, which has already suffered much in maintaining the independence and spirituality of the Redeemer's kingdom upon earth, feels constrained to bear public testimony against this defection of our late associates in the truth. Nor can we, by official correspondence even, consent to blunt the edge of this our testimony concerning the very nature and mission of the Church as a purely spiritual body among men.

"2. The union now consummated between the Old and New Assemblies, North, was accomplished by methods which, in our judgment, involved a total surrender of all the great testimonies of the Church for the fundamental doctrines of grace, and at a time when the victory of truth and error hung long in the balance. The United Assembly stands of necessity upon an allowed latitude of interpretation of the standards, and must come at length to embrace nearly all shades of doctrinal belief. Of those falling testimonies we are the sole surviving heirs, which we must lift from the dust and bear to the generations after us. It would be a serious compromise of this sacred trust to enter into public and official fellowship with those repudiating those testimonies; and to do this expressly upon the ground, as stated in the preamble to the overture before us, 'that the terms of reunion between the two branches of the Presbyterian Church at the North, now happily consummated, present an auspicious opportunity for the adjustment of such relations.' To found a correspondence professedly upon this idea would be to indorse that which we thoroughly disapprove."

No special pleading can take out the offensiveness of such charges which were wrought up in individual speeches, even to the length of insisting that we were " chained to Cæsar's car." To make retractions and confessions ourselves while we require no withdrawal of, or regret for, such charges against ourselves, made by those to whom we tender our confessions, is virtually to admit their truth; an admission which our Southern brethren would be the last to respect, or to judge a good ground for establishing fraternal relations.

The fact remains that there can be no restoration of fraternal relations while humiliating conditions are demanded on either side, or any basis but that of perfect equality and reciprocity. And we see no reason to change the opinion we have entertained since the rough repulse of our advances in 1870, that the surest and shortest way to them is to remain quiet, and wait till some sign is given that our Southern brethren are ready to enter upon these relations on terms of mutual equality and reciprocity. Such appears to have been the judgment of the Assembly.

COMMUNION WINE—TEMPERANCE.

We regret to observe that an effort was made to commit the Assembly to the recommendation of the unfermented juice of the grape as the only drink fit for the communion. We do not see how such a movement can inure to the benefit of religion or temperance. We are very confident that it will be to the advantage of both not to complicate them with any principle having so slender a scriptural basis, or likely to gain so few adherents as the doctrine in question. We are glad the Assembly disposed of the matter by making the following wise deliverance:

That the control of this matter be left to the Sessions of the several churches, with the earnest recommendation that the purest wine attainable be used.

By other action the Assembly happily cast its whole influence in favor of the great temperance movement now in progress, and appointed delegates to the convention of representatives from Christian churches in furtherance of this cause, soon to be held. We trust that this convention will not fall under the lead of extremists who will repel the co-operation of earnest temperance men by a platform of fanatical extravagance on the one hand, or of those lukewarm supporters whose help consists more in applying brakes than in clearing the track.

THE McCUNE CASE

came before the Assembly on no less than seven appeals and complaints. This number itself was appalling, and enough to tempt a body of six hundred men, preoccupied with other business quite sufficient to tax them to the utmost during the brief fortnight of their session, to shrink from undertaking to grapple with them. With the number now constituting the

Assembly, and in the absence of any regular judicial commission, it is almost a matter of course that all judicial business which is not deemed of absolute necessity, or which is not supposed to involve some point of doctrine or order that widely stirs the church, should be switched off on some ground, technical or substantial. And a judicial committee is deemed expert and efficient which succeeds in so disposing of matters before it as to consume the minimum of the Assembly's time. In regard to seven separate appeals or complaints, all virtually belonging to one controversy or issue, it was a forgone conclusion, therefore, that they should all, or nearly all, be dismissed or remanded to other tribunals. Such was the result in this case. They were all disposed of without actual trial by the Assembly; the reasons assigned, so far as we can see, being in some cases sufficient, in others of questionable validity.*

On these cases the Judicial Committee reported as follows, and the Assembly adopted the report:

Judicial Case No. 5.—In the case of the appeal of Thomas H. Skinner and others from the Presbytery of Cincinnati, the Committee recommend that, inasmuch as the so-called appellants were not an original party, they were not entitled to an appeal (Book of Discipline, Chapter vii., Sections 3, 17), and that, therefore, the case be dismissed.

Judicial Cases Nos. 6, 7, 8, and 9.—In the case of the complaints of (1) Nathaniel West and Thomas H. Skinner against the Presbytery of Cincinnati, for alleged judgment against the said West; (2) the same against the same, for adopting a resolution of its Judicial Committee; (3) E. D. Ledyard and others against the same, for the same proceeding; (4) Thomas H. Skinner and others against the same, for not sustaining the charges against Rev. W. C. McCune, the Committee recommend that, as the reasons for direct complaint to the General Assembly as presented to the Committee, and in their hands, are deemed insufficient, and as the constitutional jurisdiction and rights of the Synod over its lower courts are to be sacredly respected, therefore these several complaints be referred to the Synod of Cincinnati.

Judicial Case No. 10.—In the case of the complaint of Nathaniel West and Thomas H. Skinner against the Synod of Cincinnati, in a case of review and control, the Committee recommend that, it being a question of mere review of records, a judicial complaint does not lie, and that the case be dismissed.

Judicial Case No. 11.—In the case of Thomas H. Skinner and others against the Synod of Cincinnati, for not taking up and issuing a complaint of Dr. Skinner against the Presbytery of Cincinnati in the

McCune case, then pending, the Committee recommend that, as there had been no judicial action of the Synod in the case against which a complaint could lie, but simply and only a postponement of action on a report of the Judicial Committee of the Synod, therefore the case be dismissed.

To this a long protest, too long for insertion here, was offered by several members, and received to record. So far as we are advised, no answer was made to it. That brings to view the ground of the dissatisfaction of the appellants and complainants with these several findings of the Assembly, and with its general attitude in thus ruling out the whole subject.

In regard to No. 5, they protest that by the term "original party" in our constitution is not meant merely a party to a strictly judicial trial, but a "party aggrieved" by any judgment of the Assembly, whether judicial or non-judicial. We cannot agree with the position either of the Assembly's minute or of the protest.

We think that the whole 3rd section of Chapter vii—in the Book of Discipline implies that the "original parties" were each and all of the parties litigant, and that this follows alike from the interior reason of the case, and from any consistent construction of the different parts of the section. A public prosecutor may certainly be "aggrieved" by the manner in which the judicatory has treated him and the cause which he represents, and because in his judgment and those who agree with him, if there be no redress by appeal, "justice is fallen in the streets and equity cannot enter." One may suffer as much from a "lost cause," and more from what he deems the defeat of vital truths of religion, than from any mere personal injury; he may suffer as a member of Christ, wounded in the house of his friends. Moreover, the reasons for an appeal assigned (Sec. 3) with a single exception, may pertain as much to the prosecutor, even if he be a public prosecutor, as to the accused. The language of the book always speaks of "original parties" as plural, not single. "The original parties *and* all the members of the inferior judicatory shall withdraw."—*Id.* 9. All this reasoning applies in full force to a committee of prosecution appointed by the judicatory in a case in which common fame is the accuser. Such a committee has been expressly declared one of the original parties in a case involving that question before the O. S. Assembly, as the protest shows by a reference

to *Moore's Digest*, p. 563. Suppose a Presbytery, through prejudice or other perverting influence, utterly unfaithful or incompetent in its treatment of the committee of prosecution, their
witnesses, proof and arguments, who are so well fitted as they
to present their case in its strength to a higher tribunal?

The legal maxim *nemo bis vexari debet*, applies no more here
than in any possible case of appeal, civil or ecclesiastical. An
appeal does not repeat a trial otherwise complete. It renders it incomplete till perfected by a higher judicatory. Nor
does the right of complaint furnish an adequate remedy in
case of improper acquittal by the lower court upon the charge
of heresy. For, although it may condemn the error, it leaves
the errorist in unimpeached standing and free to propagate his
errors, however fatal, as a minister of the Church.

But, then, as to other persons than the original parties litigant
having the right of appeal, such in our view is not the meaning of our book, either express or by implication, or according
to the drift of judicial decisions.—*Moore's Digest*, p. 592. A
complaint to a higher court is the proper relief for all other
aggrieved parties. Article 2 of Section 111, Chap. 7, on
which, as compared with Art. 1, so much stress is laid, we think
is merely designed to put it beyond all doubt or peradventure
that a defeated, and especially a convicted, party can always
appeal, no matter who or what may be arrayed against the
exercise of the privilege. The cases brought directly from
Presbytery to the General Assembly, and by the Assembly referred back to Synod, were dealt with in accordance with the
prevailing usage, from which the Assembly never departs, unless in extreme and exceptional cases, and for most stringent
reasons. The reasons for any deviation from this usage should
be at least, *prima facie*, strong and irresistible. But of their
urgency the Assembly, in its wise discretion, must be the judge.
We see no evidence that in this case it is obnoxious to just
censure for such exercise of its judicial prerogative.

The dismissal of the complaint against the Synod of Cincinnati for the improper exercise of its power of review and control in its dealings with the records of the Presbytery of
Cincinnati may have been right or wrong in view of the facts
of the case. But from the exceptions taken by the Assembly
to those records, there seems to have been at least *prima facie*
ground of complaint. The reason assigned strikes us as inade-

quate, viz., that " being a question of mere review of records, a judicial complaint does not lie." If these records are records of a judicial proceeding by a lower court serving under the review of a higher, the approval or disapproval of them may be, in substance and effect, a judicial act, and if decidedly wrong, a just subject of complaint to, and call for revision by, a higher court. Moreover, in the actual practice of the Assembly, the " decision by an inferior judicatory, which in the opinion of the complainants has been irregularly and unjustly made," has been taken in its broadest sense to mean not only "judicial," but any " decision" which, in the judgment of complainants, is "irregularly and unjustly made." The questions thus brought up and issued by the Assembly on complaint are such as the propriety of one man being simultaneously elder in two churches; the mode of electing certain ruling elders; against a reference of a case to a higher court by a Presbytery ; against a Synod for dissolving a Presbytery, etc., etc. Indeed, it does not appear how great wrongs by inferior judicatories can, in many cases, be presented to the higher courts for correction, if complaints must be confined to strictly judicial action, or if judicial records cannot be made a matter of " judicial complaint." Suppose these records omit the vital elements in a case ; what then ?

Into the original merits of the case as a whole, to which the above mentioned acts refer, we have neither time nor space to go. Even the matter of the complaints and appeals above referred to is not before us. We have touched only the reasons which the record presents for the Assembly's manner of dealing with them, and some of the objections of the protestants.

As all such decisions, or the expressed reasons for them, by the Assembly, tend to acquire authority and harden into precedents, especially when they pass unquestioned, we have deemed it worth while to discuss, not the decisions themselves, of the justice of which we have no means of judging, because we have no adequate authoritative knowledge of the facts, but the sufficiency of the reasons assigned for them. The literature of the case has already become so enormous as to be extremely difficult to collect and digest. Mr. McCune is now out of our Church, and we can hardly believe that a case that has issued in making our communion too uncomfortable for him and such as he, will afford permanent encouragement to future impugners of any part of our order within our Church.

We think Mr. McCune has abundantly shown that " he went out from us because he was not of us." As so often occurs in such cases, he turns against his protectors. His doctrine that no Christian Church has a right to maintain or make a condition of ministerial standing anything but that minimum of truth which is left after excluding what is peculiar to each Christian denomination, cannot be carried out without starting one more new sect and distracting existing churches. As a Presbyterian minister he undertook, without sanction of his Presbytery, to form a church which, in its very constitution, was a constant witness against Presbyterianism. What but confusion and disorder could ensue? His scheme is a chimera which cannot be realized this side the millennial or heavenly church, in which all see eye to eye, and know even as they are known. As long as we know only in part, different Christian denominations are a necessity.

Any criticism of the proceedings of the various parties judicial and litigant in this case would now be unprofitable and superfluous. The case seems to have been complicated by more or less mistakes and indiscretions, which tended to protract it. But we do not think the experiment out of which it all grew is likely often to be repeated by ministers of the Presbyterian Church.

We think that on these matters our Church will hold no uncertain attitude, and that whatever else may be true, the "rationalism and liberalism" which the last number of the *Southern Presbyterian Review* charges us with harboring, can be found, if at all, only in homeopathic drops of the millionth dilution.*

Other great subjects occupied the Assembly which we have no space to note. The questions of Chinese and German evangelization, of Sustentation, and other problems in the Home and Foreign Field, Education, and much more, were vigorously grappled and, in general, wisely concluded.

L. H. A.

---

* We have received, at the last moment, *The Process, Testimony and Opening Argument of the Prosecution, Note and Final Minutes of the Judicial Trial of Rev. W. C. McCune, by the Presbytery of Cincinnati, from March 6 to March 27, 1877.* A well-printed pamphlet of 180 pages, in which the substantial elements in the case, with the views of the Prosecution and the Court, are fully exhibited. It will be found convenient for reference. Cincinnati: Robt. Clark & Co.

Art. XI.—CONTEMPORARY LITERATURE.

THEOLOGY.

Macmillan & Co. publish the second edition of *Salvation Here and Hereafter*, sermons and essays, by Rev. JOHN SERVICE, an English clergyman. This volume is a vigorous and plausible expansion of the author's paraphrase of Pope's famous couplet in the following terms : "For modes of faith it is obvious to common sense that senseless bigots fight, and they alone," p. 154. All theological tenets, creeds, doctrinal positions are his abhorrence. Moral purity and uprightness of life, independently of all those evangelical and supernatural truths which form the groundwork of Christian salvation and true holiness, are wholly irrelative to the author's view of "salvation here and hereafter"; nay, worse, they are scouted as if they were the dregs of an obsolete and pestilent dogmatism. The author is as Broad Church as it is possible to be without repudiating the very name and pretence of Christianity. Of future perdition, limited or unlimited in duration, he recognizes none except that of continuance in an immoral or depraved state. The highest salvation here and hereafter is that of self-sacrifice prompted by love. The revelation of anything in the Bible, beyond the intuitive truths of morality or natural religion, is denied by the author. He says:

"This was the way in which it was felt that Christ had authority : He ignored in his teachings those things for which authority was required; he insisted upon those things that speak for themselves, and carry authority along with them. These were—these are—the great principles, goodness, morality, or whatever you like to call the nobler way of life. When it is day no man needs to go about saying, 'It is not night, it is not night.' No more when it is said, 'Blessed are the good,' do you need to prove that it is quite true. Preachers who preach a system of theology need to appeal to authority. They are impressive, if at all, not from what they say, but from the authority they claim for saying it. It is different with preachers and teachers of religion—with those whom God ordains to prophecy, line upon line, precept upon precept, that to love God and man is all the law and the prophets. They don't need authority to recommend their word. There is authority in it. It matters not who said it first or who says it last, because it is the truth."—Pp. 106-7.

"Be pure, be true, be just, be generous, be magnanimous, be unselfish and unworldly. This is the sum and substance of what Christ says. In a word, it is morality, of course, the highest and purest, and connected with faith in God as the Father and Saviour of all, but still it is morality. Blessed are the good. Cursed are the evil. This is what all Christ's sayings here, his blessings and his reproofs, and his exhortations, amount to. Not a word about justification by faith, or the doctrine of atonement, or church-membership, or conversion in a moment, or a deathbed repentance, or any one of all those things of which, as concerning salvation, we hear so much. Not a word about these things."—P. 104.

This, although said of the Sermon on the Mount, is given as the representative characteristic of Christ's teachings universally.

So, denying that view of the inspiration of the Bible which holds that "it was directed by God just as it was written," he finds the only inspiration it contains in its unequalled exhibition of the "highest wisdom and noblest humanity." No wonder that such a writer makes some exceptional hypocrites typical of the whole class of people who obey the Bible in all its parts as the word of God, and not merely in its self-evident moral axioms; and that he also makes them the occasion for a monstrous caricature of those Christians who keep their allegiance to the word and church of God as supernatural and divine. It is quite consistent for such a man to say of them, "Their goodness is churchy, not human or divine. They hold a man in greater detestation for heresy than for villany, for a theological opinion which is supposed to be wrong than for a life in which there is nothing right. They subscribe to heathen missions, neglect their poor relations, and are unmannerly with their neighbors. They make money by tricks of trade, build churches which are tombs of the prophets, and museums of their dry bones, and condemn the poor to live in hovels. They hold a man in esteem if he is rich and goes to church. If a man be a steady church-goer he is a good man, though he deals in worthless goods, or cheats every market-day, or is a faithless servant, or a heartless acquaintance. If a man is ever so honest and industrious and kind, he is only a moral man unless he make a great profession of religion. Are these Christ's ideas of truth and goodness as they are here expressed? Is this goodness anything like Christ?"—Pp. 115-16.

We discover no standard in this book higher than the ethics and religion of heathenism. Its animus toward the evangelical and supernatural in Christianity is so bitter as to be its own antidote; indeed it gives us Christianity without Christ. For although it often refers to him, it recognizes him only as Teacher, Exemplar, Martyr. He is divine, as we see in him "all that we have ever conceived of in the way of goodness; since divine is a name for the highest and best, this is divine." This is what Christ's divinity amounts to, according to this volume.

Chas. B. Cox, of St. Louis, publishes seven discourses by Dr. JAMES H. BROOKS, entitled *Is the Bible True?* which defends it against the infidel attacks of Strauss, Renan, *et id genus omne*, as these worm themselves into the minds of that part of the community which is inclined to welcome the skeptical arguments now or lately in fashion. This volume is fitted to do good among persons and communities infected with this epidemic. It presents the arguments for the inspiration and canonicity of the books of the Bible in a clear, compact and cogent form, and gives a vigorous refutation of objections. We are especially struck with the overwhelming impression produced by ·the author's array and collation of texts to prove that the Bible asserts itself to be the word of God, however it may immediately proceed from the mouth, or pen, of men employed as instruments for its utterance. It is none the less the Lord that speaks, though he speaks with the tongue, or pen, or in the peculiar style of any man.

George Bell & Sons, London, publish a work, of which Scribner, Armstrong & Co. have imported a special edition for use in this country at $3.75, entitled *The Doctrinal System of St. John Considered as Evidence for the Date of his Gospel,* by the Rev. J. J. LIAS, M.A. The object of the author is to show that in John's Gospel our Saviour sets forth in forms more or less complete, at all events in germ and substance, the doctrines more extensively and minutely elaborated in the epistles, and to some extent referred to in the synoptical gospels. This is ably done. It is in some respects very much like some of the treatises published from time to time on the

Theology of Christ. For this is most largely given out in St. John's Gospel. The author shows this to be so in regard to the great doctrines of the Trinity, Incarnation, Atonement, Sin, Grace, Regeneration, Justification, Sanctification, Election, in a word, Anthropology, Soteriology and Eschatology. He also shows that Christ in this Gospel furnishes many of the forms of language and imagery for the due expression of the great truths of Supernaturalism and Redemption which pervade the Epistles. We notice that the author, while thoroughly evangelical in tone, nevertheless is a little confused on an occasional point of cardinal moment. He holds to justification by imparted as well as imputed righteousness. But his book is, on the whole, learned and discriminating, and an important addition to Johannean literature and the supports of sound Scriptural doctrine. Of course, if the Epistles presuppose St. John's gospel, this must have been of an earlier date. For sale also by McGinnis & Runyon, Princeton.

Questions Awakened by the Bible, by the Rev. JOHN MILLER, published by Lippincott of Philadelphia, was received just after all the matter of our last number had gone to press. Meanwhile the Presbytery of New Brunswick, of which the author is a member, have taken it in hand and found unanimously that it denies certain important doctrines of our standards, and have accordingly suspended its author from the ministry. It consists of three monograms respectively in answer to the questions, "Is the soul immortal?" "Was Christ in Adam?" "Is God a Trinity?" In regard to these severally the Presbytery unanimously found: 1. "That Mr. Miller teaches that the soul is not immortal; that at the death of the body it dies and becomes extinct." 2. "That Christ, as a child of Adam, was personally accounted guilty of Adam's sin; that, like other children of Adam, he inherited a corrupt nature, and that he needed to be and was redeemed by his own death." 3. "That there is but one person in the Trinity." This is the last of a comparatively recent series of books published by the author, which certainly indicate a quite eccentric astuteness, subtlety and industry. They have enforced a transient attention by the amazement they have caused that such extravagances should proceed from Princeton, and from the son of so illustrious a defender of the faith they impugn as the Rev. SAMUEL MILLER, D.D., one of the earliest professors of the Seminary. One of his books, which is written for the purpose of branding the systematic theology of Dr. Hodge as a system of Fetichism, under the title of "Fetich in Theology," sufficiently reveals some strange mental bias or disturbance. In undertaking the role of a great originator and discoverer of new light in philosophy and theology, it will be fortunate if he comes to agree with most of those who have examined his writings most closely, that he has mistaken his vocation.

Scribner, Armstrong & Co. publish, and McGinness & Runyon have on sale, *Christianity and Islam, the Bible and the Koran.* Four Lectures by the Rev. W. R. W. STEPHENS, Prebendary of Chichester. They treat of the origin of Christianity and Mohammedanism, the life and character of

Mahomet, the contrast between the theological teaching of the Bible and the Koran, also between the moral teaching of the two, and, what is not the least important, the practical results of Christianity and Islam. It is done in a calm, discriminating, judicial manner, and presents the grand points of distinction between the two systems with more justice and in a shorter compass than any other easily accessible book known to us. These lectures do not run into original investigation or speculation, but rather present the results reached by Newman, Smith, Gibbon, Milman, and others, in a condensed and popular form. The author justly states their drift thus:

"To the great prophet of Arabia, and to the marvelous work which he accomplished, I have endeavored to do justice, in opposition to the false and calumnious estimate which in a past age condemned Mahomet himself as a kind of malicious fiend, and his religion as a diabolical invention. On the other hand, I have sought to show that Christianity and Islam are radically diverse in the nature of their origin, in the character of their sacred books, and in their practical effects on mankind; that the difference between them is one not of degree, but of kind, according to the wise saying of Dr. Arnold, that while other religions showed us man seeking after God, Christianity showed us God seeking after man; a maxim which students of the crude science of comparative religion are apt to forget. I have endeavored, lastly, to point out that if there be these real and vital distinctions between the two religions, it is worse than folly to try and ignore them; that while there ought to be, and might be, peace and good will between the believers in rival creeds, it should not be placed on a rotten foundation—the rotten foundation which would be laid by those who see imaginary resemblances, and are blind to real distinctions; for if indiscriminate antagonism is mischievous, indiscriminate concession is mischievous also, and can only lead to confusion and disaster."—Pp. 7, 8.

The two treatises of the late Dr. HORACE BUSHNELL, on the *Vicarious Sacrifice*, originally published at successive times, and the latter partly in correction and amendment of the former, have now been published by Scribner, Armstrong & Co., uniform as one work in two volumes. The brilliancy, originality, ingenuity and earnestness of the author are conspicuous in these volumes, as in all his works. The work abounds in instructive and edifying passages. But the greatest prodigy of all, which his genius proved inadequate to explain, is how a sane mind, however grand and magnificent, could have undertaken to show that a strict vicarious sacrifice of Christ as the sinner's substitute should "involve the loss or confusion of all moral distinctions" in God, while, at the same time, "this simplest form of absurdity" constitutes that "altar form," under which the soul must work itself in Christian cultus if it would flourish in the Christian life. It is hard to see how two such states of mind could coexist without a prodigious strain upon the faculty of reason. It is well that he saw cause to somewhat modify his earlier views.

The Christian Way: Whither it Leads, and How to Go On. By WASHINGTON GLADDEN. New York: Dodd, Mead & Co., 1877. We heartily welcome this little volume. It is designed as a sequel to "Being a

Christian," by the same author, which was an excellent help to enter the Christian way, and we join in the devout wish of the writer that this one may lead many from the joy of beginning into " the glory of going on." It is undoubtedly true that " some clear and definite religious teaching is needed by those who have entered the church, as well as by those who seek to enter it. . . . It is important to know how to begin to be a Christian; and it is equally important to know how to go on." Hence this little vol. ume. The titles of the several chapters will show its scope : The Chris. tian's Aim, The Christian's Calling, The Christian in the Church, The Christian as a Witness, The Christian in Business, The Christian in Society, The Christian's Quiet Life.

Our Theological Century: A Contribution to the History of Theology in the United States. By JOHN F. HURST, D.D. New York : A. D. F. Randolph & Co., 1877. This essay was originally prepared for public delivery, and was so used on several occasions. It has been revised and enlarged, and is now given to the public in its present fixed form. Dr. Hurst is too well known as a writer to need commendation from us. This contribution to the history of American theology covers considerable ground, and presents the theo. logical conditions of the beginning of our national era, the American de. velopment of theological thought, theological results, and present theological necessities. It is, of course, only an outline, and is popular in form. Still it contains much that is worth reading and pondering. " Adherence to pure Christian doctrine, and growth in that doctrine—these have been the forces of our highest and purest national life." The author claims a very high place for American writers and thinkers in the theological field, and thinks before " another generation shall pass away we shall see the new phenomena of European masters in theology referring the young men who are to suc- ceed them to the productions of the American theological mind ; and a little later, the still greater phenomena of German and British aspirants for ex- cellence in theology coming to this country, as the early theological students to vigorous young Alexandria and Corinth, for the completion of their studies at these sources of advancing doctrinal thought."

The Children of Light, by Rev. WM. W. FARIS. Boston : Roberts Brothers, 1877. 12mo, pp. 312. The Hon. Richard Fletcher, LL.D., of Boston, made Dartmouth College his residuary legatee, and provided for a special fund to be under the care of the trustees of said college, from the avails of which they are to offer biennially a prize of $500 for the best essay on the subject indicated in the following extract from his will :

" In view of the numerous and powerful influences constantly active in drawing professed Christians into fatal conformity with the world, both in spirit and practice; in view also of the lamentable and amazing fact that Christianity exerts so little practical influence, even in countries nominally Christian, it has seemed to me that some good might be done by making permanent provision for obtaining and pub- lishing once in two years a prize essay, setting forth truths and reasonings calculated to counteract such worldly influences, and impressing on the minds of all Christians a solemn sense of their duty to exhibit, in their godly lives and conversation, the beneficent effects of the religion they profess, and thus increase the efficiency of Christianity in Christian countries, and recommend its acceptance to the heathen nations of the world."

We have given this extract not only to indicate the scope and character of the essay in this volume, to which this prize was awarded, but because the language sets forth so clearly and truthfully one of the most marked and alarming tendencies of the times. We honor the noble purpose of the giver, and trust that these biennial prizes will be worthy of the high end in view, and prove eminently useful.

The work before us is admirably written. It is methodical in arrangement, pure and simple in style, evangelical in spirit, and scriptural in its teaching. The author divides his essay into five parts, after a brief survey of the Lights and Shadows. *Part First.*—Coming to the Light. 1. Starting Out. 2. Locating the Light. *Part Second.*—Mistaking Darkness for Light. 1. Stumbling. 2. Falling. 3. Maimed. 4. Reproved and Recalled. *Part Third.*—Standing in the Light. 1. Learning to See. 2. The Fellowship of Light. 3. The Secret of Light. 4. The Laws of Light. *Part Fourth.*—Walking in the Light. 1. Christian Conduct, What? and Why? 2. In the Home. 3. In the Church. 4. Among Men. *Part Fifth.*—Working in the Light. 1. Responsibility. 2. Hindrances. 3. Motives. 4. What to do. This analysis of the contents will give the reader an intelligent idea of the book, which we earnestly commend as a timely and admirable contribution to our practical religious literature.

BIBLICAL LITERATURE.

Scribner, Welford & Armstrong respectively publish and sell at $6, a second edition, revised and improved, of *The Training of the Twelve; or, Passages out of the Gospels, exhibiting the Twelve Disciples of Jesus under Discipline for the Apostleship*, by ALEXANDER BALMAIN BRUCE, D.D., Professor of Theology, Free Church College, Glasgow. Like Prof. Bruce's more recent work on the Humiliation of Christ, this has decided value. It brings to view and opens out the meaning of the various discourses, parables, teachings, incidents, in the course of our Lord's ministry in connection with his Apostles, which served in any degree to train them for their great mission. This constitutes a very large part of our Lord's life and ministry. While this volume has the general merit of sound exegesis, it brings the added light which results from surveying the Saviour's teachings from a special standpoint, and with special respect to their convergence toward one great end. They have a good deal of exegetical theology, and are rich in homiletical applications of it to ministers and people. For sermonizers and exhorters they are especially rich and suggestive, in helping preparation alike for topical and expository discourses.

Scribner, Armstrong & Co. publish, and McGinnis & Runyon have for sale in Princeton, another volume of the Great Commentary of Lange, edited by Dr. SCHAFF. It is on the Books of Samuel, by Rev. Dr. Chr. Fr. DAVID ERDMANN, Professor of Theology in the University of Breslau, and is translated, enlarged and edited in an able manner by Rev. C. H. TOY, D.D., LL.D., and Rev. JOHN A. BROADUS, D.D., LL.D., Professors in the Theological Seminary in Greenville, S. C. We welcome this addition to our apparatus for the due interpretation and application of this particular book of Scripture in itself, and as an earnest of the speedy completion of the publication in English of the exhaustive and encyclopediac work of which it is a part.

Outlines of Hebrew Grammar, by GUSTAVUS BICKELL, D.D., Professor of Theology at Innsbruck, revised by the author, and annotated by the translator, SAMUEL IVES CURTISS, JR., Ph.D., with a lithographic table of Semitic characters, by Dr. J. EUTING, Leipzig, 1877. This little book of 140 pages contains a great deal of instructive matter with reference to the history and etymology of the Hebrew language. It is not an introductory grammar to vie with Davidson, Green or Seffer, or, indeed, a text-book of a more advanced character. It is rather an outline of the principles of Hebrew grammar from the standpoint of comparative philology, and thus designed for advanced students. As such it has its appropriate place among the constantly increasing number of Hebrew grammars. The principles of Hebrew accentuation ($18–20) have been prepared by Dr. Franz Delitzsch, the very best authority on this subject. Dr. Curtiss has done excellent work both in his translation and notes. We can only express our regret that Hebrew syntax receives so little attention, for this subject demands more labor, and needs that more light should be thrown upon it.

The Apologies of Justin Martyr, and the *Epistle to Diognetus,* with an introduction and notes, by BASIL L. GILDERSLEEVE, Ph.D., LL.D., Professor of Greek in the John Hopkins University, Baltimore. Harpers, 1877. This new volume of the Douglas series of Christian Greek and Latin writers is an admirable one. The introductions are full and satisfactory; the analysis thorough, and the text carefully edited. The notes are the chief features of the book, and these are models of conciseness, completeness and scholarship. The points of syntax, especially, are worthy of careful consideration, as Dr. Gildersleeve brings into comparison with the Greek of Justin, the classic authors, the LXX, the New Testament, and Hellenistic writers generally, as well as the Hebrew idiom. There are three indices: Greek terms, texts of Scripture, and subjects. This work will be even more useful to theological students and the studious ministry than to students of Christian Greek in the college course.

T. & T. Clark of Edinburgh and Scribner, Welford & Armstrong publish, at $3.00, another volume of Meyer's Critical and Exegetical Commentary on the New Testament, being Vol. I. of the *Critical and Exegetical Handbook to the Acts of the Apostles,* extending through chapter xii; translated by the PATON J. GLOAG, D. D., and revised and edited by Dr.

WILLIAM P. DICKSON, Professor of Divinity in the University of Glasgow. The high merits of this commentary are recognized among exegetes and biblical students, and it is eagerly sought for their libraries by all of this class who can afford to purchase them. For sale in Princeton by McGinness & Runyon.

HISTORY AND BIOGRAPHY.

Ex-President Maclean's History of Princeton College. One of the most important among recent historical productions has reached us at the last moment. It is entitled the *History of the College of New Jersey from its Origin in* 1746 *to the Commencement of* 1854, by JOHN MACLEAN, the tenth President of the College, in two handsome octavo volumes; published by J B. Lippincott & Co. of Philadelphia, in a style as creditable to the publishers as the contents are to its honored and venerable author. It is the first and only thorough history of Princeton College that has yet been written. Interesting and valuable historical fragments and monograms have been published, but this is the first complete and continuous history of one of the earliest and largest of the great historical colleges of the country. It is from the hand above all others qualified for the task. President Maclean, himself the son of an eminent early professor of the institution, born and reared within its classic shades, personally connected with it as student, tutor, professor, president, for more than half a century, a resident of Princeton since his retirement from office, has had means of knowledge, and access to trustworthy sources of information, possible to no other man. The preparation of it has afforded him becoming and useful occupation during his declining years; and it is fortunate that he has had leisure to test the truth of his narrative, to work it up thoroughly and well, and to make an enduring monument for himself and the college out of materials that were fast passing into an oblivion from which they could not otherwise have been rescued.

Of course these volumes will be precious and attractive, not merely to the graduates and immediate friends of the college, but to all lovers of high education, and especially those interested in the successive stages of its development in our larger and elder seats of learning. But this is not all. These volumes shed great light upon important epochs and passages of American history, civil and ecclesiastical—particularly the Revolutionary epoch, with the periods preceding and following it. Old Nassau Hall was alternately barracks for one or the other of the contending armies. Dr. Witherspoon, its president during the Revolutionary era, was equally conspicuous as a civilian, a divine, and an educator; and was among the foremost of the Revolutionary statesmen that declared our national independence and brought our nation to its birth, as also of the divines that framed the Constitution of the Presbyterian Church. His line of predecessors, Dickinson, Burr, Edwards, Davies, Finley, contains the most illustrious names of early Presbyterian and ecclesiastical history, while those that follow were among the burning and shining lights of the church. Indeed, the college was founded, first of all, in the interest of religion—to raise up a learned ministry for the church, and trained leaders in the State, and in every sphere of professional life. Indeed, it grew more immediately out of the great revival of 1740, and was especially founded and fostered by friends and supporters of that work. Its history is therefore very largely the history of the early and formative era of the American Presbyterian Church. The very mention of the names of i.s presidents will show that the history of their successive administrations involves matters of the highest moment in the religious development of our country.

We trust that this work will command the attention and the circulation it richly deserves.

Historical Sketch of Presbyterianism within the bounds of the Synod of Central New York. By P. H. FOWLER, D.D. Utica: Curtiss & Childs; p.? 7;; 1877. This work was a labor of love, and was prepared and published at the request of the Synod. whose history it records with fullness of detail, and in so lucid a manner, and in a style so pleasing, as to make it a book of no ordinary interest even to the general reader. The work could not have fallen into more competent hands; and most worthily and conscientiously has the task been performed. The history covers a period of seventy years; and all will agree with the author that the " dealings of the Spirit with the churches of his own loved denomination on that field have been remarkable and even wonderful."

Presbyterianism in Central New York was born and nurtured under the happiest auspices. "The best of ministers waited upon it, generally the alumni of Eastern colleges and seminaries, intelligent and disciplined, earnest and faithful, orthodox and orderly; and they saw to it that their succession was kept up, and candidates for ordination and applicants from foreign bodies were thoroughly examined as to their piety and literary and theological attainments." * * "Great stress was laid on doctrinal truth, and it entered largely into preaching and conversation as the prime and principal element of Christian experience and living." * * * "Calvanism being the system that was accepted and exacted,"

While the sketches of individual churches and institutions on the field are a prominent feature, no little space is devoted to revivals, "the jewels and crown of Presbyterianism in Central New York." They began with "the great revival of 1799," and have kept up almost continuously down to the present time. In these revivals originated many, if not the majority, of the churches on this favored field. This region was the scene of Mr. Finney's remarkable ministry, which began in 1824, and was the occasion of "violent discussions and animosities in the Presbyterian Church throughout the land." Dr. Fowler treats this branch of the subject with intelligent discrimination and sound judgment. His sketch of Mr. Finney, as a man and a preacher, and the wonderful effects of his preaching, is exceedingly graphic and interesting. He freely admits his faults and errors, both of manner and doctrine, some of which were serious; but he claims for him a distinguished place in the regards of the Church, and attributes no small part of the growth and prosperity of the churches of Central and Western New York to the revivals which were connected with his preaching. At the same time his remarks on the whole subject of Revivals and Evangelists are pregnant with meaning; they are timely; they deserve to be studied and pondered; they are the expression of a sound philosophy ; the mature reflections of one who has carefully observed and studied the subject.

We regret that we cannot do better justice to this valuable history, but it came to hand at the last hour.

The book also contains an address delivered before the Synod of Central New York in October last, entitled *The Presbyterian Element in our National Life and History*, by Prof. J. W. MEARS. The theme was a fitting one for our Centennial Year, and is here handled with ability and effect.

A History and Manual of the Second Presbyterian Church in Troy, N. Y., prepared and published in its semi-centennial year, July 2d, 1876, by its pastor, Dr. WILLIAM IRVIN, is a most cheering and creditable record. It is the history of one of our largest churches, which, although not without vicissitudes of trial, has, on the whole, been steadily prosperous, growing itself while giving birth to and nourishing to the point of self-support flourishing daughter churches. Its history is what might have been expected from its noble succession of pastors, which includes some of the brightest names that have adorned the Presbyterian pulpit.

Scribner, Armstrong & Co. publish *Charles Kingsley, his Letters and Memories of his Life*, edited by his wife, and abridged from the London edition. It awakens additional tender memories as it reminds us of the life and death, the literary ability and activity, and the marked Christian virtues of the author of the abridgment, Mr. EDWARD SEYMOUR, whose recent sudden decease is so great a loss, not only to the eminent publishing house of which he was an honorable member, but to the wide circle of authorship and letters. This volume is in all respects the better for the abridgment. It is a rich and welcome contribution to that luxuriant issue of memoirs, biographies and autobiographies of eminent literary and professional men, which constitute so salient a part of recent literature.

Charles Kingsley united in a remarkable degree the poet, novelist, radical, socialistic reformer, political agitator, theological innovator, the earnest and vigorous preacher and active pastor in the Anglican Church; he was, in short, a genius, setting himself at work in all directions to remove real or seeming abuses in Church and State, which he saw clearly and felt keenly. In religion he was the broadest of Broad Churchmen. He takes no pains to conceal, but is ever eager to obtrude, his intense antipathy to that concrete system of doctrines known as Evangelical. There are few established truths, doctrines or institutions which do not undergo more or less of skeptical searching and testing at his hand. While his sincere and unselfish spirit, in dealing with the great concerns of God and man, is as conspicuous as his originality and brilliancy of treatment, yet it is manifest that his mind had a one-sidedness, a tendency to detect and magnify the evils, weaknesses and faults, rather than duly to appreciate the strength, merit and excellence of accepted systems and existing institutions. Yet, it is gratifying to observe that as he advanced in life and experience he became more awake to the substantial claims of much in the existing social, political and religious organizations to which he was before blind, and to the fallacies of the ideal, speculative and unpractical, in his *Alton Locke* and other early publications. Maurice seems to have been, beyond all others, at once his master and his ideal. Writing to him, Mr. Kingsley said :

"As to the Trinity, I do understand you : you first taught me that the Trinity was a live thing, and not a mere formula to be swallowed by the undigesting reason ; and from the time that I learned from you that a Father meant a real Father, a Son a real Son, and a Holy Spirit a real Spirit, who was really good and holy, I have been able to draw all sorts of practical lessons from it in the pulpit."—P. 357.

He appears to have fluctuated very much in his ideas as to the binding force of assent to the articles of a creed, and at times to have come nearer the truth than Maurice, to whom in one case he writes thus :

"I don't quite understand one point in your letter. You say, 'The *Articles* were not intended to bind men's thoughts or consciences.' Now, I can't help feeling that when they assert a proposition, *e. g.*, the Trinity, they assert that that and nothing else in that matter is true, and so bind thought ; and that they require me to swear that I believe it so, and so bind my conscience."—P. 358.

But he clearly avows his unwillingness to be bound by any popular, however obvious, interpretation of the articles, or to be denied the liberty of placing any "non-natural sense" upon them he may like, in the following deliverance :

"For myself I can sign the Articles in their literal sense *toto corde*, and subscription is no bondage to me, and so I am sure can you. But all I demand is, that in signing the Articles I shall be understood to sign them and nothing more ; that I do not sign anything beyond the words, and demand the right to put my construction on the words, answerable only to God and my conscience, and refusing to accept any sense of the words, however popular and venerable, unless I choose. *In practice* Gorham and Pusey both do this and nothing else whenever it suits them. I demand that I shall have the same liberty as they, and no more."—Pp. 358-9.

It is very obvious that this mode of subscription would be elastic enough to admit almost any grade of dissent and skepticism. It virtually overrides the true understanding and intent which measures the obligation of the parties; the true construction of all such subscriptions and assent to creeds being the understood mind of the church which requires them, *animus imponentis*. Yet the experience of Mr. Kingsley at length taught him the necessity of some such anchorage to hold him from being set adrift, without rudder or compass, by his own dreamy fancy. He says to Maurice:

"I feel a capacity of drifting to sea in me which makes me cling nervously to any little anchor like subscription. I feel glad of aught that says to me, 'You must teach this and nothing else; you must not run riot in your own dreams.'"—P. 360.

Nor did he fail to learn wisdom from experience in reference to his early socialistic and radical theories. Speaking of natural political equality and universal suffrage, he says:

"I have some right to speak on this subject, as I held that doctrine strongly myself in past years, and was cured of it, in spite of its seeming justice and charity, by the harsh school of facts. Nearly a quarter of a century spent in educating my parishioners, and experience with my own and others' children—in fact, that schooling of facts brought home to the heart, which Mr. Mill never had, have taught me that there are congenital differences and hereditary tendencies which defy all education from circumstances, whether for good or evil. Society may pity those who are born fools or knaves, but she cannot, for her own sake, allow them power if she can help it."—P. 374.

The Life of the Rev. George Whitefield, by Rev. L. TYERMAN. In 2 vols., 8vo. New York: A. D. F. Randolph & Co., 1877. The author of this work is well and favorably known to the public by his biographies of the Wesleys, Charles and John, and his history of "The Oxford Methodists." In their preparation he naturally accumulated much original and valuable material for a new and standard life of Whitefield, the early friend of the Wesleys, whose itinerant services promoted Methodism to a large extent. The studies and services of Mr. Tyerman in this field have fitted him preëminently for the task he has here undertaken and so creditably achieved.

The world has a right to know all that can be told of such a man. While innumerable sketches, and at least half a dozen lives, of Whitefield have already been published, we have in the present biography "a large amount of biographical material which previous biographers had not employed, and much of which seems to have been unknown to them." The work is not written with special reference to the interest of any denomination. Whitefield called himself a minister of the Church of England; but in fact he belonged to the Church Catholic. He loved all who loved Jesus Christ, and was intent only on the salvation of souls. The author claims and shows that "the friendship between Whitefield and the Wesleys was much more loving and constant than it had been represented by previous biographers; and that Whitefield's services to Methodism were more important than the public generally had imagined." Whitefield is here made as far as is possible his own biographer. The book is mainly one of information. It has the substance of his journals—journals which, unlike those of the Wesleys, have never been republished, and which are almost unknown. In this day, when God is so signally honoring the ministry of Evangelists, such a biography is timely, and may be read with great profit. Whitefield's power was not in his talents or oratory, but in his piety. In prayer and faith and religious experience and devotedness to God, and in a bold and steadfast declaration of the cardinal doctrines of the Gospel, he may have many true successors. God has, indeed, raised up some in this generation who are doing as great a work for Christ and the souls of men as even Whitefield accomplished.

St. Augustine, a Poem in Eight Books, by HENRY WARWICK COLE, Q. C., is published at $4.50 by the Clarks of Edingburgh, Scribner, Welford & Armstrong of New York, and for sale by McGinness and Runyon of Princeton. It is really a biography of the illustrious divine in verse, which gives it whatever attractiveness may be thus imparted to a narrative in which we detect very little poetry, but a very fine biographical portrait of the greatest name in Christendom since the Apostles. It abounds in just and beautiful sketches, and estimates of the salient points in his career and works.

MISCELLANEOUS.

Scribner, Armstrong & Co. have issued and have on sale with McGinness and Runyon of Princeton, a third series of Mr. FROUDE'S *Short Studies on Great Subjects*, being a collection of papers previously given to the public in various British and American periodicals, with the addition of two, one on Divus Cæsar, and another entitled Leaves from a South African Journal, never before published. The latter is an animated description of his own travels in that country. The titles of the others are: Annals of an English Abbey, Revival of Romanism, Sea Studies, Society in Italy in the Last Days of the Roman Republic, Lucian, The Uses of a Landed Gentry, and Party Politics. All these are treated with brilliancy and power. They display, too, a versatility as great as the variety of topics handled. We rarely open a page which is not glowing with the warmth and brightness of his genius for pen-painting, live discussions, vivid portraitures of the present and the past. We give an extract from the essay on the Uses of a Landed Gentry. We should like to give a dozen from almost every one of his papers, in which the greatest blemish is a certain rationalistic tinge in his treatment of most religious topics that come in his way:

" Every step of what has been called progress for the last thousand years has been the work of some man, or group of men. We talk of the tendencies of an age. The tendencies of our age, unless it be a tendency to mere death and rottenness, means the energy of superior men who guide and make it; and of those superior men who have played their parts among us at successive periods, the hereditary families are the monuments. Trace them back to the founders, you generally find some one whose memory ought not to be allowed to die. And usually, also, in the successive generations of such a family you find more than an average of high qualities as if there was some transmission of good blood, or as if the power of discrediting good blood was a check on folly and a stimulus to exertion. In Scotland the family histories are inseparable from the national history. How many Campbells, for example, have not established a right to be remembered with honor? How many hundred Scotch families are there not who have not produced, I will not say one distinguished man, but a whole series of distinguished men? Distinguished in all branches—as soldier, seamen, statesmen, lawyers, or men of letters.

" It is true that the highest names of all will not be found in the peerages and baronetages. The highest of all, as Burns says, take their patent of nobility direct from Almighty God. Those patents are not made out for posterity, and the coronets which men bestow on the supremely gifted among them are usually coron ets of thorns. No titled family remains a coronet for Knox or Shakespeare. They shine alone, like stars. They need no monument, being themselves immortal. A dukedom of Stratford for the descendants of Shakespeare would be like a cap and bell upon his bust. Of Knox you have not so much as a tomb; you do not know where his bones are lying. The burial place of Knox is in the heart of Protestant Scotland."—Pp. 302-3.

From the "Leaves of his South African Journal" we take the following account of a thunder-storm which overtook him while traveling in a mail-cart:

"Between four and five o'clock (he writes) the storm began; and, between the darkness and the blinding effects of the lightning, in the intervals of the flashes, we could scarcely see ten yards from us. Even in South Africa I never saw such a display of celestial fireworks. The lightning was rose-color, deepening at times to crimson. Each flash appeared like a cross, a vertical line seeming to strike the earth, a second line crossing it horizontally. The air was a blaze of fire. The rain fell in such a deluge that the plain in a few minutes was like a lake. Of course we could not move. The horses stood shivering up to their fetlocks in water. At one time there was no interval between the lightning and the report, so that we were in the very centre of the storm. The sense of utter helplessness prevented me from being nervous; I sat still and looked at it in mere amazement. In two hours it was over. The sky cleared almost suddenly, and, with the dripping landscape shining in the light of a summer sunset, we splashed on to the river." —P. 382.

A. D. F. Randolph & Co. publish *Our National Bane; or, the Dry-rot in American Politics. A Tract for the Times touching Civil Service Reform.* By GEORGE L. PRENTISS. Dr. Prentiss has done capital service in publishing this tract, which is, after all, a volume of over 100 pages, every sentence of which is as pointed and telling as its title-page in regard to the great pest of our politics, which beyond any cause, with the possible exception of intemperance, an evil not by any means disconnected with it, is working not only the political, but moral and religious demoralization of our country, and beyond all else threatens to be the instrument of national disintegration and dissolution. We wish it could be read, not only by every statesman, official and politician, but by every voter in the country.

Only one thing needs to be added to give an adequate view of the subject, and show what cannot safely be overlooked by those who aim at any permanent cure or mitigation of this dreadful evil. We refer to universal suffrage in connection with the vast accession of ignorant and debased persons to the franchise through the constant relaxation of naturalization laws, along with the vast increase of the immigration of degraded people from foreign countries, and the emancipation of the slaves of this country. The debasement of the civil service, and the prevalence of the doctrine that public offices are the spoils of party triumph have gone on *pari passu* with the increase of the vote of the vile and worthless. Upon this the dema-gogues so graphically sketched by Dr. Prentiss play and thrive. And so long as fifty votes from the slums balance fifty votes from Union Seminary, the demagogue who obtains this vote for any Senator or Representative, by fair means or foul, makes that official sensible of dependence on him for-getting or keeping office, and unwilling to deny him the reward he demands. Here is the true *fons et origo malorum.*

The Necrological Report of the Alumni of Princeton Seminary, for the past year, including three trustees—the brothers John C. and Chancellor Henry W. Green, and Dr. J. M. Macdonald—and thirty-three who had been students in the institution, contains the names of the late Bishop Johns, Drs. Wm. B. Sprague, G. S. Boardman, J. B. Waterbury, Robert Davidson, John S. Hart, Nathaniel H. Griffin, M. W. Jacobus, and several others of note, which of themselves are sufficiently indicative of the high work done by such institutions. It is worth the consideration of life-insurance com-panies and actuaries that the average age of this list at death was 68. This also deserves the attention of those who feel that they have a special vocation to harp upon the peculiar hardships and trials of this noblest of professions.

The Rights, Powers and Duties of Members in Communion of the Re-formed Protestant Dutch Church of the City of New York, is a pamphlet originating in some recent controversies between the consistory and a por-tion of the membership of that wealthy ecclesiastical corporation known as the Collegiate Dutch or Reformed Church of the City of New York. It probably sets in the strongest light the utmost privileges and powers which can be plausibly claimed by the membership of that church, if, unhappily, any controversy arise between them and the elders.

The Report of the Commission to devise a Plan for the Government of Cities in the State of New York, presented to the Legislature of the State of New York, is an exceedingly able and valuable document on one of the most urgent and difficult of the vexed questions of the times. It is printed at the *Evening Post* office. This Commission, consisting of twelve of the most eminent pub-licists of the city of New York, the Hon. Wm. M. Evarts chairman, was appointed by Governor Tilden, under the authority of the Legislature given at his recommendation. It is well worthy of the study, by its readers, which it has evidently cost its authors. It subjects to a searching review the existing evils in the government of cities, which are patent enough to all, and which chiefly arise from the fact that their taxation, expenditures and officers are determined and allotted by those who own not their property, but comprise the larger portion of their ignorance and vice. The Commission rightly judge that all but one of the remedies proposed or tried are at best mere palliatives, often aggravations of the disease. The one remedy is to restrict the right of suffrage in respect to questions of municipal taxation and expenditure to the possessors of the property taxed, protected and affected by the outlay. This judgment is all the more weighty as emanating from a commission composed in nearly equal proportion of members of both the great political parties.

Two Addresses before the American Colonization Society at its meeting in January, 1877, one on the *Christian Civilization of Africa,* by the Hon. H. B. LATROBE, the other entitled *Patriotism, Philanthropy and Religion,* by ALEXANDER T. MCGILL, D.D., L.L.D., are contributions toward the solution of the "color question" with collateral issues in this country, and the problem of Christianizing and civilizing Africa, which will repay careful perusal.

The Carters issue *Servants of Christ,* by the author of "A Basket of Barley Loaves"; *A Hero in the Battle of Life and other Brief Memorials,* by the author of "Memorials of Capt. Hedley Vickers," two small and attractive volumes for the young, and for Sunday-school libraries ; also, *A Wreath of Indian Stories,* by A. L. O. E., Honorary Missionary at Amritsar, author of "The Young Pilgrim," "Rescued from Egypt," etc., etc.

The Presbyterian Board of Publication have added the following works to their catalogue : *The Maiden Martyr of Scotland,* by MATTHEW MOWAT (an admirable little book for the family or the Sunday-school) ; *The Pocket Hymnal* (a very neat and convenient edition) ; *Giving in Hard Times: A Word to the People and their Pastors,* by Rev. JOHN ABBOTT FRENCH, published by request of the Synod of New Jersey, which we wish could be read and its lessons laid to heart by all who complain of the hard times and make them often an excuse for not giving, and who by their sins, as the author boldly and justly charges, helped to bring these times upon us. *Alypius of Agaste,* by Mrs. WEBB, 12mo, pp. 379. *Pomponia; or, the Gospel in Cæsar's Household,* by the same author, 12mo, pp. 480. Mrs. Webb has fairly won a good reputation in the field of religious fiction. She writes sensibly, and with an earnest purpose. Her books not only interest, but tend to elevate the mind. The two works before us are similar in scope and aim. The scene of the first is laid in Egypt in the fourth century. Agaste was the birthplace of the great Augustine, and he and Alypius were companions in their boyhood. The scene of the other is laid in Rome in the reign of the emperor Claudius. Seizing on a few of the salient facts of history and making them the basis of her narrative, Mrs. Webb weaves a story in each case full of interest and instruction, not only to the young, but to mature minds.

Hours with Men and Books. By Prof. WM. MATTHEWS, LL.D. Chicago : S. C. Griggs & Co. 1877. 12mo, pp. 384. The author of this volume has achieved remarkable success. His style is captivating, and he has the rare faculty of adorning his pages with apt and telling illustrations. His "Getting on in the World," and "The Great Conversers," made his name familiar to thousands, and the present volume will add to the number. Some of the world's great authors—DeQuincy, South, Spurgeon, and Judge Story—are passed in review by him; and nearly a score of topics, among which are Moral Grahamism, The Illusions of History, The Morality of Good Living, Homilies on Early Rising, Literary Triflers, Writing for the Press, A Forgotten Wit, Book Buying, Working by Rule, and Too Much Speaking, are discussed with wit and spirit and good sense. The book is highly entertaining, and abounds with valuable criticisms. We have nowhere seen so full and satisfactory a paper on Spurgeon—the elements and secret of his wonderful power and success.

Chedayne of Kotono, a story of the early days of the Republic. By AUSBURN TOWNE. New York: Dodd, Mead & Co. 12mo, pp. 606. This is evidently the author's maiden effort, and hence the critic must not be severe. It is to its credit to be able to say that it does not belong to the sensational school. There is not much plot in it, and no sharp and discriminating character-drawing, and very little philosophy. Still it is a book which many will read with interest and pronounce good. The most that we can say of it is, that it gives promise of better performance in the future.

Fridthjof's Saga; a Norse Romance, by ESAIAS TEGNER, Bishop of Wexio, translated from the Swedish by THOMAS N. E. HOLCOMB and MARTHA A. LYON HOLCOMB. Chicago: S. C. Griggs & Co., 12 mo., pp. 213. 1877. This celebrated poem—"one of the most remarkable productions of the age," according to a high critical authority—has run through numerous large editions in Sweden, and also in Norway. It has been reproduced in all European languages, even in Russian, Polish, and Modern Greek. The present translation is the *nineteenth* English, but the *first* American translation. One special feature of it, which gives it interest, is that every canto is rendered in the same metre as the Swedish original, and the feminine rhymes are everywhere preserved. Such a poem needs no praise of ours, when no less a poet than Longfellow says of it: "The legend of Fridthjof, the valiant, is the noblest poetic contribution which Sweden has yet made to the literary history of the world."

Miss Corson's Cooking Manual of Practical Directions for Economical, Every-day Cookery. New York: Dodd, Mead & Co., 1877. Miss Corson is the Superintendent of the New York Cooking School, and this little volume is the fruit of her practical knowledge of the subject. It is simple, concise, sensible, and embodies in a brief compass just the information which every good and economical housekeeper needs. She admirably answers the question, How well can we live if we are moderately poor?

Scribner, Armstrong & Co. publish *Alcohol as a Food and Medicine. A Paper from the Transactions of the International Medical Congress at Philadelphia, September,* 1876, by EZRAS M. HUNT, A.M., M.D., who has achieved distinction, not only by his contributions to medical and sanitary literature, but also in religious and biblical publications. This volume was the answer of the International Medical Congress to the Memorial of the National Temperance Society asking for a deliverance on the subject of which it treats. It very ably contests the claims so often made in behalf of the nutritious and medicinal virtues of alcohol. Without denying some extreme cases, in which the stimulus of alcohol may spur the vital functions to a needed exceptional and abnormal activity, it conclusively proves that the free and ordinary use of it as a support or stimulus to flagging vitality is a remedy worse than the disease.

The Russo-Turkish War. This little work, costing but fifteen cents, and published by the *Christian Union Print*, gives the information which everybody needs just now in reference to this absorbing subject. "Who Are the Turks? What is Russia? The Christian Provinces, The Two Religions, How the War Began, The Seat of War, Prospects and Probabilities, are the several points discussed. A map also accompanies the work. We do not see how it were possible to compress more important information bearing on the subject in the same space than we have here. No intelligent man can afford to forego a thorough knowledge of this great movement, the full significance and probable results of which cannot well be overestimated, and may essentially affect the political condition of the old world, and inaugurate a new state of things throughout the Eastern Church.

THE

PRESBYTERIAN QUARTERLY

AND

PRINCETON REVIEW.

NEW SERIES, No. 24.—OCTOBER, 1877.

Art. I.—DOGMA AND DOGMATIC CHRISTIANITY.

By Prof. THOMAS CROSKERY, Magee College, Derry, Ireland.

THERE is a class of thinkers both in Britain and America who assert that the time has come for recasting all the issues of our theological thought, and for seeking a more thorough reconciliation of our religious aspirations with the higher criticism and advanced culture of the age. They admit that the old creeds were good things in the past, and especially at the Reformation, when the ferment of new spiritual life needed guidance, consolidation and restraint; but they have now outlived their original use, and earnest minds can be no longer content to dress themselves out in the faded garments of forgotten speculation, but must seek, by a fresh and catholic study of truth, to work out the *renaissance* of modern theology, and secure the energy and triumph of a lofty spirituality. The creeds are worse than useless. They have become prolific sources of evil to the church. They have arbitrarily arrested the development of Christian thought, and restrained the free play of the higher reflective energies on which the continued existence of Christianity, as a living and progressive power, depends. We have now, therefore, to restore living thought to its due place, and allow it to operate freely as a modifying dynamic force amidst the statical energies of modern ecclesiastical life. Besides, the concessions must be made to satisfy the demands of science and philos-

ophy, so as to give to Christianity such an aspect of ration-
ality as will win back to the faith those anti-Christian speculators who are now doing their best to uproot it from the
earth. Christianity must be freed from all the lumber with
which it has been encumbered, though it may still be unchanged in essence, and really purer in form than it was in
days which are vaunted as the ages of faith. It is thus confidently expected that the common sense and the inborn reverence of mankind will strike a healthy balance between the
aggressive dogmatism of superstition on the one side, and the
aggressive dogmatism of science on the other. It will be a
happy day, it is said, for Christianity when its moral and spiritual elements shall be seen apart from the symbolic refinements of ritual, and from metaphysical elaborations of doctrine.

If not the most distinguished, at least the most persistent
advocate of this project for remoulding the theology of the
churches is the very Rev. Principal Tulloch of St. Andrew's.
in Scotland, a professor of theology in one of its ancient universities, and one of the chaplains of Her Majesty Queen Vic-
toria. Though a fascinating writer, with a certain skill and
force of literary expression, he has no great power as a thinker,
mainly because he has nothing of that systematizing intellect
which traces leading ideas into their connections and consequences, and gathers them all up into unity of plan and principle. His writings show no promptings of a dialectic impulse,
no powerful interest in the logical aspects of the questions he
discusses; while he is singularly deficient in that quickening
and impulsive energy of thought such as makes some negative
thinkers very effective educators of their age. It is, perhaps,
this deficiency in logical faculty that has led Principal Tulloch
to oppose with such vehemence the very idea of a systematized
theology. We can appreciate the charm of his highly polished diction. Every work of his pen shows the measured
tread and artistic finish of the most accomplished scholarship;
but the sounding sentences that fill our ear are fundamentally
meagre and unsatisfying both to heart and intellect. His work
on *The Leaders of the Reformation,* published in 1859, was
his first open attack upon the theology of the Reformation;
but as Principal Cunningham complained in his trenchant review

of the book, the author made no attempt to grapple with a single doctrine, but coolly proposed to get rid of the whole mass of sixteenth-century theology without any argument at all, on the simple ground that it had become obsolete and inapplicable to our more cultivated age. "The old *Institutio Christianæ Religionis* no longer satisfies, and a new *Institutio* can never replace it. A second Calvin in theology is impossible." In 1873 Principal Tulloch published his work on *Rational Theology and Christian Philosophy in England in the Seventeenth Century*, the object being to glorify the memory of Hales, Chillingworth, Lord Falkland, Stillingfleet and the Cambridge Platonists; but he utterly failed to prove that they formed a school of theology at all, much less one of Broad Church or rationalistic tendencies. In 1874 he published two papers in the *Contemporary Review* on "Dogmatic Extremes," and "Dogma and Dogmatic Christianity," exactly in the track of his earlier work, and in the present year he has brought out an interesting and able volume of sermons entitled, *Some Facts of Religion and Life*, in which he remains true to his earlier convictions of the hurtfulness of dogma in religion.

We need hardly say that Dr. Tulloch has been ably supported and encouraged in his continued attack on creeds by allies greatly more distinguished than himself. Dean Stanley has come to his help once and again with addresses and sermons delivered at St. Andrew's and Edinburgh. The great object of the Dean of Westminster is to bring about the unity of Christendom; but as he speaks to us out of the high and misty atmosphere of a theology which is not strong in dogmatic propositions, the unity in question, if ever realized, would be only the unity of a landscape wrapped in mist. In March last he delivered an eloquent and characteristic address at St. Andrew's on "Progress in Theology," which contained much that was sound, but much, also, that was false in speculation. Mr. Froude, the historian, has epitomized the whole question in a sentence: "God gave the Gospel; it was the father of lies that invented theology." Matthew Arnold, taking up the challenge of M. Renan, that "Paul is coming to an end of his reign," says that "the reign of the real St. Paul is only beginning," and he repudiates the idea of our understanding the divine enthusiasm of the apostles by merely drawing out a diagram of their belief in its logical bearings and connections. The Rev. John Hunt, a Broad Church writer of ability, expressly repudiates a dogmatic basis for Protestantism.

The design of all this opposition to a dogmatic Christianity is very apparent. All the writers referred to advocate a general softening of lines, a blending of colors, a cutting off of salient angles—the removal, in a word, of all that has a distinctive character; but the effect of any attempt to embrace in one body diversities so wide that they should effectually neutralize each other and turn the creed into an " inorganic conglomerate of ineffectual concessions," would be to provoke a counter movement in high sacerdotal and ritualistic directions. Such views threaten to act as a solvent of theological thought. It is no wonder, therefore, that Dr. Goold, the editor of John Owens' works, in his address from the moderator's chair, this year, in the Free Church Assembly, declared emphatically, " the Church must not go fishing for a creed in this nineteenth century of the Christian era."

We shall proceed in this article to examine the position of Principal Tulloch, and endeavor to vindicate against him the validity of dogma and the competency of theological system. The question is not as to the validity or truth of this or that theological system; nor as to whether we can form a theological system that shall be exhaustive, either of principles or details; nor is it a question of narrowness or intolerance of tone in advocating this or that system, as if any one party had got a monopoly of the wisdom that is needed to thread one's way through the difficulties of theology. The question is, Can there be theology at all? Is it possible to get rid of dogma and yet retain Christianity? Dr. Tulloch answers the last question very confidently in the affirmative: " It is possible to teach the Christianity of the New Testament without any formal theology, and still more without any sectarian dogmatism." "Long before Christian theology took its rise in the schools of Alexandria, or its primary dogma formulated in the Nicene symbol, Christianity not only existed, but was more of a living power than it has been ever since." " Dogma is the aftergrowth, and not the moving spring of the Christian spirit; and dogmatic Christianity is the Christianity of the schools, and not that gospel which is the power of God." " The apostolic teaching is in the highest sense authoritative, but it is not theological. It is popular, and not formal or systematic." " With all their dogmatism none would have resented more than they (the Westminster divines) the thought that Christianity was not something more, something higher than their dogmatic system ; or, in other words, that there was not a religion of the New Testament independently of the creeds or summaries of dogma which men have made out of it." (*Contemporary Review*, May, 1874.) " The idea of a free faith, holding to very different dogmatic views, and yet equally Christian, and the idea of spiritual life and goodness apart from theoretical orthodoxy, had not dawned upon the sixteenth century, nor long afterwards." " Men thirst not less for spiritual truth, but they no longer believe in the capacity of *system* to embrace and contain that truth, as in a reservoir, for successive generations. They must seek for it themselves afresh in the pages of Scripture and the ever-dawning light of spiritual life." (*Leaders of the Reformation*, pp. 87, 169.)

It is evidently necessary that we should, at the outset, understand what Dr. Tulloch means by " dogma," for it seems to us that he has given forth two difficult and altogether inconsistent accounts of it. He says: " Take any view you like of the genesis of dogma, it cannot be denied that it is not the original, but a derivative form of Divine Truth, an expansion or development of it. . . . Dogma is not Scripture, but only a deduction from it." " This," he says, " is the sense in which the word is understood by all theological writers." Certainly not. The Germans have a special department of theological science, known as *Biblische Dogmatik*, and the divines of every country speak familiarly of the " dogmas" of Scripture exactly after the manner of the early Fathers. In another place he says: " To the Protestant, dogma is not an authoritative or accepted statement of Divine Truth, but the reasoned or formulated statement of this truth. In other words, it is Divine Truth in a deductive or logical form." But, then, in an article in the *Contemporary Review*, published five months earlier, on " Dogmatic Extremes," in which he seeks to depreciate dogma, on account of its imperfection and partial error, as dealing more or less with the insoluble, he says: " That which cannot be adequately expressed in human language, can never have any more than a persuasive or moral claim upon human acceptance. It can never take rank with *a generalization of science or a proposition of logic,* which clearly addresses itself to all intelligence, and is capable of verification in all circumstances. It belongs to a different order of truth, and has its own tests of verification ; but, *transcending the sphere of logic or scientific definition,* it can never be formulated so as to demand universal assent. In other words, Christian dogma can never be anything but imperfect." That is, dogma, at one time, is a reasoned or formulated statement of truth, and, at another, it transcends the sphere of logic, and can never take rank with a proposition of logic. Dogma is fallible, because it is a deduction of logic, and dogma " can never be formulated so as to demand universal assent," because it is *not* like logic or science, which " clearly addresses itself to all intelligence, and is capable of verification in all circumstances." Dr. Tulloch really has no fixed views on the subject. The universally accepted view of dogma is that it is authoritative doctrine— that is, resting on Divine authority, and springing out of Divine revelation ; and it derives its essential character, not from its logical or systematical development, but from the ultimate data on which it is based. It is, therefore, questionable whether it is correct to represent " dogmatic form" as identical with what is even scientifically or systematically set out.

We are, then, naturally brought to consider the oft-repeated statement of Principal Tulloch, that "Christianity is a life, not a dogma." We are all familiar with this statement in the writings of German divines and in those of Bushnell, Morell and others. Dr. Tulloch speaks of it as " the most subtle and pervading error which has infested Christianity" ; that religious parties have changed "the centre of the religious ideal from *life* to *thought.*" But, after all, is it not utter puerility for him to speak as he does of the living spirit of religion existing apart from the dogma? for where is the living spirit to be found but in the dogma? Eliminate the dogma : where is the living spirit ? Christian graces can only be the fruit of certain dogmatic apprehensions, and so far as a man's life is Christian at all, it must be in virtue of his acceptance of Christian dogma.

Even if we suppose it to spring out of the constraining force of Christ's love, must not this love have been previously apprehended in its true doctrinal significance? Certainly, if the Scriptures do not favor a religion of " bare dogmas," they lend as little countenance to a religion of blind and vague feelings, without any presiding element of sound judgment to regulate and control it. Spiritual beliefs furnish the most powerful motives which influence human conduct. Is it not, in fact, to deny a fundamental law of our nature to say that religious life can be originated in us without belief of religious truth? There is no foundation for moral character at all without the exercise of the understanding and the heart in receiving what furnishes the requisite motives to operate on life. Dr. Tulloch's system of psychology is certainly somewhat peculiar.* It is foolish to say that theology, by aiming at the scientific investigation of revealed truths, necessarily robs them of their elevating and affecting power. It is not the necessary effect of any science investigating the phenomena of physical nature to strip them of those natural features of attraction that strike the eye of all observers. But Principal Tulloch denies that their are any dogmas in Scripture: there are " religious truths that are capable of being put into a logical or propositional shape"; but as dogmas, they belong to the theology of the churches. Really, this is a most extraordinary statement. If the teaching of the Scriptures is not propounded on a dogmatic basis, let us ask what is its basis? It is not reason. An anonymous writer makes the following pregnant remarks: "If the spiritual life in man can be propagated and sustained apart from the dog ma, that certainly is a discovery for which modern theologians may take credit; but if it be a truth, it seems to have

---

* Even an Agnostic like Mr. Leslie Stephen sees the weakness of this position: " We are told with abundant eloquence that belief in Christ, and not the acceptance of certain dogmas about Christ, is that which is imperatively required. And yet, when we try firmly to grasp this rather vague statement, we find that the most abstruse dogmas convey truths unspeakably refreshing to the soul, and that belief in them is the salt of the earth. The logical conclusion to which these thinkers are tending would be that the emotion, and not the opinion, is of vital consequence; but frankly to accept that conclusion would be to part company with Christianity of the historical kind." (*Fraser's Magazine*, Feb. 1872, p. 161.)

escaped St. Paul and St. John. These primitive teachers of Christianity are to the full as dogmatic as Calvin and Owen. Their writings are, it is true, not systematic, like the Institutes of Calvin, or the Confession of Westminster, and are, besides, owing partly, it may be, to their unsystematic form, suscepti- ble of such various interpretations that it has sometimes been questioned whether rigid consistency be one of their merits : but dogmatic they are beyond question. Their teaching is not scientific—it is neither a deduction from reason nor an appeal to reason ; but it is authoritative, based upon miracle as its credential, starting from the supernatural as its premises, exacting assent, and intolerant of unbelief or indifference, and even of suspense."* But Dr. Tulloch says: "Dogmatic Christianity is the Christianity of the schools, and not that gospel which is the power of God." But was that gospel not dogmatic in the sense that it was an explicit, articulate and categorical announcement of the will of God? Remember, the question is not one of degree. It is not a question con- cerning the more or less of the theological element there may have been in primitive Christianity. Was it there at all? Was it there as the source and spring of spiritual life? We should like Dr. Tulloch to point out the distinction in kind between "the apostle's doctrine" and Calvin's Institutes. We challenge him to produce a single instance in which some statement falling strictly within the category of theology was not manifestly the means of evoking the religious sensibilities that characterized that golden age.

But Dr. Tulloch makes a wide distinction between the facts that lie at the basis of Christianity, and the "dogmatic theo- ries" with which the facts have been "overlaid "; and is very angry with one of his critics for suggesting that, according to the learned Principal, it might or might not be true, that Christ rose from the dead. In justice to him we concede

---

* *The Religious Difficulty in the Education Question.* By a Parish Minister, Edinburgh. One apostle says: "Take heed to thyself and to the doctrines"; "charge some that they teach no other doctrine." And another says : "If there come any unto you and bring not this doctrine, receive him not into your house, neither bid him Godspeed." Yet Dr. Tulloch has the audacity to say: "The idea of the church, as based upon opinion, is a mediæval and not a primitive idea. The church subsists in communion of spirit, not in coincidence of doc- trine."

that he has always sharply distinguished between facts and doctrines, as if facts were alone worthy of being exalted into solid matters of faith, and the doctrines only worthy to rank as nebulous matter of opinion. This is, of course, to destroy the idea of theology. It reminds us, indeed, of the strange and startling limitation Morell assigned to "facts" in theology, when he spoke of the death of Christ as "a fact of sense." Are there no other facts than those of sense? Are there facts of testimony, human or divine? We see two men meeting in the street: that is a fact of sense; but the one is brother of the other. That is a fact, too, but it is not a fact of sense. But, after all, is it really possible to separate the facts from the doctrines? Is not the doctrine the soul of the fact, without which it is simply worthless? Take the facts of Christ's life: how differently they appear on the Arian and Trinitarian suppositions respectively! Apart from dogma, the death of Christ tells nothing of the atonement, as the Incarnation is simply a birth under extraordinary conditions. If we accept the facts, we accept the doctrines, for the doctrines are implied in the facts, and constitute all their significance.* The savage and the philosopher see exactly the same thing when an apple falls to the ground; but for the one there is nothing but an outward appearance, for the other there is the doctrine of gravitation. To be ignorant of the doctrines is to be incapable of true knowledge of the facts. How many of Paul's doctrines in his Epistles are but generalized statements of fact! The able writer already quoted has the following observations upon this exceedingly shallow distinction between fact and doctrine: "It is the dogma that gives form to the supernatural, and meaning to the facts; and we can no more conceive Christianity apart from the dogma than apart from the facts. It is through it that the facts of gospel history have given a religion to the world."

But Dr. Tulloch has a very grave objection to the manner in which "dogmas" are constructed. He is of opinion that the old divines went to the Bible for the sake of making their sys-

---

* If the doctrines of Christianity have a fallible element, because they reach us in a logical shape, how can the facts escape? Has not our reason to be employed in getting the facts out of Scripture?

tems out of it or finding their systems in it, and that the majority of men learn their theology, not by independent study, but from tradition, authority and other similar guides. The latter remark may be perfectly true, but it applies equally to the way in which we acquire our knowledge of astronomy or any other science. But it is not an objection to the point, when the question is not concerning the actual history, but the scientific method of any study. We are not quite sure, however, that dogmatic divines went to the Bible to find in it their systems. Dr. Tulloch assures us that "an attentive study of the Institutes of Calvin reveals the presence of Augustine everywhere, and great even as Calvin is in exegesis, his exegesis is mainly controlled by Augustinian dogmatic theory." But what of Augustine himself? We may trace the genesis of his opinions from one father to another, but do we not at last come upon a man who had a Bible but no system? and how his theological ideas have come to be twisted and distorted by system we are quite at a loss to discover. The Bible was there before the systems. How could the first systematist go to it with a system already prepared? Surely, there is a weakness in the logical faculty here.

But Dr. Tulloch has an invincible repugnance to logic in theology, and has been congratulating the world and the Church for years back that "logic is no longer mistress of the field," and that "a second Calvin in theology is impossible." It appears there is "a new spirit of interpreting Scripture, which could hardly have been intelligible to Calvin," which, "while it accepts with awe the mysteries of life and death, refuses to submit them arbitrarily to the dictation of any mere logical principle."* Now, we maintain that logic has a true place in theology, because it has a true place in the Bible. Even Morell admits that Paul has given us the first example of systematic theology. The logic of the epistles is unquestionable. Of course it is possible, under the pretense of reasoning, to deduce from Scripture what is really not in it ; but in that case there is no introduction of logic into theology, but rather a delusive counterfeit of it, and a true logic is imperatively needed to detect and expel what is false. Dr. Tulloch does not believe in grounding our theology upon an induction of individ-

---

* Leaders of the Reformation, p. 168.

ual texts, independently of the spirit of the whole. He makes
sarcastic allusion in the case to a single text being made the
support of the ruling eldership. Now, even were there but
a single text, it ought to be decisive according to the degree
of clearness and appositeness; and it is no more illogical to
draw a conclusion from a single text in theology than from a
single fact in science itself. How did we come to know that
light was progressive, and not instantaneous in its motion?
The eclipse of Jupiter's satellites settled the question. But
no theologian objected to the conclusion because it was based
upon a single, indisputable, physical fact. The mind of the
Spirit in Scripture is to be ascertained as the mind of any
author is gathered out of his writings, by putting together all he
says—in various detached portions, perhaps—on any particular
subject, and honestly endeavoring to make out his meaning on
the whole. No interpreter of Scripture, worthy of the name,
disregards the " spirit of the whole"; for is there not the analogy of faith for his guidance? Dr. Tulloch falls into the error
of Morell, who held that individual texts have no divine authority—" we must take their whole spirit"; but unless ten false
parts can make one true whole, we cannot imagine how an interpreter can extract the meaning from any book of Scripture.
For if the parts do not mean what they say, we cannot possibly
ascertain the meaning of the whole.

Dr. Tulloch is very emphatic upon the imperfection dogma,
and says truly enough that "the divine relations which it
has to express are really inexpressible, or only proximately
expressible, in human language." He admits that dogmas are
serviceable notwithstanding, for "dogmas bring the divine
near to us, and help us to understand it, and so every vagrant
mind will regard them with reverence and learn from them
with humility." But the objection to dogma on the ground
of its necessary imperfection holds equally decisive against all
other knowledge. An acute critic of our author has forcibly
remarked: " It is not special to dogma, as he would seem to
imply, because it arises from the nature of the apprehending
faculty, and not from the nature of the object with which the
faculty is engaged. The simplest plant that grows, the stone
under our feet, the paper on which we write, foil our attempts
at complete and exhaustive knowledge. There is no object in

Nature of which our conceptions or our language is adequate.
The Divine is infinite, and therefore our finite thought cannot
contain it, nor human language render it. But a crystal or a
pea is infinite, as well as the universe, and the tiniest and com-
monest things of daily life, no less than its most stupendous
facts, are to us in a sense ' insoluble.' Whatever imperfection,
therefore, attaches to Christian dogmatism in this respect, belongs equally to every generalization of science, because to our
knowledge of the objects on which that generalization is founded."* But scientists and philosophers do not, on the ground
of the imperfection referred to, imitate the folly of Principal
Tulloch in relation to dogma. They draw conclusions; they
construct systems; they correlate all knowledges within man's
reach. One of the most notable characteristics of the present
age is the eager craving for exacter methods of thought. Is it
not strange, therefore, that in regard to the most important
of all subjects the philosophic discipline and methods so
greatly desired in other departments of knowledge should be
contemptuously set at nought? Why should the process of
systematizing, so invariably followed by the human mind in
dealing with every complex subject, become unlawful and unwarrantable as soon as it is applied to revealed religion? We
forget, however, that Dr. Tulloch actually pleads for haze in
theology. " The religious thought," he says, " is always and
necessarily indefinite. Haze (if you choose to use the expression) is of its very nature." But would not this make the
imperfection greater? If the thought is cloudy and the language vague, can we have any religious ideas at all? It does
not help us to come nearer correct views, as a writer observes,
to blur over all the lines and forms. There may be risk of
error in theological system, but is our position in any degree
improved by breaking away from all systems? There are no
books so full of errors as those loose and desultory works
written by men who profess to set all systems at defiance,
while they have this special mischief attaching to them, that
the errors in question are less easily detected and exposed
on account of the vague and indefinite mode of their presentation.

But if we resolve Christianity into an affair of spiritual

* *Frazer's Magazine*, " Liberal Protestantism," July, 1874.

affection and life—if "the centre of religious ideal" is to be *life* rather than *thought*—if logic is to give way to the moral and spiritual faculty, how is our position improved? There is no provision made, no guarantee provided, for this spiritual life realizing or maintaining itself. Is not this view a return to Schleiermacher's doctrine of the Christian consciousness as a *regula regulans?* A consciousness that includes natural as well as spiritual feeling—the consciousness of a Jowett, a Strauss and a Colenso, as well as of a Chalmers, a Calvin or a Hodge—but not based on the prior necessity of regeneration. May we not apply to the theological mixtures of such a consciousness what Vaughan, the author of *Hours with the Mystics*, applied to the speculations of the Mystics: "This intuitional metal, in its native state, is mere fluent, formless quicksilver; to make it definite and serviceable you must fix it by an alloy; but, then, alas! it is pure reason no longer, and, so far from being universal truth, receives a countless variety of shapes, according to the temperament, culture, or philosophic party of the individual thinker." The tendency of such a system must be to pollute rather than purify, to mix and compound rather than produce a living harmony; while it is easy to see that the fragments of a creed it continues to hold are liable to be assailed on the same grounds as the tenets it has abandoned. Let Christianity become a thing merely of life and sympathy: worship will survive; but how is worship to be maintained without reference to the character of the Being we worship? For we must "believe that He is, and that He is a rewarder of all them that diligently seek Him." Does not this involve a return to Christian dogma? We must know something of God's character and perfections, as well as of our relations to Him. But can anybody seriously dream of a church based upon pious sentiment and brotherly affection apart from creed or dogma? To use the words of Dr. Goold: "Without a common faith there can be no common worship, and if the rights and privileges of membership are dependent on the frail temper and fluctuating moods of human beings, church power might be prostituted into an engine of spiritual despotism."

This whole discussion brings us at last to this point, that in Dr. Tulloch's principles the church has yet her creed to find.

If this be so, then the church is not, and has never been, the
"pillar and ground of the truth." If it has failed in eighteen centuries to extract from Scripture a creed essential to
salvation, it has failed to serve the very purpose for which it
was founded. "Ye are my witnesses, saith the Lord," but if
it has no creed, it cannot be a witness for him. It has yet no
message to deliver, because it has not been able to agree upon
its scope and substance. This view nullifies the office of the
Holy Spirit as the teacher of truth; it palsies preaching; it
reduces the guilt of unbelievers to an infinitesimal point, as
the articles of belief are so difficult to ascertain; and it makes
it impossible for ministers to judge a heretic or cast him out
for false doctrines. We make bold to affirm, in answer to all
the liberal divines in the world, that not only has the church
formed a creed, setting forth the "one faith" of the gospel, but
that we do not expect any new discoveries of a fundamental
kind in theology, any radical revolution in the common faith
of the church, any new dogmas to be added to the circle of
faith. Professor Flint, of Edinburgh, perhaps at this moment
the foremost living theologian in Scotland, says: "Were a
man to tell me that he had discovered a divine attribute which
had never been previously thought of, I should listen to him
with the same incredulous pity as if he were to tell me that
he had discovered a human virtue which had escaped the notice of all other men. In a real and important sense, the revelation made in Scripture, and especially the revelation of God
in Christ, is most justly to be regarded as complete and incapable of addition. But there may be no limits to the growth
of our apprehension and realization of the idea of God there
set before us perfectly as regards general features." We believe
that we are not to look for any large additions to the fundamental principles of theology, or that they will be the subjects
of radical modification, either in regard to their specific statements or to the adjustment of their parts. Particular forms
of argument and defense may be abandoned, the consistency
of what is presented for belief may be set in a clearer light,
the meaning of the sacred text may be brought out more intelligently by deeper learning and critical insight, all that is of
real value in current philosophies may be utilized, and the
round of truth may be exhibited in a more symmetrical and

harmonious proportion ; but the great principles of theological belief—those principles by which God saves the soul—like the principles of mechanical force, the laws of chemical affinity, and the axioms of mathematics, are unalterably fixed, and are exactly the same from age to age. But as every generation must sow its own seed and reap its own harvests, instead of living upon the stores accumulated by its ancestors, so we must continually reproduce what is needed for our spiritual nutriment, only remembering that religion, from its very nature, supposes a basis of objective truth, which, though capable of being verified by research and criticism, does not derive its validity from the reasonings and convictions of the inquirer.

This view of the matter touches one of Dr. Tulloch's main objections to dogma, that it strangles free inquiry. On his principles we do not see, however, what need there is for inquiry at all, for if "the centre of the religious ideal"—to use his rather hazy expression—has been wrongly shifted by religious parties from life to thought, he must consistently demand a reversal of the movement. If the true centre is life, what have we to do with *thought* at all? And if thought is needful to sustain life, is not this to concede everything in the matter of dogma? But we have to deal with other opponents than Dr. Tulloch. It has been maintained by many, as a sort of axiom or postulate, that the love of truth cannot coëxist with fixed opinions, and that we must have boundless intellectual liberty if we are to make real advances in truth. But it is hard to see how free inquiry and love of truth can be incompatible with fixed opinions in a church, when they are not incompatible in an individual. But the idea is wholly absurd. It might as well be argued that the acceptance of Euclid implied the rejection of the differential calculus and quaternions. Canon Liddon puts the matter tersely thus: "You admit that revealed truths are true, but you dislike their being stated dogmatically. Why? If they are true, why not state them dogmatically? You reply that in this form they check independence of thought. Certainly, in a sense, it is true that they do check it. But after you have admitted the truth of a position, you are not at liberty to deny it. You cannot wish to do so. You cannot be loyal to known truth, and at the same time ignore or defy her. When you have discovered a fact of experience, you are not at liberty to deny that fact ; and you so

far forfeit your intellectual independence by your discovery.
. . . To believe the dogma that God exists is inconsistent
with a liberty to deny his existence; but such liberty is, in the
judgment of faith, parallel with denying the existence of the
sun or the atmosphere."* Are we always to be in the attitude
of seekers who had found nothing? If so, then our position
is as unphilosophical as it is untheological, and is only consistent with that universal skepticism which has been well called
the suicide of the soul. Free inquiry is one of the duties of
the church—" Prove all things"; but it is a fatal mistake to cut
the passage in two, and render our liberty hollow and imperfect by forgetting the counterpart—"Hold fast that which is
good." It is a significant commentary on the text that the
greatest additions have been made to theology by the Calvins,
Turretines, Witzinses, Edwards—men trained in a definite
creed, and not by the liberal divines, whose contributions have
usually been more or less Socinianized interpretations of Scripture, or a return to the Neo-Platonism of the early centuries.
Notwithstanding all the boast or pretence of free inquiry, those
who use it to the disparagement of a settled theology add little
to our knowledge, and throw but little light upon the elucidation of Scripture problems.

We maintain the right and the duty of theologians to pursue their inquiries fearlessly but reverently into all the questions that arise in the wide sphere of Bible study. Theology
is not a stationary science, though Lord Macaulay maintained, in his celebrated essay in Ranke's *History of the
Popes*, that it differed from all other sciences in the fact that
what it was in the early ages it was now in the nineteenth
century, and must be to the end of time. But this brilliant
writer had evidently in view the matter or substance of the
science of theology, not the instrument in its construction.
Anatomy is a progressive science, but the materials it deals
with are unchanged, being the bones and sinews of the human
frame. Chemistry is one of the most astonishingly progressive of modern sciences, but the things the science handles
are the same; the contents of its crucible are what they ever
were. Progress of this sort we do not refuse to own in the
study of theology; to deny it is an error that would deaden

---

* *Some Words for God.* Oxford, 1865, p. 80.

all enthusiasm and destroy all hope in the heart of the theologian. Systematic theology is the natural outgrowth of Scriptural investigation, always tending toward greater definiteness as to particular doctrines, and toward clearer views of their relations and interdependence. There are no limits to the growth of our apprehension of the idea of God. None of the fathers or schoolmen or reformers could have written a work like Dorner's *Development of the Doctrine of the Person of Christ*, simply because, apart from its own distinguished merits, the author, from his higher point of view, was able to take a more comprehensive survey of all preceding centuries. There is no reason to believe that our knowledge of the Atonement or other great articles of faith may not grow wider and deeper with every fresh realization of their inexhaustible preciousness. The history of theology, on the whole, has been a history of progress. But it is only in the line of what has been done in the past that there can be theological progress in the future; the old dogmas or creeds must not be discarded to make way for the new, for that would be to discard all that the Christian intelligence of the church had been able for ages to extract from the Divine revelation, to reject all the light that each generation had been privileged to throw upon some particular aspect of Divine truth. It has been well said : " All true progress in nature brings the new out of the old by the continuous growth and elaboration of the germs of life into organic completeness. The only true progress in theology also is that continuous and consistent development which brings the new out of the old, instead of parting with the old for the new, which increases knowledge for the future through retaining, applying and utilizing the truth which the past has brought down to the present." To part with our old dogmas, as a condition of theological progress, would be as foolish as it would be to discard all the laws and institutions of an ancient civilization, and revert to Rousseau's dream of a return to nomad life as a condition of human progress.

There cannot be the slightest doubt that the course of modern discussion has done much to strengthen and to widen the foundations of theology. The Bible is better studied now than it ever was. Dean Stanley himself sets forth the advantage theology has gained from diving below the surface and discovering the original foundations: "All the instruction, inward and outward, which we have acquired from our discovery of the successive dates, and therewith of the successive phases, of St. Paul's epistles, was lost almost until the beginning of the last century, but has now become the starting point of fresh inquiry and fresh delight. The disentanglement of the Psalter, the Pentateuch and many of the prophetic books from the artificial monotony in which, regardless of time and circumstances, a blind tradition had involved them, gives a significance to the several portions of the respective books which no one who has once grasped will ever willingly part with." Even the most negative German scholarship has established conclusions of the greatest importance to theology. How significant is the admission of Winer as to the interpretation of the text of Scripture: "The controversies among interpreters have usually led back to the admission that the old Protestant views of the meaning of Scripture are the correct ones." And, also, the testimony of Meyer, one of the ablest of living interpreters: "The older men have seen the day when Dr. Paulus and his devices were the vogue. He died without leaving a disciple behind him. We passed through the tempest raised by Strauss some thirty years ago, and with what a sense of solitariness might its author now celebrate his jubilee! We saw the constellation of Tübingen arise, and even before Baur departed hence its lustre had waned. A fresh and firmer basis for the truth which had been assailed, and a more complete apprehension of that truth, these were the blessings which the waves left behind, and so will it be when the present surge has passed away." How important the concession of Baur in relation to certain Pauline epistles as affecting the whole case for Christianity! Have not philosophers and scientists likewise strengthened the position of theology? We have much to learn from both classes of inquirers, for all knowledge runs up at last into the domain of theology. There is a complete stairway of thought from the one to the other. Yet do we not know how Darwin, in his very attempt to exclude marks of design from a world of organic beings, has supplied us with the most impressive and indisputable proofs of their existence; how the Pantheists have advanced the cause of true theism, and how the Pessimists.

like Arthur Schopenhauer, have commanded a more thorough study of the moral government of God, with its cardinal facts of sin and suffering? How much, indeed, there is still to be reaped from the speculations of anti-Christian thinkers?

We have said enough, we think, to justify the church in holding hard by its old theology, not merely because of its intrinsic value, but as a necessary condition for its own continuous progress. It may be interesting to consider for a moment the value of such a theology—if the name, indeed, is to be at all allowed—as Dr. Tulloch will consent to give us in exchange for what has been our precious possession for so many generations. What is the probable value of an undogmatic Christianity? Divines of the Liberal School are very confident that it would conciliate anti-Christian thinkers who are repelled by the rude aspect of our ancient dogmas. Why are they so confident? Is it because Christianity would be more acceptable if it were made more rational? Happily, however, we have evidence that a plan of this sort must be very thorough indeed to please the thinkers in question; so very thorough that Christianity itself must be left out of the question. The author of *Supernatural Religion*, speaking of this Liberal School of divines, says it is characterized by " a tendency to eliminate from Christianity, with thoughtless dexterity, every supernatural element which does not quite accord with current opinion, and yet to ignore the fact that in so doing ecclesiastical Christianity has practically been altogether abandoned :" and he graphically describes them as endeavoring " to arrest for a moment the pursuing wolves of doubt and unbelief by practically throwing to them, scrap by scrap, the very doctrines which constitute the claims of Christianity to be regarded as a divine revelation at all." Nothing can be more just or more decisive than this statement, and it ought certainly to open the eyes of those divines who imagine that it is possible to give up almost everything in the shape of doctrine without its making very much difference to religion.

Perhaps, however, the Liberal divines imagine that they will have more success with the masses of society. They imagine, perhaps, that they have a religion to offer, independent of dogma, that all will accept, because its leading principles

will be found to commend themselves to the moral and spiritual faculty in man.   But the misfortune is that it is not a
religion in hand ; it is a religion of the future ; and what is to
be done for the supply of present wants?   It has been said,
and certainly with some truth, in reference to Broad Church
divines, that "in proportion as they are true laborers for the
church of the future are they less true servants to the church
of the present."   Probably Mr. Maurice had this idea before
his mind when he so distinctly stated the qualification under
which he would allow himself to be ranked as a Broad Church-
man at all.   He would not consent to allow an attitude of
intellectual protest to weaken his hands for practical work in
the present.   But suppose the whole church of Christ were
to-morrow to surrender its entire dogmatic theology, and
take the position assigned to it by Dr. Tulloch: what
would be the result?   History is no better than an old
almanac if it has no light to throw upon this question.
Leigh Hunt once offered to form an eclectic religion, consisting of some of the simplest moralities and truths of the Bible,
to the exclusion of miracle, mystery and everything supernatural; and the comment of one of his friends was, that such
a religion would leave the higher classes theists and keep the
masses heathens.   What form of Christianity has ever penetrated to the depths of society?   There is but one answer to
this question.   It is evangelical theology alone that has established the most vital and manifold connections between itself and the practical piety and historic development of the
church.   There is much force in the observation of Vinet:
"You start at the strange dogmas of Christianity—a crucified
God, the punishment of an innocent victim, the mysteries of
free will and sovereign grace.   They are strange.   I dare not
make them a tittle less strange.   Yet it was these strange
dogmas that conquered the world.   It will be all over with
Christianity when the world has begun to think it reasonable,
or, eliminating the supernatural element, to give it a niche
among the philosophies."   A man of a very different type,
Mr. Leslie Stephen, knows better what the masses want. "The
old Puritan leaven," he says, "is working yet in various forms,
in spite of the ridicule of artistic minds and the contempt of
philosophers.   A religion, to be of any value, must retain a

grasp upon the great mass of mankind, and the mass are hopelessly vulgar and prosaic. The ordinary Briton persists in thinking that the words 'I believe' are to be interpreted in the same sense in a creed or a scientific statement. This appetite wants something more than 'theosophic moonshine.'" This is the testimony of an Agnostic. Can any one seriously believe that a liberal Christianity will ever convert the world? What definite message of mercy has it to carry to sinful men? What common ground can its teachers occupy? How is it that all the great propagating periods of the Church—those marked by revivals of religion or by missionary expansions—have not been the ages of rationalistic inquiry or Socinian speculation? How is it that there have been no revivals except in connection with the preaching of a dogmatic theology? There is but one way of answering these questions. We will go still further. Dogma has made nations. Calvinism is the strongest development of dogmatic theology the world has ever seen, and, tried by the test of history and practical utility, it has shown an immense superiority over every other system. Mr. John Stuart Mill, some years ago, spoke of Calvinism as a system which tends to crush out certain human faculties, and thus to produce " a pinched and hide-bound type of character." But Matthew Arnold has shown that the nations which illustrate the " Hebraizing" as opposed to the " Hellenizing" tendencies have been, whatever their faults, the toughest and most indomitable of races. Froude has pointed out Calvinism as the great *fact* in history—" the karl stalk of hemp," as Carlyle would say—that runs through the cable of the world's long drama, and which gives power alike to nations and individuals. It alone has conducted nations to greatness. It has given Luthers, Calvins, Knoxes to the Church, and Williams the Silent and Colignys to the State, while other systems, more congenial to the liberal divines of the present day, have stereotyped all men and all things in littleness. Well may Mr. Stephen say, in his article on Jonathan Edwards, that " the doctrine of Calvinism, by whatever name it may be called, is a mental tonic of tremendous potency."

It is evident, from the position we have taken up as to the possibility of progress in theological science, that we must uphold the right of the church, from time to time, to revise its creeds. No church should be in bondage to an instrument of its own production. We affirm the Word of God to be "the only rule of faith and practice," and we speak of our confessions and creeds as subordinate standards. All our creeds are in their nature temporary and provisional, calculated to meet existing wants, and liable, as these wants vary, to be modified in accommodation to altered circumstances. It would be inconsistent with Protestant principle to take any other position. The teaching which attempts to resist investigation, to stereotype thought, and to substitute trust in others for insight and conviction, abandons the highest elements of man's nature to the unbeliever, and renders him supreme in the domain of reason. But we must take care not to meddle needlessly with our standards, and, in any case, a very definite proposal ought to be submitted by those who demand a revision, that the church may be able to judge clearly as to the nature and extent of the change that is sought for ; the work of revision must involve risk of errors, controversy and distraction, not to speak of litigation, as well as of division among the branches of the great Presbyterian family, which still owes allegiance to the Westminster symbols. In recent discussions on the subject in Scotland, a very general opinion has been expressed, that if the work is to be undertaken at all, it ought to be done by no one Presbyterian church, but by a council of all the Presbyterian churches in the world. But no revision that may be attempted can be allowed to subvert the theological system embodied in our creeds, for that would involve not a change in our symbols, but a change in the convictions of the church, and a departure from the noble adage of Calvin, "Doctrinæ puritas est anima ecclesiæ." Much less will the church consent to discard all her creeds at the bidding of Liberal divines, to lose herself in the glow and rapture of emotional brotherhood, and to welcome a millennium of inarticulate harmony which involves the repudiation alike of our understanding and our faith. But she must take care never to divorce theology from religion, for those who study the noblest of all sciences must bring to it a profoundly spiritual discernment, and must realize in themselves the spirit and elevation of Christian life, if, as Hegel would say, the distinction between them is to be completely annulled, religion passing into theology, and theology into religion.

Art. II.—THE DEVELOPMENT THEORY.

By Rev. J. S. Beekman.

SOME scientists, in the development hypothesis, take for granted that in some far-off period, millions of ages ago, there appeared in space nebulæ, which by natural laws formed themselves into planets, satellites and suns ; that the earth, once a ball of fire, cooled down ; that, when prepared for it, plants, animals and man appeared in the succession of development and solely by natural laws—without a first cause to produce the nebulæ of our system—without a first cause to produce the different genera and species in either the vegetable or animal kingdoms —without a God to create matter or ordain the laws by which it is governed—without God to produce the multitude of different species of plants, over 2,000,000 of which are known to exist—without a God to create the multitude of different species of animals, or to exercise any providence over the earth. The theory, as held by such, simply stated is, " There is no God."

Comte, Mill, Herbert Spencer, Huxley, Tyndall, Fiske, and all belonging to their school of philosophy, show in their writings occasional longings to find a supernatural power, and to recognize for themselves an immortal existence, but are ever confronted by their scientific creed, and by it involved in the mists of doubt and unbelief. Their theory subjects them to struggles for an eternal existence, and involves them in constant warfare with the secret and powerful yearnings of the human soul, as the natural world, which they assume to interpret, has been and is a place of struggle for life. They have allied themselves with this kind of struggle, the aim of which is existence, but struggling against death and annihilation, which their own theory produces. But even if it should be proven that the bird has evolved itself from the reptile, and that varieties combine so as to form new species, yet religious faith in the Great First Cause and in the superintending divine power, need not be shaken. For if the laws of nature have been so ordained as to produce new species, it only proves the infinite wisdom of the God who made the laws. A machine which takes silk in its raw state, spins, weaves, and prints it with beautiful and varied designs, evidences the wisdom of the mind which constructed it for that end. Then, too, the machine does no more than the machinist designed it to do when he had it under course of construction. So, too, as to the effect of the laws of nature. This would be true, though it were proven that the nebulæ out of which the world has been evolved contained not only the properties of attraction, chemical affinity, electricity and the like, but also life, consciousness, intelligence, and love—and that these evolved by the force of law during millions of years. In the evolution of the world, no matter in what period we find any of the new forces, they have a cause ; and no matter if the cause be found to be a law of nature, the law evidences intelligence ; and even though law be traced back to nebulous matter, a Great First Cause must have given being to matter, and laws to matter, through which known results have been reached.

There was a time in the history of the world when there was no life, no sensation, no consciousness, no animal intelligence, no moral discernment. It requires greater credulity to maintain that these came into being through natural laws, imposed in nebulous matter when created of God, than to believe that the same power which created as a Great First Cause was present to exert his power to produce these new forces when the exact time arrived in the order of development for their being of utility. That each order of advancement appears at the fitting time, neither too soon nor too late as by sequence of law, may prove no more than the intelligence of the Great First Cause, and in no sense proves the absence of the First Cause. We need not be afraid to concede that, in all probability, God made every living creature by a process, or had method or law in creation ; that a higher order of vegetable or animal life may have been grafted on a lower, even as new spiritual life in a regenerated soul does not supercede or destroy the natural powers. Yet the Scriptures teach, and experience attests, that the new order of things comes about alone through the intervention of divine power. No sinner can regenerate himself any more than that a child has effected its own being. In like degree it is not probable that a higher order of being has produced itself from a lower. The most that law enables being to accomplish is to reproduce its own kind.   Hence the tree has its own kind in its seed, and the animal has its own kind, and no more, in its seed. We have no evidence of one species having produced another, or of the mixture of species having produced a kind which can reproduce itself. The mule cannot reproduce its own kind. So experience and reason, observation and Scripture, prove that divine power is exerted to produce both natural and spiritual development. The Word of God mentions certain periods when the interposition of the divine hand was manifest and seemed in an especial sense to be required. In the first epoch, or day, "God said, Let there be light and there was light." In the second, the most marked feature was the separation of the ærial matter from the earth. In the third, vegetable matter for the first appeared. In the fourth, the most marked feature was the shining of the sun and moon on the earth. In the fifth, living creatures were called into being; and in the sixth, beasts of the field and man. All are said to have been effected by the power of God. In all there is consistency, or development, or order. Each succeeding order is pre-supposed by the preceding. Animal life pre-supposes vegetable, and man an animal existence, as the humming-bee pre-supposes the fragrant flower upon which to feed. In the order of nature we have prophecies of what is to come, and in them God is recognized in law, or independent of law, to produce development from chaos to light, from light to order in planetary motion, from vegetable life to animal, and from animal life to man. That God's divine power may be so exercised and independent of natural law was wonderfully exhibited about 1,900 years ago in the conception of the Saviour of men. Man's need was the evening of his struggles to deliver himself from the wages of sin. Man's fruitless effort was prophetic of what God did to deliver him from moral and spiritual death. By the power of the Holy Ghost, Jesus was conceived in the womb of a virgin. This event is the morning of man's day on earth, and is the most distinctive of all the epochs of the world's history.

The Scriptures teach that God exerted his divine and omnipotent power in creation, in the incarnation, and in the abiding presence of the Holy Spirit, from the beginning up to the present, not through laws simply, or by mere influence, but by the living, personal presence of the Spirit. The Scriptures are explicit in teaching that God has never withdrawn his presence from the world. In the epochs of creation, the word is, "God said, Let there be light"; "God said, Let there be a firmament." His personal presence is distinctly stated. The Scriptures are entitled to our belief, for, though written by men, the ideas are from God; hence infallibly correct. Though written by men and in man's language, yet the phraseology in which the ideas are clothed accord with the mind of God. He was especially present in the incarnation. And after his ascension in the form of man, he did not even then abandon the earth, but reappears in the Holy Ghost, manifesting himself to his universal church, not to the eyes of the curious, but to the believing hearts. And the Scriptures warrant the belief that he will continue with man till the earth has finished her destiny.

The Darwinians, and all belonging to this school, maintain that the earth evolved itself from chaos by natural laws, and by law alone developed into its present state of perfection and beauty: that not only light came by natural law, but also life in the vegetable and animal kingdoms; from a state of no life, plants evolved from matter, and animals from plants; that each evolved from a lower into a higher order; that man evolved from an ape, and that his original progenitor is an oyster. But in the Scriptures we are told that "God *said*, Let there be light;" that "God *said*, Let the earth bring forth grass;" that "God *said*, Let the waters bring forth abundantly the moving creature that hath life:" that "God *said*, Let the earth bring forth the living creature *after his kind*, cattle, and creeping thing, and beast of the earth *after his kind*, and it was so." In short, that God not only gave the earth its being, but supervised its development from one state to another, and at certain stages exerted his divine power to advance it to higher stages, and that development has been produced through the exercise of divine power alone. When law can produce a certain effect, it is left to do it. But law is not endowed with intelligence, and can effect no more than God has ordained it should do. For example, the law of attraction can destroy life, but it cannot restore it, for it destroys life because life violates the law of its own being. If a man takes arsenic, he does not expect that the law, exacting death for being violated, will intelligently exert itself to counteract death. That would endow law with the power to do and not to do at one and the same time. So in the spiritual realm, man *unregenerated* is upon a lower platform, in an inferior stage of life ; but man *regenerated* is upon a higher, very much higher platform, or in an advanced life. If we may be indulged the comparison, the ape and man may represent both classes, but man as he came from the hand of his Creator. Hence the prohibition obtains new force, " Be ye not unequally yoked together with unbelievers." It must be distinctly noted here that God is the author of regeneration.

The Book of Genesis gives the order and progression in the creation. So far from this order and progression conflicting with science, many of our best and most learned scientists, among whom are Profs. Dana, Guyot and Dawson, have found science to agree with the account there given. Through the process of law there may be results such as claimed by some scientists, yet this only proves that the divine mind has so ordained law as to produce the end reached. Our not being able to see all the ins and outs of the laws of nature does not render the fact any the less certain, any more than the ignorant man not understanding the working of a machine invalidates the testimony its work gives of its having been designed by an intelligence to produce the thing accomplished by it.

It is supposable that there may have been development of the species. Prof. Huxley labors to prove that some varieties in species, though he cannot determine the process, have become distinct species, but agrees at the same time that there are species which through all the pre and past historic ages have remained unchanged. But if this were proven, which it is not, yet it could not impugn the fact that God, either directly or through the laws which he has ordained, has the honor and glory of the development, the method of which being simply discovered and understood. Jesus was born of a virgin, but by the power of the Holy Ghost. The fact is of revelation, but not the method. Oh! how much higher is he than any among men? man is weak, he strong ; man sinful, he sinless ; man polluted, he of spotless purity ; man lost, he the Saviour.

The same hand that has given the Matterhorn its grandeur

among the mountains of Switzerland, gives also beauty to the Eidelneiss growing in the midst of perpetual snows and bearing its velvety white flowers. Thus Jesus stands among men in divine grandeur, bearing the beauty and purity of the human, which, though insignificant compared to the Deity, is beautiful, sweet, lovely to earth and heaven. May not this holy humanity crown the Deity, which has been exhibited and in exercise from the earth's beginning?

Art. III.—SOME PHASES OF MODERN THOUGHT.*

By Rev. Wm. M. Taylor, D.D., New York.

WHEN Paul had spent a long day in earnest conference with the Jews at Rome, we are told that "some believed the things which were spoken and some believed not." So it has always been in the proclamation of Divine truth. I do not know that any one of its preachers has ever been blessed in securing the faith of all his hearers. Even on the day of Pentecost there were some that "mocked," saying, "These men are full of new wine." We need not be surprised, therefore, or imagine that "some strange thing has happened us" in these days when we are met with objections or unbelief. On the contrary, we ought to prepare for being disbelieved by some. We ought to lay our account with being questioned, and we should be ready "to give to every one that asketh a reason of the hope that is in us with meekness and fear." We must not disguise it from ourselves that there are difficulties in the way of believing the gospel, and our wisdom will be to seek to understand what these difficulties are in individual cases, to sympathize with those who feel them, and to endeavor by the help of God's Spirit to remove them.

For my own part, I am not astonished that a man should

----

* An address delivered before the New York Association for the Advancement of Science and Art, April 2d, 1877. Some of the arguments and illustrations here employed have been made use of in other connections by the writer, but he has thought it best to let the address go forth precisely as it was delivered.

hesitate to accept some of the statements of the Word of God. When I think of the incomprehensible mystery of the Incarnation, or of the bewildering effect that is produced in the mind whenever one tries to shape to himself a distinct conception of the eternity and self-existence of God, I can very well understand how some should falter at the reception of these things. Indeed, in this aspect of the case, the difficulties felt by the inquirer are more intelligible to me than the easy indifference which multitudes manifest respecting such all-important subjects, or the blind assent which is given by others to the orthodox statements regarding them without any perception of the perplexities which they involve. The English Laureate, in some such mood, has said :

> "There lives more faith in honest doubt,
> Believe me, than in half the creeds,"

but his words need to be carefully qualified. In doubt, properly so called, there can be no belief. But if the doubt be honest, it will be cherished in connection with the fullest and most candid inquiry, and usually such investigation is only the forerunner of intelligent faith. Again, if a creed be rationally and sincerely received, no doubt can possibly be more honest than such faith is, or can have more of real belief in it. But if a man believe the Bible for no better reason than that his father did so before him, or if his faith rests on no sort of personal inquiry or experience, then I have no hesitation in saying that it is mere credulity, and that it is not for a moment to be put into comparison with that intelligent conviction which may result from the inquiry of the honest doubter. Therefore, it is every way for the interest of Christianity that its adherents should seek to understand and assist the unbeliever.

Just here, however, the defenders of the faith have sometimes made a fatal blunder. They have denounced when they should have persuaded; they have condemned when they should have sympathized; they have repelled when they should have taken by the hand and led gently forward. What a touching exemplification of the right way of meeting the unbeliever has Jesus himself given us in his treatment of Thomas! That unhappy disciple had taken up a most unreasonable position. He had set himself up above all the other apostles. He had even demanded a kind of evidence of the most exceptional character; yet, how tenderly the Lord dealt with him!—meeting him on his own ground, and shaming him into the unfaltering confession, "My Lord and my God!" Nor did he utter one word of reproof, save what was in a manner veiled behind the precious benediction, "Blessed are they who have not seen, and yet have believed."

What a lesson have we here! I am far indeed from saying that every modern unbeliever is a Thomas in disposition ; and I willingly admit also that the evidences of the gospel are stronger now than they were even in the apostles' day, so that there is the less excuse for not accepting it. Yet I shall not be misunderstood when I say that the unbelief of the present day differs from that of the age of Voltaire and Paine mainly in this: that it is, to a large extent, the unbelief of men who are themselves earnest truth-seekers, and whose thoughts are deeply exercised with at least one side of the subjects which the gospel suggests. Now, it will not do to meet such unbelievers with anathemas, or to assail them with scorn. We must endeavor to understand their position. We must meet them as Jesus met Thomas, on their "own ground," and then, as in the case of the doubting disciple, their very unbelief, when removed, may lead to a new strengthening of the faith. To show how this may be done, let us look at a few of the phases of unbelief presently existing among us. The subject is one for a treatise rather than a brief address, but they who are best acquainted with its difficulties will be the most ready to make allowance for the imperfection which must characterize my treatment of it.

Take then, first, the case of those whose philosophical opinions or scientific speculations seem to lead to atheism. The Comtest, as interpreted by an eminent metaphysician, tells us "that we have no knowledge of anything but phenomena," and "that our knowledge of phenomena is relative, not absolute." He affirms that "we know not the essence nor the real mode of the production of any fact, but only its relations to other facts in the way of succession or similitude. These relations are constant—that is, always the same in the same circumstances. The constant resemblances which link phenomena together, and the constant sequences which unite them as antecedents and consequents, are termed laws. The laws of phenomena are all we know respecting them. Their essential nature and ultimate causes, either efficient or final, are unknown and inscrutable to us." * Now it is easy to see that, if these principles be established and received, there is no place for faith in God. But what if, in this generalization of phenomena, there is no account taken of those which are presented by the soul itself? Is not human nature a part of the universe? and in an interpretation of natural phenomena are we to ignore the instincts and intuitions of the soul? We know phenomena only because we instinctively believe the testimony of our senses; but do we not look for a final cause for all things with an instinct as strong and as real as that which impels us to believe our senses? Nay, is not that instinct strengthened within us by the consciousness that we are ourselves causes, and are daily producing effects which we can distinctly trace to the free play of our own volitions? Can it be, therefore, that this instinct, so strengthened by personal experience, is delusive, or is it not rather to be taken as the witness within us to the existence of him " of whom and through whom and to whom are all things"?

Hence, we meet the views of the Comtest by contending that the phenomena of human consciousness must be included in an investigation, and we cordially agree with a recent author when he says: " Let no one think that because science has no place for final causes, therefore there is no place for them in philosophy or religion. As an anatomist, or a botanist, or a geologist, the student may be very right in saying, ' I have nothing to do with final causes; my business is with observed appearances and ascertained connections.' But as a man, he cannot help himself; final causes will obtrude upon him whether he likes it or not. For, as a man, he not only sees and classifies, but he wistfully thinks and wonders. There are relations between himself and the universe which no analysis of sensuous observations can exhaust. The starry sky has some nameless grandeur which no results of mathematical calculation can express. The tender clouds whose colors he analyses with his prism speak a language to his heart which no prismatic chart can interpret, and among such incalculable relations between himself and the universe is the

---

* Mill's *Auguste Comte and Positivism*, p. 6.

wistful longing after inner meaning and ultimate aim which ·the enigma of creation always excites in the contemplative soul. Most natural is the artless hymn which represents the young child appealing to the little star on high, and exclaiming ' How I wonder what you are ! ' So all life long we stand and gaze at the vision expanding from a star to a universe, while still all our cry is of wonder what it is. And this inquiry after what is, includes manifestly a longing after the significance and purpose of appearances—that is, it involves the hunger of the soul for a final cause of creation." *

Here, then, on the field of human consciousness, we meet the Comtest, and assert that his doctrine as to the inscrutability of final causes is in direct antagonism to the deepest and most ·cherished intuitions of the soul of man. A little more than two years ago expeditions were fitted out in various countries to go to different parts of the world for the purpose of observing the transit of Venus across the sun. The noblest astronomers of many lands, with the finest instruments which human ingenuity could devise, were engaged in this enterprise. All that intelligence was expended in order to secure, if possible, a perfect observation of certain phenomena, and yet we must not believe that there was a personal intelligence at the other end causing the phenomena to be observed, and establishing between them such relations as enabled astronomers to calculate from them the distance of the earth from the sun. *Credat Judaeus appella ;* they may believe that who can, it won't believe for me.

In a similar way we meet the atheism which bases itself on theories of development and recent speculations about the origin of species. Let us admit the hypothesis—though it is still very far from proven to be correct—the instinct of the soul immediately presses the question, Whence came the ·" primordial germ " out of which all that we see is said to have sprung? Let us concede the facts from the analogy of which ·the theory of " natural selection " has been propounded, the inquiry still arises, Must there not be, according to the analogy itself, some mind or will presiding to regulate the selection? for the pigeon breeding was under the superintendence of the pigeon breeder. Let us grant that there is some foundation

* New Theories and the old Faith, by J. A. Picton, M.A., pp. 7,8.

for the law which has been called "the struggle for existence," or "the survival of the fittest": still again the irrepressible question leaps to the lips, Is all this by chance? or is there not a presiding intelligence who, through this law, is carrying forward his processes and working out his will? There is thus within the soul itself an irresistible instinct which neither science nor philosophy can destroy, and which will not be satisfied with less than the existence of some Great First Cause. Hence we are not surprised that one of the ablest of Darwin's followers (if, indeed, according to Wallace's own showing, I should not rather call him Darwin's anticipator) has declared that his studies have given him the abiding conviction that there is, beyond the range of physical events, an intellectual guiding force in the will of the supreme intelligence, and that all force is will-force; and though still some of our men of science may dream of discovering a physical basis of life, even as in times gone by mechanics sought after perpetual motion, we may cherish the conviction that the labors of the former, as of the latter, will only add new treasures to our knowledge; that while missing the great object which they seek, they will discover much of which otherwise they had not thought, and that far from sapping the foundations of religion, they will, in the end, only strengthen and confirm them.

But, as another phasis of modern unbelief, let us take that which falters at the Supernatural. The difficulty here lies in the apparent inconsistency of miracles with the regularly observed sequence between antecedents and consequents. Science, it is said, has demonstrated the immutability of the laws of nature. We have ourselves had no experience of any suspension or variation of or interference with these laws; hence, *à priori*, we regard such a thing as improbable, and this improbability is heightened by science into an impossibility.

Now, if but the personal existence of God be granted, I do not think that it is difficult to dispose of this objection. For in man himself we have, to a certain extent and in a certain way, power to suspend or counteract in individual cases the operation of a law of nature. By his intelligence and will he can bring into play a new cause which can suspend or counteract in a particular instance the usual working of a law of

nature. That book, for example, would lie forever where it
is if no interference with the law of gravitation were possible;
but I will to lift it, and the new cause, acting through my
muscles upon the book, raises it notwithstanding gravitation.
In the will of man, therefore, as operating first upon his own
muscular nature, and second, through that upon external
things, we have, in a certain sense and to a certain extent, a
supernatural cause. But if the intelligence and will of man
are equal to such interference with nature and nature's laws,
can we deny to God a similar power? Or is it conceivable
that he has formed in the universe a vast machine, and that
he has deliberately shut himself out from all possibility
of interfering with it for any purpose whatever, no matter
how important?

Such reasonings as these appear to me to dispose effectually
of the objections to the supernatural which are founded on
the alleged impossibility of miracles, and so we are permitted
to examine into the evidence by which the miracles of revelation are supported, just as we should investigate any occur-
rences that claim to be historical. Now, of the issue of such
an examination, when fairly and candidly conducted, there can
hardly be a question, for the testimony in behalf of the Christian miracles is so full, so reliable, so varied, and withal so
inseparably associated with the highest moral excellence and
the purest holiness, that its falsehood would be a greater
improbability than any miracle. It is here, indeed, that
Christianity has its stronghold, and I would willingly peril the
whole cause on the character of Jesus Christ as a witness-
bearer to his own miracles. If that character be of the ordinary sinful type, then his miracles become improbable, and his
life presents an insoluble enigma. But if that character be in
itself divine and supernatural, then his miracles become natural to him, and are only what in the circumstances might
have been expected by us. Either he was the best of men—
and if so, we must accept his testimony that he was Incarnate
God—or he was a mere man, and of men the very worst, because while teaching highest truth he acted the vilest falsehood, and while pretending to be benevolent and sympathizing he trifled with the most important of human interests.
These are the only alternatives which the gospel history

presents for our acceptance, or which from the nature of the case are possible. But who of us can accept the latter? Surely he was God, and this being granted, all else is at once explained, and becomes not only possible or probable, but for him natural.

Here, then, we meet the deniers of the supernatural with the question, "What think ye of Christ? whose son is he? Whence came he, from heaven? or of men?" Explain to us on merely natural principles, call them " natural selection," " development," or what you will, the genesis of such a character as that which the Evangelists have given in delineating Christ, and we will give up the whole question in debate between us. Unfold to us how in this instance alone human nature should have so far risen above itself, and we shall admit that we have misread his history in calling him Divine, and in believing in his miracles. Take Rome before the advent, with Cicero as the representative of its philosophy and statesmanship, Horace as the popular exponent of its poetry, and Tiberius as a specimen of its morals. Take the philosophy of Greece, with its different sects of Stoics, Epicureans, Platonists and the like. Take Judaism, whether as represented at Alexandria by the disciples of Philo, or at Jerusalem by the formal Pharisees, the skeptical Sadducees, or the ascetic Essenes. Put these all into the crucible even of such a seething age as that undeniably was, and by what amalgam known to men could they have produced Jesus Christ? So far from being a natural development of his age, his age crucified him for being what he was; and the inscription over his cross, written as it was in Latin and Greek and Hebrew, fitly symbolized the consensus of all the three nationalities in putting him to death. He was no development of his age; but instead, everything true, and noble, and lovely, and godlike in succeeding ages, has been a development of him. The world has grown above many other instructors; it has not yet grown up to him; and when his Sermon on the Mount shall be carried out by every man, the golden age, to which mythology looks back so wistfully, shall be restored, and the Christian millennium shall be begun. But if this character is no mere human development, whence has it come? Let the mere naturalist make the reply.

Admirably has Bushnell put this thought in these eloquent words, which I extract from his chapter on the Character of Christ—one of the finest pieces of writing of which the English language can boast: " The character and doctrine of Jesus are the sun that holds all the minor orbs of revelation in their places, and pours a sovereign, self-sacrificing light into all religious knowledge. We have not far to go for light, if only we could cease debating and sit down to see. It is no ingenious fetches of argument that we want ; no external testimony, gathered here and there from the records of past ages, suffices to end our doubts; but it is the new sense opened in us by Jesus himself—a sense deeper than words, and more immediate than inference—of the miraculous grandeur of his life, a glorious agreement felt between his works and his person, such that his miracles themselves are proved to us in our feeling, believed in by that inward testimony. . . . If the miracles, if revelation itself, cannot stand upon the superhuman character of Christ, then let it fall. If that character does not contain all truth, and centralize all truth in itself, then let there be no truth. . . . This it is that has conquered the assaults of doubt and false learning in all past ages, and will in all ages to come. No argument against the sun will drive it from the sky. No mole-eyed skepticism, dazzled by its brightness, can turn away the shining it refuses .to look upon ; and they who long after God will be ever turning their faces thitherward, and either with reason or without reason, or if need be against manifold impediments of reason, will see and believe."* Let us try this mode of meeting those who deny the supernatural. Let us give distinctness and vividness to our own conceptions of the perfection of Christ, and let us endeavor to set it before them in all its beauty and completeness. Let us seek to impress them with the divinity of his life, and then his miracles will seem to them to be as natural to him as the splendor of his beams is to the noonday sun.

Akin to that unbelief in the supernatural of which I have just spoken, is the skepticism regarding the value and efficiency of Prayer, whereof in recent years we have heard so much. To me. however, it seems as if there were no room for much argument upon this particular subject, for if a man do not believe that there

---

* Nature and the Supernatural, p. 285.

is a personal God who stands to his people on the earth in the
relation of a father to his children, there is no use in reasoning
with him about prayer. You have to begin with him farther
back. You have to convince him first of the folly of his atheism, and so you are thrown upon those intuitions and facts of
consciousness to which we have already referred in dealing with
the Comtist. If, again, a man does really believe that God is,
and is the Father of his people, we will not need to argue with
him about prayer, for, as naturally as the child goes with his
troubles and wants to his mother, he will repair to God. He
will say, and no philosophy in the world will hinder him from
saying, "Since God is my Father, then if my earthly parent
hears my cry and gives me my request, much more will my
heavenly." This whole debate about prayer, therefore, is but a
skirmish round one of the far outposts in the field whereon the
battle between belief and unbelief is being waged. The centre
of that field, the key to the whole position on the side of faith,
is the existence and Fatherhood of God. Until men can say,
believingly, "Our Father," they will never pray in any real sense
of the word; when they can say that sincerely, they will pray, no
matter who forbids. It is easy to go through the entire Lord's
Prayer, including even the petition for daily bread, when we
have accepted the first two words, "Our Father." Hence, in
attempting to meet all such objections as those which have
recently been brought against the efficacy of prayer in the
region of physical affairs, I should choose to proceed Socrati-
cally, and settle first with my adversary the prime questions of
the existence of God as opposed to atheism, and the personality
of God as opposed to pantheism. It may seem, indeed, as if this
were to evade the entire difficulty. But in reality it is not so ; for
personality centres in will, and the will of God is omnipotent,
so that if the personality of God, as God, be admitted, the
question as to prayer resolves itself into this, whether the will
of omnipotence cannot answer prayer in physical things
through the ordinary operations of what we call, somewhat
ambiguously, the laws of nature.   It has been rather too hastily
assumed by our opponents here that the answer to prayer for
material blessings involves an interference with, or interruption
of, the regularly noted sequences of antecedents and consequents, which are called laws. How do our men of science

know that these laws have not been so adjusted as to admit of God's answering prayer through their operation? We challenge any of them to prove that they have not. We believe as firmly as they do in the uniformity of what they call the laws of nature, yet it is quite possible to think of them as arranged by omniscient wisdom, so that prayer can be answered, not by their suspension or by an interference with them, but simply through them. Some time ago I was at Binghamton, fulfilling a preaching engagement, and I took the opportunity of inspecting the water supply of the city. In a small building on the bank of the Susquehanna there is an engine which goes night and day, pumping water out of the river for the inhabitants. It is so arranged that the demand of the town acts as a governor, the engine moving with greater or less rapidity according as the water is taken off in larger or smaller measure. Then when a fire occurs in the town, an alarm bell struck in the city rings in the engine-room, and immediately the engineer gears on some extra machinery which is ready for the purpose, and by which the existing mains are charged to their fullest capacity, so that an amount of pressure is brought to bear upon them that is sufficient, when the hose is attached to the hydrants, to send the water to the tops of the loftiest buildings in the place. As I looked upon the engine and heard the intelligent explanation of the man in charge of it, my thought was, Here is a piece of mechanism erected for the supply of the ordinary wants of the community, yet so arranged that in an extraordinary emergency the cry of the people for help can be heard and answered through the regular channels. Well, if man can construct a fixed engine through which he can thus answer prayer, why should not God be able to do the same in the vast machine which we call the universe? All you need to admit is the personal existence and adequate skill of the Divine Engineer.

Thus, from the very achievements of science, we derive an illustration which refutes the skepticism of some leading scientific men, and clears the way to every one for the offering of prayer. We may be sure that he who planted in the human breast the instinct of prayer, can do for us according as we ask. But it needs to be repeated that this whole debate is not simply between prayer and no prayer. It is a question between theism and atheism, or which comes virtually to the same thing, between theism and pantheism. If in your view God be a distinct spiritual person, "for whom are all things and by whom are all things," you will pray, no matter who ridicules or forbids; but if in your vocabulary the word God is nothing more than "a fine name for the universe," prayer will have for you neither significance nor efficacy. But what is there in such a dreary, starless creed to attract you? In the caves men turn toward the sunshine, but what folly is theirs who leave the light of revelation to grope in the blackness of this outer darkness!

As another phase of modern unbelief, I would mention that of those who reject the Bible because of its apparent inconsistencies with the discoveries of scientific men. Now, in dealing with this class of objections, we have two regrets to express. The first is that scientific investigators have not had the advantage of a theological training. The tendency of their pursuits, as Souffroy has well said, is "to concentrate all their minds in their eyes and hands." They are consequently apt to have no right and proper appreciation of moral evidence, or of the value of spiritual and unseen things; and so, from the habit of their minds, they are but ill fitted to give due weight to the statements which are made to them by theologians.

But our second regret is, that in theologians themselves we have precisely the opposite evil. They have had, for the most part, no scientific training, and in their vivid realization of the absorbing importance of spiritual truth they are apt to depreciate the labors of the physical philosopher. It would be desirable, therefore, as contributing to a better understanding between them, that the scientific man should give himself somewhat to the study of theology, and that the theologian should, as a part of his professional training, make himself well acquainted with science. Thus they would place themselves *en rapport* with each other, and be better able to understand and make allowance for each other's difficulties.

We, of course, cannot in any way influence, save by the expression of our opinion, the training of our men of science, but as members of Christian churches we may be able very materially to modify the training of our theologians; and few things in my judgment would contribute more to the meeting and removing of scientific unbelief than the institution, as part of the regular furniture of every theological seminary, of a professorship whose incumbent should devote himself to the discussion of scientific subjects in their relation to the Word of God. Surely there are among our theologians enough men of scientific acquirements, or among our scientists enough men of devout and reverent faith in the Word of God, to furnish occupants for such professorial chairs, while with the abundant wealth of our Christian merchants, and the generous liberality by which many of them are distinguished, the endowment of such teachers might easily be obtained.

But apart from this difference in the point of view occupied respectively by theologians and scientific men, it is well that we should see distinctly wherein the alleged discrepancies between them lie. The scientific man believes in the infallibility of nature; the theologian believes in the infallibility of Scripture; but, observe, the differences of which so much is made by modern objectors lie not between nature and revelation in themselves, but between human interpretations of them. The man of science interprets his facts in a certain way, and makes certain deductions from them. These interpretations and deductions, however, are not infallible; they are not yet all received unquestioningly and unanimously by scientific men themselves. It is too soon, therefore, to speak and act as if men's interpretations of nature were absolutely correct. Again, the theologian's interpretations of Scripture are by no means infallible. Many of them which were accepted in past days have been disproved and others substituted for them, and of many more it must be said that they are still unsettled. For instance, he would be a rash man who should assert that he has discovered with infallible accuracy the meaning of the first chapter of Genesis, or should affirm that he can satisfactorily unravel the chronology of the early chapters of that book. These questions, and many others like them, are still *sub judice*, and the wise course for both parties in this modern misunderstanding is to wait with mutual respect for each other until God, in his providence and by his Spirit, shall lead to such interpretations of Nature and of Scripture as shall make manifest their perfect harmony. Let the man of science go on with patient perseverance, and let him not take any mischievous delight in flinging his hypotheses at the Word of God. Let the theologian also prosecute his inquiries with diligence and devoutness, and let him give over calling the men of science by evil names.   They seem often, indeed, to be working against each other, but they are in reality working for each other and for the truth.   As in the formation of the tunnel through Mont Cenis, the workmen began at opposite ends and approached each other with driving machines apparently directed against each other, but met at length in the middle to congratulate each other on the completion of their great undertaking, because they were working under the same supervision. So, I feel confident, it will be with our theologians and men of science.   God, the great architect of providence, is superintending both, and by and by, through the labors of both, the mountain of difficulty will be tunneled through, no more to form a barrier to the progress of the candid inquirer.

For the rest it is well that all parties should remember such simple principles as these—namely, that the Bible was not designed to be a revelation of physical science; that its references to scientific subjects are incidental and in popular language; that if it had alluded to such subjects in other than popular language it would have been unintelligible to those to whom it was first given, and would have been rejected by them for containing that which some modern philosophers complain that it does not contain; that, considering the fact that it refers only incidentally to these topics, its language concerning some of them is occasionally very striking and in harmony with modern discoveries; and, finally, that considering the course of science in the past, in such instances, for example, as astronomy, and how what seemed at one time in hopeless antagonism to God's word is now held by all parties intelligently and consistently therewith, the wise course for both sides will be, as I have already hinted, to wait before the one tries to prove that there is a contradiction, or the other to enforce a harmony.

Nor should we allow it to be forgotten, that notwithstanding all advances of modern science, there will ever be deep, solemn, all-important experiences in the human soul which only God's Gospel can meet.   There will still be the sense of sin, the poison of the arrow, a conviction which no earthly antidote can neutralize, and which can be counteracted only by the blood of the Redeemer's cross.   There will still be the

dark sorrow of bereavement, to be removed only by the vision
of the angel at the door of the sepulchre, and the hearing of the
soothing words, " Why seek ye the living among the dead?
He is not hère, he is risen as he said ; come see the place where
the Lord lay." There will still be the sense of weary lone-
someness stealing over the heart, even amid the bustle and the
business and the prosperity of the world, to be dispelled only
by the consciousness of the Saviour's presence. There will
still be the spirit-shudder at the thought of death, which only
faith in Christ can change into the desire to depart and to be
with Christ, which is far better. For these things science has
no remedy and philosophy no solace ; and strong in its adaptation to these irrepressible necessities of the human heart, the
Gospel of Christ will outlive all philosophical attacks, and survive every assault of scientific skepticism. But I cannot think
of the religion of Jesus and of science as if they were destined
to remain in perpetual antagonism. They are like elder and
younger sister in the one family, and though occasionally they
may seem to be at variance and to fall out with each other, let
but some deep grief enter into the home, or some heavy calamity fall upon the dwelling, and then every appearance of misunderstanding will disappear, while the younger finds her resting place on the bosom of the elder. With such feeling we bid
our men of science " God-speed." Their triumphs, we are sure,
will be ultimately ours as well as theirs, for is it not written "all
things are yours"? and we may calmly wait the result in the
devout persuasion that truth in one department can never
falsify that which has been already ascertained to be true in
another.

I pass now to a brief consideration of the skepticism which
is connected with what has been called the higher criticism of
the original sacred writings. And here let it be noted that we
have nothing but gratitude for and delight in the results of
Biblical criticism, properly so called. The labors of Bengel,
and Mill, and Griesbach, and others in former days, to which
such men as Tischendorf and Tregelles in our own times have
so worthily succeeded, have been fraught with the richest
blessings to the Church of Christ. They have brought us
nearer to the exact words of the sacred writers, and in so doing
they have brought us just so much nearer what Ellicot has

called "the inner shrine," and given us "a clearer view of the thought of an apostle, yea, a less dim perception of the mind of Christ." For them and their disciples, therefore, we have the utmost reverence; they must be carefully distinguished from those who presume to set themselves up in judgment upon the style of the sacred writers, and to tell us with infallible exactness what they did and did not write. They discover, as they suppose, differences in modes of expression between one portion of a book and another, and forthwith they leap to the conclusion that it was not all written by the author whose name it bears. They find some words in one epistle which do not occur in another letter bearing the name of the same apostle, and they rush to the inference that he could not have written both—so limited was his vocabulary. They are perfectly certain that whoever wrote the 53d chapter of the book of Isaiah, it was not the same person as composed the earlier portion of that book. They are positive that if John wrote the fourth gospel, he could not have written the Apocalypse; and ever and anon they cut out portions of the epistles of the apostle of the Gentiles because, in their judgment, they are not Pauline either in their spirit or their style. In a word, they set themselves up as infallible experts, who can declare with as much certainty as that which is furnished in physics by a chemical analysis whether the true Isaiah wrote or did not write a particular passage.

Now, this process is purely destructive, and if carried to its issues it would fritter away the Word of God, and leave us with nothing worth possessing in its place. Intuitions have their value, but in matters of style and taste they are as various as the individuals in whom they exist are distinct, and they can furnish no sure criteria in such a department as that to which we are now referring. Some years ago, in England, there was a very eager controversy carried on in the columns of the *Times* and elsewhere touching the authorship of a poem which had been discovered in the British Museum, and which was alleged to be the production of John Milton. There were illustrious authorities on both sides, and it was most amusing to observe how one found the genuine Miltonic characteristics in certain lines which others as confidently fixed upon as utterly unlike any of the productions of that great poet. From all this the inference of Stanley Leathes seems to me inevitable when he says : " If, some two hundred years after Milton's death, a number of educated Englishmen, versed in the many known writings of Milton, cannot agree about the authorship of a certain poem upon internal evidence, are we to believe that great weight should be attached to the assertion of German critics who some twenty-five centuries after the death of a Hebrew prophet declare positively, upon internal evidence alone, that a series of poems are not by him ? * The assertion is a pure conjecture, and has nothing in it that commands an assent.

Besides, these critics make no allowance for the change of style which comes over a writer with the lapse of years, or which may be induced by the different nature of the subjects which the same author is treating at different times. Suppose we were to apply their principles to the works of a living author, then it would be easy to prove either that Thomas Carlyle never wrote that Essay on Burns, which is remarkable for its pure and classic English, or that he did not produce those other writings which go by his name, in which, to use his own words of Richter (if they be really his own words), " he deals with astonishing liberality in parentheses, dashes and subsidiary clauses ; invents hundreds of new words, alters old ones, or by hyphen chains, pairs and packs them together into most jarring combinations—in short, produces sentences of the most heterogeneous, lumbersome, interminable kind." † Are there then two Carlyles ? or how shall we account for this apparent incongruity ? These critics are forever insisting that the Bible should be treated like any other book : a demand which, as we have well said, " is itself a witness to the fact that it is felt to be unlike any other book." But we would turn the tables upon them, and ask them to treat other books precisely as they treat the Bible, that men may see and know to what a chaos they would reduce the fair fabric of our literature by the legitimate application of their own principles. Indeed, we may go further still, and say that if we were to deal with Ewald's History of the people of Israel, as he him-

---

* The Witness of the Old Testament to Christ.   Preface xv.
† Carlyle's Essays and Miscellanies.   Essay on Richter.

self has dealt with the historical books of the Old Testament, we might make it appear that the hands, not of two merely, but of many authors were in his own production.

It is always perilous to attempt to declare on mere internal or æsthetic grounds the authorship of a literary production; and when the attempt is made, we are reminded of a ludicrous incident which some time ago went the round of the newspaper men. Dr. Willett, lecturing in Boston, told that at one time, when he was a connoisseur in bird-stuffing, he used to criticise other people's bird-stuffing very severely. Walking with a gentleman one day, he stopped at a window where a gigantic owl was exhibited. "You see," said the doctor to his friend, "that there is a magnificent bird utterly ruined by unskillful stuffing. Notice the mounting! Execrable, isn't it? No living owl ever roosted in that position. And the eyes are fully a third larger than any owl ever possessed!" Just at that moment, however, the bird raised one foot and with his big eyes solemnly blinked at his critic, who said very little more about bird-stuffing that afternoon. The owl was there to protest against the caviling of his critic, and assert his right to roost as he pleased. That silenced his reviewer, and brought him down from the altitude of the higher criticism to the lower level of a mere observer of facts. The writers of the sacred books, however, cannot appear thus for themselves to claim their own productions, but such incidents ought to rebuke their critics for their arrogance, and to cause them to turn their attention from conjectures as to how they should have written, to the careful examination of the works which they have actually produced.

It may seem that this is a matter of comparatively small importance, and it would be easy to put it into a ridiculous light, but it concerns the most sacred treasures of our holy religion, and we must never forget that within certain limits the question of the authorship of the books which form the Bible is inseparably associated with that of their inspiration and authority. "*Hypotheses non fingo*" is a maxim which is as safe for the critical student of the sacred books as it is for the scientific observer of the facts of nature, and we must meet all such assaults of the higher criticism by a demand for some

more tangible proof than the unsupported assertions or conjectures of those who make them.

I intended to have referred to the unbelief which professes
to stumble at inspiration, and at the doctrine of atonement
which the Scriptures reveal; but I have exceeded the limits
of my time before I have reached the boundary of my theme.
Let me only say, in conclusion, that one means of meeting
prevalent phases of unbelief is open to every Christian. We
can all strive " to adorn the doctrines of God our Saviour in
all things." When one told an ancient philosopher that another
was slandering him, he replied, " What does it matter? I shall
live so that nobody will believe him." So, when the faith of
the gospel is assailed, let Christians resolve to live in such a
manner that nobody will believe the statements of its critics.
The good man's life is, after all, the best book of Christian evidences. It is " manifestly declared to be the Epistle of Christ,
written not with ink, but with the Spirit of the living God;
not in tables of stone, but in fleshly tables of the heart." It
is, besides, open to constant inspection, and may be " known
and read of all men." Even, therefore, if we should not be
able to deal with subtle philosophy, or to keep ourselves
abreast of science, or to repel with cogent reasoning the arguments of unbelievers, we shall be doing much to counteract
skepticism if we only live like Christ ourselves, and succeed by
the help of God's Spirit in forming Christ-like characters in
others. Let us aim after these two things, and we shall do
much to keep ourselves above the mists of skepticism, while
at the same time we furnish others with new evidences of the
truth.

Art. IV.—GOD'S SEVENTH DAY'S REST.

BY A LAYMAN.

AT the close of the account of the creation it is said that God "rested on the seventh day."* We shall endeavor to show that this seventh day, with its rest, still continues, and is coextensive with the human period of the world.

The proof of this is found mainly in the discussion about God's rest in the third and fourth chapters of the Epistle to the Hebrews, in connection with the ninety-fifth Psalm, the expressions on the subject in the Pentateuch, the reasons annexed to the fourth commandment, and the position of the seventh day in the same class as the six days of creation preceding it, which are believed, from comparing God's two histories of the earth, to have been long periods.

God never rested literally. He worked in the material world on the next day of twenty-four hours after the creation ended, just as he has worked during every day since, and (except in creating new matter or new species) just as he had worked before—on the same materials, by the same laws, and with the same results. This is abundantly shown by an examination of his works done before and since the last act of creation. After he made plants on the third day and fishes on the fifth, he sustained, reproduced and controlled them, before and on the literal day after he ceased to create, just as he has done ever since.

In whatever sense God rested during the twenty-four hours after he ceased to create, he rests still. If it only means that he ceased to create, then it was not for a literal day only, but the cessation still continues, for he made all things in the six days. If it means that he then looked with complacency on his works, he looks so still. If it means that he then entered on some course of divine action different from creation, such action still continues. We do not found our argument on this evident truth, but our conclusions recognize it.

The Scriptures represent God as now especially occupied in using and displaying his perfections in the government and for the benefit of the human family. We maintain that God's

---

* Gen. ii: 2.

rest in Genesis, in the fourth commandment, in the ninety-fifth Psalm, and in Hebrews, is such present divine occupation. The impression that the seventh day was a day of twenty-four hours, and that the rest spoken of in Hebrews means rest in heaven, is so deep on the minds of Christians that we are aware that we shall seem to be arguing against facts. "Enter into rest," and "Go to heaven," have become as fully synonymous in many minds as "Protestant" and "heretic" in many other minds. To prove in either case that they are not the same thing seems to them like attempting to prove that a tree is not a tree.

In discussing the passage in Hebrews we shall use Alford's translation, the authorized version being so very erroneous as entirely to alter the sense. Alford, in most cases, gives the correct rendering, notwithstanding its opposition to his theory.

We propose to show that God's rest in Hebrews is the rest he himself takes, that it is something positive, spiritual and active; that believers participate in it; that this participation is all along represented as present; that this rest is the same as that spoken of in the ninety-fifth Psalm, and the same as the spiritual blessings offered to the Israelites, and the same as the rest of the seventh day, and that it is coextensive with that day, and with the human family on earth.

The main object of the Epistle to the Hebrews was to impress on the Jewish Christians the superiority of Christi,* and the sufficiency of his work on earth and mediation in heaven,† without any help from those legal observances on which they had always relied; and so to hold fast and boldly avow their confidence in him ‡ and his sufficiency. The object was not to guard them against apostacy in general, such as into idolatry or wordliness, but as in the Epistle to the Galatians, to guard them against falling back into Jewish ritualism. Almost everything in the epistle bears upon this one point.

The discussion in which our subject is involved is introduced by saying that Christ, superior to angels, was superior to Moses as the head of God's house,§ and the writer adds: "Whose

---

* Ch. i: 1–8.   ii: 9.   iii: 1, 3, 6.   iv: 14, 15.   vii: 17, 22.   viii: 1.
† Ch. iii: 6, 14.   vii: 25.   viii: 3.   ix: 14, 28.   x: 1, 2.
‡ Ch. iii: 6, 14.   iv: 14, 16.   vi: 11.   x: 22, 23, 29, 35, 38.   xii: 1, 2.
§ Ch. iii: 6.

house are we if we hold fast the confidence and the boasting of our hope firm unto the end." "Wherefore,"* that is, in view of the possibility implied that some are not in God's house, he holds up a terrible warning from their own scriptures, and exhorts them to "take heed." They might fail of being partakers in God's house from want of confidence in God's Son (implied by want of confident and boastful hope), just as the Holy Ghost says or implies in the ninety-fifth Psalm that their fathers had failed from want of confidence in God. He then quotes the warning from the psalm in full.†

In the passage quoted God says of the disobedient Israelites, "They shall not enter into my rest."‡ This is the text of the whole discussion. We shall first inquire whose and what this rest is, and what entering into it means. Further on we shall inquire where and when it is to be enjoyed.

It is generally assumed that the rest spoken of in the psalm is different from that discussed in Hebrews. We propose to show that it is the same. This rest is God's rest. He, being the speaker, calls it "My rest."§ He being spoken of, it is repeatedly called "his rest."‖ It is called "the rest"¶ (not "rest" in general, any rest, as in A. V.) and "that rest"; that is, the particular rest under consideration, God's rest. The word here translated rest, always in the New Testament and nearly always in the Septuagint, means God's rest; man's rest in the original is a different word. God's rest naturally means that which he takes, though it is possible for it to mean that which he gives. We shall show that it means that which he takes. By common consent, this rest is not mere cessation from labor or conflict, but a spiritual rest; not a negative but a positive condition; not rest in the general sense, but in a special sense. It is a Sabbath keeping,[2] which it is a great calamity to miss,[3] into which believers[4] enter, which remains for the people of God,[5] and which we should strive to enter.[6] The word Sabbath had long been used to mean not a time of mere rest, but worship.

---

* Ch. iii : 7.   ‖ iii : 18. iv : 1.   [3] iv : 1.
† iii : 7-11. Ps. xcv : 7-11.   ¶ iv : 3.   [4] iv : 1, 3.
‡ iii : 11.   [1] iv : 11.   [5] iv : 9.
§ Ch. iii : 11. iv : 3, 5.   [2] iv : 9.   [6] iv : 11.

(*New Series, No 23.*)   40

What is meant by entering into God's rest? To enter a place is to go into it; to enter into a feeling or condition of our own is to begin to have it. This is a single, often momentary, act. If rest means heaven, as commonly assumed, then entering it is a single act. But to enter into a state or feeling or employment of another is to participate in it; for example, "Enter thou into the joy of thy Lord";* "Ye are entered into their labors";† that is, participate in that joy, or those labors, or their results. So we often say we enter into a person's views, feelings, objects or pursuits, meaning that we participate in them. This is not a single act, but continuous action. If rest means the rest God takes, to enter into it means to participate in its spirit, objects and enjoyments; and it is not a single act, but continuous action. We shall find that "enter into" here means to participate in, not for a moment, but continuously, and that the rest intended is the rest God takes. By substituting for the figurative expression "enter into," its literal equivalent "participate in," its meaning and its relations to the context become much clearer. Participation in God's pursuits, character and enjoyments is in entire harmony with other Scriptural representations. The idea runs through this epistle, and especially this part of it. Believers are partakers with Christ of flesh and blood,‡ partakers of the heavenly calling,§ partakers of Christ,| partakers of the Holy Ghost,¶ partakers of his holiness;[1] and, though the word is not used, the thought is there, partakers in his house.[2] So elsewhere we hear of partakers of the divine nature,[3] of Christ's sufferings,[4] and of his glory;[5] laborers with God,[6] co-workers with Christ,[7] helpers of the Lord against the mighty.[8]

Partaking of the heavenly calling makes us partakers of

---

* Matt. xxv: 23.

† John iv:38. "Enter into life," Matt. xviii: 8, xix: 17; "Enter into temptation." Mark xiv:38; "Enter into his glory," Luke xxiv:26; "Enter into the kingdom of God," not only come under it as subjects, but participate in it as kings. Participation is more or less an element in all these.

‡ Ch. ii:14.　　　[1] xii: 10.　　　[5] 1 Pet. v: 1.
§ iii: 1.　　　　　[2] iii: 6.　　　　[6] 1 Cor. iii:9.
| iii: 14.　　　　　[3] 2 Pet. i: 4.　　　[7] 2 Cor. vi: 1.
¶ vi:4.　　　　　　[4] 1 Pet. iv.: 13.

[8] Jud. v: 23. See also John xv: 1–7; xvii: 21–23; Eph. iii: 6; 1 Cor. xii: 27.

Christ, and he being partaker of our flesh and blood, that makes us partakers in God's family, and partakers of the Holy Ghost ; and, as will appear more and more clearly as we go on, partakers in God's rest. The six participations are all steps or phases, or parts of the same thing. The writer's mind being full of that idea, it was natural that he should develop the germ of it found in the psalm. This association of this rest with other present things is some evidence that it is present also.

After the exhortation suggested by the full quotation from the psalm, the writer calls attention to the value of the blessing at stake. He tells them to exhort one another, for " we have become * partakers of Christ, if we hold [or held] fast the beginning of our confidence steadfast unto the end."† This cannot mean that their becoming partakers of Christ was contingent on their holding fast, for they are spoken of as having become so already. A fact already existing cannot be contingent on a future condition. Their holding fast (and the tense of the verb contemplates past as well as future) must therefore be the *test* of their being partakers of Christ. So also must " be hardened"‡ in the previous verse be a test. So also must " holding fast the confidence and boasting of the hope" in the 6th verse be a test, for there the persons addressed were supposed to be God's house already, and holding fast could not be a condition of what already existed. This test seems to be in view throughout the following discussion.

After exhorting the Hebrews to hold fast their confidence to the end, and for this purpose to exhort each other§ " while it is called to-day,"‖ as the psalm says, he goes over some expression used there not bearing on our argument, and concludes that the Israelites in the desert failed to enter God's rest " because of unbelief." The history shows that it was just the phase of unbelief against which he is warning their descendants, *i. e.*, want of absolute, unhesitating confidence in their divine leader. This was at the bottom of their murmurings and

---

* In A. V. incorrectly translated " are made."

† Ch. iii : 14.   ‡ Ch. iii : 13.

§ To keep each in countenance when withering under the contempt of their old associates for deserting the religion of their fathers.

‖ Ch. iii : 13.

disobedience. For example, their crowning offence was refusing to advance against the enemy from Kadesh Barnea, because they had not confidence in God's promise of success against fortresses so strong and enemies so terrible.*

In view of the vital importance of entering God's rest, and of the inference from the psalm that it was still open, though their fathers had failed to enter, and they might fail, the apostle says, " Let us fear . . . lest any one of you may seem to have come short of it."†

The test before mentioned twice over of being of God's house, and of being partakers of Christ, was holding fast their confidence. " The sin which so easily beset "‡ them was wavering in their confidence. This would be indicated by a resort to legal observances, so fatal to the Jew-taught Galatians,§ instead of•depending on Christ alone, or by shrinking from the bold avowal that Jesus of Nazareth, held in such contempt by their old friends and their countrymen, was their only hope, or by the feebleness of that hope, which, when strong, even in presence of such contempt, maketh unashamed. Any one not holding fast his confidence would be likely to show it to all observers by these and other indications, and so would "seem to have come short" of participation in God's house or in Christ. From the repeated mention of this test, and from the usual habit of the apostle, we are led to look for some warning against failure in the test, and so of seeming not to be in Christ. This view suits the drift of the epistle, the argument of this part of it, the thoughts and expressions of the context, and the known circumstances.

But instead of giving his warning in the terms used in the reasoning that led to it, the apostle takes up the phrase used in his quotation from the psalm, entering into God's rest, and substitutes it in the warning for participation in God's house and in Christ. This intimates that entering God's rest—that is, partaking in it—and partaking in Christ are substantially the same things. We shall see more and more clearly as we go on that this is so; and as, being of God's house and being partakers in Christ, the things he is warning them to make sure of are unmistakably things present, we

---

* Numb. xiii: 28-33.   xiv: 1-4, 10, 21-23, 29.   †Ch. iv: 1.
‡Ch. xii: 1.   § Gal. i: 7, 8; iii: 1-3, 10-13; iv: 9-11; v: 3, 4.

may fairly expect to find that the expression substituted for them, entering God's rest, also means something present.

The word "seem" is in the present tense, the tense not being uncertain as in A. V. "To have come short" (not to come short as in A. V.) is previous to the present time. Whether our views of the connection of this verse with what precedes are correct or not, or whatever entering into God's rest means, it is something present on earth, and to have come short of it something perceptible. The thing already come short of is the rest itself, not any condition of entering it hereafter.

The authorized version, in order to make sense on its theory that this rest is future in heaven, mistranslates the tense of the second verb, making "to come short," instead of "to have come short," and has given both verbs the force of the future. Alford, to make sense on the same theory, gives to the present tense of the first verb (we mean the English tenses) the force of the first future, and to the perfect tense of the second verb the force of the second future. This is not admissible unless required by the context, which it is not, or necessary to be consistent with known facts, which it is not. The language is not to be interpreted by assumed but unproved facts, but the facts are to be ascertained by the language.

But even this does not mend the matter. Alford makes "seem" mean "to be found" at the day of judgment. But there is no authority for any such meaning. Seem means not to be, or be found, but only to appear to be. If rest means heaven, seem to have come short at the day of judgment must mean seem to the eye of God. But this contradicts the uniform representation of Scripture that to God nothing "seems," but, as the apostle impresses on his readers in this very connection, "all things are naked and opened."* Others make seem mean nothing at all, because cases can be hunted up where it appears to be pleonastic. But this denial or perversion of meaning cannot be resorted to without absolute necessity. This necessity does not exist, for on our natural and obvious theory it means just what it says.

The only escape from the conclusion that the rest is pres-

---

* Ch. iv : 13.

ent is the traditional assumption that the writer softens his intimation that at the day of judgment some of his readers may be found to have come short, by using the mild word "seem" instead of "be found." This does not cure the tense difficulty; and it is not only entirely gratuitous, but out of keeping with the whole tone of the epistle, and especially with that of the context. To eradicate the deeply-rooted reliance on Jewish rites and enforce reliance on Christ alone, the writer found it necessary, as in the case of the Galatians, to be almost savage. He had just been holding up the most terrible examples with the most frightful plainness, quoting the most awful denunciations with the most unflinching directness, and exhibiting the most horrible pictures in their harshest coloring. Elsewhere in this epistle he speaks of "our God a consuming fire,"* of "fiery indignation,"† and here of the "bitter provocation"‡ of their evil hearts of unbelief,§ and of their fathers' "carcasses,"‖ which we seem to see lying around and rotting on the sands of the desert. After the sight he forced on them of divine vengeance and of ancestral crime and ancestral carrion, it is incredible that he softened anything. On the contrary, his object evidently was to strike terror into the doubtful and wavering. His harshness toward their faltering was heightened by contrast with his tenderness toward their persons.¶

The common theory that rest in heaven is intended, is all through a misfit of the text. It requires the meanings of words and the tenses of verbs to be changed, and the logical connections to be disregarded. Our authorized version all along mistranslates to fit the popular theory. Our theory fits all the ins and outs of the text, and takes the meanings, tenses and connections as they are. The more literal the translation, the better for us.

The connection of the first three verses of the fourth chapter seems to be this: Let us fear lest we seem to have come short of entering into God's rest, the promise of which is still left open to us; for (in proof that it is still left open) the gospel promising it is made known to us, as it was to them; for

---

* Ch. xii: 29.   ‡ Ch. iii: 8, 15.   ‖ Ch iii: 17
† Ch. x: 26–31.   § Ch. iii: 12.   ¶ Ch. iii: 1.

(in further confirmation of the offer being still open) we who believe do in fact enter into the rest.

It is generally supposed that the rest spoken of in the 95th Psalm, as quoted in Hebrews, was the temporal rest from wandering and conflict in Canaan. The history tells us that God swore that the generations that had provoked him should not "see the land"* he had promised to their fathers. Moses speaks of coming to Canaan as "to the rest"† God was giving them; and there God would give them rest from‡ their enemies. Joshua speaks of their having "rest" in Canaan.§ So we cannot deny that the history calls the quiet possession of Canaan "rest," though not in any special sense. As God's gift it possibly might be called his rest, though it is nowhere so called in the history. We admit that at first blush, and looking at the psalm only, the rest spoken of seems to have been the temporal rest of Canaan.

But the following considerations show that the rest spoken of in the psalm must be something entirely different from that temporal rest. In all the apostle's discussions about rest he unquestionably means the spiritual state so called, either on earth or in heaven. It is still open to believers. To come short of it is something to be feared.‖ Believers do enter it.¶ It remains for the people of God.[1] We should strive to enter it.[2] It is the keeping of a Sabbath.[3] It is, therefore, a great spiritual blessing. In both quotation and argument, it is all along God's rest. There is no intimation that the writer uses the word in his comments in a different sense from that in which it is used in the text commented upon. That would have made his reasoning as inconclusive as that against bonnet ribbons from the text "top not come down."[4] On the contrary, when the writer says, in the first verse of the fourth chapter, that a promise is left of entering into "his rest," he evidently means the same rest that he had called "his rest" just before,[5] and that clearly refers to "my

---

* Num. xiv: 21–24, 26–35; xxxii: 10–13. Deut. i: 34–35; ii: 14, 15.
† Deut. xii: 9.   ¶ iv: 3.   [3] iv: 9.
‡ Deut. iii: 20; xii: 10.   [1] iv: 9.   [4] Matt. xxiv: 17,
§ Josh. i: 15; xxi: 44; xxii: 4; xxiii: 1.   [5] Ch. iii: 18.
‖ Ch. iv: 1.   [2] iv: 11.

rest," *i. e.*, God's rest, in the psalm.* "My rest" in the psalm, and "his rest" in the argument from it must be the same, and therefore both spiritual, as all admit "his rest" in the fourth chapter of the Epistle to be. The rest believers "do enter into" is identified in the third verse with that which the Israelites did not enter into. So the rest that it remains "that some enter," is identified again in the sixth verse with that which was preached to those who entered not in because of unbelief. The same pronoun implied by "therein" and "in" in this verse represents the rest of both. The rest in the psalm was not that into which Joshua led Israel,† and therefore not the temporal rest of Canaan.

It may be said that the rest of Canaan was a type of the other, and so the apostle, while in terms he speaks of the literal type, reasons upon the spiritual antitype. There is no Scriptural ground for any such supposition. By such devices anything can be proved on any side of any question. That convenient way of disposing of a difficult thing by calling it a type often prevents us from even trying to find out what the real meaning of it is, by satisfying us, or at least diverting our attention by a fanciful meaning. If types were admissible in this argument at all, we might claim that the rest of Canaan was a type of the spiritual rest of the Christian in this world, from which it is much less dissimilar than from the heavenly state; and so we might support our position that God's rest is present. But we see no warrant for supposing any such type was intended. The discussion under consideration is not declamation, or flights of fancy, or loose talk, or mere argumentative hints, but close and rigorous reasoning.

Some say the rest in question is only like that of Canaan and that after the creation. But this contradicts the plain meaning of the language and invalidates the argument. We cannot reason about a thing from something else that has merely some similarity or analogy to it, especially when, as in this case, the similarity or analogy claimed is so remote.

God did offer the Israelites two kinds of rest, as we shall show: a spiritual rest, his rest, described in the history, but not there called by that name; and the temporal rest of

---

* iii : 1.   † Ch. iv : 8.

Canaan. It is only the first of these which the psalm mentions and the Epistle argues about. As the sinning generation refused to trust God, he excluded them both from his
rest and from their own. In the second verse of the fourth
chapter the apostle goes on to say, in proof that God's rest was
still open, "For unto us was the gospel preached as well as
unto them." The word translated "gospel," whether in form
of noun or verb, whatever its use in other books or other
Greek, has in nearly, if not quite all, the hundred and twenty
or thirty places where it occurs in the New Testament the
technical meaning of good tidings of spiritual blessings, and
not merely good tidings in general. It appears from the use
of this technical word that it means the same thing in both
cases, and not that one kind of good tidings was preached in
one case, and some other kind in the other. This gospel was
preached both to the Hebrew Christians and their ancestors
alike—that is, the blessings here summed up as entrance into
God's rest were offered alike to both, though in one case
through a Saviour to come, in the other through the Saviour
already come, and of course much more clearly in the last
case than the first.

What is thus asserted in the Epistle is abundantly recorded
in the history. God offered to make the Israelites "a kingdom of priests, a holy nation, a peculiar treasure,"* which
terms are nearly the same as those that Peter uses to express
the status of Christians.† They were to be "holy unto
God,"‡ "holy chosen peculiar,"§ the Lord's "inheritance,"‖
just what Paul calls Christians.¶ They were to be assimilated
to God: "Be holy for I am holy."[1] The covenant between
him as sovereign and them as subjects—that is, their constitution, as we would call it—was the moral law;[2] and they were
to imitate, or, as we insist, participate with him in keeping a
Sabbath.[3] Of course all these spiritual blessings were on condition of faith. Their temporal blessings were promised on
condition of obedience, and that, as the apostle infers and the

---

* Ex. xix: 5, 6.
† 1 Peter ii: 9.
‡ Num. xv: 40.
§ Deut. xiv: 2.

‖ Deut. iv: 20.
¶ Eph. i: 11. See Alford's Translation.
[1] Lev. xix: 2.
[2] Ex. xxxiv: 28.   [3] Ex. xx: 11.

history shows, was dependent on confidence in God. So temporal and spiritual blessings were alike contingent on faith.

We maintain that these spiritual blessings, and especially this assimilation to God and imitation of him, though not called so in history (unless rest, in Ex. xxxiv : 14, means spiritual rest), are the same as those summed up in the psalm and in the epistle under the name of entering into God's rest. If this means, as we claim that it does, participation in his character, objects and occupations, almost the exact idea is contained in the passages above cited.

It is no objection to this theory that the history does not call these spiritual blessings by the name of rest, or entrance into it, unless in the single passage cited in the foregoing paragraph, any more than it is to the other theory, that the word rest does not occur in any recorded oath. The things are fully stated in the history ; whether the words afterward used to express them were spoken at the time is immaterial.

The generation that showed such want of confidence in God at Massah, Meribah and Kadesh thereby indicated their refusal of the spiritual blessings offered, and which in the psalm and epistle are called entering into or participating in God's rest. To make his disapprobation and their loss more conspicuous, God excluded that generation from the place where those blessings should have been enjoyed. This general exclusion from Canaan does not imply that the exclusion from the spiritual rest was equally general. It was proper that the generation that had rejected God's spiritual rest should be excluded from the place specially appropriated to its enjoyment.

The word rest in the psalm means, as we shall show, God's rest after creation. The object of the psalm is to induce men to worship God,* who made sea and land,† and who is our Maker‡ and Proprietor.§ The Holy Ghost (not David) follows up the exhortation with a caution to the Israelites not to harden their hearts as their fathers had done, and refuse to worship him who created, lest they should fail of participation in the rest he took after he ceased to create, as their fathers had failed.|

The threat implied in the psalm could not be failure to

---

* Ps. xcv : 6.   ‡ Ps. xcv : 6. || Ps. xcv : 11.
† Ps. xcv : 5.   § Ps. xcv : 7.

enter Canaan, for in David's time it was already occupied and fully enjoyed.*   Any reference to the temporal rest of Canaan would not have been relevant.   The epistle to the Hebrews, as we shall see, requires us to understand this rest as the rest after the creation.   We do not forget that the word translated rest in the psalm is different from that in Genesis, but it is the same as that in the reason annexed to the fourth command- ment, which shows that the two mean the same thing.   There might have been a difficulty in supposing the psalm referred to rest after creation, if David had been expressing his own thoughts, but he was not, as we shall now point out.

This passage from the 95th Psalm is the only one in the Old Testament that any New Testament writer quotes directly from the Holy Ghost, except, perhaps, the passage quoted in this discussion from the second chapter of Genesis.   True, the Holy Ghost is sometimes said to have taught something through some particular person or thing, and many sayings are attributed directly to God in the Old Testament, and recognized as his in the New.   In almost all cases the New Testament writers attribute the saying cited to Scripture gen- erally, or to some book or author, implying, of course, but not then stating, that it is inspired.   A reference so unparalleled leads us to suppose that the passage in question was spoken more directly and exclusively by the Holy Ghost than com- mon, not through, but above the faculties of his human aman- uensis.   We should not be surprised in such a case to find things spoken of that neither the inspired writer† nor any one else would fully understand till God's revelation should be completed, and his works and providence more fully known. We should expect to find in language treated as so extraor- dinary, written from Divine dictation, expressions which David might not have understood.   The inspired writer of the Epis- tle recognizes in the words " rest" and "day," quoted not from David, but from the Holy Ghost, meanings far above and be- yond what is obvious on the face of the passages quoted.

The rest in the psalm could not have been that of Canaan, for the apostle distinctly implies or infers in the eighth verse that Joshua did not give the Israelites rest; that is, the rest

---

* I. Chr. xxii: 18; xxiii : 25.   † 1Peter i: 11.

he did give them was not the rest in question. In the middle clause of the third verse of this fourth chapter the apostle, after saying, "We who believed do enter into the rest," defines what rest he means by *the* rest. First, it is the rest spoken of in the 95th Psalm; second, it is the rest God took after creation. The last we shall consider hereafter.

"We who believed do enter into the rest, even as He said, As I swear in my wrath, they shàll not enter into my rest." The force of "as," or "even as," or "just as," is, believers do enter, just as God said certain unbelievers should not enter. The assignment of a reason why they should not implies that but for that reason they would. The exception is quoted to prove the rule. Now, the rest in the two cases must be the same, for if they were not, but were different rests, the inference from the psalm that somebody might once have entered one would be no confirmation of the statement that anybody else could now enter the other.

"We who believed do enter into the rest." By two mistranslations in this short sentence our A. V. has entirely changed its meaning. By leaving out the definite article they substitute rest in its general sense for rest in the special and, as we shall more fully see, entirely different sense, the rest under consideration, changing it from God's rest to man's. By changing the tense of the first verb they unsettle that of the second, so as to make it possible to seem future.

The aorist tense of believe is a puzzle to commentators who consider the rest as future. It fits our theory exactly. Its obvious meaning is, "We who believed at any time in the past do enter (or rather are entering) the rest now." Supplying the necessarily implied terms, substituting literal for figurative language, and substituting for the definite article what it points out, the statement means, "We who at any time believed are now participating in God's rest." To avoid this conclusion, our A. V. puts "believe" in the perfect instead of the imperfect tense, so as to allow "do enter" to refer to the future. Even then it cannot be understood to be future without some affirmative evidence, which there is not. But with "believe" in the imperfect tense, as it ought to be, "do enter" is in form and in fact unmistakably present. Entering God's rest is therefore something present.

As this actual entrance into God's rest is adduced as evidence or illustration that the promise is still left open, it must be something perceptible as well as present. Rest in heaven could not be so adduced. The fact of this entrance could in their case be ascertained by the test beforenamed and all along kept in view. Entering into the rest, being something present, it must be something continuous, not merely momentary. If it was a single momentary act, the first verb should have been in the perfect tense, "We who have believed up to this moment enter at this moment"; or the second verb should have been in the same tense as the first, "We who believed entered." But as the second verb is in the present tense, the action is still going on, "We who believed are now entering." We claim, as a separate argument, that this heretofore puzzling incongruity of tenses recognized an essential characteristic of entering into God's rest if it means participation in his pursuits ; its continuity. Believing is the initial step of a continuous course.

The writer of the epistle goes on in the latter part of the third verse, and in the fourth, and verses further on, to show what rest he means and when it began. This we shall consider hereafter. In verse six he repeats, as a step in his reasoning, or toward his exhortation, the fact that some do enter this rest. That is, it is an observable fact that some are entering all the time. Our A. V., instead of the present tense, "it remains that some do (or did) enter," in order to suit the theory that the rest is future, puts it, "it remains that some must enter." This constant repetition of the present tense shows that entering into the rest is something that takes place now ; and the necessity for the repeated mistranslations to make it appear future shows that it is not so.

In the ninth verse of this fourth chapter the conclusion is formally repeated, "There remaineth, therefore, Sabbath-keeping for the people of God." Sabbath-keeping in the conclusion must be the same thing as rest in the argument, and in the previous conclusions now repeated. Rest being here so called, must be not mere repose, but positive holy occupation. "Remaineth" means left over, still unexhausted. It implies previous existence, and the argument recognizes previous use. Though it is so old and has been so much used, it is not exhausted. The word is in the present tense, and the argument shows that what remains unexhausted is available now, not merely in the far future.

In the eleventh verse, in view of all the facts shown, the apostle gives his concluding exhortation as follows: " Let us hasten therefore to enter into that rest." Whether the verb whose primary meaning is " hasten" should be so translated, as in the Vulgate, or its secondary meaning, " strive," adopted, as Alford has it (not labor as in A. V.), it appears from its use elsewhere that one element of its meaning is commonly, if not always, speedy action. For example, " I was forward,"[*] *i.e.*, hastened ; " I endeavored to see your face,"[†] *i. e.*, I was urgent. "Give diligence,"[‡] *i. e.*, Be not only energetic, but speedy. Whether it should be hasten or strive, it is to be done immediately. This is in accordance with what was said before about doing it " to-day," and so is in harmony with the context.

Now, if " enter into that rest " means enter heaven, then to hasten to do it seems to recommend suicide. We can only hasten to do something present, and so entering that rest must be present. We can strive or hasten to effect some present means toward getting to heaven, such as "to enter in at the strait gate," " repent," " believe," but never to hasten to get to heaven. What looks most like an exception is, " work out your salvation." But this appearance of exception comes from our commonly speaking of salvation as future, while the New Testament commonly speaks of it as present. It means, Work out your progressive salvation now as you go along, not work out its final completion at death, which is the province of God alone.

But as this exhortation is addressed to believers, " holy brethren," " partakers of the heavenly calling," we may fairly be asked how they could strive to enter God's rest, when, on our theory, they were in it already. The difficulty disappears when we consider that entering into God's rest means participating in it, and that it is not a single momentary initial act, but progressive action, to be repeated and intensified.

One great design of the apostle was to show the superiority of Christ and his religion over Moses and the national religion.

---

[*] Gal. ii: 10.   [†] 1 Thess. ii : 17.   [‡] 2 Peter i: 10.

Subordinate to this the present argument was to show not the superiority of heaven, for nobody disputed that, but the superiority of what Christians enjoyed over the Jewish ritual, and that the real spiritual blessings promised to the Israelites remained unexhausted to the Christians. Any reference to rest in heaven would have been irrelevant.

The middle clause of the third verse, and the fifth verse of the fourth chapter, do not necessarily mean that the rest is present, but by fitting that supposition exactly, they corroborate it. As the Israelites had failed so long before to enter into this rest, on account of disobedience arising from unbelief, it is all along implied that but for that, they would have entered in at the time they failed. This shows that the rest intended is in this world.

We call attention to the fact that the foregoing evidences and arguments are independent and cumulative. The conclusions from the first, third, sixth, eighth, ninth and eleventh verses of the fourth chapter are each sufficient without the others to show that the rest in question is on earth, not in heaven. Neither of them depends on either of the others, nor on the correctness or incorrectness of our views on other points.

As participation in God,[*] in Christ,[†] of the Holy Ghost,[‡] of the divine nature ;[§] as God's family,[‖] assembly,[¶] spiritual building,[1] kingdom,[2] temples of the Holy Ghost,[3] the body of Christ ;[4] as being in God,[5] in Christ,[6] co-workers with God,[7] the saved;[8] as fellowship with God,[9] and the spiritual rest Christ gives,[10] are all in this world, we are not surprised to find God's rest, another phase of very much the same thing, in this world also.

God's rest in another sense is spoken of as in this world,[11] and saints speak of a spiritual rest,[12] evidently in this world,

---

[*] 1 Thess. i : 1.
[†] Ch. iii : 14.
[‡] Ch. vi : 4.
[§] 2 Peter i : 4.
[‖] Ch. iii : 6.
[¶] Matt. xvi : 18.
[1] 1 Peter ii : 5.
[2] Ex. xix : 6.

[3] 1 Cor. vi : 19.
[4] Col. i : 24.
[5] 1 Thes. i : 1.
[6] Rom. xii : 5.
[7] 1 Cor. iii : 9.
[8] Acts ii : 47. God added the saved to the church daily.
[9] 1 John i : 3.
[10] Matt. xi : 28.

[11] Ps. 132 : 8, 14.   Isaiah lxvi : 1.
     Acts vii : 49.
[12] Ps. cxvi : 7.   Is. xviii : 4. Jer.
     vi : 16; xxx : 10. Mic. ii : 10.

and the glorious rest of the root of Jesse,* Christ, is evidently
in this world.   We have not felt authorized to use these as
arguments, but they corroborated the idea that in some ways
God and man enjoy spiritual rest in this world, *possibly* with
some allusion to God's rest now in question.

We deduce no argument from the tenth verse, but the
statement in it is entirely consistent with our view.   If " he,
that hath entered into his rest " means Christ, then he hath
ceased from his own works of redemption, as God did from
his of creation, and has entered on his application of that
redemption with the very same objects for which God has
entered on his spiritual rest.   And this is the reason, indicated
by " for," why there remains this Sabbath-keeping ever open
to the people of God.   Or if he means a believer, then he has
ceased from his own sinful works and efforts at justification
by works, as God did from mere creation, and now partakes of
God's rest.

Our conclusion is that God's rest spoken in the psalm was
the same as the spiritual blessings offered to ancient Israel, and
refused by the generation that came out of Egypt ; and the
same as that discussed in Hebrews ; and that believers participate in it in this world.   On this theory each expression
used in the discussion has its natural and not unusual meaning, and the same meaning throughout ; each particle has its
proper force ; each tense is just what it should be ; each remark
is relevant ; each argument is rigidly logical and tends to support the conclusion ; the features and terms of the discussion
are suggested by what has gone before, and the whole flows
naturally with the drift of the epistle, and tends to establish
its grand conclusion.   On any other theory all this is reversed.

The evidence and the scriptural analogies are all on one side.
Heaven is never called rest, and we never hear *in the Bible*
of rest as one of its characteristics.   On the contrary, the
four living creatures supposed to represent the redeemed in
heaven, " have no rest day nor night."†   True, certain saints
are said to " rest for a season,"‡ but that expresses mere delay.   Certain others are said to " rest from their labors,"§ but

---

* Is. xi : 10.   ‡ Rev. vi : 11.
† Rev. iv :8.   § Rev. xiv : 13.

that seems to express only exemption ; neither expresses the heavenly bliss, and in neither case does the original word mean, as in Hebrews, God's rest.   Once a different word, expressing relief from persecution, is in the authorized version rather inaccurately translated rest,* not in heaven, but at the day of judgment.   Saints are said to sleep† after death, and Job speaks of the weary being at rest ;‡ but these refer not to their souls in heaven, but to their bodies in the grave.

If the rest of heaven is not a Bible representation, why is it so generally accepted, and why is our devotional literature so full of it ?   We cannot tell, any more than we can tell why we hear so often of the *straight* and narrow path, of *Mount* Calvary, of the *sinful* Mary Magdalen, of feminine angels, or a hundred other things that are not in the Bible.   The images in the public mind do not come from the Bible, but from poetry and pictures.   Good men too often use representations, not that are true, but that will make an impression.

We shall now show that God's rest, spoken of in the psalm, and said by the apostle still to continue, is the rest of God's seventh day.   After pointing out in the first two clauses of the third verse of the fourth chapter that "the rest," *i. e.*, God's rest, still continued, the apostle adds in the third clause, according to our translation, "Although the works were finished from the foundation of the world."   Now, such juxtaposition of such correlative things as rest and work finished, indicates, if the contrary does not appear, that that rest is from those works. So we saw not long ago on the sign of a German workshop the words, "Tinschmit and Repaired."   Now, the juxtaposition of the two words made it just as certain, as if expressed in the fullest and clearest English, that there tin-work was repaired as well as made.   But we are not left to such inference.   The connective "although" distinctly fixes the relation between the works and the rest.   "Although" means that the thing just said may seem to be opposed, but really is not, to the admitted fact mentioned after that word.   The thing said here is that God's rest still continues ; the fact admitted after

---

*2 Thess. i : 7.

† Job vii : 21. Dan. xii : 2. John xi : 11. 1 Cor. xi : 30 ; xv : 51. 1 Thess. iv : 14.

‡ Job iii : 13, 17; xvii : 16.

" although" as apparently contradicting it or making it unexpected is, that the works, *i. e.,* God's works, " were finished
from the foundation of the world." If " the rest" was not
the same rest as that from the works spoken of, nothing said
about the one could seem to be opposed to anything said about
the other. It would make the use of " although" as improper
as in the statement " two and two make four, although
water runs down hill." It cannot merely mean that one was
like the other, for then there could have been no seeming
contradiction or opposition between the present continuance
of the one and the early commencement of the other. It
would have been to no purpose to say that there is a rest
into which believers enter, for God rested in some other sense
on some other occasion.

The reason why the present continuance of God's rest might
seem to be opposed to the fact that the works were finished
so long ago was not its mere antiquity, for it had already been
shown to go back to Moses' time ; but that the sacred account
says that God's rest was on or during the seventh day, which
was generally supposed to have ended thousands of years before. This is shown by the way " the seventh day" is introduced in the next sentence by " for," which necessarily connects the thing about to be said with something said or implied
about it before. Some scholars, instead of " although," render
" namely" from the works, etc. This word shows that what is
next to be said defines the thing just spoken of, and requires
the name of that thing to be expressed or understood after
" namely." Applying this rule, we paraphrase " God's rest continued," namely, the rest from the works of creation.

" From the foundation of the world." If world here means
earth or material world, then the expression " a laying down,"
translated " foundation," must include the whole construction ;
and the starting-point must be not the laying down, but the
finishing up of the structure ; otherwise the statement would
not be true. But this does not give the expression its proper
or usual meaning, which is the beginning of something, not the
whole of it, much less the very end of it. True, a measurement may be described as from something extended without
specifying from what point in it ; but then nobody would call
the extended thing by the name of some other point remote

from the real starting-point. The entire hull of a ship is some-times called a bottom, sometimes a keel; but no one would say a certain object was so many feet above the bottom, meaning the ship, when he meant so many feet above the ship. But, aside from this, suppose " laying down" means, as is usu-ally supposed, the whole construction of the works, then the starting-point being really the time when they were finished, the statement only means the works were finished from the time the works were finished. We must look for an explanation requiring less violence to the language, and which makes the statement mean something.

The word translated " world," used about 180 times in the New Testament, unmistakably means the earth or material world not more than one time in twenty, while it unmistak-ably means human society, or some part, phase, state, period, pursuit or characteristic of it, about fifteen times in twenty. In most other cases it means the scene of human action, refer-ring not so much to the earth itself as to the people on it, so that the phrase " in the world" is equivalent to " among man-kind." When the meaning does not otherwise appear, the chances are, therefore, perhaps ten to one that it means human society or something about it. Foundation, used as a date, means the beginning of something.

All the foregoing considerations raise separate probabilities, which concur in showing that the phrase means " from the foundation of the social world," or of human society, or of the present state of things. It certainly has that meaning in three[*] out of the six[†] other places where the phrase " from the foun-dation of the world" occurs, and may have the same meaning in the others.

Three ancient eras seem to be recognized in the New Testa-ment: one from eternity, one from the beginning of the mate-rial world, and one from the beginning of the social world, as here and in many other places.[‡]

If God's rest means the employment of his perfections in the moral government of the human race, then we see how

---

[*] Matt. xiii : 35. Luke xi : 50. Heb. ix : 26.

[†] Matt. xxv : 34. Rev. xiii : 8; xvii : 8.

[‡] Matt. xix : 4, 8; xxiv : 21. Mark x : 6; xiii : 19. Acts iii : 21. Eph. iii : 6-9.
2 Peter iii : 4. Rom. xvi : 25.

accurate the representation is, that it began just when the race began, that it still continues, and will continue as long as the race continues in this world. In striking but undesigned coincidence with this representation, geology reads in God's stone history that he ceased to create just at the commencement of the human period of the world. The apostle, having in the third verse identified the rest in question with the rest from the works of creation, and recognized an apparent inconsistency between the present continuance of this rest and the implied date of its commencement, goes on in the fourth verse to explain that the difficulty arose from what was said about the seventh day. " For," in indication of the reason or cause of the difficulty just recognized, " He spake in a certain place of the seventh day on this wise, And God did rest the seventh day from all his work."* The subject of this quotation is not the works or the rest from them, but the seventh day which God spoke of, or concerning. " For" shows that this subject, this seventh day, was in contemplation in what had just been presented. What was said about the seventh day was therefore quoted to account for, or point out, the difficulty. God's rest was on or during that one day, and so it was difficult for the Hebrew Christians, and possibly for the apostle himself, to conceive how it could still continue.

God has temporarily permitted some things in his word and in his works to be misunderstood, some statements in his word to be in apparent conflict, which even the inspired man through whom they were made could not reconcile, and the conclusions of some arguments to remain unexpressed, till a fuller understanding of his works, word and providence should make all plain. The object of the apostle in the third and fourth verses may have been honestly to state the difficulty without attempting to answer it; or it may have been to lay the foundation for a conclusion which it would have been premature to express in the then state of knowledge, and which is that the seventh day still continues. This is the only possible answer to the difficulty presented. On this theory all is clear and consistent. On any other this passage is inex-

---

* Gen. ii : 2 .

plicable, as is seen by the numerous unsuccessful attempts of commentators to explain it.

It is clear from these verses that the name God's Rest, into which believers enter, comes from his ceasing to create, not from man's temporal or even spiritual rest in Canaan. We should expect God's condition or course of action to be named from his own acts, not man's; and it is fit that a universal thing should be named from a universal, not a local, circumstance.

It is said in the fourth and fifth verses, "He (God or the Holy Ghost) says in a certain place," *i. e.,* in Genesis, "God rested the seventh day," and in this place again (*i. e.,* in the psalm), "If they shall enter into my rest." The object of bringing together these two passages which speak of rest is obviously to confirm what had before appeared, the identity of the rests. "Again" shows that the same thing is spoken of that had been spoken of before. As if he had said, "He spoke of the rest in Genesis, and spoke of it again in the psalm." The passage in Genesis is not attributed to any human author, but, like the psalm, directly to God or the Holy Ghost. From this we should expect that it might contain something above the knowledge or even conception of the writer, or any one else for many generations to come.

After resuming the thread of his discourse in verse sixth, the writer interrupts himself in verse seventh to say something more about the day. "Again he limiteth a certain day," saying in David, "To-day," after so long a time, "To-day if ye will hear his voice, harden not your hearts." The way the writer breaks in upon his general subject shows that his object is to explain or confirm something said before and dropped before it was fully disposed of. This explanation is about a certain limited, definite day, the day before spoken of. We may paraphrase thus: Besides specifying in Genesis the day when God rested, the Holy Ghost limits or specifies the same day in David, calling it "to-day" with God, still continuing after so long a time, as from Adam to David.

Day means time, as "day of the provocation." To-day means the present time. God's to-day, his present time, here "limited" or defined, is his seventh day, his day of rest, his day of giving grace, extending throughout the human period of the world. Man's to-day is his day of receiving grace, of entering God's rest, extending at farthest through his individual lifetime. It is very likely that David did not understand this, but the real author, the Holy Ghost, did.

In the eighth verse it is implied that Joshua did not give Israel rest; that is, the rest he did give was not the rest now under consideration. If he had given it, it would have been exhausted, and the Holy Ghost would not afterward have spoken of "another day" when it was still unexhausted. There is no indication that the word "day" was used in giving the promise to ancient Israel; but the expression "another day" refers back to some occasion when it was used. That occasion is pointed out in the fourth verse.

God created the earth in six days, and on the seventh he occupied it for the purposes for which he had created it. His natural government extends from the first act of creation till the end of time; his spiritual government over the human family from the last act of creation till the end of time. It is this which is called his rest. And it continues on during or throughout his seventh day. "He rested on the seventh day."* He blessed the seventh day, "because that in it he rested,"† not "had rested," as A. V. "In six days the Lord made" all things, "and rested the seventh day."‡ "In six days the Lord made heaven and earth, and on the seventh day he rested and was refreshed."§

If the preposition translated "in" or "on" in these passages means throughout or during the six days, it must mean the same thing when applied to the associated event in the same sentence. As God blessed the entire seventh day he rests the entire seventh day. The fourth commandment represents God and man as both working throughout six days; man's rest was to be throughout the seventh day; and the parallel requires us to understand that God's rest was also throughout or co-extensive with his seventh day. To rest is not merely to stop, but to take refreshment after stopping. "God rested and WAS REFRESHED."‖ It is not a mere point, but continuous occupation. The day was blessed on account of the

---

* Gen. ii: 2.   ‡ Ex. xx: 11.   ‖ Ex. xxxi: 17.
† Gen. ii: 3.   ‡ Ex. xxxi: 17.

rest, which shows that the rest was a holy state. The rest is not longer than the day, nor the day longer than the rest.

The day during which God rested has generally been understood to be one of twenty-four hours. But if so, it seems strange to represent the rest of that day as peculiar when God has rested in the same manner every day since. And if that is the meaning of day there, his rest in different parts of the earth, if simultaneous, was at different hours of the day in all the different degrees of longitude. And such a day is not of the same kind as the preceding six of the same series with which it is consecutively numbered. As God's rest spoken of in Hebrews evidently extends throughout the human period till the end of time, and the rest of the seventh day is the same rest, we infer that the seventh day extends throughout the human period.

The name rest was doubtless given to God's present holy occupation from his ceasing to create. The name does not describe the thing, but one of its landmarks or boundaries. So a document is often named from its first word or from the indentations at the top of the parchment on which it is written.

On our theory the reason annexed to the fourth commandment becomes plain. Man during his seventh day is to desist from his own pursuits, and devote himself entirely to those of God's seventh day—contemplation of the Divine perfections, making them known among mankind, and increasing holiness in the world. Man's rest of the Sabbath is not merely like God's, not mere imitation or commemoration, but participation.

A comparison of the account of the formation of the earth found in God's Word with that found in his works gives good reason to believe that the six days of creation were indefinitely long periods. If this was certain, it would make it all but certain that the seventh day is a long period, for it is called by the same name, placed in the same series, and numbered consecutively with the others, and thus recognized as being the same kind of day that they are. If God's rest in Genesis means a divine Sabbath-keeping, it must continue throughout this day. And as the epistle to the Hebrews speaks of a divine rest or Sabbath-keeping in which believers partake, it must be the same as that in Genesis, or else there would be two rests of the same kind, of the same name, and of the same person.

Again, if it was certain from the discussion in Hebrews, and what is said in the Old Testament, that God's seventh day extends throughout the human period of the world, then it would be all but certain that the preceding six days were also long periods. Whatever probability there is that the six days were long periods, there is therefore like probability that the seventh is also a long period, and *vice versa.* The grounds of these probabilities being entirely independent and different in kind from each other, we are entitled to the aggregate weight of all in favor of either conclusion.

Whatever weight may be accorded to our arguments in favor of our separate subordinate propositions, and whatever weight may be allowed to those propositions as arguments for our main conclusion, should not simply be added, but multiplied together. A great number of even slight probabilities, all pointing the same way, tending to establish conclusions which, when put together, fit each other and form a symmetrical whole, and that whole in entire harmony with what we otherwise know, may have all together almost the force of certainty.

Art. V.—WHO WROTE THE EPISTLE OF JAMES?

By Rev. Samuel Dodd, Hangchow, China.

We learn from the four lists of names (Matt. x : 2–4 ; Mark iii : 16–19 ; Luke vi : 14–16 ; Acts i : 13) that there were two Jameses among the apostles, viz., James of Zebedee and brother of John, and James of Alpheus ; and that, besides Judas Iscariot, there was a Judas of James. We learn also (Matt. xiii : 55, Mark. vi : 3) that, in the opinion of the people, our Lord had four brothers, and at least two or three sisters ; they are not only called his brothers and sisters by the people, but by the sacred writers as well. In New Testament usage, as with us, " brother " may be a son of the same parents, or almost any near relation, natural or moral. Neighbors, friends, associates, fellow-Christians, fellow-laborers, and fellow-ministers are all called brothers sometimes.   Among the brothers of our Lord there was one named James and another Judas.

After the death of James of Zebedee, as reported Acts xii : 2, a James is still found among the apostles—no longer, however, as James of Alpheus, but, the necessity for the distinguishing title having ceased, as James simply.   We learn (Acts ix) that when Paul visited Jerusalem the first time after his conversion, the disciples, as a class, were afraid of him ; but Barnabas took him and introduced him to the apostles.   Paul himself, speaking of this first meeting with the apostles, tells us (Gal. i : 19) that he saw only Peter, and no other of the apostles except James, the Lord's brother ; so the apostles to whom the recent convert Saul was introduced by Barnabas were Peter and James.   Death not yet having entered the ranks of the apostles, Paul tells us that the James whom he saw at that time was the " Lord's brother," thus distinguishing him from the other James of Zebedee.   This (Gal. i : 19) is the last time the phrase " Lord's brother" is found in the New Testament. Of the various visits which Paul made to Jerusalem after his conversion, the chronological order of no one can be placed more definitely beyond dispute than that of the first, and this is the visit which of all others is of special importance in enabling us to answer the question at the head of this paper. Luke (Acts ix : 26) tells us that when Saul essayed to join himself to the disciples at Jerusalem they were afraid of him and believed not that he was a disciple.   " But Barnabas brought him to the apostles," after which he was recognized by them as a Christian teacher.   The fear on the part of the disciples, shared probably by the apostles, could only have taken place at his first visit, and at no subsequent one ; and when the apostle Paul is showing (Gal. i.) his independence of all human instrumentality, whether apostolic or other, in his calling to the apostleship he shows that he had been preaching the gospel for three years or so before he ever went near Jerusalem—language that he could not have used had he made a previous visit—and that even then he only saw Peter, and no other of the apostles except James.   It is true that the language used by the apostle Paul would not prove that James was an apostle ; but neither would it prove the contrary.   It is such as he would have used whether James was or was not an apostle, which question must be settled on other grounds than the εἰ μή of Galatians (i : 19). Neither will it help to say, with some who would find a place for James the Lord's brother outside of the twelve, that the plural form *apostles* in Acts (ix : 27) " must not be pressed." This is true ; but we do not need to press it. Luke says Barnabas brought Saul to the apostles; but Paul says there were only two, viz., Peter and James: therefore Peter and James were apostles without pressing, which is required to make Luke, or Paul either, say there was only one apostle.

After the death of James of Zebedee we find James still holding a chief, if not the chief, place among the apostles at Jerusalem. Peter, on his release from prison (Acts xii: 17), says, " Go show these things to James and the brethren," and the decision of James settled the discussion in the apostolic council (mentioned in Acts xv) held about A. D. 51, at which time we learn not only from Acts that James presided, but from Galatians (ii : 9) that he takes precedence of Peter and John. When Paul made a subsequent visit to Jerusalem (Acts xxi), less than ten years after the council (Acts xv), he seems to have gone first to James, and reported to and consulted with him in reference to the work of God among the Gentiles. From all of which it seems plain that the James who, even before as well as ever after the death of James of Zebedee, occupies such a prominent place in Jerusalem, cannot possibly be any other than James the apostle, son of Alpheus, with whom we became acquainted in the gospels and the early part of the Acts, and which apostle, James of Alpheus, the apostle Paul calls the Lord's brother—a title, however, which, on examination, only confirms the above conclusion, viz., that James the Lord's brother (of Galatians i: 19) is none other than James the son of Alpheus.

Had Paul used only the name James in the two places (Gal. i : 19; ii : 9) it would have been impossible to say whether he referred to one man or two; as it is, it is impossible to doubt. In the first instance the two Jameses were still living; therefore, Paul distinguishes the James whom he saw as " the Lord's brother." At the visit mentioned in the second chapter, James of Zebedee was dead, and there being then no need for a distinguishing title, Paul uses none—another of the thousand-fold proofs, if one were still needed, that the sacred writers are anything at all but slip-shod or careless in the use of language. In fact, the language of no lawyer's brief is capable of putting its subject matter more thoroughly beyond dispute than is the language of the New Testament in settling, as far as need be settled, this subject of the Lord's brother, over which, and the questions growing out of it, there has been so much debate. Nor did the last will and testament of any man ever more evidently need to be tampered with, in order to be made to say something that the testator never meant it should say, than does the language of the Acts and Epistles in order to create confusion as to whether there really was in the early church at Jerusalem a prominent man named James, the Lord's brother, different from the apostle James of Alpheus. Let us come without any preconceived theories as to church government or church history, and we will find wonderfully little confusion, the expectation of which grows out of the widespread, insidious fallacy that the sacred writers are not particular in the use of language; that when they put the main facts concerning salvation in the possession of their readers, the thread of their narratives may then be either orderly or in hopeless confusion; and the names of persons and places may be given either with the accuracy and definitiveness that would characterize the writings of any other respectable and competent historian; or with the mixture of knowledge and ignorance, care and negligence that may be found in Shakespeare's "Two Gentlemen of Verona," or any other work intended rather to display the fine imagination of the writer than his conscientious regard for stubborn facts. As the views entertained in this paper must be much modified by the opinion which the reader entertains of the evangelist Luke's carefulness as a narrator, it may be as well to give that subject a very brief examination. And in that examination we cannot find a case better suited to our purpose than one brought forward to strengthen their position by those whose opinions on this question are entirely different from our own. We are told that it is "Luke's way" to introduce new characters in development of his plot, and that he might "introduce a third James without giving any account of his antecedents and origin," because "the self-same Luke introduces in the same manner Philip." If there is a Philip, there may be a James introduced in the Acts, who, as far as any specific statement in the narrative is concerned, may or may not be one of the twelve. If there is no such Philip, it will be vain to call on him for aid in persuading us that there is such a James. It should be borne in mind, too, here, that the phrase "James the Lord's brother," is used only by Paul (Gal. i : 19); that the passage to which he (Paul) refers in Acts (ix : 27) only says there were apostles present on the occasion, but gives the names of none. If, then, there should be, as there is not, a doubt on our mind as to the agreement between Paul and Luke, the benefit of the doubt, as far as Acts is concerned, must be given not to the apostle, but to the evangelist, who is responsible for his own book, and who succeeds in giving what he undertakes to give, *i. e.*, an orderly, intelligible and consistent "declaration of all things of which he had a perfect understanding from the very first."

If we bear in mind that the New Testament nowhere says that either Mary or Joseph had other children besides Jesus, and then examine the exegetical and historical proof for the thus supposititious offspring, we will find that so much must be taken for granted, without evidence, at every step of the investigation, that, like Prospero's banquet, they

> "dissolve,
> And, like an unsubstantial pageant, faded,
> Leave not a rack behind."

The question whether James was or was not among the twelve is not touched by the mention of the names of the brothers in the synagogue at Nazareth (Matt. xiii : 55, Mark iv : 3); whether, some time before, Jesus while at or near Capernaum had chosen twelve from among his disciples to become apostles, and whether the brother James was or was not among these twelve, are questions that we cannot suppose the bulk of the Nazarenes to have been much interested in or affected by in mentioning his kindred. The enumeration thus casts neither light nor darkness on the subject. If we take, then, Galatians i : 19, the ordinary unprejudiced reader will regard the passage as implying that James was an apostle; if, *e. g.*, instead of "James, the Lord's brother," we had met the name of John, Thomas or Andrew, no one would ever have thought of showing that the passage in the original does not prove that the one thus named was an apostle. We grant here, however, that the language in the original does not prove that he was ; but grant no more, as it does not prove the contrary. We go back next to Acts ix : 27, and find that Saul was introduced to *apostles*, and we learn from Gal. 1 : 19 that there were only two men, viz., Peter and ·James, at the meeting with Saul. We naturally infer again that the two were both apostles, but are told* that this passage must not be regarded as proof that they were. However willingly we yielded the request based on the ει μη of Gal. 1 : 19, we feel here that we must begin to make a stand for the truth ; and though believing that the fair import of the language is that the men were both apostles, we will, for the sake of argument, yield the point for the present, and ask, What next? We then go back to the gospels (Matt. xiii : 55, Mark vi : 3), and find the names of four brothers, the first two names in both lists being James and Joses. The same evangelists, without mentioning any other pair of brothers with these names, tell us that Mary, one of the witnesses of the crucifixion (Matt. xxvii : 56, Mark xv : 40), whom from another gospel (John xix : 25) we learn to have been the wife of Cleophas, was the mother of James and Joses, and we are told† that this pair of brothers are to be distinguished from the brothers of our Lord. Here we absolutely rebel against such an unwarranted assumption, and reply, No; they are not so mentioned to be distinguished from, but, on the contrary, to be identified with the Lord's brothers mentioned by name in only these two gospels ; otherwise why mention Joses at all, of whom we know nothing except that he was one of those called the brothers of the Lord! It is all well enough for the evangelist Luke, who had not given the names of the four brothers, to mention only one of the sons of Mary, viz., James, *i. e.*, one of the two Jameses whom he had already mentioned, not the brother of John and son of Zebedee, but James of Alpheus. But supposing Matthew and Mark to have been sufficiently well informed and honest, and not wanting to mislead, they could have had only one object in coupling the name of Joses, as they both do, with that of James, viz., to identify

---

* Dr. Lightfoot.   † By Dr. Alford.

them as two of the four brothers of the Lord. We next go
to 1 Corinthians xv : 5, 7, and learn that "Christ appeared
to Cephas, then to the twelve. .   .   .   . After that he
appeared to James, then to all the apostles." And though
Cephas is permitted to pass unchallenged, we are told by a
recent commentator* that "it was this manifestation of the
risen Saviour" to James "that proved for him and his brethren the turning point of their lives, so that they at once became his decided followers." Such a comment might be found
fittingly enough among the cabala of the ancient Jews; but
certainly sorts badly with the scientific accuracy expected from
Christian scholars of the present century. Even supposing that
there was, as there was not, a James the Lord's brother, not of
the twelve, it is certainly an unwarranted assumption to say
that the James of 1 Corinthians xv : 7 was he and neither of
the other two Jameses who were among the apostles ; while to
go on and say that "this appearance proved for James and his
brethren the turning point of their lives," is a flight of fancy un-
surpassed by anything of the kind outside of the "Arabian
Nights" or "Robinson Crusoe"! The next request is much more
unreasonable than any or all that have gone before ; but while
it remains ungranted, as it forever must, the others are entirely
valueless toward introducing the third James; it is to believe that it would not be contrary to what we know of the
evangelist Luke's habits as a writer to suppose that he introduced James not of the twelve in his narrative of the Acts.
After having given the book of Acts a somewhat careful examination, to discover, if possible, the reasonableness or otherwise
of this assumption, we hesitate not to affirm that it would not be
a greater insult to the literary character of Washington Irving
to suppose that the George Washington who, he tells us, in 1781
prescribed the terms of capitulation at Yorktown, Va., was a
changeling, having only the name in common with the man
who he tells us in 1755 displayed such intrepidity and coolness
on the field of Braddock's defeat, than it would to the character of the evangelist Luke, as a writer, to suppose that James,
who ever after Acts xii : 2 appears as James simply, could pos-

---

* Dr. C. F. Kling, in Lange's Commentary on Corinthians.

sibly be any other than the James of Alpheus, to whom we are introduced in the beginning of the book.

In presenting this subject to our readers, we cannot find a more fitting example than one brought forward by those whose views of the matter are entirely different from ours. We are told* that it is Luke's way to introduce new characters in the development of his plot—as, *e. g.*, Philip.

Philip, one of the seven deacons (Acts vi : 5), cannot possibly be one of the twelve. Two of said seven seem to have regarded the relative worth of preaching and distributing alms very much as the apostles did, *i. e.*, that it would be better to let the poor Greeks and others be neglected, even wronged if need be, than for themselves to abstain from preaching. Stephen finished his brief but glorious career in the next chapter (vii) after the one that records his ordination. A persecution arose thereupon, which scattered them all abroad, "except the apostles"; when Philip went down to the city of Samaria and preached Christ there. This could not possibly have been one of the apostles, who, the chapter tells, were still at Jerusalem and sent a deputation to recognize and confirm this man's work. It could have been no other than the deacon Philip, turned evangelist, whom we next encounter on the way to Gaza (viii : 26), and next at Azotus, preaching in all the cities till he came to Cesarea (viii : 40). The name is not mentioned again till some time after, when the apostle and his companions are in Cesarea, and find their way to the house of Philip. We would naturally suppose that this was the Philip whom we left there some few pages back, but no supposing is necessary; the careful historian tells us that it was the deacon turned evangelist, "Philip one of the seven." His name never occurs in any place where it could possibly be confounded with that of the apostle. And this is "Luke's way." Now, let a James, "not of the twelve," be introduced with the same clearly drawn features that Philip is, and we will accept of him, but not before. Neither will it aid the introduction of a third James to tell us that Philip is a special case. He is brought forward according to the evangelist's custom, who mentions at least four Simons, viz., Simon Peter, Simon

---

* By Drs. Lightfoot, Alford and Mombert.

Zelotes, Simon the sorcerer, and Simon the tanner—all carefully distinguished from each other; five Judases, viz., Judas
Iscariot, Judas of Galilee, a ringleader in a tumult (Acts v:
37), Judas with whom Paul stayed in Damascus, Judas Barsa-
bas, and Jude of James—no possibility of confusion here ; three
Johns, viz., John of the kindred of the high priest at Jerusalem (Acts iv: 5, 6), John Mark, and the apostle John the
brother of James—no confusion ; two Pauls, one the Apostle
Paul, another the deputy of the country at Paphos (Acts xiii:
7), whose name our translators have unnecessarily and inconsistently rendered Paulus, perhaps to distinguish him from
the apostle Paul, as though such an act were necessary in
dealing with the writings of such a clear-headed, careful penman as Luke ; there need be no fear of confounding the deputy
Paul with the apostle Paul.   Paul's name was originally Saul,
but the change is not to be conjectured by us.   Luke says
Saul who is also named Paul.   After such carefulness the
theory must be well-nigh hopeless that relies for support on
the inaccuracy, carelessness or omission of important statements with which Luke introduces the actors in his story.
It had been better if some uninspired writers on this subject
had been careful to verify their statements before drawing
conclusions from them.   We are told, *e. g.*, that " James mentioned in Acts xii: 2 and onward is already sufficiently distinguished from James of Alpheus by being spoken of without
any distinctive title."   He is distinguished by being extin-
guished in that verse under the name of James the brother of
John, and never appears afterward in this world.   We are told
that " James the Lord's brother . . . is expressly distinguished from James of Alpheus."   Let us have the proof of this
and it settles the whole controversy.   We are told that " the
brothers of Jesus were really members of the holy family, and
under the care of Joseph and Mary, in whose company they
constantly appear."   This statement, like others, as far as
Joseph is concerned, must be denied *in toto*.   The brothers
never once appear in Joseph's company, who disappears after
the visit to Jerusalem when Jesus was twelve years of age.

Let us consider the all but impossibilities in the way of
any other conclusion than that supposed to be arrived at
above, viz., that James, the Lord's brother (of Galatians i:

19) could not possibly have been any other than the apostle James of Alpheus. The brethren of our Lord are referred to often in the sacred narratives, and the list of their names is given twice, as noticed above. The alleged discrepancy between the two lists is scarcely worthy of notice; both contain a James and a Jude; and the four lists of the apostles contain each, as we have seen, in addition to James of Zebedee and John his brother, a James of Alpheus; and two of the lists, omitting the Lebbeus or Lebbeus Thaddeus found near the James of Alpheus in the other two, give in his place a Jude of James, translated in the English version, Jude *the brother* of James. If, then, we might suppose that the James mentioned in the lists of our Lord's brothers was a uterine brother, different from James of Alpheus, who was appointed an apostle by our Lord himself, and is so introduced by the writer of the Acts in the first chapter, it is entirely insupposable that he should be permitted by the same writer, ever after the death of his at first more prominent namesake, to drop out of the history without note or comment, and have his place taken in the apostolic college by some other James " unawares brought in," and of whose call to the apostleship the New Testament says nothing ! It is even more insupposable that the apostle Paul, who determined to know no man after the flesh, and was forced to prove so plainly that his own call to the apostolic office was "not of man, neither by man, but by the Lord Jesus Christ," should have paid the deference that he certainly did pay to James merely on the ground of his being a brother of the Lord according to the flesh. And it is even more insupposable that if our Lord had a uterine brother named James, who, whether an eminently good man or otherwise, must have been extensively known in the early church, the apostle Paul should have called the apostle James of Alpheus. as he assuredly does, the Lord's brother. Whether we may be able to discover why he was so called is an entirely different subject, and one which brings up the whole question of " The Brethren of our Lord " and " The Perpetual Virginity" of his mother, to which subjects we must now turn.

We may approach every such subject, however, with the full assurance that if, after a fair and full collection of all the texts of Scripture which bear upon it, entirely irrespective of unin-

ired ecclesiastical history, we are still unable to arrive at a
satisfactory conclusion, it is one on which the Holy Spirit did
not intend to enlighten us while here, and is to be regarded
as one of those foolish questions which the apostle warns us to
avoid.   The brethren of the Lord, however, would seem to
present themselves too often in the sacred narrative to warrant us *a priori* in regarding them in such a light.   We are
satisfied, as is shown in the above explanation, that James of
Alpheus is James the Lord's brother, and if he is not a uterine
brother, then neither is Joses, Simon, nor Jude.   James and
Joses had the same mother, Mary, who is introduced twice as
the mother of these two sons, who were doubtless the oldest
members of the family ; once she is the mother of James and
Joses, and once the mother of James the less and Joses (Matt.
xxvii : 56 ; Mark xv : 40).   The Mary of Joses and the Mary
of James (Mark xv : 47 ; xvi : 1) are probably the same person ; but as no relationship is expressed in the original, it may
have been either wife, mother or sister ; and as the cases are
not at all necessary for the purposes of the present paper, they
may be dismissed without further notice.   Bearing in mind,
then, that the evangelists Matthew and Mark both furnish the
names of James, Joses, Simon and Jude as brothers, it should
not be assumed that they refer to another James and Joses
when they mention the two men in connection with their
mother, or because they mention only two of the brothers ;
therefore the remaining two were not sons of the same mother.
Should we come across some old English newspaper, published
in the first quarter of the present century, and read in it that
the mother of the Duke of Wellington had been present at
some civic or religious gathering, we should neither infer therefrom that she was not the mother of the Duke's other brother,
nor that the writer of the article was ignorant of the fact that
she had other children besides the Duke.   James and Joses
(Matt. xxvii : 56 ; Mark xv : 40) must be in fairness regarded
as two brothers (Matt. xiii : 55 ; Mark vi : 3).   And although
Jude of James (Luke vi : 16 ; Acts i : 13), as remarked by
others, need not necessarily be Jude the brother of James, yet,
since the evangelists Matthew and Mark say that James and
Jude were brothers, and as the author of the Epistle of Jude
calls himself the brother of James, it should be admitted with-

out any reasonable doubt that the four men, James, Joses, Simon and Jude, were all brothers, of whom certainly two, James and Jude, possibly though not probably three, James, Simon and Jude, became apostles, but none of them the sons of Mary the mother of Jesus. The two Marys are distinguished from each other on several occasions.

That Cleophas and Alpheus are but different names of the same individual might almost be gathered from our translation of the gospels. John (xix : 25) tells us that there stood by the cross of Jesus his mother and his mother's sister: Mary the wife of Cleophas, and Mary Magdalene.* Matthew, describing doubtless the same group, says (xxvii: 56) there were Mary Magdalene, Mary the mother of James and Joses, and the mother of Zebedee's children. Mark says (xv: 40) Mary Magdalene, Mary the mother of James the less, and of Joses and Salome. The mother of our Lord appears only in the group given by John, who introduces the women during the agony on the cross, but at the commendation of Jesus takes the bereaved and stricken mother ἀπ' ἐκείνης τῆς ὥρας to his home, thus saving her from being an eye-witness of the last agony and gloom of her Son. The other two evangelists, Matthew and Mark, show us after the death has taken place, and the darkness passed away, and the veil of the temple been rent in twain, and the graves opened, the same group of women still there with the single exception of our Lord's mother, whose absence is accounted for by John, who alone mentions her. All the three evangelists tell us that other women were present, but give the names of only a very few ; those whom they mention had doubtless some special connection with the gospel history ; and it would be only natural that the same persons who on this account were mentioned by one evangelist should be mentioned by them all. Taking, then, the groups after the darkness, we have the Magdalene common to all three. The sister of our Lord's mother (John xix : 25) is in all probability Salome (Mark xv: 40), the mother of Zebedee's children (Matt. xxvii: 56). The mother of James the less and Joses (Mark xv : 40) is certainly the mother of James and Joses (Matt. xxvii : 56), and almost certainly Mary of Cleophas (John xix : 25). The name Alpheus does not occur in the gospel of John ; but that

---

*Two pairs of women.

James the less is James of Alpheus there can be no reasonable doubt ; and it has been shown by the above comparison of texts that the mother of James was the wife of Cleophas or Alpheus, either of which names, it is alleged, would be an equally good transliteration of the Hebrew. But it is only natural to believe that the mother of James and Joses was the mother of their brothers Simon and Jude, and of their sisters ; and there are thus left no sons, or daughters either, to claim the relation of child to Mary the wife of Joseph, save Jesus only. We are led to this conclusion by bringing together the texts of the New Testament, without note or comment, and for the most part as they appear in the English version.

The $Aειπαρθενια$ is a subject that we are persuaded may as well be left undiscussed, for the reason that the Scriptures do not furnish sufficient data for its solution. The very few texts that bear on the subject would certainly seem to be against it rather than in favor of it ; and yet the words " first-born" (Luke ii : 7) and " not till " (Matt. i : 25) prove absolutely nothing, though the words "thy father and I " (Luke ii : 48) would scarcely have been used had Joseph and Mary not lived together as husband and wife.

A brief quotation from ecclesiastical history may be introduced here on the subject of " the brothers." Hegesippus, who is quoted by Eusebius, though quoted here from Dr. Lightfoot and the *Princeton Review* for January, 1865, tells us that Cleophas was the brother of Joseph, the husband of Mary, the mother of Jesus ; that Simon, the son of Cleophas, was made bishop of Jerusalem after the death of James. He tells us, also, that *Jude* was called the Lord's brother. From the gospel history we see that *James, Joses, Simon* and *Jude* were brothers. Now, if we might render the celebrated passage from Hegesippus (Eusebius H. E. 4 : 22) as follows : " After James had suffered martyrdom for the same cause as his Lord, Simon, another son of his (the Lord's) uncle, Cleophas, was made bishop," etc., we would have from the pen of one who wrote only a very few decades of years after the death of Simon, the son of Cleophas, but no part of whose purpose was to shed light on the question of "the brothers," a wonderful harmony with the views presented in this article.

Grant even that Hegesippus did not express himself so neatly as he might have done, and that the above translation of the original is forced, it must be confessed, we think, by all who examine the subject for themselves, that the force requisite to bring out this idea is not a drop to the ocean of force requisite to make us believe that Luke, who introduces "the twelve" so particularly in the beginning of his work on the Acts of the Apostles, and distinguishes the two Jameses so that we could never mistake the one for the other, and tells us (Acts xii: 2) when one of the Jameses died, and how he died, and what James it was, viz., the brother of John, should nevertheless permit the other James of Alpheus to slip out of, and another James to slip into the history, nobody knows when, where, why, or how; and should permit this upstart James, not of "the twelve," to be forced into the apostolic seat from which the true apostles, Peter, Paul, and John, had been forced out! That would have us believe that the acquaintances (referred to in Luke xxiii: 49) included our Lord's unbelieving brothers, who were such a hard-hearted, hopeless set that Jesus could not commit their own mother and his to their care; notwithstanding the fact that, according to the common theory, some of them were men grown and married, while others again must have been daughters not more than half-way through their teens. That in a very few days after his mother had been committed to another household that she might there find truer, deeper sympathy and a better sphere of usefulness than she could find among her own seven or eight children, he should become so pre-eminent for faith and good works that in a very few years, while the apostles were all living, and while Jerusalem was still the centre of apostolic influence, he should be consecrated the bishop of the Mother Church there; and though not one of "the twelve" should receive as great deference from the apostles Paul, Peter, and John as any modern bishop receives from his inferior clergy!—while poor James of Alpheus, who had mysteriously disappeared to clear the way for the accession of this new James, should remain in concealment for about fourteen centuries, after which his bones were exhumed and identified in the wilds of Africa somewhere by Nicepharus, a Greek historian of the fifteenth century, "who added unreliable traditions of the last days of the apostles"!

The assumption is a bold one, but thoroughly groundless, unnatural, inconsistent in its several parts, as well as with the facts of sacred history ; and unsubstantiated by any competent historian of the first two centuries.   It will not do to say here that Thomas and other apostles disappear from the Acts immediately after their first introduction, and why might not James of Alpheus?   There is no reason that we know of why he might not, had he only done so !   After reading the first chapter of the Acts, had we found a Thomas still among the apostles, or wielding apostolic influence, we would have believed him to be Thomas of " the twelve" unless there had been something to indicate the contrary.   So with James; until there has been produced proof that has not yet been, and we are persuaded never can be, we must believe that James of the latter Acts is one of the two Jameses of the first chapter.

Even without the aid of Hegesippus we are warranted in believing that the four brothers of the gospels (Matt. xiii : 55, Mark vi : 3) were the sons of Alpheus Cleophas, some near relation of the holy family : according to the gossipers the brother of Joseph, who is mentioned but does not appear in history after Jesus is twelve years of age.   He died doubtless before, according to old tradition, long before our Lord entered on his public ministry. After the death of Joseph, his widow and her son would, according to oriental custom, as in China to-day, go to live with her late husband's brother, Cleophas Alpheus, where the lads or young men, Jesus, James, Joses, Simon and Jude, and the sisters, would grow up as one family.   Perhaps no theory need be expected to explain everything at this late day.   This one, however, conflicts with no established fact, and it sheds light on many.   Some of those which it is thought to conflict with are (1. Cor. xv : 7)—" He was seen of James, then of all the apostles."   But Acts v : 29 says, " Peter and the apostles answered."   Then we have " other apostles, the brethren of the Lord and Cephas," and " the women and Mary, the mother of Jesus, and his brethren" (Acts i : 14) ; which passages go just as far toward proving that Peter was not an apostle and Mary not a woman as that James or the brethren of the Lord could not have been among the apostles.   A more serious difficulty at first sight is presented by the passage in John vii : 5, " Neither did his brethren believe on him."   But even though his brethren had been all among the apostles, which we know was not the case, there is no more inconsistency in the saying, with only a temporary and partial unbelief on the part of the brothers, than with the rebukes administered often by the Master, sometimes to individuals and sometimes to the entire body of his disciples, including even his mother and John the Baptist. By only a very little forcing, the benediction said to be in store for those who should not be offended in the Saviour could be shown to have no place for John the Baptist, while the rebuke administered to the very chief of the disciples, " Get thee behind me, Satan, thou art an offence unto me, for thou savorest not the things that be of God but those that be of men," might be shown to be incompatible not only with the primacy, but even with discipleship. There is room for doubt whether our Lord may not have meant the multitude together with the twelve in Matthew (xvii : 17), where he calls them a " faithless and perverse generation," and the case may be dismissed. But there can be no doubt in regard to Mark (iv : 40), and no amount of scholarship will ever succeed in persuading Christendom that if the οὐκ ἔχετε πίστιν of the latter place is compatible with discipleship, the οὐδὲ ἐπίστευον of John (vii : 5) is incompatible with it.   The life of our Redeemer presented itself in many aspects to the disciples for their faith, which in many cases expanded from the most simple to the most sublime.   But that which led them first to follow the Master, or go at his bidding through the country preaching the gospel of the kingdom, was very different from that which ten years later, in the house of Cornelius, convinced the first of the apostles of that which doubtless had never entered into the mind of any mere man before—viz., " that God is no respecter of persons, but in every nation he that feareth him and worketh righteousness is accepted with him."

Joses of the four brothers was never one of the apostles ; it is almost certain Simon was not. A Simon is mentioned in the lists of the apostles near James of Alpheus, but never said to be any relation to him ; they doubtless became believers, and were the brethren (Acts i : 14) who continued with one accord in prayer and supplication with the women and with Mary the mother of Jesus. The brethren appear for the most part in company with our Lord's mother, who was a widow, and whose

home, what home she had, was in the house of Cleophas, or Clo-
pas, which are both probably the same name. Mary of Clo-
pas had probably a husband, and had household cares. She
does not appear till near the close of the scene. And if we might
suppose that the Cleophas of the journey to Emmaus was the
foster-father of our Lord, the contemplation of the experience
through which he passed, from the time when some trivial act
of the stranger during the meal reminded him of something
in Mary's son until, in the "breaking of bread," the conviction
flashed full upon him that their guest was none other than the
risen Saviour, will awaken in us a strange, mysterious feeling of
sympathy and wonder.

Though the evangelists adopt the modes of expression in
current use, they stop sometimes to give such explanations as
are necessary to prevent important mistakes (John iv: 1, 2).
They did not do so in reference to "the brothers," because the
relations, as far as it is necessary for us to know them, are discoverable from what is already written. It would, moreover,
not have mended matters to say they were not his brothers,
but his cousins. On our theory, they were no more his cousins
than his brothers; they were the sons of Joseph's brother, no
blood relation to Jesus, who, so far as we know, never acknowledged any natural relation to any man or woman. He never
called any man master, father or brother, or any woman
mother or sister, in any sense which was not open to all mankind. His relations were with humanity, as such, not with any
private person, family or nation (Matt. xii: 49, 50). If the wid-
owed Mary went to live with her brother-in-law, Alpheus Cleophas, and if the uncle's older children were considerably the
seniors of Mary's son, this fact would go far toward explaining why "the brothers," whether among the apostles or not,
were forward on several occasions to express their doubts or
disapprobation of our Lord's conduct; if Mary the mother of
Jesus, and Salome the mother of John were sisters, and if
Mary was bereaved at the cross of her only son, there was a
kind and filial reason for sending her to live with John, thus
providing her with a more homely home than she would have
found in the house of her brother-in-law or husband's nephews.
This reason would not have existed had she had sons and
daughters of her own—the youngest of whom must have been

quite young—according to the " own children" theory of Mark vi : 3 ; nor would it be affected by their being believers or un- believers, married or unmarried. The theory does not require us to embark on some shoreless sea in search of the authors of the Epistles of James and Jude outside of the twelve apostles, among men however good and holy. A recent commentary* on the first verse of Jude tells us that " Jude and James omit ἀπόστολος after their names. The simple reason of this omis- sion is that they were no apostles." Are we to conclude then that John, who never calls himself an apostle, and Paul, who calls himself only the *servant* of Jesus Christ to the *Philippians,* and the *prisoner* of Jesus Christ to *Philemon*, and claims no official relation to the Master to the *Thessalonians*, are silent in regard to their apostleship because it has no existence? Nay, verily! The relation was well enough known from other sources, and did not need to be again stated.

We have found that James, whom Paul met on his first visit to Jerusalem after his conversion, was the apostle James of Alpheus; but he was called the Lord's brother, therefore he was James (of Matt. xiii : 55, Mark. vi : 3) the brother of Joses, Simon and Jude. His home was at Jérusalem, and his every word, whether recorded in the Acts or Epistles, shows him to have been the Israelite indeed who strove to win Israel back to the service of God, rather by manifesting the excellency of the law than the necessity of the cross and its sacrifice. His bishopric being thus the circumcision, it is only to be expected that his apostolic epistle, which, while it does not conceal the fact that its author is a servant of Jesus Christ, yet does not utter one word or employ one illustration calculated to wound the national or religious feelings of Israel, should be addressed to his *Brethren of the twelve tribes.* And the fact that no Christian church or society is mentioned in the address is only in harmony with what we know of the man, his personal desire and official position. In becoming a Chris- tian he did not feel that he had ceased to be an Israelite ; he had only attained to that which had been the hope and solace of the nation in the darkest periods of its history. And he felt that God had returned now " to build again the tabernacle of David, which was fallen down ; to build again the ruins thereof,

---

* Dr. Thranmuller in Lange .

and set it up, that the residue of men might seek after the
Lord, and all the Gentiles upon whom my name is called, saith
the Lord God, who doeth all these things." It would have
been terrible to him to think that God had cast away his people whom he foreknew. And when his brother Jude—doubtless much the junior of the two—came to write his brief but
burning epistle, we need not wonder that he regarded it quite
a sufficient guarantee of its canonicity to all readers of the
Gospels and Acts to sign himself simply "*the servant of Jesus
Christ and the brother of James.*" Hence it follows that we
are not to look for the author of either of the two epistles (of
James or Jude) to any man, however good and holy, or however prominent his position in the early church, if he is outside
of the twelve apostles of the Lamb. They—the twelve—alone
received the keys; what they opened of the mysteries of the
kingdom of heaven remains open to us and to our children;
what they left closed will remain closed till the Lord comes.
It follows, also, that the idea of augmenting the sacred number
—twelve—of the apostles by the introduction of any man,
whether the brother of the Lord according to the flesh or other,
is without foundation in the New Testament. The case stands
thus: Our Lord chose twelve, from whom "Judas by transgression fell." In fact, Judas never entered on the work of an
apostle; but the Lord, who alone had the right and power, supplied his place by Paul. Suppose Matthias had been called on
to prove his apostleship as Paul was; to the best defence he
could have made his enemies could have replied: "That impulsive man, Peter, before the outpouring of the Spirit, while
there was not one particle more reason for believing that he
was inspired than when, on a previous occasion, he took his
Master and began to rebuke him—though right in feeling that
twelve was the requisite number to bear witness to the foundation facts of the gospel history, yet, so far as the record goes,
acting without divine warrant in undertaking to supply the deficiency—proposed one day that an apostle should be chosen.
Two men were set forth, and the lot fell on one of them, as it
must have done unless a miracle had been wrought to prevent
it." The apostleship of Barnabas and others could be similarly
disposed of. Twelve were chosen in the beginning; no more,
no less; and after all the sinful strife and turmoil of the world

has passed away and the New Jerusalem appears (Rev. xxi.), we find in her twelve foundations the names of the twelve apostles of the Lamb, which compels us to choose between the non-official use of the word *apostle* when applied, as it assuredly sometimes is, to others outside of the twelve, or to its poetical, meaningless use when seen on the foundations of the New Jerusalem

To sum up: We have found that the Book of Acts knows only two Jameses, both apostles, of the original twelve, one of these, by no possibility the son of Zebedee, therefore the son of Alpheus, called the Lord's brother ; therefore, beyond all con-tradiction, one of the quaternion of brothers mentioned by the two evangelists (Matt. xiii : 55, Mark vi : 3). He had a brother called Jude, and Jude the apostle had a brother called James; therefore the authors of the two apostolic epistles of James and Jude need not be looked for and cannot be found outside of the two apostle brothers who bear those names among the apostles and brothers of our Lord.

Hence, it follows that a James who, though not of "the twelve," yet because of his blood relation to the Lord, or for any other reason, was elevated to the episcopal seat in Jeru-salem before the destruction of the city by the Romans (about the year 70), is a myth, a creation of the imagination, for proof of whose existence it would be as vain to look on the pages of the New Testament as for the existence of Thor or Woden on the pages of Hume or Macaulay !

We have found that the number of apostles whom our Lord ordained in the beginning of his ministry was twelve; when one of these fell, the Lord Jesus filled the place in his own time and way, giving the new incumbent signs and seals of his appointment that no other man outside of the twelve ever possessed. And after the ministry of reconciliation has finished its work and the redeemed have all been gathered home to glory, walking in white on the golden streets under the shade of the trees of life, and by the fountains of living water that adorn the new Jerusalem, the number of apostles is still what our Lord appointed during his ministry on earth—only twelve. And we have found that three of the very few women who are mentioned as last at the cross and first at the sepul-chre were in all probability (1) Salome, our Lord's maternal aunt, and mother of the two apostles, John and James; (2) the wife of his supposed father's brother, Mary Cleophas, the mother of the two brother apostles, James and Jude ; and (3) the Magdalene, bound to her Saviour by no natural or common tie, but loving much because she had been much benefited.

And we have found that the Only Mediator is not only the Only Begotten, but the Only Son as well.

To return to the brother of the Lord, the apostle James, the son of Alpheus. He is said to have been quite old, between ninety and a hundred years of age, when he died, some time during the seventh decade of the first century of our era. His great age, which is said to be mentioned by Hegesippus, may be in part apocryphal. [As to the manner of his death the early accounts vary; but that it was violent there can scarcely be a doubt.] And we cannot but admire the mercy and justice of God in appointing this apostolic Hebrew of the Hebrews to preside over the early church at Jerusalem, who, by meeting Israel on their own ground, *i. e.*, the excellency of the law, should leave no effort untried to convince the nation as such that their only safety and glory could be found in the hearty service of their father's God, by faith in *Our Lord Jesus Christ, the Lamb of Glory !* We sympathize with the old, faithful servant of Jesus Christ in his loving, unintermittent, though often apparently hopeless labors for the benefit of his kindred according to the flesh. And we feel that he needed a sympathy more powerful than ours to sustain him, especially in his latter years, when he could not but see the signs of the coming storm; and question sometimes perhaps whether, after all, as " Israel would not be gathered," his life work had not been in vain. And we heave a sigh of relief and gratitude, not unmixed with envy, when, even at the blood-stained hands of the mob, enraged because he bore testimony to the divinity of Jesus the Son of God, his tears and toils were ended. And from the wearied, worn-out body, left all bleeding, bruised, ghastly, distorted, dishonored in the dust, James escaped to rest on the bosom of his cousin-brother, the Lord Jesus Christ our Saviour.

Art. VI.—THE INDUCTIVE SCIENCES OF NATURE AND THE BIBLE.

By Rev. E. R. Craven, D.D., Newark, N. J.

NATURE and the Bible are objects in the study of which the thoughtful minds of Christendom are, to a greater or less extent, engaged. Christians believe that both are the works (either mediately or immediately) of a personal God; multitudes who admit that Nature proceeds from such a Being deny that the Bible does so; others deny, or at least do not affirm, the existence of a personal Creator. Of those who, while they admit that Nature is the work of a personal Being, deny that the Bible also proceeds from him, there are many whose denial arises from what they regard as erroneous utterances of the first chapter of Genesis concerning the origin of Nature; and many who still profess to hold the Christian faith are, for the same supposed reason, either shaken in their belief as to the Divine origin of Scripture, or are disposed to regard the entire (so-called) Mosaic cosmogony as a myth. This article is written from the Christian standpoint, in full recognition of the doctrine of the inspiration of the Holy Scriptures, and in complete opposition to the alleged mythical character of the first portion thereof. One of the ends designed is to show that there is no vital contradiction between the established facts of Nature, and the established facts of Scripture.

It seems to be taken for granted by the opponents of the Divine origin of the Bible, that there cannot be an inductive science of that Book in all respects similar to the inductive sciences of Nature. On the contrary, we affirm, not merely that there may be such a science, but that to a certain degree it already exists.

Perhaps there is no term in the English language used in more variant though allied senses than the word *Science*. To this variance in use, often by the same writer and in the same paragraph, are largely due, in our judgment, much of the confusion that now exists in the public mind on the subject of science, and many of the conflicts between (so-called) science and (so-called) religion. Science properly means *knowledge*, which, in its highest sense, is possessed only by God. By common consent, however, it is used to designate human knowledge only, and not merely human knowledge, but such knowledge systematized and unified in accordance with the rules of right reason. This is, in substance, Webster's second or technical definition of the term, viz., "In *philosophy*, a collection of the general principles or leading truths relating to any subject, arranged in systematic order." It is, however, by multitudes subjected to the further restraint of designating only the inductive sciences, and by many of these to the still further restraint of designating only the inductive *physical* sciences. That the term is mainly used in the most restricted of the above senses by Dr. Draper, in his work entitled *Conflict between Religion and Science*, is manifest from the concluding paragraph of the first chapter. He writes (the italics are ours): " The Museum of Alexandria was thus the birthplace of modern science. It is true that, long before its establishment, astronomical observations had been made in China and Mesopotamia ; the mathematics also had been cultivated with a certain degree of success in India. But in none of these countries had investigation assumed a connected and consistent form ; in none was *physical* experimentation resorted to. The characteristic feature of Alexandrian, as of modern science, is, that it did not restrict itself to observation, but relied on a *practical interrogation of Nature.*"

The last mentioned restraint of the term, the effect of which is to produce largely in the popular mind the idea that Nature is the only field of science, is measurably due to the widespread influence of Whewell's *History of the Inductive Sciences*, and still more largely, we think, to the fact alluded to by him in what may be styled his apology for the misnomer of his work. He wrote in the preface to his first edition (italics his own): "To some it may appear that I am not justified in calling *that* a history of *the* inductive sciences which contains an account of the *physical* sciences only. . . And if there be branches of knowledge which regard morals or politics or the fine arts, and which may properly be called inductive (an opinion which I by no means gainsay), still it must be allowed, I think, that the processes of collecting general truths from assemblages of special facts, and of ascending from propositions

of a limited to those of a larger generality, which the term
induction peculiarly implies, have hitherto been more clearly
exhibited in the physical sciences which form the subject of the
present work, than in those hyperphysical sciences to which
I have not extended my history." The facts that the processes.
of induction have hitherto been more clearly manifested in the
realm of Nature than in any other field, and that they have
achieved their greatest triumphs therein, are freely admitted ;.
and, further, we believe that to these facts is due, mainly, and
in measure excusably, the restraint of the terms *science* and *in-*
ductive science to the inductive sciences of Nature. We cannot, however, admit the propriety of the restriction.

That the phrase *inductive science* is as properly applicable
in other fields as it is in Nature, will appear from a consideration of what inductive science implies, and what it is. It implies an object in which unapparent truths are concealed beneath phenomena with which they are connected—which
unapparent truths are discoverable through the study of the
individual or special phenomena. It is the result of a complex process of investigation, conducted on established principles of reason (the scientific process), which consists in, *first*,.
the careful observation of the phenomena of the object ;
secondly, the imagination (hypothesis) of a possible truth
which will give unity to the phenomena observed ; *thirdly*,
the deduction from the hypothesis of certain facts, which, if
the hypothesis be correct, must exist ; *fourthly*, the determination by investigation (in Nature, by physical experiment)
whether such facts do exist, resulting in, *fifthly*, the confirmation of the hypothesis, or its modification, or its total abandonment and the imagination of a new one ; *sixthly*, continued investigation by deduction and investigation (experiment), resulting, *finally*, in the establishment of some original or modified
hypothesis as a theory ;—the theory thus established, it should
be noted, may be itself but an elaborated hypothesis, liable to
be displaced by a more extended investigation.* In the use
of the inductive process, many positive facts are arrived at
which no subsequent investigation can overthrow, as, for in-

---

* The so-called *theory of gravitation* is now generally regarded as unsatisfactory,.
and will probably ere long be supplied by another more in accordance with the de--
mands of established facts.

stance, in astronomy, that the earth revolves around the sun; the highest possible reach of that process, however, is still more advanced *theory* until complete knowledge is attained. Now, the inductive science of any department of inquiry, at any given period, is the complex of knowledge, positive, theoretical and hypothetical, arrived at by the inductive process at that period.* Manifestly, such a science may exist in reference to any conceivable object, such as was above declared to be implied, "in which unapparent truths are concealed beneath phenomena with which they are connected—which unapparent truths are discoverable through the study of the phenomena." It matters not whether these phenomena be physical, as in Nature, or the words and phrases and figures of a Divinely inspired Book.

It should here be noted that the phenomena of the Bible, viz., words, phrases and verbal figures, may be as obscure as the phenomena of Nature. The most common terms are frequently the most ambiguous. The word *science*, for instance, as we have seen, is one of the most ambiguous terms in the English language. It is often a difficult problem to determine in what sense it is used in the writings of even such men as Herbert Spencer and Professor Huxley. And thus, manifestly, is it with some of the terms employed in the Scriptures. The Hebrew םוֹי (*yom*), translated *day* in Gen. i : 5 and ii : 4, has, like the term that translates it, several meanings; it indicates sometimes a period of twenty-four hours, sometimes the period of sunlight as distinguished from night, and sometimes a period of indefinite length. That it is used in the last of these senses in Gen. ii : 4 is manifest, for there it includes the *six creative* days of the first chapter. As to the meaning of the term in the first chapter, it is a problem for the inductive scientists of Scripture to solve. And, still further, a word having a fixed and definite meaning according to its derivation and in the mind of him who employed it in writing, a meaning discoverable through study of its derivation or the context (*i. e.*, through scientific investigation), may, through the ignorance, often unavoidable, of the reader, have an entirely errone-

---

*Such a science, manifestly, must be ever growing until it reaches completeness; it casts aside to-day as fallacy that which yesterday it set forth as theory, and will possibly adopt as theory to-morrow what to-day it ridicules as unfounded fancy. It is not *science* in the most absolute sense.

ous interpretation put upon it. Every student, in reading scientific works, has often placed upon terms meanings which, after further study, he has found to be erroneous ; and then, after still further investigation, he has discovered that the true, though obscure, meaning was etymologically correct. Such a term is רקיע (*rakkiah*) in Gen. i : 6. We do not wonder that the Septuagint translators, in the light of the apparent teaching of Nature, rendered it στερέωμα, and that the English translators, after the Vulgate, rendered it *firmament ;* the inductive science of Scripture, however, has shown that it properly means *expanse*, and now the Scripture scientist may meet with confidence the student of Nature, and affirm that if the nebular hypothesis of La Place be elevated to the dignity of a theory, it has been for ages casketed in that old Hebrew term. It seems here in place to remark that had Prof. Huxley recognized the fact of almost essential obscurity in the writings of inductive scientists of Nature—even of masters of language and inductive science—he would have foreborne uttering the sneer against the Bible : " A person who is not a Hebrew scholar can only stand by and admire the marvellous flexibility of a language which admits of such diverse interpretations."

Before proceeding further, it is proper to call attention to another concealed, and often confusing, ambiguity in the use of the term science or inductive science. By it may be indicated, and often *is* indicated on the same page without the distinction being noted, either *subjective* or *objective* science ; the former having respect to knowledge as it exists in the mind, the latter to a system reduced to writing and published for the information of others. It is specially in the former application of the term that it will be employed in this article.

It is, of course, legitimate for us to hypothesize the existence of a personal God, and that he is the author (immediately or mediately) of Nature and Scripture. Now if, upon this hypothesis, it can be shown (1) that it is rational to suppose there should be an inductive science of Scripture similar to that of Nature ; (2) that the preceding conclusion is measurably supported by facts ; (3) that the past and present postures of these (so-called) inductive sciences toward each other is that which is demanded by the hypothesis ; (4) that the advance of each has, in its publication, thrown light upon the other, causing therein, to a greater or less extent, a corresponding advance ; (5) that the tendency of both is toward unity ;—if these things can be shown, then certainly much has been done toward the establishment of the truth of the hypothesis that there is a personal God, the author of both Nature and Scripture, and its corollary that there should be an inductive science of Scripture. The effort will be made to establish (on the basis of the hypothesis) all the above mentioned points, although not in the exact order indicated.

Nature and Scripture differ in many respects, three of which will be specified as proper to the following discussion :

1. Knowledge is to be derived from Nature by the study of physical phenomena ; it is to be derived from Scripture by the study of discourse, as presented in words, phrases, verbal figures and symbols.

2. The knowledge to be derived from Nature has respect principally to man's physical necessities ; that to be derived from Scripture has respect principally (as alleged by theologians) to his spiritual needs.

3. Nature nowhere *directly declares* the existence of a personal Creator ;* Scripture begins with the assumption that such a Being exists.

Not only do Nature and Scripture differ in the foregoing respects, but they also resemble each other in two important particulars :

1. All of knowledge *essential to life* in the realm of either lies at or near the surface respectively of one and the other. In the realm of Nature it is patent to every intelligent observer what is essential to the support of *physical* life. The savage, as well as the sage, knows that fire will warm him, that corn will nourish, and that water will quench thirst. In Scripture it is equally apparent what is essential to *spiritual* life. It is a noticeable fact that, on the fundamentals of Christianity, all Christians, who regard the Scriptures as the only divinely inspired rule of faith and practice, agree.

2. Upon all subjects not *essential* to the ends specified, both Nature and Scripture are full of hidden truths. This is, con-

---

* We hold of course, that it *impliedly* declares it, in accordance with the teaching of Psalm xix.

fessedly by all, the case in the realm of Nature, and that it is so in the realm of Scripture is acknowledged by all students of the Bible, and is made manifest by the differing opinions of confessedly honest and able students of the Word of God in matters admitted to be non-essential.

It should also be remarked, as involving both a resemblance and a difference between Nature and Scripture, that, within certain narrow limits, and within those limits only, both occupy a common field. Nature, according to theologians and many inductive scientists of Nature, implies under its phenomena, to a certain extent, religious truth ; and Scripture, confessedly by all, contains a brief account of the origin of Nature.

It is manifest that it is the fact of the existence of hidden truths in the realm of Nature that affords ground for the exist- ence of an inductive science of Nature—*i. e.,* the continual advance in knowledge of the hidden truths that underlie apparent phenomena by rational observation and investigation. Were nothing *hidden* there could be no *search.* And further, it is held by many inductive scientists of Nature that the concealment of truths under phenomena was designed by the intelligent Creator to meet the demands of man's nature for continual increase of knowledge, and also by exercise in patient investigation to develop his intellectual powers. That such development is the result of such investigation no one can deny. The search after truth is the most potent means of intellectual growth. Upon the hypothesis of an intelligent Creator (which is the hypothesis on which we are now proceeding) the opinion that such a result was designed is most rational. On the one hand we have a being capable of unlimited development, and on the other we have not only an unlimited, but an attractive, gymnasium to give him that development.

Now, upon the supposition that the Bible also is from God, it is but rational to conclude that it also will contain, under the phenomena of *words,* hidden truths ; and especially is it rational to conclude that that portion which contains an account of the origin and development of Nature will contain such hidden truths. It cannot be supposed that an intelligent God would spread out before man in Nature a field of mystery, in order to his attraction unto study and his development thereby, and at the same time place in his hand a book which, by clearly explaining the mysteries of Nature, should preclude the developing study. And here is to be found the explanation of that much misunderstood and misapplied, but, in a right sense true, saying, "The Bible was not given to teach men science." It was not given as a text-book of completed science, and far less as a text-book of any one stage of the ever-advancing inductive science of Nature. And still further is it rational to conclude that that portion of the Word of God which speaks of the origin and development of mystery-embosoming Nature should itself contain mysteries; that, in the similarity of workmanship and in the light of their harmony as the mysteries of each should be unraveled, evidence should be given to his intelligent creatures that both proceeded from one all-wise and beneficent Creator.

It is but rational to suppose that if Nature and Scripture are placed before the observation of man by the same personal God, while all that is *essential* to the physical and spiritual life of man will lie on the surface respectively of one and the other, there will be in Scripture, as in Nature, those hidden truths which will not only afford ground for, but demand, an inductive science of Scripture similar to that of Nature. Thus rational considerations lead us to suspect what becomes evident upon investigation—that there are hidden truths in the written Word of God as well as in his physical kosmos. Possibly in both Nature and Scripture there are masses of undeveloped truth hidden under phenomena, physical or verbal, to which all that has been brought to light bears as slight a proportion as does the exhumed coal bear to that which lies unmined in its native beds. We as little believe that the Westminster Assembly of Divines formulated all of Scriptural truth as that Copernicus systematized all of natural truth included within the field of his gigantic researches. In the declaration that there are hidden truths in the Bible no new theological doctrine is announced. The Church in all ages has acknowledged it; her creeds and confessions, elaborated, modified and extended in successive periods of her history, are the manifestation of her acknowledgment. More than two hundred years ago the great pastor of the Pilgrim Fathers declared, just before the embarkation on the Speedwell, that "he was very confident that the Lord had more truth and light to break forth out of his holy Word." Doubtless it was in recognition of this truth that the Great Master exhorted his disciples, "*Search* (examine, investigate) the Scriptures."

It should here be remarked that the inductive scientist of Nature does not regard it as a slur upon Nature—as manifesting that she could not have come from the hand of a personal God, or that she is unworthy of notice—that he reads her teachings differently, in some points, from the inductive scientists of a former age. Why then should a similar fact in reference to the past and present interpretations of the Bible prove that it is not from God or that it is unworthy of notice? In connection with the foregoing, it should be carefully noted that the Latin, French, German and English *versions* of the Scriptures are not the Scriptures. Every version is to a large extent a commentary; it presents the translator's interpretation of the Scripture. No more is the English version the Bible itself than was the Ptolemaic interpretation of Nature Nature itself.* Had Prof. Huxley recognized this fact he would not, in his recent lectures in New York, have made as a point against the Bible that the word *whales* occurs in the account of the fifth period or day of creation (Gen. i : 21). Had he been acquainted with Hebrew, of which language he confessed his ignorance, he would have known that the Hebrew תנגים (*tanninim*), translated *whales*, means properly *sea-monsters.*

It should now be remarked, and also be carefully noted by the reader, that naturally the portion of Scripture that would be last subjected to scientific investigation by theologians is the account of the origin of Nature. This forms but the portico to the great work which the inductive scientist of Scripture has to study. His main duty is to investigate those portions which immediately relate to man's condition, duty and destiny. Beyond the bare statements that God created the world, and that he created man in his own image, the first chapter of

---

* This remark has reference to identity of substance, not to comparative correctness of representation (or interpretation). It is in recognition of the fact set forth above that the Westminster Confession of Faith declares (Chap. I. Art. 8) " The Old Testament in Hebrew (which was the native language of the people of God of old,) and the New Testament in Greek (which at the time of the writing of it was the most generally known to the nations), being immediately inspired of God, and by his singular care and providence kept pure in all ages, are therefore authentical; so, as in all controversies of religion, the Church is finally to appeal unto them."

Genesis has no primary interest for theologians *as theologians*. It was perfectly natural that their attention should not be specially directed to it, until the progress of the inductive science of Nature had rendered it probable that the popular interpretation of that chapter was erroneous; and, when their attention was called, it was perfectly natural that the old interpretations, which had for ages been embalmed in systems of theology, should be reluctantly abandoned. It has been remarked that no man in England over thirty years of age adopted the conclusions of Newton's *Principia* on the first publication of that great work; certainly but few adopted them. The general diffusion of a newly promulgated theory of physical inductive science is not so much in the minds of the leading existent scientists as in those of the uprising generation. Is it strange that a similar state of things should exist on the first promulgation of a new conclusion of inductive scriptural science? Here, however, it is proper to call attention to the fact that the first promulgation of the idea that the processes of creation (or, as it may be styled, kosmical development) occupied immense periods of time was by the great Augustine, an inductive Scriptural scientist of the fifth century, as the result of his study of the first chapter of Genesis.* Augustine, however, was, in many respects, a man before his time; his conclusion seems to have effected no change in the views of his contemporaries, and it remained for the inductive scientists of Nature to incite the inductive scientists of Scripture to investigations in what was to the latter an outlying field.

It is but natural, as appears from the consideration presented above, that in the field common to Nature and Scripture, so far as the origin of Nature is concerned, the main and inciting advance of scientific research should be made by inductive physical scientists. There is another reason for this which should be mentioned. The great object of the theologian is to act upon the *popular* mind in reference to spiritual things. Not only to him as a *theologian* and to the people, is it of no mo-

---

* *De Genesi ad Literam*, Lib. ii : ch. 14; *Contra Manichaos*, and *De Civitate*, referred to by Prof. Tayler Lewis in his " Special Introduction to the First Chapter of Genesis," in the American edition of *Lange on Genesis*, p. 131. We are under the impression that Origen, in the end of the *second* or beginning of the *third* century, preceded Augustine in the publication of this idea. We have been unable, however, to verify the fact.

ment whether the universe was created and developed in six natural days, or in six indefinite periods, but the mooting of that question in the pulpit, unless forced upon him in the defense of the inspiration of the Scripture, would accomplish evil rather than good. He would naturally and properly turn aside to the study and presentation of other topics.

But the progress of the inductive science of Nature did force this study upon theologians, and the result was, not merely an increased knowledge of the hidden truths of the Word of God, but a beneficial reaction upon the study of Nature. More than seventy years ago Dr. Chalmers, then a young man, made the following utterance in a lecture at St. Andrew's: " There is a prejudice against the speculations of the geologist which I am anxious to remove. It has been said that they nurture infidel propensities. It has been alleged that geology, by referring the origin of the globe to a higher antiquity than is assigned to it by the writings of Moses, undermines our faith in the inspiration of the Bible and in all the animating prospects of the immortality which it unfolds. This is a false alarm. *The writings of Moses do not fix the antiquity of the globe.*" Other distinguished students both of Scripture and of Nature came to the same conclusion, so that Hugh Miller, not himself inferior to any whom he mentioned, declared fifty years later[*]: " Even in this late age, when the scientific standing of geology is all but universally recognized, and the vast periods of time which it demands fully conceded, neither geologist nor theologian could, in any new scheme of reconciliation, shape his first proposition more skilfully than it was shaped by Chalmers a full half century ago. It has formed since that time the preliminary proposition of those ornaments of at once Science and the English Church, the present venerable Archbishop of Canterbury, Dr. Bird Sumner, with Drs. Buckland, Conybeare, and Prof. Sedgwick; of eminent evangelistic Dissenters, too, such as the late Dr. Pye Smith, Dr. John Harris, Dr. Robert Vaughn, Dr. James Hamilton and the Rev. Mr. Binney—enlightened and distinguished men, who all came early to the conclusion, with the lecturer of St. Andrew's, that ' the writings of Moses do not fix the antiquity of the globe.' " It is beyond question that these men, who were among the

---

[*] Testimony of the Rocks, Lect. III.

most efficient workers, in their day, in the upbuilding of the
inductive science of geology, preparing the way for further advance, were both beneficially restrained and directed by their
study of the Divine Word. A similar beneficial reaction might
be shown to have taken place in other fields of Nature, especially in astronomy, did space permit. In the hyper-physical
inductive sciences, however, of psychology, morals, law, ethnology, history, philology, the influence of the study of the
Scriptures has been most widely and beneficially felt.

There is still another important fact to be considered, namely,
that the independent investigations of the inductive scientists
of Nature and Scripture begin not merely at different, but at
opposite standpoints. The student of Nature (the completed
work) labors *ab extra ad intra*, from the circumference, so to
speak, to the centre; the student of the book of Genesis (the
description of the formation of the work) labors *ab intra ad extra*,
from the centre to the circumference. The final results of their
completed studies may perfectly agree; the first results of independent studies must necessarily be variant and opposed. Were
the inventor and manufacturer of some strange instrument to
place in the hands of two equally intelligent men for study—in
those of one the instrument, and in those of the other a brief description of the mode of its manufacture;—in the first conclusions of these students there would be variance of opinion as to
the construction and use of the machine. Years might elapse
before they would arrive at unity in judgment; probably
never would they so arrive, if neither consulted the other.
Such differences would exist as now exist between those students of the Bible who refuse to consider the conclusions of
the students of Nature, and those students of Nature who refuse to consider the conclusions of the students of the Bible.
If the one to whom was committed the description should also
study the instrument, whilst the other should persistently refuse
to look at the description, differences would still exist, though
in a less degree—such differences as now exist between the
more liberal inductive scientists of Scripture who recognize that
an inductive science of Nature does exist, and mere inductive
scientists of Nature who refuse to seriously examine the Bible,
denying its Divine origin because, in their judgment, it does
not, at first glance, support in all respects what they regard as

the established facts of Science.*   The existing differences are precisely what might be expected (on the hypothesis that both Nature and Scripture come from God) between the mere inductive scientists of Nature who deny the Divine origin of the Bible, and those students of Nature and the Bible who admit that both are the workmanship of God.

But while there are still differences between the apparent teachings of Nature and the Bible, as interpreted by the inductive scientists of each, a wonderful harmony has already been made manifest in the reaction of one inductive science upon the other.   Both Nature and Scripture seem to agree in teaching the truth of what is known as the nebular hypothesis; that the work of forming the existing kosmos was carried on throughout several immense periods of time; that light was first evolved from chaos through motion; that the separation of the sun and stars as " light-holders" was not in one of the first periods of development; that the order of appearance of fish, reptiles and mammalia, as set forth in the first chapter of Genesis, is substantially correct; that man was the last created (or developed) of the mammalia.   Many other harmonies might be mentioned.   All *apparent* differences between the books of Nature and Scripture are not yet reconciled, and that for the sufficient reason that the inductive scientists of Nature and Scripture have not yet reached their goal.

The tendencies of both inductive sciences, however, are toward still greater harmony.   May we be permitted to forecast two or three probable future coincidences?

The trend of the inductive science of Nature is toward the theory that what we now call *elements* are but modifications of one primal substance.†   We have long believed this to be a truth set forth in what we regard as a mistranslated word in Gen. i: 2, viz., בֹהוּ (*bohn*), translated *void*.   The whole passage, as it seems to us, should be translated: " The earth (there, *the material universe*) was formless and *pure* (or *simple*)."   The term is derived from the obsolete root בהחי (*bahah*), defined by Gesenius as probably, *to be clean, pure.*

---

* As well might we reject Nature as veracious because, at first glance, she seems to declare that the sun revolves around the earth.

† See *Popular Science Monthly*, Feb. 1876, p. 463.

The pureness, uncompoundedness, homogeneousness, of the primitive mass is, we think, referred to.

Again, inductive scientists of Nature are now divided into what are styled evolutionists and catastrophists—the present trend being toward the adoption of the doctrine of evolutionism (or development). In the *status* of the existing controversy, we are reminded of the old struggle between the Neptunians and the Plutonians. · The result of that struggle was the establishment, within limits, of the probable truth of both hypotheses. Such, it seems to us in the light of God's Word, will be the result of the present controversy. Within limits, we ourselves hold the doctrine of development, upon what seems to us Scriptural and natural foundations; but, upon the same grounds also, we hold the doctrine of catastrophe. The march of Nature has not been in one unbroken development. In the beginning there must have been a catastrophe which began development, and the book of Nature seems to us to teach that, like the setting and rising of the sun, there have been a series of catastrophes, ending the old and beginning the new light and life periods. In the end, as it seems to us, the inductive scientists of Nature will agree with those of Scripture in declaring that the evenings and mornings formed the days of development; and, further still, that the days of natural *development* were six, followed by a *resting* period, the seventh—the day that now is.

And yet again, inductive scientists of Nature look forward to the time when the existing light and life period shall cease to be. Scripture long ago foretold, ere modern (so-called) science had existence, that the existing heavens and earth shall pass away; and still further, that the coming night shall be followed by another morning, that from the bosom of the new chaos shall arise another kosmos—even the new heavens and the new earth wherein shall dwell righteousness.

In conclusion we would remark,

1. For obvious reasons this discussion has contemplated only those portions of Scripture which treat of the origin, development, and final destruction of the existing kosmos. It can hardly be denied that the facts set forth (not including, of course, our own forecastings) are true, and that they are in strict accord with the hypothesis that there is a personal God,

the author of both Nature and those portions of the Bible that have been referred to. We will now ask if any other hypothesis can be imagined that will satisfy the demand of the facts?

2. The discussion brings prominently to view another concatenation of facts, which not only supports but demands the hypothesis of a personal Creator and Author, and its corollary that there must be an inductive science of Scripture.

The book of Genesis is confessedly one of the oldest in existence. It was gray with antiquity long before the Museum of Alexandria, which Dr. Draper declares to have been "the birthplace of modern science," was dreamed of. Of all the ancient cosmogonies it alone continues to hold the respect of any of the learned. The modern rigid and concurrent criticisms of Nature and the Book have but served to bring out unimagined harmonies between them. Far more accurately does the first chapter of Genesis represent the established conclusions of the inductive science of Nature of the present day, than do the writings of (so-called) scientists—in astronomy before La Place, and in geology before the present century. Whence came that Book, written in the unscientific period of human history, which is so analagous to Nature in its embosoming, and so concealing unessential truths under apparent phenomena, and which is the verbal counterpart of Nature in the character of the truths which it embosoms?

3. Whilst this article has respect to the inductive science of Scripture in reference to one of the fields common to Nature and Scripture, it is not to be supposed that the researches of the inductive scientist of the Bible are confined to that field. Scripture, in its theology, anthropology, ethnology, history, ecclesiology, prophecy, spreads out before its students, as before hinted, fields as broad and rich in as yet hidden truths as are the natural fields of astronomy, geology, physics, chemistry and biology. In continuance and limitation of this remark, it should be said that there is as little danger that the surface facts of Scripture, those that are essential to spiritual life, will be shown to be false by scientific investigation, as that such investigation in the realm of Nature will ever show that water and corn are not the essential elements of physical nourishment, that arsenic does not destroy life, and that fire does not warm.

4. Between inductive science (Natural or Scriptural) and religion, *properly* so called (*i. e.*, the activity of the human soul in reference to God), *conflict* can no more exist than between such science and the activity of mind and body in reference to Nature.   Between inductive science and religion, *improperly* so called (*i. e.*, a human systematization of supposed Scriptural truth), there is no more *conflict* than between the natural inductive science of the present age and the objective systems put forth by the natural inductive scientists of a former age. In the accepted systems, both of Biblical and Natural (supposed) truths, there are grand surface doctrines, comprising all that it is necessary man should know in the realm of either, — doctrines, as declared in the preceding paragraph, that no investigation can overthrow ; in both, there are hypotheses concerning embosomed truths—the knowledge of which *truths* is interesting, essential to the completeness of knowledge, more or less important it may be, but not essential to either physical or spiritual life—some of which *hypotheses*, doubtless, will be modified while others will be overthrown.   The march of the inductive sciences of both Nature and the Bible will ever be, like the curve of the hyperbola toward its unchanging asymptote, toward SCIENCE, rightly so called, *i. e.*, completeness of knowledge.

Art. VII.—THE BRAHMO SOMAJ.*

By REV. A. BROADHEAD, D.D., Allahabad, India.

IT may be questioned whether the Brahmist movement in India has assumed sufficiently definite proportions to enable one to form a correct judgment as to its value. It is certain, however, that it may be regarded as a permanent quality among the forces that are to act upon the Hindu mind and assist in determining the form of religious development in the Indian Empire. As yet the area in which the influence of this new religion is felt is limited. It had its origin in Bengal, and for the most part its progress thus far has been confined to that province. The word *Somaj* may be taken as the equivalent for our word Church, used in its generic sense. There are, probably, not more than one hundred individual Brahmo churches—or Somajes, to form from the word an English plural—throughout India, and none of these have a very large membership. The intensely conservative nature of the people of India, which manifests itself not more in their unwillingness to forsake the manners and customs of their forefathers than in their antipathy to any change in their religious views, leads to the belief that a rapid extension is not to be expected for Brahmism or any other system which differs radically from that which has been so long cherished by the Hindus.

The person of greatest prominence at present connected with this departure from the orthodox Hindu faith, is Bábú Keshab Chandra Sen. Although he is not to be regarded as the originator of the movement, he, perhaps, more than any other, has given it an impetus; and it is probably true that its destiny for good or evil is within his control, since much, if not all, of its vitality is due to his personal magnetism. Although it is less than fifty years since Brahmism claimed any place among the religions of India, nevertheless it bears the impress of three leading minds. First among these stands Rájah Rám Mohan Roy, to whom must be accorded the merit of breaking with his caste-fellows and announcing a creed, the mere statement of which raised an insuperable barrier between him and the vast

---

* *The Brahmo Somaj.* Rev. Dr. Jardine, Allahabad Conference, 1872.
Indian Evangelical Review, October, 1875.

majority of his countrymen.   Rám Mohan Roy was a man of considerable culture, having acquaintance with the literature of the West, as well as with that of his own country.   There can be no doubt that he was assisted to the position he was enabled to take, not only by the study of writers of the Unitarian school of belief, but by his familiarity with much of the ortho- dox literature which came into his hands in his own country and in England ; and doubtless he was an interested student of the Bible during the latter part of his life.   Dr. Jardine, speak- ing of a publication of the Rájah's entitled "The Precepts of Jesus," says that it is evident that the writer looked upon the teachings of Christ as being the supreme guide to life eternal.

The first Brahmo Somaj was organized in Calcutta in 1830, three years before the death of Rám Mohan Roy.   The word Brahmo, if chosen with any reference to its derivation, seems to be an unfortunate one, and subjects those who bear the designation to the charge of cowardice in adopting for them- selves a name which, if it has any significance, conveys an idea which is repudiated by the adherents to this new faith. At the Allahabad Conference the late Dr. Wilson of Bombay, than whom no one was better fitted to pronounce upon this subject, passed some severe strictures upon these religionists for adopting the word Brahmo, which, he stated, was used in the Hindu-pantheistic philosophy to denote the deity viewed as the sole existence.   This doctrine, although rejected by the Brahmos of the present day, seems to have found some favor with Rám Mohan Roy, who quotes from the Upanishods and other Vedantic writings such passages as the following : "A wise man knowing God as perspicuously residing in all creatures, forsakes all idea of duality ; being convinced that there is only one real existence, which is God."   "The Veda (Védánta) says all that exists is indeed God."   "The soul is a portion of the Supreme Ruler: the relation is not that of mas- ter and servant—ruler and ruled—but is that of whole and part."   Since the Brahmos have fully adopted the Theistic idea, it certainly seems as though they might have chosen a designation less encumbered with pantheistic notions.

Rám Mohan Roy did not seem ambitious to form a sect, and it was reserved for Debendranath Tajore, and after him Keshab Chandra Sen, to give the movement a permanent shape.   Previous to the advent of Debendranath Tajore in 1839, the accessions to the new church had not been numerous; perhaps the larger number of disciples were obtained from among the graduates of the Government schools, the tendency of whose curriculum was to destroy their ancient faith without supplying any other in its stead. The influence exerted by the new leader was in the direction of conservatism and an exaltation of the Hindu shastras, rather than in the taking of any radical positions or showing the superiority of evangelical truth over the errors of the Hindu system. In the year 1857 Keshab Chandra Sen joined the Brahmos. He early began to show adaptation as a leader of men, and since the tendency of his mind was progressive, it was not long before he found himself at the head of a party within the church which was opposed to the tardy methods of the then leader of the Somaj. If we examine the sources from which the three guiding minds among the Brahmos appear to have drawn their inspiration, we shall find that Rám Mohan Roy had been led to drink largely at the fountain of divine truth. Debendranath Tajore, on the other hand, adhered with great tenacity to the sacred books of the Hindus, and clung to as much of the ancestral faith as was consistent with his somewhat advanced views, while Keshab Chandra Sen evidently pursued an eclectic course ; for while he fails to grasp the distinguishing truths of the gospel and denies the inspiration of the Scriptures, rejecting altogether the idea that God communicates his will to men by means of a written revelation, nevertheless he emphasizes the two great truths, of the fatherhood of God and the brotherhood of man—truths which could have been revealed to him by the Bible alone, and which cut at the root of polytheism and caste, the twin supports of the fabric of Hinduism.

Keshab Chandra Sen, in his attempt to dissever himself and his co-religionists more entirely from the Hindu faith, which, he contends, differs from the facts of the Vedas, advanced three propositions, and the defense of these, especially the first of the three, finally led to the separation of the Brahmo Church into two sections ; that adhered to by Debendranath Tajore and the more conservative portion of the Brahmos, taking the name of the Adi (original) Somaj, and that of which Keshab Chandra Sen espoused the leadership, being called the Brahmo Somaj of India.

The three propositions announced by Keshab Chandra Sen are as follows :

1. That the external signs of caste distinctions—such as the brahminical thread—should not be used.

2. That none but Brahmos of sufficient ability and good moral character, who lived consistently with their profession, should be allowed to conduct the services of the Somaj.

3. That nothing should be said in the Somaj expressive of hatred or contempt for other religions.

The struggle between the two parties in the Somaj has proved rather an unequal one, and whether due, as before remarked, to the personal influence of Keshab Chandra Sen, or to the fact that his position was a rebound from the stiff, stern, orthodox Hinduism as it had come down through the ages, it is certain that the conservative school rapidly lost ground, and the progressives everywhere are in the ascendant.

It was natural that Evangelical Christendom should regard such a movement as this with great interest, and it may be admitted that possibly too much was expected from this departure from a system which had remained intact for centuries. But Keshab Chandra Sen disappointed the hopes of those who, standing on the advanced posts of Christendom, noted with eagerness everything that might indicate weakness in any part of the enemy's stronghold. In an essay entitled " Jesus Christ : Europe and Asia," delivered in 1866, the Babu took advanced ground in favor of Christianity and its founders, but, as though fearful that he had gone too far, he seized an early occasion to recall some of his more advanced positions, and in his estimate of Christ was careful to give him a place no higher than that of the most perfect among creatures. A few extracts from the writings of the. reformer are given. From these it will be apparent that, while having a confused and very imperfect idea of the way of salvation, he is indebted to the Bible for many of the terms which he employs.

1. " Whether we look up to the heavens, or whether we look round to the various objects lying scattered on the amplitudes of nature, every object tells us that the Creator of the universe is one; all historic life, all creation tells us that He who 'guides the universe and the destinies of nations is One and Infinite." (K. C. Sen's English Visit, p. 552.)

2. "To believe in the Fatherhood of God is to believe in the brotherhood of man ; and whoever, therefore, in his own heart and in his own house, worships the true God daily, must learn to recognize all his fellow-countrymen as brethren.   Declare a crusade against idolatry and   . . .   the very sight of that will drive caste to desperation." (Lectures and Tracts by K. C. Sen, p. 211.)

3. "If every individual were to realize this great fact, and feel that God is near to him as *his* Father, while as the Universal Father he looks to the grand purpose of the universe as a whole, then, but not till then, would religion be a source of comfort on the one hand and of purity on the other." (English Visit, p. 164.)

4. "There is something in the Bible which has staggered many who stand outside the pale of orthodox Christianity and made them inimical to Christ ; I mean his sublime egotism and self-assertion.   It is true Christ says, ' Love God and love man, and ye shall have everlasting life;' but does He not also say, ' I am the way, I am the light of the world ?' Does He not say, ' Come unto *me*, all ye that are weary and heavy laden, and *I* will give you rest ?' He who said that the only way to eternal life is the love of God and the love of man, also says, ' *I* am the way.' Jesus Christ, then, truly analyzed, means, love of God and love of man." (*Ibid*, p. 240.)

5. "It would be an insult to the majesty of God's throne—it would be a blasphemy against Divine mercy, to say that He will wrathfully condemn any sinners to eternal perdition." (*Ibid*, p. 175.)

6. "If we pray in a humble spirit, if we kneel down and open up the depths of our hearts, our longings, our sorrows, our afflictions, unto the One Living God, He who is plenteous in mercy will hear us and grant our prayers." (*Ibid*, p. 68.)

7. "In the religion of the world man is his own guide, and to a great extent, his own Saviour.   He depends upon his own faculties and powers for the attainment of truth, and for deliverance from sin.   Its prayer is, that man's will may be done on earth in the name of God. (In the religion of heaven) God's will is absolute and immutable law, and his judgment final and irreversible." (Lectures and Tracts, p. 100.)

8. "True penitence humbles man to the dust, and makes

him put his entire trust in the Lord for the purpose of salvation. As such, repentance is essential to faith; for not till man's proud head is humbled down under an overpowering sense of his own unworthiness would he cling to God's feet—not till he distrusts himself would he trust the redeeming and all-sufficient grace of God. Repentance begins the good work of conversion, which faith and prayer carry on. By opening the eyes of the sinner to his iniquities, it fosters a longing for deliverance; faith and prayer act as guides, and safely lead the penitent sinner unto the kingdom of heaven, where he is regenerated by divine grace." (Lectures and Tracts, p. 116.)

As before remarked, the Brahmos reject the idea of a written revelation. This position seems to have been taken when the disciples of this School were forced to yield their belief in the divine origion of the Vedas, this being held by their founder Rám Mohan Roy.

In one sense the Brahmos may be regarded as the Protestants of India. They protest against polytheism, against idolatry, against caste, and preëminently against pantheism, which enters so largely into the Hindu systems of belief—a dreadful creed, as one remarks, that has eaten out the heart and soul of India. Besides this, the Brahmos regard with much concern the dissemination throughout India of works tending to undermine any and all faith. Speaking of positivism, Keshab Chandra Sen remarks: "This alone was wanting to complete the miseries of my country." Nor are the Brahmos backward in pressing social reforms. They have adopted advanced ideas with reference to the re-marriage of widows, they would greatly extend the opportunity for the education of females, and strenuously insist upon the abandonment of many of the evil social practices so rife in India.

But after all that may be said in favor of this new religion, the consideration of it can leave only a feeling of sadness in the minds of those who long for the day when the peoples of India shall accept Christ in his fulness. The most that can be said of this faith is, that it despises one which, so long as held, kept the soul at an infinite distance from Him who alone can save. But in this reform there is far more of human than of divine wisdom. The merit upon which it rests is that of the sinner, rather than that of the Saviour; it anchors the soul upon itself rather than upon Christ, and in its pride it says: We will not have this man to rule over us. If it has a destiny to work out, we can only hope that it may speedily yield its present beliefs, and, rejecting its "intuitions," cling alone to Him who is the Life and the Light of men.

Art. VIII.—FAITH AND TRUST.
By Prof. Edward A. Lawrence.

WHAT do these words mean? Are they synonymes or are they moral opposites? A sermon by a popular evangelical Boston minister expresses regret that "trust in Christ was being substituted for faith in Christ." It had been announced as "not a close secret" that the intelligent Christian people of Boston, "even those who are classed as evangelical, have followed with much concern the development of the plan of salvation presented and explained by Mr. Moody at the Tabernacle meetings;" and that the discourse was prepared "with special reference" to what the preacher "regards as some of the misleading utterances" of the evangelist. And it has passed into history as one of the marked features of events in connection with Mr. Moody's labors, and the remarkable work of God in Boston. It protests "against the error that trusting, simple reliance on and confidence in the goodness of another, and the love of another, without personally imitating that goodness and being born into the same love, could save men." The only idea which the word trust symbolizes is that "of repose"—simple, "babe-like, inactive, unenergetic dependence;" of "an eaglet carried on its mother's back, without motion or thought on its part—with only the capacity to lie still, enjoy and be carried." The eaglet may enjoy lying still and being carried, but it is strange that such a babe-like, thoughtless, careless dependence could be mistaken for Christian trust, though only those who "become as little children" can enter into the kingdom of heaven. And it is certain that Mr. Moody has no such conception, and no desire to

> "be *carried* to the skies
> On flowery beds of ease."

In a graphic picture of this imputed impotence and laziness
of trust, the sermon represents that the word has " no *wings*"
and "no *legs*." But Isaiah says that the trusters who " wait upon
the Lord" have both, and that "they shall mount up with
wings as eagles, shall run and not be weary, shall walk and not
faint." It says that trust "never does anything and never
wants to do anything, any more than love wants to move or
act when at rest on the bosom of infinite supply and infinite
contentment, and finds its heaven in simply lying there." But
is love, too, a mere nerveless, selfish passivity, that finds its
heaven in a lazy, luxurious lounging on the bosom of supply?
Those are infelicitous figures of speech, and that mischievous
rhetoric which so discredits these Christian graces. The only
evidence of love is obedience; and of trust, energetic, holy action where it is in place. " If a man love me," he will keep
my words. And respecting the truster, Jeremiah exclaims:
" Blessed is the man that trusteth in the Lord: he shall be as a
tree planted by the waters, that spreadeth out her roots by
the river: her leaf shall be *green*, neither shall it cease from
bearing *fruit*."

The discourse contains a somewhat elaborate philological
argument to prove the essential *unlikeness* of faith and trust.
The two words " have no similitude," and " differ in their parentage." One comes " from the Latin tongue, the other from
the old Norse language." They "are not twins," and " you
cannot put one into the cradle of the other without fraud."
There is such " a world-wide distinction between them" that
Jesus never used the word *trust* " but three times in his life."
" It is only used in the Gospels three times," "in all the rest
of the New Testament only sixteen times;" Cruden mentions
its use thirty-one times. On the other hand, *faith* is employed
as a noun " in the New Testament over two hundred times;"
and *believe* is found eighty-six times, the past form *believed*
" sixty-five times," and *believeth* " thirty-two times," while in
the Old Testament the verb *beleved* occurs " but eleven times,"
and *believeth* " but three times." This critical elucidation is
made that it might be seen " how weak is the emphasis put
upon the word *trust* in the Word of God."

This argument from philology would be more satisfactory if
it rested on the *original* of the Old and New Testament instead

of the translation. The preacher says: "We are orthodox enough to stand squarely on the texts of the Scriptures, and we don't think there can be any improvement of the text in the Tabernacle or anywhere else." But what is the text of the Scriptures? Is it the English version, admirable as it is, or the German of Martin Luther, or the Latin of Jerome? No; but that written in the Hebrew and Greek under the influence of the Divine Spirit. Properly speaking, Jesus did not make use of the word *trust* or *faith* once in his life; nor did the evangelists or the apostles. None of the words which they employed descended from the Latin or Norse stock, but, with few exceptions, all belonged to the opulent and classic Greek family.

It is true the word *faith* has a Latin parentage, and *trust* a Norse, but how does this prove dissimilitude of signifi-, cance? Faith is the softened form *fiducia*, the meaning of which Andrews in his lexicon gives as " trust, confidence, reliance"; and *fiducia* and *fides* come from the verb *fido*, which the same authority defines—" to trust, confide, place confidence in a person or thing." Still further, the lexicographer says that *fido* is the softened form of the Greek verb πειθο, which in its intransitive use signifies " to trust, to confide in." The Greek noun which in the New Testament is rendered into English by the translators over two hundred times by the word *faith*, is πιστις, which, according to Liddell and Scott, means " trust in others, faith," and by Robinson is defined as "faith, belief, trust." The word used by Jesus in opening to Nicodemus the way of salvation through faith is πιστεύω, the meaning of which Liddell and Scott give as "to believe, to trust in." Passing from the New Testament to the Old, there is found the same law of language and unity of thought. בָּטַח, the Hebrew verb, Gesensius renders " to trust, to confide, to place hope or confidence in any one"; and the noun בֶּטַח, means trust, confidence. And Isaiah, in the spirit of the saints of both Testaments, exclaims: " Behold, God is my salvation; I will trust in him and not be afraid."

Instead, therefore, of faith and trust being " world-wide apart " in natural significance, " they lie close together, if indeed they are not identical in these Hebrew and Greek words which the Old Testament writers employed in foreshadowing

Christ and the apostles in announcing the great, glad tidings, and the word faith, by the law of inheritance, through its double Latin and Greek lineage, is brimful of the life of trust." It is " a muscular word," the sermon says ; " it suggests man's power and the use of his power." Its " first significance is reliance on testimony." But just this is the root-thought of *trust.* It relies implicitly on the testimony of " the Faithful and True Witness." After having examined the records of his life and been satisfied with the evidence of his sufficiency as a Saviour, it uses its power in trusting *to* him all man has to give, and in trusting *in* him for remission of sins, illumination, repentance, and all the soul needs to *receive* from him in order to the complete salvation. Yet, with an earnestness that looks like alarm, the sermon appeals to Christians, " by every consideration of safety, to protest against the dropping of this strong, energetic, holy, adequate and efficient term by religious teachers when addressing the impenitent," and against " the substitution in its place of a weak, nerveless, inadequate term which Jesus himself never used, his apostles never used, the teachers of the church have never used, and which has scarcely a mention in the Bible." To many who listened to the teachings of the Tabernacle or carefully perused the reported sermons delivered there, and who recall how constant was the use of the energetic term and how comparatively infrequent, except in a single sermon " On Trust," was the nerveless one, this note of alarm will appear not only groundless, but as exciting unjust suspicions against one who has drawn to the cross during the last two or three years masses of the English-speaking people as no other one has for a century. In the sermon on " Free Grace," the word faith appears seven times in the space of twenty-four lines, in explaining the plan of salvation in the case of the centurion, and *trust* does not once occur in the whole discourse.

In his zeal for the orthodoxy of faith, the preacher affirms that " historical faith is not enough " ; nor is a historical trust. " Speculative faith is not enough "; nor is speculative trust. " Only the faith that works by love can save a human soul." Only the trust that works by love can save a soul, for the plain reason that nothing else is either faith or trust. It is *dead* if it does not thus work. It may be hypocrisy or a blinding delusion, but if it is loveless and workless, if it does not "establish the law" by a sense of its equity and the aim at perfect obedience, it is a sham, by whatever name it may be called.

"Saving faith," it is further said, "has two sides : a negative, and a positive one. It means negatively, *reliance ;* positively it means *self-help and co-operation*." A negative, according to Webster, implies a *denial*, something that is opposed to the positive. Reliance—"reliance on testimony," which is the "first significance" of the word faith—is therefore *opposed* to the self-help and co-operation which are the positive side, and the only side or "significance," it is affirmed, which has any relation to Christianity." Reliance on testimony—the testimony of Christ and the apostles—"no relation to Christianity." Is Christianity an intuition, or a mere whatever one believes to be Christianity? Self-help! What is it with no reliance on the great and only Helper? Co-operation! With whom? how? except in dependence on him who works in the soul of man all it works out of penitence and prayer and of victory over the world ; reliance on him who says, "Without me ye can do nothing."

The word faith "has scarcely a place in the Old Testament, for the reason that the salvation men receive through it as a means of reception was not known to the ancient world." "The blessed person had not been born." But was he utterly unknown to those worthies of ancient time, Abel, Noah, Abraham, Moses, David, Isaiah—that seed of the woman which was the foretold victor over the satanic realm ; the promised seed of Abraham, in whom all the families of the earth should be blessed, who was David's son and David's Lord, "the only name under heaven whereby we must be saved." The apostle in the Epistle to the Romans, and writing of the Epistle to the Hebrews, concluded very differently: "Without faith it is impossible to please God." But "by faith Enoch was translated, and before his translation had this testimony that he pleased God ;" and Noah "became heir to the righteousness which is by faith." By faith Abraham "rejoiced to see my day," said Christ ; "he saw it and was glad," for he looked for a city which hath foundations—offered up Isaac, and became the father of all them that believe, his faith being reckoned to him for righteousness.

Archbishop Magee, in his elaborate work on the Atonement, says: "Holy men of old, although they were not named Christians, yet exercised Christian faith, seeking as we do all the benefits of God the Father through the merits of Christ the Son." Pres. Dwight, in treating of the nature of faith, says, "The faith of the gospel is the faith of Abraham," and he thinks that no person acquainted with the Scriptures can hesitate to admit that the exercise of mind mentioned in passages which he cites from the Old Testament under the name of *trust* is the same which in the New Testament is called *faith*.

The sermon finally asserts that trust "is not a theological term," and "has gained no higher dignity in Christian discussion than to be employed by exhorters, lay and clerical, when hurrying on in the swift, impetuous torrent of hortatory speech." Theologically, "the word has no recognition." Theological means *pertaining to God*, and a glance at the Old Testament will show that no word there stands in closer connection with God, or is more frequently used to express the condition of his protecting, saving love, than this. "The devils believe and tremble." But trusters never tremble, for "they that trust in the Lord are as Mount Zion." Cruden in his Concordance defines justifying faith as "a grace whereby we receive Christ, and trust in and rely upon him and his righteousness alone for justification and salvation," and "this trust is called faith," he says, "because it relies upon the truth of a promise."

But this word has reputable theological use outside the Bible, not as a negation of faith, nor merely in the impetuous torrent of hortatory speech. Wesley, in a sermon on Justification by Faith, preached while he was in connection with the Church of England, says: "I cannot describe the nature of this faith better than in the words of our own Church, 'a sure *trust* and confidence that God both hath and will forgive our sins, that he hath accepted us again into his favor for the merits of Christ's death and passion.'" And his own words are, "Christian faith is a full reliance on the blood of Christ—a *recumbency* on him as our atonement and our life as *given* for us and *living* in us." Pres. Edwards says, "Christian faith is a trusting in Christ," and that "there is a trust in Christ in the *very essence* of faith." And, that he did not regard it as a nerveless, lying-down grace that never does anything, he declares: " They may be said to trust in Christ, and they only, that be ready to *do* and *undergo* all that he desires." Dr. Bellamy explains saving faith as that " entire trust, reliance or dependence on Jesus Christ which the humble sinner has, whereby he is encouraged to look to and trust in God through him for the complete salvation which is offered in the gospel." Pres. Dwight defines the faith of the gospel as " that emotion of the mind which is called trust or confidence, exercised toward the moral character of God, and particularly of Christ." Dr. Woods, in explaining the apostle's statement of faith as the substance of things hoped for, says the word ὑπόστασις which literally signifies what *stands under*, is here " used metaphorically, and denotes the *firm trust* or *confidence* in which the mind rests, and which gives to spiritual, invisible objects a substance and reality as if they were present. " Faith," says Lange, "is trust, and not sight." And Dr. Charles Hodge, " The primary idea of faith is trust." But what place does trust hold in the theology of the sermon? That "which a blossom holds to the tree of which it is an ornament, and of whose strong, generous life is the result." " It is not the root of Christian experience, it is one of the topmost blossoms of it." But if trust is not in the beginning, how can it become even an ornament of the Christian life? If faith and trust are "world-wide apart " at the root, how can they come together in the topmost blossoms? " Don't let us teach that you can plant a blossom in the soil, and have what you can get by planting a root—for your effort will be a failure, and your revival will be only the sensation of a month." What kind of faith in Christ would that be which had in it no trust in him?

It is not, therefore, scholarly correctness to say, as the sermon does, " Only by those who know nothing about letters could the blunder be made " of confounding these two words, nor a safe polemic adventure, in opening a theological controversy on the plan of salvation, to risk *ex cathedra* statements respecting words which Christ and the apostles used in unfolding that plan on the derivation of words which they did not use. It is not critical exactness to represent that Webster " gives the word trust no place in theology," when, in defining and illustrating it by reference and quotations, he makes use of nine passages of Scripture, and gives besides the following theological illustration in his own words, " Trust your Maker with yourself and all your concerns." And it is not historical accuracy to state respecting the word trust that " Protestant theology has never tolerated it as a synonym for faith," when so many Protestant theologians and interpreters have employed the two as nearly or quite identical in import ; and to affirm that this idea " that faith, in the sense of simple trust, is able to save a man, is an old error which Paul encountered and overthrew, and which James met and smote indignantly to the ground," since it was only the dead faith and work-less, no-trust dogma that Protestantism and the apostles could not endure, and which all their genuine successors have ever since been encountering, overthrowing, and smiting to the ground. But it is safe and eminently Christ-like to say, " If any one tells you that trusting in Jesus will save you from your sins, I advise you to look to your Testament and see if you find any such phrase in it." And, as I go to the Old Testament, I find just *such* phrases as these : " *Look* unto Me, and be ye saved, all ye ends of the earth"; " Son, give Me thine heart—trust it to Me "; " As for God, He is a buckler to all them that trust in Him." And in the New Testament I catch from the lips of the Master : " Seek and ye shall find "; " Come, for all things are ready"; " Come unto Me all ye that labor and are heavy laden, and I will give you rest." And as I look, and seek, and come, and give my heart, and trust, I am saved—saved from the guilt and love of sin to the love of God, my neighbor, and of perfect holiness.*

---

* The first of Archbishop Leighton's " Rules for Holy Living" is this : " Put all your trust in the special and singular mercy of God, that He, for His mercy's sake and of His mere goodness, will help and bring you to perfection."

Art. IX.—"THE FIRST DAY OF THE WEEK."

By Rev. JOHN M. LAYMAN.*

THERE are eight places in the New Testament in which occur certain Greek phrases, substantially the same which are translated in our received English version by the phrase, " the first day of the week." This translation has been quite generally accepted as correct by English versionists, critics and commentators. Almost all other versionists have adopted the same idea. There are doubtless some difficulties attending the phrases. There seems to be some misunderstanding of some of the terms, some little dissent from the commonly received version. As evidence of this we refer to an article on the Sabbath in the January number of this REVIEW. Now, the more these texts are studied in their *form* and *terms*, the greater will appear the need of being well versed in the standard usage of the language, in order to a full understanding of them. Without claiming to have made any special attainments in this line, we may still be allowed, in view of the importance of the subject, to give the results of some investigations made to satisfy our own minds on this subject. We have to thank the author of the article on " The Sabbath Question" for stirring us up to this investigation.

In the article thus alluded to the " literal English signification" is given as " On one of the Sabbaths." This might perhaps be called a word-for-word translation, but certainly not a truly literal one, since it violates the grammar of the original, as we shall presently see. We conceive that a *true* literal translation must not do this.

I.—PRELIMINARY INVESTIGATIONS.

1. It will be observed that there are four distinct forms of designating the Sabbath day: σάββατον, σαββάτα, ἡμέρα σαββάτου and ἡμέρα σαββάτων. In the New Testament the first form is by far the most common; the second is frequent; while the others are used each a few times. In the Septuagint and Apocrypha the second and fourth forms predominate largely, the second being most common. The various authors differ much as to the particular form they use. The form

---

* Revised by Prof. D. S. Gregory at the Author's request.

ἡμέρα σαββάτου is, perhaps, used when it is intended to emphasize the *design* of the day as one of *rest*. In the fault finding of the Jews, when they imagined that Christ had violated
the Sabbath, they declare that there are six days in which men
ought to come to be healed, and not on τῇ ἡμέρᾳ τοῦ σαββάτου, on " the day of *rest* (Luke xiii : 14). It has been suggested
that ἡμέρα σαββάτων is used in allusion to rest in *all* callings
and *every* particular.

The two latter forms are Hebraisms, and can, of course, be
best understood in the light of the original language. The
signification of the original Hebrew word, שַׁבָּת, *Shabbrath*,
passes over to the Greek version and to the New Testament,
and has much to do with determining the Greek linguistic
usage. If, therefore, we keep in view the original signification
of σάββατον, we shall be much helped in seeing the propriety
and force of some of these Hebraisms. This is especially true
in *some* connections. The expression, " the first day of the
Sabbath," is harsh; but put "rest" for "Sabbath," and the
harshness disappears.

2. It is also necessary to consider, briefly at least, that part of
the sentence, in Matthew xxviii, which precedes our phrase.
This necessity arises from its bearing on what follows. There
is a variety of sentiment on this first phrase : ὀψὲ δὲ σαββάτων.
The difficulty is chiefly with ὀψὲ, but partly with σαββάτων·
ὀψὲ is an adverb, kindred to several words denoting " evening,"
" evening-like," " late," etc. Some translate it " evening"; some
"late"; still others make it the subject of τῇ ἐπιφωσκούσῃ.
The last translation violates the grammar of the original, and
is therefore clearly inadmissible. That the word often has the
signification of " after" may be seen from the usage of Plutarch,
Philostratus, Elian, Ammonius. This would evidently seem
to be the appropriate meaning in the passage under consideration. One *point* of time is spoken of in view of *another* that is
gone. Finding many examples of ὀψὲ in the sense of "after,"
we adapt it in the present instance. The Greek δὲ has here
the full force of " but." By recurring to the preceding record, we
find that certain persons came to Pilate on the Sabbath, wishing
him to have the sepulchre guarded till after the third, the prophetic day, lest the disciples should steal away the body of
Christ. Their request was granted and the guard placed.

" But," adds the historian, " after the Sabbath, in the dawning" morning of the next day, the tomb is *found empty*; not by stealth however. The Greek σαββάτων is but one of the more usual forms to denote the Sabbath. The true idea, then, is simply this : " But after the Sabbath" or, as Mark very positively says, " the Sabbath being past." This of course implies that *another day* is begun ; or, at least, is the beginning, and, *if so*, is really begun. This idea Matthew still further carries out, adding: τῇ ἐπιφωσκούσῃ εἴς, "in the dawning into" the next day. In completing this construction, ἡμέρα must be supplied, according to well-established usage, rather than ωρᾳ or πρωίᾳ, or ὀρθρίνη ; although one of the latter words is sometimes used. The time marked is then already in the day-dawning of Sunday, Jewish style. The Sabbath is past, the first day of the succeeding week is begun. This conclusion is reached by giving to the words of the original such significations as are found in common usage ; and the meaning of this first expression conforms to the teachings of the other records of the same event.

3. Another theory has been presented and advocated by high authority. It is, that the *night* of feast days was counted *with* the day. This, it is maintained, was customary in that age. See Lightfoot, Selden, Poli Syn., *et al.* Admitting that this was the custom to a greater or less extent, it is nevertheless inadmissible here. These critics would translate our phrase : " But late of the Sabbath," *i.e.*, Sabbath night. It is the closing (*clausula, point*) of the Sabbath (its night) and the beginning-point of the next day. And as there is no such thing as a substantial *now*, they strike the balance in favor of the following day. This theory might be made to accord with the one we have maintained ; but it seems *unnecessary*, in the face of the command to observe the Sabbath " from even *to* even," and would *seem* to put the resurrection of Christ on the second day after his burial. It is true that an occasional interpreter has said that the resurrection did occur Sabbath night, and has then fallen back and asserted that the Sabbath really ended at the preceding sunset, so that, after all, it was on the third day; but we wholly dissent from such reasoning in a circle. Luke says that the women rested the Sabbath day, according to the commandment, *i. e.*, till its evening. Mark says

that the Sabbath had fully passed, using διαγενομένου (xvi:
1.) This *seems* to have been in time to make some further
purchases of spices before the night had fully set in (xvi : 1).
It is clear, therefore, that the evangelists had no such conception before their minds as that of the theory under consideration, and we should not have said so much concerning it,
had not the custom alluded to been maintained by such eminent authorities. Certain it is that, however common it may
have been to count the night with the day, these authorities
do not show that it is here either necessarily or actually followed by the evangelists.

II.—INVESTIGATION OF THE PHRASES.

The phrases usually translated "the first day of the week"
are found with trifling variations in the eight different passages.
The writer above alluded to translates them one for all : " On
one of the Sabbaths." Leaving his translation without explanatory analysis, he virtually says that this is the true rendering and *intention*, this and nothing else.

The same idea occurred to the writer many years since ; but
he soon found that it was neither sustained by philology nor
by an induction of facts. We reject the version as violating
the grammar of the original, and therefore as not a possible
rendering of the Greek text so long as any grammatical rendering can be found out.* In order to this translation the partitive of the conjoined genitive plural must agree with the numeral in gender. Thus " one of the days " is equivalent to " one
day of the days." In Greek, μία τῶν ἡμερῶν is equivalent to
ἡμέρα μία τῶν ἡμερῶν. Now μία is feminine gender, and
σάββατον neuter. Hence the μίαν, in Matthew xxviii: 1,
cannot govern σαββατων as a partitive. But ἡμέραν understood governs it by another rule well known to all Greek scholars. In order to make this rendering (to which we object) possible, it would be necessary to go still further and supply τῶν
ἡμερῶν, in which case the phrase would read " the first day of
the Sabbath days." But so bungling does this course appear,
and so foreign to the analogy of Greek grammatical usage, that
no critic has ever ventured to suggest it in explaining the
phrases under consideration. The rule for partitives is obvi-

---

* See *Commentary of Dr. J. Addison Alexander, Poli Syn, et al.* (Shall we say
et omnes ?)

ously the only rule which meets the requirements of the case ; and in every case of a numeral governing the genitive plural (of which examples abound), the partitive of such genitive plural *will*—and, we may say, *must*—agree with the numeral in gender.

In this connection we give a passing notice to a *claim* and a *charge* contained in the above-noted article. The *claim* is that Calvin gives "this identical construction" in his notes on 1 Corinthians xvi: 2.* Indeed, Calvin argues against such a construction, in his notes on the various passages containing the phrase. He would not, as a scholar, do otherwise. Almost all—versionists, revisionists, commentators, lexicographers and critics—virtually agree to the principle of the English version. The *charge* to which we refer is that Dr. Robinson says that "wherever the word σαββάτον is preceded by a numeral, it has the signification of *week*." We find nothing of the kind in the Andover edition of Dr. Robinson's Lexicon, published in 1825. In the New York edition of 1850, we find that Dr. Robinson says that the word Sabbath is "put for the interval" from Sabbath to Sabbath; hence, *a sen'night, week,* and refers to Luke xviii: 12 as an example. He goes on to say that this usage occurs "elsewhere *only* after numerals *marking* the days of the week." No man of Dr. Robinson's accurate scholarship could ever make such an assertion as that attributed to him. What he says is as far as possible from it. Peradventure the charge came of an oversight and we pass it.

1. The numeral μία, which occurs in each of the texts in question with one exception (Mark xvi : 9), needs to be particularly considered in its usage and construction. It is a cardinal number taken by our English translators as an ordinal. The following particulars may be elicited by an examination of its usage.

a. The use of cardinal numbers as ordinals is more or less common to all languages. This holds especially of the cardinal number one. This construction is particularly common in the Hebrew, and hence those texts in the New Testament in which it occurs are often spoken of as Hebraisms. A similar use of the cardinals is found in classic Greek and Latin, and is not uncommon in English.

---

* See *Tholuck's Edition of Calvin's Commentaries.*

b. The cardinal εἷς (one), particularly the feminine form of it, is often used in what may be termed a semi-ordinal manner. Thus: μία, ἑτέρα or δευτέρα, τρίτη—one, another or second, third. Genesis iv: 19, in the Septuagint version, is an example in point. In all such cases—and they abound—the cardinal εἷς, μία ἕν is really an ordinal in construction, however it may be translated as a cardinal.

c. There are other connections where it is strictly used as an ordinal; as when it is said that "Daniel continued even unto the first year (ἔνους, ἑνὸς) of King Cyrus (Dan. i : 21). " The first day of the month" (μία τοῦ μηνός) is a very common usage. " The first day of creation" (ἡμέρα μία) occurs in Genesis i : 5.*

d. Μία and πρώτη are frequently used interchangeably in speaking of the same subject, showing that the original authors regarded the cardinal as having the force of the ordinal. This is illustrated in Genesis viii : 5, 13 ; 2 Esdras vii : 9, 10; and Mark xvi : 1, 9. In view of the facts and examples, we have all the authority desirable for translating μία as an ordinal in our texts. In fact, the interchangeable use of μία and πρώτη, in Mark xvi : 1, 9, two of the phrases under consideration, shows that all of them should be rendered with an ordinal.

e. Since the word ἡμέρα, in its proper case, is to be supplied after μία in these texts, it will be proper and profitable to consider its construction with other words.

a. Whenever μία is employed to designate "a" or "one" day, the construction is invariably, in the Septuagint and New Testament, ἡμέρα μία, or μία ἡμερα, in their proper case, without the article. It occurs in a score of passages in the Septuagint, specifying the first day of the month, and is found without the article in all cases except one (Apocryphal Esther i : 2), in which example, instead of being followed by τοῦ μῆνος as usual, it is followed by the name of the month, τοῦ Νισάν. Ἡμέρα is left to be supplied, with perhaps two exceptions. The dative case is used according to the rule for the expression of time. Of course, conjoined governing words will change the case.

b. The cardinal εἷς, μία, ἕν occurs in the New Testament some three hundred times, and stands without an article in all

---

* See Schaff; also Pool's Synopsis on this passage.

cases except two, where it is specially emphatic (Matt. vi: 24;
1 John v: 8).

c. In the phrases under consideration the following construction obtains. The numeral is preceded by the article in all cases except two (Matt. xxviii: 1; 1 Cor. xvi: 2), where it is excluded by the preposition.* Σαββάτων is attended by the article in four of the passages, which is about the usual proportion with genitives when governed by another noun. The strict partitive plural *always* has its article, so far as we can find. The presence of the article before the cardinal in the greater part of our phrases, contrary to general usage in the Scriptures, is doubtless owing to the special emphasis laid upon the resurrection *time.* On the other hand, the ordinals are quite generally attended by an article.

A construction very similar to that in our phrases occurs in speaking of the Passover; but πρώτη is there invariably used: πρώτή τῶν ἀξύμων, "the first day of unleavened bread."

In all other constructions than those referred to above the ordinals are used, and very often also in those we have been considering.

III.—TRANSLATION OF THE PHRASES.

The preceding investigation has prepared the way for a translation of the phrases under consideration. Taking one for all, we translate Matthew xxviii: 1, literally, "into the one [day] of the Sabbaths" [rests].†

1. In considering this division of our subject, we note that Σάββατον is placed in the plural, according to a customary method of designating festivals and holidays. The Sabbath was regarded and spoken of as a festival. In this case, by custom, the *specific name* of the seventh day is given to the *term of days* till the next Sabbath, the *chief day* of the week covering, so to speak, the whole term.‡ This usage of the plural affords an apt method of reckoning the revolving sevens (weeks). It was a Hebraistic or Rabbinical method of numbering the

---

* See *Bengel on 1 Cor. xvi: 2.* Compare Titus iii: 10.

† Mark xvi: 9, in its literal translation, differs somewhat from the others. It is as follows: "On the *first* [day] of the Sabbath" [rest]. The ordinal number is here used, and Sabbath is in the singular number.

‡ See *Pool's Synopsis* on these passages.

days of the Sabbath (week.)   It was well understood by the
Greek and Latin Fathers, and is still in use among Jewish
scholars.*

Accordingly, " the first day of the Sabbath," " the second day
of the Sabbath," " the third," etc., meant the first, the second,
the third day, etc., unto the next Sabbath.† A similar construction prevailed in the reckoning of the Sabbaths unto Pentecost.‡ To illustrate : if, after the mention of the ending of
a certain day, it be necessary to record some fact of the succeeding day, of which an exact account and date must be given,
it would be natural and necessary to designate such day either
as the *next* day, as is often done, or to give it its name if it
has one, or to give it its number in the seven. The last of
these was the customary method of enumerating the successive
days of the Sabbath festival, culminating in the seventh day,
the head, the Sabbath indeed.§

An occasional critic would supply $\dot{a}\pi\dot{o}$ $\dot{\eta}\mu\dot{\epsilon}\rho\alpha\varsigma$ before $\sigma\alpha\beta$-
$\beta\dot{a}\tau\hat{\omega}\nu$. This seems an unnatural conjecture, though the ren-
dering be good and the reckoning the same that we have
adopted, except in this, that it reckons *from* the *past* Sabbath,
while we reckon *toward* the *approaching* one. It is quite obvious, however, that the very construction of the phrase looks
forward, and does not necessitate the supplying of any proposition.

2. It will be observed that we have not introduced the term
"week" into our translation of the phrases. We have not done
it for a two-fold reason :

First, we have desired to conform our version as nearly as
possible to the original, which is easily enough understood.

Secondly, it has been alleged that $\sigma\dot{a}\beta\beta\alpha\tau o\nu$ cannot have
the signification of $\dot{\epsilon}\beta\delta o\mu\dot{a}\varsigma$. Now it is true that a name is
only a name, and it matters little so that we have the thing.
But let us look into this objection.

a. In the Hebrew Bible, whence we get the original ideas,

---

* See *Pool's Synopsis.* The writer of this article recently had these views confirmed by a learned Jewish Rabbi, who was familiar with the entire range of Jewish
learning on this subject.

† See *Lightfoot, Selden, Pool's Synopsis,* and others.

‡ See *Cruden's Concordance.*

§ See the same authorities as before.

שַׁבָּת, *shabbath* (sabbath) is used for שָׁבוּעַ (week), a denominative from שֶׁבַע *sheba* (seven). This use of the Hebrew "Sabbath" (rest) for "week" is exemplified in Leviticus xxiii : 15, 16, and in xxv : 8 (twice). The usual term for "week" had already been used by the writer of the Pentateuch at least three times in Genesis and Exodus, but in these texts he sees fit to use the proper word for Sabbath as equivalent to week. So the Seventy in their translation take the term and translate it by ἑβδομάς. The Seventy were Jews used to the Greek language.

That שַׁבָּת in these texts is used for *week* is further evident in that *complete* Sabbaths are to be counted. There is no force in conjoining this term to "Sabbath" as a day, but much force in joining it to a week consisting of several days.

A *complete* week is its seven days. The Seventy do not indeed use σάββατον in their translation of these texts. In making a version of a language, an *important* term may be *transferred* with slight lingual variation, as σάββατον, *sabtathum*, Sabbath, for שַׁבָּת ; or the term may be *translated*, as ἀναπαυσις, *sabbathismus*, rest. The Seventy have *translated* in the texts above. Once in the above texts they use ἀναπαύσεις for שַׁבָּתוֹת, thus virtually using σάββατον for ἑβδομάς. Had they translated literally, they must have done it *thrice*. It is to be remarked that they often use ἑβδομας for שַׁבָּת. On the other hand, in the Apocrypha ἑβδομάς is occasionally used for σάββατον; as in 2. Mac. vi : 11, and xii : 38.

In the translation which we have given above, both literal and free, we have simply *transferred*, or *literally translated* the term. If it be said that the English version gives different meanings to σάββατον as occurring in the two parts of the sentence (Matt. xxviii : 1), it will be seen that we have avoided that. But we have found that it comes to the same thing at last, and after all, if we have the thing, the name used gives us little concern.

b. Turning now to the New Testament, there are two passages in which σαββάτον is taken by most critics as equivalent to week. Are they right in so taking it?

The first of these passages is Luke xviii : 12 : Νηστεύω δὶς τὸυ σαββάτον, is the language of the Pharisee in his prayer, "I fast twice of the week." It certainly seems entirely unnat-

ural to speak of fasting twice a day. Rather we would expect
to find him stating that he omitted *two meals*. But as there
were only two meals a day, it would mean, according to the
view we are considering, that he simply fasted all day on the
Sabbath. But the text is certainly not a natural expression
of that idea.* The natural interpretation must therefore be
reached in another way and in accordance with the facts of
history. We know that there were two customary fast days
in the week (according to English style), the first and fourth
(Monday and Thursday) observed by the hypocritical Pharisees, and the third and fifth (Wednesday and Friday) by
the Gentile Christians, who avoided the Jewish customs.†
Says Alford on this passage: " This was a *voluntary* fast on the
Mondays and Thursdays." This is the only natural and common-sense interpretation.

. The second of these passages is found in Acts xiii : 42. In
our version it reads : "And when the Jews were gone out of the
synagogue, the Gentiles besought that these words might be
preached to them *the next Sabbath*." The Greek phrase in
question is : $\epsilon \iota \varsigma \tau \grave{o} \ \mu \epsilon \tau \alpha \xi \grave{\upsilon} \ \sigma \grave{\alpha} \beta \beta \alpha \tau o \nu$, literally, " in the between of the Sabbath," *i. e.*, on the intervening week days.
So Scaliger and the older critics understood it, and Dr. Joseph
Addison Alexander, in his commentary on this passage, clearly
presents and abundantly vindicates the same view. It evidently cannot signify " the between Sabbath." Between what ?
Shall it be replied, between the Sabbath of verse 14 and the
$\epsilon \rho \chi o \ \mu \acute{\epsilon} \nu \omega \ \sigma \alpha \beta \beta \acute{\alpha} \tau \omega$ of verse 44 ? But Biblical history and
the early church sedulously avoid denominating the first day
of the week $\tau o \ \sigma \acute{\alpha} \beta \beta \alpha \tau o \nu$. The preposition $\acute{\epsilon} \iota \varsigma$ would also
seem to have a force not sufficiently noticed in this interpre-
tation, *i. e.*, " in," " into," " during," rather than " on." Obviously the phrase would have been put in the dative, as at
verse 44, had a *particular* day been noted. But understand their request to be for preaching " during" the week,
and the use of $\acute{\epsilon} \iota \varsigma$ and the accusative is obvious. If it be replied that $\sigma \acute{\alpha} \beta \beta \alpha \tau o \nu$ should be put in the genitive plural, as
conjectured by some, we reply, by no means, if it be taken to

---

* See *Smith's Bible Dictionary* under " Fasting and Meals."
† See Epiphanius, Theodosian, Clement and others.

designate "week." The week was denominated שׁבֻע, σάββατον, because there was a Sabbath in each week and because it was the chief, the *culminating*, day of the week.* Their request may have been, for preaching on those days (2d and 5th) of the week, observed more or less by the church of that time. Those days were denominated in the Rabbinical language " additional days," more literally, perhaps, " sprung up days," and were said to have been arranged by Ezra. Hellenistic Jews used μεταξύ to express the same idea.† The other sense meets the historical requirements of the occasion. After the Sabbath mentioned in verse 14, many Jews and proselytes followed Paul and Barnabas, who spoke to them during the week as they had been besought to do. Then on the coming Sabbath almost the whole city came together, as we would naturally have expected on a *Sabbath-day*. All this was in accordance with the custom of the apostles, who preached a great deal on week days.

In both these passages, therefore, σάββατον appears clearly to be equivalent to "week." The Pharisee fasted two days in a week. The apostles preached during the week. On the whole, therefore, the English version, " on the first day of the week," is fully justified, both by grammatical principles and by Scriptural (Hebrew and Greek) usage.

IV.—DESIGN OF THE PHRASES.

The article in the January number, already so often referred to, plainly intimates that the evangelists, in the phrases under consideration, affirm the *ending* of one series of Sabbaths— the Jewish—and the beginning of a new one—the Christian. Connected with this view are certain unwarranted assumptions, a careful review of which will prepare us for the fuller appreciation of the truth.

1. While we believe that the ending and beginning, above referred to, actually occurred, it can readily be shown that this was neither the evangelists' intention nor their affirmation.

(1.) It is obvious that any intimation that the day *following* a Sabbath was also a Sabbath would be so unexpected, that to be received it must be taught authoritatively. Much more

---

* See *Rosenmüller, Com. on. Lev. xxiii : 15, 16; xxv : 8*, etc.
† See *Conybeare and Howson, Life and Epistles of St. Paul*, vol. 1, p. 178, note.

the intimation that it was the *first one* of a *new series* of Sabbaths, the old to cease at once and forever. What was needed and demanded in such a case may be seen from what the evangelists have given us in the case of the Lord's Supper, instituted in the place of the Passover. Had we any of the fullness of specification found in Exodus xii, where an account is given of a change in the series of the months of the year, all would be perfectly plain. And might we not expect it in this seemingly more important matter? Such a change in the series of Sabbaths, from the Jewish to the Christian, must, we say, have direct and positive establishment, or meet with constant energetic resistance.

(2.) Moreover, the structure of the sentence in the cases under consideration is not such as to affirm this change. The proper phrase in the original Greek for " one of the Sabbaths" would be ἐν τῶν σαββάτων. The phrases for " on the first Sabbath," according to New Testament general usage, would be τῶ σαββάτῳ τῷ πρώτῳ. This term, almost universally used to designate the day abstractly, in the New Testament, is σάββατον. To declare a change in the series of Sabbaths from the seventh day of the week to the first, we might suggest the following, using as much of the original sentence as possible, and conforming to Scriptural Greek usage: ὀψὲ δὲ παλαιας τῆς ταξεως τῶν σαββάτων τῇ ἐπιφωσκούσῃ εἰς πρῶτον σάββατον μιᾶς καινῆς ταξεως τῶν σαββάτων, " but after the old order of Sabbaths, in the (day) dawning into the first Sabbath of a new order of Sabbaths." Doubtless other Jews might teach the same thing, but obviously the text in hand fails to do it.

The positions thus established show how the text in Acts xx: 7 must be taken. The phrase is: Ἐν δὲ τῇ μιᾷ τῶν σαββάτων. It is not the form for "the Sabbath"; no one takes it to be so. It is not the form for "a Sabbath" or "one Sabbath"; this has already been shown. Nor is it the form for "one of the Sabbaths." Besides, Paul was at Troas *only one* Sabbath. It is simply, "On the *first day* of the (revolving) Sabbath," *i. e.*, " weeks." This is the only natural and common sense interpretation. It may also readily be seen how the apostle's charge to lay by alms, 1 Corinthians xvi: 2, is to be taken. The phrase is: κατὰ μίαν σαββάτου. It is not the form of expression for "a" or "one Sabbath," nor for "each Sabbath," nor for "every first Sabbath," nor for "one of the Sabbaths." The construction is identical with that of Matthew xxviii: 1, and the phrase evidently signifies "according to the first (day) of the Sabbath," *i. e.*, on every first day of the week, the rising, first-day Sabbath.

Of course, it is plain that the next day after the Sabbath was in no sense a day of rest until set apart as such, and of such setting apart there is no hint given in connection with the eight phrases considered in this paper. In no one of the eight is the form used the proper one for a Sabbath day. This may be seen by a comparison with Acts xiii: 14; xvi: 13; Matthew xxv: 20.

(3.) That five different authors should make use of so brief a sentence, employing a construction in common use for designating another idea—the enumeration of the days unto the next Sabbaths, *i. e.*, the days of the revolving week—to teach a great *change* in the series of the days of the week, seems quite inadmissible. It could not have been the *present* design of the evangelists to teach anything on the Sabbath doctrine. This is further evident when we consider how long it was before the first-day Sabbath came to be *fully* and *only* recognized as the day of rest, even in the Christian Church. And yet all four evangelists declare it *the* Sabbath, according to the *theory* we have been considering.

(4.) It may thus be seen how baseless is the assumption in the article so often referred to, that "we find two Sabbaths coming together at the resurrection of Christ." That the sacred writers do not declare the resurrection day to be "one of the *Sabbaths*" is clear from the following considerations:

a. It is never termed the Sabbath in the subsequent records of the New Testament. Apart from these phrases, which for the present may be regarded as in dispute, it is never mentioned except under some other title than σάββατον. And in every place where σάββατον is used, it seems *clearly* to refer to the Jewish Sabbath. Would not inspiration have given the new day its *distinctive* name? This it was the more necessary to do if there was an abrupt change being made, which must be explained or authoritatively laid down in order to be assented to. Instead of this, the inspired writers continue to designate the seventh day as the Sabbath, and the first day of the week by some other title.

b. The immediate successors of the apostles applied other titles than Sabbath to this first day of the week. They strove to neglect or reject all Jewish observances and names. This was partly for distinction's sake, but chiefly from antipathy to Jewish practices. The Fathers were explicit in speaking of Sunday or Lord's day, sometimes declaring that it was a Sabbath as to duties. Now, had the doctrinal charge been given, surely apostles and church, fathers and all, would have vied with each other in efforts to establish it as a fact. Yet it is a fact that until the fifth century the seventh day is still in use unrejected. Justin Martyr affirms the eighth (*i. e.*, the first) day to be the true Sunday. He does not say Sabbath, for that was a Jewish name for the seventh day. See his Comments on Psalm xcii. St. Barnabas asserts the same (Epist. c. 15). Isocrates makes the same assertion in his Ecclesiastical History (lib. 8, c. 22). During the early ages the first day of the week is *never* termed the Sabbath. That was the distinctive name of the seventh day.* Surely had inspiration so clearly denominated the first day *the Sabbath*, and enjoined its observance as such in every particular, the church would at once have taught and observed accordingly. Evidently the church did not at once "find two *Sabbaths* coming together at the resurrection of Christ."

2. We are thus led to inquire what was the real design of the sacred writers in the phraseology adopted in the passages under consideration. An understanding of this will aid in arriving at a true translation of the phrases.

Evidently their design was to declare the exact fulfilment of Christ's prophecy concerning his burial and resurrection, *i. e.*, that he should be in the heart of the earth three days, and that he should rise again on the third day. He must lie in the tomb three days, not less in number and not more. He must rise on the third day. Was the prophecy, thus given, exactly fulfilled? The evangelists would plainly and positively set forth the facts as they occurred. This we conceive to be their *very* design.

---

*See *Coleman's History of the Ancient Church ;* also, *Gilfillan, The Sabbath.* p. 377.

Now, Christ expired on the preparation day (Saturday) afternoon, Jewish style, at three o'clock, and was laid in the tomb before the day ended. This, according to the customary method of reckoning, counted *one* day. Further: Mark says that the " Sabbath was past" (through); Matthew says, " But after the Sabbath" ; Luke says that the women, after purchasing some spices, " rested the Sabbath day according to the commandment," *i. e.*, the whole day, " from even to even." This counts as the *second* day. Christ is yet in the tomb. Further: Mark affirms that he arose early (in the morning) the *first* day of the week (Sabbath), Mark xvi : 9. We take πρωὶ in this verse to signify *morning* in the general (John xx : 19). It is often translated *very early* when it scarcely seems to admit of it. The adding of λίαν to it in Mark xvi : 2, points to the earlier hour referred to by Luke and John. We also understand πρωὶ to refer to Christ's resurrection, and not to his appearance to Mary. This is clearly the most obvious construction. But to return from this digression ; the four evangelists teach, with trifling lingual variations, that the resurrection was early on the day after the Sabbath. Thus the third day is begun. These early hours, however few (really since sunset of the preceding evening), count as the *third* day according to the usual custom. This *must all be*, or Christ lay not in the grave three days, nor any part of third and last day of the triad.

The prophecy is thus seen to have been literally fulfilled, and the fact is abundantly and plainly testified to by the evangelists. Plainer language could scarcely have been selected to declare the exact fulfillment of these prophecies. The inspired record minutely specifies the passing days and hours from the arrest of Christ till his resurrection. This we conceive to have been the design of the evangelists.

3. The subject of the *intercalation* of the first Sabbath of the Christian series calls for a brief remark. Where is the authority for it ? None is claimed. What does it amount to ? It does not satisfy the seventh-day Sabbatarian. It still leaves an abrupt change in his series of Sabbaths. It does not accord with later records. If this day is the Sabbath as before in every respect, why is it not named as the Sabbath was, instead of being termed "the first day of the Sabbath"? *i. e.*, of the week ? The fact is that both days seem to have been ob-

served more or less till after the destruction of Jerusalem,
even in the Christian Church. The Jewish Sabbath is more
frequently mentioned in the Acts than the other. The Jewish element, perhaps, held rather to the seventh-day Sabbath,
while the Gentile held rather to the first-day Sabbath, which
at length entirely supplanted the old Sabbath.

4. Finally, if it be said that the conclusion we have reached
deprives us of a most direct proof for the change of the Sabbath from the seventh to the first day of the week, we console
ourselves with the reflection that if inspiration has not given
us this particular form of proof, we can well afford to do without it. We can still fall back on the old proofs, generally regarded as abundantly sufficient to establish the change of the
day. ·Adherence to the strict grammatical construction is the
true and only way of avoiding such topsy-turvy derangement of
sensible literary productions and forms. We are always glad,
therefore, to find the scholars and the grammars in accord with
our view, or at least not in opposition to it. We do not "deny
to the Christian Sabbath its title." We demand its title for
higher reasons than ever. The first day of the Sabbath (week)
is become the head of the Sabbath (week)—the Sabbath itself.

It was not our purpose to say anything in this article on the
Sabbath question, except so far as might tend to point out
and elucidate the intended meaning of the phrases under consideration. It may be remarked, however, that whatever
view may be taken, whether we consider the creation week,
the Jewish week, or the Christian week, we find each containing its Sabbath of rest, the one-seventh of its time, *set apart
and sanctioned by Divine authority and example.*

The results of this investigation may be briefly summed up
as follows :

1. We have seen that the evident design of inspiration in
our texts is to set forth a clear and positive account of the fulfillment of Christ's prophesy, oft repeated, that he should lie in
the tomb three days, and that he should rise again on the third
day. And we have seen that the language is such as to do this.

2. We have seen that the version given in the article referred
to is untenable.

3. We have found that our English version of these phrases
is virtually correct.

Art. X.—THE GREAT RAILROAD STRIKE.

By L. H. Atwater.

THE great railroad strike, culminating in the riots, arson and murder which turned the city of Pittsburgh—more than almost any other the metropolis of a dense evangelical and even Presbyterian population—into a pandemonium, and a bright summer Sabbath from being a foretaste of heavenly rest into an " abomination of desolation," and foretaste of the diabolism of the world of despair, if terrible in itself and its immediate effects, was still more so as a revelation. It partially uncapped the crater of a social volcano over which we have been sleeping, nearly all of us without suspicion or alarm, while a few have been aware of its existence. These were the less surprised when it burst forth, because they had long seen its smouldering fires, ready to rage on the slightest gust of provocation, and come forth in fury and devastation in a time unlooked for, even as a thief cometh in the night. They have seen this to be the inevitable danger of the so-called trades-unions into which nearly all the skilled laborers, or manual laborers in special occupations, are organized. How and why they stand related as cause and effect will be made to appear in its proper place. The vast increase of tramps, idlers, and the scum of Old World communism lately cast among us, enhances the danger.

But even to these, not less than to the whole country, the scenes of that dread week, the last in July, were a revelation in another respect. None had adequately realized the extent to which our railway system is interlocked with our whole industrial, commercial, social and political life, so that its stoppage, even for a single week, paralyzes industry by preventing its products from reaching their consumers, or the raw materials from reaching their workers, thus consigning them largely to uselessness or waste ; imperils the subsistence of millions, whose daily food is supplied by the matchless rapidity of railway transportation over hundreds and thousands of miles ; arrests that transmission of intelligence by postal and other railroad communication which is the bond of modern society and underlies all the arrangements and ongoings of modern life; palsies the arm of government itself by stopping the conveyance of intelligence, supplies and resources—forces on which its power and efficiency depend. In short, the enforced stoppage of railway movement is and was seen to be to the body politic just what stoppage of the circulation of the blood is to the natural body; and the stoppage of movement on any part of a great trunk line is, for most important purposes, the stoppage of movement from end to end of itself and branches, extending hundreds and thousands of miles. The knowledge that a few desperate and infuriated men could in this manner lay their hand upon the throat of the country, and griping it almost to the very point of strangulation, keep its hold for days and weeks, was indeed a revelation of direst portent to those who, having thought they foresaw the impending evil, were thus rudely taught that they had only imagined the speck in the sky which spread, and thickened, and lowered, until it discharged itself far and wide in lightning, thunder, tempest and tornado. No event since the bombardment of Sumter has struck the country with such startling and ominous dismay, or been accepted as so loud a summons to rally to the defence of our altars and firesides as the mobocratic reign of terror in the latter part of July under the lead of railroad strikers. The periodical press of the country, almost without exception, has felt called to the duty of contributing its quota of light upon the causes and cure of the portentous social phenomena, of which these events, unless rightly improved for the prevention of their recurrence, or evils equivalent, if not worse, are not the end, but only the beginning. The subject has so many sides—economic, industrial, social, ethical, governmental and political—that we cannot do justice to them all. We can only touch upon the more salient points presented by them in the space at our command.

The topics directly or indirectly involved are so numerous and varied, and so variously interlinked with the main topic and with each other, that the precise order of treatment must be left largely to evolve itself freely as we go on, without any previous minute mapping out. Perhaps there is no more natural and logical beginning than a consideration of the alleged grievance, to redress or remedy which the strike was professedly undertaken, and its attendant crimes perpetrated.

This alleged grievance, it is needless to say, was the reduction of the wages of the employés, including the highest officials, of most of our principal roads ten per cent. In some cases this had been preceded by some previous reductions that have followed the great financial panic of 1873. But, unless in cases the most rare and exceptional, it is also true (*a*) that the wages still paid by the railroads to their employés remained, after the reduction, higher than the average of those paid for analogous services in other walks of life, and that the reduction had been less than in other departments of labor ; (*b*) that others were willing and eager to take the places vacated by the strikers at the reduced rate of compensation ; (*c*) that the reward of the laborer had declined far less than the profit or dividend upon the capital employed, which largely consists of the unspent savings of previous labor, embodied in said railroads and their furnishings, which afford the very support, opportunity and only possibility for the labor and wages of these employés. All this is eminently true of the Pennsylvania Railroad, on which the great strike and riot occurred. The wages still remained far better, not only than the average in other employments, but even in the total railroad service of the country, while the dividends upon the capital, which means, as we know, very extensively the unspent savings of the labor of others, put there for the support of widows, orphans, the aged and decrepit, have been reduced in a far greater ratio. (*d*) The reduction was rather in the nominal than in the real wages, considered with reference to their actual purchasing power, or value in procuring other things or means of subsistence and comfort. If the price of labor has been reduced from the inflated paper standards during and following the war, when a dollar of legal-tender currency was worth from one-third to one-half a gold dollar, it is because it was then raised to meet the inflation, and having swollen from the old coin price, as was just, it now shrinks back toward that standard where a paper dollar is worth almost a gold one—more than a silver one. It is quite as high, occasionally higher, than in the ante-war times. Now, as the prices of other commodities or products of labor have shrunk in proportion, it is equally available for subsistence and comfort as the same gold wages before the war, or twice or thrice the same number of paper dollars during and immediately after the war. This is true of food, fuel, raiment and shelter taken together, if not of each and every item taken separately. It is proper, however, to say that in regard to food this statement is more nearly true in this year of bountiful harvests than in the last, which gave a much poorer crop return in breadstuffs, and especially that poor man's resource, the potato. This esculent was so burnt out by the tropical heats of the summer of 1876 as to rise to double the ordinary, and four times its present price. It is also true that, at the time of the occurrence of the strike, the bountiful crops of this year had not been sufficiently matured and marketed to produce any very marked effect on prices. But all this was easily seen to be exceptional. The grievance alleged, therefore, did not exist in reference to the chief railways smitten by the strike. Indeed, this is so obvious that it is well known that most of the strikers on the Pennsylvania Railroad went into the measure very reluctantly, and only on the order of those chiefs of the Brotherhood of Locomotive Engineers to which they belonged, and whose behests they had bound themselves to obey by vows— better kept in the breach than the observance—which they dared not violate. As it was, scarcely one-tenth of the men in the employ of that colossal corporation joined in the strike, which it is thus abundantly proved had no substantial grievance to justify or even palliate it. We say this, not in any sense which questions the right of each and every employé to cease working for his employer, when he thereby violates no previous obligation or contract, express or implied, and does not become an idler and pauper, casting himself and family on public or private charity for support, or when his manner of doing it, or of combining with others to do it, does not amount to an unrighteous conspiracy against public interests and private rights.

Nor do we question the right of laborers to combine for lawful purposes and in lawful ways to further and defend their own interest, to support each other in times of adversity or destitution, to coöperate in preventing abuses or extortions practiced by their employers, whether singly or in combination, by the use of righteous and lawful means. But we hold that attempts to do it by unlawful means, by conspiring, suddenly or without notice, simultaneously to stop the trains of a road at a given hour, no matter where they are, leaving them and the property on board of them to injury or destruction, and the persons traveling on them to the danger, pain and loss incident to such a catastrophe, to be of the nature of a conspiracy against society and the individuals involved in violation of all right and law, human and divine; in short, an outrage to be punished by the judges and crushed by the strong arm of the law. So the laws of New Jersey treat it. To abrogate or prevent such laws is now a cardinal plank in trades-union and labor-reform platforms. But more especially do we hold that all attempts to force employers to accede to the demands made upon them by the forcible prevention of others from laboring for them, or, in other words, all forcible interference with the liberty of others to labor in any lawful occupation they may choose, to be an invasion of the fundamental rights of man and society, which ought to be prevented, if need be, by the extremest exercise of the powers of the State.

And just here we touch the main issue between strikers and all other classes. They, like the trades-unions which resort to them, are impotent unless they can forcibly prevent other laborers from taking the places they have deserted. Their very life and success depend on this. They therefore depend on measures which invade the rights of their fellow-men, and which the utmost power of society ought to be exerted to suppress. It is no justification of such violence that employers, whether railroads or others, whether individuals or corporations, may have come to an agreement to reduce wages for any given kind of labor they employ, so long as they violate no previous contracts, express or implied, give due notice of the intended reduction, and use no coercion to compel parties to work for them at such rates. It may justify concerted action among the employés to resist such reduction by all lawful means, but by no other in any circumstances; much less in a case in which the reduction proposed does not exceed the rate of reduction of wages generally prevalent.

We have looked at the alleged grievance which provoked the strikes and riots. We do not intend to intimate, as will in due time appear, that the railroads were faultless, or do not need great reform. Let us, however, now look for a little at the methods of redress; and first of all at the great instrument or organization employed by laborers, and especially railway laborers, for the redress of the alleged grievances. We refer, of course, to trades-unions generally, and those among railroad engineers and train laborers in particular.

So far as these unions or brotherhoods are benevolent organizations for the purpose of amassing funds to aid their members or their families when overtaken with sickness or destitution, they are eminently proper and commendable; all the more so in the case of occupations as perilous as the running of railroad trains. So far as they are organized for mutual helpfulness in lawful ways and for worthy ends, they deserve countenance, and should encounter no opposition. But they all, or nearly all, have certain features designed to enforce monopoly privileges which are utterly unjustifiable, and amount to little less than an organized conspiracy against the rights of man.

First among these is the insisting on equality of wages for all of their craft, no matter how unequal their skill, faithfulness and efficiency. This is a conspiracy against the just rights of the higher class of laborers, and takes away all motive to aim at a high standard of workmanship and efficiency. It encourages sluggish, incompetent and faithless workmen. We have been credibly informed of cases in which the members of a trades-union compelled an employer to continue the employment of drunken and dissolute fellow-members of their league, by threatening to cease working for him, at a time when such cessation of work would be ruinous, if he did not restore them to their places in his service. In pursuance of this policy they forbid the employer to give work to any outsiders, even in order to deliver them from starvation and vagrancy, on pain of deserting him in circumstances which would entail upon his business the greatest loss and destruction. Not many years since the secretary of a great Steamship Co. in New York set at work a ship-carpenter who begged for work in order to get his bread. The secretary was informed at once that all the other workmen would instantly quit his employ unless this outsider to the union was dismissed, although they had engaged to labor, and their services were indispensable in order to fit the vessel for sea within the time appointed and advertised for her sailing.

It is a part of the same system, and indispensable to carry

it out, that all work by the piece or the hour should be pro-hibited. Otherwise, a difference of reward would arise as be-tween the better and poorer laborers, and competition would defeat the system of equal wages for all workmen, good, bad and indifferent. Since the paralysis of business, which has struck no class more severely than builders, a contractor for-tunate enough to obtain a contract for the construction of a large building, employed a considerable number of stone-cut-ters in dressing the stones for his building by the piece. While they were thus earning bread for themselves and their hungry families, they and their employer were waited upon by a committee from a trades-union fifty miles off, and informed that piece-work was not permitted by the laws of the guild. The contractor replied that he should manage his own busi-ness without their superintendence. Some of his workmen continued at their work, others left it at the behest of the in-truding committee, and their places were promptly filled by others. The next resource of the trades-unionists was to loiter and stroll around, threatening and annoying the work-men who persisted in their work, till at length the contest ended, as in such cases it ever should end, in the employer causing the intruders and disturbers to be arrested and bound over to keep the peace. All this illustrates and proves the fact that these organizations cannot carry out their monopoly policy without lawless and violent interference with the inalien-able right of men to engage in honest labor. And this fact proves the very end as well as means they have in view to be utterly unwarrantable.

This policy of enforced monopoly further requires the pro-hibition of apprentices from learning the trade of the guild ex-cept in numbers the most limited. Hence it is a fundamental article of every such guild, that its members will allow no man who employs them to have more than an insignificant number of apprentices for a large number of journeymen, lest by in-creasing the number who become skilled in the craft, competi-tion should lower the rates of wages toward the level of other occupations. This is a conspiracy against the fundamental rights of men to choose the occupation for which God and na-ture have fitted them, and of society to enjoy the most advan-tageous use of the faculties of its various members. Nay, more; by depriving the rising youth of the opportunity for right and wholesome employments, it forces them to grow up as idlers, augments the dangerous classes, or, at all events, to swell the ever-increasing ranks of unskilled and poorly paid laborers, thus forcing down their wages by increasing the competition among them.

While productive, however, of all these wrongs and social and industrial evils, it defeats itself. Extreme wages in any trade are sure to attract craftsmen and experts from other countries to share them, and fill the places which would otherwise be occupied by Americans learning the craft in this country. It thus works unmixed wrong and evil to the growing youth and the whole laboring class of the country, without a solitary compensatory advantage to the guilds which inflict it.

But still further. The success of such unions is not so much, as it is often described, a successful struggle of labor against capital as of laborers against laborers,—of a comparative small set of laborers against all other laborers,—inasmuch as its success lies in compelling the latter to pay out of their wages, thus reduced by increased competition, the monopoly prices extorted from all classes for the commodities or services which embody the labors of the monopolists. This is the most favorable view that can be taken of its effects on society in general.

These monopoly wages cannot, however, be long enforced without strikes. In the long run they are impotent unless enforced by the violent prevention of other laborers from taking the place of the strikers, and thus infringing, as already indicated, on the fundamental rights of man in a manner which no government can fail to crush out by the last exertion of its power, without being recreant to its trust.

It is further demonstrable that strikes, while they involve all these evils, even if successful, cannot permanently, or on a large scale, accomplish their object. It is admitted that in particular cases they may extort temporary wages, whether just or unjust, greater than would otherwise be attainable, because such disasters would ensue to the employer from even the briefest loss of his hands, in a certain stage of his work—as in planting, harvest time, critical conditions in the process of manufacture, building or the fulfillment of contracts—that the employer must submit to the extortion, or to intolerable losses. But such cases are exceptional, and unjustifiable unless the strike is in response to an unexpected lowering of wages, in violation of the contract, express or implied, under which they entered into the work. But in the long run it is impossible that strikes should effect any advance in wages which would not have been sooner and with more advantage accomplished without them. Such strikes must occur upon a falling, stationary, or rising labor market. If upon a falling labor market, this simply means that employers cannot pay existing wages without loss, and the number seeking employment at existing rates exceeds the wants of employers. To refuse to work in order to compel employers to pay rates which would make their business unprofitable is about as wise as to attempt to reverse the law of gravitation or stop the ebb-tide. The strikers only deprive themselves of employment and wages during the period of enforced idleness; and in most cases only relieve their employers of the embarrassment of accumulating an unprofitable and unmanageable surplus stock. On the other hand, if the labor market be stationary, *i. e.*, if there be merely a demand for the existing amount of labor at present prices, then those who pay more than this rate will be undersold by others who procure labor for making the commodities they produce at current market rates. Those who make labor scarcer and higher by refusing to work, do so at the cost of losing more wages during their idleness than they can possibly make up by any increase of wages they thus obtain on returning to their work.

In a rising labor market strikes are wholly unnecessary to secure the rise of wages to which this properly entitles the laborer. If labor can be profitably employed at an advance of rates, the competition of employers for this labor will lead them to bid against each other for it till the highest point is reached at which it can be profitably employed. Beyond this it cannot permanently rise or continue, any more than water can rise above its own level. The only permanent equilibrium is that of the equality of supply and demand. Free competition will compass this with far less friction and greater benefit to all parties than the violent and disturbing agency of strikes, irrespective of the evils and wrongs, before enumerated, which they bring in their train.

The foregoing considerations apply to trades-unions and to strikes as remedies for the grievances of laborers in all occupations. They apply in full force to them when applied to that industry which is occupied in running railway trains. But they suggest only the merest minimum of the mischief, wrongs and devastation they occasion when brought to bear in enforcing control of this particular branch of industry.

Here let it be borne in mind that this control for the purpose of enforcing monopoly wages beyond the average for equivalent service, quantity, quality and responsibility considered, which the labor market can sustain, can only be effected by disabling the road in some way from running. It is not enough that the strikers themselves refuse to run its trains. They must prevent others from running them, either by direct lawless coercion, or by taking violent and lawless possession of the road, or its rolling stock, or putting the latter into conditions or positions in which it cannot be used, or used only by the strikers, or under their direction. Rails may be torn up, switches spiked, locomotives put out of gear or left deserted, with cars, passengers and freight far from round-houses, water-tanks, fuel, so that the road cannot be restored to use till great loss and injury, if not suffering, have been inflicted, not merely upon its owners, but the public who use it. Now this not only damages the particular road concerned and its immediate patrons, but the whole network of roads of which it is a part, including in it such railroad property, amounting to hundreds of millions, and not only this, but the hundreds of millions of property that depends upon the quick railroad transportation, on the faith of which it has been produced. It stops the respiratory and circulatory organs of the body politic, and inflicts upon them as certain prostration and disablement as taking the breath and blood out of the natural body. All industrial, social, commercial, and even governmental agencies are shaped with reference to the locomotive, and its lines of movement over the vast stretches of our national territory, just as much as with reference to the continued flow of our great navigable water-courses, and the winds and currents, the steam and seamanship which render them the facile motors of man and his products where they can meet his wants and desires. The violent seizure and stoppage of them by mobs is a menace and defiance of government itself, and, if carried out, would more effectually disable it than an invading army. It would paralyze its coercive power—thus its sovereignty. For in war everything depends on the mobilization of armies and the material of war by railroads. A large part of the battles in modern warfare are waged for the possession of railroads which are the key to the issue, because the key of access to soldiers and supplies. During the late great strike the State and National Governments were in a number of instances not only defied, but temporarily disabled by the strikers from transporting troops on the railroads to the points where they were needed to suppress the riots; and this to an extent which shocked and alarmed the public. Where, then, would our Government be, if its railroads were once in the hands of those who could and would prevent their use by the public authorities for the movement of the troops necessary to preserve public order, and the persons and property of the people? But this is precisely what the great Brotherhood of Locomotive Engineers assert to be their right and prerogative if the railroads do not concede their demands. They can enforce them by piercing the jugular vein, and striking death into the business, the industry, the subsistence of the people, nay, of the Government itself. And this is to be determined by their head-centre and a few confederates and satellites, whose edict, issued from some secret chamber, ordering the cessation of railroad trains and the seizure of them by the marauders who wrest them from their owners, strikes as much consternation through the heart of this great nation, as the most despotic ukase of the Czar of all the Russias spreads among his subjects.

And is a free people about to sit tamely under such a despotism, and allow their persons, property, liberty, government to be dependent on the beck, the caprice of a junto of men, who stand ready to strike in the dark, from their secret conclave, at everything we hold dear, our very altars and our firesides, no one knows when? Can we endure such an organization among us, reaching with its iron sceptre and Briarean arms over the country, and deserve the name of freemen? And whatever else may be necessary in the way of railroad reform, whether at the hands of our State or National Governments, should we rest until this monstrous usurpation, and fomenting cause of social disorganization, of mobs and riots, of evils, of which the experience of last summer gave us a fearful lesson, be abated and abolished ?

Even as we now write, some ominous mutterings of an intended railroad strike this autumn, to be planned and ordered by this junto, and made universal through the country, sends a shudder through the heart of the people. Will they tamely endure such a tyranny and bear such a yoke thus ? If they will, who shall say that they do not deserve it ? To no class of people are railways such a boon as the poor. These can least afford to be deprived of them. Will they assist in such deprivation ? Dr. Chapin well said, " The locomotive is a great democrat."

This brings us at once to the question forced upon the attention of the country by the late strikes and riots, " What is the relation of the railroads, and of those who in any capacity run and control them, to the Government, whether that of the States through which they pass, or of the nation ?" Thus far railroads have been chartered, and controlled exclusively by the laws of the States in whose territory they are ; and originally, in nearly all instances, they have been chartered with reference to the interests and convenience of the people of the States in which they are respectively located. But, from the necessity of the case, the people of each State desired roads having a continuous connection with roads running through conterminous States and Territories. Hence it has resulted that these roads, in themselves and their connections, run continuously through the country in great trunk, with manifold branch lines. Whatever different corporations may have the original control of the sections of the trunk, or the several branch lines, it is apt to result in this, that any given system or net-work of roads constituting trunk and branch lines comes virtually under the great original trunk line, of which all the rest are branches or extensions. This is a natural result of the far greater economy and efficiency of a single and harmonious, than of a fragmentary and discordant control.

Hence, it has come to pass that, although *per se* State institutions, they are the great arteries of inter-State commerce; so that vastly more commodities pass through them from State to State, and through States and Territories from ocean to ocean, than through navigable streams and water-courses. This being so, it of necessity follows that *so far forth and no further* they come under the jurisdiction of the General Government, through that clause of the National Constitution which gives it control of commerce between the States. This has long been evident to thoughtful publicists ; as, also, that exigencies must ere long arise which would make it clear to all, that the General Government could not long delay the assertion and exercise of that control. This truth has been thrust upon the mind of the country by the recent strike and riots, and has compelled recognition from many who leaned to the extremest views of State sovereignty, and therefore could brook no interference by the General Government with railroads. It is perfectly evident that if States allow mobs and lawless men, by the illegal seizure of railroads, to stop inter-State commerce through them, to prevent the transmission of mails or of Government military forces and supplies, the General Government cannot permit it. It is in duty and by the Constitution bound to re-open communications, to protect its mails and its contractors in carrying them, alike in justice to itself and other States whose prerogatives and just rights are thus infringed. Would it tolerate for a moment any parties or States in obstructing the navigation of our great rivers ? and can it tolerate them in causing or permitting the obstruction of railroad transit after it has become so established and so vast, that the stoppage of it works vastly greater wrong and injury to other States than would result from the damming up of the Delaware, Ohio, or Missouri Rivers ? Is it said that it is time for the General Government to interpose when asked to do so by the State Government ? But suppose the State Government, owing to the sympathy of many of its voters with the mob, refuses to suppress the riot, or open the obstructed railroad on which vast numbers of the people of other States and vast quantities of property and the mails themselves are dependent for movement to their destination ! Is the General Government to suffer all this without failing in its duty to protect inter-State commerce ? On what ground, then, did the U. S. Supreme Court, in the great case of Gibbons *vs.* Ogden, deny to New York, in a decision which has ever since been the unquestioned law of the land, the power to prevent the steamboats of other States from traversing its navigable streams? What is to be done, if the municipal authorities of the States indict the soldiers who fire upon' the mobs as murderers, as they have already done in Scranton and Pittsburgh?

But care must be taken not to stretch this Governmental control of inter-State commerce beyond its due intent and proper limits. It certainly involves the right and duty, when other means are unavailing, of protecting these corporations in the possession and use of their roads and their belongings for those great public and private uses for which they were constructed and their charters given. It includes the power of police, when the States fail to exercise it, and of guarding them against perversion, even by their owners or others who would frustrate the very ends for which they were chartered and invested with corporate powers. But does it go further, and warrant such a disposal or regulative control of this property by the Government, State or national, as essentially to impair or virtually to destroy it?

It is quite natural that much crude thinking and speaking should appear, on the introduction of this subject to the public mind, which will give way to juster views as the subject comes to be more thoroughly discussed and carefully digested. Thus, one scheme that has been proposed is the establishment of a bureau by the Federal Government to adjust the controversies between labor and capital, or at all events between railroads and their employés. But how can such a bureau settle these controversies authoritatively, without infringing on the rights of the owners of the railroads and their employés? How can they compel laborers to accept of given wages, and what right have they to compel railroads or other capitalists to pay any given wages to their employés? And would not the admission of such a right be tantamount to the admission of a right on the part of this bureau to destroy the value of this species of property altogether? And if by this process railroads become bankrupt, as the feebler ones certainly will, what then? What then? What but that they will be abandoned by their owners, and practically withdrawn from use or annihilated? And who will risk capital in building any more railroads, if the result is only to expose them to legislative confiscation? And where does the Constitution confer any such right as this?

Because the Federal control of internal commerce invests Government with the right and duty to keep navigable waters open to water-craft owned in any of the States, does this confer the right to determine the wages that shall be paid to the seamen who man the vessels, or the mechanics who build them, or the owners of the docks which accommodate them, so as to render them worthless? This, so far from regulating, would ruin inter-State commerce. The same is true of railroads, many of which are, at the present wages of workmen and with their present business, on the verge of ruin.

Some journals, whose general ability and soundness only render such a proposal the more astounding, actually propose that the National Government shall apply the Granger legislation of some Western States, which has already ruined several railroads and permanently stopped the construction of new ones, to the whole railroad system of the country. No project could be more visionary or ruinous, and, as we firmly believe, unconstitutional. What clause in the Constitution gives such a right as this? Is it said that the U. S. Supreme Court has upheld such legislation in the Granger States? It has only upheld it in those whose constitutions expressly confer the power of fixing freight and passenger rates on the legislature, and with reference to railways chartered since the adoption of these constitutional provisions. These thus became a part of the provisions of the charter of every road afterward chartered or constructed. But it has not been pretended that such legislation could be applied to other roads not chartered or built subject to such conditions, without violating that article of the National Constitution which prohibits any State from passing laws impairing the obligation of contracts, and from taking private property for public uses without compensation. If the State governments which gave them being cannot impose such exactions upon them, how can the National Government?

If it would be unconstitutional, it would also be in the last degree inexpedient, unjust and ruinous. It is impossible to fix on any rate of charges, which, if reasonable at some times, places and circumstances, would not be utterly unjust and ruinous under other conditions. Thus some roads or sections of them are built at immense cost through deep rock cuttings or tunnels, or by means of enormous embankments, expensive bridging, or with heavy outlays for right of way, while others, in whole or in part, are built over level tracts of cheap land, with little bridging, so that the cost of their road-bed is but a tithe of the former. Then the grades may be so steep and the curves so sharp as to render the cost of moving trains and keeping the road up, double in the one case what it is in another. Then, still further, the business on one road, or part of the same, may be double, triple, or ten-fold that of some other part, rendering it practicable to do a paying business on this part at a vastly lower rate of charge than on the other. These grounds for different charges on different roads, or sections of the same road, have been immensely enhanced by our vicious and fluctuating currency. This renders the same nominal rates of transportation at different times very different in reality, since the same number of legal-tender dollars at one time are worth twice as much as at others—and the railroads themselves must in the latter case pay double the quantity of them for the same service, materials, and other outlays in the maintenance of roadway and transportation. The imposition and enforcement of any uniform rate of transportation upon different roads, or section of the same road, would be in the last degree unjust, oppressive and ruinous. If carried out, it would demoralize and largely sweep away most of the railroad accommodations of the country.

No legislation or interference of the General Government is needed beyond the protection of the property, so that its owners can possess and use it for the purposes for which it was authorized to be constructed—the transportation of persons and commodities for a reasonable compensation, and the protection of those who are ready and willing to labor upon them and run their trains, against all molestation and mob-violence in this useful service. This once thoroughly done, all other questions will be adjusted on the principle of free competition for public patronage and the desire to obtain a remunerative business. It is quite certain that the road will be kept open for the convenience and accommodation of the public to the full extent for which the public is willing to pay. This is the contract made by the State with the investors in railroads, as understood by, and therefore binding upon, all the parties, when no other express stipulation or condition is put in their charters: viz., that, as a consideration for risking or investing their capital in these hazardous enterprises for the public accommodation, they have the State's right of eminent domain conceded to them to the extent of taking for public use the land necessary for its construction, on making due compensation therefor, and of determining the charges to be made for transportation. Unless the abuse of this power be flagrant, so as to frustrate the very ends for which the charter of the road was given and its franchises conferred, the State cannot, except as an act of mere despotism, wrest these privileges from them, unless in the exercise of its power to take private property for public uses, on making, and only on making, due compensation. But one remedy the State and the people always have which is sure to be applied in cases of flagrant and incorrigible abuse, and this is the building of competing roads. These are sure correctives, vastly more efficient and reliable than all other forms of legislative interference or usurpation. This is evident enough when we consider that already the principle has been carried so far in causing the construction of competing roads that they are rapidly not only checking, but consuming each other, until scarcely one-quarter of the railroads in the country pay any interest on their stock, and vast numbers are defaulting on their bonded indebtedness.

And just here we come in sight of the boundary beyond which competition itself gets overdone, and, like so many things good within proper limits, becomes evil when carried beyond them. This has come to pass in respect to the four great trunk lines which compete for the immense carrying trade between the Atlantic cities and those great northwestern and central produce and trade marts, Chicago and St. Louis. By their internecine contest for the through business which centres at these points, they force it down to rates below the mere expense of transportation, leaving out of account remuneration of the capital employed. Such a process continued long enough must force the roads into bankruptcy, unless offset by proportionate charges at other non-competing points. Hence they are constrained at points where they have the power, to exact to the uttermost the privileges of monopoly, or the highest charges for serving the public which can be imposed without driving away their patronage. This works

wrong and evil every way.   The people of the non-competing
points chafe under'such exorbitant charges, not only as such,
but because they are thus put at a disadvantage in comparison with those on the same line of road more distant from
market, and who use twice or thrice, in some cases ten times,
the length of road used by themselves in moving their products
to market.   And here, it may be admitted, is just cause of complaint and irritation.   That the farmers and manufacturers of
Central and Western New York should see their own railroads
used to enable the cultivators of the cheap lands of the West
to get their grain and other commodities to market at less cost
than themselves, and thus virtually to undersell them, is too
much to be borne patiently.   Very much of the prevailing discontent with railroads is due to precisely this cause.   And it
has been said, we know not how justly, that the supineness of
the authorities and inhabitants of Pittsburgh in the first outbreak of the riot, whose unrestrained progress has cost them
so dearly, was largely due to the discontent with high prices
they were compelled to pay for transportation in comparison
with places far more distant from the seaboard.   Other causes
were at work and powerful, such as the trades-unionism of
public officials and the laborers who swelled the mob, and the
desperate malignity of the tramps, communists and criminals,
who were drawn to the riotous assemblages like tigers attracted
by the scent of blood, and who seized the chance for high carnival afforded by the riot for their own demoniacal orgies and
depredations. But undoubtedly the first cause largely explains
a certain degree of that at least passive sympathy with the
strikers and rioters, at which, more than all else, thinking men
stood aghast.   Surely this evil of excessive competition at certain points, always inducing oppressive and offensive monopoly
at others, must be corrected before railroads can be on a right
and secure footing with their employés and the people.   The
reduction of freights from this cause was one of the main
causes which necessitated the late reduction of wages on the
great lines, out of which the strike grew.   Excessive competition at competing points thus aggravates monopoly at non-
competing points.   What is the remedy?
   One is, that the competing roads pool their earnings, on the
basis of fair charges, at competing points, so as to do each a

fair business for a fair compensation. This they attempt every now and then; but some direct or indirect breach of the contract by one of the parties re-opens the strife in more than its former intensity and destructiveness. It is to be hoped that dire necessity will constrain the great companies to agree in adopting this as a permanent remedy. But if they do not, a simple enactment that no rates should be charged at non-competing points higher, *all things considered*, than from competing points, would probably cure the evil. Proper statutes, tribunals and methods would need to be provided to show what is and what is not a violation of this rule. Such legislation, the necessity for which is to be deprecated, and which we trust the wise precautions of these great corporations will hereafter render needless, would rather be regulative for the purpose of insuring the proper uses of railroads as public institutions for the benefit alike of their owners, employés, and patrons, than the assumption of that arbitrary determination of rates by the legislature, which amounts to a power of confiscation, and would be quite certain to gravitate toward that result, unless arrested by the salutary fear of stopping all further investments of capital in railroads. Such arbitrary enactments would, when not specifically provided for in the charter, become a breach of faith.

And here we may say that while we have been strenuous to defend railroad property, not less than all other, against all agrarian and communistic exposure to confiscation, whether direct or indirect, by mobs or under the forms of legislation, and to insist on the same protection for it in the possession and control of its owners as for all other property, yet we fully recognize that, consistently with all this, railroads are public institutions for the public benefit, and therefore, so far subject to public regulation, that they may serve the public uses for which they were chartered, in a degree in which private corporations are not; but not in any such way as subjects them to direct or indirect confiscation any more than manufacturing corporations. They are invested with certain high prerogatives. Like other roads, they can take the property of others for their own uses, upon due compensation, because they are also, and primarily, for public use. They are invested with such other powers as are necessary to their accomplishing the ends for which they were chartered—the rapid and safe transportation of passengers, mails and freights. This gives the State the right, and imposes upon it the duty, of both protecting them in the discharge of these functions and of preventing and stopping abuses, which, so far from aiding, hinder the purposes of their creation, and are alike hostile to the interests of their owners, employés and the public. Thus, one present source of embarrassment to many railroads is the incubus of private companies, made up largely of their managers—such as palace car, fast freight, railway stores and supplies companies—which sponge out the profits of the companies and contribute much to their present embarrassments. It is reported that the Pennsylvania Company is putting an end to this. There is no doubt, still further, that some of our hitherto wealthiest and most prosperous corporations are now prostrated by the magnitude of their fixed obligations to leased lines, which by no means earn what they cost, and by the leasing of which, at rates far beyond any market value, some of the managers of the great roads leasing them made vast sums of money, by buying up the stock at low rates before other parties became aware of the intended lease. The power to leech roads by their managers in such ways does not belong to the original franchises which are necessarily conferred by railroad charters. Legislatures should be slow to grant such power, unless clearly required for the public good ; and when given, this should be on terms which prevent its being made a fraud on the public and on stockholders. Its policy should be to restrain and prohibit all arrangements which fleece the stockholders and the public for the benefit of managers, or other parasites which have fastened upon them to eat out their substance.*

---

* We find the following in a Pittsburgh journal:

The Chicago *Tribune* publishes the report of an interview with a prominent railroad official of that city, in which he says that if the trunk lines would establish a fair schedule of freights, and firmly and honestly adhere to it, they could all do a living business. Being asked if the roads would abide by any compact they might make, he replied : " There is the rub, the rock upon which we have so often split. If we could do away with this throat-cutting business and enter into honorable competition, every line could afford to pay its servants twenty per cent. more than it does now, declare a dividend twice a year, reduce its indebtedness, and in a few years run its stock up to par value." He gave as another reason of the present small profit in the railroad business that the roads maintain so many expensive " suckers," or fast freight lines. On this point he said:

If in these ways some of the managers of railroads or portions of them have thrived at the expense of the roads or their owners; if in such ways and by such means their ability to keep up the accustomed wages of employés has been lessened or destroyed, or has so appeared to these employés, it is no wonder that the latter should take such a reduction ill at the hands of such employers, and feel strongly impelled to resist it by all means in their power, without stopping to consider very scrupulously the lawfulness of their methods. And all the more so, if they see the officials retaining without material decrease the enormous salaries which many of them succeeded in procuring to be voted to themselves in flush and extravagant times. There is no reason why the salaries of officers and heads of such corporations should remain at the same number of dollars at which they were put in inflated times, when a dollar was worth but half what it was previously and is now, and the companies themselves were receiving a high-flown income; why, having been raised from five to ten, and from ten to twenty, and from twenty to forty thousand dollars in such circumstances, they should not revert to somewhat of their former proportions, under a still greater shrinkage in the business and profit of the companies, and in the income of stockholders and of people generally. A mere ten per cent. reduction of a twenty or twenty-five thousand dollar salary leaves its subject in a very different relative position from a reduction of like percentage upon wages running from one to five dollars per day. Making all allowance for difference of station, re-

---

"The expenses of a road appear on the surface to be light, but when you come to consider the innumerable auxiliaries to a well regulated road—the whole grist of 'suckers'—you will be astonished to know that even a nickel is earned above expenses. Each railroad has three or four or more 'lines" hanging to its skirts, and these lines have separate establishments, and separate managers, officials, clerks and runners. They are in themselves, to all intents and purposes, thoroughly organized institutions, and are only secondary to the railroads on whose tracks they run. It costs money to run these lines, but competition has created them and made them appear as a necessity. Are they? That is the question now agitating railroad circles. If the roads would pool east and west bound earnings, then these lines would be short-lived, since there would appear to remain no field for their operations. They are, to all intents and purposes, the drummers of the railroad companies, and they engage in the vocation with the same pertinacity of purpose as do the brass-jeweled gentlemen known as 'commercial travelers.' This line question is one of the nuts which railroad corporations will have to crack ere long."

sponsibility, gifts, expenses and the like, it still remains true that in the former case it cuts far less to the quick than in the latter. We dislike, but none the less feel bound, to say this. Without being experts ourselves, or expressing a positive judgment of our own, we only repeat a very wide expression of the declared judgment of most competent men, that no man's services are in these times worth to any company $30,000 per year, or so valuable that others equally competent and faithful may not be found ready to discharge them for a less sum. While taxes and business depression are eating out the income and destroying the dividends and threatening the safety and solvency of vast numbers of corporations, the question ought to be pressed, Have the salaries of their head officials been adjusted to the times, or shrunk from the swollen dimensions of inflated times, as they should have been?

When, at a recent meeting of the stockholders of a company which, after long and high prosperity, had by imprudent expansions been hurled down to the verge of bankruptcy, it was announced that the president's salary was $25,000 per annum, with no hint of any reduction, it was no wonder that the stock forthwith fell in the market, notwithstanding the emphatic endorsement of the management by the stockholders. We have no doubt that a searching reformatory process is called for in connection with evils and abuses that have stealthily crept into railroad construction and management, as well as other corporate institutions and enterprises, and which it required something like the recent catastrophes to lay bare and correct. It would be strange if, in the unprecedented sudden growth of this great interest, which has fairly gridironed this vast country with iron tracks, and brought fabulous fortunes to many of their builders and managers, it had not been so; not merely as such opportunities attract unprincipled schemers and grabbers as surely as the carcass will draw the vultures, but because so many who would shrink from all direct plunder, all that has the aspect of positive fraud, dishonesty or theft, are not slow to avail themselves of opportunities of enrichment, which, though not a direct or palpable trespass upon the property of the stockholders, are indirectly and really such, even if not seen or suspected to be so. What vast quantities of railroad bonds have been sold, the impression being conveyed to the buyer that they were backed and secured by a large *bona-fide* paid-up stock capital—the real fact being that they were backed by stock on which little or nothing had been paid, but which, if it became valuable, would enrich the holders who had paid nothing; if the enterprise proved unsuccessful the bondholders would be the only losers, thus reversing the true, honest order, and giving the chances to the stockholders or mortgagors while throwing the risk upon the bondholders or mortgagees? And while there have been justifiable cases of stock dividends representing earnings used in construction, undoubtedly there have been great abuses in watering stock.

Here is a wide range for thorough reforms in order to weed out from these corporations all extravagance, nepotism, indirect sponging of their profits, and frauds upon their owners, and to put them upon the most strict and rigid business footing. All mismanagement of this sort, however, is a wrong done by managers to the stockholders, not to the employés. The former suffer a thousand grievances compared with the latter. Indeed, the latter suffer only indirectly, and in some small reduction of their wages; the latter suffer directly and immensely. As a consequence, probably nine-tenths of the railroad stock, and a large proportion of the debentures of the railroad companies of this country are unproductive, and have for the most part, only a nominal or remotely prospective value. This acts, indirectly, indeed, upon railroad employés, by diminishing the ability of the companies to pay generous wages. Yet, so long as the wages are actually up to or in advance of the average wages paid in other employments, as was the case with the operatives who struck last summer, we can see no justification for the strike, much less for the mobs and violence called into being to enforce it.

Yet the responsible nature of railroad service requires a certain grade of capacity, skill and fidelity in the employés. And in order to this, they must have wages adequate to that sort of support which will keep body and mind in a healthful condition. It will not do, therefore, to follow the labor market down to any and every depth to which it may sink, in gauging the wages of trainmen. The safety of the lives and property conveyed on them cannot be ensured without the exercise of that watchfulness which strains attention to the utmost. This cannot · be expected of half-fed or overworked men. It is essential, too, that engineers, conductors, and leading operatives on trains feel alike a pride and interest in their roads, their trains and engines, if the highest efficiency be secured.

Now this loyalty to their vocation and high fidelity to the interests entrusted to them are never secure so long as they are under superior obligations to any other organization so shaped as to be liable to antagonism with their employers. On the other hand, these may well be secure if they are detached from their fealty to these outside and hostile bodies, and if their interests come to be bound up inseparably with the prosperity of the companies which employ them.

In order to this, it is desirable that the employés of the great companies should have, in connection with the company employing them, an accumulating provident fund, furnished partly by contributions from the company, and partly by a small percentage on the wages of the employés, which shall combine some of the essential features of savings-bank and life insurance, and from which, in case of disablement or death, they or their families will receive a certain proportionate allowance or pension. Let vacancies as far as possible be filled by the promotion of the most meritorious from the lower to the higher positions, and as far as possible let new recruits for the service be from the families of existing employés, so that they will look to it with considerable confidence as affording a field for their children after them ; these privileges, of course, all to be forfeited by those who leave the service for any cause but disablement or death. Let this, or some substantially equivalent arrangement, be the basis of the relation between railroad employers and employés, and with this identity of interest, antagonism between the railroads and their employés would cease, and the fell spirit of trades-unionism and strikes would be exorcised. The special hazards of running railroad trains also call for some such provision. The Reading Railroad has already initiated something of this system, and, although in the very centre of strikes and riots, has kept up an unprecedented activity of production and transportation, with low wages for labor. This method has long been practised with marked success on the Eastern Railroad of France. We are glad that the attention of railroads in this country has been directed to the system employed on this French road, in general and in detail, in a lecture delivered in Paris in 1867, by M. F. Jacqmin, manager of the road, a translation of which has recently been pubished in the *Railroad Gazette* of the City of New York. See also *New York Times* of Sept. 18, 1877.

It is quite common to speak of these, and other collisions arising from the unrest of laborers, as outworkings of the conflict between labor and capital. They are not such at all. There is no conflict between these as such. They are mutually auxiliary; capital supports labor, and labor utilizes capital. Either is useless and helpless without the other. The more there is of each, the higher is the bid or reward it will offer for the help of the other. The real conflict is between employer and employé, either of whom may or may not be a capitalist. The carpenter's tools are capital—his own capital. He can do nothing without them. Yet he may be employed by one who has less capital than he. The employer may even borrow capital of his employé, and such loan may have been the consideration inducing such employment of him at certain wages. As between employer and employed, of course, each wishes to make the best terms he can—the one to get the best service he can for his money, the other the most money he can for his service. But what can be more insane than to destroy capital, to burn up property, for the purpose of increasing wages or bettering the laborer? It were as wise to kindle a fire around a powder-house in order to protect it.

There is but one solution of the labor question, and that is, for all to go to work forthwith at the best rates and in the most agreeable occupations open to them which employers can afford to offer them. This will bring production to its maximum in forms and at rates that are marketable—it may be at low rates—so that working at low prices, numerically, they can exchange their labor for commodities likewise as low as the labor which produces them. While men remain idle and produce nothing, they can of course have nothing. The effort to prevent the wages of labor from falling to what employers can pay for it without loss, has done more than all else to aggravate and protract the financial distress, the depressed condition of labor and capital, for the past four years.

To this may be added as next in baleful influence our fluctuating currency, which, now that it has so nearly reached the standard of the honest money of the world through causes beyond the control of politicians or speculators, is certain, if not interfered with by Congressional tinkers, to be soon once more convertible with coin. But a large, and we fear preponderant body are striving to debase our money again to its former depreciated and fluctuating condition. What does it mean ? Was ever such madness ? Has God delivered us over to judicial blindness that we should be unable to see that a promise to pay a dollar binds us to pay it ; or that we should be left to believe that an enactment of our rulers can make permanently irredeemable paper, silver worth ninety per cent. of gold, and gold itself equally valuable, and capable of floating side by side as currency ? *Quem Deus vult perdere, prius dementat.*

Art. XI.—THE TYPICAL SIGNIFICANCE OF ELIJAH AND ELISHA.—2 Kings ii.

By Rev. W. G. Keady, Savannah, Mo.

THAT the career of these two prophets has a more important significance than has usually been accorded to it is a conviction that many have felt.   Our commentators pass over as a problem not to be touched any consideration of the peculiar place which both Elijah and Elisha fill in the development of God's designs of mercy to lost mankind.   Elisha is considered as taking up the unfinished work of Elijah, and the work of both as having importance only as concerns Israel.   The place of Elijah is considered as adequately established when it is said that he was the restorer to Israel of God's covenant, and that he is to be placed side by side with Moses as one of the ruling and representative characters of the old dispensation. This position is assigned him because he was with Moses at the transfiguration ; and the significance of both these men appearing on that occasion is felt to be met when we regard them as representatives of the law and the prophets testifying of the Christ.   But admitting the correctness of these views, which is by no means certain, they certainly do not exhaust the hermeneutical demands of the position either prophet holds in Scripture.   The two questions, " What is there in the new dispensation of which they were the type ? " and, " Was the type fulfilled adequately in John the Baptist ? " have not been satisfactorily answered.   This article is an attempt to find at least materials for an answer.

We will take up the case of Elijah first.   The passages of Scripture in which he is mentioned are few, and we will confine our view to Scripture, without levying upon Jewish tradition for light.   Once only is his name mentioned by the prophets that succeed him, and that is in Mal. iv: 5, 6, the very last utterance of the Old Testament : " Behold, I will send you Elijah the prophet," etc.   It is the *prophet* who is to be sent, not the Tishbite ; so that whether he is to come in person or not, it is his official, not his personal character, that is to be manifested.   In this sense John the Baptist was *an* Elijah in spirit.   Before John's birth it was announced that " many of the children of Israel shall he turn to the Lord their God.

And he shall go before him in the spirit and power of Elijah"
(Luke i: 16, 17). When John was asked, " Art thou Elijah?"
he answered, " I am not." " Art thou that prophet ? " " No."
Now John knew, from the angel's announcement to his father,
that he *was* referred to by Malachi, and no doubt assumed the
dress of Elijah as symbolic of his mission ; yet he evidently
knew, by inspiration, that *he* did not exhaustively fulfill all
that was included in that prophecy, and that there was to be
a future and a fuller fulfillment.

Just after the transfiguration the following conversation
took place between Jesus and his three disciples : " Tell the
vision to no man until the Son of man be risen again from the
dead." They asked, " Why, then, say the scribes that Elijah
must first come?" He replied, " Elijah truly shall come first
and restore all things; but I say unto you that Elijah is come
already, and they knew him not, but have done unto him whatsoever they listed; likewise shall also the Son of man suffer of
them." They understood that he spoke of John the Baptist.
The plain sense of this, taken in connection with John's denial,
which was honest and true, is that Elijah's coming was still
future, in one sense, but that he had already come in another
sense—in the person and mission of John. As there is to be another consummating coming of the Messiah himself, so there
is to be one of his forerunner, Elijah; perhaps in person, as at the
transfiguration, and as intimated in Rev. xi: 3–12; or, more
likely in spirit and in power, as in John the Baptist. The words
" Before the great and dreadful day of the Lord," show that
John cannot be exclusively meant; for he came just before the
day of Christ's coming in grace, though he did indeed appear
previous to " his coming in terror, of which the last destruction of Jerusalem was but the type and the earnest." Elijah's
coming was to " turn the heart of the fathers to the children,
and the heart of the children to the fathers." The angelic
announcement of John's coming explains this by changing the
latter clause to "and the disobedient to the wisdom of the just,
to make ready a people prepared for the Lord ;" implying that
" the reconciliation was to be effected between the unbelieving,
disobedient children and the believing ancestry." The threat
in Malachi is that if this reconciliation is not effected, Messiah's coming would prove a curse to the earth, and not a bless-

ing.   It proved so, at his first coming, to guilty Jerusalem and
the land of Judea when it rejected him, though he did bring
blessing to "as many as received him." Thus, many were
delivered from the common destruction of the nation through
John's preaching—the "remnant" of Rom. xi: 5.   It will
prove so again at his second coming to "those who obey not
the gospel of God," though he comes then to be glorified in
his saints.   But when and who is to be the forerunner of that
event ?

This prophesied coming of Elijah is the very thing that
gives point to the problem of Elijah's place in Scripture, and
we certainly fail to learn the lesson of his life by leaving that
problem to a future solution.   Especially is this the case as we
try to find the significance of the events recorded in the 2d
chapter of the 2d Book of Kings.   What is the significance of
Elijah's "taking up"?   Has it only reference to him personally, or is there not a typical or representative reference?
There is only one parallel case in the Old Testament, the case
of Enoch before the flood.   Is there anything parallel to it in
the New Testament?   It is generally taught, and we believe
correctly, that Elijah, in his appearance at the transfiguration,
in that body on which death had never passed, is the forerunner or first-fruits of the saints who shall be found alive at
the Lord's second coming.   If that be so, then the New Testament parallel to Elijah's "rapture" is found in 1 Thess. iv:
16, 17; "For the Lord himself shall descend from heaven
with a shout, with the voice of the archangel, and with the
trump of God, and the dead in Christ shall arise first.   Then
we which are alive and remain shall be caught up together with
them in the clouds to meet the Lord in the air ; and so shall
we ever be with the Lord."   Now, if Elijah in the transfiguration scene is the forerunner, and, therefore, the type of the
Church of Christ alive at the second coming, was he not that
type in all his career?   When on earth was he not the type
of the Church, or the body of Christ alive at any one time on
the earth?   We are inclined to think that just here is the key
to Elijah's position in sacred history.   The condition of the
Church of Christ (not the professing Church, but the body of
believers in Jesus, the body of Christ, scattered through all
creeds) finds analogy and illustration in all the conditions of

Elijah's life.   The mission of the Church in the world and to
the world "out of Christ," is wonderfully analogous to the
mission of Elijah to degenerate Israel.   The seeming failure of
that mission and its assured accomplishment in God's time is
illustrated in the scene on Horeb; while the witness-bearing
of the Church to the crucified Christ is illustrated by the
prophet's position at Carmel.   The hope of the Church which
shall be alive at the coming of the Lord is to be "caught up" to
heaven as Elijah was.   Whether Elijah is to come in person
or not, is it not true that the Church now living on earth, from
her very position, is *an* Elijah, "to make ready a people prepared for the Lord?"   Is she not, as much as John was, "a
voice crying in the wilderness"?   Does she not fulfill the
prophecy and type of Elijah as much as John did?   The
Church, as the ingathering of the Gentiles, has still before it a
prophetic work.   Israel is under the curse.   Is it not probable
that she shall be as successful at least as John was; nay, may
not to her be given the full completion of Elijah's work—the
bringing back of Israel to the broken covenant, to their rejected
Messiah?

If the rule is a good one which we apply in interpreting
nearly all the other Old Testament personages, making them,
either in their characters or peculiar circumstances, to serve as
typical or representative of New Testament characters or circumstances in these gospel times, then there is no reason why
Elijah should be excluded from its operation.   The view we
have taken shows that his position has a much higher significance and one that has been overlooked.   The place we would
find for him in the history of redemption, authorized, as we
believe, by all that is said of the place of the Church on earth
as the body of Christ, gives each of us who are believers in
Jesus a personal interest in Elijah and a connection with his
wonderful history that are full of instruction.   It enables us to
realize our dignity and importance as witnesses for Jehovah, in
a way that no definite statement of a fact could equal.   Elijah's
career is, as it were, an acted allegory of our position as in the
world and not of it.   It materializes for our inspection the hidden forces that are carrying forward Christianity to its ultimate
triumph.   Christianity is what it is as the consequence of the
union of Jesus, the living Head, to his living body, the Church,

in the one Spirit. The results have not come from the efforts of the Church as individuals, but from the power that is hid in her—the hidden life. It is as true of the Church in her work on earth, as it is true of each believer in working out his own salvation, "that it is God who worketh in her, both to will and to do of his good pleasure."

But, as before intimated, the position of the Church now living on earth (which may be "*we* which are alive and remain") does not fulfill *all* that is meant by the prophesied sending of Elijah "before the great and dreadful day of the Lord;" so neither does the history or the position of Elijah fully represent what the Church is in the world. As is frequently the case, the type needs here to be supplemented. As it required the several kinds of offerings—the burnt, the trespass, the meat, etc.— to set forth fully in various aspects the one great atoning sacrifice, so there was necessity for an additional character to fill up the type of the Church, *sent* into the world. This is furnished by the history of Elisha. Elijah and Elisha form together *one type;* and only as so considering can we get a clear, intelligible view of the mission of either. Elisha does not *supersede* Elijah; he carries on the same work; the same Spirit works; one work, the one purpose of God. The Church in one generation does not supersede the Church of a preceding generation, for it is the same Church; the "One Spirit" carries on by the Church, in all ages, "all that Jesus *began* both to do and teach."

It is the opinion of many who have been interested in the study of Elijah that his mission as prophet practically ended at Horeb. We are inclined to think that he there for the first time really understood what his mission was, and that instead of ending it with the appointment of his successor, he really began to do that for which he was sent—his appointment of his successor being the chief part perhaps of his work. Horeb was his Pentecost. That period of Elijah's life prior to the scene at Horeb, full of grand and imposing incidents, was the period of God's manifesting *himself,* and therefore of divine attestation to Elijah's mission. It was as necessary for Elijah that such a state of things should cease, as it was for the Church that Jesus should go away that the work of the Spirit might begin. The period after Horeb was that of quiet, unrecorded work in the carrying out of the prophet's mission, which could not have been done but for the previous divine manifestations. The analogy is borne out in the history of the Church before and after the ascension of Jesus. His display of divine power had apparently no greater effects than that of Elijah, yet it was the foundation and beginning of all that followed; and the forty days between death and ascension were days at Horeb to the disciples. For nearly ten years after Horeb, Elijah was quietly doing his work. There is no record of it, it is true, just as for ages there is no great record of the work of the Church; yet she was in the world and at work, and to-day we but carry on what was then begun; and the work will go on till he comes to receive his own to himself. We get a hint in this chapter of what formed perhaps the larger part, perhaps the distinctive part, of Elijah's work, and that is in the incidental mention of "the sons of the prophets." There were at least three schools of the prophets, located in the very centres of idol worship. If we bear in mind the former hatred of Jezebel against the prophets, and the wholesale slaughter she made in their ranks, we cannot avoid the impression that the general strength of the apostasy had been already broken by Elijah. The "seven thousand" had no doubt increased, and here were communities formed for the purpose of raising up instructors to feed and comfort and strengthen God's little flock. Elijah had set in operation the machinery which the Spirit of God uses that the truth may be witnessed for and disseminated. Here were found those who were "the salt of the earth" to Israel, the presence of the few righteous for whose sake the whole nation was not cut off. That the formation and nourishment of these schools formed the part of his work upon which his heart was set, is evident from the fact of his visiting them just before his departure.

And the end crowns the work—an end that was hardly in unison with a life of inactivity, or a mission that had been forfeited. The providence of God has always in it what we partially recognize as "the fitness of things." The closing scene of the prophet's career has a magnificent appropriateness in view of its typical significance. We think we can read between the lines here, that, so far as the latter part of Elijah's life was in the sight of God, it was grander than the former part ; just as the first and unrecorded part of the life of Jesus was as well pleasing to the Father as the latter part, wonderful as it is to us.   Elijah's life may be condensed in the same words as that of Enoch's : " And he walked with God, and he ` was not, for God took him."

Now Elisha enters upon the scene and takes up the thread of Elijah's work.   It will not do to say it was an *unfinished* work.   Had Elijah had no successor, we see clearly how his mission would have been rounded off by his " taking up into heaven."   The same may be said of the Church's mission in the world.   She still has her commission to perform, a commission without limit in the world. and she thinks it is not all fulfilled as yet; and yet, if the Lord should come to receive her to himself *now*, we know she would not leave an unfinished work.   It is better to say Elisha took up the same work.

As Elijah is the type of the Church's being in the world, witness bearing for her Lord, so Elisha is as truly the type of the Church, as bearing the gospel of God's love to ruined men. Elijah illustrates the meaning of the very existence of the Church in the world, her *passive* teaching.   Elisha illustrates her activity—the Church as a force in the world.   Elijah partially found his prototype in John the Baptist ; Elisha partially found his in the earthly life of Jesus.   Their names are significant in this connection ; Elijah means " My God·is Jehovah," or, " the strength of the Lord ; " Elisha means " My God is the Saviour," or, " the salvation of God."   The former proclaims *who* God is ; the latter proclaims *what* God is ; and this is precisely expressive of what the Church does.

The difference in the personal characteristics of the two men is significant.   To use the words of Dr. Taylor, " There is a striking contrast between them.   Mystery and majesty were the warp and woof of the Tishbite's career.   His course was one of startling appearances, defiant utterances, and mysterious hidings.   He·had no domestic surroundings, no ties to earth, apparently no settled place of abode, and so when he went up to glory, his translation is felt to be the fitting termination of his meteoric career."   Just so it may be said of the earth-living part of the body of Christ, " not of the world," while in it ; her only home, her abiding city, is not here.   But, on the other hand, " Elisha was of a social nature.   He came from a

happy household in Abel-Meholah, and had his dwelling in
the city of Samaria. Sometimes he is found amid the solitudes of Carmel, but generally he sought the haunts of men,
and he seems to have been equally at home in the courts of
the princes and in the colonies of the sons of the prophets."
He fitly illustrates the very position the Church assumes "in
the world," while not of it. Again, "the predominant feature
of Elijah's ministry was sternness. He had, indeed, a spring
of tenderness in his heart, but his work was mainly that of
judgment": and such is one feature of the Spirit's office in
the Church. "And when he is come, he will reprove (convince)
the world of sin, of righteousness, and of judgment ; of sin, because they believe not on me ; of righteousness, because I go to
my Father and ye see me no more ; of judgment, because the
prince of this world is judged."* "But Elisha was almost
always throughout his ministry a healer. His life was like a
stream which irrigated the land with blessing." And this is
the influence of the active life of the Church. Two diverse, but
not conflicting characters has she, according to the standpoint
from which she is viewed ; Elijah and Elisha combined. Her
office is like the gospel, a two-edged sword, to condemn and
to save. Just so is her office diversely intimated in the words
of her great Head: "God sent not his Son into the world to
condemn the world" (for it was condemned already), "but
that the world through him might be saved" (John iii: 17).
"Now is the judgment of this world : now shall the prince of
this world be cast out. And I, if I be lifted up, will draw all
men unto me." Is it not true, that the only way the cross of
Christ *now* draws all men unto it is in *judgment ;* some in condemnation, because they "have not believed in the name of
the only begotten Son of God ;" some in "no condemnation,"
because they "are in Christ Jesus"?

Though the circumstances of the death of each of the prophets were dissimilar, yet the record furnishes an "undesigned
coincidence," which inspiration may have designed to link
them in one type. When Elijah was taken up, Elisha cried,
"My father, my father, the chariot of Israel, and the horsemen thereof." When Elisha was about to die, "Joash, the
King of Israel, came down to him, and wept over him and

---

*John xvi : 8-11.

said, Oh, my father, my father, the chariot of Israel, and the horsemen thereof." These prophets had been the channel through which flowed to Israel all the good and blessing it had enjoyed, and when they were gone, it was as if its strongholds had been broken down, its dependence removed. "When Lot was taken out of Sodom, Sodom was blotted from the world." When the Church is taken out of the world, then comes judgment and destruction.

We need not go out of this one chapter to find illustrations for our views. The incidents connected with the opening of Elisha's career seem to be specially intended to *identify* his errand and authority with those of his predecessor. He receives Elijah's mantle—symbol of the identity of spirit, and spiritual work and spiritual power—a symbol as were the tongues of fire at Pentecost. It was a visible token to Elisha that his request had been granted. We never hear of his using it but once, and that was at the moment when he actually took up his predecessor's work by invoking Elijah's Lord, and repeating Elijah's last act of faith as the first act of faith in God and in his mission. He advanced at once into the exact line of his predecessor's undertaking. Over Jordan, to Jericho, to Bethel, to Carmel he went, recognized everywhere as he upon whom "the spirit of Elijah was." We have here as perfect an illustration as could be given of the true apostolic succession; the individuals of the living Church change and give place to their successors, but the Church lives on, the living body of Christ.

The first acts of Elisha's ministry signally favor the view we have taken. Those first acts showed him as the depository of the power of God in mercy and in judgment. The two miracles, in one of which he was an active agent, in the other passive, present the two leading features that characterize the mission of the' Church in the world. They, moreover, by the diversity in their character, identify him again with Elijah in one type; for the first miracle was characteristic of his ministry in the main, and the latter of Elijah's. In the first miracle we have the removal of the curse from Jericho—illustrative of the removal of the curse from the world. Elisha took a new cruse with salt in it, and cast the salt into the fountain-head of the waters whose destructive qualities rendered a pleasant situation a barren waste.

The " thus saith the Lord" makes this act of more than a local significance. The curse on Jericho, though it occasioned the death of the rebuilder's family, was not removed by the execution of the penalty. The curse attached to the broken law, which fell on the human race, would not be removed by the death of the whole race. The Son of God himself must go to the fountain-head, sin itself, and " put away sin by the sacrifice of himself." And this is the *gospel*, " preached before" unto Jericho, which the Church bears to a sin-cursed world.

The other miracle, in which Elisha was not the agent, is of solemn import, for it is one of judgment. Our version, by designating the scoffers as " little children," when they were young men, is suggestive of an unintentional irony (" he that sitteth in heaven shall laugh"), that describes, more aptly than words can do, a certain class of men, not always young, who deem it "very smart" to be skeptical, yet who are indeed *very* " little children" in intellect. They were counterparts of the Jews who blasphemed the Spirit's testimony to Jesus ; the judgment in both cases is alike : " Wherefore I say unto you, All manner of sin and blasphemy shall be forgiven unto men ; but the blasphemy against the Holy Ghost shall not be forgiven unto men." " The word ' cursed,' " says Tayler Lewis, " is too strong a translation, as *reproved* would be too mild. It should rather be *denounced;*" he denounced them for their great sin— an offence committed not against him, but against Jehovah ; an inherited sin, their parents having rejected the Lord, for which they had already incurred God's displeasure, " condemned already." Such is the thought suggested by the words, " in the name of the Lord." Elisha went to Bethel with a blessing, just as he had gone to Jericho. Jericho received him in the name of the Lord, as a man of God, and was blessed. The manner of his reception at Bethel brought down judgment " that had waited." Such are the consequences that follow the reception of the gospel which the Church has to bring. If men refuse Jesus Christ and salvation, they receive the punishment to which they are " condemned already." If they receive him, the very receiving opens up all the resources of God for blessing ; the curse is removed, and life and soul-health and fruitfulness given in its place.

Art. XII.—CONTEMPORARY LITERATURE.

THEOLOGY.

Bibliotheca Symbolica Ecclesiæ Universalis. The Creeds of Christendom, with a History and Critical Notes. By PHILIP SCHAFF, D.D., LL.D., Professor of Biblical Literature in the Union Theological Seminary, New York. 3 vols. Pp. 941, 557, 880. Harper & Brothers, 1877.

We have here a massive work, in three stout volumes, of some 2,400 pages, on a subject which is not only important in itself, but also lies at the root of many burning questions of the day in all the lands of Christendom. We know of no one else who could so well produce a work of this character as Dr. Schaff, whose intimate acquaintance with many different nationalities and churches, and whose broad and catholic spirit, and thorough historical training, enable him to truly appreciate the historical individualities of the various branches of the Church of Christ, and trace them in their growth from the common root. The work is stored full with treasures of learning, yet is not scholastic ; it is critical in its discriminations, yet is not polemical. Still less does it with a superficial, irenic spirit undervalue important things and overestimate little things, stretching and straining for harmony where it does not and cannot exist; but with a manly, truth-loving and sympathetic spirit, the author states the difference fairly and clearly, without misrepresentation, and accompanies the statements with the material itself and ample authorities. The work satisfies a demand of the times that has constantly been growing stronger, and which such special collections as Walch, Müller, Niemeyer, Denzinger and Dunlop, and such comparisons of symbols as we find in Mohler, Winer, Guerike, Hoffman and Oehler, written with more or less polemic spirit and sectarian bias, have only made more apparent.

Dr. Schaff gives us in Vol. I. a history and critical account of the various creeds of Christendom, and in Vols. II. and III. the creeds themselves in the original texts, with translation and critical notes.

Vol. I. treats the History of Creeds. After discussing some general questions in Chapter 1, such as the name and definition, origin, authority, value and use and classification of creeds, the author passes over in Chapter 2 to the consideration of the Œcumenical Creeds, and justly condemns the damnatory clauses of the Athanasian Creed. Chapter 3 treats of the Creeds of the Greek and Oriental churches, including the Nestorians, Jacobites, Copts and Armenians, giving also an account of the correspondence between the Anglo-Catholics and the Russo-Greek Church. Chapter 4 deals with the Roman creeds, discussing very fully the Syllabus of 1864, the Vatican decrees and the Old Catholic movement. Chapter 5 considers the Evangelical Creeds in general, distinguishing first between the *evangelical* or *orthodox* Protestantism and *heretical* or *radical* Protestantism; the latter are very properly ruled out of the creed formation of Christendom. Evangelical Protestantism is then considered in its essential principles, and divided into the Lutheran, Reformed, and other evangelical denominations.   These are then considered in the following chapters: Chapter 6 shows the creed formation of the Lutheran Church from the Augsburg Confession to the scholastic Formula of Concord and Saxon Articles.   Chapter 7 exhibits the historical development of the numerous Reformed confessions.   (1) The Swiss from the Zuinglian Creeds through the Calvinistic to the scholastic Helvetic Consensus Formula.   (2) The French and Dutch from the Gallican to the Synod of Dort.   (3) The German Reformed confessions in the various German States.   (4) The Reformed confessions in the border lands of Bohemia, Poland and Hungary.   (5) The Anglican Articles of religion from the doctrinal formula of Henry VIII, to the Articles of the Reformed Episcopal Church in 1874.   (6) The Scotch Confessions.   (7) The Westminster Standards.   These are regarded as the fullest and ripest symbolical statements of the Calvinistic system.   The Confession is carefully analyzed and its comparative merits brought out, and is then on the other hand criticised as embodying too much metaphysical divinity and overstepping the limits which divide a public confession of faith from a scientific treatise of theology, and still further, as making the predestinarian scheme to control the historical and Christological scheme.   The history of the Westminster standards in America is finally considered, and the relation of the Cumberland Presbyterians thereto.   Chapter 8 gives an account of the creeds of the modern evangelical denominations, including the Congregationalists, Baptists, Friends, Moravians, Methodis's, Irvingites, concluding with the Evangelical Alliance and a carefully composed statement of the consensus and dissensus of Christendom.

Vol. II gives the creeds of the Greek and Latin churches.   Chapter 1, the Scripture confessions of Nathanael, Peter, Thomas, the Eunuch, the baptismal formula, and other allusions to creeds in the epistles.   Chapter 2, the anti-Nicène and Nicène rule of faith and Baptismal Creeds, with a comparative table of them as related to the Apostles and Nicène Creeds.   Chapter 3, the Œcumenical Creeds, showing the process of the formation of the so-called Apostle creed, and giving the Nicene and Athanasian. and closing with the Creed of the Sixth Council.   Chapter 4, Roman Creeds of Trent and the Vatican.   Chapter 5, Russian and Greek Creeds.   Chapter 6, Old Catholic Union Creeds.

Vol. III gives the Creeds of the Evangelical Church.   Part I, the Lutheran.   Part II, the Reformed.   Part III, the modern Protestant Creeds, with an appendix containing an evangelical union catechism.

This volume is enriched with numerous fac-similes of the first edition of the confession and with the critical text and variations of the principal editions. Each of the volumes is accompanied with an index.   No Christian minister, no intelligent layman, can afford to do without a work which is a masterpiece of theological learning, and a treasury of information with reference to all branches of the Church of Christ.

The New York Religious Newspaper Agency, 21 Barclay Street, publish *Lectures by Joseph Cook*, on—1. *Certainties in Religion ;* 2. *The Atone-*

ment; 3. *God in Natural Law;* 4. *New England Skepticism;* 5. *Tri-unity and Tritheism.*

Mr. Cook has already become famous, and these lectures are among the chief works that have, and we may say justly, made him so. Their celebrity is due partly to the place and circumstances of their delivery, but still more to their inherent power, without which no adventitious aids could have lifted them into the deserved prominence they have attained. They constitute really a bold and strong defence of some of the fundamental articles of evangelical truth and catholic Scriptural theology—the very bulwarks of Christianity—against the incessant assaults they have so long suffered in front, flank and rear from the various grades of skepticism, rationalism, and nihilism, whose literary and polemical centre is also that of their intellectual, numerical and material support—the metropolis of New England. Here the vaunted religion of culture, progress, refinement, in forms now transcendental and now materialistic, has for more than half a century lifted up its head, and looked down in scorn upon, while it has spawned out its caricatures of, the religion of Christ crucified, which is to the Jews a stumbling-block and to the Greeks foolishness; but to them that are called, both Jews and Greeks, the wisdom of God and the power of God. With their resources of wealth, ancestral prestige, learning and culture in that city, they have undoubtedly more or less stifled the evangelicals into undue reticence, timidity, softliness or complaisance toward all these hosts of adversaries, in contending for the faith once delivered to the saints. The very atmosphere is repressive and dispiriting to the friends of truth. In the past it required the thunder-tones of Griffin and Lyman Beecher to stir and retone the murky air, breathe new life and courage into orthodoxy, and take down the empty pretentiousness of the cultivated caricaturists of the true religion. And we think the time had fully come for Mr. Moody in the great tabernacle, and Mr. Cook in the lecture hall, to proclaim and defend the unvarnished gospel with a ringing clearness and boldness which, while it infused new courage into the friends of truth, learned and unlearned, their adversaries were not able to gainsay or resist.

Mr. Cook has read to good purpose, and digested the current literature that could be of any service in exposing the flippant pretensions of Unitarianism and its affiliated heresies, whether the productions of friends or foes. His style, if here and there overdone in the way of conceits and oddities, is, on the whole, quite fresh, breezy and bracing. He is a great master of analysis. He probes to the bottom the pretensions of adversaries, and boldly exposes their futility in a manner which cannot fail to make its way to thinking minds—whether from the rostrum or the press. We have no doubt that for Mr. Cook's special work and field, with its surroundings, the lecture-stand is a far better *pou sto* than the pulpit, and the week-day more opportune than the Sabbath. We augur great good from these discourses, and hope they will be still further followed up as occasion may require.

It does not detract from the great merit of these lectures that all their utterances are not equally ripe and well poised. The lecture on the Atonement is generally just, able and unanswerable. He is right in saying that Christ never in any such sense bore the punishment of our sins as to be himself personally a sinner. But he is mistaken in supposing that it was left for any modern theological discoverer, whether in or out of New England, to detect and make known that fact: or that any forms of the doctrine of vicarious sacrifice which have been extensively held or set forth by standard theologians, or in recognized symbols, countenance any such idea, or have led those who embraced these views to entertain it. They are no more obnoxious to it than those passages of Scripture which represent Christ as bearing our sins, becoming a curse—nay, becoming sin for us—while yet he knew no sin. How did he become sin, or bear sin, otherwise than by bearing its curse in our stead?

But we think, on the whole, that Mr. Cook shows singular justness of view in his manner of treating the most difficult and perplexing themes, *e. g.*, God in Natural Law, and the Triunity.

T. & T. Clark of Edinburgh, and Scribner, Welford & Armstrong of New York, publish, at $2, *Outlines of Biblical Psychology*, by J. T. BECK, D.D., Prof. Ord. Theol., Tübingen. Translated from the third enlarged and corrected German edition, 1877. The author has worked to good purpose a mine which will bear working still further. The Germans have done much more on this subject than the English. Such treatises especially as Coos' *Fundamenta Psychologiæ ex Sacra Scriptura Collecta* will richly repay careful study. But beyond all others this little volume is *multum in parvo* on this great subject, which no one can be ignorant of, or in serious error about, without forfeiting all title to be counted a master of exegetical, systematic, or biblical theology. The relation of the soul to the body and spirit, as set forth in the Scriptures, is carefully exhibited and profoundly treated. The great chapter of the volume is the last, entitled "Life of the Human Soul as centred in the Heart." The light which a careful collation and exegesis of the passages of Scripture in which the word "heart" is used sheds on this subject, is surprising. It is clearly shown to be in Scriptural usage the centre, seat, substance of man's moral nature, faculties and states. We are strongly of opinion, without endorsing all the positions or interpretations of the author, that scarcely any other work within so short a compass helps more to an insight into the inner meaning of Scripture, directly in respect to its anthropology, and indirectly in regard to its soteriology.

The same houses also publish, at $6, *The Scriptural Doctrine of Sacrifice*, by ALFRED CAVE, B.A., a solid and exhaustive treatise, in which the manifold beams of Scriptural light upon the subject are gathered to a focus. While he defines a sacrifice as "a gift to God, a surrender to Jehovah of that which has cost the offerer something," and maintains the true sacrificial and substitutional character of our Lord's death, he also exposes the falsity of the theories of McLeod Campbell, Bushnell, and Dale. He maintains his positions with learning and ingenuity. But he carries his views to the extreme length of supporting the sacrificial character of the Eucharist. He contends that the Lord's Supper is not simply a memorial or sign of Christ's sacrifice, but is itself a true and proper sacrifice.

Scribner, Armstrong & Co. publish *The Religious Feeling a Study for Faith*, by NEWMAN SMYTH. Although this is our first introduction to Mr. Smyth, it raises the hope that we shall hear more of him and from him hereafter It gives promise of high service in philosophico-religious authorship, and is certainly a valuable contribution toward the solution of the controversy in regard to the origin and nature of the moral sense and religious feeling in man, particularly in the form which has been given it by the idealistic and materialistic, the transcendental and evolutionary systems of philosophy, alike at their respective points of confluence and of conflict.

Mr. Smyth first urges, and we think unanswerably demonstrates, that the feeling of dependence on a Higher Power is natural and universal; is the under-basis or prime constituent of religious feeling; that it is variously recognized by such evolutionists as Spencer and Tyndall under the titles of " Unknown Cause," " The Unseen Reality," " The Ultimate Existence," " The Inscrutable Power ;" that the existence and operation of this feeling cannot be accounted for by any evolution from other forces, elements or experiences of our nature ; that it is no development from matter, or any experiences, sensations or modifications of mere material organisms ; that it is therefore original, and is immediately implanted in the human soul as to its germ by its Maker ; and is itself a presumption and guarantee of the truth and reality of the Being or Power toward which this feeling of dependence points.

The author then proceeds with a similar analysis in reference to our moral feelings and ideas. He shows that they are not developed or compounded from other ideas, feelings or experiences, from which Materialists, Hedonists and Associationists undertake to derive them. He presents a powerful defence of Intuitionalism against the assaults of Epicureanism and Utilitarianism.

He next shows how the moral and religious feelings imply, support, and interpenetrate each other—a matter which is too much overlooked or ignored by ethicists and theologians. He then goes forward to show the relation of religious feeling to religious cognition— an important and difficult subject. We sometimes thought Mr. Smyth had a tinge of mysticism in his tendency to ground religious cognition in feeling as its ultimate ground. The truth undoubtedly is that all rational, moral or religious feeling must be evoked and guided by the corresponding objects, or truths seen by the intellect—else it is blind, fortuitous, aimless, and can have no moral or religious character. But at the outset, doubtless, these views of the intellect are more or less dim and indistinct, and become more and more clarified with our moral, religious and intellectual growth. In this respect, moral and religious knowledge and feeling are not peculiar. The feeling of beauty, for example, involves as its condition some cognition of this beauty, or it would be impossible. This may be ever so dim and rudimental at first, but for all that, it is none the less real, and susceptible of indefinite culture in respect to distinctness and adequacy. Mr. Smyth very justly applies Hamilton's maxim in regard to sensation and perception to this whole subject, viz.: that feeling and cognition, whether in the sense or above the sense, sustain to each other an inverse ratio—as one increases, the other decreases. Still, they both coexist; and the latter first in order, as the basis and guide of the former.

In the concluding chapter Mr. Smyth applies the tests and verifications which vindicate his view against the objections of adversaries. Throughout the whole he shows a learning, acuteness, and fairness which must command their respect, if not their assent to his positions.

Macmillan & Co. of London issue the following additions to the means at our command for the better knowledge of primitive patristic literature: 1. *A Dissertation on the Epistle of Barnabas,·including a Discussion of its Date and Authorship*, by the Rev. WM. CUNNINGHAM, *together with the Greek Text, the Latin Version, and a New English Translation and Commentary.* The substance of it, in a slightly different form, obtained the Hulsean prize in 1874, and is published in consequence of the conditions imposed by the trustees of that prize. The author has been aided in the recasting by his friend Mr. G. H. RANDALL, Fellow of Trinity College. The latter has also edited the texts, and furnished an English translation and commentary, which add much to the value of the book. The dissertation is very scholarly and thorough. The text, translations and typography are excellent.

The result of the investigation, so far as the question of authorship is concerned, is that Mr. Cunningham deems it "certain that this epistle could not have been written by the companion of St. Paul; but that its author was a Gentile, and probably connected with Alexandria, who had come under many Jewish influences, and who had not shaken off those influences so thoroughly as St. Paul had done, and who accordingly regarded the old dispensation in a spirit of active opposition rather than of serene superiority. He was infected with Alexandrian philosophy to a slight extent, at least in so far as it had borne fruits in the allegorizing of the Old Testament, and wrote about A.D. 79. He cannot be quoted as an independent witness of the truth of any facts of gospel history, for he made use of the gospel of St. Matthew, and for anything that the epistle shows to the contrary, of that gospel in its present form. His mode of quoting this book seems to show that he ranked it along with the Old Testatament Scriptures and the Apocrypha. There is no certain testimony to be drawn from his work in regard to any other books comprised in the canon of the New Testament."—P. 105.

2. The other book issued by the above house is entitled *St. Clement of Rome; an Appendix containing newly recovered portions, with Introductions, Notes and Translations*, by J. B. LIGHTFOOT, D.D., Professor of Divinity, Cambridge. It is a supplement to the edition of Clement's Epistles by the same author, published in 1869. It supplies the new matter requisite to complete Clement's works, since the only source of previous editions were from the Alexandrian MSS. now in the British Museum, and which are so badly mutilated that about one·tenth of the original is lost. Scholars had given up all hope of the complete restoration of the original. But within a short time two distinct, complete copies of this have come to light,

which had previously eluded the search of scholars and antiquarians, and have been published. The first is a manuscript found in the Library of the Most Holy Sepulchre at Constantinople. This was published, with prolegomena and notes, by Philotheos Bryennios, Metropolitan of Serrae, in 1875.

A few months after the results of this important discovery were given to the world, a second authority for the complete text of Clement's two epistles came to light. It was a manuscript copy of them in Syriac, which, being advertised for sale as a part of the Oriental library of M. Julius Mohl of Paris, was purchased by the Cambridge University Library. It was the only Syriac MS. in M. Mohl's collection. Although it had most singularly escaped the notice of French Orientalists, it was found by both internal and external evidence to be entitled to great consideration in revising and completing the text of the Clementine Epistles. The present volume, printed in the best style, is a continuation of Prof. Lightfoot's previous edition of them, and is paged accordingly. It adds whatever these recently-discovered manuscripts furnish for giving value and completeness to his previous edition.

Origin and Doctrines of the Cumberland Presbyterian Church, by E. B. CRISMAN, D.D.   St. Louis, 1877. This work was first published in 1856, in pamphlet form, and in 1858 was enlarged and issued in a volume. The demand for it has been such that the author has now issued a new edition, greatly enlarged and improved. While the book possesses special value to the denomination whose History and Doctrines it so clearly and ably sets forth, it is also of interest to every branch of the Christian Church. The high position of Dr. Crisman in the Cumberland Church gives a semi-official character to his book, which is recognized as authority by the denomination which he so worthily represents. If we were called upon to criticise his Doctrinal Statements, we should take exception to many points, especially in the chapter defining the "Theological Position" of his branch of the Church, as contrasted with "Calvinism" and "Arminianism." But this is not the place for adverse criticism on such a subject.

The Higher Life Doctrine of Sanctification tested by the Word of God, by HENRY A. BOARDMAN, D.D., is published by the Presbyterian Board of Publication. We have evinced our sense of the importance of this subject, and of its thorough discussion at the present time, in the space we devoted to it in our July number. Almost simultaneously this excellent volume, by one of the venerable masters in our Israel, was issued by our Board, showing that the importance of meeting the present phases and aspects of this doctrine had come to be widely felt among those most likely to know the wants of the Christian community. For our own sentiments in the premises we can only refer to the article before mentioned. Our estimate of this book is best expressed by saying that had it been published before that article had gone to press, we should have deemed it unnecessary to have put ourselves to the trouble of preparing it. The antidote to this one-sided and distempered form of Christian doctrine and life is so thoroughly and ably presented in this volume that we hope it will receive a wide circulation.

The Presbyterian Board also issue *Pastoral Theology—The Pastor in the Various Duties of his Office*, by THOMAS MURPHY, D.D., pastor of Frankford Presbyterian Church, Philadelphia, a solid and handsome octavo, which is replete with sound and judicious suggestions for the appropriate and successful discharge of every class of pastoral duties. There are few young pastors or candidates who may not profit by attention to the counsels and hints here given. These are largely infused with the instructions received by the author from those great pastors and professors, Samuel Miller and Archibald Alexander, amplified by frequent quotations from other eminent pastors or teachers of Practical Theology. The whole is pervaded by that good judgment and common sense, the lack of which gives rise to more frequent failures in the pastorate, and brings to grief more ministers not wanting in solid and brilliant gifts united to marked fidelity, than any other cause. This volume is valuable because it shows the application of sanctified common sense to every department of pastoral and church life, and makes evident the vast benefits thereof.

In Christ; or, the Believer's Union with his Lord, by A. J. GORDON, pastor of the Clarendon Street Church, Boston. Gould & Lincoln, 1872. This is an excellent unfolding of a theme which, however familiar, never loses its freshness and interest in competent hands. It is lucid, devout and edifying. We regret to observe that a book which has so much to commend it to general and catholic use should take the ground that immersion alone is baptism, and that it alone is fitted to symbolize the efficacy of Christ's death and resurrection.

BIBLICAL LITERATURE.

The Homilist. Conducted by DAVID THOMAS, D.D. Religious Newspaper Agency, 1877, New York. This is an exact reprint of the London edition of a work which has attained to great popularity and a wide circulation abroad. It is Vol. XII of the Editor's Series, and Vol. XXXVII from commencement. It is sold at about half the price of the English edition. Few living men have done more than Dr. Thomas in the line of this book, which embraces a wide range of homiletic topics, treated briefly, sometimes exegetically, and sometimes in sermonic form, but always with the view of shedding fresh light on the Bible, and aiding in its true exposition and practical enforcement. It contains the "seeds" of sermons, and cannot fail to prove highly acceptable and useful to the ministry. It is undenominational.

We learn from the publishers—and are not surprised at the fact—that it has been received with great favor, and the first edition of 3,000 copies is already nearly exhausted. It speaks well both for our friends, the enterprising publishers, and the ministry of the day, that they are meeting with such decided success in the several works they have undertaken. A year since they started *The Metropolitan Pulpit*, which has already reached a circulation of 6,000 copies, and is to be doubled in size in future issues. Six months ago they issued the first number of *The Complete Preacher*—a much larger work—which has already reached a circulation of about 4,000 copies. And now they have published the "Homilist," which bids fair to attain to something of the immense popularity which it has in Great Britain.

The success of such works is a marked indication of a new and rapidly developing interest in the methods of preaching. Happily our preachers of all denominations are not content with the modes and attainments of the past, but are reaching after all the light and help available in order to improve upon them.

The Clarks of Edinburgh, and Scribner, Welford & Armstrong of New York, bring out, at $3.00 per volume, the 2d volume of the *Commentary on St. John,* translated from the Second French Edition of F. GODET, D.D., Professor of Theology, Neuchatel, by M. D. CASIN and S. TAYLOR. It extends from verse 19 of Chapter I, through Chapter X—the first volume, which we have previously noticed, having been taken up with introductory matter. The value of this contribution to Johannean exegesis literature is generally conceded.

They also publish at the same price the first volume of *Meyer's Critical and Exegetical Handbook to the Epistles to the Corinthians,* extending from Chapter I to XII, inclusive, of the First Epistle, translated by Rev. Dr. DOUGLAS BANNERMAN, and revised and edited by Dr. WILLIAM P. DICKSON. This, when complete, makes Parts V and VI of his Critical and Exegetical Commentary on the New Testament. The standard and sterling character of these commentaries makes them an important part of the minister's library.

The same houses also publish, at $3.00, *The Symbolic Parables, or the Church, the World, and the Anti-Christ ; being the Separate Predictions of the Apocalypse, viewed in their Relation to the Truths of Scripture.* The author's name does not appear, but he has wrought out an elaborate, searching, closely-reasoned work, in which he analyzes all the symbolic figures and pictures of this closing book of the Bible, which has baffled so many interpreters, and which Calvin refrained from commenting upon becau e he frankly avowed he did not understand it. This, however, should not deter us from studying and seeking its meaning. If it be the Word of God addressed to us, we are bound to try to understand it, and hear what the Spirit saith unto the Churches. No one who is searching the meaning of this book can fail to get important aid from this carefully prepared volume. The author comes to a pause as he reaches the sublime portraitures of the heavenly state which close the book. He hardly touches upon the first and second resurrection.

God's Word ; Man's Light and Guide. A course of Lectures on the Bible, before the New York Sunday-school Association. American Tract Society, 1877. Pp. 275. In announcing this work we might content ourselves with giving the table of contents ; for, from the character of the several topics and the ability of the lecturers, the reader might readily infer that it is a book worth buying and reading. Contents : " The Inspiration of the Scriptures," by Rev. William M. Taylor, D D. ; " The Languages of the Bible," by Rev. Charles A. Briggs, D.D. ; " The Unity and the Variety of the Bible," by Rev. R. S. Storrs, D.D. ; " Ancient History in its connection with the Old Testament," by Rev. Howard Crosby, D.D. ; "The Adaptation of the Bible to the Universal Needs of the Soul, and the Witness of Christian Men to its Divine Authority and Power," by Rev. Robert Russell Booth, D.D. ; "Miracles and Prophecies which show the Bible Divine," by Rev. Noah Porter, D.D. ; "Method of Jesus Christ as Teacher," by Rev. Geo. D. Boardman, D.D. ; "The Right and Responsibility of the Christian Conscience in the Study of the Scriptures," by Rev. E. A. Washburn, D D. ; "Majesty and Holiness of the Bible," by Rev. M. Simpson, D.D., LL.D. But we are not satisfied with simply giving so inviting a bill of fare. There is not a commonplace or irrelevant lecture in the volume. They are timely, pertinent, able, and admirably fit into each other, and singly and as a whole make a good and strong impression. But instead of commendation, we will let these lectures speak for themselves so far as our limited space will allow. We give an extract or two from Dr. Brigg's Lecture on the "Languages of the Bible."

"The Hebrew language," he says, "has a wonderful *majesty* and *sublimity*. This arises partly from its original religious genius, but chiefly from the sublime materials of its thought. God, the only true God, JAHVEH, the Holy Redeemer of his people, is the central theme of the Hebrew language and literature, a God not apart from nature and not involved in nature, no Pantheistic God, no mere Deistic God, but a God who enters into sympathetic relations with his creatures, who is recognized and praised, as well as ministered unto by the material creation. Hence, there is a *realism* in the Hebrew language that can nowhere else be found to the same extent. The Hebrew people were as *realistic* as the Greek were *idealistic*. Their God is not a God thought out, reasoned out, as an ultimate cause, or chief of a Pantheon, but a personal God, known by them in his association with them by a *proper name*, JAHVEH. Hence the so-called anthropomorphisms and anthropopathisms of the Old Testament, so alien to the Indo-Germanic mind that an Occidental theology must explain them away, from an incapacity to enter into that bold and sublime realism of the Hebrews. Thus, again, man is presented to us in all his naked *reality*, in his weakness and sins, in his depravity and wretchedness, as well as in his bravery and beauty, his holiness and wisdom. In the Hebrew heroes we see men of like passions with ourselves, and feel that their experience is the key to the joys and sorrows of our life. So also in their conception of nature. Nature is to the Hebrew poet all aglow with the glory of God, and intimately associated with man in his origin, history and destiny. There is no such thing as *science ;* that was for the Indo-Germanic mind ; but they give us that which science never gives, that which science is, from its nature, unable to present us: namely, those *concrete* relations, those expressive *features* of nature that declare to man their Master's mind and character, and claim human sympathy and protection as they yearn with man for the Messianic future. Now the Hebrew language manifests this realism on its very face. Its richness in synonyms is remarkable. It is said that the Hebrew language has, relatively to the English, ten times as many roots and ten times fewer words (Grill, in l. c.) ; and that while the Greek language has 1,800 roots to 1)0,000 words, the Hebrew has 2,000 roots to 10,000 words."

In summing up he says :

"These are some of the most striking features of the Hebrew language, which have made it the most suitable of all to give to mankind the elementary religious truths and facts of divine revelation. The great body of the Bible, four-fifths of the°sum total of God's Word, is in this tongue. It is no credit to a Christian people that the Hebrew language has no place at all in the most of our colleges and universities, so-called ; that its study has been confined, for the most part, to theological seminaries and the students for the ministry. It is not strange that the Old Testament has been neglected in the pulpit, the Sabbath-schools, and the family, so that many minds, even of the ministry, have doubted whether it was any longer to be regarded as the Word of God. It is not strange that Christian scholars, prejudiced by their training in the languages and literature of Greece and Rome, should be unable to enter into the spirit and appreciate the peculiar features of the Hebrew language and literature, and so fail to understand the elements of a divine revelation. Separating the New Testament and the words and work of Jesus and his apostles from their foundation and their historical preparation, they have not caught the true spirit of the gospel, nor apprehended it in its unity and variety as the fulfillment of the law and the prophets. But this is not all, for I shall now attempt to show you that the other languages of the Bible, the Aramaic and the Greek, have been moulded and transformed by the theological conceptions and moral ideas that had been developing in the Hebrew Scriptures, and which, having been ripened under the potent influence of the Divine Spirit, were about to burst forth into bloom and eternal fruitfulness in these tongues, prepared by Divine Providence for the purpose. The Hebrew language is, as we have seen the language of religion, and moulded entirely by religious and moral ideas and emotions. The Greek and the Aramaic are of an entirely different character ; they were not, as the Hebrew, cradled and nursed, trained from infancy to childhood, armed and equipped in their heroic youth with divine revelation ; but they were moulded outside of the realm of divine revelation, and only subsequently adapted for the declaration of sacred truth."

Dr. Storrs' Lecture on " The Unity and the Variety of the Bible," is characteristic of this eloquent preacher and writer.

"Observe how utterly fearless it is ! It puts its incidental historical narratives by the side of ancient records, wherever these are found, on brick cylinders, graven in rocks, traced upon the parchments, carved upon obelisks, built into imperial structures ; and it challenges comparison ! No matter how other records have come to us, the Scripture puts its record beside them, asserts this true, and waits for centuries for its vindication. The ancient historians tell us, for example, that the king of Babylon, when that city was taken and destroyed by the Persians, was not Belshazzar, but Nabonadius or Labynetus, as the names are given differently in different languages; that he was not captured in the city, or killed, but that he escaped from it ; that he fought a battle after the capture outside of the city; that he was defeated, and was then taken prisoner ; that he was made satrap under the conqueror ; that he lived for years afterward, unmolested ; lived in abundance and died in peace. Berosus and Abydenus agree in most of this, and history laughs at the story as told in the Book of Daniel. It is an unhistoric legend, idle, worthless, because contrary to facts. The Book of Daniel puts forward its record and patiently waits. Twenty years ago there were dug up the cylinders from the remains of the ancient Ur of the Chaldees, from the mounds which mark the almost forgotten site of that renowned city of the East, which explain at a glance the seeming inconsistency.

They show that Belshazzar was the son of Nabonadius, and the Regent under him; that Daniel's record is therefore as true as was that probably of Herodotus or Berosus. They were simply writing of different persons."

HISTORY AND BIOGRAPHY.

Scribner, Armstrong & Co. publish *Thomas De Quincey, his Life and Writings, with Unpublished Correspondence*, by H. A. PAGE, in two volumes. The brilliant author of *Confessions of an Opium Eater* will not pass into oblivion until the literature of the nineteenth century fades from the memory of men. He was not only
"Linked with bright Coleridge and with opium's fame,"
but with most of the British literati of the first half of it, especially with the Lake School and their associates and friends. To know De Quincey's life is to know very much of Coleridge, Wordsworth, Southey, Hazlitt, Lamb, Hood, and their coteries. Although the creations of his genius are as fragmentary and fitful as brilliant, yet they are so magnificent that they will never cease to fascinate and enchant. Even the drug which nearly shattered his mind and body, while it momentarily soothed the latter, often stimulated the former to flashes of preternatural brilliancy, as appears in that most unique prodigy of morbid genius, the "Confessions of an Opium Eater." No such picture of the physical, mental and moral ruin wrought by the habitual use of this narcotic, or of the alternations of abnormal soaring and ecstacy of soul, like the meteors which ever and anon shoot ablaze over the darkest skies, can be found in all literature, as in the weird self-portraitures of this strangely brilliant genius. In the light of these sketches we find a clue to the idiosyncrasies of many a man of genius who flashes out with a transient brilliancy of thought or action which gives promise of a grand future of achievement in the realms of literature or life; a promise, however, which only tantalizes us, and is redeemed at best by occasional and fitful efforts, without enduring or satisfactory result. We have seen many instances of these men, young and old, who now and then do splendid things, and raise expectations which are only mocked by habitual failure and prevailing impotence, and in nearly every instance the ultimate explanation has proved to be bondage to this narcotic. It is quite worth while for all who are tempted to indulgence in this habit, except under most competent and stringent medical prescription, to study its effects as they are here depicted by a master hand from dire experience.

The admirers of the "poet-philosopher," Coleridge, have often bewailed his failure to work out those systematic treatises of which he so often gave the promise, and of which he seemed to possess the germ and potency, as shown in numberless aphorisms and outbursts seldom matched in our language. That the performance came so far short of the promise is largely accounted for by his dreadful enslavement to this narcotic. The following passage, which we find among the many valuable relics and memorials of De Quincey gathered by Mr. Page in these volumes, tells a tale which will interpret itself to all. It is from a letter to a friend:

"With respect to my book (The Logic of Political Economy, which appeared in

1844), which perhaps by this time you and Professor Nichols will have received from the publishers, I have a word to say. Upon some of the distinctions then contended for, it would be false humility if I should doubt they are sound. The substance I am too well assured is liable to no dispute. But as to the method of presenting the distinctions, as to the composition of the book, and the whole evolution of a course of thinking, then it is that I too deeply recognize the mind afflicted by my morbid condition. Through that ruin, and by the help of that ruin, I looked into and read the latter states of Coleridge. His chaos I comprehend by the darkness of my own, and both were the work of laudanum. It is as if ivory carvings and elaborate fretwork and fair enameling should be found with worms and ashes amongst coffins and the wrecks of some forgotten life or abolished nature. In parts and fragments eternal creations are carried on, but the nexus is wanting, and life and the central principle which should bind together all the parts at the centre, with all its radiations to the circumference, are wanting. Infinite incoherence, ropes of sand, gloomy incapacity of vital pervasion by some one plastic principle, that is the hideous incubus upon my mind always. For there is no disorganized wreck so absolute, so perfect, as that which is wrought by misery."—Vol. I., p. 325.

The second volume, in an appendix, gives a very able medical view of De Quincey's case by Surgeon-Major W. C. B. Eatwell, Fellow of the Royal College of Physicians, London, and formerly Principal of the Medical College, Calcutta, which is well worth the study of all interested in such subjects. It warrants the charitable and comfortable conclusion that, enormous as were the evils of his opium-eating, it was the only antidote to certain diseases or morbid tendencies in De Quincey's constitution, which would, if unchecked, have terminated his life in his early prime.

Scribner, Armstrong & Co. publish another volume of their admirable Series of Epochs of Modern History, being *The Age of Anne*, by EDWARD E. MORRIS, M.A., of Lincoln College, Oxford, with Maps and Plans.

All the preceding publications from the houses of Scribner & Co. and Macmillan & Co. can be had of McGinness & Runyon, Princeton.

MISCELLANEOUS.

Coronation: A Story of Forest and Sea. By E. P. TENNEY. Boston: Noyes, Snow & Co., 1877. *The Silent House*, by the same author, was received with marked favor by the Christian public. But we confess to an inability fairly to apprehend the scope and aim of the present work. Is it a dream or a reality? Is it fiction or painful experience? We are unable to answer. We suspect it combines all these elements. The style, however, is fascinating. It has a high moral and spiritual aim. The life and character sketched in so odd, if not fanciful a way, we suspect will find counterparts in the actual experience of mankind. The spirit and aim of the book are well expressed in the closing words of the Introduction: " And when I myself go down to sleep in the silent valley, I shall not think that I have lived wholly in vain if this story of Cephas leads one human soul to a higher appreciation of the comfort, spiritual quickening and power to be gained by hours of sweet communion and holy striving with the Lord, in those closets which God himself has made in the solitudes of the earth."

Law for the Clergy: A Compilation of the Statutes of the States of

Illinois, Indiana, Iowa, Michigan, Minnesota, Ohio and Wisconsin, relating to the duties of clergymen in the solemnization of marriage, the organization of churches and religious societies, and the protection of religious meetings and assemblies, with notes and practical forms, embracing a collation of the *Common Law of Marriage*, by SANFORD A. HUDSON, Counsellor at Law. Chicago: S. C. Griggs & Co., 1877. We have given the full title of this book, which sufficiently indicates its scope and purpose. We wish it embraced all the States of the Union. The subject is important and practical. Clergymen are often ignorant of the laws under which they live in relation to matters of such vital interest, and fail in their duty in consequence, and cause mischief and injury.

The Presbyterian Board of Publication have issued in neat form the *Proceedings and Addresses at the laying of the Corner-Stone and at the Unveiling of the statue of John Witherspoon, in Philadelphia.* Compiled by REV. WM. P. BREED, D.D. Also, *We Three*, by KATE W. HAMILTON. 12mo, pp. 270. Also, a *Manual of Forms* for Baptism, Admission to the Communion, Administration of the Lord's Supper, Marriages and Funerals, conformed to the Doctrine and Discipline of the Presbyterian Church. By ARCHIBALD ALEXANDER HODGE, D.D.

The titles of these several works indicate their character. The first is a fitting memorial of one whom the Presbyterian Church will ever hold in respectful and grateful remembrance. The second is a story of decided interest, written in a pleasant and lively style—as are all the books of this authoress—and makes a good impression. The other cannot fail to prove acceptable and useful to pastors and ministers throughout the Presbyterian Church. Dr. Hodge has shown skill and sound judgment in its preparation. The "Order" for each subject is brief, pertinent and scriptural. We heartily agree with the author that "the very spirit of liberty which opposes the authoritative recommendation of such formulas by the General Assembly will approve as legitimate such offerings to the brethren as the present, made by private persons, and thoroughly conformed to the doctrinal principles of the 'Confession of Faith,' and to the regulative injunctions of the 'Directory for Worship.'" Certainly any approximation to a uniformity of method in the administration of Baptism, the Lord's Supper and the celebration of Marriage, which can be secured without the sacrifice of freedom and adaptability to varying circumstances, will be generally welcomed.

We can barely announce, what we received too late for the more extended notice it deserves, an important contribution to Philosophy, from PROFESSOR FRANCIS BOWEN of Harvard College, entitled, *Modern Philosophy, from Descartes to Schopenhauer and Hartmann*, published by Scribner, Armstrong & Co., and for sale by McGinness & Runyon, Princeton.

Hitchcock & Walden of Cincinnati publish the *Future of the Religious Policy of America; a Discussion of Eleven Great Living Questions*, by WILLIAM RILEY HALSTEAD. These questions are handled with various ability, and have some bearing, direct or indirect, upon the title which the book bears. They hardly amount, however, to a direct treatment or solution of the problem.

Lightning Source UK Ltd.
Milton Keynes UK
UKHW020309051218
333419UK00008B/369/P